MULTILEVEL CONSTITUTIONALISM FOR MULTILEVEL GOVERNANCE OF PUBLIC GOODS

This is the first legal monograph analysing multilevel governance of global 'aggregate public goods' (PGs) from the perspective of democratic, republican and cosmopolitan constitutionalism by using historical, legal, political and economic methods. It explains the need for a 'new philosophy of international law' in order to protect human rights and PGs more effectively and more legitimately 'Constitutional approaches' are justified by the universal recognition of human rights and by the need to protect 'human rights', 'rule of law', 'democracy' and other 'principles of justice' that are used in national, regional and UN legal systems as indeterminate legal concepts. The study describes and criticizes the legal methodology problems of 'disconnected' governance in UN, GATT and WTO institutions as well as in certain areas of the external relations of the EU (like transatlantic free trade agreements). Based on 40 years of practical experiences of the author in German, European, UN, GATT and WTO governance institutions and of simultaneous academic teaching, this study develops five propositions for constituting, limiting, regulating and justifying multilevel governance for the benefit of citizens and their constitutional rights as 'constituent powers', 'democratic principals' and main 'republican actors', who must hold multilevel governance institutions and their limited 'constituted powers' legally, democratically and judicially more accountable.

Multilevel Constitutionalism for Multilevel Governance of Public Goods

Methodology Problems in International Law

Ernst Ulrich Petersmann

·HART·
PUBLISHING
OXFORD AND PORTLAND, OREGON
2017

Hart Publishing
An imprint of Bloomsbury Publishing Plc

Hart Publishing Ltd
Kemp House
Chawley Park
Cumnor Hill
Oxford OX2 9PH
UK

Bloomsbury Publishing Plc
50 Bedford Square
London
WC1B 3DP
UK

www.hartpub.co.uk
www.bloomsbury.com

Published in North America (US and Canada) by
Hart Publishing
c/o International Specialized Book Services
920 NE 58th Avenue, Suite 300
Portland, OR 97213-3786
USA

www.isbs.com

HART PUBLISHING, the Hart/Stag logo, BLOOMSBURY and the Diana logo are trademarks of Bloomsbury Publishing Plc

First published 2017

British Library Cataloguing-in-Publication Data
A catalogue record for this book is available from the British Library.

ISBN: HBK: 978-1-50990-912-4
ePDF: 978-1-50990-906-3
ePub: 978-1-50990-907-0

Library of Congress Cataloging-in-Publication Data

Names: Petersmann, Ernst-Ulrich, author.

Title: Multilevel constitutionalism for multilevel governance of public goods : methodology problems in international law / Ernst Ulrich Petersmann.

Description: Oxford ; Portland, Oregon, USA : Hart Publishing, an imprint of Bloomsbury Publishing Plc, 2017. | Includes bibliographical references and index.

Identifiers: LCCN 2016037915 (print) | LCCN 2016038122 (ebook) | ISBN 9781509909124 (hardback : alk. paper) | ISBN 9781509909070 (Epub)

Subjects: LCSH: International and municipal law—Political aspects. | Constitutional law. | International organization. | International law and human rights. | Law and globalization.

Classification: LCC K302 .P48 2017 (print) | LCC K302 (ebook) | DDC 342/.042—dc23

LC record available at https://lccn.loc.gov/2016037915

Typeset by Compuscript Ltd, Shannon
Printed and bound in Great Britain by CPI Group (UK) Ltd, Croydon CR0 4YY

To find out more about our authors and books visit www.hartpublishing.co.uk. Here you will find extracts, author information, details of forthcoming events and the option to sign up for our newsletters.

Contents

Preface

During my 40 years of practising law in German, European, UN and GATT/WTO governance institutions, and of teaching international law in universities throughout the world, I adopted the habit of reflecting on my professional experiences and academic challenges in numerous books and other publications. Nobel Prize laureate Mario Vargas Llosa—in his *Letters to a Young Novelist*—described the motive for writing literature as 'rebellion' against the daily realities of human life. Adam Smith published his *Theory of Moral Sentiments* before his empirical *Inquiry into the Nature and Causes of the Wealth of Nations*; and my former economics professor Friedrich von Hayek published *The Road to Serfdom* and *The Constitution of Liberty* besides his numerous publications on economics. Similarly, this monograph, *Multilevel Constitutionalism*, explores the moral and constitutional foundations of the countless, regulatory problems of multilevel governance of transnational public goods. It reflects a kind of protest against over-specialized, all too often 'path-dependent' studies—and intergovernmental discourses of 'experts' in UN, WTO, regional and national governance institutions—on the 'management' of international relations, as if protection of public goods can be secured piecemeal through thousands of tariffs, quotas, subsidies, local content rules, labour standards, product and productions standards, other technical regulations (eg of the environment and other scarce resources), safeguard measures, 'unfair trade' regulations (like anti-dumping and countervailing duties), government procurement, monetary, financial, health and other safety regulations, and related rights and duties of governments and citizens (eg intellectual property rights). My monograph *International Economic Law in the 21st Century* (2012) gave an overview of this complex labyrinth of multilevel regulation—and of related 'rent-seeking' and 'governance failures' to reduce unnecessary poverty in so many UN member countries—using the cover image of a painting by Diego Rivera of *El Vendedor de Alcatraces*: the dignity of a poor woman selling flowers in a Mexican market place seemed to be an appropriate starting point for analysing international economic law and governance. The importance of this perspective had been confirmed by the human rights revolution in Tunisia in 2011, triggered by the street vendor Mohammed Bouazizi and his protests against arbitrary market restrictions. The cover image of this book uses one of Picasso's 'peace doves' as an illustration of how protection of international public goods must build on the ruins of past governance failures. The inquiry of this book into the 'principles of justice' underlying modern international legal systems is *not* motivated by some vain hope of discovering objective truth on the way towards utopia.

My guiding motive was rather the need for justifying law and governance vis-à-vis citizens (including the eight children in our family) by respecting the diversity of procedural, constitutional, distributive, corrective, commutative 'principles of justice' and equity; it is ultimately the respect for human dignity, the need for social cooperation and the legitimacy of 'reasonable disagreements' that require stronger multilevel constitutional protection of human and constitutional rights in multilevel governance of public goods.

I thank Dimitri van den Meersche (doctoral candidate at the European University Institute at Florence) for his critical comments on previous drafts of this book. I am grateful to my wife and our children for their patience vis-à-vis my academic addictions. As discussed in this book, the history of constitutionalism in European political and legal thought and governance practices is much older than in other parts of our world. Even though the republican constitutionalism emerging during earlier periods of 'globalization' and 'renaissance' (eg in the Florentine and Venetian merchant republics during the fifteenth century) and the motto of the French Revolution (*liberté, égalité, fraternité*) have become incorporated into European law (eg Article 2 of the Lisbon Treaty), they continue to be resisted by authoritarian rulers in many UN member states. Having taught international economic law in African, American and Asian universities, I remain convinced that non-European readers and citizens will also benefit from exploring the need for multilevel constitutional restraints on multilevel governance of public goods from historical, legal, political and economic perspectives; for respect for 'inalienable human rights' of all citizens has become the universally recognized 'foundation of freedom, justice and peace in the world' (Preamble to the Universal Declaration of Human Rights of 1948); and it cannot become effective without 'multilevel constitutionalism' limiting abuses of power in a globally integrating world.

At the age of 70, authors not only appreciate the slowness of sunsets before darkness falls. We also more easily understand the Kantian insight that answers to the three basic questions of philosophy—What can I know? What shall I do? What can I hope for beyond the limits of human knowledge?—depend on our conception of human beings. This insight is crucial in the human search for improving multilevel governance of public goods by limiting rational egoism and 'animal instincts' through reasonable self-commitments to equal rights of citizens and constitutional restraints on all multilevel governance agents, so that rulers can be held more accountable for the ubiquity of abuses of public and private powers. If this book should make some readers more aware of the need for supplementing 'state citizenship' with 'economic citizenship' and 'cosmopolitan citizenship' rights as legal incentives for—and constitutional safeguards of—collective supply of public goods in the twenty-first century, the aim of this account of multilevel constitutionalism in multilevel governance of public goods will have been realized.

Abbreviations

ACHR	American Convention on Human Rights
ACP	African, Caribbean and Pacific Developing Countries
ACTA	Anti-Counterfeiting Trade Agreement 2011
AJIL	American Journal of International Law
AJWH	Asian Journal of WTO & International Health Law and Policy
ASIL	American Society of International Law
BATNA	best alternative to a negotiated agreement
BIS	Bank for International Settlements
BISD	Basic Instruments and Selected Documents of GATT 1947
BIT	Bilateral Investment Treaty
BRICS	Brazil, Russia, India, China and South Africa
CAFTA	Central American Free Trade Agreement
CBD	Convention on Biodiversity
CEDAW	Convention on the Elimination of All Forms of Discrimination Against Women
CETA	Comprehensive Economic and Trade Agreement Canada–EU 2016
CJEU	Court of Justice of the EU
CML Rev	Common Market Law Review
CSR	corporate social responsibility
CUP	Cambridge University Press
DDR	Doha Development Round
DSB	Dispute Settlement Body of the WTO
DSU	Dispute Settlement Understanding of the WTO
EC	European Community
ECB	European Central Bank
ECHR	European Convention on Human Rights and Fundamental Freedoms

ECJ	European Court of Justice
ECR	EU Court of Justice Reports
ECSC	European Coal and Steel Community
ECT	Energy Charter Treaty
ECtHR	European Court of Human Rights
EEA	European Economic Area
EEC	European Economic Community
EFTA	European Free Trade Area
EJIL	European Journal of International Law
EU	European Union
EUCFR	EU Charter of Fundamental Rights 2007
EUI	European University Institute
EURATOM	European Atomic Energy Community
EYIEL	European Yearbook of International Economic Law
FAO	Food and Agriculture Organization
FET	fair and equitable treatment
FCTC	WHO Framework Convention on Tobacco Control
FRA	EU Agency for Fundamental Rights
FSB	Financial Stability Board
FTA	Free Trade Agreement
GAL	Global Administrative Law
GATT	General Agreement on Tariffs and Trade 1947
GATS	General Agreement on Trade in Services
GDP	gross domestic product
GMOs	genetically modified organisms
GSP	Generalized System of Tariff Preferences
G20	Group of 19 Countries (G7 plus 12 additional states) plus the EU
HRL	human rights law
IBRD	International Bank for Reconstruction and Development 1944
ICANN	Internet Corporation for Assigned Names and Numbers
ICAO	International Civil Aviation Organization

ICAT	International Convention Against Torture 1984
ICERD	International Convention on the Elimination of All Forms of Racial Discrimination
ICC	International Criminal Court
ICCPR	International Covenant on Civil and Political Rights
ICESCR	International Covenant on Economic, Social and Cultural Rights
ICJ	International Court of Justice
ICN	International Competition Network
ICRC	International Convention on the Rights of the Child 1989
ICSID	International Centre for the Settlement of Investment Disputes 1965
IDA	International Development Association 1960
IEL	international economic law
IFC	International Finance Corporation 1956
IHR	International Health Regulations of the WHO
IIA	international investment agreement
ILC	International Law Commission
ILM	International Legal Materials
ILO	International Labour Organization
IMF	International Monetary Fund
ISDS	Investor-State Dispute Settlement
ISO	International Organization for Standardization
ITLOS	International Tribunal for the Law of the Sea
ITO	International Trade Organization
JIEL	Journal of International Economic Law
LDCs	less-developed countries
LLDCs	least-developed countries
MEAs	Multilateral Environmental Agreements
MEP	Member of the European Parliament
MERCOSUR	Common Market of Southern Countries in Latin America
MIGA	Multilateral Investment Guarantee Agency

NAFTA	North American Free Trade Agreement
NAMA	Non-Agricultural Market Access
NCDs	non-communicable diseases
NFIDC	Net-Food Importing Developing Countries
NGOs	non-governmental organizations
OECD	Organization for Economic Cooperation and Development
OJ	Official Journal
OUP	Oxford University Press
PCA	Permanent Court of Arbitration
PCIJ	Permanent Court of International Justice
PG	public goods
PIL	public international law
PTA	plurilateral trade agreement
REDD	Reduced Emissions from Deforestation and Forest Degradation
RTAs	regional trade agreements
SADEC	Southern African Development and Economic Community
SDT	special and differential treatment
SPS	Sanitary and Phytosanitary Measures (Agreement)
TBT	Technical Barriers to Trade (Agreement)
TCE	Treaty Establishing a Constitution for Europe
TEU	Lisbon Treaty on European Union 2007
TFEU	Lisbon Treaty on the Functioning of the EU 2007
TNCs	transnational corporations
TPP	Trans-Pacific Partnership
TPRM	Trade Policy Review Mechanism (of the WTO)
TRIPS	Trade-Related Aspects of Intellectual Property Rights (Agreement)
TTIP	Transatlantic Trade and Investment Agreement EU–USA
UDHR	Universal Declaration of Human Rights
UN	United Nations

UNCITRAL	United Nations Commission on International Trade Law
UNCLOS	United Nations Convention on the Law of the Sea
UNCTAD	United Nations Conference on Trade and Development
UNEP	United Nations Environmental Program
UNESCO	United Nations Educational, Scientific and Cultural Organization
UNFCCC	UN Framework Convention on Climate Change
UNGC	UN Global Compact
UP	University Press
VCLT	Vienna Convention on the Law of Treaties
VER	voluntary export restraints
WHO	World Health Organization
WIPO	World Intellectual Property Organization
WTO	World Trade Organization

'Justice is the main pillar that upholds the whole edifice. If it is removed, the immense fabric of human society ... must in a moment crumble into atoms'

Adam Smith (*The Theory of Moral Sentiments*, 1759)

'Justice is the end of government. It is the end of civil society. It ever has been and will be pursued until it is obtained, or until liberty be lost in the pursuit.'

James Madison (*The Federalist* 51, 1787)

'In the exercise of his rights and freedoms, everyone shall be subject only to such limitations as are determined by law solely for the purpose of securing due recognition and respect for the rights and freedoms of others and of meeting the just requirements of morality, public order and the general welfare in a democratic society'

Article 29:2 Universal Declaration of Human Rights (1948)

'All that is valuable in human society depends upon the opportunity for development accorded to the individual.'

Albert Einstein

'Like slavery and apartheid, poverty is not natural. It is man-made and it can be overcome and eradicated by the actions of human beings. And overcoming poverty is not a gesture of charity. It is an act of justice. It is the protection of a fundamental human right, the right to dignity and a decent life.'

Nelson Mandela (speech at the 'Make Poverty History' rally in Trafalgar Square, February 2005)

Introduction

From Democratic and Republican to Cosmopolitan Constitutionalism in Multilevel Governance of Public Goods

I. OVERVIEW

STATES, GOVERNMENTS AND international organizations justify themselves by their collective supply of public goods (PGs) demanded by citizens. Yet even though globalization continues to transform most national into transnational PGs, there is not a single legal monograph analysing how global PGs—like human rights, the rule of law, democratic peace, monetary stability, undistorted financial and trade systems, protection of the environment, 'sustainable development'—can be produced more legitimately and protected more effectively in a world without 'global democracy'.[1] The legal interrelationships between constitutional protection of national PGs (eg equal liberties of citizens, judicial remedies) and international legal protection of regional and worldwide 'aggregate PGs' (eg human rights, economic liberties, judicial remedies) are often neglected by international lawyers, for instance if UN human rights lawyers overlook that many constitutional liberties in national and European constitutional law (eg Article 2 German Basic Law, the EUCFR) go far beyond those in UN human rights law (HRL) and in common law countries committed to

[1] My monograph on *International Economic Law in the 21st Century. Constitutional Pluralism and Multilevel Governance of Interdependent Public Goods* (Oxford, Hart Publishing, 2012) focused on international economic law (IEL), and used economic and political theories on PGs (*res publica*) without exploring the relevance of *constitutional republicanism* for UN law and multilevel governance of PGs. This book explores concepts, theories and collective action problems of PGs more systematically (notably in ch 2, sections I–II below); it explains the relevance of democratic, republican and cosmopolitan constitutionalism for reforming international and European law and governance of transnational 'aggregate PGs' also beyond economic law (eg in human rights law, public health law and environmental law). The terms 'human rights', 'fundamental rights' and 'constitutional rights' overlap unless fundamental and constitutional rights are limited—eg in the EU Charter of Fundamental Rights (EUCFR)—to citizens or EU residents (eg Arts 42–44 EUCFR apply to EU citizens and residents, most other guarantees of the EUCFR protect the rights of everyone).

'parliamentary sovereignty' rather than to 'constitutional democracy'.[2] This doctrinal neglect by international lawyers and governments of the interrelationships between national, regional and worldwide protection of transnational PGs is also surprising in view of the increasing recognition that human, fundamental and constitutional rights 'constitute general principles' (Article 6:3 Treaty on European Union (TEU)), corresponding policy objectives and duties of multilevel governance institutions to respect, protect and fulfil human rights (eg as recognized in Article 51 of the EUCFR). The seventieth anniversary of the United Nations (UN) and the twentieth anniversary of the World Trade Organization (WTO) in 2015 prompted many citizens to ask why so many international organizations and so many UN member states fail to realize their declared policy objectives of protecting human rights, sustainable development and other PGs.

This book emphasizes that lawyers, political scientists, economists, government officials and other participants in multilevel governance of transnational PGs—even if, as in my own case, they have worked for 40 years in private and public, national and international governance institutions, and have lectured and published extensively on UN, WTO and regional governance problems and challenges—need to re-think their path-dependent, methodological premises. For instance, why does constitutionalism—notwithstanding its universal recognition as the most legitimate and most effective legal methodology for transforming agreed 'principles of justice' and the 'law in the books' into socially effective 'law in action' so as to protect human and constitutional rights of citizens—remain so neglected and opposed by diplomats and rulers in global governance institutions like the UN and the WTO? What are the policy lessons from the 'Brexit' referendum of June 2016, in which a majority of British voters gave up their 'constitutional rights' and benefits under EU law in view of their fears of immigration and their preferences for financing *national PGs* (like the National Health Service) rather than European PGs? If citizens have reasons to prioritize *national* over *transnational PGs*, can the agreed 'principles of justice' underlying UN, WTO and regional law be transformed into more coherent democratic legislation, administration, adjudication, international implementing regulations and 'public reason' that democratic citizens can accept as 'just' (eg in the procedural sense of being 'justified' by constitutional, participatory and deliberative, democratic and judicial decision-making processes)? This monograph acknowledges the non-ideal reality of 'limited

[2] On my criticism of interpreting international guarantees of 'liberties' (eg in UN HRL and IEL) one-sidedly from the narrow perspective of 'common law freedoms' in Commonwealth countries with 'parliamentary sovereignty' (like Australia), without adequate regard to multilevel constitutional protection of much broader 'equal freedoms' in European constitutional law, see EU Petersmann, 'Taking Human Dignity, Poverty and Empowerment of Individuals More Seriously: Rejoinder to Alston' (2002) 13 *EJIL* 845–51.

reasonableness' (eg of Brexit advocates' opting for 'rational ignorance' towards European PGs) and of intergovernmental power politics, which often justifies a deferential stance vis-à-vis under-theorized 'principles of justice' recognized in modern international law. Yet enhancing the normativity of international law as a necessary instrument of multilevel protection of transnational PGs—in a non-ideal world without 'global justice'—requires a better understanding of why respect for 'reasonable disagreement' on the interpretation of modern HRL and of other 'principles of justice' is often a pragmatic precondition for advancing necessary, political and legal 'piecemeal reforms' of international law and governance.

A. Legal Methodology Problems in the Transition from Democratic and Republican to More Cosmopolitan Constitutionalism

This book argues that—due to the universal recognition of 'inalienable' and 'indivisible human rights' by all UN member states—the customary law requirement (as codified in the Preamble to and Article 31 of the 1969 Vienna Convention on the Law of Treaties (VCLT)) of interpreting treaties and settling related disputes 'in conformity with principles of justice' and human rights, requires review of path-dependent, *power-orientated* by *citizen-orientated*, legal methodologies in the interpretation and development of international law and the judicial settlement of related disputes.[3] As explained in Chapter 1, democratic Constitutions and European and UN HRL—by protecting civil, political, economic, social and cultural fundamental rights, related human interests and PGs, and requiring their mutual reconciliation through democratic legislation, administration and judicial remedies in courts of justice—offer comprehensive legal frameworks for democratic deliberation and regulation of the new legal challenges of 'globalization', with due regard to the fundamental interests of all affected citizens and other stakeholders. Chapters 2 and 3 explain why—in order to limit the 'disconnect' between UN and WTO governance and national legislation, administration, adjudication and 'public reason' in many UN/WTO member states, and reconcile the inevitable 'piecemeal engineering' in fragmented legal regimes (like health law, environmental law and regional integration law)—multilevel governance of transnational PGs must be 'connected' more effectively by transnational democratic, republican and cosmopolitan constitutionalism. The term 'constitutionalism' is used here for

[3] Cf EU Petersmann, 'Justifying "Fragmentation" and Constitutional Reforms of International Law in Terms of Justice, Human Rights and "Cosmopolitan Constitutionalism"' in A Jakubowski and K Wierczynska (eds), *Fragmentation vs the Constitutionalisation of International Law. A Practical Inquiry* (London, Routledge, 2016) 163–82.

the process of constituting legislative, administrative and judicial governance powers and of transforming constitutionally agreed rules and principles of a higher legal rank into legislation, administration and adjudication aimed at constituting, ordering and directing a people. Democratic constitutionalism focuses on the self-constitution and emancipation of a people or of its ruling elites (eg in democratic city states in ancient Greece). Republican constitutionalism aims at limiting arbitrary domination and protecting additional PGs for the benefit of citizens (like the Roman legal system in the ancient Roman republics). Cosmopolitan constitutionalism—proceeding from constitutional protection of human rights and other fundamental rights of everyone at national and international levels of governance (eg in the EUCFR)—promotes individual and democratic self-development and collective protection of transnational PGs beyond national frontiers. As illustrated by the multilevel legal and judicial protection of human and fundamental rights of citizens in European law, transnational democratic, republican and cosmopolitan constitutionalism can limit the flaws of national, single-polity perspectives, for instance by constituting, limiting, regulating and justifying multilevel governance of transnational PGs more effectively than national constitutionalism if the latter focuses on local and state polities and national boundaries without adequate protection for all human rights, externally affected interests of non-residents and of transnational legal communities committed to protection of transnational PGs. While the spread of industrial technologies beyond Europe took centuries in the past, modern information technologies have offered unique opportunities for promoting not only economic and social, but also democratic and legal development worldwide in only a few years, as illustrated by the lifting of hundreds of millions of people out of poverty in China since the 1980s and in India since the 1990s. This book argues for legally protecting '*cosmopolitan citizenship*' not only as a bundle of rights and duties of all 'citizens of the world', but also as a status of membership in 'overlapping', self-governing local, national and transnational polities responsible for multilevel protection of transnational PGs that are necessary conditions for human autonomy and well-being. It suggests distinguishing between the *demos*, composed of citizens having the franchise, and a broader '*cosmopolitan citizenry*', including all those who have a stake in being members of a transnational polity responsible for protecting functionally limited, transnational PGs.

Due to the transformation of national into transnational PGs, democratic, republican and cosmopolitan constitutionalism complement each other by offering synergies that—as in the story of the blind men describing an elephant depending on the different body parts they touched—enable a more coherent understanding and regulation of the collective action problems in multilevel governance of transnational 'aggregate PGs', for instance based on inclusive representation of all interests that are actually affected by democratic regulation, and of the rights of all who are subject to the jurisdiction of government decisions and whose individual autonomy depends on participation in collective self-government. Transnational legal communities (eg citizens and peoples cooperating in transnational common markets) must constitute themselves as a legitimate, self-governing polity and multilevel *demoi*-cracy, rather than letting themselves be dominated by path-dependent, intergovernmental power politics that risk undermining the legal, democratic and judicial accountability of government executives vis-à-vis domestic citizens. Due to the often 'reasonable disagreements' on how to interpret, reconcile and prioritize human and constitutional rights (eg freedom of speech, privacy rights, economic, social and cultural rights), HRL and democratic discourse in 'communities of rights' need to be supplemented—as explained in Chapter 1—by theories of justice and of constitutionalism aimed at coherently clarifying indeterminate legal concepts and functional treaty regimes among states for collective protection of transnational PGs.

Following the financial crises since 2008 and the Euro-crises since 2010, the European Union (EU)—which was for a long time considered as a potential model for reforming international law—also continues to be confronted with systemic violations of the rule of law, for instance of the budget and debt disciplines in Article 126 of the Treaty on the Functioning of the European Union (TFEU) and of the 'Schengen' and 'Dublin rules' for the treatment of immigrants and refugees at the borders of the EU. The widespread perception of 'governance failures' in worldwide, regional and national governance institutions—as illustrated by more than one billion people living on $1 or less per day without effective access to protection of their human rights, or by the now 65 million displaced persons and refugees triggering the biggest transnational migration crisis since World War II—is accompanied by the increasing dissatisfaction of voters with the 'democratic deficits' of 'disconnected' UN, WTO and EU governance dominated by government executives, who negotiate and ratify—and subsequently violate—international agreements on grounds of 'political realism' and alleged 'national interests'. The British 'Brexit vote' of June 2016 to leave the EU illustrates how majoritarian governance—also in constitutional democracies like the USA and in the EU—is increasingly 'polarized' by emotions and interest-group politics, for instance in order to resist international migration and redistribute domestic income by violating international trade rules (eg on the rule of law, science-based 'risk assessments' and carbon reductions aimed at climate change prevention).

National governments in continental, resource-rich democracies (like Australia, Canada, India and the USA) operate differently from multilevel governance among democracies in vertically integrated, supranational 'PGs organizations' like the EU. Hence, American and European political and legal analyses of the need to adjust national legal and governance systems to the globalization challenges of the twenty-first century often lead to diverse policy recommendations, not to mention the different 'world order conceptions' of the BRICS countries (Brazil, Russia, India, China and South Africa). 'Legal fragmentation' (as illustrated by the 'Grexit' and 'Brexit' discussions about whether Greece and the United Kingdom should exit from EU integration) and claims to specificity of particular legal regimes (like economic law) can be considered as inevitable 'Hegelian dialectic processes' driving national as well as international legal systems (as discussed in Chapter 1, section III). This study emphasizes the need for 'constitutionalization' of 'fast rationality' (eg by the *homo economicus*) and of power politics through 'constitutional mind-sets' and 'slow reasonableness',[4] as illustrated by the 'constitutionalization' of European economic regulation in order to limit its politicization and instrumentalization by powerful lobbies. Responding to 'fragmentation' by constitutional 'checks and balances' can promote 'public reason' and convergence of diverse democratic, republican and cosmopolitan traditions of law and governance for the benefit of citizens. The laboratory of EU law also reveals tensions between varied national constitutional identities and centralized EU institutions committed to protection of under-defined European PGs (like a 'competitive social market economy' and 'economic and monetary union' pursuant to Article 3 TEU). Similarly, 'teleological' interpretations by the European Court of Human Rights (ECtHR) of the European Convention on Human Rights (ECHR) as a 'living constitutional document' have provoked criticism that judicial 'multilevel human rights constitutionalism' disrespects national democratic processes. Such tensions between national and multilevel constitutionalism raise difficult questions of legal methodology and conflict resolution (eg on the basis of the 'rules of recognition' of competing jurisdictions, or of common principles governing 'overlapping jurisdictions').

B. From 'International Law Among States' to Vertical 'Integration Law' for Multilevel Governance of Transnational Public Goods

'Globalization' refers to the global movements of goods, services, persons, capital and related payments, the global recognition of human rights, international law and multilevel governance institutions, and to the closer integration of countries. It affects the daily lives of people (eg through communications, climate change, health pandemics), transforms national into international PGs, and requires far-reaching changes in multilevel

[4] On the difference between individual rationality and 'reasonableness' balancing egoist self-interests with the legitimate interests of all others, see D Kahneman, *Thinking, Fast and Slow* (London, Penguin, 2011). The universal recognition of human rights requires justifying also international law from the moral perspective of free and equal citizens rather than only from utilitarian perspectives.

governance of transnational PGs like security and the global division of labour. The more governance decisions by governmental and non-governmental organizations (NGOs) have effects beyond states, the stronger the need for coordinating and regulating multilevel governance not only in 'horizontal relations' among states, but also in 'vertical relations' among citizens, (non-)governmental and international organizations.

The adjustment pressures generated by globalization entailed structural transformations of international law and governance institutions:

1. The '*Westphalian international law of coexistence*' (1648–1945) was driven by power-orientated conceptions of state sovereignty, international law and of the often 'anarchic' international relations. Transnational actors regulated international commercial and financial cooperation primarily through private law (*lex mercatoria*) and national 'conflict of law rules', and through the extension of national law to colonial territories that were demarcated through international agreements among states. Yet the changing conceptions of 'national welfare' led to regulatory paradigm changes (eg from 'mercantilism' to 'embedded liberalism' following World War II) that also changed foreign policies and the structures of international law.
2. In the wake of the 'Cobden-Chevallier trade agreement' between England and France (1860) and following World Wars I and II, the '*international law of cooperation*' increasingly provided for institutionalized cooperation among states (eg in the context of the League of Nations, the UN and UN Specialized Agencies, GATT 1947 and the WTO). The only progressive decolonization, the non-democratic nature of many UN member states and the domination of intergovernmental cooperation by government executives entailed, however, that UN/WTO law and governance have often not been effectively implemented inside UN member states. UN law recognizes and protects human rights, popular self-determination, international rule of law and peaceful settlement of disputes. Yet due to the 'domestic implementation deficits' in many areas of UN law and governance, it has failed to protect many international PGs effectively.
3. Such 'disconnected intergovernmentalism' and domestic 'legal dualism' often impede multilevel governance of transnational PGs for the benefit of citizens and their human rights. Many UN/WTO member state governments remain unwilling to effectively constitute, limit, regulate and justify delegation of limited legislative, executive and judicial powers to multilevel governance institutions in terms of protecting rights of citizens, such as labour rights protected by the International Labour Organization (ILO, 1919), health rights protected by the World Health Organization (WHO, 1945), rights to food protected by the Food and Agriculture Organization (FAO, 1945), rights to education protected

> by the UN Education, Scientific and Cultural Organization (UNESCO, 1945), and additional civil, political, economic, social and cultural rights protected by worldwide, regional and national human rights institutions and national Constitutions. The universal recognition of human rights by all UN member states increasingly challenges 'Westphalian conceptions' of 'international law among sovereign states' by alternative conceptions of an 'international law of peoples' (eg insisting on decolonization and democratic self-determination), 'cosmopolitan international law' deriving its legitimacy from human and constitutional rights of citizens (eg European common market law and HRL), and multilevel governance of transnational PGs through functionally limited 'PGs agreements' (eg protecting international air transport, maritime transport, postal communications and telecommunications). Especially in regional economic integration organizations like the EU and the European Economic Area (EEA), the 'legitimacy deficits' of the 'international law of coexistence' and 'international law of cooperation' (Friedmann) are progressively reduced by also providing for multilevel parliamentary and judicial institutions that protect human and constitutional rights of citizens. Such constitutional reforms—by empowering citizens to invoke and enforce 'PGs treaties' in domestic jurisdictions, rendering multilevel governance (eg of the common market among 31 EEA member states) more accountable, and by justifying international rules and institutions in terms of human and constitutional rights—can transform fragmented 'horizontal international law among states' into more legitimate and more powerful 'vertical integration law'.

Such functionally limited 'constitutionalization' of multilevel governance of transnational PGs remains contested. Many countries continue to prioritize 'constitutional nationalism' based on Hobbesian conceptions of 'international law among sovereign states' and of international relations as power-orientated rivalries that necessitate 'realist foreign policies'.[5] This study argues not only that 'Hobbesian social contracts'—based on an assumption of human incapacity for peaceful, democratic cooperation (*homo homini lupus est*)—have become inconsistent with the universal acceptance of human rights and democratic governance principles in international law and constitutional democracies, but also that multilevel governance of transnational 'aggregate PGs' can be successfully 'constitutionalized' for the benefit of citizens and their constitutional rights, even if 'global democracy' or a 'world republic' remain *utopias*. Human rights law and corresponding duties of governments to protect transnational PGs for the benefit of

[5] Cf J Goldsmith and D Levinson, 'Law for States: International Law, Constitutional Law, Public Law' in (1999) 113 *Harvard Law Review* 1–75. The competing conceptions of international law aimed at limiting realist pursuits of national self-interests without attending to moral issues (eg Rawls's 'Law of Peoples' and cosmopolitan conceptions of international law) are discussed in ch 1, sections I–III.

all 'citizens of the earth' (Kant) entail that international law and multilevel governance must become parts of 'evolutionary' or, if necessary, 'revolutionary constitutionalization' in order to constitute, limit, regulate and justify multilevel governance of transnational PGs. Even though national and regional HRL and constitutionalism (eg European constitutional law) depend on functionally limited, international agreements in order to protect global PGs for the benefit of citizens, such treaties among states and intergovernmental rules—in order to protect human needs and related entitlements effectively—need to be embedded more strongly into rights-based, national and regional constitutional systems. Yet path-dependent international lawyers and diplomats with 'statist mind-sets' continue to avoid discussing international law in constitutional terms. Hegemonic states (like China, Russia, the USA) pursuing 'realist foreign policies' continue to prioritize 'national interests'; they ratify and implement far fewer UN human rights conventions and ILO labour rights conventions than, for example, the 31 EEA member states, which have been more willing to accept UN and European HRL as multilevel, constitutional restraints on foreign policy powers.

C. 'Multilevel Constitutionalism' as a Functionally Differentiated, 'Interactional' Process of 'Constitutionalization'

In contrast to the democratic use of 'constituent power' by 'We the people' at particular constitutional moments that gave rise to national (big 'C') 'Constitutions' (eg during the revolutionary American and French constitutionalism during the eighteenth century), European constitutional law continues to evolve dynamically in the context of functionally limited treaty regimes like the EU Treaties, the ECHR and the EEA Agreement. At both national and European levels of governance, the dynamic processes of 'constitutionalizing' legislation, administration and adjudication were shaped not only by democratic law-making, but also by civil society struggles, judicial clarifications of the law, and progressive development of constitutional and legal systems.[6] This book also argues that the increasing number of regional and worldwide 'PGs treaties' beyond Europe—by constituting, limiting, regulating and justifying legislative, administrative and judicial powers for multilevel governance of functionally limited, transnational PGs, and by offering

[6] See, eg, M Poiares Maduro, *We the Court: the European Court of Justice and the European Economic Constitution* (Oxford, Hart Publishing, 1998). Maduro's methodological proposals of 'contra-punctual legal techniques' reconciling legal and judicial interpretations of overlapping legal regimes (like national, EU and EEA law) are discussed in ch 2, section V. Even though political and legal theories identify regulatory problems of international law (like the 'borrowing' and 'resource privileges' enabling non-democratic rulers to exploit their peoples), they fail to elaborate 'constitutional approaches' to limiting unjust international rules and institutions, as explored in this book.

incentives for democratic and judicial control of multilevel governance—contributes to the emergence of 'multilevel constitutionalism' for multilevel governance of PGs, for instance by limiting multilevel governance powers by individual rights and judicial remedies. Just as EU constitutional law can be better understood as a functionally differentiated process of progressive 'constitutionalization'—giving rise, *inter alia*, to an 'economic constitution' (eg based on the 'micro-economic constitution' of the EEC Treaty and the 'macro-economic constitution' of the Maastricht and Lisbon Treaties) that can be distinguished from the EU's 'political constitution', 'security constitution' and 'foreign policy constitution'[7]—so is the much less developed 'constitutionalization' of international law and governance beyond Europe characterised by functionally differentiated treaty regimes that dynamically evolve and interact with other international and national legal regimes and common constitutional principles (eg based on the human rights obligations and judicial remedies accepted by UN member states in hundreds of national and international legal instruments).

Hence, this study discusses 'constitutional pluralism' not only as 'vertical interactions' between international and national, but also as 'horizontal interactions' among functionally diverse, international and regional legal regimes acknowledging common constitutional principles. For instance, the 'constitutionalization' of the European common market was shaped not only by *national* constitutional guarantees of fundamental rights, democratic legislation and judicial remedies; the common treaty obligations of EU member states under GATT/WTO law also required the foundation of European common market law on a 'customs union' with free movement of goods (cf Articles 28 et seq TFEU) and a common commercial policy based on compliance with the GATT/WTO legal and judicial obligations of all EU member states and of the EU (cf Articles 206 et seq TFEU). 'Multilevel constitutionalism' is understood as 'interactional' and 'relational law' that dynamically evolves in functionally complementary, 'horizontal' and 'vertical' legal relations; for instance, national and international HRL and international economic law (IEL) often prioritize different 'jurisprudential' and 'doctrinal principles' due to the diverse democratic preferences of the countries involved and diverse regulatory priorities (eg common market freedoms and guarantees of undistorted competition in the EEC Treaty of 1957, as interpreted and developed by the European Court of Justice (ECJ) since the 1960s).[8] As all UN member states have accepted

[7] Cf K Tuori and S Sankari (eds), *The Many Constitutions of Europe* (Aldershot, Ashgate, 2010).

[8] Cf K Tuori, 'The Relationality of European Constitution(s). Justifying a New Research Programme for European Constitutional Scholarship' in U Neersgard and R Nielsen (eds), *European Legal Method—towards a New European Legal Realism?* (Copenhagen, DJOF Publishing, 2013) 23–36, 27: '*constitution* should be understood through the *constitutional*

'inalienable' and 'indivisible' human rights and other 'principles of justice' aimed at protecting citizens, the many 'functionally different constitutions' involve common 'rights dimensions', as explicitly acknowledged in the 'constitutions' (*sic*) establishing some UN Specialized Agencies (like the ILO, the WHO and UNESCO). Yet such 'surface-level constitutional law'[9] is often not effectively transformed into 'constitutional culture', for instance due to the domination of UN and GATT/WTO institutions by intergovernmental power politics and 'reasonable disagreements' about the interactions among economic, legal, political and social constitutionalism (eg among WTO members that have not ratified—and oppose—some UN and regional human rights conventions). In regional and worldwide courts of justice, such conflicts are often reflected in conflicting claims of civil, political, economic, social and cultural rights of citizens, of corresponding duties of governments and of 'judicial comity' among diverse jurisdictions on how to construe common 'constitutional principles' (eg of rule of law, non-discrimination, necessity, proportionality, transparent governance) in different jurisdictions. Even though regional and worldwide market liberalization, market regulation and 'economic crises' (like the financial, monetary and debt crises since 2008) remain important driving forces of 'constitutionalizing' multilevel governance,[10] this monograph focuses on 'constitutionalism' in the relationships between economic and *non-economic PGs* like health law, HRL, environmental law, judicial protection of fundamental rights, democratic governance and transnational rule of law.

Chapter 1, section II explains why the customary law requirements of interpreting treaties 'in conformity with the principles of justice', including also 'human rights and fundamental freedoms for all', continue to be neglected in intergovernmental practices and judicial decisions by many international courts of justice. International judges increasingly conceive of the multilevel legal order as one big system comprising sources of law stemming from national and international sub-systems (eg as defined in Article 38 of the Statute of the International Court of Justice (ICJ Statute)), and agree on the need for 'legal positivism' and 'legal realism' in their

relationship which *constitutional law* establishes with a *constitutional object*, that is, either an extra-legal object of regulation or, in case of the *juridical constitution*, with law itself ... [I]n France, the constitutional revolution aimed at constituting a new socio-economic system, whereas in America, the emphasis was on reaffirming the traditional "liberties of the Englishman".' Tuori's distinction between economic, juridical, political, social and security constitutions is discussed further below in section V of this Introduction.

[9] On the distinction between 'surface level constitutional provisions' and a 'legal cultural level' at which constitutional rules, principles and precedents are interpreted and applied, see Tuori (n 8), at 30.

[10] Cf Petersmann (n 1). Also J Rawls's theory of justice later emphasized that the 'stabilizing function' of his proposed 'constitutional contract' on 'principles of justice' required to institutionalize 'public reason' (eg in a 'basic legal structure' protected by a Supreme Court) in order to maintain a 'well-ordered society'; cf J Rawls, *Political Liberalism* (New York, Columbia UP, 1993).

exploration of 'what the law is'; yet they remain reluctant to ask 'why the law is as it is', how interpretations of international law can be justified vis-à-vis citizens in terms of 'principles of justice', and whether modern HRL requires the legal rights of citizens to be taken as constitutional foundations of modern legal systems and legal methodologies. Chapter 1, section III discusses 'legal fragmentation' and 'legal reintegration' as dialectic methods for progressively reforming international and domestic legal systems. As 'global democracy' remains a *utopia*, and intergovernmental power politics remains a constant threat to multilevel constitutionalism, this study argues for 'bottom-up struggles' by civil society for cosmopolitan and republican rights and democratic and judicial remedies against the ubiquity of abuses of public and private powers in multilevel governance of international PGs. In view of the 'relational nature' of 'functional constitutionalism'—ie the dependence of constitutional rules and problems on their regulatory objects and on the 'constitutional sociology' underlying constitutionalization processes beyond states—Chapter 2 engages in a number of case studies (eg of multilevel tobacco control aimed at protecting health rights, environmental protection aimed at protecting human rights, and transnational judicial remedies aimed at protecting transnational rule of law). These empirical case studies of ongoing constitutionalization processes confirm, *inter alia*:

— the diverse sociological preconditions for 'constitutional reforms' in different policy sectors (like multilevel health and environmental regulation);
— the diversity of legal methods actually used by multilevel actors;
— the changing relative importance of the various sources of law (like general principles of law) and of the related 'rules of recognition';
— the changing nature of 'legal positivism' and of 'constitutional interpretations' of international law (eg concerning inherent powers of international courts of justice); and
— the need to clarify the methods of treaty interpretation in view of the fact that many international treaties use deliberately indeterminate, legal concepts and 'incomplete rules' (like GATT Article XXIII on 'violation complaints', 'non-violation complaints' and 'situation complaints' under GATT/WTO law).

Furthermore, the customary law requirement of interpreting treaties 'in good faith in accordance with the ordinary meaning to be given to the terms of the treaty in their context and in the light of its object and purpose' (Article 31:1 VCLT) does not offer a coherent theory of how these interpretative principles and the changing paradigms of UN treaty law (eg HRL, communitarian 'global PGs treaties') should be applied in 'legislative' and 'judicial' interpretations of international law and related dispute settlement procedures.[11] There are three basic approaches to international treaty interpretation derived from the customary law rules codified in Articles 31–33 VCLT, ie:

1. clarifying the ordinary meaning of the words used in the applicable treaty provisions 'in their context', which also comprises (in addition to the text, preamble and annexes) any agreements and instruments relating to the treaty, further taking into account any subsequent agreements, practices and relevant rules of international law applicable in the relations among the parties;
2. exploring the common intentions of the contracting parties as expressed in the agreement, for instance by respecting any special meaning given by the parties to a legal term and resorting, if necessary, to 'supplementary means of interpretation' as provided for in Article 32 VCLT; and
3. looking at the object and purpose of the agreement as agreed in its text and relevant context.

Yet as the parties to a dispute disagree on how to interpret the textual and 'extrinsic materials of interpretation' (like subsequent agreements, practices and relevant rules of international law), judicial interpretations often depend on clarifying the 'jurisprudential' and 'doctrinal principles' underlying the relevant treaty rules through 'judicial administration of justice' and due process of law. If the 'legislative branch' of an international organization (like the WTO) is no longer capable of adjusting the treaty rules to new regulatory challenges (like climate change prevention), judicial interpretations and dispute settlements must explain and justify their legal and judicial methodologies even more carefully and convincingly.

D. Need for Normative and Empirical Review of Legal Methodologies

As explained in section V of this Introduction, in order to understand the changing structures and regulatory challenges of international law and multilevel governance, this study focuses on legal methodology problems in UN,

[11] On these tensions between bilateral and communitarian approaches in applying international rules on treaty interpretation, treaty conflicts, 'evolutionary' and 'systemic interpretations' of 'incomplete agreements', see E Cannizzaro (ed), *The Law of Treaties Beyond the Vienna Convention* (Oxford, OUP 2011). On the neglect of 'constitutional interpretations' in WTO dispute settlement practices, see I Van Damme, *Treaty Interpretation by the WTO Appellate Body* (Oxford, OUP 2009) 92, 109. On the 'systemic integration principle' (Article 31:3(c) VCLT) complementing 'supplementary means of interpretation' and subsequent practice as a means of interpretation in WTO jurisprudence, see also AH Qureshi, *Interpreting WTO Agreements. Problems and Perspectives*, 2nd edn (Cambridge, CUP, 2015) 48, 145.

WTO and European law from both normative and consequentialist perspectives. Chapter 1 discusses how the universal recognition of human rights and of 'multilevel constitutionalism' affects not only the 'primary rules of conduct' in international law, but also the international and national 'secondary rules of recognition, change and adjudication', for instance by requiring interpretation of state-centered 'principles of justice' (like 'necessity' and 'proportionality') in conformity with person-centered 'principles of justice' (like human rights and 'access to justice'). Chapter 2 applies economic and other consequentialist methods of social sciences for evaluating multilevel regulation of the three main types of international 'policy externalities':

— *coordination problems* calling for coordinated policy responses to specific policy concerns in order to enhance mutual welfare through 'positive externalities' (eg by internationally agreed product and production standards reducing transaction costs in the international division of labour);
— *cooperation problems* calling for more efficient, international rules and institutions limiting harmful 'negative externalities' (eg caused by inadequate national regulation of bankruptcies in the financial sector, harmful tax competition, environmental pollution or international terrorism); and
— *global PGs* as a special coordination problem if the benefits of regulatory measures are non-rival and non-excludable (eg limitations on overfishing, on ozone-depleting measures or on carbon emissions aimed at protecting 'global common resources'). Public goods entail collective action problems such as incentives for free-riding and for sub-optimal production of PGs (like prevention of global warming). 'Public bads' involve overproduction of 'negative externalities' (eg pollution) that are not 'internalized' (eg not reflected in prices).

Chapter 1 explains from normative and empirical perspectives why the universal recognition of human and constitutional rights (including also freedom of contract, private property rights and private arbitration) as 'positive law' requires 'normative bottom-up review' of state-centered rules and institutions from the point of view of reasonable citizens and their individual and democratic rights (eg as 'agents of justice', 'constituent powers', 'democratic principals' of governance agents with limited 'constituted powers', main economic and 'republican actors' in the global division of labour). 'Human rights', 'rule of law', 'democracy', 'sovereignty' and other 'principles of justice' (like non-discrimination, equality, necessity, proportionality) referred to in UN law and EU law remain indeterminate concepts. Their legal clarification may legitimately differ depending on the respective value premises, legal methodologies and legal contexts. The governance challenges resulting from globalization require review of path-dependent jurisprudential, doctrinal and judicial methodologies; regulators may learn more from the multilevel, instrumental use of law in European integration than from the different experiences in federal democracies (like Australia, Canada, India and the USA).[12] This study uses the term 'constitutionalism' both for:

a) the *normative proposition* that law and governance—in order to be accepted by citizens as legitimate and voluntarily complied with—need to be justified vis-à-vis citizens through agreed principles, rules and institutions of a higher legal rank that must be transformed into constitutional and democratic legislation, administration, adjudication, international 'PGs treaties' and 'public reason', so as to induce citizens to cooperate peacefully in the collective supply of PGs; and
b) the '*six-stage constitutionalization processes*' of law and governance by transformation of (i) agreed 'principles of justice' (eg in the US Declaration of Independence of 1776, the Universal Declaration of Human Rights of 1948) into (ii) constitutional, (iii) legislative, (iv) administrative, (v) judicial and (vi) international rules and institutions that protect equal rights of citizens and promote 'constitutional mind-sets' limiting rational egoism by 'constitutionalizing' law and governance.[13]

[12] Cf M Cappelletti, M Seccombe and J Weiler (eds), *Integration through Law*, vols 1 and 2 (Berlin, de Gruyter, 1986), who explored lessons from the 'American federal experience' for European integration law; EU Petersmann, *Constitutional Functions and Constitutional Problems of International Economic Law. International and Domestic Foreign Trade Law and Policy in the United States, the European Community and Switzerland* (Fribourg, Fribourg UP/Boulder, CO, Westview Press, 1991) (exploring lessons from the common market regulations in the liberal 18th-century US Constitution, the 19th-century Swiss Constitution, the 20th-century post-war German Constitution and EU law for multilevel regulation of international trade). This study focuses on 'legal integration through multilevel protection of PGs' rather than on the 'integration through law' paradigm as recently revisited by D Augenstein, *Integration through Law Revisited: The Making of the European Polity* (Aldershot, Ashgate, 2012). As both European law and UN/WTO law face the challenge to protect transnational PGs more effectively for the benefit of citizens and their constitutional and human rights, global governance of PGs can learn from the European experiences of limiting the legitimacy deficits of international regulation by multilevel protection of constitutional rights, rule of law, democracy and distributive justice (eg through social rights and a 'social market economy'). The failures of the EU projects to adopt a 'European Constitution' and 'European Civil Code' reflect the criticism that the EU commitment to 'creating an ever closer union among the peoples of Europe' (Art 1 TEU) no longer reflects the view of many EU citizens.

[13] Both propositions—a) + b)—are based on interpretations of the *positive law* of constitutional democracies (like the USA and EU member states) and of transnational 'treaty constitutions'. The additional claim of this study—that modern constitutional democracies have a historical record of protecting PGs for the benefit of their citizens more effectively than non-democracies—is a different empirical claim. The terms 'constitution' and 'constitutionalism' are used differently in legal and political philosophies; Kant, for instance, postulated 'cosmopolitan rights' (eg to visit other countries and communicate with their citizens) that were expected to promote transnational cooperation among 'cosmopolitan citizens' and contribute to the progressive emergence of a 'cosmopolitan constitution'; cf J Bohman and M Lutz-Bachmann (eds), *Perpetual Peace. Essays on Kant's Cosmopolitan Ideal* (Cambridge, MA, MIT Press, 1997). My discussion of 'principles of justice' in international law (see ch 1) is, likewise, based on *positive international law* (eg UN human rights law) rather than on Kantian

This dynamic process of 'constitutionalization' may start with exceptional 'constitutional conventions' elaborating constitutional documents codifying 'constitutional contracts' among citizens in the name of 'We the people'. 'Constitutionalization' and related exercises of 'constitutive power' may, however, also be initiated *ex post*, for instance by jurisprudence and judicial interpretations of rules that are subsequently accepted as higher constitutional law (eg EU member states, their national peoples and citizens accepting ECJ jurisprudence as clarifying constitutional principles in EU law). This is often so in less-developed countries that initially rejected human rights as 'Western ideas' before their own peoples insisted on adopting democratic Constitutions, ratifying UN human rights conventions and 'constitutionalizing' authoritarian government practices. Formalistic claims that 'constituent power' can only be exercised by 'We the people' for creating a *national Republic*, which subsequently consents to 'international law among states', are neither theoretically nor empirically convincing: the US Declaration of Independence (1776), for instance, justified the right to abolish unjust government by 'certain unalienable rights of all men' and 'the right of the people ... to institute new government' on universalizable grounds that were equally applicable to citizens and peoples outside the USA. The German 'Basic Law' (1949) and its extension to eastern German states following the fall of the Berlin Wall (1989) were adopted in the context of international agreements (eg with the Allied Powers preceding approval of the Basic Law in 1949, the 1990 German Reunification Treaty between West and East Germany) that were subsequently validated by the peoples through legitimate exercises of constitutional power. Regardless of whether the 'international community' is construed—like the European Community—as consisting no longer only of states but also of non-governmental and intergovernmental organizations, peoples and citizens, the universal recognition of human rights also requires exercise of legitimate 'constituent powers' for justifying international law (eg in the case of withdrawal from the EU pursuant to Article 50 TEU and the related termination of EU guarantees of fundamental rights in the jurisdiction concerned).

moral 'duties of justice' to promote 'constitutional justice' by setting up institutions that recognize and protect the equal status of all persons. Also, my assumption that 'global democracy' remains a utopia and that multilevel *governance* must be legally organized differently from *democratic governments*, is not inconsistent with the positive law argument in this study that, in the 21st century, the legitimacy of all multilevel governance institutions should be derived from respect for the 'inalienable human rights' of citizens and the corresponding obligations of all UN member states. As discussed in ch 1, even though European and UN human rights law also protect 'democratic rights', these rights have not prevented non-democratic governance in many UN member states and international institutions.

E. Empirical Case Studies and Policy Conclusions

Chapters 1 and 2 engage in case studies of the 'six-stage constitutionalization processes' of transnational PGs, to examine why internationally agreed principles of justice (eg health rights protected in UN human rights law and WHO law) are so often inadequately protected in constitutional laws, democratic legislation, administration, adjudication and international regulation (eg of tobacco consumption and other health pandemics):

— Chapter 1, sections II–IV examine the impact of 'human rights constitutionalism' on treaty interpretation, multilevel adjudication, the 'principles of justice' and the 'rules of recognition' underlying international law.
— Chapter 1, section III uses the examples of international investment law and multilevel economic adjudication to illustrate how multilevel 'republican constitutionalism' can justify 'legal fragmentation' as an instrument for rights-based reforms and 'reintegration' of international investment law and related adjudication.
— Chapter 1, section IV illustrates the growing impact of democratic and 'cosmopolitan constitutionalism' on European integration law in order to better 'reconnect' citizens and the peoples as 'constituent powers' with the limited 'constituted powers' of multilevel governance institutions to protect PGs (like the EU's common market).
— Chapter 1, section V uses the example of the EU's 'cosmopolitan foreign policy constitution' to illustrate why 'constitutionalization' of discretionary foreign policy powers has failed if national and international courts of justice do not protect the rights of citizens and transnational rule of law.
— Chapter 1, section VI concludes that the legitimacy of international law and of multilevel governance of transnational 'aggregate PGs' depends on embedding constitutional democracies into multilevel republican and cosmopolitan constitutionalism, limiting 'Hobbesian interpretations' of foreign policy powers and 'collective action problems' in multilevel governance through stronger protection of constitutional rights and judicial remedies of citizens.

Chapter 2 offers additional social science analyses (eg applying economic and 'public choice' methods to legal analyses as proposed by 'law and economics') of how international law constitutes, limits, regulates and justifies multilevel governance of 'aggregate PGs':

— Chapter 2, sections I–II use economic and political 'PGs theories' for analysing multilevel trade and environmental governance of PGs.
— Chapter 2, section III examines multilevel health regulation and adjudication in the context of the WHO Framework Convention on Tobacco Control (FCTC).

— Chapter 2, section IV explains why the EU negotiations on 'transformative' transatlantic free trade agreements risk undermining the 'cosmopolitan principles' that the Lisbon Treaty prescribes for EU external relations (eg in Articles 3, 21 TEU).
— Chapter 2, section V describes how national and international courts of justice should use their 'constitutional mandates' to protect transnational PGs in the context of multilevel judicial protection of cosmopolitan and republican rights and remedies.

The empirical case studies proceed from 'methodological individualism', ie the assumptions that (i) rational individuals seek to maximize the achievement of their preferences, and (ii) the only valid source of preferences (values) is individuals.[14] Rational pursuit of individual self-interests by private and public actors (eg of politicians pursuing their political re-election) often conflicts with 'public reason' and 'social welfare' as defined by human rights, constitutional law and impartial adjudication limiting rational pursuit of self-interests. Moreover, the normative premises of welfare economics (eg that under perfect competition and absent transaction costs the market allocates resources efficiently) often do not exist in real-world conditions without perfect competition. Hence, 'positive economic analyses' of human behaviour must be supplemented by political science, legal sociology and social psychology analyses of how law and social institutions affect human behaviour. For instance, economic analyses are about efficient realization of existing preferences in certain circumstances; yet they do not offer objective standards for evaluating these preferences (eg to benefit from global economic integration) that may conflict with other preferences (eg to maintain individual and national autonomy and democratic self-governance).

Chapter 3 concludes by explaining why 'civilizing' and 'constitutionalizing disconnected governance' of transnational PGs in UN, WTO, European and national institutions requires stronger legal and judicial protection of state citizens, transnational 'market citizens' and 'cosmopolitan citizens' in multilevel PGs regimes, notably by linking the functional constitution, limitation, regulation and justification of multilevel governance institutions through international treaties to the empowering, limiting, regulatory and justificatory functions of constitutional and cosmopolitan rights (Chapter 3, section I). There are good reasons why constitutional democracies and national and international courts of justice increasingly integrate the competing conceptions of international economic regulation as (i) public international law, (ii) global administrative law, (iii) international private law, (iv) multilevel economic regulation or (v) multilevel constitutional law

[14] On the use of 'law and economics tools' for analysing international law, see J Trachtman, *The Economic Structure of International Law* (Cambridge, MA, Harvard UP, 2008).

in order to protect citizens as 'constituent powers', 'democratic principals' and 'agents of justice', who must hold all multilevel governance legally, democratically and judicially more accountable. Comparative 'positive' (ie descriptive) legal and economic analyses of competing 'PGs regimes' (eg national 'PGs regimes' in democratic and non-democratic countries, multilevel economic, health, environmental and related legal regulation and adjudication in different regional and worldwide legal regimes) confirm that the existing allocation of governmental authority does not maximize efficient protection of agreed PGs. Hence, this study also uses the historical experiences with 'democratic, republican and cosmopolitan constitutionalism' for advocating legal and policy changes in order to empower citizens and their democratic institutions and 'courts of justice' to protect more effectively equal individual liberties (eg as defined by national and international human rights and constitutional rights) and economic preferences (eg for lower prices of good quality goods and services in competitive markets). Further empirical 'cost–benefit analyses' and normative casestudies are needed to support the 'constitutional hypotheses' and policy recommendations in this study.

II. DOES MULTILEVEL GOVERNANCE REQUIRE MULTILEVEL CONSTITUTIONALISM?

This study focuses on multilevel governance of transnational 'aggregate PGs' in the twenty-first century, and draws lessons from the history of democratic, republican and cosmopolitan constitutionalism in Europe and North America for constituting, limiting, regulating and justifying multilevel governance of transnational PGs for the benefit of citizens. Due to this policy-orientated focus on limiting the 'collective action problems' in modern UN, WTO and regional governance of PGs, the study neglects other dimensions of multilevel governance (eg the evolution of state jurisdictions and authoritarian governance in past Greek, Roman, Byzantine, Ottoman, British, Soviet or American empires). In order to evaluate national and international PGs (like human rights, common markets, prevention of health pandemics and of climate change) and related legal regimes, the study combines normative, legal 'bottom-up approaches' with context-specific, empirical case studies. Chapter 1 explains why HRL, constitutional democracies and also UN law require justification of the legitimacy of international law and governance no longer only in terms of 'sovereignty' and the equality of states, but also in terms of human rights, democratic self-government and transnational rule of law for the benefit of citizens as legitimate 'constituent powers', 'agents of justice', 'democratic principals' of governance agents with limited 'constituted powers', main economic and 'republican actors' in multilevel governance of PG. Chapter 2 focuses on empirical case studies of multilevel governance of 'aggregate PGs' like public health, regional and global markets, and protection of the environment. As the interaction between normative and empiricial analyses is crucial for a better understanding of multilevel governance, the study evaluates the case studies (eg of multilevel trade and health governance in the context of UN, WTO and EU law) in the light of the normative standards of HRL and of democratic, republican and cosmopolitan constitutionalism. Chapter 3 summarizes the main policy conclusion, for instance that the transformation of national PGs into transnational aggregate PGs requires supplementing democratic and republican constitutionalism with cosmopolitan constitutionalism in order to constitute, limit, regulate and justify multilevel governance in terms of equal rights and remedies of citizens. In order to render the human rights obligations of all UN member states more effective, the increasing number of 'international PGs treaties' need to be 'constitutionalized' through democratic legislation and judicial protection of fundamental rights, empowering citizens to hold multilevel governance of transnational PGs legally, democratically and judicially accountable.

In their recent bestseller on *The Fourth Revolution—The Global Race to Reinvent the State*, two Anglo-American political analysts justify their call for a 'fourth revolution' on essentially utilitarian grounds:

1. the '*political revolution*' during the sixteenth and seventeenth centuries justified the sovereign state on the basis of a 'Hobbesian social contract', transforming the civil wars among individuals (the 'state of nature') into governmental protection of law and order;
2. the '*democratic revolution*' during the eighteenth and nineteenth centuries advocated the need for protecting equal freedoms against unjustified governmental restrictions;
3. the '*social revolution*' in politics during the twentieth century aimed at protecting social welfare inside nation states and beyond (eg through labour laws, human rights and decolonization);
4. the '*fourth revolution*' must 'reinvent' national governance and the state in the twenty-first century in response to globalization (eg global communication technologies). It needs to review the past regulatory paradigms, such as Hobbes's ideal of authoritarian order, Mill's ideal of a liberal state, and the 'lost paradise' of socialist ideals of globalizing welfare states. In order to limit majoritarian interest group politics and protect the liberty of citizens also in transnational cooperation, the two political analysts emphasize the need for 'handing over some powers to technocrats and others to micropowers' like local governments.[15]

[15] J Micklethwait and A Wooldridge, *The Fourth Revolution. The Global Race to Reinvent the State* (London, Penguin Books, 2014) 266 f.

> Yet even though 'this revolution is about liberty and the rights of the individual',[16] the needed changes in national, regional and worldwide *legal systems* are not discussed, possibly also in view of the unpopularity of human rights discourse in 'realist' foreign policies of hegemonic countries.[17]

This book offers the first *legal monograph* exploring—from historical, legal, political and economic perspectives—the relationships between constitutional democracies, republican constitutionalism and cosmopolitan constitutionalism in multilevel governance of transnational aggregate PGs. It argues that 'globalization' and its transformation of many national into transnational PGs require embedding 'democratic constitutionalism' into multilevel republican and 'cosmopolitan constitutionalism', in order to constitute, limit, regulate and justify multilevel governance institutions more effectively for the benefit of citizens and their human and constitutional rights. Historically, democratic constitutionalism (since the ancient 'Constitution of Athens'), republican constitutionalism (since the ancient Roman, Florentine and Venetian republics) and cosmopolitanism focused on different values, like democratic governance, collective supply of PGs (like Roman private law and its transformation into a *jus commune* in Europe), and the equal moral rights and duties of all human beings. Each of these approaches to 'constitutionalism' (eg in the sense of legal prioritization of agreed 'principles of justice' and their collective transformation into legislation, administration, adjudication and multilevel governance) prioritized different values (eg democratic participation of male property owners in the ancient Athenian democracy, aristocratic protection of public goods for the benefit of Roman citizens, protection of 'inalienable human rights') and entailed different forms of distribution of welfare gains. Following the return to humanism in the Renaissance and in 'enlightenment philosophies' of man (as illustrated by the focus on the dignity of man founded on man's freedom and reasonableness in the Renaissance philosophy of Pico della Mirandola and the enlightenment philosophy of Kant),[18] the increasingly universal recognition of human rights entailed the emergence of ever more 'constitutional democracies' that protect human and constitutional rights, the rule of law and other PGs demanded by citizens in more integrated and more effective ways than non-democratic governance regimes. Yet extending 'constitutional democracy' beyond states has proven difficult, for instance in view of the lack of a 'transnational *demos*', the inadequate

[16] *Ibid*, 270.

[17] Cf J Peck, *Ideal Illusions: How the US Government Co-Opted Human Rights* (New York, Metropolitan Books, 2010).

[18] Cf E Cassirer, PO Kristeller and JH Randall (eds), *The Reniassance Philosphy of Man* (Chicago, IL, Chicago University Press, 1956).

constitutional restraints of many multilevel governance institutions and the reality of intergovernmental power politics (eg in UN and WTO institutions) resisting citizen-orientated proposals for multilevel *demoi-cracy*. Also the multilevel 'human rights constitutionalism' based on national, regional and UN human rights conventions and functionally limited, international 'treaty constitutions'—like the 1919 Constitution (*sic*) establishing the International Labour Organization—has failed to protect human rights effectively in many parts of the world, notably in Africa and Asia.[19]

A. From 'National Governments' to Multilevel Governance of Global Public Goods

The term 'governance' (*gubernare*, meaning 'to steer' and 'to regulate') refers to the image of steering a ship (eg the 'state ship') and the method by which organized society directs, influences and coordinates public and private activities to supply goods and services. Even inside states with a centralized government authority controlling the state, there are many diverse forms of indirect and decentralized governance (eg through market competition, judicial litigation), centralized governance (eg through hierarchically structured governments, courts and regulatory agencies), multilevel governance (eg in federal states) and 'mixed' governance (eg network governance, public-private partnerships). National governments operate through rule systems, institutions, sub-delegation of powers (eg to 'trusteeship institutions' like central banks and international courts of justice), 'co-optation' of NGOs, 'orchestration' of decentralized supply of PGs (like international criminal justice, climate change prevention), and continuous adjustment of rules and policies in response to demands by civil society. Governance differs from government by its different performance of government functions and its coordination of social relations without a unifying authority (eg decentralized performance of information, allocation, coordination and sanctioning functions through market competition and intergovernmental network cooperation). These governance structures and processes tend to differ among policy areas, and depend on the respective constitutional and political systems of states.[20]

[19] For instance, the 'Arab Charter on Human Rights' (2008) and the ASEAN Human Rights Declaration (2012) have been criticized for protecting human rights only selectively without providing for effective judicial remedies, and for systemic monitoring of national implementing legislation. Also the African Court for Human and Peoples Rights—which was established by a Protocol to the African Charter on Human and Peoples Rights (in effect since 1986)—came into being only in 2004 and delivered its first judgment on the merits only in 2009.

[20] Cf EU Petersmann, 'Framework of Analysis: Towards Multilayered Governance in Monetary Affairs' in T Cottier, RM Lastra and C Tietje (eds), *The Rule of Law in Monetary Affairs* (Cambridge, CUP, 2014) 434–61.

Also in democratic states with a central government authority representing the 'nation state' as a legal person under international law, governance remains a 'multilevel task' involving citizens (eg as 'constituent powers', 'democratic principals' and 'agents of justice'), legislative, executive and judicial governance institutions with delegated 'constituted powers', and diverse 'third party intermediaries' (like political parties, the media, business, trade unions and other NGOs) participating in indirect and decentralized forms of governance. 'Principal-agent theories' emphasize that 'delegation' of governance powers (eg to legislative, executive and judicial institutions, independent regulatory agencies)—even if necessary for enhancing the 'governance capacities' of the 'governors' through use of decentralized information, specialized expertise, additional resources and credible commitments (eg to avoidance of inflation through central bank autonomy)—entails 'principal-agent problems' (eg of limited *ex ante* and *ex post* control of governance 'agents' by their 'principals', diverging goals of agents, choices among alternative governance modalities); they require legal regulation in order to limit 'agency costs' and 'governance failures'. Due to globalization, not only do the levels of legal regulation, 'government dilemmas' (eg security risks) and multilevel forms of governance continue to multiply, for instance in view of the enhanced capacities of citizens to circumvent national regulations (say, through the Internet, by means of relocating business to 'tax havens' for purposes of tax avoidance, relocation of polluting production abroad to countries with less stringent environmental regulations), but also the substantive regulatory challenges change, for instance due to the globalization of production through global supply chains of goods and services, and the increasing move from trade liberalization to international regulatory cooperation on economic and non-economic issues. Globalization may increase the regulatory autonomy of non-governmental actors (like transnational corporations (TNCs)), but it limits the regulatory autonomy of states and their democratic governance. The more transnational PGs (like the global division of labour) are regulated through international treaties rather than through national legislation, the more difficult becomes inclusive, democratic participation in multilevel governance, regulation and rule implementation. The 2007 Lisbon Treaty responded to the multilevel governance challenges by committing the EU to 'strict observance of international law' and 'protection of its citizens' and their human rights in the external relations of the EU (Article 3 TEU). Yet the Comprehensive Economic and Trade Agreement (CETA) between the EU and Canada was negotiated from 2009 until September 2014 in almost complete secrecy. The public fears of intergovernmental interest group politics have increased civil society opposition to the EU–US Transatlantic Trade and Investment Partnership (TTIP) since 2013; this induced the EU Commission to announce, in 2015, a new 'transparency strategy' for international economic agreements, so as to enhance parliamentary and democratic support of such 'PGs treaties'. The complaints raised in the 'public consultations' of EU citizens—eg of inadequate accountability of 'insiders' (like commercial arbitrators in secretive investor-state arbitration), 'information asymmetries' disadvantaging 'outsiders' (like taxpayers affected by investor-state arbitration), and risks of corruption (eg in order to be included in 'stakeholder meetings' with treaty negotiators so as to obtain 'strategic information' and influence rule-making)—forced the EU's political institutions to change their legal positions in the CETA and TTIP negotiations on investor-state dispute settlement (ISDS). Parliamentary *ex post* consideration of draft agreements secretly elaborated among governments during many years of negotiations (eg US 'fast track procedures' allowing for only 'yes' or 'no' votes) is increasingly criticized as coming too late for effective democratic involvement.

The more parliamentary democracy reveals itself as being ineffective in multilevel governance of global PGs without a single *demos*, the more the supplementary forms of constitutional, participatory and deliberative democracy must be extended beyond state borders. As discussed in Chapter 2, empirical evidence confirms that *multilevel republican* and *cosmopolitan constitutionalism*—by empowering citizens through civil, political, economic, social and cultural rights and remedies to hold multilevel governance institutions legally, democratically and judicially accountable—have protected PGs more effectively (eg in European economic and constitutional law and HRL, international commercial and investment law and arbitration, international criminal law) than path-dependent forms of intergovernmental power politics.

B. Constitutional Principles of Conferral, Subsidiarity, Proportionality and Justice

National and international societies enable individuals to increase their welfare through mutually beneficial cooperation and the creation of organizations (eg private firms, states and international organizations). From this economic perspective, national and international markets and legal systems emerge from interactions among utility-maximizing individuals, firms and governments exercising, coordinating and limiting their respective freedoms and power through welfare-enhancing contracts and agreements establishing institutions (eg property rights, governance institutions, judicial and state jurisdictions) so as to facilitate transactions and the efficient achievement of preferences. For instance, private and public actors (eg states as mediators of private and public interests) negotiate international rules, institutions and transfers of authority in order to maximize the participants' net gains (eg 'Kaldor-Hicks efficiency' resulting from economies of scale and scope).

Reasonable actors are likely to prefer international rules only in sectors and at efficient 'subsidiary levels' of regulation that enhance their individual welfare, for instance by mitigating collective action problems in collective supply of PGs by redistributive measures. Public choice theory emphasizes that—as organizations have no rationality of their own—government actors (politicians, bureaucrats) are likely to maximize their own interests (eg in political support, limited accountability) rather than the reasonable preferences of the citizenry. Yet even if government officials aim at maximizing their own 'political welfare' rather than 'public welfare' (say, in terms of general consumer welfare or voter welfare), and international trade, financial, environmental and tax regulation are influenced by the political search for domestic policy coalitions, the search for efficiency remains an important objective. Domestic politics and inadequate constitutional restraints and accountability may explain why politicians favour economically suboptimal rules, for instance subsidies and reciprocally agreed rather than unilateral trade liberalization, in order to please domestic lobbies and strengthen domestic political coalitions through reciprocal export opportunities that induce domestic export industries to politically support domestic politics for import liberalization. Constitutional and economic theories postulate that—as states are instruments for promoting the welfare of their citizens—reasonable citizens will engage in transnational cooperation and delegate powers to international institutions only subject to principles of conferral (ie limited delegation of power to restrict individual rights), subsidiarity (ie delegation of powers to restrict individual freedoms only to the extent necessary for achieving individual preferences more efficiently) and proportionality (eg authorization of only least-restrictive governmental measures that avoid disproportionate restrictions of equal rights of citizens). Article 5 TEU explicitly incorporates these national constitutional principles into EU law:

1. The limits of Union competences are governed by the principle of conferral. The use of Union competences is governed by the principles of subsidiarity and proportionality.
2. Under the principle of conferral, the Union shall act within the limits of the competences conferred upon it by the Member States in the Treaties to attain the objectives set out therein. Competences not conferred upon the Union in the Treaties remain with the Member States.
3. Under the principle of subsidiarity, in areas which do not fall within its exclusive competence, the Union shall act only if and in so far as the objectives of the proposed action cannot be sufficiently achieved by the Member States, either at central level or at regional and local level, but can rather, by reason of the scale or effects of the proposed action, be better achieved at Union level. The institutions of the Union shall apply the principle of subsidiarity as laid down in the Protocol on the application of the principles of subsidiarity and proportionality. National Parliaments ensure compliance with the principle of subsidiarity in accordance with the procedure set out in that Protocol.
4. Under the principle of proportionality, the content and form of Union action shall not exceed what is necessary to achieve the objectives of the Treaties ...

As discussed in Chapter 1, the principles of conferral, subsidiarity and proportionality pertain to the need for *constitutional justice* and *distributive justice* that must be distinguished from questions of *commutative* and *corrective justice* and of *equity* in relations among individuals, peoples and states.

This study argues that adjusting national constitutionalism to the reality of multilevel governance requires integrating the complementary republican, democratic and cosmopolitan constitutional traditions into new kinds of 'multilevel constitutionalism' with due respect for the legitimate reality of 'constitutional pluralism', as illustrated by the very diverse forms of European integration law (as discussed in Chapter 2) based on:

— 'multilevel constitutional *demoi*-cracy' (eg among the 28 EU member states);
— more deferential forms of 'multilevel cosmopolitan democracy' respecting the 'dualist constitutional traditions' in some of the member states of the EEA (like the Nordic EEA member states Iceland and Norway);
— respect for 'direct popular democracy' in Switzerland (whose population rejected membership of both the EU and the EEA); and
— authoritarian forms of governance in some other member states of the Council of Europe and of its ECHR, like Turkey and Russia.

Similar to the experiences inside constitutional democracies, multilevel republican and cosmopolitan constitutionalism can compensate 'democracy deficits' in UN, WTO and regional governance by committing multilevel governance agents to republican PGs (like the rule of law), corresponding cosmopolitan rights (like individual judicial remedies) and to respect for diverse democratic preferences (eg to withdraw from EU membership pursuant to Article 50 TEU). Even if—as inside the EU—'democratic principles' (as defined in Articles 9–12 TEU) have become legally protected in regional integration law, additional constitutional commitments to specific PGs (as defined in numerous EU treaty provisions) and to cosmopolitan rights (eg as protected in the EU Charter of Fundamental Rights and in the jurisprudence of EU courts) can render multilevel governance of PGs more legitimate and more effective. Empirical comparisons of Europe's functionally limited 'multilevel republican constitutionalism'—for example, for the common market of the 31 EEA member states, the monetary union among 19 Eurozone member states, and the 'area of freedom, security and justice' among the 28 EU member states—seem to confirm the proposition of this study that protecting democratically defined, transnational 'aggregate PGs' in terms of democratic, republican and cosmopolitan rights can set incentives for 'republican support' by citizens and for holding multilevel governance institutions more accountable for 'market failures' (eg challenged through decentralized enforcement of common market and competition rules by private economic actors and citizens in domestic and European courts) as well as for 'governance failures' (eg challenged by citizens in national and European courts).

Yet constitutional principles of distributive, commutative, corrective justice and equity remain contested in multilevel governance of PGs (eg due to discrimination of former colonies in the post-World War II Bretton Woods and GATT practices). The universal recognition of human rights and the needed 'institutionalization of public reason' in the twenty-first century require 'constitutional' treaty interpretations and stronger judicial protection of individual rights of citizens—as 'agents of justice', 'constituent powers', 'democratic principals', and main economic and republican actors—in multilevel governance of PGs, as discussed in Chapter 1. While some global institutions have become more representative of the global changes in governance systems (like the G20 and the WTO), reforms of others (like the UN Security Council, IMF governance institutions) have been prevented by the self-interests of 'insiders' to share their veto powers with 'outsiders'.[21] The challenge of also 'constitutionalizing' public-private partnerships in multilevel governance (eg the 'corporate social responsibilities' and human rights obligations of non-governmental actors) requires functionally limited 'republican' and 'cosmopolitan' constitutionalism in order to empower citizens to hold multilevel governance institutions more accountable. Even where such constitutional reforms have been prevented by power politics (eg in the UN Security Council), there is a need for pragmatic 'piecemeal responses' to the legitimacy deficits in multilevel governance, as illustrated by the decentralization of global governance tasks (eg by means of humanitarian interventions by regional security systems) and by the 'transparency initiatives' in European governance, as discussed in Chapter 2. European constitutionalism suggests that the 'micro-economic common market constitution' of the EU and the EEA and the 'multilevel human rights constitution' of the ECHR were more successful in protecting equal rights of citizens and the rule of law across state borders than efforts at constitutionalizing the EU's 'monetary constitution' and 'security constitution'.[22] Also in UN and WTO governance, constitutionalization of specific decision-making institutions (like the ICJ and the WTO Appellate Body) has been easier to achieve than that of the 'macro-dimensions' of global governance (like democratic participation of citizens and parliaments in multilevel governance and its democratic control and accountability).[23] Since there is no single

[21] For instance, the amendments of the Agreement establishing the IMF providing for larger voting rights of China and other developing countries were approved by the US Senate only in December 2015.

[22] Cf K Tuori, *European Constitutionalism* (Cambridge, CUP, 2015) ch 5.

[23] Cf C Caroll and E Bécault, 'Global governance and the challenge of diversity' in J Wouters *et al* (eds), *Global Governance and Democracy. A Multidisciplinary Analysis* (Cheltenham, Elgar, 2015) 191–225.

demos legitimating global governance arrangements, this study argues in favour of bottom-up approaches to improving democratic participation and accountability in global governance, so as to limit the democratic deficits of political representativeness in intergovernmental rule-making and bring multilevel governance closer to the citizens and to affected stake-holders.

C. From National to Multilevel Constitutional Restraints of Governance

The plurality of private and public, national and transnational legal orders and legally constituted governance authorities inside and beyond states raises the question of how multilevel, overlapping governance powers (eg to restrict the freedom of citizens and other actors) can be legally justified, coordinated and controlled so as to limit abuses of power and promote voluntary compliance with rules and 'rulers' that are recognized as legally and morally 'legitimated'. This study avoids exploring utopias like 'global constitutionalism' and 'global democracy'. It proceeds from the *normative premise*—as empirically confirmed by the history of republican and democratic constitutionalism—that the universal recognition of human rights (eg in national Constitutions and UN law) calls for citizen-driven 'discourse justifications' of law and governance and 'bottom-up struggles' for extending the 'trias' underlying constitutional democracies (ie human and constitutional rights, rule of law, democratic governance) to multilevel governance of transnational 'aggregate PGs' (like the world trading system) in order to justify international law and institutions vis-à-vis citizens. European integration law confirms that republican, democratic and 'cosmopolitan constitutionalism' can also succeed in 'constitutionalizing' *multilevel governance* of transnational PGs like the European common market. The Lisbon Treaty provisions on 'democratic principles' (Articles 9 et seq TEU) illustrate the need for supplementing parliamentary democracies by multilevel participatory, deliberative and representative, democratic governance and cosmopolitan rights beyond state borders, with due respect for the constitutional principles of conferral, subsidiarity, proportionality and the rule of law (cf Article 5 TEU). The EU's 'cosmopolitan foreign policy constitution' (eg based on Articles 2, 3, 21 TEU and the EUCFR) extends the same constitutional principles to the EU's external relations; yet it has failed to effectively 'constitutionalize' most external agreements of the EU, with the notable exception of the EEA. Chapters 1 and 2 argue that this 'constitutional failure' is due to 'governance failures' of EU institutions, such as:

- their non-compliance with 'strict observance of international law' (as required by Article 3 TEU) and with judicial protection of the rule of law (as required, for example, by Articles 2, 19 and 21 TEU);

- their authoritarian 'disempowerment' of EU citizens in international trade and investment agreements, by intergovernmental exclusion of private rights and remedies (contrary to the Article 3 TEU requirement of 'protection of its citizens' in EU external relations);
- the non-transparent and non-inclusive 'executive dominance' in external relations that often circumvents effective parliamentary, democratic and judicial control;[24] and
- the decreasing legitimacy and 'democratic support' by EU citizens of certain EU practices, such as EU import restrictions on bananas in violation of GATT/WTO obligations (1992–2012), persistent violations of EU budget and debt disciplines by some Eurozone member states since 2010, and, more recently, treatment of foreign migrants and asylum seekers in violation of the 'Schengen' and 'Dublin rules' agreed among EU member states.

From the perspective of national and European 'constitutionalism' (eg in the sense of national and European constitutional restraints on governance powers so as to protect the EU's constitutional 'values' as defined in Article 2 TEU), such 'constitutional failures' reflect inadequate 'constitutionalization', for instance in the sense of ineffective transformation of national and EU 'constitutional principles' into multilevel legislation, administration, and judicial and democratic protection of human and constitutional rights of EU citizens. How should reasonable citizens—as 'democratic principals' of all multilevel 'governance agents'—respond to such 'constitutional' and 'governance failures' in order to better protect the agreed 'constitutional principles', 'policy objectives' and PGs demanded by them? Why has the WTO legal and trading system proved to be so 'resilient' (eg as illustrated by its more than 500 WTO dispute settlement procedures since 1995), in spite of the failure of WTO members to conclude their Doha Round negotiations since 2001? As international legal regimes may not offer clear solutions to unforeseen crises (like the fiscal and debt deficits of Euro-member states triggering the 'Euro crises' since 2010), which properties and features of multilevel legal regimes facilitate speedy adjustment measures and problem-solving? Are private law systems more flexible (eg due to their decentralized incentive structures) and national public law systems more capable of speedy adjustments than public international law regimes based on state consent

[24] For instance, the EU's non-compliance with 'strict observance of international law' and 'dis-empowerment' of citizens in free trade agreements have only rarely been challenged by national parliaments and the European Parliament. A recent example of the European Parliament rejecting EU Commission proposals for violating WTO obligations related to the disapproval—on 28 October 2015—of a draft regulation giving EU member states the power to ban the use of genetically modified food ingredients even if such genetically modified organisms (GMOs) had been approved by the EU's risk-assessment procedures.

and veto-powers? What are the legitimate powers of courts of justice to clarify and develop indeterminate principles (like 'fair and equitable treatment' requirements in international investment law) and incomplete rules of international law, even against the will of individual states, for instance on the basis of 'principles of justice' (like transparent exercise of public authority) that are part of the domestic legal systems of the states concerned?

D. Normative and Empirical Hypotheses and Five Policy Propositions of this Study

In order to limit 'governance failures' and protect equal rights of citizens and PGs more effectively beyond national borders, this study calls for stronger 'republican' and 'cosmopolitan' constitutionalism in constituting, limiting, regulating and justifying regional, UN and WTO governance of transnational PGs. There is vast sociological evidence supporting the normative hypothesis of this study that globalization requires 'embedding' constitutional democracies into multilevel republican and cosmopolitan constitutionalism protecting transnational PGs by empowering citizens, national parliaments and courts of justice to hold multilevel governance institutions more legally, democratically and judicially accountable. For instance:

— As discussed in Chapter 1, the 'principles of justice' underlying UN law (eg in terms of human rights) are not effectively transformed into UN and WTO governance and institutions.[25] Human rights law also protects individual and democratic diversity, and the legitimate reality of 'constitutional pluralism' at national and international levels of governance (eg diverse '*demoi*-cracies' in the governance of regional common markets in Africa, Europe and Latin America). Yet HRL requires 'constitutionalizing' the 'disconnected UN/WTO governance' in order to limit abuses of powers, protect rights of citizens more effectively, and justify multilevel governance vis-à-vis citizens as 'agents of justice' and 'democratic principals' of all governance institutions.

— As discussed in Chapter 2, multilevel governance of PGs must learn from 'comparative institutionalism' by empirically exploring why certain 'PGs regimes' (such as the compulsory WTO dispute settlement system) have succeeded in protecting transnational PGs more

[25] On the distinction between 'principles' (for maximizing values through a process of weighing and balancing against competing principles) and 'rules' (characterized by 'if-then-commands' which, if applicable, prescribe a precise conduct), see R Alexy, *A Theory of Constitutional Rights* (Oxford, OUP 2002) 44 ff; M Scheinin, 'Core Rights and Obligations' in D Shelton (ed), *The Oxford Handbook of International Human Rights Law* (Oxford, OUP 2013) 532–35.

effectively than other treaty regimes. Parliamentary control of the 'executive dominance' in intergovernmental, worldwide institutions is likely to remain ineffective; hence, cosmopolitan constitutionalism is a necessary substitute for enabling citizens and courts of justice to hold multilevel governance institutions more legally, democratically and judicially accountable. Empirical evidence confirms that 'cosmopolitan PGs regimes'—like international commercial, investment, human rights, criminal law and adjudication, the WHO FCTC, regional common market law in the EU and in the EEA—protect transnational rule of law and equal rights of citizens more effectively (eg through multilevel judicial protection of cosmopolitan rights in regional common markets, free trade areas and human rights courts) than 'disconnected UN/WTO governance' excluding rights of citizens to hold governments accountable by invoking and enforcing UN/WTO rules in domestic courts.

— Chapter 3 concludes that law—as an instrument of social regulation and 'legal culture' whose social effectiveness (the 'law in action') depends on the voluntary acceptance of the 'law in the books' by citizens, peoples, states, intergovernmental and non-governmental actors as being a 'justified' and 'reasonably coherent *legal system*'—must learn from the history of civil society struggles for 'republican constitutionalism' since the ancient Athenian democracy and Roman republic more than 2,400 years ago. The progressive 'constitutionalization' and 'socialization' of legal systems offers important policy lessons for limiting 'collective action problems' in multilevel governance of PGs. Contrary to claims by 'radical pluralists' that 'no coherent normative practice arises from the assumptions on which we identify international law',[26] republican and democratic constitutionalism succeeded not only in 'constitutionalizing' national and European legal systems (like EU common market law and HRL); they also laid the foundations for the post-war emergence of multilevel 'cosmopolitan constitutionalism' (eg multilevel commercial, trade and human rights law and adjudication) that empowers citizens and courts of justice to support transnational rule of law and 'socializes' international legal practices for the benefit of citizens by institutionalizing 'public reason' and multilevel protection of human, economic and constitutional rights.[27]

[26] M Koskenniemi, *From Apologia to Utopia: The Structure of International Legal Argument* (Cambridge, CUP, 2005) 69.

[27] This policy conclusion is in line with the recent studies of how the ICJ has contributed to the convergence and strengthening of international law as a unitary legal system; cf M Andenas and E Bjorge (eds), *A Farewell to Fragmentation: Reassertion and Convergence in International Law* (Cambridge, CUP, 2015).

This study proceeds from the constitutional insight—as already observed in Tocqueville's analysis of *Democracy in America*[28] and advocated much earlier by 'republican constitutionalism'—that individual rights and local, republican institutions are to liberty what primary schools are to education and science: they empower people to develop republican virtues and to actively participate in republican governance, for instance by holding government agents accountable for their failures to protect PGs and by offering citizens 'countervailing rights' against abuses of power and judicial remedies enabling 'struggles for justice'. This Introduction and Chapter 1 draw lessons from the historical civil society struggles—from the ancient Greek constitutional democracies and Roman 'constitutional republicanism', up to the American and French 'human rights revolutions' during the eighteenth century and the post-war recognition of human rights by all UN member states—for transforming the ancient communitarian forms of democratic and republican governance into modern 'human rights constitutionalism' for democratic supply of national PGs. The main claim of this monograph is that—due to globalization and its transformation of most national PGs into transnational aggregate PGs—national constitutionalism must be transformed into 'multilevel constitutionalism', empowering citizens through cosmopolitan rights to hold multilevel governance institutions more accountable for their failures to protect PGs effectively. The 'domestic implementation deficit' is one of the main weaknesses of UN and WTO law; promoting stronger rule of law requires interdisciplinary methodologies in multilevel governance research, as recalled in the famous statement by US Justice Louis Brandeis that 'a lawyer who has not studied economics and sociology is very apt to become a public enemy'; economic resources and incentives, democratic deliberation and persuasion, and republican constitutionalism as a systemic, inclusive approach to 'socializing' and 'constitutionalizing' multilevel governance of PGs are of crucial importance for rendering UN, WTO and regional governance of PGs more effective and more legitimate.

The remainder of this Introduction summarizes the main *five propositions* that are elaborated in this legal study, but which continue to be neglected by lawyers and diplomats, even though they explain many of the 'failures' in UN and WTO governance. It concludes (in section V) with an overview of the legal methodology challenges of moving from 'constitutional nationalism' for collective supply of national PGs to functionally limited, multilevel constitutionalism, constituting, limiting, regulating and justifying multilevel

[28] Cf A de Tocqueville, *Democracy in America*, vol II (JP Mayer ed, London, Fontana Press, 1994 reprint of the 1840 edn) 63.

governance of transnational 'aggregate PGs' more effectively and more coherently for the benefit of citizens.

Proposition 1: Globalization Requires Extending Democratic, Republican and Cosmopolitan Constitutionalism to Multilevel Governance of Public Goods

Since the ancient, democratic Constitution of Athens (eg as discussed by Plato and Aristotle) and the republican Constitution of ancient Rome (eg as discussed by Polybius and Cicero), the evolution of law and politics in Europe has been influenced by civil society struggles for improving democratic and republican constitutionalism in order to protect PGs for the benefit of citizens. Modern globalization transforms *national* into *transnational PGs*, whose collective supply depends on international law and institutions. This study explains why the more the 'collective action problems' in multilevel governance of transnational 'aggregate PGs' change, the more national Constitutions reveal themselves as partial, incomplete Constitutions that can protect ever more transnational PGs for the benefit of citizens only by complementary use of multilevel republican and cosmopolitan constitutionalism limiting international law and justifying multilevel governance for the benefit of citizens. Designing such rules and institutions requires reviewing state-centered legal methodologies and taking into account the historical lessons from 'republican constitutionalism' that democratic and cosmopolitan rights of citizens to participate in constitutional, representative, participatory and deliberative 'republican governance' are of constitutional importance for holding governments legally, democratically and judicially more accountable for effective protection of PGs like human rights, the rule of law, democratic governance and limitation of 'market failures' as well as 'governance failures'.

While political and legal PGs theories have been discussed in Europe for more than 2,000 years, economic PGs theories are more recent; integrating political, legal and economic PGs theories and designing multilevel, democratic governance of transnational 'aggregate PGs' remains neglected due to the complexity of their 'horizontal' as well as 'vertical' interdependencies and legally fragmented evolution (eg of monetary, financial, trade, investment, environmental, health, legal, security and human rights regimes at national, regional and worldwide levels of governance). Hence, the first proposition of this study remains very general: globalization requires adjustments to local and national, democratic and republican constitutionalism in order to promote more effective, multilevel governance of transnational 'aggregate PGs' for the benefit of all citizens, whose inalienable human rights, reasonableness, conscience and 'public reason' are the primary sources of democratic legitimation of law and governance in the twenty-first century.

Proposition 2: Human Rights Require Embedding Multilevel Governance of Public Goods into Multilevel Democratic, Republican and Cosmopolitan Constitutionalism

Most international treaties for collective supply of 'aggregate PGs' (like treaties establishing the UN and UN Specialized Agencies, UN human rights treaties) use indeterminate legal concepts and 'incompletely theorized' rules and principles. The customary law rules on interpreting treaties and settling related disputes 'in conformity with the principles of justice and international law', including 'human rights and fundamental freedoms for all' (as recalled in the Preamble to and Article 31 of the VCLT), require clarification of the relevant 'contexts' and 'principles of justice' in order to promote 'public reason' and justify legal and judicial decisions more coherently, especially whenever the text, context, object and purpose of the applicable treaty provision remain ambiguous and contested. The fragmented evolution of PGs regimes means that national and international governance institutions and courts of justice often fail to justify coherently the mutual delimitation of:

- state-centered 'principles of justice' underlying international rules among states;
- citizen-centered 'principles of justice' underlying transnational private and commercial law and also HRL; and
- transnational 'principles of justice' (eg governing concession contracts between states and foreign investors and other transnational 'private-public partnerships') so as to protect citizens beyond national frontiers as holders of 'inalienable' and 'indivisible human rights' more effectively.

Also academics and legal practitioners often do not distinguish the different rationalities of these three diverse, yet complementary—international, inter-personal and transnational – dimensions of multilevel regulation, for instance in international investment law[29] and and other fields of IEL.[30] The 'principal-agent problems' in these different dimensions of multilevel governance—ie that citizens as 'constituent powers' delegate only limited 'constituted governance powers' that remain constrained by 'rights retained by the people' (cf Amendment IX to the US Constitution)—remain unduly neglected in research on governance of international PGs. Similarly, the path-dependent 'Hobbesian assumption' that justice and legal order depend

[29] Cf JW Salacuse, *The Three Laws of International Investment. National, Contractual, and International Frameworks for Foreign Capital* (Oxford, OUP, 2013).

[30] Cf Petersmann (n 1), ch I.

on authoritarian government powers and 'top-down regulation', prompt UN and WTO governance to neglect alternative, more decentralized and more citizen-orientated 'optimal policy' instruments that are more consistent with the human rights obligations of all UN member states. Many of the 'regulatory deficits' of constitutional democracies in ancient Greece, republican constitutionalism in Italian city republics and 'human rights constitutionalism' since the eighteenth century are re-emerging in the multilevel governance of international PGs since World War II, due to the latter's domination by government executives without adequate 'constitutional checks and balances'. They require:

- adjusting traditional conceptions of 'constitutional democracy' (eg by protecting parliamentary, representative, participatory and deliberative democratic rights in multilevel governance across national frontiers); and
- extending 'republican constitutionalism' to multilevel governance of transnational PGs on the basis of 'cosmopolitan constitutionalism' protecting the 'constituent powers' of citizens, limiting the 'constituted powers' of multilevel governance institutions, and regulating and justifying multilevel governance in more accountable and responsible ways.

Hence, *proposition 2* of this study is that—similar to the historical struggles for 'republican constitutionalism' for protection of national PGs, which resulted in progressively stronger, constitutional safeguards of human and constitutional rights, the rule of law and democratic empowerment of citizens inside many national republics (notably in Europe and North America)—transnational PGs also can be protected most effectively on the basis of cosmopolitan rights of citizens, judicial protection of transnational rule of law, and 'participatory' and 'deliberative democracy' empowering citizens to fight for more effective protection of transnational PGs.

The following section of this Introduction briefly recalls the structural 'globalization challenges' and explains *propositions 1* and *2* in more detail. Section IV summarizes *propositions 3–5*, which respond more specifically to the 'constitutional adjustment challenges' of multilevel governance of PGs. Section V gives an overview of legal methodology problems in multilevel governance of transnational 'aggregate PGs'. Chapter 1 elaborates these legal methodology problems (eg the need for redefining the international 'rules of recognition' of UN law) from the point of view of citizens. It explains why the universal recognition—by all UN member states—of human rights as an integral part of positive international law justifies and requires 'constitutional' interpretations and adjudication in multilevel governance of transnational PGs, in order to strengthen international law as an instrument of multilevel regulation of PGs that must be justified in multilevel governance by coherent 'principles of justice' for justifying the 'primary rules of conduct' and interpreting the 'secondary rules of recognition, change and adjudication'. Chapter 2 illustrates how worldwide and regional treaties constituting, limiting, regulating and justifying multilevel governance of PGs often fail to effectively regulate the 'collective action problems' of multilevel governance due to their domination by government executives that prioritize rights of states, diplomatic privileges and 'disconnected UN/WTO governance', without adequate accountability vis-à-vis citizens. Chapter 2 also explores the legal sociology questions of how the UN and WTO 'law in the books' can be transformed more effectively into 'law in action', for instance by bringing the 'Washington consensus' underlying the legal practices of the IMF, the World Bank Group, the General Agreement on Tariffs and Trade (GATT 1947) and the WTO into conformity with the 'Geneva consensus' underlying the law of the ILO, the WHO and of UN human rights bodies at Geneva. Chapter 2 uses the multilevel judicial invocation and enforcement of the 2003 WHO FCTC and the EU negotiations of transatlantic free trade agreements (FTAs), with Canada and the USA as case studies, to illustrate the need for stronger 'republican' and 'cosmopolitan', constitutionalism empowering citizens to hold multilevel governance institutions more legally, democratically and judicially accountable for their frequent failures to protect transnational PGs for the benefit of all citizens.

Chapter 3 concludes that citizens—as universally recognized subjects of 'inalienable' human rights and 'democratic principals' of multilevel governance agents with limited 'constituted powers'—should respond to the obvious governance failures by continuing their civil society struggles for stronger protection of 'republican constitutionalism' so as to hold UN, WTO, EU and other regional governance institutions more accountable for interpreting international treaties for collective supply of international PGs for the benefit of citizens. Local and national republicanism for collective supply of national PGs has become progressively more effective through democratic constitutionalism protecting parliamentary, representative, participatory and deliberative democratic self-governance of citizens. Similarly, multilevel governance of transnational 'aggregate PGs' must be rendered more effective through cosmopolitan rights and remedies of citizens as legal subjects of modern international law. Citizen-orientated 'cosmopolitan constitutionalism' based on 'constitutional interpretations' of international 'PGs regimes' (like EU common market law) tends to be resisted by many diplomats and government executives interested in maintaining their foreign policy discretion and limited legal, democratic and judicial accountability vis-à-vis citizens; yet diplomatic claims that UN and WTO governance should remain 'member-driven' rather than 'citizen-driven'—ie defining states and their diplomatic representatives as the 'masters of treaties' and 'principals' in UN/WTO governance—are inconsistent with the rights of citizens as 'constituent powers', 'democratic principals' and 'agents of justice' in multilevel governance of PGs in the twenty-first century. Constitutional and legal methodologies explain why responses to such global governance challenges—like 'legal fragmentation' of IEL, HRL and related adjudication in order to introduce legal reforms at national and regional levels of governance that are opposed in worldwide UN/WTO governance systems—depend on the value premises applied by governments, legislators, judges and NGOs in interpreting and designing international law and institutions, and in settling related disputes. Law as an instrument of social regulation must not only be justified by empirical social sciences (eg competition, environmental and social laws and policies) in order to limit abuses of power, and 'market failures' as well as 'governance failures'. Law and governance must also remain justifiable in terms of coherent 'principles of justice', so that citizens voluntarily comply with law as a matter of justice and republican virtue. As 'principles of justice' are about 'discursive justification' of law and governance through democratic discourse and 'due process of law', with due respect for different 'contexts of justice' (like procedural, distributive, corrective, commutative justice and equity)—rather than about 'objective truths' that elude human beings in view of their limited 'cognitive capacities'—this study is essentially about *methodological legal problems* of multilevel governance of transnational 'aggregate PGs'. Legal methodology problems continue to be neglected and need to be addressed in order to reform the 'disconnected' and often ineffective UN/WTO governance of transnational PGs. The book concludes that person-centered 'cosmopolitan constitutionalism' is often more appropriate for civilizing and constitutionalizing fragmented UN, GATT, WTO and regional legal regimes than one-sidedly state-centered, power-orientated intergovernmentalism that risks undermining constitutional, representative and deliberative democracy.

III. WHY 'GLOBALIZATION' REQUIRES CONSTITUTIONALIZING MULTILEVEL GOVERNANCE OF PUBLIC GOODS FOR THE BENEFIT OF CITIZENS

Why is it that—as postulated in *propositions 1* and *2*—the fact of 'globalization' requires the complementing of national with multilevel constitutionalism (eg in the sense of extending the principles, rules and governance institutions constituting national democratic legal orders to multilevel governance of 'aggregate PGs')? Since ancient times, 'realist conceptions' of law (eg as advocated by Machiavelli and Hobbes) as power-orientated instruments of social regulation (eg for limiting abuses of power, 'market failures' and 'governance failures') have been challenged on the ground that voluntary rule compliance depends on justifying law and governance not only on utilitarian grounds (like peaceful order), but also by 'principles of justice' that citizens understand and support. Yet even though all modern legal systems refer to 'principles of justice' for rationalizing legal rules, such principles are also criticized for reflecting subjective values and being capable of manipulation, such as in the case of:

— the 'legal idealism' advocated by ancient philosophers like Plato and Aristotle, analysing legal systems from the point of view of justice as an eternal ideal;
— 'legal theologies' criticizing positive law systems from the justice perspective of Christian, Jewish or Islamic interpretations of God's law; and
— diverse natural law schools like ancient Stoic theories of natural law or Rousseau's advocacy for a 'social contract' restoring the natural freedoms and equality of human beings.

A. How to Justify Law and Governance vis-à-vis Citizens?

The common dilemma of such diverse theories of justice is their insistence on the need for supplementing *empirical* justifications of law (differing, *inter alia*, in their respective conceptions of human beings as rational egoists or reasonable human beings) with 'meta-physical' (ie non-empirical), *normative* justifications of law; citizens should not only respond to law and governance as 'rational utility maximizers', but actively support the collective supply of PGs (like human rights, the rule of law, public order and social welfare) as a matter of justice and of republican virtue. Plato, in his *Republic*, famously proposed that rule by philosophers or philosophizing by rulers were the most important changes necessary and sufficient for making the 'good city' based on harmony and unity (also within the souls of citizens) a reality. As knowledge of the good implied being good, only philosophers could grasp the order and harmony they found in external reality, once they had succeeded in leaving the human condition of 'life in a dark cave'.[31] It was only in his later book on *The Laws*, following Plato's tragic adventures with political tyranny in Sicily, that Plato acknowledged the need for embedding authoritarian governance pursuing ideal 'principles of justice' into a 'mixed constitution' based on division of powers, legislation and rule of law, also protecting free discussion about the human and political virtues that citizens needed to develop.

[31] Plato's cave allegory explaining the 'human condition' is narrated by Socrates in book VII of Plato's *The Republic*.

Plato's disciple Aristotle expanded the empirical and normative research into individual and political, natural and conventional justice by analysing and comparing more than 160 city constitutions, so as to discover the most successful rules for transforming natural justice into positive law guided by principles of distributive, commutative, corrective justice and equity.[32] The Aristotelian claim that justice was both natural (eg one form of justice being complete virtue in an individual) and conventional (eg city republics constituting justice in the polity by regulating power relations and distributing to each citizen what was due to him in view of his particular human capacities) illustrated an early recognition of legal methodology problems, notably the need for constitutional limitations of legislation and of discretionary regulation based on principles of natural justice as a virtue of individuals as related to others. The happiness of individuals remained subordinated to the happiness of the city as the highest end of politics and to the law demanding justice (understood as complete virtue).[33] The proper end of Aristotelian politics was the happiness and virtuous actions of the citizens, rather than their individual protection from harm or Plato's prioritization of the happiness of the city as a whole (instead of the happiness of individual citizens). This social and political conception of the person also explains the ancient neglect of individual rights protecting the individual against state authorities. Aristotle's empirical research distinguished just and unjust constitutions, depending on whether the rulers protected the common good (thereby enabling just individuals to act as just citizens in a virtuous city) or only their own good. But the justice of the constitutional structure of the polity was, for Aristotle, a matter of fairness to individual citizens, rather than a matter of natural rights.[34] The historical success of the constitutions of Athens and Sparta was seen as empirical evidence that republican constitutionalism and 'virtue politics' could improve social cooperation and republican virtues, even if the socio-anthropological reality of individual, 'rational egoism' might not change.

[32] Aristotle's writings about justice are found chiefly in the fifth book of the *Nicomachean Ethics* and the third book of his *Politics*; on Aristotle's use of comparative constitutional and institutional research, see C Rowe, 'Aristotelian Constitutions' in C Rowe and M Schofield (eds), *Greek and Roman Political Thought* (Cambridge, CUP 2005) 366 ff.

[33] On this Aristotelian conception of justice being exercised by persons playing their proper role in a political community and ensuring proper concern for the happiness of the other members of the community (ie individuals as social and political human beings who can live a just and self-sufficient life only in a community), see J Roberts, 'Justice and the Polis' in Rowe and Schonfield (eds) (n 32) 344 ff.

[34] This interpretation remains contested; cf FD Miller, *Nature, Justice and Rights in Aristotle's Politics* (Oxford, OUP, 1995).

B. Value Pluralism Underlying Democratic and Republican Constitutionalism

In his *Politics*, Aristotle described Athenian democracy in the following terms:

> The basis of a democratic state is liberty; which, according to the common opinion of men, can only be enjoyed in such a state—this they affirm to be the great end of every democracy. One principle of liberty is for all to rule and be ruled in turn, and indeed democratic justice is the application of numerical not proportionate equality; whence it follows that the majority must be supreme, and whatever the majority approve must be the end and the just. Every citizen, it is said, must have equality, and therefore in a democracy the poor have more power than the rich, because there are more of them, and the will of the majority is supreme. This, then, is one note of liberty which all democrats affirm to be the principle of their state. Another is that a man should live as he likes. This, they say, is the mark of liberty, since, on the other hand, not to live as a man likes is the mark of a slave. This is the second characteristic of democracy, whence has arisen the claim of men to be ruled by none, if possible, or, if this is impossible, to rule and be ruled in turns; and so it contributes to the freedom based upon equality.
>
> Such being our foundation and such the principle from which we start, the characteristics of democracy are as follows: the election of officers by all out of all; and that all should rule over each, and each in his turn over all; that the appointment to all offices, or to all but those which require experience and skill, should be made by lot; and that no property qualification should be required for offices, or only a very low one; that a man should not hold the same office twice, or not often, or in the case of few except military offices; that the tenure of all offices, or of as many as possible, should be brief; that all men should sit in judgment, or that judges selected out of all should judge, in all matters, or in most and in the greatest and most important ...; that the assembly should be supreme over all causes, or at any rate over the most important, and the magistrates over none or only over a very few.[35]

According to Constant's famous essay on 'The Liberty of the Ancient and the Liberty of the Moderns' (1819), the 'ancient liberties' in the Greek and Roman republics protected democratic participation in the rule of the public sphere rather than individual rights and freedoms in the private and social sphere (like 'negative liberties' left to the rule of the private will).[36] While

[35] Aristotle, *Politics* and *The Constitution of Athens* (S Everson (ed), Cambridge, CUP, 1996) 154 f (para 1317b); Aristotle enumerates other characteristics of democracy, like payment for services.

[36] Cf P Pettit, *Republicanism. A Theory of Freedom and Government* (Oxford, Clarendon Press, 1997) 18. Pettit argues for a 'communitarian character of freedom as non-domination', recognizing that 'the freedom of a community is as basic a notion as the freedom of individuals' (at 275).

the ancient Greeks emphasized democracy and the need for legal philosophy justifying law and governance (eg based on Aristotelian 'principles of justice' and 'virtue politics'), the republican tradition is often said to have more of a Roman character and to have focused more on PGs like the Roman legal system, its—compared with Greek constitutionalism—more complex 'constitutional checks and balances', and its development and codification by professional jurists.[37] Roman republicanism was aristocratic rather than democratic, and differed from Greek republicanism in many ways (eg the central role of the Roman Senate, aristocratic election procedures, and appointment of officers through elections rather than by lot).[38] This study argues that the democratic and republican heritage of European states—since the ancient city republics in Greece and Italy—remains an important theoretical and empirical-political source of knowledge for justifying civil society advocacy, designing citizenship rights for collective supply of PGs, and 'democratizing' not only *national republics* but also *multilevel governance* (eg UN, WTO and regional governance) of transnational PGs, like common markets in federal states and regional communities like the EU and its EEA with European Free Trade Area (EFTA) states.[39]

Following the Kantian 'enlightenment revolution', demonstrating the relativity of all human cognition (eg in terms of time, space, causality of human reasoning, subjectivity of human senses) and the need for respecting human autonomy ('dignity') and reasonableness (eg the 'categorical imperative' of protecting maximum equal freedoms and legitimate diversity of individual conceptions of a 'good life' and 'truth'), social contract and constitutional theories of law emphasized the need for justifying positive law not only as facts (eg in terms of authoritative issuance and social effectiveness of rules), but also in terms of reasonable 'principles of justice' (eg as explained by social contract theories) and historical processes of justification (eg in terms of Hegelian claims of dialectic transformation of legal

[37] *Ibid*, 283 ff. On the Roman republic as the common property of the public, see Cicero, *The Republic and the Laws* (Oxford, OUP 1998) 19. For a 'neo-Athenian' interpretation of republicanism emphasizing the need for democratic elections and participatory democracy (which were also part of the Roman Constitution), see M Sandel, *Democracy's Discontent: America in Search of a Public Philosophy* (Cambridge, Harvard UP, 1996).

[38] For detailed comparisons, see Rowe and Schofield (eds) (n 32); and U Wessel, *Geschichte des Rechts in Europa. Von den Griechen bis zum Vertrag von Lissabon* (Munich, Beck, 2015), eg at 20–53 ff.

[39] Cf M Van Gelderen and Q Skinner, *Republicanism: A Shared European Heritage*, 2 vols (Cambridge, CUP, 2002). On the diverse legal traditions of republicanism and the disagreement on whether the core values of republicanism should be defined in terms of liberty (non-domination), republican virtues of active citizenry finding self-realization in political participation and collective supply of PGs, communitarianism, social and political equality, or deliberative democracy, see S Besson and J Luis Marti (eds), *Legal Republicanism: National and International Perspectives* (Oxford, OUP, 2009). These historical controversies are left open in this study.

systems through public reason).[40] Arguably, the most important result of these continuing debates about legal philosophy is the universal recognition of 'inalienable' and 'indivisible human rights' and of national Constitutions (written or unwritten) by—today—almost all UN member states. In the twenty-first century, human rights have become the most important 'people-centered' discourse on justice and the most legitimate 'legal source' for justifying law and governance vis-à-vis citizens, with due respect for the reality of 'constitutional pluralism' due to the diverse democratic preferences and constitutional traditions of peoples.[41]

C. Need for Embedding Constitutional Democracies into Multilevel Republican and Cosmopolitan Constitutionalism

As discussed in Chapter 1, the more UN human rights treaties are implemented through multilevel regional and national human rights guarantees and judicial remedies, the more 'human rights constitutionalism' requires review of the rules of recognition, change and adjudication in international legal practices. Modern constitutional democracies in Europe and North America have progressively limited past 'market failures' and 'governance failures' by integrating democratic, republican and cosmopolitan constitutionalism, as illustrated by the multilevel judicial protection by national and European courts of the human rights guarantees of the ECHR and of the EUCFR, with due respect for national 'margins of appreciation' in different national constitutional contexts. Yet beyond the EU and the EEA, the legal and political relevance of the diverse democratic, republican and cosmopolitan traditions for designing multilevel governance of transnational 'aggregate PGs' for the benefit of citizens in response to the modern 'globalization' of formerly national PGs continues to be neglected. Citizens of the EU increasingly criticize the EU crises resulting from persistent disregard by EU member states and EU institutions for the 'rule of law' as defined by national parliaments in EU treaties (eg the Eurozone crises related to violations of the agreed budget and debt disciplines of the Lisbon Treaty; immigration and terrorism crises have related to persistent violations of the Schengen und Dublin rules on controlling immigration).

The less people are self-sufficient in a globally interdependent world, the more they depend on economic, legal and social cooperation for collective

[40] On the relevance of Kantian legal theory for justifying 'cosmopolitan constitutionalism' and multilevel regulation of IEL, see Petersmann (n 1), ch III.

[41] On human rights advocacy and 'legal construction' of human rights at local, national, transnational and international levels, see K Nash, *The Political Sociology of Human Rights* (Cambridge, CUP, 2015).

supply of transnational PGs like consumer welfare, public health, food security, climate change prevention, democratic peace, transnational rule of law and political security. Both on empirical as well as on normative grounds, the democratic, republican and cosmopolitan traditions of empowering citizens to develop their 'republican virtues' and exercise republican rights remain of crucial importance not only in the emerging 'global network society', so as to induce citizens, for instance:

— to participate in multilevel economic governance;
— to hold multilevel governance institutions legally, democratically and judicially accountable; and
— to limit the ubiquity of abuses of public and private power and violations of the rule of law.[42]

Republican, democratic and cosmopolitan constitutionalism also refute claims that 'law is incapable of providing convincing justifications to the solution of normative problems'.[43] Related claims that 'no coherent normative practice arises from the assumptions on which we identify international law'[44] are inconsistent with the universal recognition of human rights and of international organizations like the EU that protect community interests (eg in legal and judicial protection of fundamental rights, welfare-enhancing common markets, a European 'social market economy' and other PGs) and limit abuses of power politics advocating outdated 'Westphalian conceptions' of 'international law among sovereign states'. Yet the current crises in EU law and governance (eg regarding the 'Brexit' referendum of June 2016, the Dublin rules on immigration, debt and unemployment problems in the EU's monetary union, political extremism and terrorism) also show that 'constitutionalization' of law and governance in the EU remains a perennial challenge due to inadequate transformation of human rights, the rule of law, democracy and other 'principles of justice' into multilevel government practices and 'republican virtues' of EU politicians and citizens.

Chapter 1 explains why the universal recognition of human rights continues to transform the 'Westphalian community of states' into a global community, including citizens, peoples, (non-)governmental and

[42] Cf JGA Pocock, *The Machivallian Moment: Florentine Political Thought and the Atlantic Republican Tradition* (Princeton, NJ, Princeton UP, 1975) (emphasizing, eg, at 67, that the republican ideal of cultivating and exercising individual virtues remains central to the collective supply of PGs as explained by Aristotle and Cicero). For a classical explanation of the importance of the four cardinal virtues (prudence, justice, courage and temperance) for citizenship as a public office that is essential for protecting PGs, and of the different forms of representing citizens (eg by monarchy, aristocracy or democracy) that risk being transformed into tyranny, oligarchy and ochlocraty if citizens lack 'civic virtues', see Cicero, *De officiis*; cf Rowe and Schofield (eds) (n 32), 477, at 505 ff.

[43] Cf Koskenniemi (n 26) 69.

[44] *Ibid.*

international organizations as legal subjects of international law. The related methodological challenges of multilevel governance require a 'republican philosophy' of international law (notably of its 'rules or recognition') justifying the constitution, limitation and regulation of multilevel governance of transnational 'aggregate PGs' in terms of citizen-orientated, 'constitutional' and 'cosmopolitan principles of justice' and rights of citizens rather than only of states. Chapter 1 argues that the text, context and objectives of UN law are sufficiently open-ended and justify 'constitutional interpretations', for instance of the 'rules of recognition' as defined in Article 38 of the ICJ Statute. As most international agreements use indeterminate legal terms and regulate transnational relations in incomplete ways, the Preamble to the VCLT recalls that 'disputes concerning treaties, like other international disputes, should be settled … in conformity with the principles of justice and international law', especially if the text, context, object and purpose of the applicable treaty provisions remain indeterminate and have to be clarified in conformity with the legal principles underlying incomplete treaty rules. The proposed paradigm shift in interpreting the 'rules of recognition' of international law (as codified in Article 38 of the ICJ Statute) aims at reinterpreting state sovereignty and state consent from the perspective of democratic consent and the human and constitutional rights of citizens and 'republican responsibilities' for multilevel governance of PGs. National, regional and also worldwide courts of justice increasingly acknowledge that interpreting international law requires doctrinal and judicial justifications, which must no longer one-sidedly focus on state-centered 'Westphalian justice' governing 'international law among sovereign states'. Yet due to the domination of UN/WTO institutions by government executives and their 'path-dependent legal reasoning' prioritizing state sovereignty and 'member-driven governance' as defined by diplomats, most UN and WTO lawyers continue to neglect this impact of HRL on the 'rules of recognition' governing modern HRL and IEL. Whereas national courts in democracies decide in the name of 'the people' and act as guardians of human rights and constitutional democracy, the more limited mandates and 'applicable law' of UN, WTO and regional courts—created by treaties among states with under-theorized 'principles of justice'—render the legitimacy of international court judgments, and the role of international judges as 'guardians of the fundamental rights of the individual',[45] more contested.

Modern 'republican constitutionalism' and the adoption of national Constitutions by almost all UN member states resulted from 2,500 years of political deliberations and practical experiences with collective supply of

[45] Cf H Krunke, 'Courts as protectors of the people: constitutional identity, popular legitimacy and human rights' in M Scheinin, H Krunke and M Aksenova (eds), *Judges as Guardians of Constitutionalism and Human Rights* (Cheltenham, Elgar, 2016) 71–93.

local PGs since the ancient city republics in Greece, Roman republicanism, Renaissance republicanism (eg in Italian and Hanseatic city republics) and 'Enlightenment republicanism' (eg since the American and French 'human rights revolutions' in the eighteenth century). The major 'political inventions' emerging from these political 'trials and errors' were the need for 'mixed constitutions' at local and national levels of governance that combine *mono-*, *oligo-* and *democratic* structures of political governance. The 'checks and balances' among multilevel legislative, executive, judicial powers and regulatory agencies also protect decentralized, participatory and deliberative governance methods (like economic markets, democratic politics, constitutional rights, judicial litigation). Human rights law requires recognition of citizens as 'constituent powers' that must hold abuses of public and private 'constituted powers' legally, democratically and judicially accountable.[46] One-sidedly nationalist focus on protecting individual and communitarian liberties inside states as the main concern of republicanism risks impeding the transformation of most national PGs into international PGs (like the international monetary, financial, trading, development, environmental, legal, communication and security systems) that no government, no single state and no national legal system can secure unilaterally in the global economy of the twenty-first century.

Hence, Chapter 2 argues that protecting republican constitutionalism in multilevel governance of transnational 'aggregate PGs' also requires stronger cosmopolitan rights and multilevel 'checks and balances', enabling citizens to hold multilevel governance institutions legally, democratically and judicially more accountable. Politically determined *state borders* impose territorial and jurisdictional rather than moral limits on government policies vis-à-vis individuals and communities that increasingly cooperate beyond state borders with other individuals and communities in collectively supplying transnational PGs (like protection of 'inalienable' human rights and transnational rule of law). Chapter 2 explains how the legal, political and economic interdependencies between local, national, regional and worldwide rules and institutions entail 'knowledge gaps', 'governance gaps' and other 'collective action problems' in multilevel governance of 'aggregate PGs'. It argues that the path-dependent paradigms of 'state sovereignty' and 'executive dominance'[47] in multilevel UN, WTO and regional governance

[46] For a historical overview, see A Riklin, *Machtteilung. Geschichte der Mischverfassung* (Darmstadt, Wissenschaftliche Buchgesellschaft, 2006). Most advocates of republicanism continue to neglect the need for extending 'rights-based republican governance' to multilevel governance of transnational PGs; due to globalization, republican governance of PGs is no longer possible without international law and multilevel governance institutions.

[47] Cf EA Posner and A Vermeule, *The Executive Unbound: After the Madisonian Republic* (Oxford, OUP, 2010).

need to be limited by stronger constitutional and democratic 'checks and balances' so as to extend rights-based 'republican governance' to transnational rights of citizens to participate in multilevel governance of transnational 'aggregate PGs'. This is of particular importance for global 'economic network governance' influenced by millions of economic actors in diverse jurisdictions, as illustrated by 'global supply chains', Internet governance and financial market regulations coordinating the autonomous actions of producers, investors, traders and consumers all over the world. The legal dimensions of 'collective action problems' in multilevel governance of transnational 'aggregate PGs' continue to be neglected in legal research. Empirical use of *comparative institutionalism* (eg comparing the diverse UN and WTO multilevel governance institutions) and normative use of the lessons from *republican* constitutionalism can contribute to reducing the 'research gap' in the legal and political literature on multilevel governance of international PGs. Even though republican governance of PGs has been discussed by political philosophers since the ancient Athenian democracy in 500 BC, there is—surprisingly—not a single, multidisciplinary legal monograph elaborating a coherent legal theory for how citizens, peoples, governments and states can collectively provide transnational 'aggregate PGs' demanded by citizens in the new context of a globally integrating world, where PGs regimes interact both 'horizontally' and 'vertically'. This study hopes to induce more academic, political and legal research on how human and constitutional rights of citizens can be protected more effectively in multilevel governance of transnational PGs.

IV. CONSTITUTIONAL FAILURES OF 'DISCONNECTED' UN, WTO AND EU GOVERNANCE

Chapter 1 challenges the prevailing 'realist conceptions' of international law from the perspective of the constitutional insight that human rights and other agreed 'principles of justice' cannot become effective unless they are transformed into democratic legislation, administration, adjudication and international 'PGs regimes' that protect constitutional and cosmopolitan rights of citizens to engage in mutually beneficial cooperation across frontiers, and to hold multilevel governance agents legally, democratically and judicially accountable for their failures to protect PGs for the benefit of all citizens. In his recent book on *World Order*, Henry Kissinger claims that the Westphalian order ending the 30-year war in Europe (killing almost one-third of Europe's population) remains the scaffolding of the international order as it now exists.[48] He defines world order as 'the

[48] H Kissinger, *World Order* (New York, Penguin Press, 2014).

concept held by a region or civilization about the nature of just arrangements and the distribution of power thought to be applicable to the entire world'. He admits that power is a necessary but insufficient tool of government; for any successful world order rests on a 'balance between legitimacy and power': the legitimacy of 'a set of commonly accepted rules that defines the limits of permissible action'; and a 'balance of power that enforces restraint where rules break down'. This dual concept of world order based on power and legitimacy prompts Kissinger—like most UN and WTO diplomats—to prioritize 'realist respect' for the UN principle of state sovereignty over the 'idealism' underlying the universal recognition of human rights and corresponding, governmental 'duties to respect, protect and fulfil human rights'. Most realists concede that governmental failures to protect human rights and other PGs do not justify foreign interventions unless they produce harmful externalities abroad, threatening essential interests of foreign states and peoples (eg Al Qaeda's attacks inside the USA on 11 September 2001 justifying US destruction of Al Qaeda's headquarters in Afghanistan). Yet World War II and the Holocaust demonstrated that avoiding systemic, worldwide risks of intergovernmental power politics requires limiting national sovereignty and power-orientated security policies by human rights and multilevel protection of PGs through international law and organizations. Political realists—including Kissinger's policy recommendations for protecting 'world order'—often unduly neglect the 'human rights revolution' and the economic, social and environmental challenges in the twenty-first century, which require 'constitutionalizing' multilevel governance of transnational PGs in order to empower citizens to struggle for stronger protection of their human rights and transnational rule of law. Even if the 'European model' of multilevel 'judicial constitutionalization' of EU law, EEA law and of European HRL cannot be repeated by worldwide courts (like the ICJ, the Law of the Sea Tribunal, the International Criminal Court, the WTO Appellate Body), the case studies in Chapters 1 and 2 suggest that multilevel judicial cooperation among national and international courts beyond Europe can clarify and protect cosmopolitan rights and judicial remedies of citizens, and thereby promote transnational 'republican constitutionalism'.

A. Why 'Cosmopolitan Foreign Policies' are No Longer Unrealistic Utopias

Chapters 1 to 3 refute—on both normative as well as empirical grounds—the prevailing wisdom of UN and WTO diplomats that state-centered power politics, 'member-driven top-down governance' and 'constitutional nationalism' are more 'realistic' than citizen-orientated, 'bottom-up governance' of international PGs based on multilevel legal and judicial protection of rights of citizens. The empirical case studies discussed in Chapters 1 to 3—like EU and EEA law, HRL and IEL, UN environmental conventions, the WHO FCTC and 'transformative transatlantic FTAs'—confirm the normative need for 'cosmopolitan foreign policies', empowering citizens to invoke and enforce international treaty regimes. Regional free trade area, customs union and environmental agreements in Europe and North America, regional human rights treaties in Europe and Latin America, international commercial law, intellectual property law and investment treaties, international criminal law and consular treaties protecting individual rights across national frontiers, all have been supported by citizens and courts of justice as more legitimate and more effective protection of PGs (like transnational rule of law, respect for human and constitutional rights in the implementation of UN Security Council 'smart sanctions') than 'disconnected governance' based on intergovernmental rules that treat citizens as mere legal objects and—due to 'diplomatic *fiat*'—are not enforceable inside countries. 'Cosmopolitan treaty regimes'—like the common market law of the EU and of the EEA, regional human rights conventions in Europe and Latin America, multilevel competition rules, international investment and commercial law and arbitration—have often succeeded in limiting abuses of powers and in promoting the inclusive 'public reason' necessary for collective supply of PGs. Human rights law and constitutional democracies suggest that treating citizens as legal subjects—rather than as mere legal objects of UN and WTO law, without individual rights to hold governments legally, democratically and judicially accountable (eg by invoking and enforcing precise and unconditional UN/WTO rules in domestic courts)—should be recognized as a *legal requirement* of the human rights obligations of all UN member states that is fully consistent with 'political realism' aimed at protecting citizens against abuses of power.

In constitutional democracies, citizens and people are the legitimate holders of 'constituent powers'; they delegate only limited powers to international organizations. The ineffective implementation of UN HRL inside many UN member states suggests that stronger democratic and cosmopolitan rights of citizens are essential for holding multilevel governance institutions more accountable for their frequent failures to protect human rights and other international PGs for the benefit of citizens. In view of the resistance by many governments against citizen-orientated reforms of global UN and WTO agreements, it is mainly through citizen-driven 'fragmentation' of treaty regimes (eg by means of regional human rights treaties, thousands of trade, investment and double-taxation agreements) and incremental judicial reforms (eg based on 'judicial rebalancing' of public and private interests in interpreting the 'exception clauses' in trade, investment and human rights agreements) that international law continues to be progressively transformed for the benefit of citizens and their constitutional rights.

Modern constitutional democracies (like the EU and EEA member states) have become successful by integrating the different democratic, republican and cosmopolitan traditions of constitutionalism in the context of functionally limited, multilevel constitutionalism. This study concludes that the necessary limitation of the existing 'implementation deficits' in UN/WTO governance of transnational PGs likewise requires extending 'republican' and 'cosmopolitan' constitutionalism, so as to empower citizens to insist on more effective legislative, administrative and judicial implementation of UN/WTO rules and transnational rule of law. This empirical as well as normative policy conclusion is based on 'constitutional premises' and 'policy propositions' that remain contested; as outlined in *propositions 3–5* below, they need to be clarified in order to improve multilevel governance of PGs.

Proposition 3: Multilevel Economic Governance Can be 'Constitutionalized' Beyond Supranational EU Law and the More Deferential EEA Law

All national democracies have experienced how institutionalizing human rights through democratic, legislative, administrative and judicial institutions for the protection of PGs demanded by citizens requires some form of 'constitutionalism' that constitutes, limits, regulates and justifies limited government powers for the benefit of citizens. In constitutional democracies, citizens—in order to hold 'constituted powers' legally, democratically and judicially accountable—delegate only limited legislative, executive and judicial powers to separate branches of government and regulatory agencies, and limit such powers by the rights and judicial remedies of citizens and other constitutional and institutional 'checks and balances'. Due to globalization, national Constitutions have turned out to be 'partial constitutions' that can no longer unilaterally secure the supply of many transnational 'aggregate PGs' demanded by citizens without increasing use of international law for constituting, limiting, regulating and justifying multilevel governance institutions protecting transnational PGs. In order to collectively protect such PGs, national constitutionalism—as the historically most legitimate and most effective method for supplying national PGs demanded by citizens—needs to be complemented by multilevel 'republican governance' of transnational aggregate PGs. Arguably, the multilevel constitutional and legal regulation of the EU's common market and its multilevel, democratic governance through EU law and EU institutions—like the EU Commission, the EU Council, the EU Court of Justice (CJEU), the European Parliament, the EU Central Bank and other independent EU regulatory agencies—for the benefit of more than 500 million EU citizens, are empirical illustrations of the political feasibility of extending functionally limited, 'multilevel constitutionalism' to multilevel governance of transnational PGs enhancing the constitutional rights and economic welfare of citizens beyond state borders. The more deferential, constitutional and legal regulation of the extension of the EU common market to EFTA states by means of EEA law, or to third states by customs union agreements (with Turkey) and bilateral FTAs (eg with Switzerland), illustrates the political reality of 'constitutional pluralism'. Are similar, functionally limited approaches to 'constitutionalization' of multilevel governance of PGs also possible beyond European democracies?

As illustrated by the WTO membership of 'illiberal states' (like China and Russia), authoritarian governments asserting 'Hobbesian principles of justice' and hegemonic foreign policies also recognize their national self-interests in rules-based, multilevel governance of the global economic division of labour. Their participation in multilevel commercial, trade, investment and Internet regulation, and in its multilevel judicial enforcement (eg through WTO dispute settlement rulings, commercial, investment and Internet arbitration), demonstrates their willingness to submit to functionally limited, multilevel 'economic constitutionalism' based on judicial protection of cosmopolitan rights and transnational rule of law. Due to the rational self-interests of citizens and governments in mutually beneficial economic cooperation across national frontiers, the 'constitutionalization' of citizen-driven, transnational *economic cooperation* has also proved to be possible among governments that strongly reject *political integration*, as illustrated by the functionally limited economic integration in Europe during the 1950s (eg based on the 1951/52 European Coal and Steel Community and the 1957/58 European Economic Community), in spite of the French rejection of proposals for a European Political and Defence Community. The now almost 600 regional FTAs and additional 'plurilateral trade agreements' (PTAs, eg on government procurement, information technologies, financial and telecommunications services) among WTO members confirm the political feasibility of progressive 'bottom-up reforms' through 'legal fragmentation' (eg FTAs and PTAs) if worldwide legal reforms are blocked. The increasing recognition of individual rights and common constitutional principles in multilevel economic, environmental, Internet governance and human rights regulation illustrates the transition from a 'community of states' to a global community of citizens, peoples, governmental and non-governmental institutions, with more complex, multilevel rights and obligations.

Comparative research of the creation of common markets in federal states and of their dynamic legal evolution confirms that decentralized, legal and judicial accountability mechanisms have proved to be of crucial importance for limiting 'market failures' as well as 'governance failures' in the creation of national and regional common markets not only in Europe, but similarly in economic and legal integration in the Americas, Africa and Asia.[49] 'Cosmopolitan rights' protecting citizens across national frontiers—like human rights, EU citizenship rights, rights of free movement of persons beyond state borders (eg due to liberalization of services), multilevel EU parliamentarianism and recognition of transnational rights of migrants (eg to take up employment and receive social security benefits while residing in another common market member country)—are no longer 'unique European experiments' in rights-based, regional common markets and integration law. Their 'enabling', 'legitimating', 'enforcement' and 'republican functions' (eg as decentralized means for limiting implementation deficits of PGs regimes), and their often 'derivative nature' (eg common market freedoms and investor rights linked to state citizenship rather than to human rights), are increasingly also recognized in African, Latin American and Central American integration regimes.[50] This study's advocacy for 'cosmopolitan interpretations' of UN and WTO law acknowledges the continuing necessity for states, their centrality in international law and the need for interstate treaties for multilevel governance of PGs. Yet 'horizontal' conceptions of international law focusing on the 'sovereign equality of states' and on the 'balance of power' between sovereign states must be complemented by 'constitutional checks and balances' protecting constitutional, democratic and cosmopolitan rights of citizens vis-à-vis the ubiquity of abuses of foreign policy powers in UN, WTO and other international institutions neglecting protection of human rights and other PGs, for example on the ground that 'statesmen' should keep moral considerations separate from foreign policies. The 'Brexit' referendum of June 2016 illustrates that—even in constitutional democracies—multilevel constitutionalism risks being reversed by democratic majority decisions.

[49] Cf G Anderson (ed), *Internal Markets and Multilevel Governance: The Experience of the EU, Australia, Canada, Switzerland and the US* (Oxford, OUP, 2012); Petersmann (n 12); this book explained why the constitutional legitimacy of multilevel economic regulation could be enhanced by interpreting the multilevel guarantees of equal freedoms, non-discrimination, rule of law and access to justice in national, regional and worldwide economic law in mutually coherent ways for the benefit of citizens and their constitutional rights in domestic legal systems. Such 'mutually consistent interpretations' promote the legal and judicial accountability of multilevel governance agents that are often inadequately controlled by citizens, civil society, parliaments and courts of justice, and which fail to effectively protect PGs demanded by citizens).

[50] On the increasing recognition of transnational economic, labour, social and political citizenship rights (eg in the EU, the EEA, the Andean Community, MERCOSUR, the Central American Common Market, the Economic Community of West African States, the Gulf Cooperation Council) and of regional parliamentary institutions, see C Closa and D Vintila, *Supranational citizenship rights in regional integration organizations* (Florence, EUI, 2015) (unpublished manuscript on file with the author). On the related problems of 'plural citizenship', see PJ Spiro, *At Home in Two Countries: The Past and Future of Dual Citizenship* (New York, NYU Press, 2016); PJ Spiro, *Beyond Citizenship: American Identity after Globalization* (Oxford, OUP, 2008).

Also, WTO law illustrates the advantages of recognizing private and public non-state actors at sub-national and supra-national levels of governance (like Hong Kong, Macau, Taiwan, regional organizations like the EU) as increasingly important legal subjects of multilevel governance of PGs. The 'constitutional functions' of such WTO rules for peacefully reintegrating legally separate customs territories—like China, Hong Kong, Macau and Taiwan as separate WTO members, using WTO and FTA rules for progressively re-creating a single 'Chinese common market'—are recognized outside Europe too.[51] The *Decision on Advancing the Rule of Law in China*, adopted by the fourth plenary session of the 18th Communist Party of China Central Committee meeting on 23 October 2014, aims at promoting law and the independence of judicial review from local political influences (eg by central financing of national and local courts). China's Trade Minister, in an article on 'Strengthening Trade Policy Compliance and Promoting Rule of Law in China' of 31 December 2014, explicitly acknowledged the linkages between China's compliance with WTO rules and dispute settlement rulings, including systemic checks of the 'WTO compliance' of national and local trade regulations, with the broader promotion of the rule of law in China.[52] The legal and institutional 'checks and balances' among legislative, executive and judicial governance powers in WTO law aim at limiting trade politics by 'rule of law', in conformity with the approval of WTO agreements by national parliaments in WTO members. Some WTO agreements also recognize rights of private actors like holders of intellectual property rights (protected by the WTO Agreement on trade-related intellectual property rights (TRIPS)), pre-shipment inspection companies (protected by the WTO Agreement on Preshipment Inspections), or foreign companies participating in government procurement tendering procedures and protected by the WTO Agreement on Government Procurement. The WTO requirements for legislative and administrative good-faith implementation of WTO law and for its judicial protection inside domestic legal systems too, serve to 'ensure the conformity of laws, regulations and administrative procedures' with WTO obligations (Article XVI:4 WTO Agreement) so as to provide 'security and predictability to the multilateral trading system' (Article 3:2 Dispute Settlement Understanding of the WTO (DSU)). China's 'rule of law' strategy, however, does not seem to limit the 'primacy of communist

[51] On the autonomous WTO memberships of the four customs territories of China, Macau, Hong Kong and Taiwan—and on their incentives for peaceful reduction of the economic and legal divisions of China as a single sovereign country, eg due to rules-based FTAs progressively recreating a common market—see CH Wu, *WTO and the Greater China: Economic Integration and Dispute Resolution* (Leiden, Nijhoff, 2012).

[52] Cf G Yang, 'China in the WTO Dispute Settlement: A Memoir' in (2015) 49 *Journal of World Trade* 1–18.

party politics'; even though China continues to comply with WTO rules and WTO dispute settlement rulings, China's Constitution and judiciary do not effectively limit the political powers of the Communist Party and its 'rule by law' (eg using police powers and criminal proceedings for sanctioning political dissenters).[53] Moreover, while China effectively implements some of its other international legal obligations (eg to limit tobacco consumption and other health pandemics in conformity with the FCTC)[54], it does not effectively implement its human rights commitments, labour law and certain other international legal obligations (eg under the UN Convention on the Law of the Sea).[55]

Proposition 4: Effective 'Constitutionalization' of Functionally Limited 'Treaty Constitutions' Depends on Republican Rights of Citizens and Their Multilevel Judicial Protection

Following the American and French human rights revolutions of the eighteenth century, national constitutionalism has become progressively accepted by most UN member states as the most legitimate and most effective method of governance for constituting, limiting, regulating and justifying government powers for the collective supply of PGs. Yet even though international treaties assume ever greater 'legislative functions' for collective supply of transnational PGs, many UN member states do not effectively transform ('constitutionalize') 'PGs treaties' through democratic legislation, administration and judicial remedies protecting PGs and rights of citizens. Only a few UN Specialized Agencies have been established through functionally limited (small 'c') 'treaty-constitutions' (*sic*) that explicitly link their respective multilevel governance of international PGs—for instance, in the ILO, the WHO, FAO and UNESCO—to corresponding human rights, such as labour rights and human rights to protection of health, food, education and rule of law, that are protected by legal and/or judicial remedies. Yet with the exception of the 'tri-partite' composition of the ILO institutions (by representatives of governments, employers and employees), all UN institutions are dominated by intergovernmental decision-making without effective democratic participation and accountability vis-à-vis citizens. They fail to provide for effective 'republican rights' and remedies for the effective

[53] On the lack of judicial independence, see Z Tong, 'A Comment on the Rise and Fall of the Supreme People's Court's Reply to QI Yuling's Case' in (2010) XLIII *Suffolk University Law Review* 669–79.

[54] Cf LA Jacobs, 'Global Tobacco Control Law and Trade Liberalisation: New Policy Spaces?' in D Drache and LA Jacobs (eds), *Linking Global Trade and Human Rights. New Policy Space in Hard Economic Times* (Cambridge, CUP, 2014) 131, at 140–43.

[55] Cf L Biukovic, 'Is There Space for Human Rights Linkages in China's Trade and Investment Network?' in Drache and Jacobs (eds) (n 54) 274–97; and PB Potter, 'Human Rights and Social Justice in China' in Drache and Jacobs (eds) (n 54) 299–316.

enforcement of transnational PGs regimes. Chapters 2 and 3 criticize the 'disfranchisement' of citizens and inadequate democratic and judicial accountability mechanisms in UN/WTO law—and increasingly also in EU external relations law, due to pursuit of bureaucratic self-interests without effective democratic control—as being contrary to the 'democratic imperative' that citizens must be recognized as 'constituent powers', democratic principals and legal subjects of democratic law on protection of PGs.

Human rights law suggests that, in the twenty-first century, international law also derives its constitutional legitimacy from protecting equal rights of citizens and individual 'access to justice' for reviewing abuses of power. As discussed in Chapter 2, the multilevel restriction of tobacco supply and consumption through the FCTC in the context of the WHO—by linking tobacco control to human and constitutional health rights, judicial remedies and multilaterally agreed 'best practices' for the implementation and coordination of tobacco regulation in the WHO, WTO and regional organizations like the EU—confirms the experience of regional trade and investment agreements that republican rights and related 'principles of justice' (like public health protection) can be enforced most effectively 'bottom-up', by empowering individuals and economic actors to invoke and enforce multilevel economic and health regulations in domestic courts. Chapters 1 to 3 also discuss the more recent ICJ jurisprudence on protecting human rights and other individual rights (eg to receive consular assistance pursuant to Article 36 of the 1963 Vienna Convention on Consular Relations); similar to the multilevel judicial protection of human and constitutional rights by the CJEU, the EFTA Court and the ECtHR in cooperation with national courts, this jurisprudence confirms that multilevel constitutionalism at regional and worldwide levels of governance can become more effective and more legitimate by empowering citizens through individual rights and judicial remedies.

Regional IEL, HRL and related jurisprudence by national and regional courts of justice illustrate the legal methodology problems of 'republican interpretations' and multilevel judicial protection of cosmopolitan rights of citizens. Even though most citizens continue to exercise their *civil* and *political rights* in local communities, the worldwide division of labour and globalization of communications increasingly induce citizens to exercise their *economic*, *social* and *cultural rights* by participating in the global economy (eg as consumers and producers of traded goods and services) and in the emerging global society resulting from global communication networks, international migration, transnational citizenship rights and other civil society cooperation beyond national frontiers. For example:

— as consumers of foreign goods (such as food, medicines, books, newspapers, automobiles) and services imported from abroad (eg music, films, news, medical services);

— as users of global communication networks (eg telephone, Internet and television services) cooperating through NGOs;
— as tourists, migrants and workers travelling abroad (eg in response to arrangements by transnational corporations and regional FTAs); or
— as investors, depositors, shareholders or workers in international banks and other transnational corporations (TNCs),

citizens constitute functionally limited, transnational communities supporting transnational PGs (like the elaboration of international human rights, environmental, criminal law and other 'PG treaties').

All related economic and social transactions are subject to multilevel governance and multilevel legal regulation (eg of the Internet, global supply chains) that affect the individual lives of billions of people. The regulatory capacity of individual nation states not only declines due to globalization; it also increasingly depends on participation in multilevel governance institutions for the collective supply of transnational 'aggregate PGs'. Even though UN and WTO agreements focus on the rights and obligations of governments, national and international courts of justice are increasingly confronted with claims of citizens to interpret indeterminate, incomplete and under-theorized UN and WTO provisions not only as legal constraints on governments, but also as corresponding rights of citizens (eg to legal and judicial remedies). Republican constitutionalism calls for empowering domestic citizens and 'compliance communities' (like the international trading community participating in and benefitting from the global division of labour) to assume 'republican responsibilities' for 'legal socialization' and domestic implementation of transnational PGs regimes. This study argues on both normative and factual grounds that—just as human rights, the rule of law and democratic self-governance are recognized inside constitutional democracies as mutually complementary 'pure PGs' (eg in the sense of being non-excludable and non-exhaustible for the benefit of domestic citizens) that are necessary for protecting 'human dignity' (eg in the sense of human reasonableness, conscience and autonomy)—multilevel governance of transnational PGs must also be protected and justified vis-à-vis citizens in terms of these very same constitutional principles, in order to limit 'market failures' and 'governance failures' and legitimise law and governance, so that they are voluntarily supported by citizens.

Proposition 5: 'Constitutional Justice' Justifies 'Constitutional' Treaty Interpretations and Adjudication in Order to Protect Rights of Citizens to PGs and Accountability of Governments

As discussed in Chapter 1, modern theories of justice justify respect for equal freedoms as the 'first principle of constitutional justice' in very diverse (eg moral, procedural and substantive) ways. Problems of treaty interpretation and adjudication arise if the parties construe existing rules and principles in mutually conflicting ways. If interpretation of treaty provisions on the basis of their text, context, object and purpose remains unclear or disputed, the customary rules of treaty interpretation (as codified in the VCLT) require settling 'disputes concerning treaties, like other international disputes, ... in conformity with the principles of justice and international law' (Preamble VCLT). Legislative, administrative or judicial clarification of the applicable treaty provisions in conformity with the legal principles underlying treaty rules may also be required if general legal concepts (like national treatment, most-favoured-nation treatment, 'fair and equitable treatment', human rights, democracy, rule of law) were left indeterminate and incompletely regulated. Yet there is often no agreement among the 193 UN member states and their citizens on how to define the 'principles of justice' mentioned in numerous treaties (eg the UN Charter, human rights treaties); also, the 'balancing' of state-centered principles (like state sovereignty) and person-centered principles (like human rights and democratic sovereignty) in national Constitutions and in the jurisprudence of national and international 'courts of justice' often remains contested. This study uses the distinction of 'four stages of legal theory' by the American legal philosopher Ronald Dworkin, in order to develop a coherent methodology for clarifying the legal interrelationships among different principles and incomplete rules of multilevel regulation:

— At the *semantic stage* of law, many legal terms remain indeterminate 'interpretive concepts' that may be used by different actors with different meanings.
— At the *jurisprudential stage*, multilevel regulation (eg of the economy and health protection) requires justification in terms of 'principles of justice' (eg state-centered versus cosmopolitan, constitutional or global administrative law conceptions of IEL) and elaboration of a convincing theory of 'rule of law' that citizens can accept as legitimate.
— At the *doctrinal stage*, the 'truth conditions' have to be constructed of how particular fields of law-making and administration (eg competition rules based on economic theories of undistorted competition) can best realize their values and justify their practices and ideals (eg insisting on competition, environmental and social law limiting 'market failures' as a pre-condition of a well-functioning 'social market economy' as required by EU law).
— *Judicial administration of justice* must apply, clarify and enforce the law in concrete disputes by independent and impartial rule clarification that institutionalizes 'public reason' and protects equal rights and social peace.[56]

[56] Cf R Dworkin, *Justice in Robes* (Cambridge, MA, Harvard UP, 2006) 9 ff.

Dworkin convincingly criticized the 'conservative bias' of too many legal positivists claiming, like Professor Hart, that 'the existence and content of law can be identified by reference to the social sources of law'[57] without reviewing path-dependent, traditional legal practices in the light of 'principles of justice' as reflected in constitutional laws.[58] Yet even though 'principles of justice' are integral parts of modern national and international legal systems, their legal definition risks being influenced—or even manipulated—by subjective value premises.[59] Since Aristotle, procedural, distributive, corrective, commutative justice and equity continue to be recognized as diverse 'spheres of justice' in the design of legal and dispute settlement systems (eg, for 'violation complaints', 'non-violation complaints' and 'situation complaints' pursuant to GATT Article XXIII). Post-colonial IEL also includes 'principles of transitional justice' based on preferential treatment of less-developed countries (eg, in Part IV of GATT and in the dispute settlement system of the WTO), as well as 'cosmopolitan principles of justice' based on the universal human rights obligations of all UN member states. In contrast to the 'freedoms of the ancient' (Constant), which protected only limited freedoms of a privileged class of male property owners (eg in the republican constitutions of Athens and Rome 2,500 years ago), modern constitutional democracies and international law proceed from 'inalienable', equal human rights, constitutional rights and judicial remedies of citizens as preconditions for 'constitutional justice'.[60]

The 'rules of recognition' discussed in Chapter 1, and the 'collective action problems' in multilevel governance of the different kinds of 'aggregate PGs' discussed in Chapter 2, confirm that legal and judicial clarification of the relationships between state-centered 'principles of justice' (like the UN Charter principles of 'sovereign equality of states' and 'rule of law' among states) and citizen-orientated 'principles of justice' (like human rights and democracy) remains the central problem in the interpretation and judicial enforcement of multilevel economic and health regulations. From the point of view of moral and legal cosmopolitanism underlying modern HRL and also increasing parts of IEL, the state-centered UN and WTO governance fails to protect 'cosmopolitan justice' and international PGs effectively for the benefit of citizens. The multilevel governance of the world trading system and of other PGs (like public health) requires more coherent legislative, administrative, judicial and international legal protection of cosmopolitan

[57] Cf HLA Hart, *The Concept of Law*, 2nd edn (Oxford, OUP, 1994) 269.

[58] Cf R Dworkin, 'Hart's Postscript and the Character of Political Philosphy' in (2004) 24 *OJLS* 1.

[59] Cf M Sornarajah, 'Introduction' in AD Mitchell, M Sornarajah and T Voon (eds), *Good Faith and International Economic Law* (Oxford, OUP 2015) 1.

[60] Cf EU Petersmann, 'Human Rights, International Economic Law and "Constitutional Justice"' (2008) 19 *EJIL* 769–98.

rights and other 'principles of justice', empowering citizens and domestic courts to insist on more effective implementation of UN and WTO legal commitments. This study focuses on the central 'constitutional challenge' of the twenty-first century, ie whether the needed 'constitutionalization' of UN, WTO and regional governance institutions is feasible in spite of the diversity of national legal and governance systems; and how it can be promoted by 'republican' and 'cosmopolitan' constitutionalism in view of the inevitable limits of parliamentary control of multilevel governance in UN, WTO and regional institutions. For instance, as discussed in Chapter 1, do the major nine UN human rights conventions and their implementation in regional and national HRL offer adequate 'universalizable principles of justice' for protecting the equal freedoms and human rights of citizens in multilevel governance of transnational PGs? As human rights also protect individual and democratic diversity, national Constitutions differ from each other, depending on the democratic preferences, resources and historical experiences of the people concerned. Does UN HRL require national constitutional democracies to be complemented by multilevel 'cosmopolitan *demoi*-cracy' that recognizes citizens not only as holders of 'inalienable' and 'indivisible' human rights, but also as 'UN and WTO citizens' and 'democratic owners' of all multilevel governance institutions for the collective supply of PGs, thereby complementing national constitutional and citizen rights by transnational cosmopolitan rights and responsibilities? How can person-orientated, 'constitutional interpretations' and adjudication be promoted in state-centered UN and WTO governance?

So far, UN and WTO governance eludes effective parliamentary, democratic and constitutional control; human rights and general consumer welfare are not effectively protected in UN law, and are not even mentioned in GATT/WTO law. How can the 'constitutional functions' of UN and WTO guarantees for protecting equal freedoms, non-discriminatory treatment, transnational rule of law and individual access to justice for citizens inside and beyond national borders be rendered legally more effective in view of the self-interests of governments to limit their legal, democratic and judicial accountabilities for not effectively implementing UN and WTO rules, for instance by invoking power-orientated justifications of 'freedom of manoeuvre'[61] of politicians to violate UN and WTO obligations that

[61] Even though the Lisbon Treaty prescribes 'rule of law' (Art 2 TEU) and 'strict observance of international law' (Art 3 TEU) for all EU institutions, the term 'freedom of manoeuvre' continues to be used by both the political EU institutions and the EU Court of Justice (eg in Joined Cases C-120 and C-121/06 P, *FIAMM* [2008] ECR I-6513, para 119) as the main justification for their disregard of legally binding UN conventions, WTO rules and WTO dispute settlement rulings. On the legal inconsistency of justifying this interpretation by the 'institutional balance' between the political and judicial EU institutions see ch 2, sections IV and V.

parliaments approved for the benefit of citizens? Even where UN and WTO agreements are incorporated into domestic legal systems for the benefit of citizens (as in EU law), they do not effectively restrain multilevel governance failures due to the inadequate protection of UN and WTO law inside most domestic legal systems. As discussed in Chapter 1, EU constitutional law, the European Parliament and the CJEU have failed to protect EU citizens against persistent violations by political EU institutions of the constitutional requirement of 'strict observance of international law' and of 'protection of citizens' (Article 3 TEU) in conformity with their constitutional rights, eg as defined in the EUCFR and in the 'cosmopolitan foreign policy constitution' of the EU (cf Articles 3, 21 TEU). Also, in most Anglo-Saxon democracies outside Europe, governmental treatment of citizens as mere objects of intergovernmental UN and WTO regulation—without rights and effective remedies to invoke and enforce UN and WTO rules in domestic courts—continues to be justified by government executives as a requirement of 'political realism'. The domination of UN and WTO governance by governments interested in accommodating political interest groups in exchange for political support (eg for re-election of politicians) entails that the governmental self-interests in preventing domestic courts from also acting as agents of the *international* order (eg in the sense of Scelle's *dédoublement fonctionnel*)[62] prevail over the 'constitutional functions' of UN and WTO law to protect transnational rule of law and other rules-based, transnational PGs for the benefit of citizens beyond national boundaries.

V. LEGAL METHODOLOGY: NEED FOR EMBEDDING CONSTITUTIONAL DEMOCRACIES INTO MULTILEVEL REPUBLICAN AND COSMOPOLITAN CONSTITUTIONALISM

Law can be divided into three diverse fields:

— first, law as an *instrument of multilevel regulation of social relations* through private and public, national and international law-making, administration, adjudication and other forms of social regulation (eg as discussed by legal philosophy, jurisprudence and empirical legal doctrines about 'law and economics');

— secondly, law as a *legal and institutional system* based on 'primary rules of conduct' and 'secondary rules' of recognition, change and enforcement (eg as discussed by legal theory); and

[62] Cf A Tzanakopoulos, 'Domestic Courts in International Law: The International Judicial Function of National Courts' (2011) 34 *Loyola of Los Angeles International & Comparative Law Review* 153–88.

— thirdly, law as *legal culture*, transforming the 'law in the books' into 'law in action' as social facts and compliance with legal rules (eg as analysed by legal sociology).

As a socially agreed effort at subjecting human conduct to the governance of 'just rules', law is voluntarily complied with by law-abiding citizens only to the extent of a 'reflective equilibrium' in the relevant moral, political and legal communities that the legal rules and governance can be justified vis-à-vis citizens in terms of their underlying 'principles of justice', like 'inalienable human rights' and constitutional agreements on the 'inner morality of law'.[63]

As discussed in Chapter 1, section II, modern international and European law explicitly recognize this need for justifying the legal coherence and legitimacy of law and governance in terms of 'principles of justice' so as to promote continuous congruence between the 'law in the books' and the social 'law in practice'. Hence, the three functions of law as (i) an instrument of social change, (ii) a coherent legal system of 'primary' and 'secondary rules' and principles, and (iii) a legal culture based on reciprocal interactions between citizens and multilevel governance institutions must complement each other. Also the legitimacy and effectiveness of international law and of multilevel governance of transnational 'aggregate PGs' (like rule of law) depend on their interactions with domestic legal practices of citizens complying with the international rules as a matter of 'justice' (as discussed in Chapter 1, section II) and of democratic self-governance.[64] The empirical

[63] On the democratic premise of citizens as 'free and equal persons' due to their 'two moral powers (a capacity for a sense of justice and for a conception of the good) and the powers of reason (of judgment, thought and inference connected with these powers)', rendering persons free and capable of individual and democratic self-legislation, see J Rawls, *Political Liberalism* (n 9) 19, 310 ff. As empirical data on *how the world is* do not tell us *how the world should be*, moral, political and legal norms need to be justified by a 'reflective equilibrium' justifying the normative propositions in terms of their underlying 'principles of justice', as discussed in ch 1, section II. On the 'two moralities of duty and of aspiration', the 'inner morality of law' and related procedural and substantive 'rule of law criteria', see LL Fuller, *The Morality of Law*, rev edn (New Haven, CT, Yale UP, 1969).

[64] On the moral and sociological need for constructing law 'bottom up' by involving all citizens and actors concerned in the making, administration and adjudication of (inter)national rules, see J Brunée and SJ Toope, *Legitimacy and Legality in International Law: An Interactional Account* (Cambridge, CUP, 2010) 86: 'Interactional law only emerges when shared understandings become fused with a "practice of legality", rooted in *Fuller's eight criteria of legality* and embraced by a community of practice that adheres to those criteria in day-to-day decision-making'. On Fuller's 'inner morality of law criteria' as constitutive elements of 'legality' and the rule of law, see Fuller (n 63) 197–200. On the interrelationships between these eight principles of *generality* (law must take the form of general rules), *publicity* (law must be published), *clarity* (law must be comprehensible and not overly vague), *consistency* (laws must not contradict one another), *feasibility* (it must be possible for people to comply with the law), *constancy* (law must not change too rapidly), *prospectivity* (law cannot be retroactive) and *congruence* (law must be administered and enforced as it is written) with human rights law, see D Luban,

fact that the intergovernmental 'management' of UN and WTO rules remains so often 'disconnected' from domestic legislators, administrators, courts, citizens and non-governmental actors—as illustrated by the more than 500 WTO disputes since 1995 over alleged non-compliance with WTO legal obligations, and by the frequent lack of effective, domestic implementation of many UN and WTO legal obligations (eg in many African countries)—reveals the major 'constitutional problem' of UN and WTO governance of international PGs: if citizens and civil society fail to understand international rules and to support their implementation in domestic legal systems in order to protect transnational PGs through coherent multilevel regulation, the rules cannot realize their declared objectives (like 'providing security and predictability to the multilateral trading system' pursuant to Article 3:2 DSU). The large number of international disputes (eg in the WTO and investment arbitration) also illustrates that many governments disagree on how the often vaguely drafted international rules should be interpreted and implemented in domestic legal systems. Such disagreements—both among the state parties to international agreements and among citizens over their rights vis-à-vis government agents with limited, delegated powers—reduce the reciprocity and effectiveness of multilevel regulation of transnational PGs, for instance by lending themselves to claims that WTO rules and dispute settlement rulings may be 'disregarded' if 'efficient breaches' of WTO law enhance 'national welfare' as defined by trade politicians.[65] The 'public consultations' of EU citizens in 2014 revealed widespread civil society criticism of investor-state arbitration rules in the FTAs of the EU (eg with Canada); this politically forced the EU institutions to suggest radical reforms of these investment rules and procedures for the CETA and Transatlantic Trade and Investment Partnership (TTIP) with the USA.[66]

The term 'legal methodology' is used here as the 'best way' for identifying the 'sources' of legal systems, the methods of legal interpretation, the 'primary rules of conduct' and 'secondary rules of recognition, change and adjudication', the relationship between 'legal positivism', 'natural law' and

'The Rule of Law and Human Dignity: Re-examining Fuller's Canons' (2010) 2 *Hague Journal of the Rule of Law* 29.

[65] On the inconsistency of such 'anti-legal' claims with WTO law (eg the WTO requirements of 'good faith compliance' and termination of illegal measures), see J Jackson, 'International Law Status of WTO DS Reports: Obligation to Comply or Option to "Buy Out"?' (2004) 98 *AJIL* 109 ff.

[66] On these interdependencies between 'legal orders', related 'interpretative communities', 'social legal fields' and communities of citizens demanding changes in international investment law, see J Pauwelyn, 'The Rule of Law without the Rule of Lawyers? Why Investment Arbitrators are from Mars, Trade Adjudicators from Venus' (2015) 109 *AJIL* 761–805. On the EU proposals for new investor-state adjudication, see A Reinisch, 'The EU and Investor-State Dispute Settlement: From Investor-State Arbitration to a Permanent Investment Court' in Centre for International Governance Innovation, *Investor-State Arbitration Paper No 2* (Waterloo, Ontario, March 2016).

'social theories of law', and the 'dual nature' of modern legal systems. The etymological origins of the word methodology—ie the Greek word *meta-hodos*, referring to 'following the road'—suggest that globalization and its transformation of most national PGs into transnational 'aggregate PGs'—like human rights, rule of law, democratic peace and mutually beneficial, international monetary, trading, development, environmental, communication and legal systems promoting 'sustainable development'—require new legal methodologies in order to enable citizens and peoples to increase their social welfare through global cooperation.[67] All three different dimensions of law—as (i) a normative ordering of social cooperation, (ii) a coherent legal system of 'primary rules of conduct' and 'secondary rules' of recognition, change and adjudication, and (iii) social facts ('living law') based on 'legal socialization' and compliance by legal subjects with legal rules and principles—need to be reviewed from the perspective of globalization, the changing context of legal systems, and the instrumental function of law as 'social engineering' and 'just ordering' of social relations. For instance:

— the traditional European legal distinctions between private law (sub-divided into regulation of persons, things and actions, contract law, property law, family law and inheritance law), national public law (sub-divided into constitutional law and administrative law) and international law are increasingly challenged by the emergence of transnational law and multilevel regulatory systems driven no longer only by states, but increasingly also by non-governmental and international actors, as illustrated by transnational regulation of the Internet (*lex digitalis*) and of global 'sports law';
— the new 'legal pluralism' based on *functional* rather than only *territorial* legal sub-systems (eg WTO membership admitting not only states but also sub- and supranational customs territories like Hong Kong and the EU) entails conflicts of jurisdiction that challenge the boundaries and cultures of national, transnational and international legal and judicial systems, and related legal pre-conceptions (*Vorverständnis*) of legal actors;[68]
— as the 'collective action problems' of the diverse kinds of 'pure' or 'impure' PGs tend to differ depending on their diverse regulatory

[67] Pure 'PGs' (like sunshine, clean air, inalienable human rights) tend to be defined by their non-rival and non-excludable use that prevents their production in private markets. Most PGs are 'impure' in the sense of being either non-rival (eg 'club goods') or non-excludable (like common pool resources). Economic, political and legal 'PGs theories' are discussed below in ch 2, sections I–II.

[68] For case studies of competing jurisdictions of national, European, international and arbitral courts, see, eg N Lavranos, *Jurisdictional Competition. Selected Cases in International and European Law* (Groningen, Europa Law Publishing, 2009).

contexts,[69] Chapter 2, sections I–IV engage in empirical case studies and also discuss international relations theories that focus on *states* (like realism, institutionalism, functionalism)—or on individual and non-governmental actors in order to disaggregate the black box of 'states' (like 'public choice', constitutional or other constructivist theories)—so as to explain the choices of *political actors*.[70]

Chapter 1 argues that the emerging 'multilevel human rights constitution' based on national, regional and UN HRL, requires a 'new philosophy of international law' that focuses on the human and constitutional rights of citizens, and on the corresponding duties of all multilevel governance agents to respect, protect and fulfil human rights and other PGs. From this 'constitutional perspective', Chapter 1 criticizes the frequent disregard for human rights and for related, constitutional 'principles of justice' in the interpretation of the 'rules of recognition' of international law as defined in Article 38 of the ICJ Statute. Chapter 2 emphasizes the need for

— *sociological legal approaches* (eg aimed at promoting rule compliance by making governance agents more legally and judicially accountable);
— *comparative institutionalism* (eg comparing the relative effectiveness of the law and governance practices of FTAs and of different international organizations); and
— *constitutional approaches* aimed at limiting 'collective action problems' by extending cosmopolitan and 'republican constitutionalism' to the constitution, limitation, regulation and justification of multilevel governance institutions.

Empirical case studies (eg of multilevel trade, tobacco and health regulation in the WHO, WTO and EU) are used for illustrating how stronger cooperation—in conformity with the 'consistent interpretation' and

[69] For instance, while 'best-shot PGs' (like the invention of pharmaceuticals against global diseases) may be promoted unilaterally through private-public partnerships in a single country, transnational 'aggregate PGs' may require universal participation of states in a worldwide 'global administrative law regime' (like the Universal Postal Union) or 'constitutional regime' (like multilevel legal and judicial protection of transnational rule of law and human rights).

[70] On 'realist challenges' of international law (eg by the BRICS) and of the 'idealism' associated with inter-war legal and political scholarship, and the emergence of alternative political science conceptions of international law (notably 'liberalism', 'institutionalism' and 'constructivism') overcoming realism's hostility to international law by explaining the mutual advantages of international rules and institutions and 'legal constructivism', see JL Dunoff and MA Pollack (eds), *Interdisciplinary Perspectives on International Law and International Relations. The State of the Art* (Cambridge, CUP, 2014). The '*status quo* bias' of American international relations theories and their frequent neglect of UN and WTO law and adjudication are often criticized by Europeans as 'an American crusade' aimed at justifying hegemonic US power politics without offering convincing strategies or leadership for collective supply of many international PGs (like transnational rule of law and protection of human rights, climate change prevention) beyond national US interests.

'integration' requirements of customary international law (eg as codified in Article 31:3(c) VCLT)—among multilevel governance institutions and protection of cosmopolitan rights through multilevel judicial remedies can strengthen 'republican constitutionalism' for multilevel supply and protection of transnational PGs.

Exploring the five propositions outlined in sections II and IV, ie

1. the 'globalization challenge';
2. related 'constitutional adjustment challenges';
3. 'constitutional' and mutually 'consistent interpretations' in multilevel governance based on 'common constitutional principles' underlying multilevel regulation of PGs;
4. transnational 'socialization' of law through 'republican constitutionalism', with due regard to the changing context of multilevel regulation; and
5. 'cosmopolitan constitutionalism' protecting rights of citizens as 'constituent powers' beyond state borders vis-à-vis multilevel governance institutions with limited, 'constituted powers',

raises numerous legal methodology questions. For instance, *propositions 3–5* are discussed by using the 65 years of 'trial and error' in European integration as policy lessons for extending 'republican' and 'cosmopolitan' constitutionalism to multilevel governance of transnational PGs in the external relations of the EU. Yet governments in Africa, the Americas and Asia rightly insist on the legitimacy of 'constitutional pluralism': the constitutional mandate of the Lisbon Treaty (eg in Articles 3 and 21 TEU) to 'export' the EU's constitutional values in the EU's external agreements with third countries may not reflect the democratic preferences and 'public reason' of peoples outside Europe; it has been criticized (eg by non-democratic rulers) as Euro-centric 'cultural imperialism', and has supported civil society struggles abroad against abuses of power (eg invoking the 'human rights clauses' in EU agreements with African countries as justification for the 'Arab Spring').

A. Lessons from European Integration Law for Multilevel Governance of Global Public Goods?

European integration law emerged in the 1950s based on the pragmatic 'Jean Monnet method', as reflected in the 'Schuman Declaration' of 1950 proposing the creation of a functionally limited European Coal and Steel Community (ECSC):

> Europe will not be made all at once ... It will be built through concrete achievements, which first create a *de facto* solidarity. The gathering of the nations of

> Europe requires the elimination of the age-old opposition of France and Germany ... The solidarity in production thus established will make it plain that any war between France and Germany becomes not merely unthinkable, but materially impossible.[71]

This pragmatic, functionally limited policy paradigm illustrates the 'normative force' of certain social realities, such as the human conflicts resulting from 'fast rational egoism' and only 'slower, reasonable human thinking'.[72] It was modified by the enlargement of the ECSC through the European Economic Community (EEC) Treaty of 1957, implementation of which was influenced by the German *ordo*-liberal conception of a common market with supranational competition rules. *Ordo*-liberalism aimed at limiting 'market failures', as well as government failures, through a multilevel 'legal community' based on transnational rule of law and constitutional 'checks and balances' (eg by the EC Court of Justice), as explained by Hallstein (the first President of the EEC Commission) and Müller-Armack (Germany's chief negotiator of the EEC Treaty).[73] European economic integration based on the EEC Treaty confirmed the 'functional spill-overs', which Jean Monnet (as President of the ECSC High Authority) had expected from prioritizing *economic* integration over *political* and *defence integration* (as rejected by the French National Assembly in the 1950s).

Another 'paradigm shift' emerged from the 'judicial transformation' of the EEC Treaty, resulting from judicial interpretation of the 'common market freedoms' and other EEC Treaty provisions (eg on gender equality) as fundamental economic and social rights of citizens to be protected by national and European courts of justice. Due to the increasing invocation of EU rules by citizens in domestic courts, European integration law no longer evolved only as 'international law among sovereign states'; it was progressively transformed into multilevel constitutional law (eg based on principles of legal primacy, direct effect and direct applicability of EU rules), protecting ever more civil, political, economic and social fundamental rights of citizens and other 'constitutional principles' derived from the common constitutional traditions of EEC member states and codified today in the EUCFR.[74]

Subsequent amendments and enlargements of the EC Treaties continued the 'twin ideas of integration and of pluralistic, participatory federalism'.[75]

71 Full text in *EC Bulletin* 5-1980, 14–15.

72 Cf Kahneman (n 4).

73 Cf W Hallstein, *Europe in the Making* (London, Allen, 1972).

74 Cf P Pescatore, *The Law of Integration* (The Hague, Sijthoff, 1974); G di Federico, *The EU Charter of Fundamental Rights. From Declaration to Binding Instrument* (Dordrecht, Springer, 2011).

75 M Cappelletti, 'Foreword' in Cappelletti, Seccombe and Weiler (eds) (n 12), vol 1, book 1, at VIII.

This expansion was both substantive, for instance by launching and progressively establishing the European Monetary and Economic Union on the basis of the 1992 Maastricht Treaty, and geographical, due to the progressive extension of the common market to (now) 28 EU member states, and additional, associated EFTA states' joining the common market through the EEA Agreement with the EU. The dynamic evolution of European integration law reflects the potential, progressive 'constitutionalization' of multilevel economic governance more clearly than the less distinct efforts at 'constitutionalizing' worldwide institutions and multilevel governance outside Europe, for example through compulsory jurisdiction for third-party adjudication of disputes among 164 WTO members, including sub-national (like Hong Kong, Macau and Taiwan) and supra-national WTO members (like the EU), and multilevel judicial governance based on cooperation among national, regional and WTO dispute settlement systems. It remains contested which policy lessons may be learnt for functionally limited UN and WTO governance from the dynamic transformations of European integration law. For instance:

— The 1951 ECSC and 1957 EEC Treaties among (initially) six member states were progressively transformed—notably through judicial interpretation of the common market freedoms and competition rules as fundamental rights of citizens—into a micro-economic '*ordo*-liberal economic constitution' that protected non-discriminatory conditions of competition among economic actors in the common market, equal fundamental rights and transnational rule of law.[76]
— The 1992 Maastricht Treaty changed this 'economic constitution' by adding a 'macroeconomic monetary constitution' for the progressive elaboration of a European Monetary Union.
— The 1997 Amsterdam Treaty provisions on a common 'area of freedom, security and justice' initiated an additional 'security constitution' that was progressively extended by additional security policy coordination (notably following 9/11).
— The 2007 Lisbon Treaty commitments to protecting human rights, democratic governance, 'strict observance of international law' and active EU participation in multilevel UN and WTO governance of transnational PGs laid the foundations for a 'cosmopolitan foreign policy constitution' (cf Articles 3 and 21 TEU), as discussed in Chapter 1, section V.
— The Eurozone crisis measures adopted since 2010 transform and 'constitutionalize' multilevel economic governance of the now 19 Eurozone member countries, thereby 'fragmenting' the European Economic

[76] Cf K Tuori and K Tuori, *The Eurozone Crisis* (Cambridge, CUP, 2014) 5 ff.

and Monetary Union among all EU member states. Even though the role of courts in macro-economic policy coordination remains more limited than in micro-economic common market regulation, Eurozone crisis measures were increasingly challenged both in the CJEU[77] and the national courts. The 'OMT decision' of 14 January 2014 by the German Constitutional Court[78]—initiated, *inter alia*, by constitutional complaints from some 36,000 German citizens who invoked their 'right to democracy' (Article 38 German Basic Law) and the democratic and judicial accountability of German government institutions to control the monetary policy powers of the European Central Bank (ECB)—requested a preliminary ruling from the CJEU on, *inter alia*, the question of whether the decision of the ECB Governing Council of 6 September 2012 on purchases of government bonds of over-indebted Eurozone member countries in 'secondary money markets' exceeded the limited monetary policy powers of the ECB. The judgment by the CJEU of 16 June 2015 specified the legal conditions (eg following from the constitutional principle of proportionality) under which the ECB decision on the OMT programme could be construed as being consistent with the limited ECB competences and the TEU prohibition of monetary financing of budgets. The final judgment by the German Constitutional Court of 21 June 2016[79] concluded that—if these conditions formulated by the CJEU in its judgment of 16 June 2015 and intended to limit the scope of the OMT programme are met—the constitutional rights of the complainants are not violated, as the ECB decision on the OMT programme did not 'manifestly' exceed the limited competences of the ECB. Even though the Constitutional Court expressed 'serious objections' to the reasoning in the judgment of the CJEU, it accepted the restrictive interpretations in that judgment as still remaining within the mandate of the CJEU under Article 19 TEU.

— The dynamic evolution of European HRL—as codified in the ECHR and in the EUCFR, and progressively clarified through the human rights jurisprudence of the CJEU, the EFTA Court, the ECtHR and national courts, the incorporation of the common constitutional principles of EU member states into EU law and the EU accession to the ECHR—illustrates how the integration of HRL and IEL has strengthened protection of civil, political, economic, social and cultural rights in all

[77] Cf Case C-370/12, *Pringle v Ireland*, judgment of 27 November 2012, EU:C:2012:756, and Case C-62/14, *Gauweiler et al v Germany*, judgment of 16 June 2015, EU:C:2015:400. For a detailed analysis of these judgments, see V Borger, 'Outright Monetary Transactions and the Stability Mandate of the ECB: *Gauweiler*' (2016) 53 *CML Rev* 139–96.

[78] On this decision (2 BvR 2728/13 of 14 January 2014) see the special issue of the *German Law Journal* 2014, 107–382.

[79] 2 BvR 2728/13; cf Press Release No 34/2016 of 21 June 2016.

28 EU member countries and associated EFTA countries by promoting a new, transnational human rights culture. The EUCFR's integrated, innovative conception of dignity rights, liberty rights, equality rights, solidarity rights, citizen rights and of guarantees of 'access to justice' differs from the fragmented protection of human rights in separate UN human rights conventions; it proves that 'integrating HRL and IEL' can *strengthen* the constitutional foundations and enforcement of human rights in and beyond IEL. Chapter 1 argues more generally that 'integration law' respecting constitutional rights of citizens (like EU and EEA law) has empirically proven to be more powerful and more effective than 'fragmentation law' based on the sovereign freedom of states to regulate transnational PGs without reference to human rights and other person-orientated 'principles of justice' (like GATT law).

B. From 'Economic Citizenship' and State Citizenship to 'Cosmopolitan Citizenship' in Multilevel Governance of Public Goods?

The rights-based, citizen-orientated conception of European integration law confirms that democracy and collective supply of PGs through republican constitutionalism depend on empowering citizens and civil society to assume responsibility for their common interests in PGs like common markets and rule of law. Without such rights-based incentives, transforming formerly authoritarian states (eg in Eastern Europe, Africa and many Asian countries) into constitutional democracies has proved difficult. The European historical experience with citizen-driven struggles for republican constitutionalism confirms the policy conclusion of this study that—just as *objective principles* and *institutions of justice* (eg courts of justice) can become effective only if citizens and government officials also practise justice *subjectively* as a republican virtue—democracy depends on democratic virtues of citizens; legal protection of constitutional, participatory and deliberative democracy must complement parliamentary, representative democracy and institutionalize 'public reason' so as to enhance the democratic capabilities of governance institutions for collective supply of PGs.

As explained by Dworkin, the adverse impact of the ideological antagonism in American society on the decreasing capacity of the US Congress to reach agreement among Republicans and Democrats on legislative compromises, reflects decreasing 'democratic virtues' to respect legitimate 'constitutional pluralism'.[80] The civil, political, economic, social and cultural human rights protected by HRL aim not only at empowering citizens to

[80] Cf R Dworkin, *Is Democracy Possible Here?* (Princeton, NJ, Princeton UP, 2006).

realize their individual and democratic self-development with due respect for different 'contexts of justice' (eg respect for the rights of refugees and economic migrants in European integration); they also reflect republican and democratic 'duties to the community', as recognized in Article 29:1 of the Universal Declaration of Human Rights (UDHR), for instance duties to respect the equal rights and personal privacy of citizens (eg their family lives, freedom of religion), and to protect political, economic, social and cultural rights against 'market failures' as well as 'governance failures' like under-supply of PGs. As discussed in Chapter 1, section II, the republican 'principles of justice' defined in national Constitutions and in numerous treaties cannot become effective without recognition of human rights to justification of governmental restrictions on individual rights; arguably, neglect of the governmental duties to justify PGs in terms of equal rights and welfare of citizens is the main cause of the current crises in European integration (eg the majoritarian 'Brexit request' to terminate the rights and benefits of British citizens under EU law and their participation in collective protection of European PGs). 'Republican virtue politics' and judicial 'administration of justice' must protect 'rights ethics' and a corresponding 'responsibility ethics' for collective protection of PGs, just as 'inalienable' and 'indivisible' civil, political, economic, social and cultural human rights require legal and judicial 'balancing' in order to promote overall coherence of legal systems.

Chapter 2 argues that the one-sided domination of UN/WTO governance by government executives—without effective parliamentary, democratic and judicial control by citizens and civil society institutions—is a major reason for many 'collective action problems' in multilevel economic and health governance (eg welfare-reducing trade protectionism, the global 'tobacco epidemic' that killed 100 million people during the twentieth century). The recognition and justification—in some treaty constitutions (*sic*) establishing UN Specialized Agencies—of health rights (eg in the WHO constitution), labour rights (eg in the ILO Constitution) and food rights (eg in the law of the FAO and its World Food Convention) reflect the insight that individual rights to protection of PGs (eg health rights) can set incentives for more inclusive, more coherent and more accountable protection of PGs (like public health), for instance by empowering citizens to challenge 'market failures' (like the sale of toxic tobacco products) and related governance failures in domestic courts. Legal history and social anthropology confirm that—as human beings have to earn a living in order to survive (*homo laborans*), and strive for social recognition in their professional lives (*homo faber*)—rights-based and citizen-driven contract law, property law, economic law (eg regulating money and trade), tort law and criminal law have been essential elements of national and international legal systems since ancient times. Such legal rules hold individuals legally accountable for what a morally indifferent *homo economicus* may perceive as 'efficient breaches' of the law. Similarly, the more individuals depend on political cooperation for the collective supply of PGs (*homo politicus*), the more must the reasonable self-interests of citizens in collective supply of PGs be protected through democratic and republican rights (*homo ordinans*). Legal anthropology and sociology can help to design rules and institutions so as to make law and governance socially more effective. For instance, the legal prioritization of economic integration and economic rights in European integration before World War I and following World War II was driven by reasonable self-interests of citizens in protecting the PG of a mutually beneficial division of labour beyond state borders through FTAs, European common market law and GATT/WTO law.

Just as European economic market integration has created incentives for complementary 'policy integration' (eg for social integration of foreign workers and their families into host states),[81] so does the acceptance by all five UN Security Council veto powers of rights-based commercial, trade and investment law with compulsory jurisdiction for the peaceful resolution of transnational economic disputes offer empirical evidence for the 'Jean Monnet method' of using mutually beneficial economic cooperation for creating *de facto* solidarity and progressive 'spill-over effects' promoting legal and policy integration. By protecting the 'direct applicability' of treaty rules by citizens and their legal enforceability through domestic courts (eg of individual trading rights, investor rights, intellectual property rights and human rights) in the internal and external relations of European states, citizens were empowered to act as transnational, legal subjects, 'agents of justice' and 'democratic guardians of the rule of law', in conformity with republican traditions of participatory citizen rights in multilevel governance of PGs. By transforming state citizenship into a 'dual citizenship' of the EU and of its member states (cf Articles 9–12 TEU; Articles 18 et seq TFEU), and also empowering EU citizens through the EUCFR, the 'democratic deficit' resulting from the lack of a 'European demos' was partly compensated for by the granting of rights to EU citizens that they had never enjoyed before in European history. Yet EU law also reflects ongoing power struggles and systemic treaty violations by governments; for instance, the EU's 'cosmopolitan foreign policy constitution' is often circumvented, due to the lack of effective judicial remedies for holding EU governments accountable for disregarding 'strict observance of international law' (Article 3 TEU) and for 'disempowering' EU citizens (eg by explicitly excluding private rights and judicial remedies in FTAs concluded by the EU since 2006).

This study argues that the necessary 'constitutionalization' of multilevel governance of international PGs beyond Europe should follow the lessons

[81] Cf M Dougan, NN Shuibhne and E Spaventa (eds), *Empowerment and Disempowerment of the European Citizen* (Oxford, Hart Publishing, 2012).

from European integration by complementing state citizenship with multilevel legal protection of functionally limited cosmopolitan and republican rights, thereby inducing citizens to assume responsibility for multilevel governance of economic and political 'aggregate PGs'. Transnational 'economic citizen rights' to participate and be protected in the global division of labour—similar to human rights vis-à-vis multilevel governance institutions—assume increasing importance for the individual and social welfare of citizens. European Union common market regulations avoid one-sided, libertarian conceptions of economic freedoms by also protecting civil, political and social rights, related responsibilities and the social needs of EU market participants. Similarly, international investment law increasingly changes in response to civil society demands to balance private and public interests more comprehensively by interpreting private property and investor rights in conformity with all other human rights obligations of the home and host states of the investor.[82] The need for such legal and judicial 'balancing' is now recognized by all European courts, as illustrated by the CJEU case law holding that the judicial presumption of a 'reasonably well-informed and reasonably observant and circumspect consumer' does not apply in contexts where the health risks of products are not sufficiently evident (eg due to tobacco addiction and other cognitive constraints on vulnerable consumers).[83] Constitutional and fundamental rights of citizens specify and strengthen governmental duties to regulate 'market failures' as well as 'government failures', for instance by protecting consumers against their individual weaknesses, cognitive constraints and bounded rationality so that public health protection can 'take precedence over economic considerations'.[84] Yet governmental limitations of economic and other human freedoms require legal justification (cf Article 114:3 TFEU) and must remain subject to judicial review at the request of adversely affected citizens and other market actors.

C. 'Methodological Pluralism' and the Need for 'Constitutional Coherence' of Public Goods Regimes

One major constitutional challenge of the twenty-first century is that neither citizens and civil society nor national parliaments effectively control multilevel governance of international PGs in worldwide and regional organizations.

[82] Cf PM Dupuy, F Francioni and EU Petersmann (eds), *Human Rights in International Investment Law and Arbitration* (Oxford, OUP, 2009).

[83] On this jurisprudence see JU Franck and K Purnhagen, *Homo Economicus, Behavioural Sciences and Economic Regulation: On the Concept of Man in Internal Market Regulation and its Normative Basis*, EUI Working Papers Law 2012/26, at 8 f, 14, 16, 18, 20.

[84] Case C-183/95 *Affish* [1997] ECR I-4315, para 43.

Responding to this challenge requires 'republican constitutionalism' based on cosmopolitan citizenship rights, enabling citizens to assume responsibility for holding multilevel governance institutions accountable for complying with international PGs regimes that parliaments approved for the benefit of citizens. As discussed in Chapter 3, the 'empowering functions', 'limiting functions', 'regulatory functions' and 'justificatory functions of cosmopolitan rights' are—both on normative grounds and in view of empirical evidence—essential for transforming 'disconnected UN/WTO governance' dominated by government executives into legally more connected and constitutionally more constrained governance protecting rights of citizens and peoples. The coordination of multilevel economic and health governance through WTO and WHO rules empirically confirms the normative proposition that multilevel 'integration law' embedded into constitutional, representative, deliberative and participatory democratic structures and judicial remedies can render multilevel governance of transnational 'aggregate PGs' more effective. European Union law, EEA law, international investment, commercial, Internet law and regional HRL likewise empirically confirm that multilevel judicial protection of cosmopolitan rights (eg human rights, EU and EEA common market rights, investor rights, commercial freedoms of contract and arbitration, Internet domain names) can transform 'disconnected, multilevel governance' into more effective and more legitimate 'integration law' protecting civil, political, economic and social rights of citizens beyond state borders. Like the construction of a multi-storied house accommodating diverse people under a common roof,[85] and similar to the 'plywood principle' (ie using complementary layers of wood reinforcing one other), the collective construction of transnational 'aggregate PGs' (like human rights and rule of law) must build on local, state, federal, regional and global levels of legal and political protection using mutually coherent 'constitutional principles' and 'intermediate PGs' that enable diversity and protect the overall legal, political, social and economic consistency and resilience of multilevel regulation and governance.

This dependence of multilevel governance of PGs on overall legal coherence is also emphasized in the 'rule of law assistance programs' provided by the UN for almost 150 member states.[86] The UN 'Declaration of the High-Level Meeting of the General Assembly on the Rule of Law at the National and International Levels' of 24 September 2012 emphasized the systemic importance of 'an international order based on the rule of law'

[85] Cf T Cottier, 'Towards a Five Storey House'; in C Joerges and EU Petersmann (eds), *Constitutionalism, Multilevel Trade Governance and International Economic Law* (Oxford, Hart Publishing, 2011) 495–532.

[86] Cf *Strengthening and Coordinating UN Rule of Law Activities. Report of the Secretary-General*, A/67/290, 10 August 2012.

as an 'indispensable foundation for a more peaceful, prosperous and just world': 'human rights, the rule of law and democracy are interlinked and mutually reinforcing and ... belong to the universal and indivisible core values and principles of the United Nations'.[87] The annual reports by the UN Secretary-General on 'The rule of law at the national and international levels' define the 'rule of law'

> as a principle of governance in which all persons, institutions and entities, public and private, including the State itself, are accountable to laws that are publicly promulgated, equally enforced and independently adjudicated, and which are consistent with international human rights norms and standards. It requires, as well, measures to ensure adherence to the principles of supremacy of law, equality before the law, accountability to the law, fairness in the application of the law, separation of powers, participation in decision-making, legal certainty, avoidance of arbitrariness and procedural and legal transparency.[88]

Yet as explained in a *Report on the Rule of Law* by the European Commission for Democracy through Law (Venice Commission), the legal provisions referring to the rule of law in UN law, European law and national legal systems—even if confirming that the rule of law is 'a fundamental and common European standard to guide and constrain the exercise of democratic power'—tend to remain very general;[89] for instance, as discussed in Chapter 1, section V and Chapter 2, section IV, EU institutions also use intergovernmental agreements to exclude individual rights and judicial remedies of citizens; and EU courts continue to condone persistent violations of GATT/WTO obligations by EU institutions, to the detriment of European citizens adversely affected by illegal import restrictions (eg of bananas, hormone-fed beef, genetically modified organisms).

Is this study's acknowledgement of the need for 'constitutional' and 'methodological pluralism' consistent with the five legal and policy propositions set out above for 'constitutionalizing' multilevel governance of transnational PGs? Just as HRL and 'constitutionalism' protect individual and democratic diversity, and require respect for the reality of 'constitutional pluralism', so must legal methodologies respect the reality of 'methodological pluralism' (eg in designing diverse kinds of 'human rights constitutionalism' and justifying 'theocratic' conceptions of law in some Muslim countries).[90]

[87] UN Declaration of the High-Level Meeting of the General Assembly on the Rule of Law at the National and International Levels of 24 September 2012, A/RES/67/1, paras 1, 5.

[88] Cf *Delivering Justice: Programme of Action to Strengthen the Rule of Law at the National and International Levels. Report by the Secretary-General*, A/66/749, 16 March 2012, para 2. The same definition was used in many previous reports by the UN Secretary-General (eg *The rule of law and transitional justice in conflict and post-conflict societies*, Doc S/2004/616 of 23 August 2004).

[89] Cf *Report on the Rule of Law* (Venice, Venice Commission, 2011) 14.

[90] Cf EU Petersmann, 'JIEL Debate: Methodological Pluralism and its Critics in International Economic Law Research' (2012) 15 *JIEL* 921–70.

Chapter 1 argues that—in view of the universal recognition of 'inalienable' human rights by all UN member states—'principles of justice' and 'democratic constitutionalism' must be discursively justified by citizens as 'agents of justice'. The universal commitment to respect for 'human dignity' (eg in terms of 'reason and conscience' as universally recognized in HRL) entitles individuals and peoples to conceive of themselves as autonomous authors and addressees of 'constitutional contracts', 'democratic self-government' and legitimate law. This study hopes to contribute to the global discourse on how to interpret the existing yet under-theorized 'principles of justice' in international law (eg UN HRL) and multilevel adjudication. Its analysis of UN and WTO governance of 'aggregate PGs' remains selective, for instance by focusing on 'constitutional problems', 'collective action problems' and the limited, yet important contribution of the EU's external relations law and policies to 'republican constructivism' in reforming UN and WTO law and governance.[91] It is written from the perspective of a German constitutional lawyer who practised European and international law for more than 35 years in German, European, UN, GATT and WTO legal and political governance institutions, and who benefitted from teaching IEL in numerous universities in Africa, the Americas, Asia and Europe. Discourse theories insist on the 'justificatory equality' of all reasonable citizens affected by the collective 'construction' and discursive justification of 'constitutional contracts' and 'principles of justice'. Hence, economists, political scientists and lawyers with different professional and academic experiences are likely to favour different worldviews and methodologies. Mutual criticism, public debate and respect for 'reasonable disagreement'—rather than a Platonic search for 'philosopher kings'—offer the best way for improving the 'human condition', for instance by overcoming stumbling blocks (such as the 'Brexit referendum' of June 2016) like a 'happy Sisyphus' (Camus). The 'dignity' of human beings 'endowed with reason and conscience' (Article 1 UDHR) and their 'inalienable human rights' justify not only the republican demand of not being dominated by arbitrary power in the search for a 'good life' and PGs; the human right to individual self-determination also requires democratic justification of governance on the basis of general and reciprocal 'principles of justice' that can be shared by all citizens affected and participating in democratic debates on equal terms. 'Practical' and 'public reason' justifying law and governance institutions must remain subject to constant review and critique in the relevant democratic,

[91] On this role of the EU as a 'policy exporter' shaping the international legal order, see more generally G Falkner and P Müller (eds), *EU Policies in a Global Perspective. Shaping or Taking International Regimes* (London, Routledge, 2014); D Kochenov and F Amtenbrink (eds), *The European Union's Shaping of the International Legal Order* (Cambridge, CUP, 2014).

republican and 'cosmopolitan communities' in order to morally justify respect for the law. As explained in Chapter 1, international lawyers focusing one-sidedly on path-dependent, state-centered 'Westphalian principles of justice' should review their value premises and accept their moral responsibility for justifying their frequent neglect of the customary law requirement to interpret treaties and settle related disputes 'in conformity with the principles of justice', including 'human rights and fundamental freedoms for all'.[92]

[92] On the controversial question of the relevance of theories of justice for a self-enforcing, constitutional democracy for justifying modern international law see, eg, T Hinton (ed), *The Original Position* (Cambridge, CUP, 2015), Introduction and ch 12. While J Rawls's 'Law of Peoples' focused on the limited question of what kind of principles of justice should guide liberal peoples in their international relations (eg with non-liberal societies and 'outlaw regimes' living in separate states that are neglecting the mainly domestic causes of the welfare of peoples), the remainder of this book argues that the fact of globalization (including also universal recognition of human rights by all UN member states) has rendered Rawls's view of the separateness of states outdated; human rights and related 'principles of justice' have become the most important justifications also of international institutions, and collective supply of most PGs requires multilevel, republican and cosmopolitan constitutionalism for limiting abuses of public and private powers through multilevel protection of PGs vis-à-vis all affected citizens.

1

Human Rights, 'Constitutional' Treaty Interpretation and Judicial Protection of Individual Rights in Multilevel Governance of Public Goods

I. INTRODUCTION

DOES THE AUTHORITY of international law derive from its validity and legally binding obligations regardless of the content of the specific rules if they have been accepted by states, as claimed by most diplomats and 'legal positivists' (eg perceiving national and international law as a single system deriving its 'legality' from higher customary or constitutional 'basic norms', 'sources of law' and consent of governments and peoples)? Or has this path-dependent 'standard view' of 'international law among sovereign states' become inconsistent with the universal recognition of 'inalienable' human rights (including a *jus cogens* core of human rights) and of democratic self-determination? Do democratic conceptions of 'international law among sovereign peoples' and cosmopolitan conceptions of 'international law among citizens' require content-dependent 'constitutional limitations' (eg individual rights of 'access to justice' and judicial remedies against 'unjust' restrictions of human and constitutional rights), as claimed in democratic and civil society struggles for human rights, decolonization and 'democratization' of intergovernmental power politics, and as increasingly acknowledged by national, European and also worldwide courts of justice in their judicial review of claims of international legal obligations?[1] Is legal positivism's claim to separate law from morality consistent with the incorporation of 'inalienable' human rights and other 'principles of justice'

[1] For a discussion of competing conceptions of international law, see B Cali, *Authority of International Law: Obedience, Respect and Rebuttal* (Oxford, OUP, 2015). On political conceptions of compliance with international law as offering a 'spectrum' of policy choices rather than only an 'either/or', see A Chayes and AH Chayes, *The New Sovereignty. Compliance with*

into modern national and international legal systems, and with the 'constitutional mandates' of modern courts of justice to identify and interpret the rules they apply in their settlement of concrete disputes in accordance with the agreed 'rules of recognition' in the jurisdiction concerned? Under what conditions must formal 'legal authority' claims of binding international legal obligations (like the customary rules of state immunity for acts *jure imperii*) give way to 'inalienable' human rights of 'access to justice', and to judicial protection of constitutional and human rights and of their underlying 'substantive justice' claims (eg to reparation of injury suffered by victims of war crimes)?[2] Should compliance with international law be governed only by 'national interests' (as defined by diplomats and national parliaments), or by democratic and cosmopolitan interests of citizens, especially if they cooperate in regional 'unions' of states, peoples and citizens (like the EU) with national and transnational citizenship rights, so as to collectively protect transnational PGs like human rights, the rule of law, common markets and monetary unions beyond national frontiers and beyond 'Westphalian international law among states'?

Multilateral (eg UN and WTO) agreements about protecting international PGs tend to be 'incomplete'; they often delegate powers to international courts to 'clarify' indeterminate legal concepts and settle disputes among states, without offering unambiguous answers to the legal methodology questions mentioned above. How are we to reconcile 'dynamic', 'systemic' and 'functional treaty interpretations' (eg based on principles of 'effectiveness' of treaty rules and agreed treaty objectives) with concerns that international political and judicial bodies lack democratic legitimacy if their subsequent treaty interpretations go beyond what national parliaments and peoples expected when they approved international treaties?[3] The Preamble to and Chapter I of the UN Charter justify UN law essentially in terms of

International Regulatory Agreements (Cambridge, MA, Harvard UP, 1998). On the increasing number of national court cases (eg in Germany and Italy) and European court cases (notably by the CJEU) giving priority to constitutional and human rights over inconsistent international law obligations, see, eg, the contributions to the symposium on 'Judgment No 238/2014 of the Italian Constitutional Court on the Constitutional Legality of State Immunity for International Crimes' (2014) XXIV *Italian Yearbook of International Law* 1–60.

[2] See, eg, F Francioni, 'From Deference to Disobedience: The Uncertain Fate of Constitutional Court Decision No 238/2014' (2014) XXIV *Italian Yearbook of International Law* 1–6. For a discussion of this judgment (finding the Italian legislation implementing the 2012 ICJ judgment on *Jurisdictional Immunities of the State* to be incompatible with Arts 2 and 24 of the Italian Constitution and the human right of access to justice in case of violations of 'inviolable' human rights), see also R Pavoni, '*Simoncioni v Germany*, Judgment No 238/2014 of 29 October 2014' (2015) 109 *AJIL* 400–06.

[3] For instance, in May 2016, the USA informed the WTO Dispute Settlement Body that it could not support the reappointment of the WTO Appellate Body judge from Korea in view of the US concern that some Appellate Body judgments during the tenure of this judge had

four principles and objectives, without specifying the legal interrelationships and ranking of these agreed 'principles of justice':

— 'to reaffirm faith in fundamental human rights, in the dignity and worth of the human person, in the equal rights of men and women and of nations large and small' by 'promoting and encouraging respect for human rights and fundamental freedoms for all without distinction as to race, sex, language or religion';
— '[t]o develop friendly relations among nations based on respect for the principle of equal rights and self-determination of peoples' and 'on the principle of the sovereign equality of all Members' of the UN;
— peaceful settlement of international disputes without threat or use of force 'in conformity with the principles of justice and international law', without intervening 'in matters which are essentially within the domestic jurisdiction of any State';
— duties to cooperate internationally and with the UN so as 'to establish conditions under which justice and respect for the obligations arising from treaties and other sources of international law can be maintained'.

A. How to Clarify the 'Constitutional Principles' Underlying UN Law?

The interrelationships between these 'constitutional principles'—human rights, democracy, transnational rule of law and peaceful settlement of disputes with due respect for the sovereign equality of states and for 'access to justice'—were left indeterminate in the UN Charter. Their legal clarification is not a matter of 'truth' but rather of 'constructing public reason' supported by agreements of citizens and their democratic institutions. Arguably, from the perspective of modern European integration law, the progressive specification of these legal interrelationships in numerous UN and regional legal

exceeded the legitimate role of Appellate Body judges by 'restricting trade agreement rights or expanding trade agreement obligations' as negotiated and accepted by WTO members and approved by the US Congress (quoted from S Lester, 'Appellate Body Drama', in *International Economic Law and Policy Blog* of 13 May 2016). On previous US complaints that the Appellate Body jurisprudence had neglected the text of Art 17:6(ii) of the WTO Anti-dumping Agreement by focusing on the 'correct interpretation' resulting from the application of the customary rules of treaty interpretation (as required by the first sentence of Art 17:6(ii)) rather than on the exploration of whether the anti-dumping rules allow—and require judicial deference—for more than one 'permissible interpretation' (as envisaged in the second sentence of Article 17:6(ii)), see D McRae, 'Treaty Interpretation by the WTO Appellate Body: The Conundrum of Article 17(6) of the WTO Antidumping Agreement' in E Cannizzaro (ed), *The Law of Treaties Beyond the Vienna Convention* (Oxford, OUP, 2011) 164–83.

instruments over the past 70 years confirms what was already universally agreed in the 1948 UDHR. For instance:

- 'recognition of the inherent dignity and of the equal and inalienable rights of all members of the human family is the foundation of freedom, justice and peace in the world' (Preamble UDHR);
- 'it is essential, if man is not to be compelled to have recourse, as a last resort, to rebellion against tyranny and oppression, that human rights should be protected by the rule of law' (Preamble UDHR);
- 'All human beings are born free and equal in dignity and rights. They are endowed with reason and conscience and should act towards one another in a spirit of brotherhood' (Article 1 UDHR);
- '[e]veryone has the right to an effective remedy by the competent national tribunals for acts violating the fundamental rights granted him by the constitution or by law' (Article 8 UDHR);
- '[e]veryone is entitled in full equality to a fair and public hearing by an independent and impartial tribunal, in the determination of his rights and obligations and of any criminal charge against him' (Article 10 UDHR);
- '[e]veryone has the right to take part in the government of his country, directly or through freely chosen representatives. Everyone has the right of equal access to public service in his country. The will of the people shall be the basis of the authority of government; this will shall be expressed in periodic and genuine elections which shall be by universal and equal suffrage and shall be held by secret vote or by equivalent free voting procedures' (Article 21 UDHR);
- '[e]veryone is entitled to a social and international order in which the rights and freedoms set forth in this Declaration can be fully realized' (Article 28 UDHR);
- '[e]veryone has duties to the community in which alone the free and full development of his personality is possible. In the exercise of his rights and freedoms, everyone shall be subject only to such limitations as are determined by law solely for the purpose of securing due recognition and respect for the rights and freedoms of others and of meeting the just requirements of morality, public order and the general welfare in a democratic society' (Article 29:1 and 2 UDHR).

The now more than 70 years of legal and human rights practices based on UN law have entailed that the international legal system—even if not always and universally enforced—is no longer based only on state consent and power politics; international lawyers and judges, as custodians of international law, increasingly construe legitimate authority in international law as being dependent on consistency with the 'inalienable core' of HRL, as illustrated by the successful decolonization of colonial territories all over the world and the acceptance of human rights obligations and of judicial remedies by all UN member states. Some countries (like China, Russia, the USA) continue to ratify and implement only few UN human rights and ILO labour rights conventions in view of their power-orientated conceptions of 'international law among sovereign states'. Yet even if they advocate narrower conceptions of HRL, they respect that other countries have ratified most UN, ILO and regional human rights conventions as promoting universal, moral and legal rights deriving from respect for human dignity.[4] The dialectic tensions and antagonistic interactions between competing principles of 'state sovereignty', 'popular sovereignty' and 'individual sovereignty' (as protected by 'inalienable' human and constitutional rights) prompt constitutional democracies and their courts of justice to insist that state power and also transnational governance powers must be democratically constituted and limited by human rights (as safeguards of freedom and equality of citizens) in order to be recognized as legitimate.

Hobbesian conceptions of 'state sovereignty' (eg justifying absolute monarchical powers by the alleged incapacity of human beings to govern themselves peacefully) have become inconsistent with HRL, and with its constitutional assumption that only democratic self-government can protect equal rights of citizens and other PGs legitimately and effectively. As democratic citizens delegate only limited powers to governments and to transnational governance institutions, *individual* and *democratic sovereignty* have more legal and political legitimacy than power-orientated claims in the name of *state sovereignty* aimed at protecting order (eg as defined by authoritarian rulers) rather than human rights and democratic self-governance. Since the entry into force of the UN Charter in 1945, human rights, democratic self-government and rule of law have been legally protected in hundreds of UN human rights instruments, human rights conventions, and national constitutional, legal and institutional guarantees in ever more UN member states and regional agreements. Arguably, in the twenty-first century, these 'constitutional principles' (like respect for 'inalienable' and 'indivisible' civil, political, economic, social and cultural human rights, the rule of law,

[4] See, eg, J Rawls, *The Law of Peoples* (Cambridge, MA, Harvard UP, 1999) 79 ff (arguing for only limited political functions of UN HRL to justify the legitimacy of states, interventions in international relations and the limitation of pluralism among peoples). The 2007 Lisbon Treaty on European Union (eg Arts 2, 3, 21 TEU) and its EUCFR recognize more comprehensive civil, political, economic and social human rights as integral parts of European law deriving from respect for human dignity. Recognition of international HRL as deriving from respect for human dignity does not entail that all moral human rights are part of UN or European HRL. Yet the moral and legal justification of UN HRL by human dignity and basic human needs (including institutionalization of 'public reason') recognizes much broader 'political functions' of HRL (eg in the context of international health law, copyright law, humanitarian and criminal law) than the narrow conceptions advocated by Rawls and by advocates of power-orientated, 'realist conceptions' of 'international law among sovereign states'. In contrast to Rawls's narrow conception of human rights, UN law also protects democratic rights and recognizes situations (eg due to humanitarian disasters, climate change) where 'burdened societies' may require comprehensive 'humanitarian interventions'.

democracy, sovereign equality of peoples and of their states) are no longer only treaty obligations but also general principles of law binding on all UN member states.[5] Globalization contributes to progressive expansion of human, constitutional and cosmopolitan rights. Due to the lack of a '*demos*' beyond nation states, the transnational protection of 'representative democracy' (Article 10:1 TEU) can no longer be separated from 'constitutional', 'deliberative' and 'participatory' democracy requiring decisions to be taken 'as openly and as closely as possible to the citizen' (Article 10:3 TEU). The more international treaties pursue 'legislative functions' for collective supply of PGs demanded by citizens, the more multilevel HRL and constitutional law also call for 'constitutional interpretations' of international rules for the benefit of citizens as 'democratic principals' vis-à-vis government agents with limited, delegated powers. As discussed below, this is increasingly recognized not only in the jurisprudence of national and international commercial, investment and criminal tribunals and European economic and human rights courts (eg deriving individual rights from international treaties among states); ICJ jurisprudence also increasingly protects human rights in multilevel governance of transnational PGs, requiring mutual 'balancing' of state-centered and person-centered principles of law.

B. 'Human Rights Constitutionalism' Requires 'Constitutional Mind-Sets'

This chapter explains why the multilevel 'human rights constitutionalism' and the customary law requirements of interpreting treaties and settling related disputes 'in conformity with principles of justice', including 'human rights and fundamental freedoms for all' (as codified in the Preamble to and Article 31 of the VCLT), require 'constitutional interpretations' of international law and adjudication. As every UN member state has recognized human rights treaties and recognized human rights as part of customary international law (or even *jus cogens*), the rights and obligations of states and international organizations under international law must be construed and protected in conformity with their respective human rights obligations, including the UN legal guarantees of the rights of all *peoples* to self-determination (cf the common Article 1:1 of the 1966 UN Covenants on civil, political, economic, social and cultural rights) and the human right of every *citizen* (eg pursuant to Article 25 ICESCR, Article 21 UDHR):

(a) To take part in the conduct of public affairs, directly or through freely chosen representatives;

[5] Cf O De Schutter, *International Human Rights Law* (Cambridge, CUP, 2010) 31 ff; P Macklem, *The Sovereignty of Human Rights* (Oxford, OUP, 2015).

(b) To vote and to be elected at genuine, periodic elections which shall be by universal and equal suffrage and shall be held by secret ballot, guaranteeing the free expression of the will of the electors;
(c) To have access, on general terms of equality, to public service in his country.

Many state representatives and their legal advisers from national ministries of foreign affairs often resist—in UN institutions (like the UN General Assembly, the International Law Commission, the ICJ) too—limitations on their discretionary foreign policy powers by 'constitutional interpretations' (eg of the general principles of international law) and 'cosmopolitan interpretations' of the 'international community' (as consisting not only of states, but also of non-governmental and intergovernmental institutions, peoples and citizens) so as to protect 'state consent' as a precondition for accepting international obligations. Yet due to the universal recognition of 'inalienable' human rights, citizens must be recognized as 'constituent powers' who, in the twenty-first century, delegate only limited powers to multilevel governance institutions mandated to protect human rights and other PGs. Constitutional legitimacy derives—in both national and international legal systems—from respecting and protecting free and equal citizens governing themselves, even if this universal legal requirement of HRL often continues to be disregarded in the practices of many governments and—due to inadequate 'constitutionalization' of international legal systems and the limited 'constitutional powers' of international institutions—democratic legitimacy of international rules derives from their voluntary acceptance by UN member states. Moreover, as the 'rules of recognition' must also be interpreted 'in conformity with human rights and fundamental freedoms for all', the 'legal validity' of 'inalienable' human rights derives from their mutual recognition among citizens even if the 'genealogy' of human rights treaties is based on state consent. Due to the universal human rights obligations of all UN member states, the moral duties of citizens to form just institutions that are necessary for respecting, protecting and fulfilling human rights, apply to relations among human beings inside and beyond state borders; they are also necessary preconditions for legitimate multilevel governance and protection of many other international PGs, even if—due to their different legal and democratic contexts—national *governments* and *multilevel governance institutions* must be designed in different ways. As discussed in section V below, in contrast to the wide foreign policy discretion acknowledged in most national Constitutions, the EU's 'cosmopolitan foreign policy mandate' (eg in Articles 3 and 21 TEU) is more constitutionally constrained (eg by limited delegation of powers, multilevel parliamentary and judicial review) and more precisely committed to 'protection of human rights' (eg as specified in the EUCFR) and 'strict observance of international law' (Article 3:5 TEU).

C. Civil Society Struggles for Justice and Human Rights

The increasing number of 'human rights revolutions' (eg in Arab countries) is also motivated by the worldwide political experience that human rights, democratic self-government, the rule of law and other PGs demanded by citizens and universally recognized in UN law cannot be effectively protected without 'democratic constitutionalism'. Monarchical conceptions of national law ('*l'état, c'est moi*') and power-orientated, 'realist paradigms' of 'international law among sovereign states' have all too often failed to protect human rights and other PGs for the benefit of citizens. In contrast to the French human rights revolution of 1789, which ushered in terror, the American human rights revolution that followed the 1776 Declaration of Independence succeeded in establishing a stable constitutional democracy. This success was due to the progressive transformation and institutionalization of the constitutionally agreed 'principles of justice' into democratic legislation, administration and adjudication that protected constitutional rights and were supported by the majority of citizens, notwithstanding temporary discriminations (eg against women and racial minorities) and related 'transitional justice principles' (eg as defined by US courts) reflecting political compromises imposed by democratic majorities. The opposition by many rulers to similar processes of transforming UN HRL into more effective constitutional, legislative, administrative and judicial remedies explains why so many governments (eg in Africa and Asia) do not effectively protect human rights. Pragmatic diplomats fear that exploring 'principles of justice'—like staring at the sun—risks blinding people to the possibility of pragmatic progress here and now.

In European law, the emerging 'multilevel human rights constitution' based on the ECHR and European constitutional law continues to progressively 'constitutionalize' human rights in European integration, thereby limiting abuses of multilevel governance powers and complementing national constitutionalism by reinforcing and strengthening multilevel protection of human rights. Human rights law and multilevel judicial protection of cosmopolitan rights—by constituting human rights beyond constitutional democracies, limiting and regulating multilevel governance powers, and justifying judicial control and constitutionalization of multilevel legislation, administration and judicial powers—challenge the traditional 'horizontal paradigm' of 'international law among sovereign states' by a 'constitutional paradigm' focusing on protection of citizens against abuses of limited, multilevel governance powers.[6] The human right 'to a social and international

[6] In the Introduction to this book, 'constitutionalism' was defined as a *dynamic process* of constituting, limiting, regulating and justifying legislative, administrative and judicial governance powers based on constitutionally agreed principles of justice and fair procedures for

order in which the rights and freedoms set forth in this Declaration can be fully realized' (Article 28 UDHR) illustrates how human rights may justify 'cosmopolitan interpretations' of IEL and call for constitutional order. Such 'human rights to have additional cosmopolitan rights' that empower citizens beyond nation states, are constitutionally necessary for limiting path-dependent 'state-centered interpretations' by 'citizen-orientated interpretations' in order to supplement 'member-driven governance' (eg of the WTO) with 'citizen-driven self-governance' in transnational markets based on decentralized self-regulation (eg commercial law inside and among TNCs), and rights of citizens to invoke and enforce precise and unconditional IEL rules in domestic courts so as to protect transnational rule of law for the benefit of citizens. The 'Brexit referendum' of June 2016 illustrates how 'civil society struggles for justice'—if manipulated by populist prejudices (like *xenophobia*) and disinformation (eg on participation in the EU common market without free movements of persons)—may also undermine agreed multilevel constitutionalism inside democracies that are committed to 'national exceptionalism' (as illustrated by the numerous exemptions of the United Kingdom (UK) from EU law).

D. The Impact of the 'Human Rights Revolution' on Legal Methodology Remains Neglected in International Law

This chapter argues that UN, WTO and many other IEL agreements remain 'incompletely theorized agreements', whose state-centered, government-driven interpretations need to be limited by cosmopolitan interpretations that promote a 'better fit' of IEL with HRL on jurisprudential grounds (like 'constitutional justice', human rights, rule of law) and doctrinal grounds (like promotion of economic efficiency, general consumer welfare, public goods). 'Constitutional interpretations' of indeterminate and under-theorized treaty terms are also justifiable from the perspective of 'legal positivism' and the judicial task of justifying legal interpretations 'in conformity with principles of justice' as the 'best fit'.[7] The cosmopolitan conception of

the collective supply of PGs demanded by citizens. Cf also S Gardbaum, 'Human Rights and International Constitutionalism' in JL Dunoff and JP Trachtman (eds), *Ruling the World? Constitutionalism, International Law and Global Governance* (Cambridge, CUP, 2009) 233–57. On the need for revealing the (implicit) preconceptions determining legal interpretations and choices of legal methods, see J Esser, *Vorverständnis und Methodenwahl in der Rechtsfindung* (Munich, Beck, 1972). Arguably, rights-based conceptions of 'constitutional contracts' are necessary for making the agreed 'principles of justice' self-enforcing, just as cosmopolitan conceptions of international law and 'constitutional interpretations' of international treaties enhance their decentralized enforceability at the request of citizens.

[7] Cf EU Petersmann, 'International Trade Law, Human Rights and the Customary International Law Rules on Treaty Interpretation' in S Joseph, D Kinley and J Waincymer (eds), *The WTO and Human Rights* (Cambridge, CUP, 2009) 69–90; R Dworkin, *Justice in Robes* (Cambridge, MA, Harvard UP, 2006) 9 ff, 20 ff.

multilevel constitutionalism as a precondition for transnational rule of law in multilevel governance of 'aggregate PGs' limits nationalist conceptions of (big 'C') Constitutionalism by establishing 'an integrative basic conceptual framework for a general theory of public law that integrates national and international law'.[8] The cosmopolitan paradigm of multilevel governance of transnational 'aggregate PGs' based on 'cosmopolitan public reason' provides a more coherent approach to regulating the 'collective action problems' in multilevel governance beyond states for the benefit of citizens. The prevailing, statist conceptions of (big 'C') Constitutionalism (eg as a 'constitutional contract' of 'We the people' delegating limited powers for governing a democratic, political community as a sovereign nation) need to be reconciled with the factual and legal limitations of state sovereignty by globalization, international law and governance of transnational 'aggregate PGs' in the multilevel, legal and political framework of UN and WTO rules and institutions.

The 'inalienable core' of human rights—such as legal respect for human dignity, individual and democratic autonomy, equal freedoms and basic human needs—is not refuted by the fact that, like traffic rules, many specific legal human rights guarantees are not effectively protected against violations of law in many UN member states. The customary rules of treaty interpretation (as codified in Articles 31–33 VCLT) not only require that '[a] treaty shall be interpreted in good faith in accordance with the ordinary meaning to be given to the terms of the treaty in their context and in the light of its object and purpose' (Article 31:1); Article 31:3 also clarifies that '[t]here shall be taken into account, together with the context ... (c) [a]ny relevant rules of international law applicable in the relations between the parties'. As all UN member states have accepted human rights obligations as well as other 'principles of justice' under the UN Charter and under additional UN conventions, the Preamble to the VCLT emphasizes

> that disputes concerning treaties, like other international disputes, should be settled by peaceful means and in conformity with the principles of justice and international law,
>
> *Recalling* the determination of the peoples of the United Nations to establish conditions under which justice and respect for the obligations arising from treaties can be maintained,
>
> *Having in mind* the principles of international law embodied in the Charter of the United Nations such as the principles of the equal rights and self-determination of peoples, of the sovereign equality and independence of all States, of non-interference in the domestic affairs of States, of the prohibition of the threat of

[8] Cf M Kumm, 'The Cosmopolitan Turn in Constitutionalism: On the Relationship of Constitutionalism in and beyond the State' in Dunoff and Trachtman (eds) (n 6) 258–325, at 264.

> use of force and of universal respect for, and observance of, human rights and fundamental freedoms for all ...

This chapter argues that—in the twenty-first century—the above-mentioned customary law rules of textual, contextual, functional and also justice-orientated, 'constitutional' treaty interpretation and adjudication require 'inclusive interpretations' of the 'rules of recognition' of the UN legal system in conformity with 'human rights and fundamental freedoms' and other 'principles of justice', so as to protect civil, political, economic, social and cultural rights more effectively and justify legal and judicial interpretations by their underlying 'principles of justice' (see section II). National, regional and UN HRL and related institutions have laid the foundation for an emerging 'multilevel human rights constitution' that limits 'legal fragmentation' in multilevel governance of transnational PGs for the benefit of citizens and their cosmopolitan rights (see section III). Rather than criticizing 'legal fragmentation' of UN law for creating 'structurally biased' and disconnected, functional regimes (eg of monetary law, trade law, investment law, environmental law or regional HRL and institutions administered by experts with often inadequate expertise in UN law), sections III and IV below argue that 'legal fragmentation' can often be justified as a necessary strategy for reforming state-centered 'Westphalian conceptions' of international law that unduly prioritize rights of governments over rights of citizens as 'democratic principals' of multilevel governance. Bilateral, regional and other plurilateral legal regimes often respect, protect and fulfil human rights more effectively by legal and judicial protection of cosmopolitan rights, judicial remedies, democratic participation, inclusive democratic deliberation and other accountability mechanisms in multilevel governance of PGs; legal fragmentation (eg of GATT 1947 through subsequent Tokyo Round Agreements) is often a necessary reform strategy for subsequent reintegration of legal reforms (eg the WTO Agreement replacing previous GATT law). European Union law illustrates that democratic legitimacy derives not from whatever 'We the people' may decide (eg through popular referenda); it is constitutionally limited by 'principles of justice' and constitutional restraints in democratic decision-making (such as transparency, inclusive participation, representativeness, democratic accountability, individual access to justice, the rule of law). Cosmopolitan paradigms of multilevel governance of international PGs focus on equal cosmopolitan rights and on respect for legitimately diverse 'constitutional pluralism' as legal limitations on 'state sovereignty', majoritarian power politics or hierarchical claims of 'monism' or 'dualism'.[9] Comparative institutional and

[9] On the 'international legal monism' proposed by the 'Vienna School' (eg Kelsen, Verdross, Lauterpacht) for explaining international and national law as one hierarchically integrated legal system that recognizes and authorizes states to govern themselves (eg through national Constitutions) within the limits of international law as a framework for resolving the 'collective action problems' in providing PGs, see J von Bernstorff, *The Public International Law Theory*

constitutional analyses tend to confirm the relative efficiency, reasonableness and social effectiveness of cosmopolitan rules and constitutional principles in diverse national and international legal systems.

II. THE CUSTOMARY LAW REQUIREMENT OF TREATY INTERPRETATION AND ADJUDICATION IN CONFORMITY WITH 'PRINCIPLES OF JUSTICE'

The references—in the Preamble to the VCLT—to interpreting treaties and settling related disputes 'in conformity with principles of justice and international law' had been inserted at the request of US representatives influenced by the 'New Haven School', committed to promotion of world public order through 'evolutionary interpretations'.[10] Yet most international trade and investment tribunals avoid references to 'principles of justice' and human rights unless such legal principles have been explicitly invoked by the parties to the dispute. The ICJ, by contrast, takes it for granted that 'Whatever the legal reasoning of a court of justice, its decisions must by definition be just, and therefore in that sense equitable.'[11] Further, '[e]quity as a legal concept is a direct emanation of the idea of justice. The Court whose task is by definition to administer justice is bound to apply it.'[12]

Similar to the deferential jurisprudence of the Permanent Court of International Justice (PCIJ) towards state sovereignty (eg in terms of presumptions against limitations of national sovereignty, narrow interpretations of such treaty limitations), the contribution of the ICJ to the development of HRL remained so limited during the first 50 years of ICJ jurisprudence that it became 'necessary to question whether the International Court is a court of law, let alone a court of justice'.[13] For since only states (ie legal constructs that empower the rulers over a population in a given territory, often without effective guarantees of democratic representation) may be parties in cases

of Hans Kelsen. Believing in Universal Law (Cambridge, CUP, 2010). See also Kumm (n 8, eg at 277 ff) on why both 'statist dualism' and 'international legal monism' (claiming primacy of international law) offer less persuasive accounts for protecting transnational rule of law than 'cosmopolitan constitutionalism' that connects multilevel 'constitutional principles of justice' in order to clarify the applicable 'conflict rules' and competent authority in case of conflicts.

[10] Cf R Gardiner, *Treaty Interpretation* (Oxford, OUP, 2010) 65 ff; M McDougal, H Laswell and JC Miller, *The Interpretation of Agreements and World Public Order* (New Haven, CT, Yale UP, 1967). On the ancient origins of 'principles of justice' in Greek and Roman legal traditions defining law as 'participation in the idea of justice' and conceiving of 'justice as a prerequisite to living a civic life, to living in community' (Plato), see CJ Friedrich, *The Philosophy of Law in Historical Perspective* (Chicago, IL, Chicago UP, 1963) chs II and XX.

[11] *North Sea Continental Shelf* (Judgment) [1969] ICJ Rep 48, para 88.

[12] *Continental Shelf (Tunisia v Libyan Arab Jamahiriya)* (Judgment) [1982] ICJ Rep 60, para 71.

[13] P Allott, 'The International Court and the Voice of Justice' in V Lowe and M Fitzmaurice (eds), *Fifty Years of the International Court of Justice* (Cambridge, CUP, 1996) 17, at 27.

before the ICJ, and the Court's jurisdiction is limited to cases submitted with the consent of the defendant state, large parts of the global social reality (eg non-state actors, including the 2 billion poor people living without effective protection of their human rights) have no effective access to the ICJ and are not effectively represented in disputes before it. Principles of procedural justice and of equity continue to be important in the ICJ jurisprudence on 'due process of law' and the settlement of border disputes (eg the delimitation of adjacent 'territorial seas' and 'continental shelves').[14] Notwithstanding references to human rights in some ICJ judgments and advisory opinions since the *Corfu Channel Case* (1949), it is only since the 1990s that—due to the quasi-universal commitment to human rights following the end of the Cold War—the ICJ has used HRL as *ratio decidendi* for limiting certain abuses of government powers.[15] In spite of the 'optional protocols' to some UN human rights conventions that enable individual complaints to political UN bodies, UN law does not offer legal and judicial remedies that effectively protect human rights and other 'principles of justice' vis-à-vis individuals and peoples if they are exploited by non-democratic rulers (eg in some African and Asian countries); such human rights violations are only rarely challenged in the ICJ.

The few investment disputes decided by the ICJ have been criticized as proving the inadequacy of ICJ proceedings for protecting investor rights and human rights by means of 'diplomatic protection', prior 'exhaustion of local remedies' and ICJ judgments more than 25 years after the contested governmental interferences with the investor rights (eg in the *ELSI* case).[16] The deliberate avoidance by the ICJ, up to its *Genocide Case* in 2007, of references to judgments of other international courts, and the limited jurisdiction for human rights treaties,[17] further illustrate narrow conceptions of procedural and substantive 'principles of justice' in UN law and in ICJ jurisprudence that focus on the 'sovereign equality of states' and the ICJ as 'the principal judicial organ of the UN' (Article 92 UN Charter), without effective judicial protection of 'access to justice' as a human right and 'judicial dialogues' with other jurisdictions in order to clarify 'principles

[14] Cf T Cottier, *Equitable Principles of Maritime Boundary Delimitation. The Quest for Distributive Justice in International Law* (Cambridge, CUP, 2015).

[15] For detailed analyses of the ICJ jurisprudence on human rights, see the two contributions by Judge B Simma, 'The ICJ and Human Rights', and Judge A Yusuf, 'The ICJ and the Development of Human Rights Law', in Società Italiana di Diritto Internazionale (ed), *La Tutela Dei Diritti Umani e il Diritto Internazionale* (Naples, Editoriale Scientifica, 2012) 3–30, 573–81 respectively.

[16] Cf Judge SM Schwebel, 'The Treatment of Human Rights and of Aliens in the ICJ' in Lowe and Fitzmaurice (eds) (n 13) 327, at 350.

[17] Only five of the major human rights conventions include a compromissory clause providing for jurisdiction, and none of these clauses seems to have been used so far by states for challenging human rights violations by other states in the ICJ.

of justice' other than 'state sovereignty'. The 2010 and 2012 ICJ judgments in the *Diallo Case (Guinea v Congo)* seem to be the first economic dispute in which the ICJ assessed breaches of human rights treaty obligations while referring to the jurisprudence of UN and regional human rights bodies.[18] The *Diallo* judgments illustrate the legal importance of interpreting international rules with due regard to the different 'contexts of justice' (eg depending on whether only rights of states or those of citizens too have been violated).

A. Formal and Procedural Principles of Justice in (Inter)National Legal Systems

Following the traditions in ancient city republics like Athens and Rome, statues of *Justitia* continue to stand today in town halls and courthouses all over the world as a symbol of justice, whose blindfolded eyes, scales in one hand and sword in the other represent 'principles of justice' like impartiality, the 'balancing' of conflicting claims, lawful authority and due process of law. Similar to 'discourse justifications' of human rights as necessary preconditions of the reciprocal recognition of the equal freedoms of discourse participants, the free and equal standing of litigants in a court of justice reflects the priority of 'constitutional justice' and 'procedural justice' over distributive, political and social justice. As recalled in numerous international treaties, 'principles of justice' remain important not only for judicial settlement of disputes, but also more broadly for justifying and regulating the 'basic legal structures' of national and international societies. Theories of justice, from Aristotelian 'virtue ethics' up to Rawls's theory of 'justice as first virtue of social institutions', emphasize that social cooperation—which produces rules and allocates benefits, burdens and social costs—requires justification by 'principles of justice' whenever the equal rights of citizens are restricted. Regardless of whether this need for justification is derived from deontological grounds (like human rights), morality (like respect for human dignity) or from 'communitarian arguments' (like mutually beneficial social cooperation and agreed exchanges), it also applies to the modern global division of labour and to the fulfilment of the human rights obligations of all UN member states under the UN Charter and HRL.

[18] For a discussion of these ICJ judgments (awarding damages as reparation for the violation of the human rights of Diallo), see A Vermeer-Künzli, 'Diallo: Between Diplomatic Protection and Human Rights' in (2013) 4 *Journal of International Dispute Settlement* 487; M Andenas, 'Reassertion and Transformation: From Fragmentation to Convergence in International Law' in (2015) 46 *Georgetown Journal of International Law* 685, at 712 ff.

i. Justice as Justification of 'Equal Treatment'

Application of the ancient ideal of 'distributive justice'—'treating like cases alike, and different cases differently' (*suum cuique distribuere*)[19]—often remains controversial in constitutional, legislative, administrative and judicial decision-making, in view of disagreements on the relevant grounds of legitimate differentiation. As already noted in Aristotle's *Ethics*:

> Everyone agrees that in distributions the just share must be given on the basis of what one deserves, though not everyone would name the same criterion of deserving: democrats say it is free birth, oligarchs that it is wealth or noble birth, and aristocrats that it is excellence. Consequently, the just is something proportionate ... Proportion is equality of ratios ...[20]

Perelman distinguished the following six 'most current conceptions of justice':

1. To each the same thing.
2. To each according to his merits.
3. To each according to his works.
4. To each according to his needs.
5. To each according to his rank.
6. To each according to his legal entitlement.[21]

The current transatlantic discussions on the legal limits of privacy rights (eg vis-à-vis taping of telephone conservations on grounds of 'public security') illustrate how different polities may construe national and international 'legal entitlements' and equal treatment (*suum cuique*, to each his own) differently in order to protect the security and self-determination of citizens against arbitrary domination. In many areas of international law, 'justice', as a 'relational concept' that protects 'just relations among persons', continues to be procedurally and substantively under-defined and in need of multilevel legal clarification through discursive justification vis-à-vis individuals as 'agents of justice', who are entitled to justifications whenever their human, constitutional and other rights are restricted.[22] As a common '*formula of abstract justice*' with an indeterminate variable for the 'innumerable values' that underlie 'concrete formulas of justice', Perelman proposed the following definition of *formal justice*: 'a principle of action

[19] Greek and Roman legal philosophy defined justice as a principle of morality: 'justitia est constans et perpetua voluntas jus suum cuique tribuendi' (justice is the constant and perpetual will to give to each one that to which he is entitled).

[20] Aristotle, *Nicomachean Ethics* (D Ross trans) (Oxford, OUP,1998) para 1131 a.

[21] C Perelman, 'Concerning Justice' in C Perelman, *The Idea of Justice and the Problem of Argument* (J Petrie trans) (London, Routledge 1963) at 6–7.

[22] On the human right to justification, see R Forst, *The Right to Justification. Elements of a Constructivist Theory of Justice* (New York, Columbia UP, 2012).

in accordance with which beings of one and the same essential category must be treated in the same way'.[23] The concept of justice focuses on 'a certain application of the notion of equality'.[24] 'Essential' refers to the chosen material criteria pursuant to which persons should be treated alike in the administration of justice, such as human beings entitled to equal human rights, citizens entitled to equal constitutional rights, or complainants and defendants entitled to the same 'due process of law principles' (like 'hear the other side') to be administered by impartial judges in judicial proceedings. As long as the 'essential categories' and different 'contexts of justice'[25] remain so inadequately defined and justified in many areas of international law, *formal justice*, in the sense of equal treatment, rule-following, correct interpretation and progressive clarification of the 'positive law', depends on agreed procedures rather than only on 'principles of justice' as the 'first virtue' of human beings and humane institutions.

Procedural theories of justice go beyond formal concepts of justice (eg in terms of avoiding arbitrary distinctions and discriminatory allocation of rights) by justifying and deriving (eg from HRL) substantive criteria for concrete *distributive*, *corrective*, *commutative* and *equity conceptions of justice*. For instance, 'Rawlsian justice as fairness' (as briefly discussed in ii. below), Habermas's concept of justice as inclusive discourse enabling reasonable agreement (iii. below), judicial administration of justice by independent and impartial courts of justice (iv. below), or 'constitutional justice' as defined in constitutional conventions and in multilevel constitutional protection of PGs (v. below) are used in national and international legal systems for justifying rules and interpretations through complementary procedures, with due respect for 'reasonable disagreement' among governments and citizens, who often use their 'moral powers' for defining their individual conceptions of a 'good life' and of 'social justice' in legitimately diverse ways.

ii. Rawlsian Justice as Fairness

Rawls's *theory of justice* offers a procedural interpretation of Kantian 'moral autonomy' through a 'thought experiment' of rational and reasonable individuals, who negotiate 'principles of justice' behind a 'veil of uncertainty' concerning their future positions in a law-complying, isolated society. In order to promote equal opportunities of self-development and limit unforeseen risks, they would agree on 'maximum equal liberties' subject

[23] Perelman (n 21) 16.

[24] *Ibid*, 12.

[25] On the need for distinguishing diverse 'contexts of justice' respecting private and public autonomy rights (such as privacy rights versus political rights to participate in democratic self-rule), see R Forst, *Contexts of Justice: Political Philosophy beyond Liberalism and Communitarianism* (Berkeley, CA, University of California Press, 2002).

to democratic legislation as the 'first principle of justice', and on 'difference principles' as the 'second principle of justice', so as to protect the least advantaged in society. Rawlsian *justice as fairness* expresses 'justice as a complex of three ideas: liberty, equality, and reward for services contributing to the common good'.[26] Yet the practical relevance of Rawls's ideal theory of a perfectly just society governed by *principles of justice* for the non-ideal reality of international law and adjudication (eg 'doing justice' piecemeal by resolving disputes and justifying judgments) remains deeply contested; only few constitutional democracies (like Germany) explicitly protect maximum equal freedoms of citizens in their Constitutions as a general constitutional principle subject to democratic legislation (cf Article 2:1 Basic Law of Germany). The reasonable disagreement (eg among liberals and communitarians) over how to define the 'first principle of justice' is also illustrated by Rawls's controversial proposals for an international *Law of Peoples*, based on limited duties of international assistance rather than on cosmopolitan principles of justice.[27]

iii. Justice as Deliberative Democracy

Democratic discourse theories (eg by Habermas) rely on inclusive, public discourse among free and equal citizens on alternative conceptions of the PG. Such discourse may enable 'reasonable agreement' in the 'public sphere', notably on constitutional, parliamentary, executive and judicial institutionalization of 'public reason' in order to limit potential abuses of majority politics (eg if lack of time and of 'ideal speech situations' prevent consensus); it promotes legitimate, democratic decision-making and self-governance of the people within constitutionally agreed limits.[28] Yet as long as cosmopolitan rights of access to justice, participation, justification and 'justificatory equality' remain so inadequately protected in international law and intergovernmental power politics, ideals of justifying international law by the reasonableness and inalienable human rights of citizens remain constrained by the reality of inadequate 'institutionalization' of democratic and cosmopolitan public reason beyond state borders. The 'democratic governance principles' acknowledged in numerous UN human rights conventions and related UN declarations are not effectively implemented in many UN member states and intergovernmental organizations. Moreover, as human rights

[26] Cf J Rawls, *Collected Papers* (S Freeman (ed), Cambridge, MA, Harvard UP, 1999) 48; J Rawls, *A Theory of Justice* (Oxford, OUP, 1973).

[27] See Rawls (n 4); T Hinton (ed), *The Original Position* (Cambridge, CUP, 2015), notably chs 11 and 12 (discussing the diverse 'original positions' proposed by Rawls for national democracies and for their international policies).

[28] Cf J Habermas, *Between Facts and Norms. Contributions to a Discourse Theory of Law and Democracy* (trans W Rehg, Cambridge, MA, MIT Press, 1998); J Rawls, *Political Liberalism* (Cambridge, MA, Harvard UP, 1993).

also protect individual and democratic diversity, 'reasonable disagreement' among citizens and governments with diverse conceptions of a 'good life' and 'social justice' is likely to remain a permanent fact.

iv. Judicial Administration of Justice

The legal institution of impartial, independent judges administrating justice continues to be the oldest paradigm of justice.[29] Its application to foreigners as well (eg in commercial arbitration since the ancient Roman *lex mercatoria*) reflects the cosmopolitan ideal of constitutional justice not only inside states, but also vis-à-vis foreigners as free and equal holders of rights that deserve to be protected against arbitrary domination in mutually beneficial cooperation (eg transnational commerce based on cosmopolitan rights as postulated by Kant). *Judicial theories of justice* explore the authority, legitimacy and legal methodology of courts of justice in their task of settling disputes by identifying, interpreting, clarifying and applying the positive law rules and 'principles of justice', so as to render justice, resolve the dispute and justify their judgments.[30] The judicial duties to clarify the often indeterminate text, context, objective and purpose of legal rules (eg on 'violation complaints', 'non-violation complaints' and 'situation complaints', and legal remedies against 'nullification or impairment' of treaty benefits or treaty objectives pursuant to Article XXIII:1 GATT) and of interpretive legal concepts (like justice, liberty, equality, rule of law, equity), derive from diverse 'principles of justice' aimed at protecting the rule of law and limiting injustices in different 'contexts of justice'. For instance, 'violation complaints' pursuant to GATT Article XXIII:1(a) reflect principles of formal, procedural, distributive and corrective justice; 'non-violation complaints' pursuant to Article XXIII:1(b) are primarily based on the 'agreed balance of reciprocal concessions' (commutative justice); 'situation complaints' pursuant to Article XXIII:1(c) GATT are also based on principles of equity.[31]

The 'semantic methods' for clarifying indeterminate legal terms, 'jurisprudential methods' for clarifying their underlying legal principles, 'doctrinal

[29] This is reflected in the public spaces (eg statues of *Justitia* in courthouses all over the world representing the virtue of justice as a constitutional restraint on 'the rule of men' and their 'rule by law'). The functional interrelationships between law, judges and justice are also reflected in legal language from antiquity (eg in the common core of the Latin terms *jus*, *judex*, *justitia*) up to modern times (cf the Anglo-American legal traditions of speaking of 'courts of justice', and giving judges the title of Mr Justice, Lord Justice, or Chief Justice).

[30] For an overview, see EU Petersmann, 'Constitutional Theories of International Economic Adjudication and Investor-State Arbitration' in PM Dupuy, F Francioni and EU Petersmann (eds), *Human Rights in International Investment Law and Arbitration* (Oxford, OUP, 2009) 137–94.

[31] Cf EU Petersmann, *The GATT/WTO Dispute Settlement System* (The Hague, Kluwer, 1987) ch 4.

methods' for promoting their coherent application and realization of agreed policy objectives (like 'fair price comparisons' in anti-dumping determinations), and 'adjudicative methodologies' for the administration of justice in national and international dispute settlement proceedings remain contested.[32] For example, judicial interpretations of civil, political, economic and social human rights (eg as universally agreed in UN HRL) as 'negative freedoms from' disproportionate governance restrictions, or as 'positive freedoms to' individual self-determination and self-realization, reflect divergent conceptions of liberty rights, human dignity, and of citizens as authors and addressees of constitutional democracies.[33] Legal restrictions on the different dimensions of autonomy rights may require different justifications in view of 'reasonable disagreement' on the legal relationships between ethical autonomy (what is good for my individual life?), moral autonomy (what is good for humanity?), legal, democratic and social autonomy (eg how to define equal rights and legal responsibilities in a polity with due regard to the social capacity of autonomous life in society?).[34]

v. 'Constitutional Justice' as Multilevel Constitutional Protection of Public Goods

Rawls's *Theory of Justice* uses the example of US constitutional law to demonstrate that the stability of constitutional democracies depends on a 'four-stage process' of constitutional agreement on 'principles of justice' (eg in the 1776 US Declaration of Independence) and of their progressive transformation into a national Constitution, democratic legislation, administrative application and judicial administration of justice institutionalizing 'public reason' among citizens and democratic institutions. As explained in Chapters 2 and 3, the transformation of most national PGs into transnational 'aggregate PGs' requires the extension of these dynamic transformation processes to 'constitutionalization' of multilevel governance of transnational PGs.

[32] Cf Dworkin (n 7). Dworkin's claim (as developed in his book on *Law's Empire*, 1986) that judges ('Hercules') must justify their judgments as the 'single correct interpretation' and 'best fit' of coherent legal systems—similarly to the claim of normative discourse theories that inclusive 'ideal speech situations' should enable finding the correct answer (cf Habermas (n 28) at 285 f)—remains contested, for instance whenever law includes indeterminate principles (eg 'justice', 'human dignity'), 'gaps' (eg defining as of which moment the human embryo becomes a 'human person' protected by law) and provisions delegating the 'burden of judgment' (Rawls) to competing political and judicial rule-clarification procedures requiring respect for compromise or for citizen-driven markets as decentralized 'discovery mechanisms'. Majority voting inside judicial bodies does not refute the moral duty of individual justices to justify their judgment as the 'correct finding'.

[33] Cf EU Petersmann, *International Economic Law in the 21st Century. Constitutional Pluralism and Multilevel Governance of Interdependent Public Goods* (Oxford, Hart Publishing, 2012) 172 ff (distinguishing four different concepts of liberty).

[34] Cf Forst (n 22), ch 5.

Such multilevel legislation, administration and adjudication must not only remain justifiable by the 'principles of justice' agreed within constitutional democracies (eg human rights, democratic self-governance, the rule of law and judicial accountability), with due respect for legitimate 'constitutional pluralism'; they must also create a 'constitutional culture' supported by the 'public reason' and the 'republican virtues' of citizens. The coexistence of more than 200 sovereign states with diverse legal systems and democratic preferences—and of hundreds of intergovernmental and of thousands of non-governmental organizations influenced by competing rationalities (eg profit maximization by TNCs)—makes 'legal fragmentation' an inevitable means for coordinating and reconciling the 'sovereign equality of states' (Article 2 UN Charter) with the reality of thousands of public and private international law regimes that provide public and private goods and services demanded by citizens in conformity with the diverse preferences of citizens. The transformation of the EC and EEA treaties, as well as of the ECHR, into 'constitutional instruments' that protect human rights and other fundamental rights beyond state borders through multilevel legislation, administration and adjudication, not only illustrates that functionally limited, multilevel constitutional protection of transnational PGs is a 'realistic utopia'; it also confirms that such 'constitutional reforms' depend on citizens, democratic governments and courts of justice insisting on transforming principles of justice into international law and institutions, like the European Parliament composed of directly elected EU citizens, and European courts of justice protecting common market freedoms and other fundamental rights for more than 500 million EU citizens invoking their rights of 'access to justice' and to judicial remedies against unjustified restrictions of equal freedoms. If 'sovereignty' remains inadequately constrained (eg in terms of parliamentary sovereignty, 'the king can do no wrong') and citizens stop invoking and defending their EU rights, populist *referenda* (eg on the 'Brexit' and 'Grexit') may unravel the multilevel constitutional structures (eg on EU membership) and guarantees of fundamental rights (eg under the EUCFR).

B. 'Westphalian Justice' as International Order Protected by State Power

The preceding distinctions between five formal 'principles of justice' underlying the justification of the legal ordering of social relations among individuals in national and European legal systems—ie justice as (i) justification of equal treatment, (ii) fair procedures, (iii) inclusive democratic deliberation, (iv) judicial administration of justice, and (v) 'constitutional justice' as agreed in constitutional conventions and progressively institutionalized through democratic legislation, administration and judicial protection of constitutional rights—remain incomplete and contested. Ancient Athens was democratic only in certain dimensions of its internal relations; it justified imperial and arbitrary exercises of power in its external relations. National 'political realism' (eg as advocated by Hobbes) focuses on states as the main international actors in a 'billiard ball model' of 'international law among egoist states' driven by power politics so as to maximize national security and other 'state interests'. Realists claim that just as state-centered international law reflects the status quo distribution of power rather than 'principles of justice', so also 'international adjudication is unable to impose effective restraints upon the struggle for power on the international scene'.[35] International courts can only be effective 'in those spheres which do not affect the security and existence of the state'.[36] 'Political disputes' over the use of force and the distribution of power that underlie the applicable rules of international law, risk eluding judicial control and being 'non-justiciable', as illustrated by the fact that the PCIJ considered only once such international dispute.[37]

Similarly, national courts were also often ineffective in constraining excesses of power prior to the democratic revolutions challenging power-orientated, authoritarian legal systems (eg in England in the seventeenth century, America and France in the eighteenth century). Colonial and intergovernmental power politics in the context of the GATT 1947 (which was not ratified by the US Congress) prior to the establishment of its Legal Office in 1982/83, illustrated the IEL dimensions of 'political realism'. Many GATT rules and GATT dispute settlement rulings were not effectively implemented within domestic legal systems (eg in the context of import restrictions on cotton and textiles from less-developed countries) if domestic interest groups and power-orientated majority politics objected to the adjustment costs that resulted from trade liberalization and trade regulation. The GATT 1947 was applied on the basis of a 'Protocol on Provisional Application', without ratification by national parliaments and subject to 'grandfather clauses' that protected GATT-inconsistent national legislation. Hence, the first and second Directors-General of GATT 1947 (Wyndam White and Olivier Long)—albeit both lawyers by training—deliberately avoided establishing a GATT Office of Legal Affairs up till the 1980s.[38] 'Political realists' conceive of IEL as 'international law among sovereign states' (eg GATT 1947) prioritizing

[35] H Morgenthau, *Politics among Nations. The Struggle for Power and Peace* (New York, Knopf, 1951/1985) 224.

[36] EH Carr, *The Twenty-Years Crisis 1919–1939* (London, Macmillan, 1946) 249.

[37] Cf Morgenthau (n 35) at 224 (discussing the PCIJ Advisory Opinion on the dispute over the German-Austrian Customs Union, PCIJ Series A/B no 41).

[38] Cf EU Petersmann, 'The Establishment of a GATT Office of Legal Affairs and the Limited Public Reason in the GATT/WTO Dispute Settlement System' in G Marceau (ed), *A History of Law and Lawyers in the GATT/WTO. The Development of the Rule of Law in the Multilateral Trading System* (Cambridge, CUP, 2015) 182–207.

rights of governments over rights of citizens, so as to enable 'pragmatic, intergovernmental management' of transnational economic relations. Even though GATT diplomacy aimed at remedying some injustices of colonial politics (eg by adding Part IV on 'Trade and Development' to GATT 1947), trade diplomats often continue expressing the view of Thrasymachos in Plato's *Republic*, that justice is merely whatever the powerful say it is. Realist conceptions of foreign power politics in a 'society of states' often fail to protect justice vis-à-vis individuals, including domestic citizens who participate in the global division of labour without effective judicial remedies against violations of UN and WTO agreements approved by national parliaments for the benefit of citizens, yet ignored by many domestic courts at the request of governments and diplomats who seek to limit their legal, democratic and judicial accountability vis-à-vis citizens for (inter)governmental restrictions of equal liberties and human rights in the foreign policy area. By committing the EU's external relations policies to the same 'principles which have inspired its own creation, development and enlargement, and which it seeks to advance in the wider world: democracy, the rule of law, the universality and indivisibility of human rights and fundamental freedoms for all' (Article 21 TEU), 'protection of its citizens' and 'strict observance of international law' (Article 3:5 TEU), EU constitutional law recognizes that multilevel protection of transnational PGs needs to be embedded into multilevel constitutionalism protecting rights of citizens against abuses of discretionary foreign policy powers. Yet, as discussed in section V, multilevel 'constitutionalization' of foreign policy powers remains resisted inside the EU too, for instance by 'realist claims' of EU diplomats that traditional foreign policy discretion (eg to engage in secretive FTA negotiations on FTA rules excluding rights of citizens) should not be hampered by naive 'legal wish lists for a better world'.

C. 'Democratic Justice' Based on Parliamentary Approval of UN and GATT/WTO Agreements

The foreign policies of constitutional democracies tend to be guided in diverse ways by their domestic 'principles of justice' and related governmental duties to protect the rights and interests of citizens. 'Integrity principles'[39] protecting the coherence of domestic and foreign policies—similar to the 'Habermasian justice as deliberative democracy' (as discussed in section II.A.iii above) as a normative ideal of democratic discourse theories—often lead to very diverse democratic practices, depending on whether the country, peoples

[39] Cf FJ Garcia, *Global Justice and International Economic Law. Three Takes* (Cambridge, CUP, 2013) 67 ff.

and citizens concerned prioritize constitutional, representative, participatory or deliberative forms of democratic governance. 'Wilsonian liberalism' believed that, following World War I, the USA could protect international peace through the promotion of liberal democratic values and institutions for peaceful resolution of international disputes. But the rejection by the US Congress of US membership of the League of Nations and of the compulsory jurisdiction of the PCIJ also illustrated that democratic people might refuse to project *national* democratic and judicial institutions onto *international* levels of governance in a world that includes non-liberal and 'outlaw states'. Under neither the League of Nations nor the UN has it been possible to institute effective 'world parliaments' and 'world courts' with universal compulsory jurisdictions. Following World War II, 'democratic approaches' to US foreign policies (eg as advocated by the 'New Haven School') contributed to persuading other states to ratify the UN Charter and other agreements establishing UN Specialized Agencies (like the Bretton Woods institutions) on the basis of drafts prepared by the US Government, which explicitly incorporated 'principles of justice' and 'human rights and fundamental freedoms for all' into the UN Charter and other UN agreements (like human rights instruments, the Preamble to the 1969 VCLT).[40]

Yet the policy-orientated 'democratic participant perspective' of the New Haven School was also invoked in order to justify US legal privileges (eg veto rights in UN and Bretton Woods institutions), unilateral military interventions, US refusals to participate in international PGs regimes (like the compulsory jurisdiction of the ICJ, the International Criminal Court (ICC), the Kyoto Convention on climate change prevention), and discriminatory economic sanctions (eg based on Section 301 of the US Trade Act). Constitutional and economic liberalism calls for protection of freedom of trade across frontiers and the correction of 'market failures' through non-discriminatory internal regulations in order to maximize consumer welfare; yet discretionary trade policy powers are often 'captured' by domestic interest groups without effective protection of 'equal freedoms' as the 'first principle of justice' (Rawls). Rawls's proposals for a *Law of Peoples* justify the *existing* principles of UN law for the national pursuit of international justice in an international society of liberal states, non-liberal but 'decent states', outlaw states and states burdened by unfavourable conditions,[41] without proposing a theory of global justice based on cosmopolitan or communitarian principles that limit the 'justice deficits' of international law. The limited 'duties of international assistance' recognized in Rawls's *Law of Peoples* for

[40] For a modern presentation of 10 'foreign policy principles' based on 'values of human dignity' advocated by the 'New Haven school', see WM Reisman, *The Quest for World Order and Human Dignity in the 21st Century: Constitutive Process and Individual Commitment* (The Hague, Hague Academy of International Law, 2012) 433–54.

[41] Cf Rawls (n 4) 59 ff.

a non-ideal 'society of states' reflect that nationalist 'democratic conceptions' of international law aim at legitimizing it in terms of parliamentary ratification and control of international agreements (eg US congressional ratification of the Bretton Woods Agreements, congressional control of financial assistance by the Bretton Woods institutions, US 'fast track authority' for negotiating and ratifying the 1979 Tokyo Round Trade Agreements). Such parliamentary majority politics often fails to protect human rights, justice and international PGs effectively across national borders. Proposals for developing 'global administrative law'[42] as a means of promoting transparency, legal and judicial accountability and 'good governance' of international organizations tend to be based on administrative law principles of constitutional democracies (notably US administrative law) that, likewise, risk being inappropriate for international institutions (eg due to the latter's inadequate democratic, parliamentary and judicial control).

D. 'Constitutional Justice' as Multilevel Constitutional Protection of Equal Constitutional Rights in UN Law and European Law

Following World War I, the Peace Treaty of Versailles included the 'Constitution of the International Labour Organisation' (ILO, 1919) so as 'to secure the permanent peace of the world', proceeding from the recognition that 'lasting peace can be established only if it is based upon social justice'; 'the failure of any nation to adopt humane conditions of labour is an obstacle in the way of other nations which desire to improve the conditions in their own countries' (Preamble to the ILO Constitution). Just as the more than 180 ILO conventions adopted by the ILO were justified in terms of protecting social and labour rights and peace, so were the post-World War II 'treaty constitutions' (*sic*) that established the Food and Agriculture Organization (FAO) (1945), the United Nations Educational, Scientific and Cultural Organization (UNESCO, 1945) and the WHO (1946) justified in terms of fundamental rights like:

— 'ensuring humanity's freedom from hunger' (Preamble to the FAO Constitution);
— 'to further universal respect for justice, for the rule of law and for the human rights and fundamental freedoms which are affirmed for the peoples of the world without distinction of race, sex, language or religion, by the Charter of the United Nations' (Article 1 UNESCO Constitution); as well as

42 Cf R Stewart and RM Ratton Sanchez Badin, 'The WTO and Global Administrative Law' in C Joerges and EU Petersmann (eds), *Constitutionalism, Multilevel Trade Governance and International Economic Law* (Oxford, Hart Publishing, 2011) 457–94.

— 'the enjoyment of the highest attainable standard of health [as] one of the fundamental rights of every human being without distinction of race, religion, political belief, economic or social condition' (Preamble to and Article 1 of the WHO Constitution).

Such functionally limited treaty constitutions for collective supply of transnational PGs are fundamentally different from national democratic Constitutions constituting a people and its collective supply of national PGs. Yet both national Constitutions and international 'PGs regimes' share the 'constitutional functions' of constituting, limiting, regulating and justifying limited governance powers for the benefit of citizens and their equal rights. Due to the domination of UN decision-making processes by diplomats interested in limiting their legal accountability towards citizens, UN law and governance—including the UN Specialized Agencies like the ILO, FAO, UNESCO and WHO—continue to prioritize rights of governments over rights and judicial remedies of citizens, without effectively protecting the 'constitutional functions' of UN rules in many UN member states.[43] Their domination by diplomats claiming to represent 'the state' often entails 'disconnected multilevel governance' that lacks effective implementation of international treaty obligations through democratic legislation, administration and judicial protection of rights of citizens.

Multilevel governance institutions that effectively empower citizens have been established so far only in certain regional economic and human rights conventions like the ECHR—adopted by (now) 47 'European countries ... to take the first steps for the collective enforcement of certain of the rights stated in the Universal Declaration', based on 'their profound belief in those fundamental freedoms which are the foundation of justice and peace in the world' (Preamble ECHR). The regional treaties establishing the EU, the EEA and the ECHR are interpreted and enforced by national and European courts as 'constitutional instruments' to protect regional PGs—like the European common market, human rights, fundamental freedoms and transnational rule of law for the benefit of citizens; each of these three treaty systems evolved through 'constitutional interpretations' (eg of 'common market freedoms' in the EU and EEA) by European and national courts that protected cosmopolitan rights of citizens and the democratic and judicial accountability of governments through 'evolutionary interpretations' and clarification of fundamental rights in multilevel, European regulation.[44] Yet in contrast

[43] Cf EU Petersmann, *Constitutional Functions and Constitutional Problems of International Economic Law* (Fribourg, Fribourg UP, 1991).

[44] For a comparison of the judicial methodologies of the CJEU, the EFTA Court and the ECtHR, see EU Petersmann, 'Multilevel Judicial Governance in European and International Economic Law' in S Besson and A Ziegler (eds), *Le juge en droit européen et international* (Geneva, Schulthess, 2013) 45–64.

to the hierarchical nature of *national* constitutional systems, the functionally limited 'constitutionalization' of European treaty law relies less on supranational legal hierarchies than on reciprocal protection of common 'general principles' (cf Article 6 TEU) in mutually beneficial, private and governmental cooperation beyond state borders. These common constitutional principles (eg of fundamental rights, the rule of law, democratic governance, transparency, subsidiarity and proportionality of governmental restrictions) and institutional 'checks and balances' are progressively clarified through 'judicial dialogues', 'preliminary rulings' and 'advisory opinions' among national and European courts of justice, thereby promoting 'consistent interpretations', the rule of law, 'judicial comity' among national and transnational courts, and inclusive cosmopolitan rather than power-orientated, intergovernmental 'public reason'. The Lisbon Treaty postulates more ambitious 'cosmopolitan constitutional principles' for the external relations law of the EU than can be found in most national Constitutions:

> In its relations with the wider world, the Union shall uphold and promote its values and interests and contribute to the protection of its citizens ... and the protection of human rights ... as well as to the strict observance and the development of international law, including respect for the principles of the United Nations Charter. (Article 3:5 TEU)
>
> The Union's action on the international scene shall be guided by the principles which have inspired its own creation, development and enlargement, and which it seeks to advance in the wider world: democracy, the rule of law, the universality and indivisibility of human rights and fundamental freedoms, respect for human dignity, the principles of equality and solidarity, and respect for the principles of the United Nations Charter and of international law. (Article 21:1 TEU)

European Union institutions have promoted some international law reforms, for instance by securing EU membership and 'regional organization clauses' in some UN and WTO agreements, and inserting human rights clauses into the EU agreements with some 130 third states.[45] Yet the EU institutions continue to claim 'freedom of manoeuvre' to violate treaties approved by European parliaments and, since 2006, have begun excluding individual rights in FTAs with third states. This limitation of legal and judicial accountability vis-à-vis EU citizens for welfare-reducing violations of the GATT and WTO guarantees of open markets also runs counter to the legal guarantees—in both WTO law (eg Article XVI:4 WTO Agreement, Article 3 DSU, Article X GATT) and EU law—of 'strict observance of international law' (Article 3 TEU) and judicial remedies for the benefit of citizens participating

[45] See T Takacs, A Ott and A Dimopoulos (eds), *Linking trade and non-commercial interests: the EU as a global role model?* CLEER Working Paper 2013/4.

in and benefitting from international trade. The EU's frequent disregard for GATT/WTO legal obligations and dispute settlement rulings—eg during the 20 years of the GATT-inconsistent EU import restrictions on bananas from 1992 to 2012, in spite of more than a dozen legally binding GATT and WTO dispute settlement rulings—illustrates that the rule of law in the context of the EU's common trade and agricultural policies may be as fragile as in a 'banana republic', whenever interest groups (including the comparatively small lobby of banana producers inside the EU) succeed in lobbying the EU institutions in order to reap 'protection rents' from EU violations of IEL and EU courts do not enforce 'strict observance of international law' (Article 3 TEU).[46]

E. 'Commutative Justice' in WTO Law

The WTO Agreement establishes multilevel legal, governance and dispute settlement networks outside the UN legal system, aimed at promoting reciprocal liberalization and regulation of multilateral trade based on mutually agreed 'commutative justice principles',[47] like reciprocal market access commitments (cf GATT Articles II, XXVIII) subject to sovereign rights to protect non-economic PGs (eg by using Articles XIX–XXI GATT). The mutually agreed 'reciprocal balance of concessions' among GATT/WTO members is protected by comprehensive legal and judicial remedies such as 'violation complaints', 'non-violation complaints' and 'situation complaints' under the GATT/WTO dispute settlement procedures.[48] Since the establishment of a GATT Legal Office in 1983, the transformation of the multilevel GATT dispute settlement system into a compulsory worldwide jurisdiction for the settlement of trade disputes through panel, appellate, arbitration and

[46] Cf EU Petersmann, 'Why Do the EU and its Court of Justice Fail to Protect the "Strict Observance of International Law" (Article 3 TEU) in the World Trading System and in other Areas of Multilevel Governance of International Public Goods?' in *European Yearbook of International Economic Law—Liber Amicorum for Horst G Krenzler* (Heidelberg, Springer, 2015) 145–89.

[47] The term 'commutative' is derived from the Latin verb *commutare* (meaning 'to exchange') and requires rendering to each contracting party what belongs to him; 'commutative justice' refers to mutual agreements on functionally limited 'treaty principles of justice' like reciprocal market access commitments and the economic efficiency principles underlying the legal ranking of economically 'optimal trade policy instruments' in GATT/WTO law (eg non-discriminatory domestic regulation and subsidies rather than border discrimination; tariffs rather than non-tariff trade barriers; sanitary regulations on the basis of science-based 'risk-assessments' rather than on the basis of discriminatory protectionism).

[48] Cf EU Petersmann, *The GATT/WTO Dispute Settlement System. International Law, International Organizations and Dispute Settlement* (Deventer, Kluwer, 1997) ch 4.

domestic judicial procedures continues to strengthen the rule of law and other 'principles of justice' in international trade relations, for instance by 'checks and balances' between the political and judicial branches of multilevel trade governance.[49]

Yet, similar to UN law, WTO law remains dominated by 'intergovernmental decision-making' and fails to protect its treaty objectives (like 'sustainable development') effectively due to inadequate regulation of 'market failures', 'governance failures' and of legal, democratic and judicial 'accountability mechanisms'. The WTO dispute settlement bodies recognize that WTO law does not constitute a 'self-contained regime'. Treaty-based IEL systems remain embedded in general and treaty law, as illustrated by the WTO provisions for cooperation with other treaty regimes (eg IMF law) and regulatory agencies (eg national, international and non-governmental risk assessment institutions in the field of technical and sanitary regulation). Even though WTO law provides for a multilevel legal and dispute settlement system that protects individual 'access to justice' in domestic courts (eg in GATT Article X and similar WTO provisions), many governments limit their domestic legal and judicial accountability for harmful violations of their WTO obligations by insisting that domestic courts should *not* protect domestic citizens against violations of WTO obligations and WTO dispute settlement rulings, even if adversely affected 'violation victims' and 'sanction victims' seek judicial remedies in domestic courts. Similarly, many FTAs (eg by the USA) remain dominated by hegemonic power politics rather than liberal and constitutional 'principles of justice'.[50] The implementation of the WTO agreements adopted at the 2013 WTO Ministerial Conference (eg on trade facilitation for less-developed countries, public stockholding for food security purposes, preferential treatment of least-developed countries) was subsequently blocked by India until October 2014. Such unilateral use of 'veto powers' illustrated how 'commutative justice' based on consensus among more than 160 developed and less-developed WTO members may be elusive in the twenty-first century, unless agreements among states facilitate consensus-based decision-making and judicial rule compliance for the benefit of all affected citizens.[51]

[49] On my experiences as first 'legal officer' ever employed by the GATT Secretariat in 1981, and as legal secretary of the Uruguay Round Negotiating Group (1987–93) that elaborated the Dispute Settlement Understanding (DSU) of the WTO, see Petersmann (n 38).

[50] Cf Garcia (n 39) 260 ff (describing US abuses of power in NAFTA and CAFTA dispute settlement procedures as illustrating 'how US trade policy is not always consistent with notions of justice', at 257, 324).

[51] On justifying trade transactions by voluntary consent as the 'essential characteristic making economic exchanges "trade" rather than theft, coercion or exploitation', see *ibid*, at 216, 220.

F. 'Cosmopolitan Justice' in Commercial, Trade and Investment Law

Cosmopolitan constitutionalism[52] and cosmopolitan conceptions of IEL and HRL aim at multilevel, legal and judicial protection of cosmopolitan rights (eg human, commercial, property rights, labour and social rights) so as to protect transnational rule of law for the benefit of free and equal citizens governing themselves through mutually beneficial cooperation and democratically legitimated, multilevel governance institutions. The WTO Agreement on Preshipment Inspection, for example, protects individual access of preshipment inspection companies and exporters to submit disputes over preshipment inspections to commercial arbitration in the WTO (cf Article 4), thereby decentralizing and depoliticizing related disputes among the importing and exporting countries concerned. Similarly, Article XX of the WTO Agreement on Government Procurement protects individual access to domestic courts that must review the legal consistency of domestic government procurement proceedings with the WTO Agreement. More than 3,000 bilateral and regional investment agreements replace 'diplomatic protection' of foreign investors by their home states through investor-state arbitration protecting individual rights and remedies of foreign investors. Diplomatic protection of foreign investors had become politically controversial (eg due to power asymmetries, the absence of individual rights to diplomatic protection) and legally inadequate, for instance in ICJ dispute settlement proceedings among states, ushering in judgments more than 25 years after the investment dispute arose. Prior exhaustion of local remedies in domestic courts, followed by lengthy intergovernmental disputes between the home and host states of the investor concerned (eg involving disputes over the nationality of the investor, the protection of foreign company shareholders, the substantive standards of legal protection), have proved to offer less effective legal remedies than individual access to justice and investor-state arbitration.[53]

Like other principles of justice, the cosmopolitan paradigm of multilevel economic regulation operates as a jurisprudential 'background principle' that needs to be specified through legal rules, institutions and democratic

[52] The Greek term 'cosmopolite' refers to a 'citizen of the world', recognizing all human beings as morally equal and constituting a single world community that should avoid national prejudices. 'Cosmopolitan constitutionalism' argues for multilevel constitutional and judicial protection of human rights and other cosmopolitan rights, the rule of law and democratic governance across national frontiers, as in European HRL and European common market law.

[53] Cf Schwebel (n 16); Andenas (n 18); P Muchlinski, 'The Diplomatic Protection of Foreign Investors: A Tale of Judicial Caution' in C Binder *et al* (eds), *International Investment Law for the 21st Century. Essays in Honour of C. Schreuer* (Oxford, OUP, 2009) 342–63; R Dolzer and C Schreuer, *Principles of International Investment Law* (Oxford, OUP, 2008).

procedures providing for precise conflict rules. For instance, whether investment disputes in FTAs should be settled through investor-state arbitration based on cosmopolitan investor rights or through non-discriminatory access of foreign investors to domestic courts of justice based on national treatment guarantees remains a policy choice, as currently discussed in the context of the EU negotiation of transatlantic FTAs with Canada and the USA. Both national adjudication and investor-state arbitration may be justifiable in terms of cosmopolitan constitutionalism and require 'judicial comity' and mutually consistent interpretations in national and international jurisdictions. Yet in relations between constitutional democracies (like the transatlantic FTAs of the EU with Canada and the USA) with impartial and independent courts of justice that guarantee due process of law regardless of the nationality of the parties to the dispute, investor-state arbitration privileging foreign investors entails 'negative discrimination' of domestic investors, and appears to be sub-optimal compared with non-discriminatory judicial remedies of all citizens in domestic courts. Arguably, cosmopolitanism requires reconciling the constitutional rights of all citizens with the need for protecting transnational rule of law and governmental treatment of foreigners as free and equal persons in multilevel protection of transnational 'aggregate PGs'.

If, according to the 'interest theory of rights', the purpose of rights is to protect basic human interests and judicial remedies, recognition of cosmopolitan rights is likely to promote 'public reason' and more inclusive participation in, and justification of, decision-making procedures, for instance by progressively clarifying the scope and meaning of equal rights through legislation, administration and adjudication. If multilevel governance institutions recognize each other as being engaged in a joint task of coherent protection of transnational 'aggregate PGs' for the benefit of all citizens, such multilevel legal and political cooperation is also likely to promote the legal coherence and quality of multilevel governance by focusing on a joint constitutional task and methodology rather than on fragmented legal texts.[54] Comparative legal and institutional analyses confirm that cosmopolitan legal regimes—like transnational commercial and investment law and arbitration, rights-based FTAs like the EEA, the EU common market and competition law agreements, cooperation among national and international criminal courts

[54] The decision of the German Constitutional Court in *Görgülü v Germany* (2004) 2 BvR 1481/04 postulates a constitutional duty of German courts to take into account relevant judgments of the ECtHR in clarifying constitutional and human rights in Germany: 'the Convention as interpreted by the ECtHR must be taken into account in making a decision; the court must at least duly consider it' (para 62); 'A complainant may challenge the disregard of this duty of consideration as a violation of the fundamental right whose area of protection is affected in conjunction with the principle of the rule of law' (para 30); 'as long as applicable methodological standards leave scope for interpretation and weighing of interests, German courts must give precedence to interpretation in accordance with the Convention' (para 62).

in holding individuals accountable under international criminal law—have protected international PGs (like transnational rule of law, fundamental rights) more effectively than 'Westphalian regimes' that lack effective legal, democratic and judicial accountability of governments vis-à-vis adversely affected citizens.[55] Multilevel judicial administration of justice and protection of individual rights have contributed to 'civilizing', de-politicizing and 'constitutionalizing' international law and transnational rule of law for the benefit of citizens, for instance through:

— cooperation between national courts and arbitral tribunals in the recognition, surveillance and enforcement of arbitral awards (eg deciding on contractual commercial rights, property rights and judicial remedies) pursuant to the 1958 New York Convention on Recognition and Enforcement of Foreign Arbitral Awards;
— cooperation among national and regional economic and human rights courts that protect individual rights and transnational rule of law for the benefit of more than 500 million EU citizens, whose individual rights are protected by EU law, EEA law, and the ECHR in domestic and European courts;
— the arbitration, annulment and enforcement procedures of the International Centre for the Settlement of Investment Disputes (ICSID) in cooperation with national courts enforcing ICSID awards on investor rights and obligations under bilateral and multilateral investment treaties; or
— the more than half a dozen international criminal courts complementing national criminal jurisdictions, and protecting individual rights and legal accountability through multilevel judicial cooperation.

G. Principles of Equity

As mentioned above, equity has been recognized by the ICJ as a general principle of law, and has been applied notably for delineating and reconciling overlapping claims of coastal states to the continental shelf and an exclusive economic zone (eg based on 'equidistance' and other principles balancing competing interests); the pertinent ICJ jurisprudence has contributed to clarifying the potential—as well as the limitations—of distributive justice in UN law and the need for correcting general rules by justifying exceptions on the basis of fact-intensive, creative judicial reasoning.[56] Judicial decision-making *ex aequo et bono* pursuant to Article 38 ICJ Statute

[55] Cf EU Petersmann (n 33) 145 ff.
[56] Cf n 11 and Cottier (n 14).

has hardly ever been authorized by the parties to ICJ disputes. By contrast, the judicial clarification of 'equitable principles' can remedy shortcomings of incomplete, general rules (the 'completing and corrective functions' of equity) and bring laws into conformity with contemporary perceptions of justice and regulatory needs (the 'adjustment function' of equity); it is recognized in both national and international legal systems as a requirement of 'administration of justice'.[57] Yet the 'judicial activism' and 'judicial rule-making' underlying 'equity jurisprudence' also raises legitimacy questions concerning the respective roles of legislative, administrative and judicial government bodies in clarifying 'equity standards' of justice (eg equity *infra legem*, *praeter legem* and, exceptionally, *contra legem*). Explicit legislative empowerment of courts, as in Article 4 of the Swiss Civil Code of 1907, to decide cases by recourse to equity in the absence of existing rules on the subject matter, remains rare in view of the frequent belief that 'judicial law-making'—even if necessary to protect 'individualized justice' by clarifying incomplete rules in particular disputes—risks undermining the 'democratic function' of parliamentary legislation. In view of the 'member-driven' traditions of GATT/WTO law, it is not surprising that 'situation complaints' (cf Article XXIII:1(c) GATT) and the underlying equity principles have so far never been used in GATT/WTO jurisprudence. Also the GATT provisions on 'equitable market shares' (cf Article XVI:3 GATT) and 'equitable commodity prices' (cf Article XXXVI:4 GATT) have remained contested in GATT/WTO practices.

Similar to the evolution of English equity principles and institutions into integral parts of the English legal system complementing the common law and legislation, many 'equity principles' have also become incorporated into explicit rules of European and international law (eg the Lisbon Treaty, UN HRL, the 1982 Law of the Sea Convention), for example regarding principles of good faith, estoppel, acquiescence, abuse of rights, proportionality, the protection of legitimate expectations and the delimitation of maritime borders. Human rights law, constitutionalism and multilevel judicial clarification and protection of individual rights continue to reduce the need for resorting to equity for remedying injustice. It is mainly in underdeveloped and contested areas of international law (like distribution of natural resources outside state territories, post-colonial claims for remedying past injustices, protection of 'sustainable development' and 'inter-generational equity') that equity principles continue to be invoked by governments and citizens as justifications for particular legal and redistributive claims and 'fair' dispute settlement taking into account specific, factual circumstances. As in the field of maritime boundary delimitation, the progressive legislative,

[57] Cf Cottier (n 14) 9; and RA Newman (ed), *Equity in the World's Legal Systems: A Comparative Study* (Brussels, Bruylant, 1972).

administrative, judicial clarification, development and 'constitutionalization' of such under-regulated fields of international relations (like climate change protection, access to resources in the Arctic) is likely to reduce the need for judicial recourse to general 'principles of justice'.

H. Need for Institutionalizing 'Republican Virtues' and 'Public Reason'

The compendium (*Digest*) of Roman law (*Corpus Juris Civilis*) compiled by order of the Emperor Justinian I during the sixth century defined justice as preceding and justifying positive law,[58] albeit not necessarily being identical with law (eg in the case of 'unjust laws'). It defined the requirements of personal justice in terms of the three categorical principles of living honestly (*honeste vivere*), injuring nobody (*neminem laedere*) and giving everyone his due (*suum cuique tribuere*). Since ancient times, citizens (like Antigone challenging the orders of the king in Sophocles' Greek tragedy of that name) have justified their 'struggles for justice' by claims that positive law and governance must remain justifiable in terms of 'higher' principles of justice. The statues representing ancient goddesses of justice (like Dike and Justitia) in court buildings all over the world recall such individual struggles towards realizing 'justice' in all legal cultures, for instance by requesting courts of justice to protect:

— the legal requirements for equal treatment and impartiality, and prohibitions on arbitrariness (as recalled by the blindfold of Justitia);
— legal and judicial 'balancing' of competing rights and protection of the due process of law (as recalled by the 'balance' carried by Justitia); as well as
— legal and judicial enforcement of the law (as illustrated by the sword held by Justitia).[59]

The evolution of legal cultures linking justice to religious beliefs (eg God's 'Ten Commandments', emperors deriving their legitimacy from God) and arbitrary government practices inside many UN member states also reveal profound disagreements, for instance regarding the divine origins of justice[60] and the fairness and impartiality of court proceedings (eg the jury trials

[58] Cf *Digest* 1.1.1.1: 'Jus est autem a justitia appellatum' ('Law derives its name from justice'). The notes added 'Sicut a matre sua, ergo prius fuit justitia quam jus' ('Like coming from a mother, justice was prior to law').

[59] Cf J Resnik and D Curtis, *Representing Justice. Invention, Controversy, and Rights in City-States and Democratic Courtrooms* (New Haven, CT, Yale UP, 2011).

[60] Greek mythology links the historical origin of impartial courts of justice to Aeschylus' tragedy of Orestes (who killed his mother, Clytemnestra, so as to avenge her killing of his father, Agamemnon), where the Greek goddess Athena protected Orestes from the Furies (goddesses of vengence) by submitting his case to an impartial tribunal that finally acquitted him on the basis of procedural rules of justice (*in dubio pro reo*).

condemning Socrates and Jesus, the church trials condemning Galileo Galilei). Republicanism emphasizes that the rule of law and law-abiding societies depend on law-abiding citizens, who defend their republican rights as a matter of justice and other 'republican virtues'. Both national and international republicanism not only aim at limiting 'domination' of people by unjustified abuses of power;[61] they also emphasize the need for promoting active citizenship based on 'civic virtues' and cosmopolitan rights, inducing citizens to assume republican and democratic responsibilities in and beyond their national polities, notably for democratic governance of transnational PGs.[62] The preceding overview of the diversity of 'principles of justice' invoked in national and international courts of justice illustrates that—in spite of the universal recognition of human rights and of related principles of constitutionalism—the individual and democratic diversity of peoples and of 'contexts of justice' excludes relying on any single, comprehensive theory of justice that can justify a uniform, practical approach to the necessary reforms of multilevel governance of transnational PGs. Even if justification of law and governance in terms of 'principles of justice' is recognized as 'the foundation of freedom, justice and peace in the world' (Preamble UDHR), 'there isn't (and perhaps can't be) a single path or approach to justice on a global scale in a globalizing world',[63] in view of the plurality of reasons for justice and for criticizing perceived injustices.

This legitimate diversity of procedural and substantive 'principles of justice' underscores the need for respecting 'methodological pluralism' and the legitimacy of 'constitutional pluralism' protecting individual and democratic diversity and 'reasonable disagreements' among citizens and governments with conflicting self-interests.[64] Yet it does not contradict the need for 'institutionalizing public reason' by transforming agreed principles of justice into democratic legislation, administration, adjudication and international 'PGs regimes'. 'Public reason' can be defined as a 'system of reasons that all can participate in' as an essential, reciprocal 'coordinating device' in societies that depend on decentralized support of rules and on their justification

[61] On 'rule of men' as domination, and 'rule of law' as non-domination, see P Pettit, *Republicanism. A Theory of Freedom and Government* (Oxford, OUP, 1997).

[62] On civic humanism and civic republicanism, see I Honohan, *Civic Republicanism* (London, Routledge, 2002).

[63] Cf Garcia (n 39) 10, 51. On the different 'grounds of justice' (like shared membership in states; common humanity; humanity's collective ownership of the Earth; shared membership in world society; and shared membership in the global trading system) justifying international rules and related 'principles of justice', see M Risse, *On Global Justice* (Princeton, NJ, Princeton UP, 2012).

[64] Cf EU Petersmann, 'JIEL Debate: Methodological Pluralism and its Critics in International Economic Law Research' (2012) 15 *JIEL* 921–70.

by 'principles of justice' for the stability and legitimacy of legal regimes.[65] For the efficient functioning of a decentralized, global division of labour among billions of producers, investors, traders and consumers in some 200 sovereign states with diverse legal and political systems, a shared 'public reason' that justifies IEL rules and their overall coherence with HRL is of constitutional importance. This justificatory need is recognized in HRL (eg Article 28 UDHR), European constitutional law (eg in Article 52 EUCFR), by the explicit incorporation of human rights and other principles of justice into UN law (eg the UN Charter; Preamble and Article 31 VCLT), and by the statutory requirements for courts of justice to render reasoned judgments. Institutionalizing public reason may also enhance the democratic capability of government institutions (eg to convince citizens of the collective benefits of participating in 'PGs treaties' like the EU treaties). Yet in view of the permanent fact of 'reasonable disagreement' among citizens over their respective conceptions of a 'good life' and over comprehensive theories of political justice, the search for transnational 'public reason' must be limited to an 'overlapping consensus' (Rawls) among people with often conflicting moral and political worldviews, and correspondingly diverse conceptions of economic regulation (eg trade unions requesting high, employers offering low salary increases). For instance, GATT/WTO law focuses on voluntary, reciprocal market access commitments, subject to 'general exceptions' reserving sovereign rights to unilaterally adopt trade restrictions necessary for protecting non-economic PGs that people may legitimately define differently in different jurisdictions. This recognition of sovereign rights of WTO members further entails that governments may also interpret what the WTO Preamble calls the 'basic principles and objectives underlying this multilateral trading system' differently, pursuant to their diverse constitutional systems. In a dynamically changing world, where citizens compete for scarce resources and often express conflicting views, legislation cannot exhaustively prescribe and specify 'just solutions' for all possible regulatory problems. Hence, even if—inspired by the republican tradition of Plato and Aristotle—justice is perceived as the most important among the four 'cardinal virtues' (along with temperance, fortitude and prudence) necessary for a just order inside the human soul as well as inside the republic, citizens, parliaments, courts of justice and governments in different countries will often continue to voice different views on the right interpretation of general

[65] On the importance for people to agree on shared reasons for just laws coordinating a 'stable equilibrium' in the decentralized application and enforcement of rules by individual agents that will support the institutions and interactions required by a political conception of justice only if they can be reasonably assured that they will benefit as a result, see GK Hadfield and S Macedo, *Rational Reasonableness: Toward a Positive Theory of Public Reason*, University of Southern California Law and Economics Working Paper Series: Working Paper 127 (2011).

'principles of justice' and on their contextual relevance for clarifying indeterminate rules. As explained already by Kant,[66] in law and jurisprudence, lawyers are likely to find it easier to identify the positive law rule applicable to a particular dispute than to justify its 'right interpretation', which may depend on jurisprudence and legal philosophy.

III. LEGAL FRAGMENTATION AND REINTEGRATION AS DIALECTIC METHODS FOR RECONCILING 'PRINCIPLES OF JUSTICE' AND DEVELOPING INTERNATIONAL LAW

As emphasized in section II.A, most international agreements and other legal instruments (like the 1948 UDHR) use indeterminate legal terms and regulate transnational relations in incomplete ways that call for progressive clarification, for instance through national and international rule-making, administration and adjudication. Moreover, international treaties tend to focus on particular general interests (eg protection of specific environmental goods) without clarifying their relationship to other PGs, for example without specifically coordinating 'fragmented' regulations pursuing 'eco-centric environmental values' with those protecting competing 'anthropocentric human rights values' or utilitarian economic values like 'efficiency'. Who should clarify—or settle disputes over—such 'fragmented regulations'? Is it a problem if different procedures and jurisdictions lead to diverging interpretative procedures, 'applicable law' and 'judicial balancing methods'?

The 'rules of recognition' of international law, as codified in Article 38 of the ICJ Statute, refer to state consent to international treaties, 'international custom ... recognized as law', 'general principles of law recognized by civilized nations', and 'judicial decisions and the teachings of the most highly qualified publicists of the various nations, as subsidiary means for the determination of the rules of law'. Yet they do not clarify the relationships between different sources of international law and between 'rules' (based on 'if-then commands') and general principles of law, including 'principles of justice' mentioned in the UN Charter and in numerous other treaties and national Constitutions. The fact that the intergovernmental prioritization of rights of states is not challenged in UN and WTO institutions dominated by government executives does not prove that the principles of 'Westphalian justice' governing the representation of member states in the UN and in the WTO can claim higher normative legitimacy than the cosmopolitan, democratic and constitutional principles of justice universally recognized in

[66] I Kant, 'The Metaphysics of Morals' in H Reiss (ed), *Kant: Political Writings* (Cambridge, Cambridge UP, 1991) at 132 ff.

UN HRL. This is illustrated by the *Kadi* judgments of the CJEU and their emphasis that effective

> judicial review is indispensable to ensure a fair balance between the maintenance of international peace and security and the protection of the fundamental rights and freedoms of the person concerned, those being shared values of the UN and the European Union.[67]

> It is also clear from the case-law that respect for human rights is a condition of the lawfulness of Community acts (Opinion 2/94, paragraph 34) and that measures incompatible with respect for human rights are not acceptable in the Community (Case C-112/00, *Schmidberger* [2003] ECR I-5659, paragraph 73 and case-law cited).[68]

As the exclusion of citizens, civil society institutions and parliaments from intergovernmental rule-making and legal interpretations entails power-orientated biases, European courts have also rightly emphasized that

> the fact that certain provisions of the Treaty are formally addressed to the Member States does not prevent rights from being conferred at the same time on any individual who has an interest in compliance with the obligations thus laid down (see Case 43/75 *Defrenne v Sabena* [1976] ECR 455, para 31). Such consideration must, *a fortiori*, be applicable to Article 48 of the Treaty, which ... is designed to ensure that there is no discrimination on the labour market.[69]

Defining the relevant 'contexts of justice' and legitimate 'interpretative legal community' in multilevel governance of transnational PGs raises numerous questions of legal methodology, especially in citizen-driven areas like HRL, IEL and other multilevel governance systems for collective supply of PGs demanded by citizens. Past experience suggests that leaving complex decision-making processes (eg on risk assessments) to group interests (eg trade diplomats, agricultural lobbies) and to specialized 'epistemic communities' (eg of climate change experts) risks non-inclusive 'balancing' of all legitimate interests. The Introduction to this book argued from an empirical and normative perspective for a 'six-stage sequence' of democratic, republican and cosmopolitan constitutionalism for (i) transforming agreed 'principles of justice' (as discussed in section II.A and postulated, for instance, in the 1948 UDHR) into (ii) constitutional and (iii) democratic legislation, (iv) administration, (v) adjudication and (vi) international law and multilevel governance institutions, so as to effectively protect transnational PGs for the

[67] CJEU, Joined Cases C-584/10P, C-593/10P and C-595/10P, judgment of 18 July 2013, para 131, EU:C:2013:518; for extensive analysis, see M Avbelj, F Fontanelli and G Martinico (eds), *Kadi on Trial* (London, Routledge, 2014).

[68] See Joined Cases C-402/05P and C-415/05P, *Kadi and Al Barakaat International Foundation v Council of the EU and Commission of the European Communities* [2008] ECR I-6351, para 284.

[69] Cf Case C-281/98, *Angonese* [2000] ECR I-4139.

benefit of citizens and their human and constitutional rights. This section argues—again from both empirical and normative perspectives—that, in a world based on 'sovereign equality of states' (eg as regards their 'veto powers' vis-à-vis international 'PGs treaties') and without 'global democracy', this 'six-stage sequence' of multilevel constitutional protection of transnational PGs makes 'legal fragmentation' (as a temporary transition to later 'legal convergence') a political necessity and frequent state practice.

A. 'Legal Pluralism' and 'Legal Perspectivism'

The legal regulation of the global economy in the twenty-first century is characterized by the coexistence of more than 200 national legal orders with thousands of public and private, transnational and international legal orders governed by hundreds of international organizations and millions of non-governmental actors (like TNCs governing production of and trade in private goods and services through interconnected 'global supply chains' coordinated through contractual, private law regimes and subsidiaries in many countries). The term 'legal pluralism' is used not only for *describing* this plurality of private and public, national, transnational and international legal orders and of their legal interactions. 'Legal pluralism' is also being used as a *normative* legal term to challenge traditional 'binary conceptions' of national and international law. For instance, the national, international and European human rights norms and related judicial interpretations by national courts, the CJEU and the ECtHR inside the national and European legal orders of the EU and of its member states, are based on a plurality of legal sources (eg national law, common constitutional principles of EU member states, EU law, the ECHR). They serve diverse, albeit complementary legal functions (eg depending on their national or European constitutional contexts) and interact in ways (eg based on multilevel judicial cooperation and judicial clarifications by national, European and international courts) that differ from traditional principles of legal primacy of international law over national law (as postulated in Article 27 VCLT), or of legal primacy of national constitutional law over international treaty law (as claimed by many national Constitutions). In response to the *Solange I* jurisprudence by the German Constitutional Court, which insisted on protecting national constitutional rights vis-à-vis European Community regulations, the CJEU recognized human rights and fundamental freedoms as general principles of Community law.[70] Even though this 'judicial law-making' prompted the

[70] On the *Solange I* (BVerfGE 37,271) and *Solange II* (BVerfGE 73,339) jurisprudence of the German Constitutional Court, and the fundamental rights and constitutional jurisprudence of the CJEU, see AM Slaugther, A Stone Sweet and J Weiler (eds), *The European Court and National Courts: Doctrine and Jurisprudence* (Oxford, Hart Publishing, 1998).

German Constitutional Court—in its *Solange II* jurisprudence—to limit its constitutional review of Community law 'as long as' ('*solange*' in the German language) Community law protected human and constitutional rights in a way that was equivalent to their constitutional protection inside Germany, the Constitutional Court continues to review whether EU law exceeds its limited scope of powers (*ultra vires* review) and does not infringe upon the 'constitutional identity' of German constitutional law.[71] In its *Bosphorus* judgment, the ECtHR likewise limited its judicial review of the consistency of EU law with the human rights guarantees of the ECHR, 'as long as' EU law and European courts protect equivalent guarantees of human rights.[72] In response to the 'constitutional jurisprudence' of the CJEU as well as of the ECtHR, all national courts in Europe recognize EU law and the ECHR as multilevel constitutional systems that interact with the diverse national constitutional systems of EU and ECHR member states in complex ways that may be described as 'constitutional pluralism' based on multilevel, legal and judicial protection of constitutional and human rights.[73]

Legal pluralism can give rise to problems of 'legal perspectivism', for instance because the implementation of international human rights obligations through constitutional, legislative, administrative law and adjudication legitimately differs among national jurisdictions. This diversity is also influenced by national 'margins of appreciation' and different democratic priorities in implementing human rights. Comparative studies of the interactions between HRL, constitutional law and foreign trade regulation in European and American constitutional democracies, in their regional economic integration agreements and in multilevel adjudication, confirm the interrelationships between 'human rights pluralism' and multilevel 'constitutional pluralism'.[74] For instance, the diverse legal and constitutional approaches to protection of human rights inside the EU, the EEA, NAFTA and MERCOSUR are not only due to the pluralism of HRL inside the member countries of these regional trade and economic agreements in Europe, North America and South America; they are also influenced by the reality of 'perspectivism', ie the fact that the perspectives and legal interpretations advocated by constitutional, administrative and international lawyers, judges, politicians and

[71] For a discussion of this jurisprudence by the German Constitutional Court (eg in its 'Lisbon judgment' of June 2009), see K Tuori, 'Transnational law. On legal hybrids and perspectivism' in M Maduro, K Tuori and S Sankari (eds), *Transnational Law. Rethinking European Law and Legal Thinking* (Cambridge, CUP, 2014) 9, 30 ff.

[72] *Bosphorus v Ireland*, App no 45036/98 (ECtHR, 2005-VI). For discussion, see S Besson, 'European human rights pluralism: notion and justification' in Maduro *et al* (eds) (n 71) 170–205.

[73] Cf H Keller and A Stone Sweet (eds), *A Europe of Rights: The Impact of the ECHR on National Legal Systems* (Oxford, OUP, 2008).

[74] Cf S Gardbaum, 'Human rights as international constitutional rights' in (2008) 19 *EJIL* 749–68.

private actors in respect of trade, investment and regional economic integration agreements are often diverse. In the 'cave allegory' of the ancient Greek philosopher Plato (comparing the 'human condition' to prisoners in a cave), the prisoners confused the shadows on the wall with the reality existing in the sunshine outside the cave entrance, and interpreted these shadows in very different ways. Similarly, national parliamentarians, government officials, judges, diplomats and economic actors often interpret the relevance of human and constitutional rights for designing and regulating regional trade and economic integration agreements from particular perspectives in diverse ways. For instance, 'realists' and 'radical pluralists' emphasize conflicts among competing legal regimes, for example due to:

— diverse, *internal value assumptions of legal actors* who justify the legal coherence, validity and hierarchy of national and international 'self-contained legal regimes' from different legal perspectives; this might be related to different (eg ontological or phenomenological) conceptions of 'basic norms', and of their legal pre-conceptions (*Vorverständnis*) in terms of Kelsen's legal theory of the legal hierarchies (*Stufenbau*) of national and international legal orders that derive their respective legitimacy from a presumed, national or international 'foundational norm' (*Grundnorm*);

— diverse, *strategic self-interests of legal actors* and institutional biases of specialized legal regimes (eg of trade law, investment law, intellectual property law, environmental law, UN HRL, UN Security Council regulations), whose respective legal priorities, legal claims and self-interests may conflict with one another; or

— different explanations of inherent inter-regime conflicts by their self-contained, '*autopoietic dynamic of social differentiations*' following the particular rationality of social sub-systems (like the economy, security protection, Internet regulation) and related, functionally orientated conflict rules and remedies.[75]

B. 'Legal Fragmentation' as a Method for Transforming State-Centered into Person-Centered Legal Regimes

Many areas of international law progressively develop through bilateral, regional or functionally limited, plurilateral agreements among 'coalitions of the willing' if worldwide legal reforms are blocked by lack of consensus. For example, GATT 1947 was progressively supplemented by multilateral

[75] For an analysis of these 'three versions of radical pluralism' (Kelsen's legal orders, Koskenniemi's imperial international law regimes, Luhmann's autopoietic social systems), see Tuori (n 71) 34–37.

trade agreements negotiated during eight 'GATT Rounds' and concluded by a limited number of GATT contracting parties until the termination of GATT 1947 in 1995, leading to the replacement of this pluralist 'GATT legal system' by the more integrated WTO legal and dispute settlement system. Similarly, since the first bilateral investment treaty (BIT) concluded between Germany and Pakistan in 1959, international investment law has been progressively transformed at the request of capital-exporting countries and their foreign investment industries, through BITs, regional investment agreements and arbitral jurisprudence deriving investor rights from investment agreements and protecting such 'cosmopolitan rights' against discriminatory, unnecessary or disproportionate 'regulatory takings', cancellation or alleged violation of contracts, and revocation or denial of licences. Until the ICJ judgment in the *ELSI* dispute,[76] many international investment disputes were decided either by recourse to domestic courts, or by diplomatic protection of the foreign investor by the home state, which, occasionally, submitted the dispute to international courts like the ICJ or its predecessor, the PCIJ. Yet, as illustrated by the *ELSI* judgment delivered by the ICJ more than 25 years after the dispute arose between the US investor and the local authorities in Sicily, most foreign investors perceive prior exhaustion of local remedies in national courts—followed by 'politicized', lengthy and costly procedures of diplomatic protection and disputes among states in international courts—as offering inadequate legal and judicial safeguards of investor rights.

The transformation of international investment law from a 'Westphalian' into a more 'cosmopolitan system' evolved, starting in the 1960s, essentially in five phases:

- Since the conclusion of the first BIT between Germany and Pakistan in 1959, the number of BITs dynamically increased to number (now) more than 3,000 agreements. Yet the 'first generation BITs' did not yet provide for direct access of foreign investors to independent international arbitration.
- The 1965 World Bank Convention that established the ICSID, which entered into force in 1966 (following 20 ratifications), offered a multilateral legal framework for institutionalized, transnational arbitration of investment disputes based on consent between the states and investors involved. The first ICSID disputes were based on investor-state contracts,[77] or on national legislation that provided for direct access of foreign investors to international arbitration.[78]

[76] *United States v Italy* (*ELSI* case) [1989] ICJ Rep 15.

[77] The first ICSID dispute based on an investor-state contract was *Holliday Inns v Morocco*, ICSID Case no ARB/72/1.

[78] The first ICSID dispute based on national legislation was *SPP v Egypt*, ICSID Case no ARB/84/3.

— Treaty-based investor-state arbitration was provided for only in the 'second generation BITs' concluded after 1969. In view of its many advantages for private investors (eg in terms of direct access to independent international arbitration, usually without prior exhaustion of local remedies, direct control of the procedures without dependence on 'diplomatic protection', availability of institutionalized ICSID procedures), most modern BITs provide for treaty-based investor-state arbitration.[79]
— In contrast to the fewer than 400 BITs concluded prior to 1989, the number of new BITs increased dramatically from the 1990s, and now exceeds 3,000 BITs or corresponding treaty provisions in FTAs (like NAFTA Chapter XI) and other sectorial agreements (like the Energy Charter Treaty, which entered into force in 1998). The number of BITs among less-developed countries also continues to increase.
— Since the 1990s, the number of treaty-based ICSID disputes, or investor-state disputes based on UNCITRAL or other commercial arbitration procedures, has increased from only one case before 1989 to now more than 600 known investor-state dispute settlement (ISDS) cases. The ISDS case law refers to the more than 600 known investor-state arbitral awards and related 'annulment decisions' or national court decisions as relevant precedents. Even though investor-state arbitral tribunals decided 37 per cent of the disputes in favour of the state and only 25 per cent in favour of the foreign investor (with 28 per cent of cases being settled), the perceived biases and lack of transparency in investor-state arbitration have prompted many countries to revise or reassess their investment treaties, and to pursue systemic reforms of investment disputes (eg in the context of transatlantic FTAs).[80]

Similar to the dialectic evolution of international trade and investment law (eg from GATT 1947, to the 1964 Kennedy and 1979 Tokyo Round Agreements, to the 1994 WTO Agreement), the UN legal system also continues to evolve in dialectic ways in response to civil society struggles towards protecting human rights and other international PGs. Due to the indeterminacy and inadequacy of many UN Charter provisions for the collective supply of global PGs, the power-orientated diplomacy in UN politics has induced the emergence of competing regional treaty regimes (eg for collective security and human rights protection), and functionally limited UN Specialized Agencies and other international organizations outside the

[79] The first ICSID dispute based on a BIT clause was *AAPL v Sri Lanka*, ICSID Report IV, at 250.

[80] Cf *Investor-State Dispute Settlement: Review of Developments in 2014*, UNCTAD IIA Issues Note No 2, May 2015.

UN system, like the WTO governing the worldwide trading system. This 'fragmentation' of international law risks legal incoherence, for instance due to structural biases and 'forum shopping' in specialized legal regimes like investment law, intellectual property law, environmental law and HRL. These dangers—as further discussed in Chapter 2, section III using the example of tobacco litigation in national, regional and worldwide legal regimes—have so far rarely materialized;[81] as discussed in the following sections, they remain legally constrained by the customary law requirement to interpret treaties and settle related disputes with due regard to 'any relevant rules of international law applicable in the relations between the parties', 'in conformity with principles of justice' and the 'human rights and fundamental freedoms' of all citizens. As the UN Charter recognizes 'judicial decisions and the teachings of the most highly qualified publicists of the various nations as subsidiary means for the determination of rules of law' (Article 38(c) and (d) ICJ Statute), civil society, democratic institutions and courts of justice increasingly insist on reinterpreting existing international rules (eg in BITs) for the benefit of citizens, so as to reduce the human rights deficits and 'governance failures' of intergovernmental politics among self-interested diplomats through legal and judicial protection of cosmopolitan rights and other 'principles of justice'.[82] The commitments of national, regional and UN legal systems to HRL and to other 'principles of justice' (eg as developed in the jurisprudence of regional courts of justice and of UN human rights bodies) are increasingly recognized as justifying limitations of power-orientated IEL rules. For instance, the governmental duties to protect human rights require reduction of the unnecessary poverty of 2 billion people without effective access to rule of law, medicines, health, water and adequate food inside WTO members; they justify legal limitations of formal conceptions of 'sovereign equality of states' and of utilitarian 'Kaldor-Hicks efficiency' by providing for 'special and differential treatment' of less-developed WTO members, especially if they comply with UN human rights conventions.[83]

[81] The most cited example is the *Tadic* case of 1999, in which the Appeals Chamber of the International Criminal Tribunal for Yugoslavia used an 'overall control standard' for the accountability of foreign states over acts of parties in civil war that differed from the 'effective control standard' developed by the ICJ in the *Nicaragua* case (cf *The Prosecutor v Dusko Tadic*, IT-94-1-A, 15 July 1999, 50, at 122).

[82] The *Belilos v Switzerland* judgment of the ECtHR, Judgment of 29 April 1988, Series A no 132, 28, is often cited as example of why HRL may justify interpretation methods different from the customary methods codified in the VCLT.

[83] For a discussion of the WTO dispute on *EC tariff preferences* and the EU reaction of differentiating its system of generalized trade preferences for less-developed countries depending on the participation of developing countries in UN human rights and ILO labour rights conventions, see Petersmann (n 33) 313.

C. 'Proportionality Balancing' as a Judicial Method Required by the 'Integration Principle'

The customary law requirement of interpreting treaties 'in conformity with principles of justice' and 'any relevant rules of international law applicable in the relations between the parties', including 'human rights and fundamental freedoms for all' (cf the Preamble and Article 31 VCLT), recognizes a legal requirement for 'consistent interpretation' through 'systemic integration' of fragmented treaty rules among the parties to an international dispute. Similar legal requirements follow from the 'indivisible' nature of civil, political, economic, social and cultural human rights, and from constitutional law presumptions that international agreements ratified by parliaments must 'contribute to the protection of citizens' (Article 3 TEU) in order to protect international PGs for the benefit of citizens (like a rules-based world trading system). Many international trade, investment and environmental agreements serve 'constitutional functions' by extending constitutional principles (eg of national treatment, the rule of law, access to justice and judicial remedies) to transnational cooperation among citizens and states in order to 'compensate' for inadequate domestic constitutional restraints on discretionary foreign policy powers.[84] International trade and investment tribunals increasingly 'balance' state-centered and person-centered 'principles of justice' and treaty rules through 'proportionality balancing'.

i. ICJ Jurisprudence

In view of the inadequate legal and judicial remedies under HRL, the ICJ has a long-standing practice of issuing provisional measures in order to protect human rights in disputes between states pending before it.[85] As stated by Judge Higgins, the Court recognizes 'the humanitarian realities behind disputes' between states.[86] The Court was also asked to decide on provisional measures to safeguard the life of certain individuals in the three cases filed against the USA for infringements of the 1963 Vienna Convention on Consular Relations, *Paraguay v USA*[87] *Germany v USA*[88] and

[84] Cf Petersmann (n 43).

[85] A Duxbury, 'Saving Lives in the International Court of Justice: The Use of Provisional Measures to Protect Human Life' (2000) 31 *California Western International Law Journal* 141–75 (discussing numerous examples since the case concerning *United States Diplomatic and Consular Staff in Tehran (USA v Iran)*, Provisional Measures, Order of 15 December 1979, [1979] ICJ Rep 7, at 19, para 36).

[86] See R Higgins, 'Interim Measures for the Protection of Human Rights' in JI Charney *et al* (eds), *Politics, Values and Functions. International Law in the 21st Century. Essays in Honour of Professor Louis Henkin* (The Hague, Brill Publishing, 1997) 101 ff, at 103.

[87] *Paraguay v USA*, Provisional Measures, Order of 9 April 1998, [1998] ICJ Rep 248.

[88] *LaGrand (Germany v USA)*, Judgment of 27 June 2001, [2001] ICJ Rep 466, paras 109–10.

Mexico v USA.[89] The provisional measures were justified by the 'extreme urgency' of the matter (Article 41 ICJ Statute) pending the decision on the merits; the ICJ ordered suspension of the execution of death sentences against nationals of the applicants. The Court interpreted Article 36 of the Vienna Convention on Consular Relations as conferring on individuals the right to receive consular assistance. Hence, it construed non-compliance with this provision as a violation of individual rights rather than only of a state's right, thus departing from the traditional approach granting diplomatic protection and entrusting the state with the right to protect its citizens abroad.[90] Despite the ICJ's stated refusal to act as an 'ultimate court of appeal in national criminal proceedings',[91] by emphasizing the legally binding nature of all Court judgments and related judicial decisions pursuant to Article 94 of the ICJ Charter, it used its powers to order provisional measures for protecting individual rights similar to a constitutional court.[92]

ii. Investment Arbitration

In investor-state arbitration, investors, host states, third parties and arbitrators increasingly raise human rights arguments (eg about due process of law, protection of private property, justification of state measures by the human rights of access to water, food and health protection, third party rights of indigenous peoples) and cite human rights jurisprudence (eg about 'proportionality balancing' of property rights with other human rights) as relevant context for the interpretation of investment treaty rules.[93] A number of arbitral awards interpreting treaty provisions on 'necessity' in the light of the restrictive customary rules on state responsibility (eg precluding invocation of 'necessity' if 'the State has contributed to the situation of necessity')[94] have been criticized or annulled by ICSID annulment committees on the ground that 'proportionality balancing' as a 'general principle of law' (in terms of Article 38:1(c) ICJ Statute) offers a more appropriate legal

[89] *Avena and Other Mexican Nationals (Mexico v USA)*, Provisional Measures, Order of 5 February 2003, [2003] ICJ Rep 77.

[90] Cf AA Cançado Trindade, 'The Humanization of Consular Law: The Impact of Advisory Opinion No 16 (1999) of the Inter-American Court of Human Rights on International Case-Law and Practice' in (2007) 4 *Chinese Journal of International Law* 1.

[91] *LaGrand*, cit *supra* n 88, para 52, at 485–86.

[92] Cf G Ziccardi Capaldo, 'Global Constitutionalism and Global Governance: Towards a UN-Driven Global Constitutional Governance Model' in C Bassiouni (ed), *Globalization and its Impact on the Future of Human Rights and International Criminal Justice* (Antwerp, Intersentia, 2015) 639–61.

[93] Cf Dupuy *et al* (eds) (n 30).

[94] Cf J Crawford, *The International Law Commission's Articles on State Responsibility. Introduction, Text and Commentaries* (Cambridge, CUP, 2002) 178 ff.

methodology for balancing all interests involved on the basis of 'suitability', 'necessity' and 'proportionality *stricto sensu*' principles, as practised by ever more national and international courts throughout the world.[95]

As a general principle of HRL (eg as codified in Article 29 UDHR) and of constitutional law (eg as codified in Article 52 EUCFR), the 'proportionality principle' not only requires transparent, systemic balancing of competing 'state interests' and of reciprocal rights and obligations among states; civil, political, economic, social and cultural human rights and other rights of citizens and NGOs must also be taken into account, including property rights of companies. Especially in economic and social crisis situations (as in Argentina 1999–2002, Greece since 2010) leading to 'regulatory takings' of foreign property rights protected under international investment law, or to international financial assistance conditional on 'austerity measures' limiting social rights of citizens, national and international judgments continue to clarify the controversial, legal 'borderlines' between 'necessary' governmental restrictions of rights of *domestic citizens* (eg social rights exceeding national budgetary resources) and 'disproportionate' restrictions of *foreign property rights*.[96] The more complainants, respondent states, third parties and judges invoke individual rights and other 'principles of justice' as applicable law in investment disputes, the more judicial rule clarification and adjudication on the basis of general principles of law can limit incoherencies among fragmented treaty regimes, especially if they are dominated too one-sidedly by 'state interests' and government executives eager to limit their own legal, democratic and judicial accountability vis-à-vis citizens adversely affected by harmful treaty violations. Yet if neither the investor nor the host state refers to human rights, commercial arbitrators often interpret their dispute settlement mandate narrowly by avoiding human rights arguments (eg on indigenous peoples' rights, the human right to water) that risk complicating voluntary compliance with the arbitral award and may trigger annulment proceedings criticizing judicial human right arguments. Ultimately, mutually agreed, *ad hoc* investor-state arbitration tribunals are economic courts with limited mandates, rather than 'human rights courts' or 'constitutional courts' mandated to protect the constitutional rights of all citizens in the polity concerned. However, such limited mandates do not justify inconsistent and non-transparent human rights approaches that take into consideration only some human rights (eg jurisprudence relating to property

[95] Cf A Stone Sweet and G della Cananea, 'Proportionality, General Principles of Law, and Investor-State Arbitration: A Response to José Alvarez' in (2014) 46 *New York University Journal of International Law and Politics* 911–54.

[96] On the different cultures and legal understandings of judicial 'balancing' and 'proportionality review', see G Huscroft, BW Miller and G Webber (eds), *Proportionality and the Rule of Law. Rights, Justification and Reasoning* (Oxford, OUP, 2014).

rights and procedural fairness) and disregard others (such as human rights to water and health protection if negatively impacted by foreign investments and invoked by host states as justification for investment regulations).[97]

iii. WTO Jurisprudence

The jurisprudence of the WTO applies 'dynamic interpretations' and 'proportionality balancing' not only in 'horizontal' relations among WTO members, but also in protecting private economic actors against disproportionate governmental trade restrictions. For instance, in *Shrimp-Turtles II*, the Appellate Body concluded that the US administration of non-transparent and discriminatory certification procedures and import restrictions on shrimp had failed to protect the rights of exporting countries and of their individual exporters to 'basic fairness and due process'.[98] In the WTO jurisprudence on the protectionist 'zeroing practices' of EC and US anti-dumping authorities, the WTO Appellate Body rightly interpreted the WTO requirement for 'fair price comparisons' from the perspective of the reasonable interests of economic actors, rather than—as advocated by some WTO panels—only from the perspective of EC and US anti-dumping bureaucracies, which claimed that they had not intended to limit their 'sovereign right' to apply discriminatory 'zeroing methodologies' by concluding the WTO Agreement on Anti-dumping.[99]

iv. Regional Economic Courts

Regional economic courts in Europe (eg the CJEU and the EFTA Court) and in Latin America (eg the MERCOSUR and Andean common market courts) increasingly interpret the regional trade and common market rules in conformity with the human rights jurisprudence of national and regional courts. For example, European courts have interpreted FTA and common market rules of the EU Treaty as conferring fundamental rights on individuals. Governmental limitations on such 'market freedoms'—eg in the case of imported laser games that simulate the killing of people, and which were prohibited in the German town of Bonn as offending 'human dignity' and public order—were accepted by the CJEU as legally justifiable and 'proportionate' even if other towns in Germany and other EU member states did not adopt similar prohibitions due to their different conceptions

[97] Cf T Meshel, 'Human Rights in Investor-State Arbitration: The Human Right to Water' in (2015) 6 *Journal of International Dispute Settlement* 277–307.

[98] *Shrimp-Turtles II*, WT/DS58/AB/R, adopted on 6 November 1998.

[99] For an analysis of this jurisprudence, see P Van den Bossche and W Zdouc, *The Law and Policy of the WTO*, 3rd edn (Cambridge, CUP, 2013) 689 ff; S Cho, 'Global Constitutional Lawmaking' in (2010) 31 *University of Pennsylvania Journal of International Law* 621–78.

of 'human dignity'.[100] The four '*Kadi* judgments' of the General Court and CJEU since 2005 can be understood in conformity with the '*Solange* jurisprudence' of the German Constitutional Court and of the ECtHR, to the effect that 'as long as' (*solange*) the higher level of law (ie UN law in the *Kadi* cases, EU law in the *Solange* jurisprudence of the German Constitutional Court) does not guarantee equivalent protection of fundamental rights, the courts at lower levels of multilevel legal and judicial systems must guarantee such fundamental rights in domestic jurisdictions. Just as the German Constitutional Court and the ECtHR refrained from exercising their jurisdiction 'as long as' the CJEU protects fundamental rights in ways equivalent to the constitutional protection under German constitutional law and the ECHR respectively, the CJEU might limit its judicial review of EU measures implementing UN Security Council sanctions once UN law offers equivalent procedural and substantive legal protection of individual rights of defence, property rights and effective judicial protection. Both the *Kadi* and the *Solange* jurisprudence suggest that, as UN and regional human rights conventions leave states 'margins of appreciation' for implementing and protecting higher standards of human rights in their national legal systems, multilevel legal regulation and judicial protection of civil, political, economic, social and cultural rights must be based on mutually consistent interpretations and 'judicial comity' (eg regarding the local remedies rule in HRL), 'subsidiarity' and 'loyal cooperation' among the different levels of governance, with due respect for the sovereign rights of states to guarantee higher levels of constitutional protection in domestic jurisdictions than at international levels of governance.[101]

The 'judicial comity', 'proportionality balancing' and references to HRL in national, transnational and regional economic adjudication reduce the 'systemic risks' of 'legal fragmentation' (eg separation of IEL and UN HRL), for example in the interpretation of international treaty exceptions (eg for reconciling economic and health rights) and 'saving clauses' (such as Article 53 ECHR recognizing sovereign rights to protect higher standards of constitutional rights in domestic jurisdictions). The 'systemic integration' principle of the customary rules of treaty interpretation requires judicial 'interpretive reintegration' of formally separate legal regimes. This

[100] Cf Case C-36/02 *Omega* [2004] ECR I-9609.

[101] Cf nn 67, 68, 70 and 72 above. On the increasing impact of HRL on MERCOSUR and Andean common market law and adjudication, see SS Schneider, *Access to Justice in Multilevel Trade Regulation: Brazil, MERCOSUR and the* WTO, EUI doctoral thesis 2014, ch IV. Due to the 2011 'human rights amendment' of Art 1 of the Constitution of Mexico, human rights treaties have become incorporated into Mexican law too, and increasingly influence adjudication and arbitration inside Mexico. Yet as neither Canada nor the USA has ratified the Inter-American Convention on Human Rights, international HRL seems to have only marginally influenced the interpretation of NAFTA law (eg NAFTA investment arbitration referring to the rights of indigenous peoples).

must be promoted through 'judicial dialogues' in the multilevel search for 'consistent interpretations', national 'margins of appreciation' in domestic implementation of human rights obligations, and 'remedial subsidiarity' of international court judgments (eg WTO dispute settlement rulings prescribing termination of illegal measures, without specifying the domestic choice of legal means and without prejudging financial reparation of injury that may be awarded by national courts of justice or investor-state arbitration in the case of violations of individual rights). Regional economic integration law in Africa, the Americas and also in ASEAN confirms the European experience that economic integration and adjudication require legal reintegration beyond the economic realm. Such 'spill-over effects' arise from the need for judicial review of—and progressive legal harmonization of national measures taken under—'exception clauses' and inherent regulatory powers to restrict trade by non-discriminatory product and production regulations (eg for tobacco control), reciprocal recognition of domestic product and production standards, and multilevel legal harmonization aimed at protecting non-economic PGs (like public health), free movement of persons and investments, and multilevel judicial cooperation. The more than 135 dispute settlement rulings under GATT 1947, and the more than 360 panel, appellate and arbitration rulings by WTO dispute settlement bodies since 1995, illustrate that—even though none of the GATT and WTO dispute settlement findings *explicitly* referred to the human rights obligations of GATT and WTO members—these GATT/WTO dispute settlement findings apparently remained consistent with HRL.[102]

IV. GLOBAL DEMOCRACY? HUMAN RIGHTS REQUIRE 'CONNECTING CONSTITUENT AND CONSTITUTED POWERS' THROUGH 'COSMOPOLITAN CONSTITUTIONALISM'

Every UN member state has ratified one or more of the nine core UN human rights treaties;[103] more than 80 per cent of all UN member states have ratified the ICCPR and/or the ICESCR. Hence, whatever the intent of the governments that voted for the UDHR as a UN General Assembly

[102] Cf Petersmann (n 33) 407 ff (discussing the various reports by the UN Human Rights Commissioner on the human rights dimensions of GATT/WTO rules and practices which, likewise, did not identify specific human rights violations in GATT/WTO legal practices).

[103] These include the 1965 Convention on the Elimination of all Forms of Racial Discrimination, the 1966 Covenants on Civil and Political Rights (ICCPR) and Economic, Social and Cultural Rights (ICESCR), the 1979 Convention on the Elimination of all Forms of Discrimination against Women, the 1984 Convention against Torture and other Cruel, Inhuman or Degrading Treatment or Punishment, the 1989 Convention on the Rights of the Child, the 1990 Convention on the Protection of the Rights of all Migrant Workers and Members of their Families, the 2006 Convention on the Rights of Persons with Disabilities and the 2006 Convention for the Protection of all Persons from Enforced Disappearance.

Declaration, the multilevel human rights practices since 1948 have transformed most rights stipulated in the UDHR into 'general principles of law recognized by civilized nations'.[104] For instance, courts of justice in Europe and in the Americas may convincingly argue that—as specified in the UDHR and confirmed in many national Constitutions and regional human rights conventions that explicitly refer (eg in the Preamble to the ECHR) to their treaty objective of implementing obligations under the UDHR—all human beings have rights to non-discrimination (Article 2), to life, liberty and security (Article 3), prohibitions of slavery, servitude (Article 4) and of torture (Article 5), rights to recognition as a person before the law (Article 6) and to equality before the law (Article 7), rights to judicial remedies (Article 8) and to a fair trial (Article 10), freedom from arbitrary arrest (Article 9), presumption of innocence (Article 11), rights of privacy and of honour (Article 12), rights to freedom of movement and residence (Article 13), rights to asylum (Article 14), to a nationality (Article 15), to marry and to protection of the family (Article 16), rights to own property (Article 17), freedom of thought, conscience and religion (Article 18), freedom of opinion, expression and information (Article 19), freedom of assembly and association (Article 20), rights to democratic self-governance (Article 21) and social security (Article 22), labour rights (Article 23), rights to an adequate standard of living (Article 25) and education (Article 26), rights to participate in cultural life and author's rights (Article 27), and rights 'to a social and international order in which the rights and freedoms set forth in this Declaration can be fully realized' (Article 28 UDHR).

It remains contested to what extent the treaty obligations of the 160 parties to the ICESCR to 'take steps, individually and through international assistance and cooperation, especially economic and technical, to the maximum of [their] available resources, with a view to achieving progressively the full realization of the rights recognized in the present Covenant' (cf Article 2), go beyond their general international law obligations as codified in the UDHR, notably as regards the right to work (Article 6), the right to just and favourable conditions of work (Article 7), trade union rights (Article 8), rights to social security (Article 9), family rights (Article 10), rights to an adequate standard of living (Article 11) and of health (Article 12), rights to education (Articles 13, 14) and cultural rights (Article 15 ICESCR). The ICESCR recognizes the 'indivisibility' and interdependence of human rights by requiring, for instance, that the right to work must be realized 'under conditions safeguarding fundamental political and economic freedoms to the individual' (Article 6); 'the ideal of free human beings enjoying freedom from fear and want can only be achieved if conditions are created whereby everyone may enjoy his economic, social and cultural rights, as

[104] De Schutter (n 5) 16.

well as his civil and political rights' (Preamble ICESCR). These conditions depend ever more on IEL's protecting a mutually beneficial global division of labour, enabling all countries and citizens to increase their access to scarce goods, services and other resources. This section argues that the emergence of 'multilevel human rights constitutionalism' and of 'multilevel economic constitutionalism' empirically and normatively confirms the need for connecting the rights of citizens to the multilevel duties of governments in order to promote the 'six-stage constitutionalization' of (i) human and constitutional rights and related 'principles of justice' through (ii) constitutional and (iii) parliamentary legislation and (iv) multilevel governance, (v) adjudication and (vi) international law and institutions.

A. 'Multilevel Human Rights Constitutions' as an Example for 'Six-Stage Constitutionalism'

The human rights obligations of all UN member states under the UN Charter, UN human rights conventions and under general international law continue to evolve and confirm that '[a]ll human rights are universal, indivisible and interdependent and interrelated'; 'it is the duty of States, regardless of their political, economic and cultural systems, to promote and protect all human rights and fundamental freedoms'.[105] The references—in human rights treaties, national bills of rights and government practices—to the UDHR support the view that most rights enumerated in the UDHR have also become part of customary international law and 'inalienable rights' of human beings that constitutionally limit all national and international governance powers.[106] Just as the EU is constitutionally founded on and limited by respect for human rights and rule of law (Article 2 TEU), HRL requires interpreting the powers of all international institutions (like the UN) as being constitutionally limited by human rights and related rule-of-law principles, as acknowledged in the *Kadi* jurisprudence of the CJEU. Neither national governments nor international governance institutions have legitimate powers to unduly restrict 'inalienable' and 'indivisible' civil, political, economic, social and cultural rights of citizens, notwithstanding their often diverse democratic priorities, diverse domestic implementing legislation, and inadequate resources for fulfilling all of these rights simultaneously in national and international jurisdictions. In the context of the ECHR and

[105] Vienna Declaration and Programme of Action adopted at the UN World Conference on Human Rights by more than 170 states on 25 June 1993 (A/CONF.157/24, para 5). This 'universal, indivisible, interrelated, interdependent and mutually reinforcing' nature of human rights was reaffirmed by all UN member states in numerous human rights instruments, such as UN Resolution 63/116 of 10 December 2008 on the '60th anniversary of the Universal Declaration of Human Rights' (UN Doc A/RES/63/116 of 26 February 2009).

[106] Cf De Schutter (n 5) 50 ff.

of the Inter-American Human Rights Convention, the close cooperation between national and regional human rights courts in their multilevel protection of human rights in response to complaints by citizens continues to promote emerging 'multilevel human rights constitutions'[107] that remain embedded in national constitutionalism as protected by national courts and legitimately differ among jurisdictions (eg depending on their respective participation in and implementation of human rights conventions in national and local jurisdictions).

Functionally limited 'treaty constitutions' have been concluded since the 1919 Constitution (*sic*) that established the ILO in order to protect labour rights and related PGs like social peace and 'justice as fairness'. Yet due to the reality of power politics, UN HRL does not effectively constrain power-orientated UN/WTO governance focusing on 'sovereign rights' of governments rather than on rights and empowerment of citizens. Member states of the UN only rarely use the UN Human Rights Council and the ICJ to *enforce* human rights vis-à-vis other governments; the UN human rights treaty bodies lack effective legal powers and judicial remedies. Human rights are neither mentioned nor effectively protected in most worldwide and regional *economic agreements* outside Europe. Most national legal systems of UN member states focus one-sidedly on protecting civil and political rights (eg in US constitutional law and practices) or economic rights (eg in Communist countries like China), without multilevel, legal and judicial protection of the 'indivisibility' and 'interdependence' of civil, political, economic, social and cultural rights as required by UN HRL. European Union law, EEA law and the ECHR offer the most developed regional legal systems for multilevel, judicial protection of integrated civil, political, economic, social and cultural rights, based on an innovative methodology in the EUCFR of 'dignity rights' (Title I EUCFR), liberty rights (Title II), equality rights (Title III), solidarity rights (Title IV), citizen rights (Title V) and access to justice (Title VI) protected by national and European courts (eg the CJEU, the EFTA Court, the ECtHR), in addition to the diverse national constitutional rights guaranteed in European states. The 'direct applicability' by citizens of their fundamental rights protected under EU, EEA and ECHR law, and their multilevel judicial protection in local, national and regional jurisdictions illustrate why 'six-stage processes of constitutionalization' can protect human and constitutional rights so much more effectively than, for instance, ILO labour rights and related conventions, which are often not effectively implemented through domestic legislation, administration and adjudication for the benefit of citizens.

[107] Cf EU Petersmann, 'Human Rights, Markets and Economic Welfare: Constitutional Functions of the Emerging UN Human Rights Constitution' in FA Abbott, C Breining and T Cottier (eds), *International Trade and Human Rights* (Ann Arbor, MI, University of Michigan Press, 2006) 29–67.

B. Need for Interpreting the 'Rules of Recognition' of UN/WTO Law in Conformity with 'Human Rights and Fundamental Freedoms for All'

All UN and WTO member states recognize UN law and IEL as 'legal systems' that comprise 'primary rules of conduct' and 'secondary rules of recognition, change and adjudication'.[108] The universal recognition and explicit incorporation of 'inalienable human rights' and other 'principles of justice' into positive international law—based on corresponding principles in national and regional constitutional systems—challenge traditional distinctions between legal positivism (eg emphasizing the authoritative issuance and enforcement of legal rules as social facts), natural law (eg emphasizing the pre-state foundation of law through 'constitutional contracts' among citizens and their reciprocal recognition of 'natural rights') and sociological conceptions of law (eg analysing the 'law in action' as a 'reality check' on the 'law in the books'). They require interpreting the path-dependent 'international law among sovereign states' in conformity with democratically evolving 'principles of justice', changing legal practices and *opinio juris sive necessitatis* not only of states (as represented by their heads of state, ministers of foreign affairs and diplomats), but also of citizens, civil society, democratic institutions and courts of justice that constitute legitimate legal systems. The jurisprudence of UN tribunals increasingly reflects these structural changes transforming the 'international community of states' (Article 53 VCLT) into a global community of citizens, peoples, governmental and non-governmental organizations. For instance:

— Since the 1990s, the ICJ jurisprudence has increasingly referred to other international, regional and also national courts of justice 'as subsidiary means for the determination of rules of law' (Article 38:1(d) ICJ Statute) and as empirical evidence that certain rules are accepted in state practice as law (*opinio juris*), eg the jurisdictional immunity of states even if *jus cogens* is involved.[109]
— The ICJ and the International Tribunal for the Law of the Sea (ITLOS) explicitly emphasize that the settlement of disputes among states must remain in conformity with their human rights obligations.[110]

[108] On the characteristics of 'legal systems' as a union of 'primary rules of conduct' and 'secondary rules of recognition, change and adjudication', see HLA Hart, *The Concept of Law* (Oxford, OUP, 1994) ch V.

[109] Cf *Jurisdictional Immunities of the State (Germany v Italy)* [2012] ICJ Rep 99.

[110] Cf *Arctic Sunrise (Netherlands v Russia)*, International Tribunal on the Law of the Sea (ITLOS), Case no 22, Order of 22 November 2013: 'The settlement of such disputes between two states should not infringe upon the enjoyment of individual rights and freedoms of the crew of the vessels concerned.'

- In judgments like *Gabcikovo-Nagymaros*, *Pulp Mills* and *Whaling in the Antarctic*,[111] the ICJ resorted to 'dynamic interpretations', developing international environmental law by acknowledging community interests.
- ICJ judgments no longer ascertain international legal practice only in terms of state consent; they also recognize individuals, corporate actors and international organizations as legal subjects of ever more fields of international law, whose rights limit traditional principles of 'international law among states', for instance:
  - in the case of applicability of human rights treaty provisions even without reciprocity;
  - recognition of *erga omnes* and *jus cogens* obligations limiting the legal relevance of state consent, and enlarging the scope of rights of diplomatic protection against human rights violations;
  - different allocation of the burden of proof in the case of certain human rights violations by authoritarian governments; and
  - the award of damages in the 2012 ICJ judgment as reparation for the violation of the human rights of Diallo.[112]

i. From Discretionary 'Diplomatic Protection' to Judicial Protection of Cosmopolitan Rights

The often very long duration of (eg of more than 20 years in the investment disputes leading to the *ELSI* and *Diallo* judgments of the ICJ) and inadequate legal remedies in ICJ proceedings further illustrate why non-governmental actors so rarely request their governments to submit trade, investment and human rights disputes to the ICJ. For instance, the ICJ's award of damages in its 2012 *Diallo* judgment was the Court's first judgment on damages in a human rights case. As there are more transnational dispute settlement bodies in IEL than in any other field of international law, multilevel economic adjudication—eg through annually hundreds of judgments by WTO, regional, arbitral and national tribunals—dynamically clarifies and develops indeterminate rules (eg of 'international custom … recognized as law') and the 'general principles of law recognized by civilized nations' (Article 38 ICJ Statute), for instance by acknowledging the constitutional limitations of IEL resulting from HRL and from common 'constitutional law principles' like proportionality balancing and citizen-orientated, impartial adjudication (eg balancing economic and intellectual property rights with health rights and other human rights). Empirical

[111] See the overview of international environmental adjudication and of human rights courts identifying human rights provisions with environmental content in PM Dupuy and JE Vinuales, *International Environmental Law* (Cambridge, CUP, 2015) 244 ff, 307 ff.

[112] For a discussion of the relevant ICJ judgments in *Congo v Uganda* (2005), *Diallo* (2010/2012) and *Belgium v Senegal* (2012), see Andenas (n 18) 712 ff.

evidence confirms that the social effectiveness and 'compliance rates' with such 'judicial law-making' by regional economic and human rights courts, WTO dispute settlement findings, investment and commercial arbitration remains high, notwithstanding criticism from diplomats that 'judicial law-making' has evolved into one of the most dynamic instruments for interpreting and progressively developing HRL, international trade and investment law, regional economic integration law and other fields of international law (like international criminal and environmental law). Practical examples in investor-state arbitration include judicial interpretation and progressive clarification of vague international investment law standards—like 'fair and equitable treatment' and limitations of investor rights on grounds of 'necessity'—in conformity with human rights, environmental law and other legal obligations of states.[113] The pertinent judgments by WTO dispute settlement bodies (eg the 'zeroing jurisprudence' of the WTO Appellate Body on reconciling public and private interests in anti-dumping law), by regional economic courts (eg the *Kadi* case law of the CJEU on reconciling UN Security Council sanctions with human rights) and investment arbitration (eg the *Continental Casualty v Argentina* arbitration of 2008 on reconciling investor interests with public interests in situations of economic emergencies and social crises) are increasingly justified in terms of citizen-orientated 'constitutional principles' and cosmopolitan rights that are common to modern legal systems (eg as explicitly acknowledged in Article 52 of the EUCFR), and limit state-centered 'principles of justice' (like 'state sovereignty').[114]

ii. Judicial Rule Clarification Can Limit the 'State Bias' of Intergovernmentalism

All UN and WTO agreements for the collective protection of PGs (like rules-based monetary, trading and development systems) are subject to 'exceptions' and 'limitation clauses' reconciling diverse PGs regimes. As explained in the discussion of 'proposition 5' in the Introduction to this book, person-orientated 'constitutional justice' administered by independent and impartial 'courts of justice' is more likely to limit state-centered interpretations of treaties among states—and to respect the customary law requirement of interpreting treaties 'in conformity with principles of justice', including also 'human rights and fundamental freedoms for all'—than power-orientated, national diplomats and 'intergovernmentalism' in UN and WTO bodies prioritizing rights and interests of states and national foreign policy discretion. Path-dependent diplomats are more likely to identify relevant rules

[113] Cf Dupuy and Vinuales (n 111).

[114] Cf Petersmann (n 33), ch VIII (identifying dozens of national and international judgments protecting cosmopolitan rights in IEL, and justifying their legal interpretations in terms of constitutional principles of law).

of positive law by focusing on past state practices rather than on human rights, constitutional rights and other rights of individuals, and on domestic jurisprudence on 'limitation clauses' authorizing limitations of individual rights by important public interests. This 'conservative bias' is confirmed by the fact that—eg in GATT, WTO and investment disputes—'public policy exceptions' in international treaties (eg on protection of public order pursuant to GATT, WTO and BIT exception clauses) tend to be exercised by governments invoking 'public interests' rather than corresponding rights of citizens and their judicial balancing in domestic jurisdictions. The increasing 'judicial dialogues' among national, regional and international courts of justice on the 'suitability', 'necessity' and 'proportionality *stricto sensu*' of public interest regulations, and on how the competing private and public interests should be weighted case by case, contribute to institutionalizing person-orientated, common 'principles of justice', for example:

— by clarifying the WTO requirement of 'fair price comparisons' in the determination of 'dumping margins' no longer only from the government perspective of anti-dumping administrations, but also with due respect for reasonable expectations of exporters to be protected against systematically biased price calculations;[115]
— by interpreting BIT requirements of 'fair and equitable treatment' of foreign investors in conformity with human rights obligations of the host and home states of the foreign investors;[116] and
— by interpreting BIT exceptions on 'necessity' of public restrictions of investor rights in conformity with citizen-orientated 'proportionality principles', rather than in the light of the customary rules on state responsibility among states.[117]

Such person-orientated jurisprudence protecting individual rights and limiting state-centered domination of international relations by government executives is also justified by 'cosmopolitan conceptions' of the sources of international law and related 'rules of recognition', which are not limited to 'international conventions ... recognized by states' (Article 38(a) ICJ Statute). The additional sources—'(b) international custom, as evidence of a general practice accepted as law; (c) the general principles of law recognized by civilized nations; (d) ... judicial decisions and the teachings of the most highly qualified publicists of the various nations, as subsidiary means for the determination of the rules of law' (Article 38 ICJ Statute)—must be construed 'in conformity with principles of justice', including also 'human rights

[115] Cf Cho (n 99).

[116] Cf I Knoll-Tudor, 'The Fair and Equitable Treatment Standard and Human Rights Norms' in PM Dupuy, F Francioni and EU Petersmann (eds), *Human Rights in International Investment Law and Arbitration* (Oxford, OUP, 2009) 339 ff.

[117] Cf Stone Sweet and Della Cananea (n 95).

and fundamental freedoms for all', as explicitly recalled in the Preamble to and Article 31:3(c) of the VCLT. Arguably, international and national HRL require subjecting state consent and multilevel governance to constitutional restraints, as illustrated by the *Kadi* jurisprudence of European courts.[118] Just as legal systems are about the establishment of a *just legal order*, as explained by Fuller,[119] modern international law can be justified by state consent only to the extent that such consent remains consistent with the human rights obligations of states. If the international 'rules of recognition' are construed in conformity with the legal duties of all governance institutions to respect, protect and fulfil human rights and other constitutional rights 'retained by the people' (in the words of the Ninth Amendment of the US Constitution), the universal recognition of human rights and the corresponding duties of all UN member states to respect, protect and fulfil human rights remain the ultimate sources of international law and political legitimacy too in the twenty-first century, as convincingly explained by the late Ronald Dworkin in his last legal analysis, published *post mortem*.[120] As citizens and democratic institutions may legitimately disagree on how to prioritize, balance and construe civil, political, economic, social and cultural rights in different legal, economic and political contexts, respect for democratic 'constitutional pluralism' and for the 'inalienable core' of human rights may be a more convincing legal justification than mere state consent and economic utilitarianism (eg in anti-dumping and intellectual property law).

International trade and investment law differ from HRL by the fact that WTO law and BITs often protect *higher standards* of economic freedoms, property rights, non-discrimination and transnational rule of law than those in *national* trade and investment legislation, which tends to permit border discrimination and welfare-reducing restrictions on foreign goods, services and investments. The 'constitutional functions' of such higher international legal guarantees of freedom, non-discrimination and rule of law for mutually beneficial economic cooperation among citizens across national frontiers may justify the interpretation of such legal guarantees as 'compensatory constitutional extensions' of corresponding domestic legal guarantees of equal freedoms, non-discriminatory competition and rule of law for the benefit of citizens.[121] The more international 'PGs regimes' take over the functions of democratic legislation for PGs, the stronger becomes the need for justifying why such transnational guarantees of equal freedoms, non-discrimination, the rule of law and judicial remedies

[118] Cf nn 67 and 68.

[119] LL Fuller, *The Morality of Law* (New Haven, CT, Yale UP, 1969) 96.

[120] R Dworkin, 'A New Philosophy for International Law' (2013) 41 *Philosophy & Public Affairs* 2–30.

[121] Cf Petersmann (n 43) and A Peters, 'Compensatory Constitutionalism: The Function and Potential of Fundamental International Norms and Structures' (2006) 19 *LJIL* 579 ff.

should not be interpreted as cosmopolitan rights of citizens, so as to set democratic incentives for holding government legally, democratically and judicially accountable for welfare-reducing violations of precise and unconditional treaty commitments.

C. Human Rights Require Transforming Cosmopolitan Principles into 'Republican' and 'Cosmopolitan' Constitutionalism

In contrast to power- and state-centered 'realist approaches' to international relations, the 'cosmopolitan principles' that underlie HRL and international private and commercial law (eg based on freedom of contract and other fundamental freedoms, private property rights, freedom of arbitration, principles of 'public order' like respect for good faith and *pacta sunt servanda*, judicial comity between national courts and transnational arbitration in protecting transnational rule of law) are based on universally agreed 'principles of justice' that emphasize respect for human dignity and human autonomy (normative individualism), reasonableness, the equal moral worth of all persons and corresponding 'duties of justice' towards all human persons (rather than only to national compatriots).[122] Yet the ongoing struggles for republican constitutionalism at national levels of governance illustrate the political difficulties of transforming moral 'duties of justice'—for instance, of helping all persons to have access to just institutions and to further just rules that are not yet effectively protected—into multilevel governance systems and institutions dominated by power-orientated foreign policies and 'executive dominance' of UN and WTO decision-making without adequate control by citizens, national parliaments and judicial institutions. Even inside constitutional democracies with participatory decision-making procedures that are less dominated by power inequalities (like the EU member states), cosmopolitan arguments for welcoming immigration of refugees, 'displaced persons' and other foreigners (eg in view of their moral equality, fairness in global labour markets) are challenged by communitarian counter-arguments that prioritization of national citizens and community interests is a legitimate part of the right to democratic self-determination, and to protecting communitarian identities and achievements (eg social solidarity inside limited communities) through border controls.[123]

[122] Cf KC Tan, *Justice without Borders: Cosmopolitanism, Nationalism and Patriotism* (Cambridge, CUP, 2004) 60; A Buchanan, *Justice, Legitimacy and Self-Determination: Moral Foundation for International Law* (Oxford, OUP, 2004) 86–87.

[123] Cf JM Valadez, 'Is immigration a human right?' in R Pierik and W Werner (eds), *Cosmopolitanism in Context. Perspectives from International Law and Political Theory* (Cambridge, CUP, 2010) 221 ff; and T Spijkerboer, 'A distributive approach to migration law: or the convergence of communitarianism, libertarianism, and the status quo', ibid, 277 ff.

i. 'Socializing States' by Strengthening Domestic Protection of Human Rights

Why is it that the domestic implementation and legal protection of UN HRL in so many UN member states is so much less effective[124] compared with regional human rights conventions establishing regional human rights courts and promoting their close cooperation with national courts of justice? Following the fall of the Berlin Wall (1989), most Central and Eastern European states acceded to the Council of Europe's ECHR and to the EU. The comparatively more effective implementation of European HRL inside these countries can be explained in terms of (i) material inducement (eg through EU membership conditional on compliance with European HRL), (ii) persuasion (eg of post-Communist political leaders and democratic majorities in these countries to respect human rights, democracy and rule of law), (iii) 'acculturation' and 'assimilation' through adoption of the beliefs and behavioural patterns prevailing inside EU institutions and democratic societies.[125] As explained in sections II and III of Chapter 1, even more important than such 'external contributions' to institutionalizing 'cosmopolitan public reason' in domestic politics and enforcing cosmopolitan rights and 'duties of justice' are domestic legislation, administration and adjudication transforming cosmopolitan principles into legal rights and duties of citizens, and into democratic and judicial, domestic institutions that protect cosmopolitan rights and 'cosmopolitan public reason'. For instance:

— As none of the UN human rights conventions offers citizens effective access to, and judicial remedies by, international courts of justice or democratically controlled accountability mechanisms, the multilevel 'European human rights constitutionalism' (eg based on the ECHR, the EUCFR and the multilevel judicial protection of common constitutional principles inside EU, EEA and ECHR member states) has been comparatively more effective than UN HRL and national 'human rights constitutionalism' outside Europe.

— WTO law and governance tend to regulate non-economic public interests (such as public health protection) without protecting corresponding rights of citizens, for instance if they move into foreign countries in the context of GATS commitments on liberalization of international movements of 'natural persons for the purpose of supplying

[124] Cf E Posner, *The Twilight of Human Rights Law* (Oxford, OUP, 2014).

[125] These three mechanisms for influencing states to comply with their human rights obligations are distinguished by R Goodman and D Jinks, *Socializing States: Promoting Human Rights through International Law* (Oxford, OUP, 2013).

services',[126] rights-based multilevel regulation of health protection and labour rights through WHO law (eg the Framework Convention on Tobacco Control), and through ILO conventions. European Union and EEA regulations, by contrast, have protected cosmopolitan rights more effectively than the WTO legal safeguards of individual access to justice inside *domestic legal systems*,[127] which, apart from a few exceptions protecting *individual access* to international arbitration (eg in Article 4 of the WTO Agreement on Pre-shipment Inspection) and *individual rights* to invoke and enforce WTO rules (eg Article XX of the WTO Agreement on Government Procurement) in domestic courts, have not been effectively implemented in most domestic legal systems. Arguably, the multilevel 'republican' and 'cosmopolitan' constitutionalism inside EU and EEA member states have enabled a comparatively stronger 'socialization' of national legal systems, as also illustrated by the arrival in Europe of millions of refugees from Africa and Asia.

ii. Transforming Antagonistic Rivalry into Mutually Beneficial Cooperation Through Trade Law

Since Kant's 'philosophical sketch' on promoting 'perpetual peace' through cosmopolitan republicanism protecting equal rights in all human interactions at national, transnational and international levels of governance, many legal philosophers have emphasized the potential contribution of rules-based trade to 'socializing international law':

> [N]ature unites nations which the concept of cosmopolitan right would not have protected from violence and war, and does so by means of their mutual self-interest. For the spirit of commerce sooner or later takes hold of every people, and it cannot exist side by side with war. And of all the powers (or means) at the disposal of the power of the state, financial power can probably be relied on most. Thus states find themselves compelled to promote the noble cause of peace, though not exactly from motives of morality.[128]

Arguably, it is no coincidence that common market regulation was the driving force in the evolution of most federal states and supranational organizations like the EU, or that GATT/WTO law has evolved into a successful

[126] Cf the 1994 'Decision on Negotiations on Movement of Natural Persons' and the GATS 'Annex on Movement of Natural Persons Supplying Services under the Agreement' in *The Results of the Uruguay Round of Multilateral Trade Negotiations* (Geneva, WTO, 1994) 353, 458 f.

[127] For instance in the field of GATT (Art X), the WTO Anti-dumping Agreement (Art 13), the WTO Agreement on Customs Valuation (Art 11), the Agreement on Subsidies and Countervailing Measures (Art 23), the General Agreement on Trade in Services (Art VI GATS), and the Agreement on Trade-Related Aspects of Intellectual Property Rights (cf Arts 41–50, 59 TRIPS).

[128] I Kant, 'Perpetual Peace: A Philosophical Sketch' in Reiss (ed) (n 66) 93 ff, at 114.

global legal system with the only worldwide, compulsory dispute settlement system accepted by 164 states, including all five permanent members of the UN Security Council. Even though the benefits from international trade are not shared equally among all trading countries and their citizens, trade has proved to be the most important incentive for mutually beneficial cooperation, creating jobs and economic growth, and lifting millions of people out of poverty. New patterns of trade (such as global value chains) are likely to further promote new legal cultures among trading nations, for instance through promoting participatory governance,[129] domestic rule compliance and judicial remedies,[130] 'reconstructing the WTO as a world trade community', and replacing, thereby, the international 'contract model' of GATT law (as a reciprocal bargain among 'contracting parties') and the anachronistic 'monolocation production/trade model' (focusing on exports of finished products among 'atomistic producers') with more realistic conceptions of multilevel, global trade cooperation.[131] A world trade community based on shared ideas and values regarding international trade, including the need for protecting legal 'security and predictability' for non-governmental economic actors too,[132] as a global PG, has proved to be one of the most powerful driving forces for transforming rational power politics and utilitarian cost–benefit maximization into long-term legal cooperation, adjudication, rules-based negotiations, science-based 'risk-assessments' and impartial 'peer review' of reasonable 'best practices' for regulating trade, market integration and 'sustainable development'.[133]

iii. Extending Republican and Cosmopolitan Constitutionalism to Multilevel Governance

Human, constitutional, republican and cosmopolitan rights are 'intermediate PGs' for the collective supply of transnational 'aggregate PGs' like the rule of law, public health, food security, public education, democratic, cultural and sustainable development, and a rules-based world trading system. In contrast to nationalist power politics (eg focusing on 'national interests' as defined by powerful interest groups and power-orientated bargaining with other governments), multilevel constitutionalism emphasizes the interrelationships between local, national, regional and worldwide 'aggregate

[129] Cf Y Bonzon, *Public Participation and Legitimacy in the WTO* (Cambridge, CUP, 2014).

[130] Cf M Yilmaz (ed), *Domestic Judicial Review of Trade Remedies: Experiences of the most active WTO Members* (Cambridge, CUP, 2014).

[131] Cf S Cho, *The Social Foundations of World Trade. Norms, Community and Constitution* (Cambridge, CUP, 2015).

[132] Cf Art 3 DSU and the WTO Panel Report on *United States—Sections 301–310 of the Trade Act of 1974*, WT/DS152/R (adopted 27 January 2000), para 7.76.

[133] Cf Cho (n 131) on the different forms of 'norm internalization' and 'socialization' through WTO law.

PGs'. While national (big 'C') Constitutions are about constituting peoples and their democratic governance of national PGs (eg by providing for equal rights, social solidarity and loyalty among citizens as preconditions for majority rule), the extension of republican and cosmopolitan (small 'c') constitutionalism to multilevel governance of functionally limited 'aggregate PGs' pursues more limited goals depending on the specific PGs concerned. Yet the functional interrelationships between the local, national, regional and worldwide components of 'aggregate PGs' entail that their respective 'building blocks' (like the republican values of 'negative liberty' from unjustified interference, 'positive liberty' for individual and democratic self-mastery, 'constitutional liberty' preventing arbitrary domination) must remain protected coherently, notably by interpreting the common constitutional principles underlying national, transnational and international guarantees of freedoms, non-discrimination and the rule of law in mutually consistent ways. Cosmopolitan thinkers often neglect how their moral cosmopolitan claims can be transformed into positive international law and institutions that continue to be dominated by intergovernmental decision-making and governmental self-interests in limiting democratic and judicial accountability of foreign policy discretion vis-à-vis adversely affected citizens.[134] Some cosmopolitan idealists perceive the state as having only instrumental value for the promotion of the cosmopolitan values and rights of all world citizens as moral equals (rather than recognizing states as also promoting legitimate non-cosmopolitan values like national 'communitarian justice'); yet the 'co-originality' of individual and democratic freedom, and the non-ideal reality of an international society of states and peoples constrained by power politics, exclude centralized concepts of a single world government protecting cosmopolitan ideals. The legitimate reality of 'constitutional pluralism' and of the 'sovereign equality' of states rather calls for multilevel governance structures based on constitutional principles of conferral of limited governance powers, subsidiarity and proportionality (eg as prescribed in Article 5 TEU) respecting human rights and limited jurisdictions of overlapping local, national, regional and global institutions that cooperate in diverse forms depending on the regulatory policy problems.[135]

The historical lessons from republican and liberal constitutionalism suggest that collective supply of PGs depends on constituting, limiting, regulating and justifying multilevel governance powers in terms of constitutional rights and corresponding government duties to protect PGs for the benefit of citizens. The Roman republican traditions aimed at limiting perceived 'governance failures' in the 'Athenian democracy' by stronger emphasis on freedom of the citizen (privileging adult male citizens over slaves, females

134 Cf Tan (n 122) 94; Pierik and Werner (eds) (n 123) Introduction, at 4.

135 Cf Buchanan (n 122) 55–56; Pierik andWerner (eds) (n 123) 5; Petersmann (n 33) ch I.

and children who had to live *in potestate domini*), the rule of law, constitutional limitations on government power by 'checks and balances', representation of different classes (including also foreigners as protected by the *praetor peregrinus*), and commitment of the republican Constitution and of the civic virtues to the common good of the people (*res publica* as the common property and community interest of the citizens). Modern, rights-based constitutionalism in Europe has progressively limited many of the 'constitutional' and 'governance failures' of the 'ancient constitutionalism' that evolved in the context of local and national Constitutions (eg of republican city states like ancient Athens and the Florentine republics during the Renaissance) for the governance of local and national peoples (*demos*).[136] Similar to past historical experiences of power politics overthrowing local democratic and republican constitutionalism (eg in Athens, Rome, Florence and Venice), World Wars I and II confirmed the Kantian insight that national republicanism remains constantly at risk as long as discretionary foreign policy powers lack adequate constitutional restraints. As discussed in section V below, the EU's 'cosmopolitan foreign policy constitution' (eg in Articles 2, 3, 21 TEU and the EUCFR) also has not prevented power-orientated abuses of EU policy powers and arbitrary interferences with the equal rights of EU citizens, for instance by persistent violations of EU commitments to 'strict observance of international law' and 'protection of its citizens' (Article 3 TEU) without judicial accountability towards adversely affected citizens cooperating in the collective supply of rules-based international PGs (like the WTO legal, trading and dispute settlement system), thereby undermining modern 'republican constitutionalism'.

As human rights also protect individual and democratic diversity and 'reasonable disagreement' among citizens and governments with often conflicting self-interests, the moral unity underlying the universal recognition of 'human dignity' (eg as a source of 'inalienable' and 'indivisible' civil, political, economic, social and cultural human rights) is limited by the legitimate reality of 'constitutional pluralism' (eg based on diverse Kantian, Rawlsian or 'discourse justifications' of basic rights and constitutional democracy); as discussed in section III above, human rights may also justify legal and institutional fragmentation of multilevel governance of transnational 'aggregate PGs' and other 'community interests'. The 1998 Rome Statute of the ICC recalls that the 'common bonds' and 'shared heritage' of 'all peoples' may not prevent 'this delicate mosaic [being] shattered at any time', as illustrated by continuing wars, genocide, crimes against humanity and war crimes against UN member states. The principal role of the US in elaborating the post-war UN Charter, UN Specialized Agencies and GATT 1947 illustrates that it is often only *after* such human catastrophes that constitutional democracies exercise

[136] On the Roman character of the republican tradition, see Pettit (n 61) 283 ff.

leadership in transforming 'public reason' into *worldwide* agreements and institutions that are explicitly committed to protecting cosmopolitan principles more effectively. The preceding survey of multilevel judicial protection of cosmopolitan rights (eg to consular protection, transnational trading and investor rights) further illustrates that the transformation of cosmopolitan principles into legal institutions can often proceed only piecemeal on the basis of bilateral and regional agreements concluded among governments and people committed to protecting 'human rights and fundamental freedoms for all' (Article 1 UN Charter) more effectively. This study argues that human rights to justification (eg as recognized in Article 29:2 UDHR) require transparent, participatory and inclusive 'discourse justifications' of governmental restrictions of equal freedoms and democratic and judicial accountability mechanisms to challenge power-orientated pursuit of utilitarian self-interests (eg of companies and diplomats arguing for promotion of economic efficiency without 'burdening' intergovernmental negotiations with human rights and distributive justice concerns); republican and cosmopolitan rights and constitutional restraints are even more necessary in multilevel governance of global PGs, due to the limited parliamentary control of intergovernmental law-making and administration. In the civil society struggles for recognition of individual rights[137] in multilevel governance of transnational PGs, political and judicial support for cosmopolitan reforms of international law and protection of cosmopolitan rights will often not prevail over power-orientated national and intergovernmental 'realism' due to non-inclusive decision-making procedures. The path-dependent 'Westphalian structures' of UN and WTO agreements favour the one-sided domination of UN/WTO governance and legal interpretations by self-interested government executives, rather than civil society struggles resisting 'injustices' and 'governance failures' in the non-ideal reality of intergovernmental power politics.

D. 'Constitutionalization' of Multilevel Governance as a Struggle for Additional Rights of 'Constituent Powers' vis-à-vis 'Constituted Powers'

In contrast to the 'reciprocal bargaining' and 'contract models' underlying GATT 1947 and the reciprocal trade concessions among 'GATT contracting parties', the UN Charter and the worldwide agreements constituting UN Specialized Agencies and the WTO share with 'constitutionalism' the long-term commitments to global principles, rules and institutions governing the

[137] Cf A Honneth, *The Struggle for Recognition. The Moral Grammar of Social Conflicts* (Cambridge, MA, MIT Press, 1995).

collective supply of PGs and the relationship between 'constituent powers' and 'constituted powers'. Since the American and French human rights revolutions during the eighteenth century, constitutional democracies and related theories of justice (eg by Rawls) have perceived citizens and 'We the people' as 'constituent powers', who delegate limited government powers to constitutional, parliamentary, administrative and judicial 'constituted powers'. The latter remain subject to constitutional restraints, like constitutional rights, the separation and limited delegation of powers, the rule of law, and democracy. Yet the more national government powers are collectively exercised in international organizations and diplomats claim to be the 'masters' of 'member-driven' international treaties, the more government executives and also political scientists like to define 'principal–agent relationships' in terms of states (represented by heads of states, ministers of foreign affairs and diplomats) delegating powers to international organizations (as agents), rather than in terms of citizens and parliamentary representatives delegating limited powers to multilevel governance institutions.[138]

i. Constitutional Pluralism

'Dualist Constitutions' that distinguish between decisions by 'We the people' and decisions by the government differ enormously, for example regarding the scope of 'rights retained by the people' (Amendment IX to the US Constitution). Some Commonwealth countries continue to define 'constitutionalism' on the basis of 'parliamentary supremacy' rather than 'popular constitutional sovereignty'. And many non-liberal UN member states (like China) have 'Constitutions without constitutionalism', ie constituting government powers internally and externally without effectively protecting citizens against abuses of power.[139] Due to decolonization, there are today more than 200 nation states with national Constitutions (written or unwritten) and hundreds of international legal instruments that recognize, specify and extend 'constitutional principles' (like fundamental rights, the rule of law, democratic governance) to multilevel governance of PGs. It remains contested whether the relationships between the hundreds of national and international legal regimes should be coordinated by formal legal criteria (eg the different 'rules of recognition' of national and international legal regimes) or in the context of constitutional principles (e.g. underlying multilevel HRL) that are common to functionally 'overlapping', national and international legal regimes.

[138] Cf H Tamm and D Snidal, 'Rational Choice and Principal-Agent Theory' in TG Weiss and R Wilkinson (eds), *International Organizations and Global Governance* (London, Routledge, 2014) 132 ff.

[139] Cf VC Jackson and M Tushnet, *Comparative Constitutional Law* (New York, Foundation Press, 1999) 222 ff.

Comparative legal research confirms that 'constitutionalism' has become the most effective governance method for democratic supply of national PGs. Yet there is no agreement on the defining elements of 'constitutionalism'. *Process-based conceptions* (eg in Commonwealth countries) focus on the rule of law, divisions of power and democratic legitimacy.[140] They often provide only for 'weak-form judicial review' (eg of economic, social, cultural and environmental rights in Canada, Ireland, New Zealand, South Africa, the UK and the USA).[141] *Rights-based constitutional approaches* offer stronger protection for constitutional and human rights through 'strong-form judicial review' (eg of civil and political rights in the USA, and also of economic and social rights in EU and EEA member countries).[142] They often acknowledge the 'constitutional functions' of international legal guarantees protecting 'constitutional principles' (eg of transparent policy-making, the rule of law, equal transnational freedoms, non-discriminatory treatment, the peaceful settlement of disputes) in transnational relations beyond state borders.[143] The universal recognition of civil, political, economic, social, cultural and other cosmopolitan rights in UN law remains limited by 'reasonable disagreement' on how particular constitutional democracies should exercise their national 'margins of appreciation' and democratic preferences, for instance by prioritizing and 'balancing' competing rights in particular 'contexts of justice', like individual privacy rights, the economy, the environment, scientific research and the polity. Also, UN HRL can effectively protect 'inalienable', 'indivisible' and 'natural rights' only to the extent that national and regional legal systems provide for effective rules, institutions and resources enabling fulfilment of its 'republican promises'.

Universalist approaches to comparative constitutional law (eg reconsidering national human rights interpretations in the light of the experiences of other constitutional democracies and international human rights conventions) and *functionalist approaches* (eg comparing the effectiveness of constitutional approaches in resolving democratic governance problems) are increasingly influencing the modern post-war Constitutions in Europe and in many developing countries (eg due to the regional human rights conventions in Africa and in the Americas). The particular context of the US Constitution (such as long-standing prioritization of civil and political over

140 Cf A O'Donoghue, *Constitutionalism in Global Constitutionalisation* (Cambridge, CUP, 2014) ch VI.

141 Cf M Tushnet, *Weak Courts, Strong Rights. Judicial Review and Social Welfare Rights in Comparative Constitutional Law* (Princeton, NJ, Princeton UP, 2008).

142 According to Tushnet (*ibid*), 'strong-form judicial review' refers to the power of courts to declare legislative acts unconstitutional and to order injunctions against further enforcement of the statute by executive officials, dismissal of prosecutions under the statute, or awards of damages for people injured by the statute's operation.

143 Cf Petersmann (n 43) ch VII.

economic and social rights, life tenure of US Supreme Court judges, lack of explicit constitutional guarantees of 'strong-form judicial review') explains the continuing dominance of 'procedural conceptions' of democratic self-governance and of 'contextualism' in some US constitutional doctrines (eg claims that constitutional ideas can be understood only in the particular institutional, social and cultural context of the USA as expressions of its self-understanding).[144] Yet this 'contextualism' of national Constitutions has not prevented the international recognition of 'common constitutional principles' governing UN, WTO and regional international law and institutions, and the delegation of limited, non-democratic decision-making powers to international regulatory agencies (eg international financial institutions). The more international law limits the policy choices available to national polities and the more international institutions decide without unanimity or consensus,[145] the more important it becomes to clarify the rights of transnational polities in the emerging world community of 'global citizens', states and multilevel governance by intergovernmental and non-governmental actors.

ii. Citizens and Democratic Peoples as 'Constituent Powers'

The UN legal principles of self-determination of peoples and human rights, including the right of 'everyone ... to take part in the government of his country' and have 'equal access to public service in his country' (Article 21 UDHR), entail universal recognition that 'inalienable' and 'indivisible' human rights and 'the will of the people shall be the basis of the authority of government' (Article 21 UDHR). The confirmation of these UN legal principles and democratic rights in hundreds of national and international constitutional and human rights instruments justifies the legal conclusion that—in the twenty-first century—human beings, citizens and democratic peoples

[144] According to Tushnet (n 141), weak-form judicial review proceeds from 'the recognition that people can reasonably disagree over the proper interpretation of a constitution's relatively abstract provisions', and 'reasonable judicial interpretations have no intrinsic superiority to reasonable legislative and executive interpretations' (at 79). Supporters of strong-form judicial review refer to examples of patently unconstitutional statutes (as discussed by Tushnet in chs 4 and 5 of his book) as historical evidence that periodically elected legislators and executive officials are often subject to political pressures that justify independent, impartial and reasoned judicial review in response to complaints by adversely affected citizens. If the objective of a 'constitution is to place limits on a legislator's natural inclinations to advance the interests of the majority at the expense of minority rights, and to adopt policies that give the decision-makers short-term gains at the expense of long-term impairment of good government' (at 85), then the different institutional characteristics of courts (such as their obligations to review complaints in public hearings and provide reasoned decisions) may enhance 'deliberative constitutional democracy' as a necessary restraint on the modern realities of majority politics.

[145] On the distinction between consensus-based diplomacy and majoritarian democracy, see DM Curtin, *Postnational Democracy* (The Hague, Kluwer, 1997) 27 ff.

must be recognized as legitimate 'constituent powers'. Neither states nor the many 'constituted power holders' inside non-democratic states and international institutions can exercise legitimate powers without a democratic mandate from citizens and democratic peoples.

Arguably, Austin's power-orientated, nineteenth-century version of legal positivism—which perceives law as commands enforced by rulers—lacks democratic legitimacy in the twenty-first century. National Constitutions that constitute, limit, regulate and justify legislative, administrative and judicial government institutions for the collective supply of *national PGs*, share 'constitutional problems' similar to those of international treaties constituting, limiting, regulating and justifying international organizations for the collective supply of *transnational PGs*. This is the case, for instance, regarding the indeterminate nature of many agreed principles and rules (eg on human rights, the rule of law, democracy, national treatment, fair and equitable treatment), the absence of centralized enforcement authorities in some areas of multilevel governance, and the constitutional limitations of all political authorities.[146] Even though treaties that establish international governance institutions tend to be concluded in the name of states, the treaty-making powers of the governments concluding such treaties remain constitutionally limited by the inalienable human and constitutional rights of their citizens. 'State sovereignty' under international law can no longer legitimately limit the democratic sovereignty and 'individual sovereignty' of citizens.[147]

iii. Global Democracy? Lack of Participatory and Deliberative Democracy in Multilevel Governance Institutions

As social human beings, humanity congregates as hundreds of local and national peoples with diverse traditions and democratic preferences. Global democracy based on a single *demos* is neither desirable nor politically feasible. As 'democracy' remains an indeterminate concept and can be defined by diverse criteria (eg democratic elections, representative parliaments, protection of human rights, constitutional, participatory, deliberative, direct and indirect forms of democracy, etc), lists of 'democratic countries' remain contested. The 'democracy index by country (2014)' identifies—on the basis of 60 indicators—24 'full democracies' and 52 'flawed democracies' among 167 countries.[148] As 'We the people' will continue to refer primarily to national peoples, a single 'global constitution' constituting, limiting,

[146] Cf J Goldsmith and D Levinson, 'Law for States: International Law, Constitutional Law, Public Law' (1999) 113 *Harvard Law Review* 1–75.

[147] Cf Petersmann (n 33) 438 ff.

[148] The Economist Intelligence Unit, *Democracy Index 2014*, available at <www.eiu.com>.

regulating and justifying a single world government appears neither desirable nor politically feasible. Because democratic preferences will continue to differ among national peoples, the participation of states in the hundreds of functionally limited, transnational PGs regimes will also differ depending on their preferences, priorities and resources. Similarly, the national methods and traditions of incorporating international law in domestic legal systems and of democratically controlling international PGs regimes inside national polities are likely to continue to differ from country to country. Yet there remain many ways of reducing the 'democratic deficits' of specialized, transnational PGs regimes.

Direct elections by citizens of representative, parliamentary bodies in international organizations remain exceptional (eg in the EU). Most parliamentary bodies in international organizations (like the Council of Europe, NATO) have only consultative rather than legislative powers; their members are selected and delegated by national parliaments in member states. In the executive organs of the Bretton Woods institutions and the IMF, Executive Directors are representing 'constituencies' of member states that empower those Executive Directors to exercise voting rights on their behalf. The tripartite structures of ILO bodies composed of representatives from governments, employers and employees reflect still another system of representation of 'stakeholder constituencies'. Representative, participatory and 'deliberative democracy' recognizing reciprocal rights between citizens and elected, democratic agents remain underdeveloped, under-theorized and inadequately protected in UN and WTO institutions. As long as UN and WTO law offer citizens no effective rights and judicial remedies against abuses of government powers, the often non-transparent and non-inclusive UN and WTO governance procedures lack adequate legitimation; from the perspective of citizens in non-democratic member countries, they may resemble (eg in case of power-orientated IMF and GATT decision-making) the 'intergovernmental feudalism' of past centuries.

How can the 'constituted powers' of international organizations be made more accountable vis-à-vis citizens (as 'constituent powers') and vis-à-vis the international 'community of humanity' that is affected by the failures of multilevel governance to protect international PGs effectively? Due to the power-orientated emergence of nation states since the sixteenth century, the formation of 'peoples' inside states and representative democracies remain limited by national boundaries. Transnational 'constituencies' are characterized by 'power and information asymmetries', for instance due to the greater mobility and concentrated interests of producers compared with consumers, who tend to remain 'rationally ignorant' vis-à-vis 'global supply chains' and related production processes for the supply of thousands of consumer products. Even in the EU, with its directly elected European Parliament representing some 500 million EU citizens, the 'political distance' between local constituencies and elected members of the European Parliament remains wide, and the democratic representation is unequal (eg a German Member of the European Parliament (MEP) represents more than 1 million voters, compared to a MEP from Luxembourg representing constituencies with only some thousands of voters). From the point of view of republican and democratic constitutionalism, decentralized forms of 'participatory', 'deliberative' and 'cosmopolitan stakeholder democracy' may offer more legitimate, constitutional approaches to hold limited, 'constituted powers' more accountable vis-à-vis 'constituent powers' than state-centered conceptions of multilevel governance institutions based on presumptions of legitimate representation of citizens by diplomats. The path-dependent obstacles to extending democratic processes of 'constitutionalization' (eg through legislative, executive and judicial 'constitutional interpretations' of international rules for the benefit of citizens and their cosmopolitan rights) to multilevel governance of international PGs call for stronger 'cosmopolitan countervailing rights', enabling citizens to hold multilevel governance agents more accountable. For instance, the particular 'constituency groups' of stakeholders actively involved in the collective supply of transnational PGs (like governments, employers and employee representatives in the ILO) must be held more accountable for their multilevel governance through 'human rights approaches' (eg as acknowledged in the ILO, WHO, FAO and UNESCO Constitutions) that protect access of all human beings to transnational PGs like health, food, human and labour rights protection. Human rights must be complemented by additional constitutional and cosmopolitan rights, and by judicial protection of 'constitutional justice' for the benefit of 'constituent power holders' in multilevel governance.[149] European law illustrates why 'constitutionalism' has proved to be indispensable for protecting equal rights of citizens not only inside national legal systems, but also in multilevel governance and collective supply of transnational PGs beyond state borders. *National constitutionalism* risks being undermined by discretionary foreign policy powers (the 'Lockean dilemma'), unless it is complemented by multilevel, albeit functionally limited *transnational constitutionalism* that limits abuses of international law in multilevel governance of PGs by protecting equal cosmopolitan rights and accountability of the holders of 'constituted powers' vis-à-vis citizens as the legitimate holders of 'constituent powers'.

iv. Cosmopolitan Constitutionalism as Never-Ending 'Struggle for Justice'

The creation of ever more 'city republics' since ancient Greece, Rome, Renaissance Italy and the 'Hanseatic League', the 'Glorious Revolution' in

[149] Cf Gardbaum (n 74) and EU Petersmann, 'Human Rights, International Economic Law and 'Constitutional Justice' (2008) 19 *EJIL* 769–98.

seventeenth-century England, the human rights revolutions since the eighteenth century and the emergence of European constitutional law (eg based on the 2007 Lisbon Treaty) can be construed as a progressive transformation and 'constitutionalization' of multilevel governance powers in response to struggles by citizens for justification and protection of their rights through constitutional, legislative, administrative, judicial and international legal protection of the rule of law and equal rights. Constitutionalism as a 'Kantian moral imperative' (eg demanding reconciliation of rational self-interests with the reasonable, common interests of all others) calls for 'constitutionalization' (as never-ending democratic processes and 'struggles for rights') of multilevel governance powers so as to prevent national constitutionalism from being undermined by foreign policy discretion and intergovernmental power politics. Domestic 'horizontal divisions' of constitutional, legislative, administrative and judicial powers inside national democracies may not be transferable to international law and international organizations. Also the diverse and often fragmented 'vertical, multilevel governance systems' may need to be coordinated and progressively 'constitutionalized' through new conceptions of 'participatory multilevel constitutionalism' with different 'functional separation' and geographical fragmentation of powers.

As explained in Chapter 2, multilevel governance approaches and 'optimal policy instruments' must target the particular 'collective action problems' of international PGs so as to ensure 'constitutional accountability' of the holders of national, regional and worldwide 'constituted power' vis-à-vis local holders of 'constituent power'. As recognized in EU law and also in UN HRL, cosmopolitan rights, democratic governance, the rule of law, and parliamentary and judicial 'checks and balances' must remain the core instruments of 'cosmopolitan constitutionalism' for holding multilevel governance accountable. As illustrated by the diverse designs of UN Specialized Agencies and WTO institutions, different functional 'treaty constitutions' may follow diverse 'constitutionalization approaches', for instance for empowering 'stakeholder constituencies' (eg in the ILO) and humanity as a 'global community' (eg in global health regulation and international criminal law based on universal recognition of human rights, corresponding 'duties to protect' and sanctions against 'crimes against humanity').[150] The 2012 high-level UN 'Declaration on the rule of law at the national and international levels' emphasizes the inevitable interrelationships between national and international rule of law.[151] Comparative constitutional and international legal

[150] Cf O'Donoghue (n 140), ch 7, for a discussion of why global constitutionalism might focus on 'international constituencies' rather than on 'international community': 'Actors affected by, and who affect, other actors within a global constitutionalising order provide the members of the international constituency' (at 248).

[151] Cf UN Doc A/RES 67/L.1 of 24 September 2012 (High-level meeting of the General Assembly).

analyses reveal, however, that UN and WTO legal guarantees of equal freedoms and rule of law remain ineffectively 'constitutionalized' and protected inside most UN and WTO member states.[152] Even though UN HRL and WTO law aim at empowering citizens to engage in mutually beneficial, rules-based transnational cooperation, and are essential for promoting general consumer welfare and other international PGs demanded by citizens, most citizens lack effective legal and judicial remedies to invoke and enforce UN and WTO rules in domestic courts in order to hold the 'disconnected UN/WTO intergovernmentalism' accountable vis-à-vis adversely affected citizens. 'Realist diplomats' justify their intergovernmentalism by the claim that foreign policy discretion is more important for protecting 'national interests' and limiting multilevel governance failures than cosmopolitan ideals for extending constitutionalism (as a governance method) to international law and institutions for the collective supply of transnational PGs. Yet, as discussed before, the UN Security Council and the ICJ increasingly recognize the need for using their powers to protect human rights (eg by UN Security Council resolutions establishing international criminal courts and ordering 'smart sanctions' against individual terrorists, and ICJ judgments ordering 'provisional measures' aimed at protecting human rights pending ICJ proceedings).

V. CONSTITUTIONALIZING UN/WTO GOVERNANCE THROUGH JUDICIAL PROTECTION OF COSMOPOLITAN RIGHTS? FAILURES OF THE EU'S 'COSMOPOLITAN FOREIGN POLICY CONSTITUTION'

Legal positivism defines national and international law by the authoritative issuance and social effectiveness of legal rules and principles of law. Yet as national and international legal systems have incorporated 'inalienable' human rights derived from respect for human dignity as well as other 'principles of justice', the traditional distinctions between 'natural law' and 'positive law' conceptions of legal systems risk being misleading. For, as already explained by Kant in his *Critique of Pure Reason* (1781), most rules do not sufficiently spell out the conditions of their own application (eg of whether the general rule or a specific exception should be applied in a particular situation). Hence, the rule of law requires 'reasonable judgments' and a 'constitutional mind-set' from the law-appliers;[153] these must be informed

[152] Cf M Hilf and EU Petersmann (eds), *National Constitutions and International Economic Law* (The Hague, Kluwer, 1993).

[153] On the importance of a 'constitutional mind-set' of the legal profession and 'courts of justice' using the international legal transformations for promoting human rights and inclusive 'public reason', see Petersmann (n 33), ch III; M Koskenniemi, 'Constitutionalism as a Mindset: Reflections on Kantian Themes About International Law and Globalization' (2007) 8 *Theoretical Inquiries in Law* 9–36.

by human rights (eg to democratic participation in government) and related principles of 'reformative justice' that justify 'evolutionary interpretations' rather than only 'conservative justice' in terms of path-dependent rule-following. By taking into account 'principles of justice'—including 'participatory', representative and 'deliberative democracy' and the constitutional limitations of 'state sovereignty' by 'popular' and 'individual sovereignty' (as protected by HRL)—and reviewing the constitutional coherence and democratic legitimacy of positive rules of law, legal interpretations often do not discover pre-existing 'right interpretations' of positive law; they rather find and apply the most reasonable and practical 'judgments' that fill 'gaps' in existing, yet incomplete and under-theorized legal texts. The more UN and WTO governance has to resort to majority decisions and directly affect the lives of individuals, the more person-orientated 'constitutional interpretations' (eg by judicial bodies)—even if they challenge state-centered interpretations and their underlying 'principles of Westphalian justice'—have been accepted as justifiable by the human rights obligations of UN member states and their corresponding 'republican duties' to protect PGs. Clarification of indeterminate rules by courts of justice is often not about discovering objective 'truth', but rather about justifying coherent interpretations on the basis of legal texts, contexts and functional arguments in conformity with human rights and other agreed principles of justice.

Hence, the changing *opinio juris sive necessitatis* and legal practices of citizens, civil society, democratic institutions and courts of justice—ie the 'law in action'—may be no less important for determining and interpreting the 'law in the books' than the legal claims of diplomats as traditional 'gate-keepers' of 'Westphalian international law among sovereign states'. The more national and transnational polities (like the EU) interact, and the more 'law in action' evolves due to changing interpretations of legal rules and judicial protection of their underlying principles of justice, the more democratic self-governance inside and beyond states may justify legal interpretations that 'constitutionalize' and limit abuses of public and private power in response to requests by citizens and judgments by courts of justice. As most EU citizens also continue to define their identity first by their national citizenship rather than by their EU citizenship, democratic legitimacy in multilevel governance of PGs derives more from compliance with international 'PGs treaties' enacted by national parliaments for the benefit of their citizens, and from recognition of corresponding rights of citizens, than from claims by diplomats to enjoy 'freedom of manoeuvre' to violate transnational rule of law.[154] The traditional distinctions and 'binary logic' of national and international law categories are also challenged by the emergence of 'transnational law' and 'multi-valued legal reasoning' that

[154] Cf n 61 in the Introduction to this book and the related text.

'balances' competing legal values and legal regimes. The necessary reconciliation of multilevel legal regimes can be achieved, for instance, by means of 'margins of appreciation' and '*solange*' doctrines, 'consistent interpretations' of national and international rules of law, 'reciprocal recognition' principles (eg based on 'equivalent protection'), judicial 'balancing' and protection of 'countervailing rights' of citizens, so as better to protect procedural justice principles (like transparency of governmental decisions) and legal accountability in multilevel governance. National, regional and worldwide legal systems increasingly justify their multilevel regulation in terms of common 'constitutional principles' (eg in Articles 2–6 TEU), for instance by limiting 'state sovereignty' as a power-orientated command structure of society by 'duties to protect' transnational freedoms, human rights, non-discriminatory treatment and the rule of law beyond state borders. The 'subsidiarity principle' of EU law, the 'margins of appreciation' principle of multilevel HRL, and the 'complementarity principle' in the ICC Statute promote multilevel legal, political and judicial cooperation in exercising the often 'overlapping jurisdictions' in multilevel governance of PGs.

A. Human Rights Law and 'Access to Justice' Justify Additional Cosmopolitan Rights

United Nations human rights law protects civil, political, economic, social and cultural rights, with due respect for state sovereignty to decide which UN and regional human rights conventions a state wishes to ratify and how democratic states exercise their national 'margin of appreciation' regarding their prioritization of civil and political rights (eg in the USA), or of economic, social and cultural rights (eg in China). Due to this 'reasonable disagreement' and related state practices, additional cosmopolitan rights continue to be protected outside HRL (eg in international trade, investment, intellectual property law and labour law). Section III above used the example of multilevel trade and investment regulation and its 'judicial reinterpretation' (eg deriving individual trading, investor and other cosmopolitan rights from international economic agreements) in order to illustrate the governmental and judicial use of 'legal fragmentation' for reforming state-centered rules of international law. The US policy of differentiating among GATT members depending on their compliance with conventions on the protection of intellectual property rights, the EU policy of granting additional trade preferences to less-developed countries complying with UN human rights conventions and ILO conventions, and BITs making promotion of capital exports to less-developed countries conditional on protection of 'access to justice' and property rights, are additional examples of how state-centered, international 'legal fragmentation' is often justified as a means for protecting person-centered 'principles of justice'. 'Constitutional' BIT disciplines of non-discrimination, 'full protection and security', 'fair and equitable treatment' and related investment arbitration raise legal problems similar to those in domestic constitutional law systems, such as identifying the relevant comparator for the purpose of establishing discrimination, the scope of police power jurisdiction for limiting private property rights, protection of due process of law, enforceability of transnational contracts and 'proportionality review' in investor-state arbitration of governmental limitations of property rights. Yet does international recourse to such 'constitutional principles' justify the conclusion of an 'emergent economic constitutional order' in international investment law?[155]

From the perspective of European constitutional law and its multilevel guarantees of judicial protection of 'inalienable' and 'indivisible' civil, political, economic, social and cultural rights of citizens, the vaguely defined 'principles of justice' exported through BITs in order to compensate for the lack of impartial and independent judiciaries in many less-developed, capital-importing countries do not adequately protect impartial and independent 'constitutional balancing' of all public and private interests involved. This is illustrated by the often one-sided domination of investor-state arbitral tribunals by commercial lawyers from big law firms that advise transnational corporations and are reluctant to interpret the 'applicable law' and 'jurisdiction' of investment tribunals as including HRL and constitutional law. In the Comprehensive Economic and Trade Agreement (CETA) between Canada and the EU, as well as in the ongoing EU–US negotiations on a Transatlantic Trade and Investment Partnership (TTIP), the 'commercial arbitration paradigm' of UNCITRAL and ICSID investor-state arbitration is being limited by reforms of substantive and procedural investment rules acknowledging the sovereign duties to regulate the economy and protect constitutional rights. Yet, as illustrated by the intergovernmental exclusion of rights and effective judicial remedies of citizens in domestic courts in Article 30.6 CETA, investor-state arbitration amounts to the provision of legal and judicial privileges to foreign investors—especially in relations among transatlantic democracies—that can circumvent constitutional commitments of governments to protect equal rights and judicial remedies for all adversely affected citizens through constitutionally constrained, permanent courts of justice. Investor-state arbitration offers advantages if compared with 'diplomatic protection' and investment disputes in the ICJ. The out-sourcing of judicial protection of the rule of law and of other public interests to commercial arbitrators is, however, justifiable only as a second-best substitute for 'transitional justice' as long as multilevel judicial protection of investor rights and of 'constitutional

[155] Cf D Schneiderman, 'Global Constitutionalism and International Economic Law: The Case of International Investment Law' (2016) 7 *EYIEL* forthcoming.

justice' remains underdeveloped in capital-importing countries, notably if the latter are ruled by despotic and corrupt governments that often collude with foreign investors in appropriating domestic resources to the detriment of general consumer welfare. Arguably, as long as BITs fail to effectively limit 'market failures' as well as 'governance failures' and 'constitutional failures' in host states, and avoid references to the human rights obligations of both home and host states of investors, they cannot effectively 'constitutionalize' international investment law.

B. The EU's Multilevel Economic Constitutionalism

European integration law illustrates more clearly how European constitutional law and HRL—notably their recognition of 'basic human rights to justification',[156] 'access to justice' and judicial protection of fundamental freedoms and other constitutional rights—justified 'constitutional interpretations' of European economic law protecting ever more comprehensive 'common market rights' and constitutional rights of EU citizens. Even though EU common market law remains based on the customs union rules of GATT Article XXIV, the inadequate competition and social rules in GATT/WTO law for the protection of 'justice in transnational economic transactions' and 'communitarian justice'[157] necessitated EU common market law's constructing a 'social market economy' (Article 3 TEU) 'bottom up', with due respect for the legitimate 'constitutional pluralism' among EU member states. The jurisprudence and cooperation of national and European courts progressively transformed the fragmented treaties among European states (eg constituting the separate international organizations of the European Coal and Steel Community (ECSC), the European Economic Community (EEC) and the European Atomic Energy Community (EURATOM)) into a multilevel constitutional order deriving its legitimacy from the protection of individual rights of 'common market citizens' and 'EU citizens'.[158] Both the preliminary ruling procedure (Article 267 TFEU) and the multilevel cooperation among national courts and the CJEU outside of this procedure (as illustrated by the *Solange I* and *II* judgments of the German Constitutional Court regarding multilevel judicial protection of

[156] Cf Forst (n 22) 1–2. The right to justification is 'what the Kantian idea of the dignity of a person as "an end in itself", as a justificatory being, implies' (*ibid* at 130).

[157] On communitarian principles of justice in the worldwide division of labour, see A James, *Fairness in Practice. A Social Contract for a Global Economy* (Oxford, OUP, 2012); Garcia (n 39) 137 ff. On 'transactional modes' for diagnosing injustice and improving the 'internal justice' of economic transactions, see Garcia (n 39) 205 ff.

[158] Cf J Weiler, 'Van Gend en Loos: The individual as subject and object and the dilemma of European legitimacy' (2014) 12(1) *International Journal of Constitutional Law* 94 ff.

human rights inside the EU) induced national and EU courts of justice to protect the 'sovereignty of EU law' in the name of fundamental rights and constitutionally limited, democratic governance.[159] Arguably, the multilevel judicial governance by the CJEU, the EFTA Court, the ECtHR and national courts not only justified their common focus on teleological and 'systemic' (eg comparative)—rather than merely textual—interpretations of European treaties, as being more in line with the customary methods of treaty interpretation than with the judicial methods applied by national courts (such as judicial deference towards parliamentary majority decisions, focus on preparatory work of statutes in order to respect the intentions of the legislator).[160] All three European courts rightly emphasized their 'constitutional embeddedness', requiring protection of human rights and other constitutional principles common to their member states.

The judicial protection of common constitutional principles justified the active use of judicial powers to limit abuses of foreign policy discretion and protect fundamental rights of EU citizens, as illustrated by the '*Kadi* case law' on protection of EU fundamental rights for the benefit of foreigners.[161] Some national courts continue to insist on sovereign rights of member states to scrutinize whether EU acts are *ultra vires*, violate the 'national constitutional identity' (cf Article 5 TEU) or fail to protect constitutional safeguards equivalent to national fundamental rights.[162] Multilevel judicial reasoning and 'judicial dialogues' promote 'judicial comity', compliance with EU law as interpreted by EU courts and the search for 'the best fit' of judicial interpretations. For instance, the *Mangold* judgment by the CJEU on age discrimination in employment was widely criticized by governments for exceeding the borderline separating law from policy; yet the German Constitutional Court reluctantly accepted it as a 'methodologically justifiable development of the law'.[163] Such conditional cooperation among supreme courts illustrates that the validity and legitimacy of legal rules may depend no less on respect for legitimately diverse legal methodologies than on the outcome of judicial decisions. By connecting novel interpretations to the

[159] Cf F Jacobs, *The Sovereignty of Law: The European Way* (Cambridge, CUP, 2007).

[160] The CILFIT formula—according to which 'every provision of Community law must be placed in its context and interpreted in the light of the provisions of the Community as a whole, regard being had to the objectives thereof' (Case 283/81, *CILFIT* [1982] ECR 3415, para 20)—is fully consistent with the interpretation methods codified in Art 31 VCLT.

[161] Cf nn 67 and 68 above and related text.

[162] Cf nn 77–79 in the Introduction and related texts regarding the 2014 request by the German Constitutional Court for a preliminary ruling by the CJEU on the scope of powers of the European Central Bank (2 BvR 2728/13 of 14 January 2014); see also the Lisbon judgment of the German Constitutional Court of 30 June 2009, BVerfGE 123, 267.

[163] Case C-144/04 *Mangold* [2005] ECR I-9981; BVerfGE 2 BvR 2661/06 of 6 July 2010 ('Dem Gerichtshof ist auch die Rechtsfortbildung im Wege methodisch gebundener Rechtsfortbildung nicht verwehrt').

aims of EU law and of national constitutional systems, national authorities may find it easier to accept the reasonableness of judicial determinations as integral parts of their existing legal obligations.[164] If the 'constitutional traditions common to the member states' or international agreements and related jurisprudence binding on the EU do not justify uniform 'autonomous interpretations' of EU legal concepts, the CJEU often deliberately refrains from interpreting EU legal terms (such as 'public order', the right of access to courts and to a fair trial) in an autonomous, uniform manner, so as to respect legitimately diverse legal traditions in member states that interpret equivalent notions in conformity with their national constitutional values in their respective legal systems.[165]

Almost a century ago, the German jurist Jhering noted that the 'life of the law' often depends on citizens struggling for their rights. He argued that such 'struggle for his rights' may be a 'duty of the person whose rights have been violated', as well as a 'duty to society'.[166] In US antitrust law, as well as in European economic law, individual plaintiffs who invoke and enforce competition and common market rules have been likened to 'attorneys general' who promote 'community interests' rather than pursuing only individual self-interests.[167] Following the recognition of human rights and other 'principles of justice' as integral parts of national and international legal systems, increasing numbers of national and international courts throughout Europe have interpreted international guarantees of freedom, non-discrimination and the rule of law for the benefit of citizens even if the international rules were addressed to states without explicitly providing for cosmopolitan rights.[168] Yet the EU policy since 2006 of explicitly excluding individual rights in FTAs with third countries—even in FTAs with democracies like Canada (cf Article 30.6 CETA)—also demonstrates that the 'cosmopolitan foreign policy constitution' of EU law (cf Articles 3, 21 TEU) protects cosmopolitan rights much less effectively than the EU's internal

[164] An example is the justification by the CJEU of the need for European 'uniform interpretations': 'According to settled case law, the need for uniform application of Community law and the principle of equality require that the terms of a provision of Community law which makes no express reference to the law of the Member States for the purpose of determining its meaning and scope must normally be given an autonomous and uniform interpretation throughout the Community; that interpretation must take into account the context of the provision and the purpose of the legislation in question' (Case C-373/00 *Truly* [2003] ECR I-1932, para 35).

[165] Cf J Gerhards, 'Judicial Argumentation in Fundamental Rights Cases—the EU Court's Challenge' in U Neergard and R Nielsen (eds), *European Legal Method in a Multilevel EU Legal Order* (Copenhagen, DJOF Publishing, 2012) 27–70, at 47.

[166] R Jhering, *The Struggle for Law* (Chicago, IL, Callaghan, 1915) chs II–IV.

[167] This conception was emphasized by the ECJ in its *Van Gend en Loos* judgment (Case 26/62 [1963] ECR 1), where the Court stated that 'the vigilance of the individuals concerned to protect their rights amounts to an effective supervision in addition to the supervision entrusted by (ex) Articles 169 and 170 to the diligence of the Commission and the Member States'.

[168] Cf Case C-281/98, *Angonese* [2000] ECR I-4139 (n 69).

common market constitution.[169] Moreover, the fact that national parliaments and the European Parliament did not even discuss this executive 'disempowerment' of EU citizens in multilevel governance of transnational PGs (like a transatlantic common market) illustrates the limited effectiveness of parliamentary control of secretive, intergovernmental rule-making without transparent democratic debate. As discussed below, the CJEU also refrains from protecting 'strict observance of international law' (Article 3 TEU) in the EU's external relations, and—for political reasons—refrains from reviewing EU compliance with UN and WTO agreements and with related UN/WTO dispute settlement findings of EU violations of international law.

C. Political Opposition to the EU's Cosmopolitan 'Foreign Policy Constitution'

The multilevel constitutional limitations of EU foreign policy powers through the national and EU legal systems (eg delegating only limited powers to the EU), and the recognition of international law as an integral part of EU law with legal primacy over other 'secondary EU law' (eg in view of EU obligations under UN and WTO law to protect equal freedoms and rule of law beyond states), can be viewed as constituting a multilevel 'foreign policy constitution'.[170] Human rights law and European constitutional law provide that '[a]ny limitation on the exercise of the rights and freedoms recognized by this Charter must be provided for by law and respect the essence of those rights and freedoms', subject to constitutional safeguards of 'necessity' and 'proportionality' (Article 52 EUCFR). This constitutional justification and protection of transnational freedoms must be also respected by national and EU institutions in the external relations law of the EU, whenever such freedoms—like the freedoms 'to choose an occupation' (Article 15), 'to conduct a business in accordance with Union law' (Article 16), to own and use private property (Article 17), and to have access to effective judicial remedies (Article 47 EUCFR)—are protected by EU constitutional law across national and EU frontiers.

European Union law (eg Articles 2, 3, 21 TEU) aims—in the external relations of the EU too—at a rule of law community with constitutionally limited powers based on principles of conferral, subsidiarity and proportionality (Article 5 TEU), and committed to 'protection of its citizens' and 'strict observance of international law' (Article 3 TEU). Hence, international

[169] Cf A Semertzi, 'The Preclusion of Direct Effect in the Recently Concluded EU Free Trade Agreements' (2014) 51 *CML Rev* 1125–58.

[170] Cf EU Petersmann, 'The Foreign Policy Constitution of the European Union: A Kantian Perspective' in U Immenga *et al* (eds), *Festschrift für Ernst-Joachim Mestmäcker* (Baden-Baden, Nomos, 1996) 433–47.

dispute settlement obligations of the EU must also be legally presumed to derive their constitutional legitimacy from protecting equal rights of EU citizens, including their rights to effective judicial remedies (cf Article 47 EUCFR). Similar to the constitutional obligations of national courts (eg pursuant to the jurisprudence of the German Constitutional Court) to interpret fundamental rights with due regard to their interpretation and protection by the CJEU and by the ECtHR,[171] the 'consistent interpretation' requirements of EU law and international law may require national and EU courts to protect transnational rights of citizens with due regard to 'strict observance of international law' (Article 3 TEU), as authoritatively clarified through international dispute settlement rulings binding on the EU and its member states. The shared legal obligations and 'constitutional functions' of national courts, EU courts and UN/WTO dispute settlement bodies, to interpret treaties and settle related disputes 'in conformity with the principles of justice and international law', including 'universal respect for human rights and fundamental freedoms for all' (Preamble and Article 31 VCLT), require multilevel judicial comity in their common mission of administrating justice, including 'individual justice' for citizens participating in mutually beneficial transnational cooperation and protection of PGs. European Union law (eg Article 52 EUCFR) requires balancing state-centered and person-orientated 'principles of justice' with due respect for 'due process of law' and judicial remedies in the EU's external relations too, so as to 'support democracy, the rule of law, human rights' and 'consistency' between its internal and external actions (cf Article 21 TEU). This calls for multilevel legal protection of civil society cooperation and democratic self-government among free and equal citizens beyond national frontiers, for instance in the world trading system based on the WTO legal and dispute settlement system, 'providing security and predictability to the multilateral trading system' (Article 3 DSU) through transnational 'compliance communities' protecting and benefitting from transnational rule of law.

i. Three Complementary Levels of the EU's 'Republican' and 'Cosmopolitan' Foreign Policy Constitution

'The Union is founded on the indivisible, universal values of human dignity, freedom, equality and solidarity', 'the principles of democracy and the rule of law', and 'places the individual at the heart of its activities' (Preamble EUCFR). European Union law also justifies itself in terms of republican 'output legitimacy' (eg a 'social market economy', Article 3 TEU) and 'input legitimacy' (eg protecting 'negative freedoms from interference', 'positive

[171] Cf *Görgülü v Germany* (2004) 2 BvR 1481/04.

freedoms' to individual and democratic self-determination, and 'constitutional freedoms' from domination). As a community of member states, peoples and EU citizens, 'cosmopolitan' and 'republican' interpretations of EU foreign policy powers 'fit better' its multilevel constitutional structures than power-orientated statist paradigms focusing on 'national interests'. European Union law explicitly protects the 'national identities' (Article 4 TEU), the principles of conferral, subsidiarity and proportionality (Article 5 TEU), and the 'constitutional traditions common to the Member States' as 'general principles of the Union's law' (Article 6 TEU). Citizens of the EU and national 'peoples' also remain the 'constituent powers' and 'democratic principals' in the EU; the directly elected European Parliament exercises limited legislative, budgetary and political powers (cf Article 14 TEU) in view of the EU's limited rights and Parliament's unequal representation of EU citizens (who lack equal voting powers).

In addition to the constitutional principles rooted in the common constitutional traditions of EU member states, treaty-based, constitutional restraints of EU foreign policy powers are prescribed in the 'common provisions' (eg Articles 1–8 TEU), 'democratic principles' (eg Articles 9–12 TEU), institutional restraints (eg Articles 13–19 TEU) and specific provisions for the EU's external actions (eg Articles 21–46 TEU; Articles 205 et seq TFEU). They require the EU to promote 'respect for human dignity, freedom, democracy, equality, the rule of law and respect for human rights', and 'protection of its citizens' in its external relations too, including 'strict observance of international law' (Article 3 TEU). The specific foreign policy mandates emphasize the need for respecting 'uniform principles' (Article 207 TFEU) and specific foreign policy goals like 'progressive abolition of restrictions on international trade and on foreign investments' (Article 206 TFEU), or 'reduction and ... eradication of poverty' as 'primary objective' of the EU's development cooperation policy (Article 208 TFEU). Compared to most national Constitutions and their often scant regulation of foreign policy objectives, EU law regulates foreign policy powers in more detail through more precise constitutional restraints and commitments to protecting transnational PGs.[172]

The third level of constitutional restraints is the most neglected and, arguably, the most important, due to the transformation of *national PGs* into *transnational* and *global PGs* (as recognized in Article 21 TEU) that can be collectively supplied and protected only through EU participation in international agreements 'binding upon the institutions of the Union and on its Member States' (Article 216 TFEU). For the national and EU law principles of 'democracy, the rule of law, the universality and indivisibility of human

[172] For details, see J Larik, *Worldly Ambitions. Foreign Policy Objectives in European Constitutional Law* (Florence, EUI doctoral thesis, 2013).

rights and fundamental freedoms, respect for human dignity, the principles of equality and solidarity' (Articles 2, 3, 21 TEU)—which are today also recognized in UN HRL—cannot remain effective in transnational relations without 'strict observance of international law' (Articles 3, 21 TEU) protecting mutually 'consistent interpretations' of the local, national, regional and global regulation of 'aggregate PGs' (like equal freedoms and human rights) in the EU's participation in multilevel PGs regimes. In order to protect overall coherence of European constitutional law, national, EU, UN, WTO and other dispute settlement procedures must also be construed coherently as instruments for protecting equal freedoms, the rule of law, democratic governance, and other human and constitutional rights of citizens as democratic sources of legitimacy of multilevel governance of transnational 'PGs regimes'. The rights-based, multilevel constitutional frameworks for EU external relations limit collective action problems through rules-based procedures (eg impartial WTO dispute settlement procedures rather than majoritarian power politics discriminating among EU citizens) based on 'cosmopolitan' and 'republican' legal assumptions that international treaties concluded by the EU (like the WTO Agreement protecting 'security and predictability' in the multilateral trading system, cf Article 3 DSU) are enacted by parliaments in order to protect the EU's 'values' (like equal freedoms and rule of law, cf Article 2 TEU) for the benefit of EU citizens. While national foreign policy discretion may need to be broad in power-orientated international relations, foreign policy powers of international 'PGs organizations' (like the EU) must remain limited to 'strict observance of international law' (cf Article 3 TEU) in order to remain democratically legitimate.

ii. Political Opposition to 'Constitutionalizing' EU Foreign Policies

Constitutional principles and rules cannot become effective unless they are transformed into democratic legislation, effective administration and judicial protection of individual rights of citizens. Just as persistent violations of the budget and debt disciplines in Article 126 TFEU undermined the EU's 'monetary constitution', so have persistent EU violations of GATT/WTO rules and of related GATT/WTO dispute settlement rulings undermined the EU's 'foreign policy constitution'. Depending on their often 'path-dependent' value premises, EU lawyers and politicians disagree on whether 'constitutionalization' of foreign policies should be welcomed[173] or criticized as reflecting

[173] In this sense: Petersmann (n 170); more recently EU Petersmann, 'Integrating Human Rights into EU Trade Relations—The EU as a Global Role Model?' in Takacs *et al* (eds) (n 45) 15–26.

'unrealistic idealism'.[174] Similar disagreements exist among political scientists and economists evaluating the EU's external relations. Some argue that the EU has evolved into a 'civilian normative power' that has succeeded in progressively transforming the 'Westphalian system' of 'international law among sovereign states' for the benefit of more than 500 million EU citizens cooperating in the common market and in a transnational rule of law system protecting human rights, democratic peace, a 'social market economy' and other PGs. Others describe the reality of the EU's common commercial and development policies as 'power politics in disguise'.[175] Empirical evidence suggests that inadequate protection of the rule of law inside some EU member states (like Bulgaria, Greece and Romania), in some areas of EU integration (like the Eurozone, migration into and within the EU, illegal financial disbursements by EU institutions as annually documented by the EU Court of Auditors) and in some external EU policies (eg persistent disregard for some WTO legal obligations) undermines the democratic legitimacy of EU law; according to the 'Euro-barometer' statistics, confidence of EU citizens in the EU was at its lowest ebb in 2014, the distance between EU institutions and EU citizens having continually widened: 'citizens believe that their voices are not taken into account by the EU, which they consider to be removed from their concerns and lacking in transparency'.[176] In response to questions of why, since 2006, EU FTAs exclude private rights of citizens and 'direct applicability' of FTA provisions (cf Article 30.6 CETA), EU trade diplomats admit their self-interest in avoiding legal, judicial and democratic accountability vis-à-vis EU citizens by following the power-orientated trade policy traditions of third states.[177] Yet is EU power politics a legitimate foreign policy option?

The historical lessons from 2,500 years of 'trial and error' with 'republican constitutionalism' since the ancient Greek and Italian city republics confirm that multilevel governance of transnational 'aggregate PGs' cannot be effective and democratic unless the multilevel rules and institutions are construed as a 'principal-agent relationship' aimed at protecting rights of citizens, including their modern entitlement 'to a social and international

[174] Cf B de Witte, 'Too Much Constitutional Law in the EU's Foreign Relations?' in M Cremona and B de Witte (eds), *EU Foreign Relations Law—Constitutional Fundamentals* (Oxford, Hart Publishing, 2008) 3 ff.

[175] Cf T Forsberg, 'Normative Power Europe, Once Again: A Conceptual Analysis of an Ideal Type' (2011) 49 *JCMS* 1183 ff; EU Petersmann, 'How to Evaluate the EU as a Normative Power in Multilevel Governance of Public Goods?' in C Kaddous (ed), *The EU in International Organizations and Global Governance* (Oxford, Hart Publishing, 2015) ch 14.

[176] J Zalc, 'Overcoming Democratic Breakdown in the EU' in Fondation Robert Schuman, *European Issues* No 333 of 18 November 2014, at 1.

[177] Cf EU Petersmann, 'Transformative Transatlantic Free Trade Agreements without Rights and Remedies of Citizens?' (2015) 18 *JIEL* 579 ff.

order in which the rights and freedoms set forth in this Declaration can be fully realized' (Article 28 UDHR). National Constitutions in EU member states are increasingly transformed into 'cosmopolitan Constitutions' recognizing and protecting transnational rights of citizens and of democratic parliaments in their transnational cooperation in European integration.[178] The functionally limited, multilevel foreign policy constitution of the EU—as an international organization with limited powers—differs from that of sovereign nation states in three important ways:

— The external relations powers of the EU are constitutionally limited to collective supply of enumerated PGs (eg in Articles 2, 3 and 21 TEU). While 'parliamentary sovereignty' and monarchical governance remain possible inside nation states (like the UK), the EU is functionally limited to '*multilevel, republican governance*' for the benefit of EU citizens as 'democratic principals' in internal as well as external EU relations.
— EU law rightly recognizes that collective supply of international PGs (eg those listed in Article 21 TEU) protecting the equal rights of EU citizens depends on '*strict observance of international law*' and EU participation in international agreements that 'are binding upon the institutions of the Union and on its Member States' (Article 216 TFEU). Transnational 'aggregate PGs' must build on mutually coherent constitutional foundations at local, national and regional levels of law and governance.
— The EU is constitutionally committed—in the exercise of its foreign relations powers too—to 'the protection of its citizens' and 'protection of human rights' (Article 3 TEU); this *cosmopolitan constitutionalism* reflects Europe's long-standing, constitutional experience that collective protection of PGs depends on republican rights of citizens to hold government agents legally, democratically and judicially accountable.

iii. Text, Context and Objectives of EU External Relations Law are Committed to 'Strict Observance of International Law'

The 'constitutional reading' of EU external relations law is mandated by the text, context and declared objectives of the Lisbon Treaty. European Union law circumscribes the external relations powers of the EU as being constitutionally limited by the EU's foundational principles (cf Articles 2, 3, 21 TEU). For instance:

— The *text of Article 21 TEU* requires the EU external policies 'to advance in the wider world: democracy, the rule of law, ... human rights and

[178] For a survey, see Larik (n 172) ch II; A Somek, *The Cosmopolitan Constitution* (Oxford, OUP, 2014).

fundamental freedoms' and 'the principles of international law'. By stipulating that 'the Union's action on the international scene shall be guided by the principles which have inspired its own creation, development and enlargement', 'in order to safeguard its values ..., consolidate and support democracy, the rule of law, human rights and the principles of international law', Article 21 TEU recognizes that EU foreign policies must remain constitutionally restrained and accountable vis-à-vis EU citizens as holders of the 'constituent powers', sources of legitimacy of EU law and 'agents of justice' entitled to effective legal, judicial and democratic remedies as confirmed in the EUCFR. The text of Article 21 TEU suggests that the EU's customs union principle (Articles 28–31 TFEU)—based on the EU's GATT obligations incorporated into EU law—should be also protected in terms of equal 'market freedoms' of EU citizens in transnational trade relations with third WTO member states, as was done by the EU until 2006 in the context of most FTAs with third states. National and EU parliaments enact international treaties as representatives of EU citizens in order to protect PGs for the benefit of those citizens. Hence, precise and unconditional FTA guarantees of freedoms and of non-discriminatory competition must be presumed to protect rights of EU citizens to invoke such legal guarantees in domestic courts too.

— The *text of EU provisions conferring specific EU foreign policy powers* refers explicitly to 'principles, objectives and general provisions' as constitutional restraints of, say, the common commercial policy (cf Article 206 TFEU) and development cooperation (cf Article 208 TFEU). For instance, common external policies must be based on 'uniform principles' (Article 207 TFEU); the Union and member states must 'comply with the commitments ... they have approved in the context of ... international organizations' (Article 208 TFEU); and they must cooperate with international organizations (eg pursuant to Articles 212 and 214 TFEU).

— The *context* of the Lisbon Treaty confirms this multilevel 'cosmopolitan constitutionalism' limiting the foreign policy powers of EU agents vis-à-vis EU citizens and democratic peoples. The explicit requirement of 'strict observance and development of international law, including respect for the principles of the United Nations Charter' (Article 3:5 TEU), is not qualified by any conferral of EU powers to violate international law. Hence, 'under the principle of conferral, the Union shall act only within the limits of the competences conferred upon it by the Member States in the Treaties to attain the objectives set out therein. Competences not conferred upon the Union in the Treaties remain with the member States' (Article 5:2 TEU). This Treaty provision confirms that the EU Commission and EU Council have no mandate to violate EU agreements (eg the WTO Agreement) approved by national and EU parliaments for the benefit of citizens and having a legal rank inside the EU superior to unilateral, 'secondary' EU regulations and decisions. Similarly, 'under the principle of proportionality, the content and form of Union action shall not exceed what is necessary to achieve the objectives of the Treaties' (Article 5:4 TEU). 'Hobbesian claims' of 'freedom of manoeuvre'[179] to violate by majority decisions GATT/WTO obligations and related dispute settlement rulings—eg during the 20 years of the EU's banana disputes, with enormous costs for EU taxpayers (estimated at $4–5 billion annually) and discriminatory trade distortions privileging a handful of European trading countries importing more expensive bananas from former colonial territories of some EU member states—are not in the reasonable self-interests of EU citizens in view of their welfare-reducing, trade-distorting effects and violations of the rule of law. Persistent EU violations of treaties ratified for the benefit of citizens—and related denial of 'access to justice' for adversely affected EU member states and EU citizens (eg as in the more than 100 national and CJEU cases challenging the EU's illegal import restrictions on bananas without being allowed to invoke the GATT/WTO rules and dispute settlement findings against the EU)—are neither 'necessary' nor 'proportionate' instruments for legitimate EU policies, as the EU's return to WTO-consistent 'banana policies' since 2013 has confirmed.

— The *object* and *purpose* of the EU external relations law are explicitly defined in terms of common pursuit of international PGs—like 'strict observance of international law' (Article 3 TEU), 'integration of all countries into the world economy', improving 'the quality of the environment and the sustainable management of global natural resources', international assistance in 'confronting natural or man-made disasters' and promotion of 'good global governance' (Article 21 TEU). Article 21 TEU and other external relations provisions recognize that collective supply of global 'aggregate PGs' (eg the WTO trading and legal system) depends on multilevel respect for 'intermediate PGs' like 'democracy, the rule of law, human rights and the principles of international law'

[179] The term 'freedom of manoeuvre' continues to be used by both the political EU institutions and the CJEU (eg in Joined Cases C-120 and C-121/06P *FIAMM* [2008] ECR I-6513, para 119) as the main justification for their disregard of legally binding UN conventions, WTO rules and WTO dispute settlement rulings. The most recent CJEU judgment (Case C-21/14P *Rusal*, judgment of 16 July 2015) justifies 'the settled case-law of the Court that, given their nature and purpose, those (WTO) agreements are not in principle among the rules in the light of which the Court is to review the legality of measures adopted by the EU institutions', essentially on utilitarian grounds such as the 'lack of reciprocity' by the EU's most important trading partners (paras 38–39). Yet, as recognized by the CJEU in its *Kupferberg* judgment of 1982, 'the fact that the courts of one of the parties consider that certain of the stipulations in the agreement are of direct application whereas the courts of the other party do not recognize such direct application is not in itself such as to constitute a lack of reciprocity in the implementation of the agreement' (Case 104/81 *Kupferberg* [1982] ECR 3644, para 18).

(Articles 2, 21 TEU) in order to coherently protect the EU's 'values, fundamental interests, security, independence and integrity' (Article 21). These values include multilevel legal and judicial protection of cosmopolitan rights of EU citizens, as recognized in the individual 'freedom to conduct a business in accordance with Union law and national laws' (Article 16 EUCFR) and everyone's 'right to an effective remedy' (Article 47 EUCFR).

iv. EU Law Requires Multilevel Rule of Law Protecting Rights of Citizens

In view of the universal recognition of human rights, 'strict observance of international law' (Article 3 TEU) must be construed in conformity with the rule-of-law requirements of EU law and of national constitutional systems, as it is in the multilevel judicial protection of constitutional and human rights by the CJEU, the ECtHR, the EFTA Court and national constitutional courts in Europe. As also illustrated by the rejection of the 2004 Treaty establishing a Constitution for Europe, the functional unity of the multilevel European constitutional rules and principles can be understood more convincingly as 'cosmopolitan' and 'republican' constitutionalism (eg protecting human rights, fundamental rights of EU citizens, the rule of law, democratic governance and other, functionally limited PGs across national frontiers) than by the statist paradigms of (big 'C') Constitutionalism (eg constituting a single, sovereign nation defending 'national interests' vis-à-vis third states through power-orientated insistence on utilitarian reciprocity principles). 'We the Peoples' governing ourselves inside the EU remain diverse national peoples conferring only limited powers on the EU. The 'public reason' justifying EU law—in the EU's external relations too, as acknowledged in Articles 3 and 21 TEU—derives from 'respect for human dignity, freedom, democracy, equality, the rule of law and respect for human rights' inside the EU (Article 2 TEU). Hence, 'rule of law' and 'access to justice'—inside the EU, as well as in the EU's external legal and dispute settlement systems committed to 'strict observance of international law' (Article 3 TEU)—must be construed in mutually consistent ways as also protecting individual 'access to justice' (eg as guaranteed in Article 47 EUCFR), and compliance with international treaty obligations and dispute settlement rulings binding on the EU and its member states. Such mutually coherent interpretations 'fit best' with the legal 'consistency requirement' that '[i]n its relations with the wider world, the Union shall uphold and promote its values and interests and contribute to the protection of its citizens' (Article 3:5 TEU). The reality of EU power politics—such as the EU's disregard of legally binding dispute settlement findings against the EU (eg in the 15 GATT and WTO 'banana disputes' from 1992–2012)—was never convincingly justified as being a 'necessary' and 'proportionate' instrument for pursuing legitimate EU policy objectives; arbitrary, majoritarian rule-violations disregarding equal freedoms of EU citizens undermine the EU's multilevel rule-of-law system.[180]

Human rights law (cf Article 29 UDHR) and EU constitutional law (cf Article 52 EUCFR) require justifying law and governmental restrictions on fundamental freedoms in terms of the rule of law, necessity, proportionality and other agreed 'principles of justice'. The customary law requirement of interpreting treaties and settling related disputes 'in conformity with the principles of justice' requires the interpretation of multilevel economic rules in conformity with multilevel 'constitutional principles' (like human rights, the rule of law, equal fundamental freedoms, access to justice, democratic governance) that have become integral parts of national, EU and UN legal systems, notwithstanding their frequent disregard inside some UN member states. The EU's 'foreign policy constitution' (eg Articles 2, 3, 21 TEU) acknowledges this Kantian 'constitutional insight' of functional interdependencies between internal and external guarantees of equal freedoms of citizens; it is because '[t]he problem of establishing a perfect civil constitution is subordinate to the problem of a law-governed external relationship with other states, and cannot be solved unless the latter is also solved',[181] that the EU's external actions 'shall be guided by the principles which have inspired its own creation, development and enlargement', and which the EU must 'advance in the wider world'. For the same reason, EU participation in multilevel legal and dispute settlement systems (eg reciprocal GATT/WTO guarantees of individual access to justice as 'integral parts of the Community legal system') should protect equal rights of EU citizens in all human interactions at national, transnational and international levels of governance. For example, the WTO obligations of 'providing security and predictability to the multilateral trading system' (Article 3 DSU) through national and international judicial remedies protecting transnational rule of law should be applied for the benefit of EU citizens in conformity with the 'consistent interpretations' requirements of WTO law (cf Article XVI:4 WTO Agreement) and EU law (cf Article 21:3 TEU).

As EU constitutional law also requires the EU 'to contribute to the protection of its citizens' (Article 3:5 TEU) in FTAs, following the positive experiences with the citizen-driven enforcement of free trade rules inside the EU's common market and EEA, precise and unconditional FTA guarantees of

180 Cf Petersmann (n 46). According to the settled case law of the CJEU, 'the principle of proportionality requires that acts of the EU institutions be appropriate for attaining the legitimate objectives pursued by the legislation at issue and do not go beyond what is necessary in order to achieve those objectives' (cf Case C-59/11 *Kokopelli* EU:C:2012:447, para 38 and the case law cited).

181 I Kant, 'Idea for a Universal History with a Cosmopolitan Purpose' in Reiss (ed) (n 66) 41, at 47.

equal freedoms were rightly protected by European courts as also conferring individual rights.[182] Such 'constitutional' treaty interpretation 'fits best' with the human rights obligations of EU member states and with their diverse 'social contract' traditions (which, from Hobbes to Rawls, are used as 'reasonable thought experiments' for justifying law and governance rather than as describing historical facts of constitutional contracts). The EU commitment to 'inalienable human rights' is more consistent with Lockean rights-based interpretations of limited delegation of powers than with Rousseau's interpretation of social contracts as constituting democratic self-governance within the limits of a fictitious 'general will' of citizens (as distinguished from their private interests as rational individuals). Kantian 'moral interpretations' and constitutional 'discourse interpretations' (eg in Rawls's 'thought experiment' of constitutional contracts in an 'original situation'; Habermas's 'discourse principle', recognizing as democratically legitimate only such rules to which all reasonable citizens could agree) of multilevel constitutional restraints as protecting equal, cosmopolitan freedoms and transnational rule of law are likewise consistent with interpreting the EU's foreign policy powers as being constitutionally constrained by individual rights (eg of access to justice vis-à-vis arbitrary treaty violations). The constitutional law of the EU may also be construed in conformity with Rawlsian justifications of 'maximum equal freedoms' and 'difference principles' governing law-abiding constitutional democracies and their 'public reason'.[183] Yet Hobbesian interpretations of the 'social contract' underlying EU law—eg as constituting and justifying 'absolute government powers' of EU institutions to violate treaties enacted by parliaments—are inconsistent with the constitutional rights of EU citizens and the EU's constitutional 'principle of conferral' (Article 5 TEU).

v. 'Hobbesian Interpretations' of EU Foreign Policy Powers are Inconsistent with EU Law

European Union law and UN law refute 'Hobbesian claims' that authoritarian top-down governance is justified by the incapacity of individual citizens to maintain peaceful, democratic order (*homo homini lupus est*). The '*Kadi* jurisprudence' of the CJEU recognizes, as a matter of principle, that UN and EU foreign policy actions also remain constitutionally restrained by human rights. Power-orientated 'Hobbesian interpretations'—eg asserting unwritten EU foreign policy powers to ignore 'strict observance of international

[182] Cf M Bronckers, 'Is Investor-State Dispute Settlement (ISDS) Superior to Litigation Before Domestic Courts? An EU View on Bilateral Trade Agreements' (2015) 18 *JIEL* 655–77, at 662 ff.

[183] For comparisons of the diverse social contract theories, see, eg, D Boucher and P Kelly (eds), *The Social Contract from Hobbes to Rawls* (London, Routledge, 1994).

law' (Article 3 TEU) to the detriment of equal rights of EU citizens—require a high burden of constitutional justification. Violations of WTO obligations and of WTO dispute settlement rulings by the EU undermine 'the rule of law' (as defined by EU and WTO law); they cannot be convincingly justified on grounds of power politics ('freedom of manoeuvre'), utilitarianism (eg lack of economic reciprocity by EU trading partners) or political opportunism (eg unwillingness of some EU member states to comply with WTO legal obligations, such as science-based 'risk justifications' of national prohibitions on genetically modified organisms). From the point of view of citizens and parliamentary democracy, the principal-agent relationship between EU citizens and EU institutions requires—as stated in Article 3 TEU—'strict observance of international law' in the multilevel EU protection of transnational PGs. Arguably, the 'constitutional functions' of incorporating international 'PGs agreements' approved by national and EU parliaments for the benefit of EU citizens as 'integrating part of the Community legal system' are to protect equal freedoms as the 'first principle of justice' legitimizing the 'rule of law' as a legal and democratic precondition for equal treatment of all EU citizens through coherent, multilevel governance of international 'aggregate PGs' at local, national, regional and international levels of cooperation. Yet without effective judicial remedies of EU citizens and 'courts of justice' protecting person-orientated rather than power-orientated 'principles of justice', the EU treaty requirement of 'strict observance of international law' cannot be effectively protected vis-à-vis EU institutions eager to avoid legal and judicial accountability for persistent rule violations.

D. Functional 'Multilevel Constitutionalism' Requires Multilevel Judicial Protection of Transnational Rule of Law for the Benefit of Citizens

The preceding three arguments set out in sections V.A–C—ie that (i) HRL justifies additional cosmopolitan rights to collective protection of PGs; (ii) the EU's economic constitution has become effective on the basis of such rights (like common market freedoms and related social rights protected by multilevel judicial remedies); and (iii) the EU's 'foreign policy constitution' prescribes 'strict observance of international law' and 'protection of citizens' and their constitutional rights for the EU's external relations too—confirm the broader 'republican argument' that 'republican freedom'[184] (as recognized as a foundational EU 'value' in Article 2 TEU) in multilevel

[184] On the mainly Roman origins of republicanism (eg in the sense of not being subject to anyone's domination and being protected by a constitution forcing the government to protect the common good: *res publica*), see Pettit (n 61) 283 ff. Pettit argues (at 49) that early republicans rejected the potentially radical definition of freedom as independence from arbitrary

governance of transnational 'aggregate PGs' cannot remain effective without 'multilevel constitutionalism' protecting cosmopolitan rights and 'republican virtues' in multilevel governance of transnational PGs too.[185]

Since the human rights revolutions during the eighteenth century, national (big 'C') Constitutions tend to be adopted at particular 'constitutional moments' in which the people (the *demos*) exercise constituent power (*pouvoir constituant*) so as to comprehensively organize democratic self-government and collective supply of national PGs. By contrast, the constitution, limitation, regulation and justification of international organizations, and of their multilevel governance powers for the collective supply of international PGs, tend to be based on functionally limited 'treaty constitutions'—like the post-war UN 'constitutions' (*sic*) that established the ILO, the WHO, the FAO and UNESCO. Such 'treaty constitutions'—including the Lisbon Treaty, in spite of its deliberate avoidance of any references to the previous efforts at adopting a 'Constitution for Europe'—continue to evolve dynamically through legal adjustments and 'piecemeal constitutionalization' of their governance systems, for instance in response to the 'globalization' and the 'constitutional adjustment challenges' described in the Introduction to this book, the demands of democratic governments and civil societies, and the 'collective action problems' of multilevel governance. The more globalization transforms formerly 'self-contained jurisdictions' into interdependent, multilevel governance regimes, the more citizens invoke their human and constitutional rights and the increasing number of judicial remedies as constitutional restraints on multilevel governance beyond the EU too. These rights are invoked both as a 'shield', in order to protect citizens against 'executive dominance' in UN, WTO and other international institutions, and as a 'sword', in order to force governments to protect PGs (like public health, cosmopolitan rights) more effectively. From a cosmopolitan perspective, the citizen-orientated reforms of regional and worldwide law and governance can be seen as a continuation of earlier emancipation processes, so as to protect 'republican freedoms' against abuses of public and private powers at national—and, in the twenty-first century, increasingly also at regional and worldwide—levels of governance of PGs demanded by citizens. As explained by Sen:

> [A] person belongs to many different groups (related to gender, class, language group, profession, nationality, community, race, religion and so on), and to see them merely as a member of just one particular group would be a major denial

power in favour of the less demanding ideal of 'negative liberty' as non-interference. On 'positive liberty' to individual and democratic self-development and 'constitutional freedom from potential domination', see also I Berlin, *Liberty* (H Hardy (ed), Oxford, OUP, 2002) (emphasizing liberalism and pluralism as interdependent and mutually supportive values protecting individual freedom of choice).

[185] On the need for transnational civic republicanism, see P Pettit, 'A Republican Law of Peoples' (2010) 9 *European Journal of Political Theory* 70–94.

of each person to decide how exactly to see himself or herself. The increasing tendency towards seeing people in terms of one dominant 'identity' ... is not only an imposition of an external and arbitrary priority, but also the denial of an important liberty of a person who can decide on their respective loyalties to different groups.[186]

i. The Need for Clarifying the 'Emancipatory' and 'Republican Functions' of Cosmopolitan Rights

Similar to the functions of constitutional rights to constitute, limit, regulate and justify individual and democratic self-governance, cosmopolitan rights (eg as defined in the EUCFR and in UN HRL) are important for constituting, limiting, regulating and justifying multilevel governance of PGs beyond state borders for the benefit of citizens. Due to globalization, citizens and NGOs increasingly use their mobility and cosmopolitan freedoms and rights, for instance as tourists, migrant workers, investors, foreign residents abroad, Internet users, refugees or otherwise 'displaced persons'. These rights serve not only individual, 'emancipatory' and 'liberating functions', for instance if they empower individuals to contest abuses of public or private power (republican liberty as 'negative freedom' from interference and 'constitutional freedom' from domination) and promote 'positive freedom' of individual and democratic self-development (eg by prompting individuals to invoke the liberating promises of human rights vis-à-vis EU governance). Cosmopolitan rights and corresponding government duties also serve 'republican functions', for instance by inducing citizens to protect national PGs (eg by assisting migrant workers to integrate into the host state's social order) and international PGs (eg by inducing EU citizens to support the EU's common market and transnational rule of law among EU member states). The progressive clarification and judicial protection of EU citizenship rights illustrates how 'positive law' dynamically evolves through progressive transformation of 'principles of justice' (like EU citizenship rights) into legislative, administrative and judicial protection of rights and related PGs.[187] Multilevel, legal protection of 'republican freedom'—as, today, an egalitarian PG[188]—continues to evolve dynamically, for instance

[186] A Sen, *The Idea of Justice* (Cambridge, MA, Harvard UP, 2009) 246 f.

[187] See D Kochenov (ed), *EU Citizenship and Federalism: The Role of Rights* (Cambridge, CUP, 2015).

[188] Aristotle held, like Plato, 'that only certain sorts of occupation are compatible with a life of virtue: soldiering, ruling (holding office, sitting in courts, etc), and philosophizing. This meant that his good man is inevitably parasitic on others, and the *Politics* accordingly assigns all other necessary occupations to non-citizens: slaves, resident aliens, and serfs of foreign origin'; see C Rowe, 'Aristotelian constitutions' in C Rowe and M Schofield (eds), *Greek and Roman Political Thought* (Cambridge, CUP, 2005) 366, at 388.

from legal protection of (i) mere 'negative freedom' as non-interference and of (ii) 'positive freedom' as individual and democratic self-mastery, to more comprehensive conceptions of (iii) 'freedom as non-domination', protected by multilevel constitutionalism preventing arbitrary interferences and (iv) also protecting transnational 'cosmopolitan freedoms' through regional and worldwide PGs treaties and institutions.[189]

The Introduction to the book discussed the dynamic evolution and progressive constitutionalization of European integration law that resulted from the 1951 ECSC Treaty, the 1957 EEC Treaty, the 1992 Maastricht Treaty, the 1997 Amsterdam Treaty, the 2007 Lisbon Treaty and the increasing number of additional, European integration treaties that promote 'enhanced cooperation' among only some of the 28 EU member states, eg:

— in the context of the European Monetary Union, among the now 19 Eurozone member countries; or
— the 2013 Agreement ratified by 25 EU member states on a Unified Patent Court.

Many of these 'constitutional reforms' had been preceded and facilitated by multilevel judicial protection of individual rights protected by EU law. The close cooperation between national courts and the CJEU, the EFTA Court and the ECtHR has proved to be a citizen-driven 'motor of European integration' by protecting individual rights, the rule of law and democratic governance in the legislative, administrative and judicial transformation of treaty law. In the EU's external relations, the CJEU's reluctance to cooperate with worldwide courts and dispute settlement procedures has impeded similar protection of cosmopolitan rights and transnational rule of law.[190] Paradoxically, even though the CJEU jurisprudence recognizes international agreements concluded by the EU as an 'integral part of the Community legal system', with a legal rank higher than other EU secondary law, the Court denies the rights of citizens to invoke and enforce even precise and unconditional UN and WTO treaty rules in European courts so as to protect its judicial independence vis-à-vis UN and WTO dispute settlement bodies.[191] Both the opinions (pursuant to Article 218:11 TFEU) and judgments of the CJEU on the participation of the EU in international agreements with compulsory dispute settlement procedures reveal a strong determination by the

[189] See Petersmann (n 33) ch III.2 (arguing for a 'cosmopolitan fourth concept of freedom' extending to the global community Pettit's argument that 'the freedom of a community is as basic a notion as the freedom of individuals'; see Pettit (n 61), eg at 275).

[190] See C Eckes, 'The Court of Justice's Participation in Judicial Discourse: Theory and Practice' in M Cremona and A Thies (eds), *The European Court of Justice and External Relations Law. Constitutional Challenges* (Oxford, Hart Publishing, 2014) 183–210.

[191] See E Cannizzaro, P Palchetti and R Wessel (eds), *International Law as Law of the European Union* (Leiden, Nijhoff, 2012).

CJEU to protect its own jurisdiction over EU law vis-à-vis concurrent international jurisdictions, even if the CJEU persistently fails to exercise its own jurisdiction and judicial duties to protect 'strict observance with international law' (Article 3 TEU) by EU institutions (eg judicial deference vis-à-vis EU non-compliance with WTO legal obligations as an 'integral part of the Community legal system').[192] The CJEU's 'double standards' in interpreting unilateral EU secondary law for the benefit of EU citizens but denying 'direct applicability' of UN and WTO treaty obligations of the EU as an 'integral part of the Community legal system' in spite of their higher legal ranking,[193] reveal a 'political question doctrine'. From a citizen's perspective, such judicial self-restraint (ie leaving treaty interpretation to the EU's political institutions and respecting their political preference for avoiding 'judicial accountability' vis-à-vis EU citizens) is, arguably, inconsistent with:

— the Lisbon Treaty's explicit requirement for 'strict observance of international law' (Article 3 TEU);
— the *Kadi* jurisprudence on judicial protection of EU fundamental rights and the rule of law as constitutional restraints on EU policy discretion; and
— the cosmopolitan mandate (eg in Article 21 TEU) and explicit objectives of the EU's external relations powers to promote 'democracy, the rule of law, the universality and indivisibility of human rights and fundamental freedoms' in all external relations of the EU for the benefit of EU citizens.[194]

ii. Transnational 'Aggregate Public Goods' Depend on Multilevel Judicial Protection of Cosmopolitan Rights and Mutually 'Consistent Interpretations'

Kant was the first legal philosopher to emphasize that the rule of law in the protection of equal freedoms of citizens and democratic legitimacy inside states depends on multilevel constitutional restraints that protect the rule of law and equal freedoms in transnational relations too, through international rules and institutions transforming the 'wild freedom' in the state of nature into 'the most precise specification and preservation of the limits of this freedom in order that it can co-exist with the freedom of others'.[195] Even though

[192] Cf B de Witte, 'A Selfish Court? The Court of Justice and the Design of International Dispute Settlement Beyond the European Union' in Cremona and Thies (eds) (n 190) 33–46.

[193] On the CJEU's WTO jurisprudence, see n 174 above; see also Case C-308/06 *Intertanko* [2008] ECR I-4057 (denying 'direct applicability' of the UN Convention on the Law of the Sea) and Joined Cases C-404 and 405/12 *Stichting*, judgment of 13 January 2015 (denying 'direct applicability' of the UN Aarhus Convention).

[194] Cf the preceding section V.C.

[195] This and the following citations are from I Kant, 'Idea for a Universal History with a Cosmopolitan Purpose' in Reiss (ed) (n 66), at 46–49.

the 'self-seeking animal inclinations into exempting himself from the law where he can' would render it impossible to realize a perfectly law-governed social order ('nothing straight can be constructed from such warped wood as that which man is made of'), Kant convincingly explained the need for constitutional restraints on external relations powers and for a 'cosmopolitan system of general political security' as necessary conditions for securing the rule of law inside states too.

Arguably, the 20 years of persistent EU violations of GATT/WTO law and dispute settlement rulings resulting from the illegal EU 'banana policies' (1992–2012, as discussed in preceding sections) empirically confirm the Kantian claim that multilevel protection of equal freedoms in transnational relations is not feasible without multilevel constitutional protection of 'strict observance of international law' (Article 3 TEU) in conformity with national and regional guarantees of equal constitutional freedoms and their judicial protection. As explained in the analysis of the EU's cosmopolitan 'foreign policy constitution' (section V.C above), it is inconsistent with the Lisbon Treaty to claim that 'the EU's external objectives lack a *telos*' and 'the EU's external policy objectives are non-teleological, non-prioritised, open-ended, and concerned more with policy orientation than goal-setting'.[196] Such 'Hobbesian interpretations' of EU law are refuted by Articles 2, 3 and 21 TEU (as specified further in the TFEU), which limit the EU's external relations powers by equal rights of citizens and rule of law requirements, without authorizing EU institutions to violate international treaties (like the WTO Agreement) that national parliaments and the European Parliament approved so as to protect transnational PGs for the benefit of EU citizens. The constitutionally required response to EU violations of international law (eg persistent EU violations of WTO dispute settlement rulings) should be to acknowledge vis-à-vis adversely affected EU citizens that '[e]veryone whose rights and freedoms guaranteed by the law of the Union are violated has the right to an effective remedy before a tribunal in compliance with the conditions laid down' in Article 47 EUCFR.[197]

The rule of law and 'consistent interpretation' requirements of national and EU legal systems are also integral parts of UN and WTO law, and of their respective guarantees of individual 'access to justice' (eg under UN HRL and GATT/WTO law) and of domestic implementation of international legal obligations (cf Article XVI:4 WTO Agreement). United Nations

[196] M Cremona, 'A Reticent Court? Policy Objectives and the Court of Justice' in Cremona and Thies (eds) (n 190) 29, 31.

[197] On the lack of judicial protection inside the EU of 'violation victims' and 'sanction victims' due to persistent denial by the CJEU of 'direct applicability' and effective judicial remedies vis-à-vis EU violations of WTO obligations, see A Thies, *International Trade Disputes and EU Liability* (Oxford, OUP, 2013); and Petersmann (n 46).

law, WTO law and EU law all regulate multilevel governance of interdependent 'aggregate PGs' in separate multilateral treaties that—according to the 'integration principle' of the customary rules of treaty interpretation (cf Article 31:3(c) VCLT)—must be construed in mutually consistent ways. Hence, as emphasized by former WTO Director-General Pascal Lamy, the 'Washington consensus' underlying the Bretton Woods and GATT/WTO agreements must remain consistent with the 'Geneva consensus' that underlies the law of the UN human rights bodies, the WHO, the ILO and other UN Specialized Agencies in Geneva.[198] The more globalization transforms *national* into *global PGs* and territorial borders into 'functional boundaries' (like common markets transcending national boundaries), the more *national Constitutions* become 'incomplete constitutions' that can no longer effectively regulate and protect 'aggregate PGs' without international law and multilevel governance institutions transcending hierarchical, national constitutional systems. Overcoming the international 'legal fragmentation' in the regulation of interdependent 'aggregate PGs' (like mutually beneficial monetary, trading, financial and environmental systems) requires mutually 'consistent interpretations' and 'judicial comity' in multilevel governance and judicial protection of transnational 'rule of law'. This must also include 'providing security and predictability to the multilateral trading system', as required by Article 3 of the WTO DSU. The reports by the Study Group of the International Law Commission (ILC) on *Fragmentation of International Law. Problems caused by the Diversification and Expansion of International Law* recognized the legitimacy of specialized legal regimes for the collective supply of diverse international PGs; it concluded that the recognition by specialized treaty regimes of their remaining integral parts of the general international law system can avoid legal conflicts and provide political and legal procedures for reducing 'legal fragmentation' if conflicts arise.[199] Even if national and regional courts of justice may have good reasons to refuse to comply with 'unjust' international law rules, they must—as in the case of the *Kadi* jurisprudence—engage in 'judicial comity' and justify the 'public reason' preventing domestic compliance with specific international treaty obligations.

iii. Human Rights Law Requires 'Constitutionalizing Disconnected Multilevel Governance'

From the constitutional perspective emphasized in sections II–IV above, '[e]ach nation has a general responsibility to do what it can to improve the

[198] Cf P Lamy, *The Geneva Consensus. Making Trade Work for All* (Cambridge, CUP, 2013).

[199] Cf UN Docs A/CN4/L.682 (Analytical Report of 13 April 2006) and A/CN/L.702 (Conclusions of 18 July 2006).

legitimacy of its own coercive government, and a responsibility to attempt to improve the organization of states in which it functions as a government'.[200] The power-orientated prioritization of rights of governments in the Bretton Woods and WTO Agreements—without even mentioning human rights, general consumer welfare and democratic accountability—is a major cause of the neglect of human rights and general consumer welfare in IMF, World Bank and WTO governance. Human rights advocates identify the legal source of individual, popular and state duties to respect, protect and fulfil human rights inside and beyond state borders—and to collectively supply international PGs demanded by citizens—in principles of *individual* and *popular 'responsible sovereignty'* and 'shared responsibilities', rather than in *state sovereignty*.[201] Similar to the adoption by most UN member states of new (big 'C') Constitutions in response to the 'human rights revolutions' and decolonization following World War II in order to define their national 'constitutional contracts' in more democratic ways, so the post-war emergence of hundreds of new international treaties and institutions for the collective supply of international PGs requires a 'new philosophy of international law' (Dworkin) and a new 'social contract for a global economy' aimed at limiting the 'governance failures' of the Westphalian 'international law among sovereign states'. The interpretation, coordination and democratic legitimacy of many of the hundreds of specialized, international legal regimes and institutions often remain contested among citizens, civil society, governments and diplomats, for instance in view of the use of indeterminate principles (like 'sustainable development'), technical rules (eg on 'risk assessment procedures'), legal and institutional biases (eg prioritizing monetary, trade, environmental, financial or criminal law and institutions), and insufficient procedures for coordinating specialized legal regimes so as to promote synergies and avoid 'regime collisions'. The ILC Report on *Fragmentation of International Law* acknowledged that 'public international law does not contain rules in which a global society's problems are, as it were, already resolved'; 'the whole complex of inter-regime relations is presently a legal black hole'.[202] Yet the Report also rightly concluded 'that legal technique [is] perfectly capable of resolving normative conflicts or overlaps by putting the rules and principles in a determinate relationship with each other'; 'if lawyers feel unable to deal with this complexity, this is not a reflection of problems in their "tool-box" but in the *imagination*

[200] Dworkin (n 120) 27.

[201] On mutual respect of human dignity as foundation of human rights and related personal, popular and international 'shared responsibilities', see Petersmann (n 33) chs III and IV; IM Young, *Responsibility for Justice* (Oxford, OUP, 2011); M Langford *et al* (eds), *Global Justice, State Duties. The Extraterritorial Scope of Economic, Social and Cultural Rights in International Law* (Cambridge, CUP, 2013).

[202] Analytical Report (n 199) 253.

about how to use it'.[203] Mutually consistent interpretations and 'balancing' of multilevel legal regulation of PGs are the 'ultimate rule of law'.[204] Multilevel 'judicial comity' is especially needed in IEL so as to better reconcile *economic freedoms* with *non-economic rights* and public interests, subject to requirements of transparency, non-discrimination, 'suitability', necessity, 'proportionality *stricto sensu*' and legal accountability. Legal and judicial protection of cosmopolitan rights promote not only more inclusive 'public reason' and democratic conceptions of the relevant 'rules of recognition' as 'tests' for legitimate interpretations of IEL and justifications of its principled coherence with human rights and other 'principles of justice'; they also justify reviewing the 'Westphalian methodologies' of WTO dispute settlement bodies and 'investor biases' in investment arbitration, in order to protect reasonable citizen interests more effectively.

National and international courts of justice, individual citizens (as 'cosmopolitan agents of justice') and guarantees of individual access to justice in constitutional law, HRL and IEL have often proved to be more effective guardians of 'principles of justice' than UN and WTO diplomats interested in accommodating political pressures from powerful domestic interest groups in exchange for their political support. Section II illustrated how 'principles of justice' recommended in ideal theories of justice (like Rawls's *Theory of Justice* for a perfectly just national society in a closed economy) remain contested in the non-ideal reality of 'disconnected UN and WTO governance', where—in order to advance justice pragmatically case by case—intergovernmental UN and WTO diplomacy often avoids discussing political disagreements on how to promote consumer welfare, human rights and other 'principles of justice'. The jurisprudence of European economic, human rights and constitutional courts confirms that even *prima facie* 'easy cases' of treaty interpretation (eg where the text of treaty provisions prioritizes rights of governments without mentioning rights of citizens) may turn out to be 'hard cases',[205] for instance whenever European courts and investment tribunals have construed treaty provisions on rights and obligations among states as also conferring *individual*, procedural and substantive rights on citizens. This chapter has argued that courts of justice must take more seriously the customary law requirement of interpreting international treaties and settling related disputes 'in conformity with principles of justice' and 'human rights and fundamental freedoms for all'. Human right law, constitutional law and IEL increasingly recognize such rights to justification and to legal remedies against unjustified restrictions of equal freedoms. In contrast to political institutions that reason in terms of power and rational

[203] *Ibid*, paras 410, 488.
[204] Cf DM Beatty, *The Ultimate Rule of Law* (Oxford, OUP, 2004).
[205] Cf R Dworkin, *Taking Rights Seriously* (London, Duckworth, 1977) 81 ff.

self-interests, courts of justice must justify their judgments vis-à-vis citizens by principles of procedural, distributive, corrective, commutative justice and equity. The boundaries of democratic and judicial law-making remain inevitably contested in multilevel governance of PGs, as illustrated by the often diverging, political and judicial conceptions of whether, to what extent and in which areas transnational market regulations should follow a 'centralized model' (based on legal harmonization), a 'competitive model' (based on competition of rules and reciprocal recognition of equivalent regulation) or a 'decentralized model' (based on non-discriminatory state regulation).[206] The successful multilevel cooperation among *national courts* and *arbitral tribunals* in protecting transnational rule of law for the benefit of citizens in international commercial and investment law illustrates that the proposed, stronger cooperation of national courts with *regional* and *UN/WTO dispute settlement bodies* is also legally practicable, for instance in 'providing security and predictability to the multilateral trading system' (Article 3 DSU) in conformity with the 'consistent interpretation' and 'judicial comity' requirements of national and international legal systems, which, at the request of governments, often continue to be ignored by domestic courts even inside constitutional democracies in Europe and North America.

VI. CONCLUSION: MULTILEVEL GOVERNANCE MUST PROMOTE THE 'SIX-STAGE SEQUENCE' OF DEMOCRATIC, REPUBLICAN AND COSMOPOLITAN CONSTITUTIONALISM

As briefly recalled in the Introduction to this book, 'republicanism' refers to diverse theories and practices for citizen-driven, collective supply of PGs. It emerged in ancient Greece, Rome and during the Renaissance as an alternative to monarchy. Republicanism emphasizes the importance of civic virtues (eg aiming for the good of the whole *polis*), political freedoms (eg in the sense of non-domination by arbitrary power), participatory governance, and the need for constitutional 'checks and balances' limiting and controlling abuses of power, so that 'mixed constitutions' and 'mixed governments' (eg combining elements of monarchical, aristocratic and democratic governance) remain representative of all major groups in the polity. Even though the ancient Greek city states were confronted with common enemies (like Persia), neither Plato's nor Aristotle's republicanism addressed the legal problems of *international law*. The political theories and government practices in ancient Greek city republics, the Roman republic, European Renaissance republicanism (eg in Italian city states and the Hanseatic League),

[206] Cf MP Maduro, *We, the Court. The European Court of Justice and the European Economic Constitution* (Oxford, Hart Publishing, 1998).

'enlightenment republicanism' (eg during the eighteenth century in the USA, France and Switzerland) and in modern republicanism were so diverse that the term 'republicanism', and its relationship to representative and majoritarian democracy (eg the principle of rule by the consent of the governed based on 'popular sovereignty'), continues to be used in diverse ways.

When Diogenes the Cynic described himself as a 'citizen of the world' (*cosmopolite*), he challenged Aristotle's *polis*-centered, ethical and political conception of human beings with the larger Stoic vision of human beings committed to universal reason. *Cosmopolitanism* proposes that citizens are not only members of local communities but also share a common humanity, which entails moral duties towards all human beings as the ultimate sources of values and of moral concern for 'human dignity' and other 'principles of justice'. Cosmopolitanism was developed in ancient Greek and Roman philosophy primarily as a moral proposition—with only few legal and institutional consequences (eg for *jus gentium* governing transnational commerce to be protected by the *praetor peregrinus* in Roman law). Even though Greek and Roman republicanism claimed to be based on universal principles, the ancients could not envisage a 'cosmopolitan world republic'. This study focuses on why globalization and its modern transformation of *national* into *transnational PGs* require supplementing democratic constitutionalism for collective supply of *national PGs* by multilevel republican and cosmopolitan constitutionalism for transnational aggregate PGs—without exploring in more detail the legal requirements of supplementing national and regional citizenship rights (eg pursuant to Articles 18 et seq TFEU) with global citizenship rights.[207]

This chapter has argued that *republican constitutionalism*—in order to effectively constitute, limit, regulate and justify multilevel governance of global PGs—must be embedded into *cosmopolitan constitutionalism* protecting equal rights of citizens across national frontiers in mutually beneficial cooperation. Just as constitutional rights have proved necessary for democratic governance of *national PGs* in order to transform agreed 'principles of justice' (eg in the US Declaration of Independence of 1776) into constitutional and democratic legislation, administration and adjudication, so are cosmopolitan rights necessary for effectively constituting, limiting, regulating and justifying multilevel governance of *transnational 'aggregate PGs'* and transforming the 'law in the books' (eg as postulated in the 1948 UDHR) into 'law in action' through the 'six-stage sequence' of multilevel constitutionalism. Empirical evidence confirms that cosmopolitan PGs regimes providing for multilevel, legal and judicial protection of human rights, commercial and investment rights, common market freedoms

[207] See P Kleingeld, *Kant and Cosmopolitanism: The Philosophical Ideal of World Citizenship* (Cambridge, CUP, 2012).

and related social rights have changed legal practices more effectively than state-centered UN and WTO governance regimes. Cosmopolitan rights to protection of related PGs (eg individual rights to public health protection) strengthen all three major functions of modern legal systems: (i) the instrumental function of law as a means of social regulation; (ii) the theoretical coherence of multilevel legal and governance systems; and (iii) the social effectiveness of law (eg in regional common markets, health law and rule of law systems).[208]

Multilevel constitutionalism in the EU limits the 'rules of recognition' by recognizing only such rules and institutions as legitimate and legally valid that respect constitutional rights and 'principles of justice' as defined in democratic law-making and judicial proceedings.[209] The modern 'multilevel republican constitutionalism' underlying the 'economic constitution', 'security constitution' and 'foreign policy constitution' of the EU is fundamentally different from the ancient Greek, Roman, Renaissance and national constitutionalism of times past. The evolution of the ECHR and of the EUCFR into a multilevel 'European human rights constitution', like the Maastricht Treaty's introduction of a multilevel 'monetary constitution' of the EU and the Lisbon Treaty's foundation of an EU 'foreign policy constitution', reflects the increasing willingness of most EU member states to protect international PGs through functionally limited 'multilevel republican constitutionalism' that continues to evolve dynamically in response to 'trials and errors'.[210] In contrast to other areas of international law, where third-party adjudication remains an exception to the rule of 'auto-interpretation' by governments, regional HRL and IEL are today characterized by a growing role for national and international courts of justice in clarifying, progressively developing and enforcing transnational rule of law and cosmopolitan rights to protection of transnational PGs. The traditional distinctions between 'international public law among states' (considering states as exclusive subjects and objects of international law) and 'international private law' (recognizing citizens as legal subjects and settling disputes over 'conflicts of laws' on the basis of national choice-of-law rules) are increasingly blurred by the emergence of 'transnational legal systems'. The latter recognize individuals as legal subjects, who can derive individual rights from international

[208] This constant interaction between 'law as a legal order' and 'law as legal practice' is emphasized by 'critical legal positivism', according to which law and its legal changes should be examined on (i) the surface level of positive law, (ii) the legal culture, and (iii) the deep structures of law; cf K Tuori, *Critical Legal Positivism* (Aldershot, Ashgate, 2002).

[209] In order to avoid legal uncertainty, only violations of human rights, constitutional rights and other forms of 'extreme injustice' are likely to affect the validity of legal rules; cf R Alexy, *The Argument from Injustice* (Oxford, OUP, 2010).

[210] Cf K Tuori and S Sankari (eds), *The Many Constitutions of Europe* (Aldershot, Ashgate, 2010).

agreements (eg on human rights, commercial, investment and intellectual property law, regional trade, economic and environmental agreements) and create autonomous, denationalized legal systems (like *lex mercatoria* regulating international trade, *lex sportiva* regulating international sports, *lex digitalis* regulating the Internet).[211]

A. 'Constitutional Contract Justifications' of International Law?

Hobbes, Locke, Rousseau and Kant—the four classical expositors of social contract interpretations of law and governance—argued for very diverse concepts of 'social contracts' and the state, due to their diverse value premises and interpretations of the human 'state of nature'. Hobbes claimed that there is no justice or injustice in the war of everybody against everybody else in the state of nature. He also denied the possibility of grounding moral and political principles in the rational self-interests of individuals asserting 'natural rights' and maximizing their individual benefits through rational choices. Hence, it was only subsequent to the 'social contract', by which citizens established civil society and political authority with absolute powers to secure social peace, that—according to Hobbes—the will of the sovereign established right and wrong. Paradoxically, because Hobbes perceived the individual in the state of nature as being also entitled to pursue his self-interests through the use of force, he interpreted the 'social contract' as an alienation of individual rights by people giving up their power to an absolute ruler securing external peace and legal order. This 'master/slave interpretation of the ruler/subject relationship' was rejected by Locke, Rousseau, Kant and modern theories of justice (eg by Rawls) on the ground that people retained 'inalienable human rights' and delegated only certain legislative, administrative and judicial government powers that must remain constitutionally limited by the equal rights of free citizens. Such 'constitutional contract interpretations' derive the legitimacy of law and governance from the voluntary consent of reasonable, free and equal individuals (as a thought experiment rather than as an historical fact); they agree that justice and injustice do not depend upon a sovereign ruler dominating citizens as a monarchical master, but rather on the reasonable consent (hypothetical or real) of free and equal citizens as holders of 'constituent powers', using government as a constitutionally limited 'protection agency' (Nozick).

[211] Cf Maduro *et al* (n 71). On the different forms of 'rights cosmopolitanism' not only in EU and EEA law, but also in the ECHR since the entry into force of its Protocol No 11 and the judicial recognition of its supra-legislative status in national legal systems throughout Europe, see H Keller and A Stone Sweet (eds), *A Europe of Rights: The Impact of the ECHR on National Legal Orders* (Oxford, OUP, 2008).

According to Grotius, Pufendorf and Locke, the social contract that establishes civil society and a legal community, remained embedded in God's moral law and the mutual recognition of human rights and moral obligations among human beings. Contrary to claims (eg by Locke and Rousseau) that the social contract only determines where sovereignty lies (eg *popular sovereignty* rather than *state sovereignty* as claimed by the rulers), Grotius and Pufendorf interpreted the social contract as including provisions on the delegation of government powers and reciprocal responsibilities vis-à-vis citizens. If the individual 'natural rights' to life, liberty and property, the moral duty of self-preservation and free consent to political authority are perceived as the foundations of social and constitutional contracts establishing protective government agencies with limited powers and constitutional duties to protect the equal rights of citizens, then the reasonable, constitutional clarification of the reciprocal rights and duties among citizens as holders of constituent powers and of the limited, 'constituted government powers' becomes the main constitutional task of democratic legislation, administration and adjudication. Modern UN and EU law explicitly recognize that citizens, peoples, governments and states must also protect—at local, national, regional and global levels of governance—transnational 'aggregate PGs' like 'equal and inalienable rights of all members of the human family [as] the foundation of freedom, justice and peace in the world' (Preamble UDHR). As argued in section II above, the universal recognition of 'inalienable human rights' of citizens as 'constituent powers' entails that all multilevel governance institutions derive only limited powers from the consent of citizens and democratic institutions that remain subject to constitutional duties to protect human and constitutional rights of citizens and other PGs.[212]

i. The Emergence of 'Cosmopolitan Constitutions' with Cosmopolitan Citizenship Rights

The political argument that a peaceful international order can be developed only through cosmopolitan law (*Weltbürgerrecht*) that transforms the classical law among nations (*Völkerrecht*) through multilevel constitutional guarantees of equal cosmopolitan rights of citizens, was only developed in the eighteenth century in Kantian legal philosophy (notably in his essay *Toward Perpetual Peace*).[213] With the post-war acceptance by UN member

[212] For a discussion of why the relevant 'recognitional community' and 'process of making and unmaking international law' must include every human being struggling for law and justice, see C Focarelli, *International Law as Social Construct. The Struggle for Global Justice* (Oxford, OUP, 2012), eg, at 65.

[213] Cf J Bohman and M Lutz-Bachmann (eds), *Perpetual Peace. Essays on Kant's Cosmopolitan Ideal* (Cambridge, MA, MIT Press, 1997).

states of human rights obligations under international and national law, the normative values underlying moral cosmopolitanism have become part of positive national and international legal systems:

— normative individualism emphasizing the moral worth ('dignity') of each person;
— 'inalienable' human rights and fundamental freedoms for all;
— derivative obligations of all governments, and the instrumental role of states, to protect the human rights of everybody and the democratic rights of peoples;
— collective protection of PGs demanded by citizens through 'republican constitutionalism' inside and beyond states, based on principles of constitutional democracy (human rights, the rule of law, limited delegation and separation of governance powers, constitutionally limited democratic self-government) empowering citizens and limiting multilevel governance institutions for functionally limited, collective supply of national and transnational PGs; and
— political subsidiarity of worldwide and regional governance institutions towards democratic self-government in local and national political communities; the EU, for instance, 'shall act only if and in so far as the objectives of the proposed action cannot be sufficiently achieved by the Member States, either at central level or at regional and local level, but can rather, by reason of the scale or effects of the proposed action, be better achieved at Union level' (Article 5:3 TEU) or at worldwide levels of governance. As political legitimacy derives from respect for human and democratic rights, international law must also be interpreted 'in conformity with principles of justice', including 'human rights and fundamental freedoms for all'.

From the ancient 'republican city constitutions' (eg in Greece and Italy) up to the eighteenth-century American and French 'democratic constitutions', constitutionalism focused on the republican supply of local and national PGs, the liberation and protection of citizens vis-à-vis domination, and the constitution of democratic peoples and civil societies subject to limited and separated government powers. Following World War II, European integration and decolonization contributed to the emergence of new kinds of multilevel 'human rights constitutions' recognizing the constitutional limitation of 'state sovereignty' and 'popular sovereignty' by multilevel human rights guarantees protecting 'individual sovereignty' inside and beyond state borders.[214] Whereas 'constitutional nationalism' ('constitutionalism 1.0' in Somek's terminology) focused on republican and democratic

[214] Cf EU Petersmann, 'State Sovereignty, Popular Sovereignty and Individual Sovereignty: From Constitutional Nationalism to Multilevel Constitutionalism in International Economic Law?' in W Shan, P Simons and D Singh (eds), *Redefining Sovereignty in International Economic*

self-determination inside city republics and states, modern 'constitutional democracies' recognizing multilevel human rights obligations (eg under regional human rights conventions) and multilevel 'cosmopolitan constitutions' (eg based on EU law) engage in multilevel 'republican constructivism' for protecting transnational PGs for the benefit of citizens ('constitutionalism 2.0' and 'constitutionalism 3.0' in Somek's computer terminology). As the 'demos' and its 'democratic governance' remain limited by state borders, transnational democracy must compensate for the inadequate parliamentary participation and democratic control by empowering citizens through cosmopolitan rights to hold multilevel, transnational governance powers legally, democratically and judicially accountable.

Modern 'cosmopolitan constitutions' in EU and EEA member states differ from 'democratic constitutional nationalism' by their commitment to international law and multilevel governance institutions as integral parts of republican governance of international PGs, such as the EU 'area of freedom, security and justice' governed by multilevel EU institutions protecting cosmopolitan rights and non-discrimination for some 500 million EU citizens.[215] In contrast to democratic constitutional nationalism establishing legislative, executive and judicial powers for nation-building (as represented by the US and French Constitutions of the eighteenth century, and the Swiss Constitution of the nineteenth century), the 'human rights constitutions' of the twentieth century (like the German Basic Law of 1949) and the emergence of 'cosmopolitan constitutionalism' (eg in EU and EEA law, regional human rights conventions with regional human rights courts) focus on multilevel legal and judicial protection of cosmopolitan rights and other constitutional restraints of multilevel governance of international PGs as instruments for 'de-fragmentating international law'.[216] The 'emancipatory

Law (Oxford, Hart Publishing, 2008) 27–60; Somek (n 178) 9 ff (describing the constitutional practice in post-war Germany as a paradigm for the shift from 'constitutional liberty' and self-determination by a nation—eg in the US Constitution—to a human rights-based Constitution committed to protecting civil, political, economic and social rights inside and beyond the state).

[215] Somek (n 178) one-sidedly focuses on national constitutional law and wrongly claims that 'the overall constitution of the multilevel system ceases to be law altogether. It is a *factum*, not a law' (at 21). Somek's treatment of 'cosmopolitan constitutionalism' as a 'form of political constitutionalism' (at 22) unduly neglects the 'multilevel republican law' and 'judicial checks and balances' characteristic of EU, UN and WTO law; he ignores the constitutional challenges examined in this book, ie the question of how citizens and democratic peoples (as 'principals') can constitutionally and democratically control multilevel governance 'agents' in a globally integrating world, where most national PGs have become international 'aggregate PGs' demanded by citizens. The political reality of infringements of EU, UN and WTO rules (eg in the handling of the current migration of millions of refugees to the EU) does not justify disqualifying EU and UN/WTO law as merely political rather than legal orders.

[216] On 'de-fragmentation of international law' through multilevel judicial reinterpretations of multilevel regulations, see K Fauchald and A Nollkaemper (eds), *The Practice of International and National Courts and the (De)Fragmentation of International Law* (Oxford, Hart Publishing, 2014).

functions' of 'cosmopolitan constitutionalism' and of European 'integration law' for constituting, limiting, regulating and justifying multilevel governance of transnational PGs raise multilevel, constitutional problems, such as 'proportionality review' of common market regulations, respect for national 'margins of appreciation' in domestic protection and 'balancing' of human rights, conditional cooperation between national and international competition, monetary and other regulatory agencies, and 'judicial comity' between national and international courts 'so long as' they reciprocally respect their constitutional minimum standards. Such multilevel constitutional problems (eg of democratic governance beyond states) tend to be far more complex than the introverted 'constitutional interpretations' (eg based on 'originalism' as advocated by the late US Supreme Court Judge Scalia) advocated by 'constitutional nationalism'.

B. 'Constitutional Treaty Interpretations' Can Justify Cosmopolitan Rights

Following the example of 'EU citizenship', diverse forms of 'cosmopolitan citizenship' (eg based on common passports, free movement rights, transnational labour rights) are also promoted in an increasing number of regional economic unions beyond the EU, notably in Latin America (like MERCOSUR, the Andean Common Market, the Central American Common Market) and Africa (like the West, East and Southern African Economic Unions).[217] This chapter has argued that—just as the history of republican constitutionalism in Europe justified and necessitated 'constitutional interpretations' progressively extending democratic, republican and cosmopolitan rights so as to protect national PGs more effectively—the task of 'constitutionalizing' multilevel governance of transnational PGs can also justify 'constitutional interpretations' of international treaties as constituting cosmopolitan citizenship rights to multilevel governance of transnational aggregate PGs. Not only national, but also multilevel constitutionalism needs to be justified through coherent 'constitutional contract theories' recognizing citizens as 'democratic principals' of multilevel governance institutions, rather than government executives asserting themselves to be 'masters of international treaties'. As in European integration law, such a 'constitutionalization' of foreign policy powers can be achieved through 'constitutional interpretations' of UN, WTO and regional agreements 'in conformity with principles of justice' and the 'human rights and fundamental freedoms' of all human

[217] C Closa and D Vintila, *Supranational citizenship rights in regional integration organizations*, EUI Working Paper (Florence, EUI, 2015).

beings, as prescribed by the customary rules of treaty interpretation. As democratic parliaments enact international treaties for the benefit of their citizens, the 'principles of justice' that underlie UN, WTO and regional agreements, the human rights obligations of all UN member states, and the 'courts of justice' interpreting and applying such agreements justify interpreting treaties no longer only in terms of reciprocal rights and obligations among states and their governments, but also in terms of protecting the rights of free and equal citizens vis-à-vis multilevel governance institutions that must remain constitutionally restrained by corresponding legal obligations to protect the equal rights of citizens.

Such 'constitutional interpretations' are particularly warranted for international agreements like the EU Treaties, which are 'founded on the values of respect for human dignity, freedom, democracy, equality, the rule of law and respect for human rights' (Article 2 TEU), including 'strict observance of international law' (Article 3 TEU), without conferring powers on EU institutions to violate international treaties approved by parliaments for the benefit of citizens. 'Constitutional interpretation' of international agreements—as constituting multiple legal layers of reciprocal obligations among states, governments, peoples and citizens—recognize citizens and their equal human rights and constitutional rights—rather than states—as ultimate sources of legal legitimacy in modern international law in the twenty-first century. They limit both Hegelian prioritization of the state as having moral, communitarian autonomy and organic unity, as well as purely utilitarian justifications of centralized state power (eg as being necessary for protecting collective security). Respect for legitimately diverse 'constitutional pluralism' and national 'margins of appreciation' entail that people will often 'reasonably disagree', for instance on whether constitutional contracts should be based on Kantian ideals of morality and justice as impartial, multilevel protection of equal freedoms under the rule of law, or whether citizens and democratic people choose alternative, 'democratic discourse' justifications and other communitarian foundations of their national Constitutions. Yet 'state citizenship' needs to be complemented by transnational 'cosmopolitan citizenship rights' in order to hold multilevel governance institutions more accountable for protecting PGs demanded by citizens. Just as national citizenship laws differ among countries, the scope and justification of EU citizenship rights and of similar rights in other regional integration systems remain likewise contested.[218] Yet neither in democratic national Constitutions nor in EU law and UN law are human rights and other cosmopolitan rights conferred top-down by the rulers, even if cosmopolitan rights are reciprocally recognized in international commercial, investment, intellectual

[218] Cf M La Torre (ed), *European Citizenship. An Institutional Challenge* (The Hague, Kluwer, 1998).

property, labour and human rights treaties among states. From the constitutional perspective of citizens with 'inalienable human rights', including their democratic rights as holders of constituent power, such treaties must be interpreted as being concluded on behalf of citizens, mutually recognizing and protecting rights of citizens vis-à-vis abuses of public and private power. If citizens do not confer on international institutions (like the EU) powers to violate treaties approved by parliaments for the benefit of citizens, then constitutional guarantees of individual rights to effective remedies and to a fair trial—as in Article 47 EUCFR[219]—must also protect individual 'access to justice' for those adversely affected by arbitrary treaty violations (eg in the case of persistent EU violations of WTO dispute settlement rulings to the detriment of EU citizens). Recognition of additional 'cosmopolitan citizenship rights' (eg in international trade, investment, environmental, criminal and human rights law) is justified so as to strengthen the constitutional foundations of multilevel governance of transnational aggregate PGs for the benefit of citizens, and the corresponding legal accountability and constitutional duties of multilevel governance institutions. Even if 'states' are valued independently from ideals of 'cosmopolitan justice' (eg by 'realist theories' of international law and Rawls's 'society of states' approach to international law), cosmopolitan rights are necessary for *strengthening* the constitutional rights of citizens, democratic peoples and multilevel governance of global PGs vis-à-vis abuses of public and private power.

C. Methodological Challenges of 'Multilevel Constitutionalism'

State-centered 'realists' prioritizing the pursuit of national interests through 'international law among sovereign states', like economic and political theories of PGs (as discussed in Chapter 2), tend to remain agnostic vis-à-vis the three methodologies used in this study:

— *Multilevel 'republican'* and *'democratic' constitutionalism*, based on the insight that the protection of human rights through legislation, administration and adjudication requires 'constitutional democracies' to protect transnational PGs through international law and institutions that must remain constitutionally accountable towards citizens and democratic parliaments; the transformation of national PGs into

[219] Art 47 EUCFR states: 'Everyone whose rights and freedoms guaranteed by the law of the Union are violated has the right to an effective remedy before a tribunal in compliance with the conditions laid down in this Article. Everyone is entitled to a fair and public hearing within a reasonable time by an independent and impartial tribunal established by law. Everyone shall have the possibility of being advised, defended and represented. Legal aid shall be made available to those who lack sufficient resources in so far as such aid is necessary to ensure effective access to justice.'

transnational 'aggregate PGs' requires extending the historical lessons from 'republican constitutionalism' to 'multilevel constitutionalism' for collective supply of international PGs.

- '*Cosmopolitan constitutionalism*', based on the universal recognition of 'inalienable' civil, political, economic, social and cultural rights and related 'constitutional principles' and PGs in the UN Charter, in UN HRL, in the law of some UN Specialized Agencies, as well as in hundreds of additional constitutional, human rights and other legal instruments, including UN resolutions and action programs like the 'Millennium Development Goals'.
- *Comparative institutional analyses* of national, regional and worldwide PGs regimes (as discussed in Chapters 2 and 3), aimed at finding empirical evidence for the most successful modes of multilevel governance of functionally limited PGs, as well as for normative justifications of multilevel 'republican constructivism' (eg in European integration law). *Comparative institutionalism* must go beyond comparing alternative social decision-making processes inside states such as:
  - economic market processes (that risk being distorted by 'market failures' like abuses or private power, external effects, information asymmetries, social injustice);
  - democratic political processes (that risk being distorted by 'governance failures' like 'majority' or 'minority biases' in majoritarian regulation and deregulation);
  - judicial litigation and adjudication (eg involving choices among judicial and political rule clarification and 'principled public reasoning'); and
  - independent regulatory agencies.

As discussed in Chapter 2, the transformation of national into transnational PGs changes multilevel governance and 'collective action' problems, for instance due to the 'executive dominance' in intergovernmental rule-making and the self-interests of UN and WTO diplomats in limiting their legal, democratic and judicial accountability vis-à-vis citizens as 'democratic principals'. *Republican constructivism* must clarify and connect the relevant 'principles of justice' justifying national, transnational and international legal sub-systems and multilevel governance institutions, so as to protect human and constitutional rights of citizens, deliberative democracy, the rule of law and 'public reason' more effectively.

D. Multilevel Constitutionalism Must Target the Collective Action Problems of Multilevel Governance of Public Goods

In view of the 'reasonable disagreement' on how to design multilevel governance institutions, there is a need for empirical, comparative studies of the rules, institutions and effectiveness of PGs regimes in order to identify 'best practices' and 'collective action problems'. Due to its challenge of the prevailing legal methodologies, this study goes beyond the recommendations of path-dependent UN and WTO reports, such as the UN Secretary-General's 'Synthesis Report' of December 2014 for the post-2015 'Sustainable Development Agenda',[220] which neither challenge the power-orientated, 'disconnected nature' of intergovernmentalism dominating UN and WTO governance,[221] nor acknowledge the need for 'multilevel constitutionalism' so as to empower citizens to press governments—not only in non-democratic UN member states, but also in democracies (including the USA, with its ambivalence towards economic and social rights and international human rights conventions) and in regional organizations—to protect transnational PGs more effectively.[222]

Chapter 2, on constituting, limiting, regulating and justifying multilevel governance of PGs regimes, summarizes research resulting from comparative studies of the different multilevel governance methods of UN Specialized Agencies, GATT/WTO regimes and other 'PGs treaties'. It confirms the need for a 'context-sensitive approach', taking into account the specific collective action problems of PGs regimes, and the diverse mandates, rules, institutions and practices of real existing institutions.[223] The transformation and judicial enforcement of tobacco control measures through national, transnational and international litigation, and the 2003 WHO Framework Convention on Tobacco Control (FCTC), ratified by 177 UN member states and the EU, are used to illustrate why coordinating and justifying multilevel economic and health governance on the basis of 'constitutional' and 'cosmopolitan principles of justice' has succeeded in limiting governmental collusions with

[220] *The Road to Dignity by 2030: Ending Poverty, Transforming all Lives and Protecting the Planet*, Synthesis Report of the Secretary-General on the Post-2015 Agenda, New York, December 2014. The Report identifies 'extraordinary progress' (eg due to the halving of extreme poverty since 1990, lifting 700 million out of extreme poverty) alongside 'unacceptable—and unsustainable—levels of want, fear, discrimination, exploitation, injustice and environmental folly at all levels' (paras 11, 17).

[221] On the 'refeudalization of the public sphere' in intergovernmental diplomacy, see J Habermas, *The Structural Transformation of the Public Sphere* (trans T Burger) (Cambridge, MA, MIT Press, 1991).

[222] As to human rights and their codification in national and international human rights instruments as reflecting historical struggles for rights in order to overcome particular existential problems at particular historical moments, see CNJ Roberts, *The Contentious History of the International Bill of Human Rights* (Cambridge, CUP, 2014). On the need for connecting the 'constitutional functions' of *international legal guarantees* of economic freedoms, non-discrimination and transnational rule of law to the corresponding *national legal guarantees* so as to better protect transnational cooperation among citizens, see Hilf and Petersmann (eds) (n 152).

[223] On the defining characteristic of PGs (eg non-rivalry in consumption, non-excludability in use) and the different kinds of PGs, see ch 2, section I. The need for context-specific analyses of PGs regimes is also emphasized by Pierik and Werner (eds) (n 123).

tobacco industries selling toxic tobacco products by persistently deceiving consumers as to the health risks of smoking. The intergovernmental negotiations on the EU's transatlantic FTAs with Canada and the USA, and their potentially adverse impact on the fundamental rights and judicial remedies of EU citizens, are discussed as illustrating the risks of 're-feudalization' of international economic relations if government executives are allowed to use trade agreements to prevent citizens from invoking their fundamental rights and effective judicial remedies (eg under the EUCFR). One-sided economic regulatory approaches based on 'separation of policy instruments' (Jan Tinbergen) risk leading to 'over-regulation' of PGs (as in certain fields of intellectual property rights as incentives for decentralized promotion of PGs such as basic research, education, public health and protection of the environment).[224] The European Parliament refused—in 2012—to ratify the draft 'Anti-Counterfeiting Trade Agreement' (ACTA), on the ground that it was negotiated by the EU Commission without public debate and adequate parliamentary consultation;[225] yet the Parliament has never discussed the democratic justifiability of the EU's initiatives, since 2006, to explicitly exclude private rights and effective judicial remedies of EU citizens under FTA agreements negotiated by the EU with third countries.

Chapter 3 illustrates the need for integrating the 'constitutional functions' of cosmopolitan rights by discussing the five competing conceptions of IEL and the need for their 'integration' through 'constitutional interpretations' and person-orientated (rather than only state-centered) adjudication. It concludes that cosmopolitan rights—as the 'transnational dimension' of state citizenship similar to EU citizenship rights, supplementing national constitutional rights and existing, multilevel human rights guarantees—need to be promoted and progressively developed, for instance by more specific constitutional and treaty provisions that clarify the transnational rights of citizens under UN, WTO and regional agreements approved by national parliaments for the benefit of citizens. The more international agreements become the main instrument for collectively providing transnational PGs, the more such agreements should be construed as part of multilevel democratic legislation that protects equal rights of citizens and justifies individual rights to invoke and enforce precise treaty guarantees of equal freedoms, non-discrimination and the rule of law in domestic courts, so as to hold governments accountable for transnational rule of law and multilevel protection

[224] For case studies on intellectual property rights (like patent rights) as impediments to follow-on innovation, competition and social welfare for all, see KE Maskus and JH Reichman (eds), *International Public Goods and Transfer of Technology under a Globalized Intellectual Property Regime* (Cambridge, CUP, 2005).

[225] Cf M Cremona, 'International Regulatory Policy and Democratic Accountability: The EU and the ACTA' in M Cremona *et al* (eds), *Reflections on the Constitutionalisation of International Economic Law—Liber Amicorum for Ernst-Ulrich Petersmann* (Leiden, Nijhoff, 2014) 155.

of equal rights of citizens and other PGs. The proposed 'cosmopolitan citizenship rights'—as integral parts of state citizenship (eg in terms of rights to 'consistent interpretation' of international agreements ratified by parliaments for the benefit of citizens)—could be progressively promoted by courts of justice and through reciprocal recognition among governments, without formal changes of national and EU citizenship regulations. Both 'cosmopolitan constitutionalism' (eg as practised in European economic and human rights law) and judicial protection of cosmopolitan rights (as practised in commercial and investment arbitration and by European courts) raise complex questions of legal methodology, which are further explored in the following chapters. Citizen-orientated 'cosmopolitan interpretations' of international law should deliberately leave open many controversies in theories of justice that are not explored further in this study, for instance whether law and governance should be justified:

— by models of communitarian cooperation (as argued by Plato and Aristotle); or
— by individualist models of social conflict resolution (as argued by rights-based social contract theories insisting on individual consent and advantages for every person rather than only for a collective);
— by conceptions of justice as fairness and impartiality (eg in Rawls's thought experiment of an 'original position' in which reasonable human beings agree on 'principles of justice', behind a 'veil of uncertainty', and prioritize maximum equal freedoms of individuals over 'equal opportunities' and 'difference principles' protecting the least advantaged); or rather
— by conceptions of 'commutative justice' as reciprocally agreed 'just exchanges' (eg in view of the fact that the private and public goods and services necessary for human survival and development first need to be produced through social division of labour based on mutually agreed contracts before they can be distributed on the basis of agreed principles of social justice).

In view of the 'burden of judgment' required by Kantian and Rawlsian justifications of constitutional guarantees of 'maximum equal freedoms' as the 'first principle of justice' inside constitutional democracies, Rawls later limited his Kantian definition of the 'first principle of justice' by replacing the 'equal right to the most extensive basic liberty compatible with a similar liberty for others' with 'an equal right to a fully adequate scheme of equal basic liberties which is compatible with a similar scheme of liberties for all'.[226] This chapter concludes similarly that multilevel constitutional-

[226] The 'evident consequence of the burden of judgment is that reasonable persons do not all affirm the same comprehensive doctrine'; cf Rawls (n 4) 60, 291 ff.

ism is necessary for governing multilevel governance of global PGs for the benefit of all citizens because reasonable people often do not share comprehensive doctrines of national and international justice (as discussed in section II) and insist on legitimate 'legal pluralism' and respect for diverse democratic preferences inside constitutional democracies (as discussed in sections III and IV).

2

Constituting, Limiting, Regulating and Justifying Multilevel Governance through Multilevel 'Republican Constitutionalism'

THIS CHAPTER DISCUSSES legal and methodological problems of multilevel governance of the international trading, development, environment and related legal systems from the perspective of economic, political and legal PGs theories. Section I gives an overview of theories concerning multilevel governance of global PGs. Section II discusses 'collective action problems' in multilevel governance, and failures in managing 'interface problems' of the world trading, environmental and development systems; through case studies, and by comparing the legal regulation of diverse 'aggregate PGs', lessons can be drawn for legal and institutional alternatives for more efficient, legitimate and effective governance of interrelated PGs.[1] Section III recalls the post-war efforts at constituting, limiting, regulating and justifying multilevel governance through UN 'treaty constitutions' (*sic*) establishing the ILO, WHO, UNESCO and FAO, in order to protect cosmopolitan labour rights, health rights, rights to education, food security and other human rights in the context of a coherent UN legal and governance system. Many of these UN 'treaty constitutions' were not effectively 'constitutionalized', for instance due to inadequate transformation of UN human rights guarantees into actionable rights and democratic and judicial remedies in the domestic laws of UN member states, and the 'disconnected' nature of UN governance. Section III uses the the WHO

[1] In order to illustrate 'collective action problems' in multilevel governance of transnational aggregate PGs empirically, sections I and II of this chapter refer to 12 case studies published in EU Petersmann (ed), *Multilevel Governance of Interdependent Public Goods. Theories, Rules and Institutions for the Central Policy Challenge in the 21st Century*, RSCAS 2012/13, Global Governance Programme Working Paper (Florence, EUI, 2012), as well as to additional case studies (eg those published in (2012) 23 *EJIL* 643–791) that were discussed at EUI conferences.

Framework Convention on Tobacco Control (FCTC) and its enforcement through national and international litigation as an example for the more general claim that—in order to protect cosmopolitan rights and other PGs more effectively—the rights and 'constitutional principles' acknowledged in the ILO, WHO, UNESCO and FAO constitutions need to be transformed into democratic legislation, multilevel administration and judicial remedies in coordination with other multilevel PGs regimes. The tobacco litigation in national and regional courts of justice, transnational investment arbitration and WTO dispute settlement rulings illustrate how 'integration law' and judicial remedies—like the regulation and coordination of economic and health rights in the WHO FCTC, their judicial clarification through WTO dispute settlement procedures, and the legal and judicial implementation of these rules in domestic legal systems—can help to make the state-centered 'Washington consensus' underlying the Bretton Woods agreements, GATT and the WTO more consistent with the person-centered 'Geneva consensus' underlying the UN human rights institutions, the ILO, the World Intellectual Property Organization (WIPO) and the WHO in Geneva. Section IV criticizes the transatlantic FTA negotiations for neglecting transparent, democratic rule-making and the protection of rights and remedies of citizens. Section V concludes that—as long as government executives continue to prioritize their own rights and interests in intergovernmental treaty negotiations—civil society will continue criticizing 'disconnected UN/WTO governance' that treats citizens as objects rather than as legal subjects of international regulation of PGs; parliaments and courts of justice should insist on stronger protection of cosmopolitan rights of citizens as 'democratic principals' in multilevel governance of PGs.

I. THE GAP BETWEEN THEORY AND PRACTICE IN MULTILEVEL GOVERNANCE OF GLOBAL PUBLIC GOODS

As the provision of PGs is the main justification of states and of other public organizations, legal and political research on PGs is much older than the economic distinction between private and public goods in Adam Smith's *The Wealth of Nations* (1776). *Private goods* tend to be produced, financed and distributed spontaneously in private markets and communities in response to supply and demand by citizens and to their coordination by price mechanisms and other economic incentives. Private goods remain scarce in relation to consumer demand, because private producers use their property rights to exclude consumers unless there is voluntary agreement on selling (or renting) private goods and services and transferring related property rights in exchange for payment of the agreed price. *Public goods* are not provided in private, commercial markets but must be provided collectively because their consumption is open to all ('non-excludable') and/or does not reduce their availability to others ('non-rival'). Apart from 'intermediate PGs', like human rights and the rule of law, non-excludable and non-rival 'pure PGs' (like sunshine) remain rare. Most PGs are 'impure', in the sense that their consumption is either non-rival but exclusive (eg 'club-goods' like the WTO trading, legal and dispute settlement system limited to WTO members, patented knowledge whose industrial use is limited to patent holders), or non-exclusive but rival (eg common pool resources like fish in the high seas).

A. Why are Transnational 'Aggregate Public Goods' Undersupplied?

Globalization continues to transform ever more local and national PGs traditionally supplied inside states into international 'aggregate PGs' that require new forms of multilevel governance, regulation and justification. Transnational, private and public governance spheres (eg of globally integrated financial markets, pollution of the environment) often lack adequate regulation and provoke systemic crises. Citizens, civil society and the newly emerging 'transnational communities' (eg of citizens communicating through the Internet and cooperating in 'global supply chains') increasingly criticize governance failures to protect transnational PGs like human rights, democratic governance, transnational rule of law, financial stability, a liberal world trading system, the prevention of climate change, and the reduction of unnecessary poverty and diseases in so many UN member states. The world financial crises since 2008, the European debt crises since 2010, the failures of the Doha Round and climate change negotiations, and the unnecessary poverty of 2 billion people living on $2 or less per day are 'public bads'; they illustrate systemic failures of the prevailing 'Westphalian model' of intergovernmental regulation of 'aggregate PGs' (eg transnational 'composite goods' like the world trading system composed of vertically and horizontally interconnected, local, national, regional and worldwide PGs). The adverse repercussions of such multilevel governance failures on national PGs inside states (eg due to destruction of jobs and private investment caused by the international financial and debt crises) also undermine the legitimacy and effectiveness of domestic governance systems for supplying national PGs. In order to remedy governance failures, it is important to identify why transnational PGs remain under-supplied even though they are beneficial for all citizens and demanded by civil society. This study argues that most 'governance failures', and many other 'collective action problems' in multilevel governance of transnational PGs, relate to a lack of 'political and legal culture' in terms of democratic, republican and cosmopolitan constitutionalism protecting human rights and the rule of law across national borders so as to provide transnational 'aggregate PGs'.

B. Utilitarian Economic and State-Centered Political Public Goods Theories

Since Adam Smith, economists have explored the incentives for producing PGs (eg through 'private-public partnerships') and the 'collective action problems' impeding their collective supply. Public knowledge about the need for correcting 'market failures' in order to promote undistorted market competition for producing private goods has increased enormously. Yet there is broad agreement today that

> the provision of global public goods occurs largely without the benefit of relevant, up-to-date theory. Public goods research often lags behind the rapidly evolving political and economic realities—marked by a state-centric and national focus and, consequently, providing poor support for advice on the provision of global public goods in today's multi-actor world.[2]

Apart from noting that the international law principle of 'sovereign equality of states' prevents *coercion* of 'free-riding states' into cooperation in the supply of international PGs, economic and political PGs theories often neglect legal theory[3] and comparative institutional research, as well as the common principles underlying the hundreds of multilateral agreements accepted by UN member states for protecting international PGs. The 'Westphalian governance practices' prevailing in most UN institutions likewise neglect alternative 'legal methodologies', for instance the fact that 'realist', ie state-centered and power-orientated, approaches to regional economic integration (eg in Africa, the Americas and Asia) have been less successful in promoting non-discriminatory market integration and transnational rule of law than rights-based governance practices (eg in the EU and EEA). Some modern political science handbooks on 'international organizations and global governance' mention neither economic and political PGs theories, nor international legal regimes for 'global commons' (such as Antarctica, the deep seabed beyond exclusive economic

[2] I Kaul *et al* (eds), *Providing Global Public Goods. Managing Globalization* (Oxford, OUP, 2003) 5.

[3] The two leading research publications on global PGs published by the UN Development Program—ie I Kaul, I Grunberg and MA Stern (eds), *Global Public Goods. International Cooperation in the 21st Century* (Oxford, OUP, 1999), as well as Kaul *et al* (eds) (n 2)—did not include legal studies. The book edited by KE Maskus and JH Reichman (eds), *International Public Goods and Transfer of Technology under a Globalized Intellectual Property Regime* (Cambridge, CUP, 2005) focused on knowledge as 'perhaps the quintessential public good' (at 47), and on its decentralized supply by means of intellectual property rights excluding 'free-riders' and setting incentives for innovation. Also, research on intellectual property rights (eg empirical justifications of the duration of exclusive patent rights) remains underdeveloped and contested.

zones, the moon) as alternatives for appropriation and competitive uses by private actors and states.[4]

The main reasons why global PGs—in spite of their non-excludable and non-rival benefits for all—remain undersupplied are related to political governance problems, such as

- 'failed states' lacking capable governments to protect human rights, or 'rogue states' circumventing nuclear non-proliferation;
- war-torn states embroiled in civil wars that harm international cooperation through adverse 'external effects';
- lack of resources, inadequate knowledge and welfare-reducing government policies;
- disagreements on the distribution of related costs and benefits (eg as illustrated by non-compliance with the EU 'Schengen' and 'Dublin' rules on treatment of foreign immigrants and refugees);
- inadequate international rules and institutions for protecting transnational PGs; and
- other 'collective action problems' impeding mutually beneficial cooperation among governments and civil societies across national borders.

'Realist' political theories admit that state-centered foreign policies aimed at maximizing 'national interests' (as defined by the rulers) often fail to cooperate, even when states have common interests in providing transnational PGs. Neo-liberal institutionalism explains why international rules, procedures and institutions can help states to overcome systemic 'prisoner dilemmas' and 'free-rider dilemmas' of international relations among states, for instance through the formation of international organizations providing information, incentives for long-term cooperation, monitoring of rule compliance and sanctions towards 'free-riders'. 'Political functionalism' aims at promoting 'low politics' (eg international economic division of labour), based on self-interests of sub-national and supra-national actors that may induce 'attitude change' ('deeds, not words') and 'spill-overs' of mutually beneficial cooperation into other areas of 'high politics'. Yet, as explained in Chapter 1, the universal recognition of human rights and of the need for limiting abuses of power through 'constitutionalism' reflect the worldwide

[4] An example is TG Weiss and R Wilkinson (eds), *International Organizations and Global Governance* (London, Routledge, 2014). The relationships and overlaps between economic, political (eg republican) and legal theories for governance and regulation of transnational PGs have been rarely discussed and empirically explored so far. Many authors use assumptions (eg of the need for centralized world governance institutions for collective supply of global PGs) that remain normatively and empirically contested and under-researched (eg in terms of comparative research on international regimes on 'global commons' and protection of the 'common heritage of mankind').

experience that—in order to promote international PGs more effectively—'*third images*' of international relations focusing on the state system must be complemented by '*first* and *second images*' focusing on rational choices by individuals, NGOs, and legislative, administrative and judicial government agents, and on 'constitutional checks and balances' for holding private and public actors more accountable for collective supply of PGs.[5] For instance, some 'single best efforts PGs' may be supplied through private-public partnerships and the support of a single state, as illustrated by the development of polio vaccines in the USA; the collective production of 'weakest link PGs' may focus on a few 'risk states', even if the latter contribute the least (like eradication of smallpox through WHO-sponsored programs in poor African countries like Somalia); and also collective supply of global 'aggregate PGs' can be facilitated through mutually beneficial, burden-sharing arrangements, with financial support from international institutions and the most developed countries.[6] Yet without 'constitutionalization' and 'socialization' of democratic governance systems transforming fundamental rights and other agreed 'principles of justice' into democratic legislation, administration and adjudication protecting the rule of law for the benefit of citizens, multilevel governance of transnational PGs cannot build on the 'intermediate PGs' that compose transnational 'aggregate PGs' as necessary legal foundations.

Public goods theory emphasizes the obvious fact (as reflected, for example, in the diverse legal systems of the 15 UN Specialized Agencies, GATT and the WTO) that the 'supply strategies' for the different types of PGs—such as '*best shot PGs*' (eg a medical invention), '*weakest link PGs*' (eg nuclear non-proliferation) and '*aggregate PGs*'—vary depending on their particular characteristics and the preferences of the citizens and governments involved (eg for 'internalizing external effects' by means of taxes, subsidies or a change in property rights, labour rights and other individual rights). Depending on their respective 'provision paths', some PGs can be supplied unilaterally by 'single best efforts' (eg an invention). The supply of some other PGs depends on the 'weakest links' (eg dyke-building, global polio eradication, nuclear non-proliferation). 'Aggregate global PGs' tend to be supplied through a 'summation process' of local, national and regional public goods. Global PGs 'differ from their national counterparts in terms of the complexity—the multi-actor, multi-sector, multi-level nature—of their provision path, as well as in terms of the policy-interdependence they entail'.[7] As the public or private character of goods is often a social construct rather than an innate

[5] For surveys of political theories of multilevel governance, see *ibid*.

[6] On the different kinds of PGs and their diverse 'production technologies', see S Barrett, *Why Cooperate? The Incentive to Supply Global Public Goods* (Oxford, OUP, 2007).

[7] These and the following quotations are from I Kaul, 'Global Public Goods: Explaining their Underprovision' in Petersmann (ed) (n 1) 41–60.

property, the policy choices and preferences of countries vis-à-vis PGs may legitimately differ. Some global PGs—like global transportation and communication systems—are better provided for than others, for instance due to:

— political market failures (like 'free-riding' in climate change prevention efforts);
— fairness and efficiency deficits in international negotiations (eg due to power politics);
— organizational constraints (eg due to path-dependent 'intergovernmentalism');
— policy stand-offs (eg due to contested distributional implications);
— inconsistency among global PGs (eg due to conflicting preferences); or
— uncertainty caused by inadequate information and time for elaborating agreed responses to relatively new collective action problems (like climate change).

Some of these impediments have prompted policy responses in terms of new principles (like 'duties to protect', 'special and differential treatment of less-developed countries', 'special but differentiated responsibilities') and new institutions (like the G20, the establishment of a Green Climate Fund for mitigation of and adaptation to climate change). Yet many reform measures achieve only incremental change, or fail due to policy stalemates. According to Kaul, a 'certain amount of … global decision-making "messiness" could well prove, in the medium and longer-term, to be the more efficient policy path because it might broaden and deepen the political consensus on which change initiatives rest'. The state-centered focus in political science analyses of international organizations (eg focusing on states as 'principals' in 'member-driven governance' of intergovernmental organizations) neglects that, as explained by 'public choice' theories, politicians and diplomats also pursue political self-interests, for instance in foreign policy discretion, diplomatic privileges, and limited accountability towards citizens adversely affected by UN and WTO governance failures. Political republican theory has failed to address the republican task of constituting, limiting, regulating and justifying multilevel governance of PGs in a systemic manner. Also, economic proposals to limit 'adverse externalities' by granting 'countervailing rights' to 'countervailing powers'—notably 'countervailing rights' of adversely affected citizens that can limit multilevel governance failures directly at 'their source' (eg as illustrated by the judicial challenges by Mr Kadi of the EU implementation of UN Security Council 'smart sanctions' violating the human rights of alleged terrorists)—are little discussed in political science research on multilevel governance. Nor do most political scientists attach importance to the legal methodology problems discussed in Chapter 1, ie the legal legitimacy of person-orientated reinterpretations of international PGs treaties by courts of justice interpreting treaties and settling related disputes 'in conformity with principles of justice and international law', including 'human rights and fundamental freedoms for all'. Political and economic PGs research neglects the importance of human rights and other 'principles of justice' in multilevel governance of transnational PGs, for instance as incentives for citizens, civil society and courts of justice to hold politicians and multilevel governance institutions accountable for their frequent failures to protect transnational PGs.

Historical experience confirms that realizing the 'cosmopolitan empowerment' proposed in this study requires 'constitutional mind-sets' and Sisyphus-like struggles for democratically constituting, limiting, regulating and justifying governance powers beyond states so as to adjust 'public reason' and 'public justice' to the constitutional challenges of the twenty-first century. As confirmed by the 'judicial constitutionalization' of European economic and human rights law, 'constitutionalizing' intergovernmental power politics has often been politically easier through multilevel judicial protection of cosmopolitan rights than through 'constitutional conventions' in exceptional 'constitutional moments'. Finding cosmopolitan support and viable 'political paths' for constitutional reforms must begin with a better understanding of the practical challenges of multilevel governance in UN law and IEL, and of the related 'why' and 'how' questions, such as *why* transnational protection of constitutional rights of citizens and of 'aggregate PGs' is necessary, and *how* it may be possible.[8] Citizens and academics must promote inclusive, public discourse on the need for cosmopolitan incentives for citizens to assume their democratic responsibilities vis-à-vis multilevel governance. For instance, the secretive policy by EU executives, since about 2006, to exclude private rights and effective judicial remedies of citizens in EU FTAs and implementing regulations was never explicitly discussed in the European Parliament, even though such 'disempowerment' of citizens in multilevel governance of PGs (like transnational markets and division of labour) runs counter to the Lisbon Treaty requirement (eg in Article 3 TEU) to protect EU citizens and their rights in the EU's external relations too.[9] Globalization requires not only legislators, governments, judges and citizens, but also lawyers, economists and political scientists to broaden their conceptions of multilevel governance of transnational 'aggregate PGs'. The more self-proclaimed 'realist policies' fail to protect transnational PGs, the

[8] My personal experiences with working in UN, GATT and WTO diplomacy for more than 35 years—both from the perspective of national government representatives, EU institutions, and UN, GATT and WTO institutions, and from the perspective of national courts and GATT/WTO dispute settlement bodies—confirm that UN/WTO diplomats are often not interested in *why* so many UN and WTO legal obligations are not effectively implemented, and *whether* and *how* their 'realist scepticism' towards cosmopolitan rights of citizens is consistent with HRL.

[9] Cf EU Petersmann, 'Transformative Transatlantic Free Trade Agreements without Rights and Remedies of Citizens?' (2015) 18 *JIEL* 579 ff.

stronger becomes the need for reviewing state-centered policy premises so as to render multilevel governance of PGs—notably protection of the human rights obligations of all UN member states—more effective.[10]

C. Insufficient Legal Research on Transnational Public Goods Regimes

Political scientists explain why the economic focus on the non-rivalry and non-exclusivity of PGs neglects many additional reasons for their undersupply, like lack of resources, inadequate regulation of property rights and 'capture' of regulatory institutions by organized interest groups: 'the conventional public goods debate offers less than it promised for the analysis of social and political problems'.[11] Economic, political and legal analyses of the different 'supply conditions' of PGs, of alternative instruments and institutional designs for constructing PGs, or for transforming PGs into 'club goods' (such as the WTO) often differ. In view of the few examples of 'pure PGs' as defined by economists, political and legal discourse uses the term 'public goods' more broadly for goods that benefit and can be consumed by all citizens and whose supply is confronted with political problems of collective action and free-riding.[12] The decentralized, private law forms of the global governance of the Internet by the Internet Corporation for Assigned Numbers and Names (ICANN), and the settlement of thousands of international 'domain name disputes' by means of arbitration procedures administered by WIPO and enforced by ICANN, illustrate the potential importance of decentralized, rights-based regimes that transform global PGs into institutionalized 'club goods' so as to limit incentives for 'free-riding' and create incentives for supporting club goods.

The diversity of environmental agreements confirms that there is no 'one size fits all' solution to the problems of 'common pool resources' (like

[10] On this educative task of academics, see MC Nussbaum, 'Cultivating Humanity in Legal Education' (2003) 70 *University of Chicago Law Review* 265–79; R van Gestel, HW Micklitz and M Poiares Maduro, *Methodology in the New Legal World*, Working Papers Law 2012/13 (Florence, EUI, 2012).

[11] F Kratochwil, 'Problems of Policy Design based on Insufficient Conceptualization: the Case of "Public Goods"' in Petersmann (ed) (n 1) 61–72.

[12] For instance, from the perspective of constitutional law or global administrative law, many 'constitutional principles' can be perceived as PGs. On expanded definitions of PGs, see also Kaul *et al* (eds) (n 2), explaining, *inter alia*, why conceptualizing and analysing global natural commons (such as the atmosphere, the high seas), global man-made commons (such as global rules, regimes and knowledge) and global policy outcomes (such as global peace, financial stability and environmental stability as global PGs) from the perspective of the 'triangle of publicness'—ie publicness in consumption (is the good consumed by all?), publicness in net benefits (are the net benefits of the good equitably distributed?) and publicness in decision-making (who decided to place the good in the public domain?)—reveal differences that may be important for regulating PGs and for the optimal 'aggregation technology'.

fisheries, bio-diversity, clean air, climate). Yet the sub-optimal supply of many international PGs (like sustainable high seas fisheries) is often related to the property regime. Changes in the design of property rights may—as explained by Kratochwil—transform the 'tragedy of the commons' by limiting membership and over-use. Rather than resolving a 'prisoner's dilemma' by focusing on the two alternatives of government intervention or privatization, legal differentiation between different types of ownership rights (eg rights of access, extraction, management, exclusion) and of legal forms of cooperation (eg among non-state actors in NGOs) may enable more effective provision of PGs. Due to the 'human rights revolution', transnational legal actors increasingly challenge path-dependent conceptions of 'international law among sovereign states' by invoking human and constitutional rights, and contesting the legality of intergovernmental measures (eg 'smart sanctions' by the UN Security Council against alleged terrorists) in domestic and international courts. As recognized by European courts, NGOs—including companies and other non-state actors—also deserve protection by fundamental rights if they collectively represent the interests of individuals that fall within the original scope of protection of fundamental rights. Similar to Ronald Coase's famous question of why the hierarchical structures of a firm exist at all in view of the alleged efficiency of free market exchanges between individuals,[13] constitutional and PGs theories must 'pierce the corporate veil' and protect the values that legitimately motivate individuals to cooperate through NGOs in transnational relations.

The 'constitutional premise' elaborated in Chapter 1—ie that the universal recognition of human rights requires extending 'republican constitutionalism', cosmopolitan rights, transnational rule of law and democratic governance to multilevel governance of transnational 'aggregate PGs'—has been progressively realized in some areas of European integration. Yet the legitimately diverse 'legal pluralism' in national and European legal systems (as illustrated by the supranational EU common market and monetary law compared with the more deferential EEA law), in UN law (eg the diverse structures of some UN Specialized Agencies like the ILO) and in the diverse legal forms of EU participation in UN institutions (eg EU membership of the FAO and UN Convention on the Law of the Sea (UNCLOS))[14] illustrates that national and international 'collective action problems' (eg impediments to EU membership in UN institutions) differ depending on their legal

[13] Cf R Coase, 'The Nature of the Firm' (1937) 4 *Economica* 386. On fundamental rights of companies, 'corporate social responsibilities' of NGOs and their direct access to European courts, see EU Petersmann, *International Economic Law in the 21st Century. Constitutional Pluralism and Multilevel Governance of Interdependent Public Goods* (Oxford, Hart Publishing, 2012), eg at 226 ff.

[14] Cf E Kaddous (ed), *The EU in International Organizations and Global Governance. Recent Developments* (Oxford, Hart Publishing, 2015).

contexts. For instance, the European Parliament's refusal—in 2012—to ratify the draft Anti-Counterfeiting Trade Agreement (ACTA) was justified on the ground that it was negotiated by the EU Commission without public debate and adequate parliamentary consultation.[15] Even if—as argued in Chapter 1—UN HRL also justifies claims of citizens (eg as recognized in Article 28 UDHR) to additional cosmopolitan and democratic rights in multilevel governance of international PGs, the model of the 'tripartite ILO composition' (governments, employer and worker representatives) may not be appropriate for other multilevel governance institutions and other 'aggregate PGs' (composed of local, national, regional and worldwide PGs).

This study argues that the 'laboratory' of European multilevel governance offers lessons for reforming worldwide governance institutions dominated by executives. As inside Europe, legitimate participation of states in multilevel governance of transnational PGs beyond Europe requires a citizen-driven, multilevel integration law in order to protect transnational PGs more effectively. Legal, economic, political and constitutional theories need to be integrated in PGs research, and to promote stronger legal, democratic and judicial accountability of intergovernmental rule-making vis-à-vis citizens on the basis of 'republican' and 'cosmopolitan' constitutionalism. The WTO and the EU—ie the two most developed, multilevel legal and compulsory dispute settlement systems for governing the international trading system—are also increasingly confronted with governance failures that undermine the global PG of a liberal (ie liberty-based) trading and legal system protecting consumer welfare and transnational rule of law for the benefit of citizens. For instance, the private and public debt crises and economic crises in the EU since 2010 were closely related to the fact that 23 out of 28 EU member states persistently violated their fiscal and debt disciplines agreed upon in the Lisbon Treaty (eg Article 126 TFEU). Citizens of the EU and parliaments inside the EU increasingly complain that multilevel EU governance lacks legitimacy due to inadequate deliberative, participatory and rights-based democracy (eg in secretive FTA negotiations, security surveillance interfering with privacy rights) and multilevel violations of the rule of law.[16] Democratic support and loyalty towards EU governance need to be promoted by giving citizens, civil society, parliaments and courts of justice more incentives to participate in multilevel governance (eg by using rights

[15] Cf M Cremona, 'International Regulatory Policy and Democratic Accountability: The EU and the ACTA' in M Cremona *et al* (eds), *Reflections on the Constitutionalisation of International Economic Law—Liber Amicorum for Ernst-Ulrich Petersmann* (Leiden, Nijhoff, 2014) 155.

[16] As loyalty to EU governance also depends on the possibilities for 'voice' and 'exit', and the Lisbon Treaty now explicitly provides for the legal admissibility of 'exiting' the EU (cf Art 50 TEU), the EU institutions and EU member states responded pragmatically to the UK's demands to renegotiate certain EU rules prior to its national referendum in June 2016 on a 'Brexit'.

of access to documents and information) and to hold EU governance legally, judicially and democratically accountable. As only citizens and people—not states—have moral and human rights, the democratic legitimacy of international law depends on transparent 'democratic discourse justifications' of international rules (eg of the 'human rights coherence' of EU agreements with third states) by EU citizens, peoples and their democratic representatives. Incentives for cooperation in collective supply of international PGs must be strengthened through stronger cosmopolitan rights, judicial remedies and 'constitutional limitations' of 'state sovereignty' by 'duties to protect' international PGs beyond state borders based on modern HRL and related concepts of 'responsible sovereignty'. For instance, HRL may justify:

— *cosmopolitan economic and social rights* for holding governments more accountable for failures to protect international PGs, as illustrated by the judgment of the German Constitutional Court of 18 July 2012, recognizing a fundamental right of asylum seekers and other foreign migrants in Germany to receive higher cash benefits for their 'dignified minimum existence', protected by their human right to dignity (Article 1, section 1 of the German Basic Law) in conjunction with the constitutional guarantee of a social welfare state (Article 20, section 1);[17]
— *additional rights of 'access to justice', to justification and judicial review of governmental restrictions*, as illustrated by guarantees of judicial remedies in regional HRL and IEL;[18] for instance, the broad guarantee of the 'right to judicial protection' in Article 25 of the American Convention on Human Rights has been construed by the Inter-American Court of Human Rights as constituting 'one of the basic pillars not only of the American Convention, but of the rule of law (*état de droit, estado de derecho*) itself in a democratic society' in the sense of the Convention;[19]
— *'duties to protect common concerns' and corresponding judicial remedies* (eg pursuant to Article VIII:2(b) of the IMF Agreement concerning the non-enforceability of exchange contracts violating IMF rules),

[17] Judgment of 18 July 2012 (1 BvL 10/10, 1 BvL 2/11).

[18] Examples include Art 8 UDHR, Art 13 ECHR, Art 47 EU Charter of Fundamental Rights, Arts 3 and 7 African Charter of Human and People's Rights, Arts 8 and 25 Inter-American Charter of Human Rights; cf F Francioni (ed), *Access to Justice as a Human Right* (Oxford, OUP, 2007).

[19] Para 1 of Art 25 reads, 'Everyone has the right to simple and prompt recourse, or any other effective recourse, to a competent court or tribunal for protection against acts that violate his fundamental rights recognized by the constitution or laws of the state concerned or by this Convention, even though such violation may have been committed by persons acting in the course of their official duties.' The text and the pertinent jurisprudence of the Inter-American Court of Human Rights are cited in AA Cançado Trindade, *The Access of Individuals to International Justice* (Oxford, OUP, 2011) 51 f.

and sanctions vis-à-vis gross human rights violations by dictatorial governments or 'free-riding countries' that refuse to participate in the joint reduction of environmental harms;[20]

— the *transformation of PGs into 'club goods'* excluding 'free-riders' (like countries unwilling to accept the legal disciplines of WTO law or regional FTAs); and
— the granting of *public or private property rights in 'common pool resources'* (like deep seabed minerals, fishery resources) so as to prevent the 'tragedy of the commons'.

II. 'COLLECTIVE ACTION PROBLEMS' AND COMPARATIVE INSTITUTIONAL ANALYSES: EXAMPLES FROM MULTILEVEL ECONOMIC AND ENVIRONMENTAL GOVERNANCE

Comparative constitutional and institutional analyses emphasize that the comparative advantages of economic markets, political decision-making, constitutional, legislative, administrative, judicial and intergovernmental processes depend on which institution is in a better position to protect the constitutional values inherent in the relevant rules and arbitrate competing legal claims.[21] Modern Constitutions increasingly acknowledge that—due to globalization—international PGs can be protected for the benefit of citizens only in cooperation with other states based on international law and multilevel governance institutions. Yet, as discussed in Chapter 1, even though international treaties serve legislative functions for collective supply of transnational PGs, treaty negotiations in the UN, its 15 UN Specialized Agencies and the WTO continue to be dominated by power-orientated policies and non-inclusive negotiations among government executives prioritizing 'intergovernmentalism' without effective constitutional safeguards of human and constitutional rights of citizens and democratic governance. Once the intergovernmental negotations among more than 160 UN/WTO member states are concluded and the draft treaties are submitted to national

[20] An example is the unilateral extension of environmental protection measures to polluters from third countries, as discussed by L Bartels, 'The WTO Legality of the Application of the EU's Emission Trading System to Aviation' (2012) 23 *EJIL* 429–67.

[21] Cf the interdisciplinary constitutional, legal, economic and 'public choice' analyses of multilevel economic regulation in M Hilf and EU Petersmann (eds), *National Constitutions and International Economic Law* (The Hague, Kluwer, 1993). On participation-orientated 'comparative institutional analysis' of alternative decision-making processes like markets, political processes and judicial procedures, see N Komesar, *Imperfect Alternatives: Choosing Institutions in Law, Economics and Public Choice* (Chicago, IL, Chicago UP, 1994); N Komesar, *Law's Limit: The Role of Courts, the Rule of Law and the Supply and Demand of Rights* (Chicago, IL, Chicago UP, 2001); G Shaffer and J Trachtman, 'Interpretation and Institutional Choice at the WTO' (2011) 52 *Virginia Journal of International Law* 1–52.

parliaments, it remains very rare that the text agreed among governments can be effectively renegotiated at the request of a few parliaments. As a consequence, many countries—notably those with 'dualist' legal systems—do not effectively implement international treaty rules, for instance because

- domestic interest groups insert legislative provisions into the implementing legislation undermining the treaty obligations;[22]
- domestic regulatory agencies continue established trade restrictions in violation of the treaty obligations;[23]
- parliaments in less-developed countries refrain from adopting effective implementing legislation due to the limited treaty obligations and resources of these countries (eg for the 1994 Uruguay Round Agreements);[24] and
- national administrative and judicial bodies in most states—including in countries with 'monist' legal systems incorporating international treaties into the 'law of the land' (eg in the USA) and into 'community law' (eg in the EU)—refuse to directly apply UN/WTO treaty rules in domestic jurisdictions, at the request of government executives eager to maintain their 'freedom of manoeuvre' in intergovernmental power politics.

As a result, the 'collective action problems' addressed by democratic, republican and 'human rights constitutionalism' at national levels of governance of national PGs continue to exist for multilevel governance of transnational PGs, such as:

- *prioritization of rights of governments* over rights of citizens in multilevel PGs legislation due to intergovernmental exclusion of private rights;[25]

[22] Cf M Schaefer, 'Are Private Remedies in Domestic Courts Essential for International Trade Agreements to Perform Constitutional Functions with Respect to Sub-Federal Governments?' (1997) 17 *NW Journal of International Law & Business* 609 ff, at 639 (explaining that the US Uruguay Round Agreements Act of 1994 prohibited 'private causes of action'—as did the preceding NAFTA implementing legislation—in violation of Art XX Government Procurement Agreement protecting private rights to invoke the treaty obligations in domestic courts).

[23] For an analysis of the illegal 'zeroing practices' by EU and US antidumping authorities as established by numerous WTO dispute settlement findings, see S Cho, 'Global Constitutional Lawmaking' (2010) 31 *University of Pennsylvania Journal of International Law* 621–78.

[24] For instance, the 1994 Uruguay Round Agreements were not effectively implemented through national legislation in many African WTO member countries; cf M Finger and P Schuler, 'Implementation of Uruguay Round Commitments: The Development Challenge' (2000) 23 *The World Economy* 511–25.

[25] On EU and US implementing rules excluding 'direct applicability' of WTO rules by citizens in domestic jurisdictions, see EU Petersmann, *The GATT/WTO Dispute Settlement System. International Law, International Organizations and Dispute Settlement* (Deventer, Kluwer, 1997) 19 ff, 233 ff. To date, the US Uruguay Round Agreements Act (19 USC §3512(c)) continues to exclude domestic judicial challenges to US compliance with the 1994 WTO Government Procurement Agreement (GPA), even though Art XX.2 GPA (and Art XVIII.1 of the revised GPA of 2012) explicitly requires member states to provide access to a forum where aggrieved suppliers can challenge 'alleged breaches of the [GPA] arising in the context of procurements in which they have, or have had, an interest'.

- *lack of rights of citizens* to invoke and directly apply UN/WTO guarantees of transnational freedoms, non-discrimination, the rule of law, judicial remedies and respect for human rights in most *domestic* administrative and judicial government bodies;
- *inadequate constitutional 'checks and balances'* due to insufficient control of foreign policy discretion and of UN/WTO rule-making by national parliaments, courts of justice and civil society;
- *inadequate representation of domestic civil society* due to 'protection biases' favouring concentrated, 'rent-seeking' interest groups over dispersed, general consumer interests;
- *inadequate 'cosmopolitan public reason'* because reasonable interests of foreign citizens are not represented in domestic decision-making processes.

The diverse forms of 'dualist separation' of national and international legal systems prevailing in most countries, the frequent disregard for the 'consistent interpretation principles' underlying national and international legal systems, and the 'remedy gap' resulting from international treaties aimed at protecting PGs without recognizing citizens as 'democratic principals' and legal subjects of PGs regimes,[26] entail that multilevel governance of transnational PGs continues to be distorted by the very same 'governance failures' that were characteristic of the ancient 'republican constitutionalism' (eg neglect of equal human rights, discriminatory limitations of citizenship rights, non-inclusive and non-transparent 'feudal governance' of PGs, welfare-reducing border discrimination, inadequate constitutional 'checks and balances' limiting abuses of foreign policy powers).

A. Non-Transparent Interest Group Politics Rather Than Democratic Governance of Public Goods

Chapter 1 explained why the universal recognition of human rights also includes rights 'to a social and international order in which the rights and freedoms set forth in this Declaration can be fully realized' (Article 28 UDHR), and limitations of human rights 'are determined by law solely for the purpose of securing due recognition and respect for the rights and

[26] Cf D Sloss (ed), *The Role of Domestic Courts in Treaty Enforcement: A Comparative Study* (New York, CUP, 2009). In his introductory chapter, Sloss argues that—in order to reduce the 'remedy gap' resulting from international treaties providing for rights without enforcement mechanisms—domestic courts should provide remedies to promote treaty compliance based on a customary law obligation of states to allow private claims for treaty violations in domestic courts. Similar arguments were developed by Petersmann (n 25) for construing national and international guarantees of freedom of trade and the rule of law in mutually consistent ways for the benefit of citizens.

freedoms of others and of meeting the just requirements of morality, public order and the general welfare in a democratic society' (Article 29 UDHR). Procedural justice (eg in the sense of a human right to reasonable justification of governmental limitations) depends on 'democratic discourse justifications' of law and governance and on due process of law (eg respecting individual 'access to justice' and to all relevant information on public governance). Hence, transparent, non-discriminatory and inclusive forms of governance (eg protecting access of citizens to all relevant information, comprehensibility of law and governance for all citizens, readability of positive law rules) are constitutional conditions of the democratic legitimacy of law and governance.[27] Parliamentary *ex post* 'rubber-stamping' of thousands of pages of secretly negotiated, intergovernmental treaty texts in the context of 'fast track procedures' is increasingly criticized by civil society as not protecting adequate democratic scrutiny of democratic legislation.

Due to their functional focus on particular PGs, most global governance institutions—like the UN Specialized Agencies and the WTO—are dominated by government executives and administrative 'experts', who search for 'technically right' solutions to international regulatory problems (eg of monetary, financial, trade, development, health and climate change policies and related risk assessments). This often happens without democratic politics and parliamentary control. As a result—similar to the focus of ancient Greek and Roman constitutionalism on the rational self-interests of powerful social groups (eg adult male property owners, soldiers and government officials defending 'republican values') and the then prevailing, non-inclusive and communitarian conceptions of democratic governance without protection of human rights—intergovernmental UN and WTO negotiations remain dominated by rational self-interests of governments and of powerful interest groups, without effective legal and judicial protection of human rights in most areas of UN and WTO governance. As discussed below in section IV, modern trade negotiations—eg on the Uruguay Round agreements and the mega-regional FTAs like the Canada–EU Comprehensive Economic and Trade Agreement (CETA) and the Trans-Pacific Partnership (TPP) among 12 Pacific trading countries—were conducted over many years in secrecy among government executives and 'stakeholders' (eg business, experts from regulatory agencies and international standards organizations), without public access to most draft texts and negotiating documents. In the words of former WTO Director-General Pascal Lamy, the prevailing 'Westphalian conceptions' of 'international law among sovereign states' and of intergovernmental rule-making postulate that 'as states are coherent and legitimate,

[27] Cf A Bianchi and A Peters (eds), *Transparency in International Law* (Cambridge, CUP, 2013).

global governance is necessarily coherent and legitimate as well'.[28] In international practice, however, 'states are often incoherent'. 'Member-driven' international organizations often lack legitimacy in the eyes of citizens. Coordination and cooperation between international organizations in order to remedy the 'coherence gap' and 'legitimacy gap' often remain weak. The 'sovereign equality' and related 'veto powers' of member states in consensus-based UN and WTO practices entail 'jurisdiction gaps', 'governance gaps', 'incentive gaps', 'participation gaps' and transnational 'rule of law gaps', which impede collective supply of global PGs.[29] The EU model of reducing such 'gaps' by regional 'communitarization', legalization and 'constitutionalization' of economic and environmental regulation in multilevel governance institutions has not been followed by most other regional economic groupings and international organizations outside Europe. Similarly, the example of EU membership in the WTO—facilitating transformation of *national* and *regional* into *global PGs*, as illustrated by the EU's leadership role in the Doha Round negotiations—has been followed neither by other regional trade organizations nor by most UN Specialized Agencies (apart from EU membership in the FAO).

As 'theory and practice do not match', Lamy calls for 'pragmatic solutions … to be found now to enhance global governance and better address the problems that our world is facing', notably by providing better leadership, more legitimacy, efficient results for the benefit of people at a reasonable cost and more policy coherence. At the national level, leadership, legitimacy and efficiency are in the hands of a single 'government'; at the international level, however, the three elements are much more complex. European integration has evolved into a unique multilevel governance model based on leadership by the independent European Commission and legitimacy promoted by democratic and judicial EU institutions that protect European PGs like the common market. But the declining participation in elections of the European Parliament and the rising scepticism in public opinion (eg vis-à-vis EU governance of the euro, refugees and illegal migration) also reveal the limits of legitimacy of the EU. Lamy supports the emerging 'triangle of coherence' based on:

— the G20 providing political leadership and policy direction;
— the UN providing a framework for global legitimacy through accountability; and

[28] WTO Director-General P. Lamy, 'Global Governance: From Theory to Practice' in Petersmann (ed) (n 1) 25–30. The following quotations in the text are from this key-note speech by Lamy.

[29] On such 'gaps', which are analysed in greater detail below, see Kaul, Grunberg and Stern (eds) (n 3) 450 ff; Petersmann (n 13) 91ff.

— member-driven international organizations providing expertise and specialized regulation, whose mutual coherence is being promoted by the increasing 'bridges' linking the G20 to the UN and to specialized organizations like the WTO.

Lamy also endorses the attempts at revitalizing the ECOSOC in order to enhance UN system-wide coherence, the increasing number of joint initiatives by the WTO and UN agencies, as well as the readjustment of voting rights in the Bretton Woods institutions. But Lamy emphasizes that 'secondary legitimacy' deriving from consent by democratic states must be reinforced by more 'primary legitimacy' deriving from direct participation of citizens. Hence, global governance must respond to the democratic criticism of 'too-distant, non-accountable and non-directly challengeable decision-making at the international level'. Another lesson from European experience is the need for basing successful integration on common principles, shared values and adequate institutions focusing on concerns of citizens. According to Lamy, the UN human rights values and regional integration are 'the essential intermediate step between the national and the global governance level' and need to be strengthened, before stronger local and 'community support' for multilevel governance institutions may emerge.[30] More 'primary legitimacy' of global governance based on support from civil society and 'global citizens'—supporting a 'global community' and the necessary building of a new 'polity'—requires 'localizing global problems'. This remains 'the main political challenge we are facing'. As illustrated by the constitutional complaints by more than 35,000 German citizens to the German Constitutional Court challenging alleged excesses of power by the European Central Bank (ECB), empowering citizens through democratic and cosmopolitan rights can set powerful incentives for promoting government accountability and for assuming 'cosmopolitan responsibility' and 'democratic ownership' of multilevel governance institutions, and of their often opaque redistribution of domestic income through non-transparent, discriminatory policy instruments (such as the ECB's indirect financial assistance to over-indebted euro member governments, whose persistent violations of the budget and debt disciplines under Article 126 TEU provoked higher interest rates (risk *premia*) that impede their access to financial markets).

B. Focus on National Interests Rather Than on Transnational Public Goods

International agreement on which—and how many—PGs to provide often depends on the 'input legitimacy' of the rule-making procedures, and on

[30] Cf 'Trade and human rights: a case for misplaced suspicion' in P Lamy, *The Geneva Consensus. Making Trade Work for All* (Cambridge, CUP, 2013) 146 ff.

the distribution of the respective costs, benefits and responsibilities. For instance, the US leadership for the elaboration and adoption of the 1944 Bretton Woods Agreements, the 1945 UN Charter, GATT 1947 and for the 1948 UDHR was not only due to the hegemonic position of the US after World War II and to the US willingness to cover most of the 'negotiating costs' (eg of the 1944 Bretton Woods, 1945 San Francisco and 1947 New York Conferences). Of no less importance for securing broad international consent were the US efforts at promoting inclusive negotiations and 'principled justifications' of a liberal post-war international order based on 'sovereign equality of states', decolonization and respect for human rights. Yet the US insistence on US veto powers in the Bretton Woods institutions, in the UN Security Council and in consensus-based GATT/WTO negotiations, as well as the US refusal to participate in many international PGs regimes (like many ILO conventions, UN human rights conventions, environmental conventions, the WHO Framework Convention on Tobacco Control, the Rome Convention establishing the International Criminal Court, the Law of the Sea Convention) also illustrate how alleged 'national interests' often prevail over a reasonable, common interest in protecting transnational PGs. Just as many ancient and Renaissance republics were overthrown by power politics (eg the three Florentine republics from the thirteenth to the sixteenth centuries), national power politics also continues to prevail too often in modern UN and WTO negotiations on protecting international PGs, as well as in subsequent domestic debates on how legislatures, administrations and tribunals should implement international treaty obligations.[31]

Views about the 'input legitimacy' and 'distributional fairness' of intergovernmental negotiations over PGs tend to differ depending on the 'observational standpoint', for instance whether the legitimacy and efficiency of multilevel rules and governance institutions are evaluated from the perspective of 'constitutional approaches', 'global administrative law approaches' or 'legal pluralist approaches' to multilevel regulation of transnational PGs.[32] The under-supply of international PGs reveals a 'leadership vacuum' in most UN and WTO institutions. Paradoxically, the evolution from the comparatively weak GATT 1947[33] into the worldwide WTO legal and compulsory dispute settlement system was more successful than the evolution of the Bretton Woods Agreements that had been duly ratified by national

[31] The example of the US Uruguay Round Agreements Act and of its hidden, statutory provision violating Art XX GPA (cf n 25 above) illustrates this influence of interest group politics on all levels of multilevel governance of international PGs.

[32] These competing 'regulatory approaches' and conceptions of the law of international organizations are discussed in ch 3, section II. See also G Shaffer, 'International Law and Global Public Goods in a Legal Pluralist World' (2012) 23(3) *EJIL* 669–93.

[33] For instance, GATT 1947 had not been legally ratified by most GATT contracting parties, had weak institutions, and 'grandfather exceptions' exempted inconsistent, mandatory national legislation.

parliaments. Yet the increasing number of trade agreements concluded outside the WTO, the failure to conclude the Doha Round negotiations and other 'governance gaps' confirm the 'legitimacy deficits' and 'constitutional limits' of intergovernmental power politics as a legitimate tool for protecting global PGs. Waiting for global consensus (eg among now 164 WTO members) has proved to be an unreasonable negotiation strategy, just as the 'single undertaking method', consensus-based amendment procedures and related veto powers in WTO law risk being impractical 'implementation strategies'.[34] The current negotiations on new 'mega-regional FTAs' (like the TPP and TTIP) pursue not only economic objectives (like trade liberalization and trade regulation), but also geo-political objectives of transforming the world trading system among 'coalitions of the willing' and circumventing the political opposition (eg from some BRICS countries) to reforming the WTO system. Similar to the replacement of GATT 1947 by the 1994 WTO Agreement in 1995, the mega-regional FTAs among the most important WTO members could ultimately be 'merged' and replace the 'WTO 1994' with a more ambitious 'WTO 2020'.

In the WTO Doha and UN climate change negotiations, some of the 'governance failures' to reach agreement are related to disagreements on the distribution of costs and benefits. For instance, less-developed WTO members have made their acceptance of the 2014 Trade Facilitation Agreement conditional on receiving technical and financial assistance and 'regulatory freedom' to decide themselves on the domestic implementation of the related legal commitments; the refusal by many less-developed WTO members to accept the WTO disciplines on welfare-reducing government procurement practices (like non-transparent government procurement) is similarly related to political concerns by authoritarian governments with maintaining their domestic 'policy discretion' to discriminate in favour of powerful domestic lobbies and interest groups in exchange for political support. The 'Paris Agreement' of December 2015 on climate change prevention leaves it to each contracting party to decide on its respective carbon reduction commitments. Harmful 'policy externalities' are often a major impediment to collective supply of PGs, as illustrated by the harmful impact of illegal US cotton subsidies on African and Latin-American cotton-exporting countries that oppose conclusion of a 'Doha Development Round' without prior US compliance with the WTO dispute settlement rulings of November 2001 on the illegality of these US cotton subsidies. The continuing US non-compliance illustrates how rent-seeking lobbies financing the election campaigns of US politicians are often politically more powerful than consumer interests

[34] For instance, it remains uncertain when and whether the 2005 amendment of the TRIPS Agreement and the 2015 amendment inserting the Trade Facilitation Agreement into WTO law will ever come into force due to the inadequate number of national ratifications to meet the two-thirds requirement in Art X:3 of the WTO Agreement.

in rules-based, liberal trade, as well as in avoidance of wasteful subsidy practices violating WTO legal disciplines.

Reconciling national and transnational self-interests requires 'responsible sovereignty' and inclusive decision-making procedures balancing all reasonable interests involved. Non-inclusive intergovernmental negotiations often induce periodically elected governments to prioritize their own political self-interests (eg in accommodating rent-seeking or polluting industry interests during times of political elections). Transformation of global PGs into 'club goods' (eg by concluding the WTO Agreement on Government Procurement as a separate 'plurilateral agreement') and sanctions against free-riding third countries (eg under the Montreal Protocol on substances that deplete the ozone layer) offer incentives for limiting such 'collective action problems'. Violations of *erga omnes* legal obligations to respect, protect and fulfil human rights, and of other 'duties to protect' internationally agreed 'common concerns' (eg the WTO prohibitions on trade-distorting subsidies) may justify recourse to international dispute settlement procedures and reprisals from adversely affected third countries.

C. Multilevel 'Constitutional Gaps' and 'Jurisdiction Gaps' Without 'Constitutional Justice'

Chapter 1 argued that the citizen-driven 'bottom-up constitutionalism' characteristic of democratic governance of PGs in constitutional democracies and European law—ie recognizing citizens and democratic peoples as holders of 'constituent power', 'democratic principals' and 'agents of justice' delegating only limited 'constituted powers' to governments—must be extended to transnational 'aggregate PGs' in order to hold multilevel governance institutions more accountable for their failures to protect transnational PGs for the benefit of citizens. Chapter 1 went on to argue that this can be achieved through 'constitutional', citizen-orientated interpretations of precise and unconditional UN and WTO rules as constituting rights not only of governments, but also of citizens; international treaties approved by national parliaments—like other democratic legislation—derive their constitutional legitimacy from protecting the 'constitutional contracts' and constitutional rights of citizens through democratic implementing legislation, administration and judicial protection. Yet the Kantian 'constitutional insight' of the interdependencies between national and international rule of law—ie that 'the problem of establishing a perfect civil constitution is subordinate to the problem of a law-governed external relationship with other states, and cannot be solved unless the latter is also solved'[35]—continues to

[35] Cf I Kant, 'Idea for a Universal History with a Cosmopolitan Purpose' in H Reiss (ed), *Kant—Political Writings* (Cambridge, CUP, 1991) 47.

be neglected in European integration law too. In the application of rational choice and principal-agent theories to international organizations, most political scientists focus on *states* as agents and on how governments can control their limited delegation of powers to international organizations, for instance in order to avoid:

- 'agency slack' (eg the agent minimizing the effort it exerts on behalf of the principal in order to pursue his self-interests);
- 'adverse selection' (eg an organization using donor money to expand the benefits of the bureaucracy); and
- 'moral hazard' (eg an agent taking risks, whose costs fall on the principal whenever the risky policy fails).

It is only more recently that principal-agent analyses have also included rational choices by multiple non-state actors in global governance, for instance by acknowledging that 'international trustees' (eg courts of justice) may exercise legitimately independent, autonomous governance powers in order to comply with the customary law requirement of interpreting treaties and settling related disputes 'in conformity with the principles of justice', including 'human rights and fundamental freedoms for all' (cf the Preamble to and Article 31 of the VCLT). Chapter 1 suggested recognizing citizens, democratic voters and national parliaments (rather than government executives and states) as legitimate 'principals', and reinterpreting the mandate of international courts as a 'principal-trustee' relationship vis-à-vis domestic citizens and government agents. This may justify judicial actions to limit state-centered conceptions of 'member-driven governance', for instance by promoting individual access to justice (eg by admitting *amicus curiae* submissions from third parties), transparent and inclusive procedures (eg in investment arbitration and WTO disputes), and judicial 'balancing' of state-centered and person-orientated 'principles of justice' in the interpretation of treaty exceptions for the protection of public interests (like health and environmental protection); WTO jurisprudence and investor-state arbitration have progressively clarified and developed indeterminate treaty provisions, and thereby complemented intergovernmental rule-making and dispute settlement.[36]

The history of constitutionalism confirms the Kantian argument that power-orientated 'top-down governance' cannot effectively protect human rights and other international PGs without being constrained by constitutional rights and remedies of citizens that limit abuses of power in all human interactions at national, transnational and international levels.[37] The 'path-dependent' focus of many national and UN/WTO legal systems

[36] Cf H Tamm and D Snidal, 'Rational Choice and Principal-Agent Theory' in Weiss and Wilkinson (eds) (n 4) 132 ff.

[37] On Kantian legal, constitutional and cosmopolitan theories, see Petersmann (n 13) ch III.

on 'foreign policy discretion' (eg veto powers by non-democratic rulers in the UN Security Council and in consensus-based WTO rule-making) confirms the 'Lockean dilemma' of inadequate constitutional control of foreign policy discretion; the inadequate, multilevel safeguards for protecting cosmopolitan rights and judicial remedies of citizens favour interest group politics (eg in WTO negotiations) at the expense of domestic consumer welfare and of other general citizen interests. Just as transformation of 'national Westphalian regimes' depended on institutionalizing democratic and republican constitutionalism (eg through democratic, parliamentary and judicial 'checks and balances') at the request of citizens struggling for constitutional protection of their rights, so does the transformation of 'international Westphalian regimes' into multilevel constitutional and democratic protection of cosmopolitan rights and PGs require multilevel constitutional reforms that limit abuses of power by protecting citizens through cosmopolitan rights and accountability mechanisms. European integration law has been most effective in those areas—like the common market, competition law, HRL and multilevel legal protection of certain social rights—where 'Westphalian international law' was progressively reformed among 'coalitions of the willing' (eg amongst initially only six EC member states, today 28 EU member countries) in favour of constitutional and judicial protection of cosmopolitan rights.

The 'constitutional deficit' that results from national foreign policy discretion (eg veto powers of UN and WTO members) without adequate constitutional restraints entails 'jurisdiction gaps', as illustrated by the incapacity of WTO institutions to conclude their Doha Round negotiations since 2001 and to secure the proper functioning of the WTO Appellate Body in light of the politically motivated disagreement (since May 2016) on the appointment of Appellate Body judges. Chapter 1 explained why UN and WTO tribunals have inherent jurisdiction for 'judicial balancing' of public and private interests and 'constitutional interpretations' protecting the human rights obligations of the parties to the dispute. Yet neither individual states nor UN and WTO institutions can unilaterally protect 'aggregate PGs'; this is possible only through multilateral cooperation among multilevel governance institutions in protecting transnational rule of law and other PGs for the benefit of citizens through coordinated exercise of sovereign powers. For instance, due to global transport, travel and communication networks, no individual state can unilaterally control the risks of health pandemics, cybercrimes, climate change, transnational pollution, migration and underregulation of global markets (eg regarding tax evasion and 'toxic' financial instruments). Nor can UN and WTO institutions secure collective protection of aggregate PGs if—due to their 'consensus' and 'state sovereignty' principles—individual governments unilaterally veto UN and WTO regulation of internationally recognized 'common concerns' (like climate change prevention, 'sustainable development'). Neither the UN Secretary-General nor the WTO Director-General has been granted 'powers of initiative' to propose global rules necessary for protecting PGs. The inadequate leadership for protecting 'community interests' and insufficient incentives for 'bottom-up aggregation of PGs' (eg promoting national, bilateral and regional 'public-private partnerships' among 'key actors' open to all countries) prompt governments in many UN and WTO member states to neglect multilevel governance of international PGs.

The focus on intergovernmental power politics in political UN and WTO institutions often fails to secure the democratic, collective law-making and governance that are necessary for protecting human rights, transnational rule of law and other PGs for the benefit of citizens. Only about one-third of UN member states have accepted the compulsory ICJ jurisdiction for peaceful settlement of disputes. And many UN member states emphasize that—in contrast to judgments by European economic and human rights courts—ICJ judgments, WTO dispute settlement rulings and decisions by UN human rights bodies are not enforceable through domestic courts. As 'diplomatic espousal' of individual rights vis-à-vis foreign states and related judicial procedures in the ICJ have often been ineffective (eg in the field of protection of foreign investors against 'regulatory takings'), most UN member states have consented to depoliticize and decentralize foreign investment disputes by providing for investor-state arbitration in the now more than 3,000 BITs and additional investment protection treaties. Many regional trade agreements strengthen judicial remedies of private economic actors as more effective and more legitimate alternatives to dispute settlement among states.

D. Multilevel 'Accountability Gaps', 'Legitimacy Gaps' and 'Remedy Deficits'

Similar to the guarantees in Roman constitutionalism for protecting the transnational *jus gentium* (eg by the *praetor peregrinus* protecting rights of foreign traders), modern Constitutions and the Lisbon Treaty include—as discussed in Chapter 1—ever more constitutional rules and institutions for protecting mutually beneficial cooperation among citizens in the external relations of the EU too. Yet the exclusion of citizens, civil society and parliaments from UN and WTO decision-making processes, and the inadequate accountability of intergovernmental UN and WTO rule-making vis-à-vis adversely affected citizens, entail *governance failures*. This is illustrated by governmental neglect of human rights, general consumer welfare and democratic accountability that are nowhere mentioned in WTO law. The UN Secretary-General's Synthesis Report on *The Road to Dignity by 2030: Ending Poverty, Transforming All Lives and Protecting the Planet*, emphasized the need for 'a new paradigm of accountability' as a core component of the post-2015 agenda for sustainable development.[38] The impunity of many governments for violating international law for the benefit of powerful interest groups (eg during the 20 years of illegal EU import restrictions on bananas (1991–2012) that redistributed income among domestic citizens through illegal distortions of trade and competition to the detriment of national consumer welfare) illustrates 'disconnected governance' and *accountability gaps* that call for stronger constitutional, democratic and judicial remedies for adversely affected citizens. European common market law demonstrates that legal empowerment of citizens, parliaments, independent regulatory agencies (like multilevel competition authorities and central banks), and national and international courts of justice can effectively limit such abuses of 'intergovernmental power politics' through 'checks and balances' that protect constitutional rights.

European law and the parliamentary and judicial responses to the euro crises also illustrate that human rights, the rule of law and democratic self-governance can be successfully extended to multilevel governance, for instance by promoting transnational parliamentary, participatory and 'deliberative democracy', judicial accountability and other 'countervailing powers' that limit the 'executive dominance' in foreign policymaking and challenge abuses of power by regulatory agencies. Multilevel constitutional restraints of 'Westphalian foreign policy discretion' can enhance the democratic and problem-solving capacities of multilevel governance, for instance through multilevel networks of monetary, financial, competition, environmental and other regulatory authorities protecting individual rights, transparent decision-making and judicial remedies. 'Intergovernmentalism' in UN/WTO institutions and secretive treaty negotiations risk entailing 'information gaps' justifying parliamentary and judicial rejection of intergovernmental rules (eg on confidentiality of documents); European courts have repeatedly challenged intergovernmental agreements that failed to protect constitutional rights (eg of 'whistleblowers' revealing illegal government activities).[39]

E. 'Incentive Gaps', 'Discourse Failures' and 'Market Failures' Distorting Multilevel Governance of Public Goods

The exclusion of private actors from UN and WTO governance and the limited role of democratic parliaments also entail incentive gaps, 'discourse

[38] Cf UN Secretary-General, *The Road to Dignity by 2030: Ending Poverty, Transforming All Lives and Protecting the Planet*, New York, December 2014.

[39] A recent illustration is the CJEU judgment of 6 October 2015 invalidating the EU–USA 'safe harbour agreement' on transfers of data, in view of their inadequate legal and judicial protection in the USA against disproportionate mass surveillance by the US National Security Agency.

failures', free-riding and 'participation gaps' in the collective supply of international PGs, whose collective production often depends on inclusive, democratic rule-making with incentives for private-public partnerships and collective burden-sharing (eg in the implementation of WTO rules on technology transfer, food aid and trade facilitation). The functional specialization of intergovernmental decision-making in UN Specialized Agencies and WTO institutions risks limiting 'institutionalization of public reason' on 'interface problems' of PGs regimes like climate change prevention, protection of biodiversity and transnational rule of law. For instance, by disregarding HRL, WTO governance unduly neglects that 'human development' often depends on respect for human rights (eg to education, health protection, food security, freedom of opinion, democratic participation), for example if cosmopolitan rights and judicial remedies are incentives for citizens to challenge abuses of power (eg corruption, anticompetitive business practices) and to assume their democratic responsibilities for promoting consumer welfare through open markets and non-discriminatory competition. Neglect for the 'systemic integration requirement' (Article 31:3 VCLT) risks rendering the coordination of specialized PGs regimes more difficult, for instance if intergovernmental rules on 'common but differentiated responsibilities' and 'duties to protect' are not effectively assigned to private and public, national and international actors due to insufficient financial and technical assistance for poor countries that provide transnational environmental services by protecting tropical forests that are of global importance for biodiversity and carbon reduction.

The WTO provisions for capacity building and trade facilitation—by assisting less-developed countries in implementing WTO rules—illustrate how legal and financial incentives for private and public participation in the supply of international PGs may limit 'governance failures' and promote equitable sharing of adjustment costs. For instance, the WTO provisions on legal assistance for developing countries (cf Article 27 DSU) and the establishment of the Advisory Centre on WTO Law have promoted 'procedural justice' in WTO dispute settlement proceedings for the benefit of less-developed WTO members with lesser 'legal resources' and financial resources. The Doha Round negotiations since 2001 illustrate the difficulties of consensus-based WTO negotiations and the need for more legal flexibility for 'plurilateral trade agreements' among 'coalitions of the willing'. Just as the Tokyo Round and Uruguay Round Agreements enabled the progressive transformation of the fragmented GATT into a more coherent WTO legal system, the new 'mega-regional FTAs' (like the TPP and TTIP) may facilitate future reforms of the WTO trading system (eg by limiting market and governance failures through additional competition, consumer protection, labour and environmental rules, and legal harmonization).

F. Regulatory Competition Promoting 'Bottom-Up Aggregation' of Public Goods

As discussed briefly in Chapter 1, respect for democratic 'subsidiarity principles' (eg in Article 5 TEU) can justify bilateral, regional and other plurilateral 'fragmentation' of treaty regimes so as to create 'building blocks' for 'bottom-up reforms' with due respect for democratic diversity. Both UN and WTO law promote regional cooperation as a second-best policy instrument for the global supply of 'aggregate PGs' (like worldwide and regional security systems, an open world trading system, monetary stability). Regional security alliances (like NATO), FTAs and common markets (like the EU) among democracies limit the collective action problems of 'aggregate PGs'. Through progressive enlargement and 'regulatory competition', they can contribute to reforming global PGs regimes (eg through EU membership of the FAO and WTO, humanitarian NATO interventions circumventing unjustified vetoes in the UN Security Council, the *Kadi* jurisprudence of the CJEU inducing reforms of decision-making in the UN Security Council).

For example, since the unilateral abolition of the English corn laws in 1846, the multilateral trading system dialectically developed through multilevel trade regulation. The 1860 Cobden-Chevallier trade agreement between England and France set a precedent for the subsequent 'multilateralization' of the European trading system through dozens of bilateral trade agreements, which were interconnected through most-favoured-nation clauses and progressively liberalized trade until the end of the nineteenth century. The post-war initiatives to negotiate GATT 1947 (based on treaty clauses used in the more than 30 bilateral trade agreements previously negotiated on the basis of the 1934 US Reciprocal Trade Agreements Act) and to progressively transform GATT into the WTO legal system, illustrated how multilevel governance of transnational aggregate PGs can be promoted through dynamically evolving 'bottom-up' legal and political processes. The 1979 Tokyo Round Agreements had been ratified by only a limited number of GATT contracting parties, and had operated in separate institutional and dispute settlement frameworks. The 1994 'single undertaking' requirement for WTO membership entailed that most Uruguay Round Agreements were integrated into one single WTO Agreement, now accepted by 164 WTO members, subject to an integrated dispute settlement system.

The benefits of the 1996 Information Technology Agreement were unilaterally extended to all WTO members after a 'critical mass' of those members had ratified the Agreement. The revised Government Procurement Agreement, which entered into force in April 2014, remains a 'plurilateral agreement' (PTA in terms of Article II:3 WTO Agreement) with a progressively increasing number of WTO contracting parties. The regulatory competition among hundreds of FTAs, customs union agreements and PTAs has increased legal convergence of multilevel trade regulation; paradoxically, it can contribute to reducing 'legal fragmentation' by initiating worldwide reforms of economic rules, for instance by influencing mega-regional FTAs and promoting future 'multilateralization' of FTA commitments among WTO members. The private 'stakeholder participation' (eg of private standard-setting organizations) and 'public-private partnerships' (eg in transforming private product and production standards into public law standards) in regional agreements have served as a model for some of the WTO agreements (eg on technical barriers to trade, sanitary and phyto-sanitary measures). The protection of individual rights in some WTO agreements (like the GPA and TRIPS agreements), and the compulsory WTO dispute settlement system, incorporate 'constitutional reforms' from regional integration agreements aimed at limiting abuses of government powers through multilevel legal and judicial protection of the rule of law. The linkage of the WTO Agreement on Trade Facilitation to technical and financial assistance commitments and transitional periods likewise reflects new governance techniques incorporated into WTO law from other legal regimes. The call for reconciling the 'Washington consensus' on promotion of non-discriminatory, liberal trade with the 'Geneva consensus' on interpreting non-economic 'public interest' and 'exception' clauses in WTO law in conformity with the UN legal obligations of WTO members, aims at promoting legal coherence of interdependent and 'overlapping' PGs regimes. As discussed in section III, the multilevel tobacco litigation on how to reconcile economic and health rights through WTO, investment law, regional and national dispute settlement proceedings illustrates the potential synergies of 'multilevel judicial governance', provided the applicable rules and procedures are interpreted in mutually consistent ways.

G. Need for Comparative Legal and Institutional Analyses of Public Goods Regimes

The diversity of UN Specialized Agencies and of other worldwide and regional PGs regimes illustrates the need for political pragmatism and legal and institutional experimentation:

- The regulatory governance problems and institutional needs of diverse 'aggregate PGs', 'best effort PGs' and 'weakest link PGs' differ, for instance depending on whether they can be supplied within more limited legal and institutional frameworks.
- The legal design of the collective supply of international 'aggregate PGs' (such as human and labour rights) may also differ depending on the decision-making procedures of UN institutions (eg the veto powers

of the permanent members of the UN Security Council), financial UN institutions (eg the weighted voting powers of members of the Bretton Woods institutions), the ILO (with its tripartite membership and voting rules) and the modalities of trade negotiations (eg bilateral 'request-offer procedures' or multilateral 'formula approaches' for liberalizing tariffs and non-tariff trade barriers).

— The 'horizontal' legal regulation of 'overlaps', cooperation and conflicts between interdependent PGs (eg the relationships of GATT and the WTO to other UN Specialized Agencies) remains incomplete and evolves in response to newly emerging regulatory challenges (like currency manipulation), as illustrated by the GATT/WTO rules (such as GATT Articles XII to XV), WTO declarations and WTO agreements on cooperation with the Bretton Woods institutions, the ILO, WIPO, WHO and environmental organizations.[40]
— The regulation of the 'vertical interactions' between international and domestic legal regimes reveals a variety of legal approaches, as illustrated by the more limited remedies for reparation of injury caused by treaty violations in the WTO compared with the rules on state responsibility applied in UN law and by the ICJ.

Comparative analysis of the existing 'international legal and institutional pluralism' suggests that citizen-driven, rights-based human rights conventions (like the ECHR) and economic integration agreements in Europe (like the EU and the EEA) have protected cosmopolitan rights, judicial remedies and transnational rule of law for the benefit of citizens more comprehensively than state-centered human rights and economic agreements (eg in Africa) without effective individual and judicial remedies against violations of *erga omnes* obligations (like human rights, fundamental freedoms of EU and EEA law). While the supply of some global PGs has been assigned to UN Specialized Agencies, the supply of other global PGs has been attributed to institutions with limited membership (such as the Basel Committee on Banking Supervision elaborating international rules on bank capital requirements). United Nations conventions that provide for legal and institutional protection of the 'common heritage of mankind' beyond national jurisdictions (like the 1972 UNESCO World Heritage Convention, the 1982 UNCLOS) appear to have been more effective than multilateral 'framework conventions' that merely recognize 'common concerns' (like the 1992 UN Conventions on Biological Diversity and on Climate Change). Multilateral agreements on the protection of the environment have been more successful if they included financial support for rule compliance in less-developed

[40] Cf A Pitaraki, *Institutional Linkages: WTO—IMF, World Bank, WIPO, WHO. A Global Administrative Law Approach as a Means for Supplying Public Goods* (Florence, EUI doctoral thesis, 2014).

countries and sanctions against 'free-riding' by third countries (as in the case of the 1987 Montreal Protocol on the Protection of the Ozone Layer). The common patterns of many multilateral environmental agreements—eg their initial design as framework conventions without enforcement powers, whose rules were progressively supplemented by additional Protocols with more precise regulations—illustrates how international institutions can promote learning processes and incentives for progressive rule clarification in cooperation with non-governmental interest groups.[41] Treaty provisions on 'enhanced cooperation' among 'coalitions of willing countries' (eg pursuant to Article 20 TEU), 'plurilateral agreements' among some of the WTO member states (like the Government Procurement Agreement) and regional trade agreements (eg pursuant to Article XXIV GATT and Article V GATS) may set incentives for 'competing regulation' and institutional experimentation. Economic PGs theory offers few criteria as to when global PGs should be regulated issue-by-issue (eg pursuant to the economic theory of separation of policy instruments underlying the separate UN Specialized Agencies) or by means of package deals that facilitate compromises over the distribution of costs and benefits (as in the 1994 WTO Agreement now incorporating more than 60 specific agreements like GATS, the TRIPS Agreement and accession protocols).

The legitimacy and effectiveness of the 1968 Treaty on the Non-proliferation of Nuclear Weapons were undermined by the fact that nuclear powers neither complied with their own commitments to phase out nuclear war materials, nor prevented strategically important countries (like Israel, India, Pakistan, North Korea) from developing nuclear bombs. Many 'weakest link PGs' (like the eradication of polio, prevention of piracy) were undermined by unwilling or unable 'failing states' that lacked the resources or the political capability to protect agreed international PGs. International assistance for overcoming such collective action problems may sometimes be solved through unilateral action by a few donor nations without necessitating worldwide governance mechanisms.[42] Yet external coercion may be an inevitable *ultima ratio* against 'rogue states' that deliberately undermine international PGs (like the Taliban government in Afghanistan and the 'Islamic State' terrorists in Syria destroying cultural world heritage like the Giant Buddha at Bamiyan and promoting terrorism abroad). Also, in

[41] More generally on how international organizations change the mechanisms and reasoning behind the making, implementation and enforcement of international rules (eg through iteration of negotiations enhancing the outcome of prisoners' dilemmas, technical expert advice from impartial secretariats, reducing information asymmetries and transaction costs, self-enforcing behaviour, creation of property rights, issue linkage, etc), see JE Alvarez, *International Organizations as Law-makers* (Oxford, OUP, 2005).

[42] Cf D Bodansky, 'What's in a Concept? Global Public Goods, International Law and Legitimacy' (2012) 23 *EJIL* 651–68.

the case of 'single best effort PGs', which may be supplied by one or few actor(s), international governance problems (eg of climate change 'geo-engineering' through injection of stratospheric aerosols) may not require global organizations with legislative and enforcement powers. Yet *unilateral* supply of international PGs may create international conflicts due to harmful externalities for states that would benefit from the under-supply of the international PG concerned (eg climate change promoting the melting of the ice-cap, entailing new opportunities for mineral exploitation in the Arctic).

H. Comparative Lessons from Case Studies and 'Piecemeal Reforms'

Reforms of global governance institutions (like the 'G20' group of 19 'systemically significant' industrialized and emerging economies plus the EU), regulations of collective action problems inside multilevel PGs regimes, and the horizontal and vertical 'interface problems' between national and functionally limited, international PGs regimes can be evaluated best by resort to case studies.[43] The following survey is limited to three illustrative, regulatory challenges.

i. Lessons from Europe for Improving Global Governance Institutions? The Example of the G20

The G20 was established in 1999 pursuant to a proposal by the G7 finance ministers and central bank governors in response to the experience, during the Asian financial crisis of the late 1990s, that the G7 structure did not enable adequate responses to global financial and economic crises. The G20 is in a powerful position to promote the global common good, and to make it prevail, at times, against narrow, short-term interpretations of national interests.[44] It is, however, much less clear whether the needed improvements

[43] Kaul *et al* (eds) (n 2) discuss (at 44 ff) 10 global PGs prioritized in a report by the UN Seceretary-General: (1) basic human dignity for all people, including universal access to basic education and health care; (2) respect for national sovereignty; (3) global public health, particularly communicable disease control; (4) global security or, put differently, a global public domain free from crime and violence; (5) global peace; (6) communication and transportation systems harmonized across borders; (7) institutional infrastructure harmonized across borders to foster such goals as market efficiency, universal human rights, transparent and accountable governance, and harmonization of technical standards; (8) concerted management of knowledge, including worldwide respect for intellectual property rights; (9) concerted management of the global natural commons to promote their sustainable use; and (10) availability of international arenas for multilateral negotiation between states, as well as between state and non-state actors. Kaul *et al* acknowledge that many of the multilateral agreements regulating these PGs 'lack even the first steps toward implementation: signature and ratification by all concerned nation-states' (at 44).

[44] Cf J Wouters and T Ramopoulos, 'The G20 and Global Economic Governance: Lessons from Multilevel European Governance?' in Petersmann (ed) (n 1) 73–87.

of 'G20 governance' should be inspired by lessons from multilevel European governance, for instance in order to institutionalize the G20 as a more effective and more legitimate global governance executive. For example, the 'competence catalogues' of the Lisbon Treaty listing various categories of EU competences (cf Articles 3–6 TFEU on exclusive, shared, parallel and supporting competences), and limiting their exercise by constitutional principles (eg in Articles 2–6 TEU), prevented neither daily turf battles on shared EU competences nor newly emerging modes of multilevel governance (eg of the debt crises in the Eurozone among (now) 19 EU member states). The EU member states have transferred more legislative and policy powers to supranational institutions than any other group of states. A comparison of the European Coal and Steel Treaty of 1951 with the 2009 Lisbon Treaty shows that the design of EU institutions evolved through trial and error. It is difficult, however, to draw general lessons from this very specific process for the provision of PGs and for the organization of global governance institutions. For instance:

- Does the transformation of the EU Council from a 'political directorate' that operated outside the EU Treaties (essentially until 1986) into a Treaty institution (Article 15 TEU) offer lessons for reforming the G20 as today's primary forum for international economic cooperation?
- How should the G20 be coordinated with alternative modes of governance (like markets, hierarchical organizations, informal networks)?
- Should the G20's currently informal mode of negotiating agreements as a 'diplomatic club' in a culture of reciprocity be changed, for instance by creating a permanent G20 Secretariat, transforming the G20 into a 'Council of Governors' of the Bretton Woods institutions and the WTO, or by otherwise promoting synergies through regular delegation of tasks to existing or new organizations (like the Financial Stability Board), thereby enhancing decision-making in UN and WTO institutions or initiating their reform?
- Could the 'representative voice' and deliberative legitimacy of G20 meetings be enhanced by stronger stakeholder involvement (such as the participation of NGOs) and by offering G20 membership to the African Union too (as South Africa remains the only G20 member from Africa)?

Europe's declining influence in global governance—as illustrated by the European debt crises that have overshadowed G20 summit meetings since 2011, and by related tendencies to renationalize European monetary and debt governance—render a 'Europeanization of the G20' unlikely. The recent use of 'military might' by G20 members (like China and Russia) as a means for 'making rights' by appropriating foreign territory (eg the Crimean peninsula) and extraterritorial maritime resources (eg in the South China Sea) reveal fundamental disagreements among G20 members on how to protect international rule of law.[45] Arguably, it also confirms the hypothesis of this study that more limited efforts at 'bottom-up constitutionalization' of regional and functional 'republican governance' are more likely to 'civilize' and protect multilevel governance of PGs than intergovernmental bargaining and coordination in global institutions like the G20.

ii. Lessons from Europe for Improving UN Governance Regimes? The Example of Environmental Law

The UN and its Specialized Agencies have the advantage of pursuing multilevel governance of functionally limited PGs through multilateral treaties, permanent institutions, expert secretariats and quasi-universal membership of states and, exceptionally (eg in the FAO), of the EU. Yet the power-orientated 'intergovernmentalism', consensus-based decision-making and 'disconnected UN governance' entail that many UN member states avoid effective legislative, administrative, judicial and democratic rule implementation inside domestic jurisdictions subject to multilevel control mechanisms. The lack of a UN Specialized Agency for protection of the environment and the inadequate financial, institutional and legal resources of the UN Environmental Program (UNEP) further illustrate the inadequacy of the 'UN system'—designed more than 70 years ago—for securing multilevel governance of transnational PGs in the twenty-first century. In Europe, environmental protection was made effective inside many EU countries in the context of EU common market and environmental legislation, EU supervision, financial assistance, promotion of public participation and 'environmental democracy' based on the rights of citizens to access to information, participation in environmental decision-making and access to justice, as also promoted through international agreements like the 1998 Aarhus Convention on Access to Information, Public Participation in Decision-Making and Access to Justice in Environmental Matters.[46] The two examples of climate change prevention and protection of biodiversity illustrate how the universally accepted goal of 'sustainable development' requires collaborative agendas and rules among national and international, economic and environmental actors.

a. Climate Change Prevention Requires Multilevel 'Integration Law'

The almost universal support of the 'Paris Agreement' of December 2015 on voluntary limitations of greenhouse gas (GHG) emissions is widely expected

[45] On the difficulties of establishing rule of law in post-conflict situations, see J Stromseth, D Wippman and R Brooks, *Can Might Make Rights? Building The Rule of Law After Military Interventions* (Cambridge, CUP, 2006).

[46] Cf G Bandi (ed), *Environmental Democracy and Law. Public Participation in Europe* (Amsterdam, Europa Law Publishing, 2014).

to provide a legal and institutional framework for progressively increasing and transforming these commitments into more comprehensive legal obligations aimed at preventing global temperatures from rising more than 2°C by 2100 (with an ideal target of keeping temperature rise below 1.5°C). Yet the limited results of previous UN conferences on climate change prevention raise questions about how worldwide and regional efforts at phasing out fossil fuels can be rendered more successful. One major collective action problem and potential tragedy of the 'global commons' (like the atmosphere) is that the latter often deteriorate before collective action on protecting the environment is able to make any real difference.[47] The harmful externalities of national GHG emissions on global warming, rising sea levels, changing rainfall patterns, and an increase in the number and force of hurricanes cannot be addressed successfully by any nation acting alone. Countries often disagree on worldwide disciplines (eg for less-developed countries like India) and on the sharing of the related costs and benefits of emission controls so as to prevent global over-exploitation of a limited resource.[48]

The reasons for past failures of the complex web of institutions and programs aimed at mitigating climate change can be grouped into three main categories: political economy considerations, negotiation roadblocks, and inadequate institutional structures ensuring adherence to shared commitments in the UN Framework Convention on Climate Change (UNFCCC). Overcoming these collective action problems requires the establishment of a Global Environmental Organization and closer coordination of the world trade and climate change regimes. The 1997 Kyoto Protocol to the UNFCCC implemented its principle of 'common but differentiated responsibilities' (Article 10) by exempting less-developed countries from binding GHG reduction commitments. The 'Paris Agreement' of 2015 envisages replacing the Kyoto Protocol with a new treaty providing for GHG reduction commitments by less-developed countries too, like Brazil, China and India, who have become major polluters. The cost–benefit calculations regarding the optimal level of GHG reduction commitments of developed and less-developed countries, as well as of individual industries and companies, differ enormously. They are bound to render difficult universal, legally binding GHG reduction commitments to ensure that the world has a net-zero emission level in 2050. Climate change policies aimed at low-carbon growth are bound to affect trade (eg in the event of carbon taxes and border carbon tax adjustments); trade policies can change and promote low-carbon growth

[47] Cf D Esty and A Moffa, 'Why Climate Change Collective Action has Failed and What Needs to be Done within and without the Trade Regime' in Petersmann (ed) (n 1) 119–30.

[48] Cf J Verschuuren (ed), *Environmental Law and Climate Change* (Cheltenham, Elgar, 2015).

(eg by removing trade barriers for climate-friendly goods and services, so as to reduce their cost and promote their availability). Hence, environmental and trade institutions (like the WTO Committee on Trade and Environment, the WTO Technical Barriers to Trade Committee) must cooperate, for instance in liberalizing environmental goods and services, regulating a global market for emissions trading, and ensuring that trade and climate change measures (eg 'green subsidies') are coherent and mutually supportive. The UNFCCC principle of 'common but differentiated responsibility' cannot become effective without involving UN development institutions for promoting the joint implementation by developed and less-developed countries of 'clean development mechanisms' and for preventing 'carbon leakage' (eg if carbon taxes and emissions trading affect the competitiveness of firms and prompt such firms to relocate to countries with less strict mitigation policies so as to maintain their market shares and trading opportunities).

Legal environmental arrangements have often failed to achieve their declared objectives (eg of carbon and other environmental pricing) and may give rise to unexpected side-effects (like trade distortions, abusive practices relating to environmental subsidies and emissions trading systems).[49] In view of the uncertainty of an effective UN convention on climate change prevention, the examination of national and regional policy alternatives is increasingly important. The worldwide recognition of climate change as a 'common concern' in the 1992 UNFCCC promoted progressive regulation at national, regional and worldwide levels of governance, including 'experimental regional climate change governance' so as to fill the 'regulatory vacuum' at the global level (eg in the UNFCCC, the Kyoto Protocol and WTO law).[50] Comparing regional emissions trading schemes in Europe and North America, and the complementary use of border tax adjustments for protecting the global PG of GHG reductions, also offers lessons for the regulation of other 'global environmental commons' that require a multitude of regulatory strategies and levels.[51] The focus on market-based environmental regulation and on out-sourcing responsibilities for achieving emissions reductions on behalf of states illustrates the 'regulatory multipolarity' and 'polycentric international regulatory order' dealing with inter-generational environmental problems that affect all states and billions of individuals. The international dispute over the inclusion of foreign airlines in the EU's carbon emissions trading system[52] confirms doubts over whether 'marketization'

[49] Cf P Martin and A Kennedy (eds), *Implementing Environmental Law* (Cheltenham, Elgar, 2015).

[50] Cf M Hartmann, 'Carbon Emission Trading and Border Carbon Adjustments in Europe, North America and Global Regimes (UNFCCC, WTO)' in Petersmann (ed) (n 1) 131–50.

[51] Cf E Wordman, M Roggenkamp and M Holwerda (eds), *Essential EU Climate Law* (Cheltenham, Elgar, 2015).

[52] Cf Bartels (n 20).

of carbon dioxide emissions is the best methodology for climate change prevention. Comparisons of European and North American regulatory approaches identify numerous problems in the implementation of the EU's emission trading system (eg over-allocation of permits in 2007/08 and inadequate incentives for reducing CO2 emissions on a larger scale), as well as in sub-federal climate change regulations at state and local levels in response to past US refusals to develop a federal emissions trading scheme. Recent proposals to link regional carbon-emissions trading systems (eg in Australia, California and the EU) have not been realized yet. 'Border carbon adjustments' may be a necessary, supplementary policy instrument and legally justifiable under WTO law, notwithstanding risks of manipulating carbon taxes for protectionist purposes. Yet polycentric, market-based regulations may neither change individual behaviour nor reduce extensive carbon emissions, unless external authorities impose enforceable rules that change the incentives faced by environmental polluters based on a 'transnational rule of law' system that protects coherence between private and public, national and international levels of governance for the benefit of citizens. Climate change prevention thereby illustrates the importance of the 'systemic integration principle' (Article 31:3(c) VCLT)—as discussed in Chapter 1—for interpreting interdependent PGs regimes (like trade and environmental law) in mutually coherent ways, as explicitly recognized in the 1994 WTO 'Decision on Trade and the Environment'[53] and in the commitment of WTO law to 'sustainable development, seeking both to protect and preserve the environment and the means for doing so in a manner consistent with their respective needs and concerns at different levels of economic development' (Preamble to the WTO Agreement).

b. Multilevel Protection of Biodiversity

The protection of biodiversity in the context of the 1992 UN Convention on Biodiversity (CBD) as the principal framework for protection in a highly fragmented, multilevel biodiversity regime, offers another case study of progressive, multilevel regulation of global PGs and 'environmental commons'.[54] The CBD's focus is less on 'command-and-control regulation' than on legal, economic and other tools to incentivise the private sector contribution as a decentralized instrument for implementing a global environmental treaty and reducing related collective action problems. The CBD aims primarily at

[53] Cf *The Results of the Uruguay Round of Multilateral Trade Negotiations. The Legal Texts* (WTO, Geneva, 1995) 469 f (recognizing, *inter alia*, 'that there should not be, nor need be, any policy contradiction between upholding and safeguarding an open, non-discriminatory and equitable multilateral trading system on the one hand, and acting for the protection of the environment, and the promotion of sustainable development on the other').

[54] Cf J Penca's analysis of 'International Incentive Mechanisms for Conservation of Biodiversity and Ecosystem Services' in Petersmann (ed) (n 1) 151–83. The citations in the text are from this analysis by Penca.

protecting *national* resources by means of instruments different from those used for climate change protection; however, the 'common concern' for protecting biodiversity as a global PG is also recognized. Some market-based, regulatory instruments overlap with the Kyoto Protocol's 'flexible mechanisms' (like the Reduced Emissions from Deforestation and Forest Degradation (REDD) mechanism). They confirm the importance of involving the private sector and changing individual behaviour by incentives for sustainable biodiversity management based on duties of 'custodial sovereignty'.

Like many other multilateral environmental agreements that are only progressively specified through additional protocols, the CBD reveals regulatory deficiencies (eg its lack of effective enforcement provisions) and related distributional problems (eg regarding 'fair and equitable benefit-sharing' arising out of the utilization of genetic resources, inadequate resources of the Global Environmental Facility). As in the case of carbon emissions trading systems, the increasing use of certification of environmental products, ecosystem services (like the REDD), 'business biodiversity offsets', environment-related codes of conduct (eg the Equator Principles and other Performance Standards used by the International Finance Corporation) and of 'green development mechanisms' illustrates that there can be commercial incentives for investing in biodiversity conservation and for promoting private-sector integration in the CBD. The increasing number of bilateral initiatives that support the implementation of the 2010 Nagoya Protocol on Access and Benefit-Sharing illustrates that—as in the case of bilateral trade agreements concluded by the EU and USA with explicit references to other worldwide environmental agreements (like the 1973 UN Convention on International Trade in Endangered Species)—unilateral and bilaterally agreed initiatives for the protection of global environmental goods can offer important 'second-best instruments' and non-judicial enforcement incentives, as long as multilateral environmental framework rules do not yet include effective worldwide compliance and enforcement mechanisms. Universal recognition of 'common but differentiated responsibilities' may justify private and public, unilateral, bilateral and plurilateral leadership initiatives for protecting global PGs.[55]

iii. *How to Improve Multilevel Governance of Global Public Goods Outside the UN System: The Example of the WTO*

Member countries of the GATT and WTO continue to insist that—notwithstanding the close cooperation of the GATT and the WTO with

[55] Cf the case study by E Morgera, 'Bilateralism at the Service of Community Interests? Non-judicial Enforcement of Global Public Goods in the Context of Global Environmental Law' (2012) 23 *EJIL* 743–68.

many UN institutions—the WTO should continue to remain legally outside the 'UN system'. Many benefits of the WTO trading and legal system are open to all countries and 'non-exhaustible' (eg in terms of legal security, access to the best markets for goods and services demanded by consumers). A liberal world trading system can be perceived as a global PG that also offers potential gains from trade for those countries that do not join more limited 'club goods' like the WTO and regional FTAs (eg North Korea, importing and benefiting from the global market protected by WTO rules). The rule-making and dispute settlement functions of international trade organizations (like FTAs and the WTO) provide 'intermediate PGs', for instance by progressively clarifying the meaning of trade rules, limiting harmful 'externalities' of unilateral trade policy actions, negotiating new trade rules on the liberalization and regulation of trade, and 'providing security and predictability to the multilateral trading system' (Article 3 DSU).[56] Trade liberalization may, however, cause adjustment costs to import-competing industries inside countries, and can adversely affect non-economic PGs (eg public health endangered by trade in toxic cigarettes). Hence, trade agreements provide for 'safeguard clauses' (like GATT Articles XIX–XXI) that protect unilateral, sovereign rights to non-economic PGs, for instance by enabling importing countries to limit 'injurious imports' and to use some of the national 'gains from trade' for alleviating the costs of adjusting to import competition (eg by granting non-trade-distorting adjustment subsidies). In order to coordinate interdependent PGs regimes, Article V of the WTO Agreement requires the WTO General Council to 'make appropriate arrangements for effective cooperation with other intergovernmental organizations that have responsibilities related to those of the WTO' (paragraph 1); the General Council 'may make appropriate arrangements for consultation and cooperation with non-governmental organizations concerned with matters related to those of the WTO' (paragraph 2).

Economists and policy-makers increasingly analyse the world trading system from the perspective of PGs theories in order to better understand the functional unity of its local, national, regional and international 'composite PGs', and the need for reconciling *overlapping PGs* (such as monetary, trading and related legal systems). This conception of the WTO as an aggregate PG is justified by WTO law, for instance in view of the WTO provisions:

— recognizing the 'systemic nature' and 'basic principles' underlying WTO rules (cf the Preamble to the WTO Agreement: 'determined to preserve the basic principles … underlying this multilateral trading system');

[56] Cf PC Mavroidis, 'Free Lunches? WTO as Public Good, and the WTO's View of Public Goods' (2012) 23 *EJIL* 731–42.

— emphasizing that 'the dispute settlement system of the WTO is a central element in providing security and predictability to the multilateral trading system' (Article 3:2 DSU);
— mandating the WTO dispute settlement bodies 'to preserve the rights and obligations of Members under the covered agreements, and to clarify the existing provisions of those agreements in accordance with customary rules of interpretation of public international law' (Article 3:2 DSU);
— requiring 'each Member [to] ensure the conformity of its laws, regulations and administrative procedures with its obligations' under WTO law (Article XVI:4 WTO Agreement), and excluding 'reservations ... in respect of any provision of this Agreement' (Article XVI:5);
— prescribing legal protection of individual access to justice also in domestic legal systems inside WTO members, for instance in the field of GATT (cf Article X), the WTO Antidumping Agreement (cf Article 13), the WTO Agreement on Customs Valuation (cf Article 11), the Agreement on Pre-shipment Inspection (cf Article 4), the Agreement on Subsidies and Countervailing Measures (cf Article 23), the General Agreement on Trade in Services (cf Article VI GATS), the Agreement on Trade-Related Intellectual Property Rights (cf Articles 41–50, 59 TRIPS) and the Agreement on Government Procurement (cf Article XX);
— providing for institutionalized review of free trade and customs union agreements (eg pursuant to GATT Article XXIV and GATS Article V), other PTAs (eg pursuant to Articles II:3, III:1 and X:9 WTO Agreement) and domestic trade policies (eg pursuant to the Trade Policy Review Mechanism (TPRM) regulated in Article III:4 WTO Agreement); and
— promoting 'greater coherence in global economic policy-making' (Article III:5 WTO Agreement) and related policy areas (eg as required by the 1994 Ministerial Decision on 'Trade and Environment') in view of the interdependencies between the monetary, financial, trade, environmental and related legal systems as 'overlapping aggregate PGs'.

From this perspective of multilevel 'aggregate PGs', the importance of regional and other PTAs is increasingly seen as creating *building-blocks* (rather than *stumbling blocks*) to develop the multilevel WTO legal and dispute settlement system further. Yet due to power-orientated conceptions of reciprocal trade bargaining among governments in the WTO, the subnational, national, regional and worldwide components of the WTO trading, legal and dispute settlement systems continue to remain fragmented. Since the repeal of the British 'corn laws' in 1846, the world trading regime has continued to evolve through dialectic processes of unilateralism, bilateralism and multilateralism. The 1994 WTO Agreement was made possible only after increasing recourse to regional and 'plurilateral agreements' (like the 1979 Tokyo Round Agreements among limited numbers of GATT contracting parties); the termination of GATT 1947 by the end of 1995 and the phasing out of the international textiles agreements set additional incentives for third countries to join the 'single undertaking' underlying the WTO Agreement. The 'legal fragmentation' under GATT 1947 that resulted from thousands of bilateral 'voluntary export restraints' (VERs) was successfully limited by WTO law, notably by the phasing out of the international textiles agreements and by explicitly prohibiting VERs in the WTO Agreement on Safeguards (Article 11). Yet, similar to the inadequate surveillance of GATT Article XXIV, the WTO legal restraints on FTAs and customs union agreements are not effectively enforced, thereby illustrating the 'political limits' of worldwide trade regulation.

In order to avoid circumvention of separate trading regimes by resorting, for example, to monetary or environmental measures that 'nullify or impair' previous trade commitments in terms of GATT Article XXIII, the 'horizontal' and 'vertical' interconnections between the international trading, environmental, 'sustainable development' and related legal systems are regulated specifically in numerous WTO rules, for example in a number of:

— GATT/WTO provisions (like GATT Articles XII–XV, XVIII on balance-of-payments and other monetary restrictions on trade) coordinating GATT/WTO rules with rights and obligations of WTO members under other agreements;
— WTO cooperation agreements with UN Specialized Agencies (like the IMF, the World Bank and WIPO)[57] and related *ad hoc* legal practices (eg of WTO dispute settlement bodies inviting advice from UN Specialized Agencies like the IMF, WHO and WIPO);[58] and
— WTO Declarations on the relations of WTO law and institutions with UN institutions (eg the ILO), and with UN policies aimed at promoting 'sustainable development' and protection of the environment.

Even though UN law conceptualizes 'sustainable development' as a collective task to provide global PGs in a network of international organizations open to all UN member states, GATT and the WTO remain formally outside the UN system. Yet the above-mentioned WTO rules and practices confirm that UN law, GATT/WTO law and domestic legal systems must be construed in mutually coherent ways in conformity with the 'consistent interpretation' and 'systemic integration requirements' of national and international legal systems, as discussed in Chapter 1. Increasingly, WTO institutions cooperate with other international organizations (like the

[57] Cf Pitaraki (n 40).

[58] Cf M Foltea, *International Organizations in WTO Dispute Settlement. How Much Institutional Sensitivity?* (Cambridge, CUP, 2012).

IMF, the World Bank, WIPO, the WHO) so as to 'limit the likelihood of a clash of regimes'.[59] In addition to referring to the customary rules on treaty interpretation and related 'conflict of law' principles (eg as codified in Article 31 VCLT), numerous WTO provisions emphasize the need for good-faith implementation of WTO obligations in *domestic legal systems*. For instance, '[e]ach Member shall ensure the conformity of its laws, regulations and administrative procedures with its obligations as provided in the annexed Agreements' (Article XVI:4 WTO Agreement). Yet the periodic review of national trade policies by the WTO's TPRM focuses on *political* and *economic problems* rather than on the inadequate *legal implementation* of WTO obligations inside many national trade laws.

Domestic courts (eg in the EU and USA) often disregard—at the request of trade politicians and vested interests—the 'consistent interpretation' requirements of national, regional and WTO legal systems. Such disregard by national and regional economic courts of WTO obligations and WTO dispute settlement rulings regarding the countries concerned is hardly consistent with the comprehensive WTO legal requirements to implement WTO legal obligations in good faith and to protect legal and judicial remedies in domestic legal systems.[60] As constitutional democracies protect *national PGs* by constitutional approaches, and justify legal protection of freedom of trade among domestic citizens in terms of 'principles of justice', multilevel governance of 'aggregate PGs' should—as explained in Chapter 1—take more seriously the customary law requirement to interpret WTO rules, and protect welfare-enhancing freedoms of trade beyond state borders, in conformity with 'principles of justice' and the human rights obligations of UN member states.[61] For instance, the

[59] Cf WTO World Trade Report 2013, *Factors Shaping the Future of World Trade* (Geneva, WTO, 2013) 15. An illustration is the joint study by the WHO, WIPO and WTO on 'Promoting Access to Medical Technologies and Innovation' (Geneva, 2013), notwithstanding its explicit disclaimer that it does not purport to present any authoritative legal interpretations of WTO rules that remain the exclusive authority of the WTO Ministerial Conference and the WTO General Council (cf Art IX:2 WTO Agreement).

[60] On WTO legal guarantees of access to domestic legal and judicial remedies, see Petersmann (n 25) 194 ff. More generally on WTO obligations regarding national law, see S Bhuyian, *National Law in WTO Law. Effectiveness and Good Governance in the World Trading System* (Cambridge, CUP, 2007).

[61] The references, eg in the UN Charter and the VCLT, to 'principles of justice' could be construed in the sense of Dworkin's arguments in favour of a 'moral interpretation' of human rights and constitutional democracy, so that collective decisions should be made by political and judicial institutions 'whose structure, composition, and practices treat all members of the community, as individuals, with equal respect and concern' (R Dworkin, *Freedom's Law* (Cambridge, MA, Harvard UP, 1996) 17. As the self-interests of diplomats (as agents) are often different from those of citizens (as democratic principals), the prioritization of rights of governments over those of citizens in WTO legal and judicial practices risks undermining 'constitutional democracy'. A constitutional interpretation of WTO rules could recognize individuals as cosmopolitan members and 'democratic principals' of the WTO, necessitating more inclusive, citizen-orientated decision-making procedures and interpretations of WTO law.

duty to provide 'security and predictability to the multilateral trading system' (Article 3 DSU) should be promoted through 'consistent interpretations' of domestic trade laws in conformity with WTO obligations and 'judicial comity' in multilevel trade adjudication. This would enable holding governments accountable to adversely affected citizens for welfare-reducing abuses of trade policy powers in violation of WTO agreements approved by parliaments for the benefit of citizens. As long as trade rules continue to be distorted by power politics, the lack of fairness and legitimacy is also bound to undermine economic efficiency, transnational rule of law and democratic support by reasonable citizens.

I. Responsibility of 'Epistemic Communities' for Reconciling Competing 'Regulatory Paradigms' and 'Diffusion of Authority'

The 'systemic integration requirement' (eg as recognized in Article 31:3(c) VCLT) reflects broader 'principles of justice' and of 'public reason' that need to be promoted by epistemic communities so as to advance the mutual coherence of governance policies.[62] The thousands of specialized NGOs and hundreds of specialized intergovernmental organizations participating in multilevel governance are necessary parts of 'aggregating' and coordinating the local, national, regional and global dimensions of 'aggregate PGs' like the international monetary, trade, financial, development, environmental and related rule of law and human rights systems. They illustrate the importance of competing 'epistemic communities' representing diverse interests and expertise in the often antagonistic processes of mutually adjusting and reforming 'regulatory paradigms', such as the neo-liberal 'Washington consensus' underlying the 1944 Bretton Woods institutions, GATT and the WTO and the more person-orientated 'Geneva consensus' pursued by the UN human rights institutions, the ILO and the WHO at Geneva, as well as by other UN Specialized Agencies like the FAO and UNESCO. Most international organizations not only reflect 'member-driven governance' and 'path-dependent' representation of state interests; they also contribute to diffusing power amongst a much greater range of international and sub-national actors shaping multilevel governance of transnational relations and constraining the capacity of states to exercise power in illegitimate ways.[63] Individually, the thousands of governmental,

[62] Epistemic communities are 'networks of professionals with recognised expertise and competence in a particular domain and an authoritative claim to policy relevant knowledge within that domain or issue-area'; cf P Haas, 'Epistemic Communities and Policy Coordination' (1992) 46 *International Organizations* 3.

[63] Cf M Barnett and R Duvall, 'International Organizations and the Diffusion of Power' in Weiss and Wilkinson (eds) (n 4) 48–59.

non-governmental and inter-governmental actors exercising power across borders, setting agendas, influencing government policies, establishing rules, implementing programs and evaluating their outcomes tend to have only limited influence on 'global governance'; they often pursue diverse and antagonistic interests. This 'diffusion of authority' limits the feasibility of 'constructivist problem solving approaches' to multilevel governance of global PGs.[64] These fragmented and antagonistic dimensions in multilevel governance of interdependent PGs are limited by the coordination of UN Specialized Agencies and the WTO through the political leadership and direction of the G20 and UN initiatives like the *2030 Agenda for Sustainable Development*,[65] which promote overall consistency in international treaty interpretation and related adjudication of disputes.

For instance, even though UN membership is based on 'sovereign equality of states' without interference with their 'domestic jurisdiction' (Article 2 UN Charter), the UN and all UN Specialized Agencies continuously increase their cooperation with business partnerships and other civil society representatives inside UN member states, in order to enhance the resources, technical expertise, coordination and legitimacy of UN activities.[66] Due to improved transparency and communication systems, civil society increases its role as a critical watchdog of global governance, for instance by monitoring the implementation of the 2000 UN Global Compact designed to align business with 10 universally accepted principles and related 'corporate social responsibilities' in the areas of human rights, labour, environment and anti-corruption. The tripartite representation of governments, employers and labour in ILO bodies has made the more than 180 ILO conventions and declarations (notably the 1998 ILO Declarations on Fundamental Principles and Rights at Work) a uniquely representative standard-setting framework. Membership of the WTO goes beyond states, including sub-state customs territories (like Hong Kong, Macao, Taiwan) and supranational organizations with common markets (like the EU), thereby also promoting 'vertical coherence' in multilevel governance (by the EU and its 28 member states).

Global monetary governance coordinated by the IMF and the Bank for International Settlements, global development governance coordinated by the World Bank and regional development banks, trade governance coordinated by WTO institutions and global environmental governance coordinated by the UNEP are all dominated by specialized government experts,

[64] Cf D Held, 'Diffusion of Authority' in Weiss and Wilkinson (ed) (n 4) 60–72; and SK Sell, 'Who Governs the Globe?' in Weiss and Wilkinson (eds) (n 4) 73–85.

[65] Cf *Transforming Our World: the 2030 Agenda for Sustainable Development*, adopted by the UN Sustainable Development Summit on 25 September 2015, which builds on the *Millennium Developed Goals* adopted in 2000.

[66] Cf C Gregoratti, 'UN-Business Partnerships' in Weiss and Wilkinson (eds) (n 4) 309–21; and JA Scholte, 'Civil Society and NGOs' in Weiss and Wilkinson (eds) (n 4) 322–34.

related interest groups and 'epistemic communities'. Even though increasingly committed to common goals like 'sustainable development', they continue to prioritize functionally different, path-dependent 'regulatory paradigms' and related 'principles of justice'. For instance, as discussed in Chapter 1:

— the UN Security Council—in view of its 'primary responsibility for the maintenance of international peace and security' (Article 24 UN Charter)—provides for the veto powers of its five permanent members (the victorious powers of World War II) as a means for protecting international order on the basis of power-orientated principles of 'Westphalian justice';
— liberalization of national restrictions of trade and related payments in GATT, the IMF and the WTO is based on principles of 'economic efficiency' and 'commutative justice' (based on reciprocally agreed 'balances of commitments' under WTO law);
— the protection of health rights by the WHO, of access to food by the FAO, of labour rights by the ILO, of rights to education by UNESCO, and of other human rights by UN human rights bodies is based on 'justice as human rights' and corresponding duties of UN member states to respect, protect and fulfil human rights as PGs;
— 'constitutional justice' in the EU goes far beyond UN HRL, as reflected by the EU Charter of Fundamental Rights and corresponding constitutional mandates and limitations of the EU's legislative, executive and judicial institutions (eg limiting EU membership to constitutional democracies).

Due to the functionally limited mandates of each UN Specialized Agency and of the WTO, the 'interface problems' of 'overlapping PGs' are often inadequately clarified and regulated (eg in Article XV GATT on mutual coherence of monetary and trade measures); they require increasing cooperation among UN and WTO institutions. Cooperation and coordination between worldwide and regional organizations (eg between national, regional and WTO dispute settlement bodies) also often remain inadequate.[67] Similar to the dialectic, historical evolution of republican constitutionalism in ancient city republics, transnational coordination of competing 'regulatory paradigms' involves 'constitutional trials and errors', as illustrated by the

[67] For case studies on the lack of cooperation between Brazilian, MERCOSUR and WTO dispute settlement bodies, as well as between national courts inside EU member states, the CJEU and WTO dispute jurisprudence, see EU Petersmann, 'Administration of Justice in the WTO: Did the WTO Appellate Body Commit "Grave Injustice"?' in N Lavranos (ed), *Multilevel Judicial Governance Between Global and Regional Integrations Systems*, Working Paper MWP 2009/41 (Florence, EUI, 2009) 41–66.

spread of 'democratic conditionality' of membership in an increasing number of regional organizations beyond the EU and the EEA. Numerous UN resolutions and the 'UN Democracy Fund' now recognize democracy as one of the universal core values of UN law; yet multilateral promotion of democracy has been more effectively pursued through regional agreements, notably in the Americas and Europe. For instance, the democratic crisis in Paraguay in 2012 led to the temporary suspension of Paraguay from the South American Common Market (MERCOSUR) based on the 'democracy clauses' in the Protocols of Ushuaia (1998) and Montevideo (2011).[68] Both 'republican constitutionalism' and 'democratic constitutionalism' are progressively accepted by ever more states for their legal design of regional integration agreements. The transformation of the EC customs union into EU constitutional law, and of GATT 1947 into the global WTO legal and compulsory dispute settlement system, confirm the earlier experiences of 'merchant republics' (like Florence during the Renaissance) and nation states that liberal trade, customs unions (like the German *Zollverein* during the nineteenth century) and transnational common markets can set important incentives for the 'constitutionalization' of legal systems for the benefit of citizens, especially if compliance with free trade and common market rules is protected by national and regional courts at the request of citizens.[69]

III. HOW TO MOVE FROM THE 'WASHINGTON CONSENSUS' TO THE 'GENEVA CONSENSUS' IN MULTILEVEL GOVERNANCE OF PUBLIC GOODS? THE EXAMPLE OF THE WHO FRAMEWORK CONVENTION ON TOBACCO CONTROL

The term 'Washington consensus' is used for describing the market-orientated economic policies underlying the 1944 Bretton Woods agreements (eg as applied by the World Bank and the IMF in their lending and financial assistance policies), GATT 1947 and multilevel trade governance in the WTO. Their focus on macroeconomic disciplines (eg fiscal and budget disciplines, tax reform, liberalizing interest rates, competitive exchange

[68] Cf A Ribeiro-Hoffmann, 'At Last: Protection and Promotion of Human Rights by Mercosur' in T Börzel and V van Hüllen (eds), *Governance Transfer by Regional Organizations* (London, Palgrave Macmillan, 2015).

[69] Cf EU Petersmann, *Constitutional Functions and Constitutional Problems of International Economic Law. International and Domestic Foreign Trade Law and Policy in the United States, the European Community and Switzerland* (Fribourg, Fribourg UP, 1991); EM Hafner-Burton, *Forced to be Good: Why Trade Agreements Boost Human Rights* (Ithaca, NY, Cornell UP, 2009), who argues that economic agreements offering material benefits for compliance with human rights, changing the 'cost–benefit calculations' of human rights violators and setting incentives for 'participatory democracy', may be more important for promoting human rights and satisfying basic needs than pushing more countries to ratify UN human rights conventions.

rates), trade and investment liberalization, privatization, deregulation and protection of property rights has come under increasing criticism from the 'Geneva consensus' underlying the law of UN human rights bodies, the ILO, WHO and other UN institutions that justify multilevel governance of international PGs in terms of civil, political, economic, social and cultural human rights (ie normative individualism) rather than only in terms of state sovereignty and economically 'optimal ranking' of neo-liberal policy instruments (eg market-based tariffs and exchange rates rather than non-tariff trade barriers, separation and market-based coordination of monetary, trade and development policies).

As discussed in Chapter 1, the 'consistent interpretation' and 'integration requirements' underlying the customary rules of treaty interpretation (cf Article 31:3(c) VCLT) legally require taking into account the citizen-orientated 'principles of justice' underlying the 'Geneva consensus' in the legal interpretation of international treaties and related dispute settlement proceedings. Yet it is often only at the request of citizens resorting to national and regional courts of justice that the legal and economic principles underlying international trade and investment law are reconciled with the constitutional and cosmopolitan principles underlying the human rights obligations of all UN member states.[70] The 'collective action problems' in multilevel UN/WTO governance of transnational PGs, as identified in sections I and II above, further suggest that—from the perspective of HRL and democratic constitutionalism aimed at limiting 'collective action problems' in the governance of PGs—the citizen-orientated 'principles of justice' underlying the 'Geneva consensus' are also important for constituting, limiting, regulating and justifying multilevel governance of transnational 'aggregate PGs' more coherently by assisting citizens, civil society and democratic parliaments to hold all multilevel governance institutions legally, democratically and judicially more accountable for their governance failures. This section uses the example of the 2003 WHO Framework Convention on Tobacco Control (FCTC) to illustrate why a rights-based 'cosmopolitan constitutional approach' to multilevel regulation of tobacco control can assist in protecting and 'constitutionalizing' public health more effectively than traditional 'Westphalian paradigms' underlying GATT/WTO rules on public health protection. This case study of national and international litigation over tobacco control measures offers practical evidence of why legal and judicial empowerment of citizens through cosmopolitan rights and judicial remedies can promote the administration of justice and compensate for

[70] See the jurisprudence of European courts discussed in Petersmann (n 13) ch VIII. See also Lamy (n 30); M Herdegen, *Principles of International Economic Law* (Oxford, OUP, 2013); H Horn and PC Mavroidis (eds), *Legal and Economic Principles of World Trade Law* (Cambridge, CUP, 2013).

inadequate parliamentary and judicial control of multilevel governance; it further illustrates how national and international legal institutions (eg national and regional courts, investment tribunals, WTO dispute settlement bodies) increasingly cooperate and compete for authority inside the same territorial and economic spaces, for instance in reviewing the consistency of national tobacco control measures with international law.

A. Can Health and Economic Governance in Fragmented Legal Regimes be Reconciled with Human Rights Through Multilevel Tobacco Control Litigation?

During the twentieth century, tobacco caused the death of about 100 million people, similar to the combined death toll of World Wars I and II. Why is it that tobacco companies can enrich themselves by selling toxic products and misleading consumers, in spite of half a century of scientific evidence that tobacco products kill half of their long-term consumers (currently almost 6 million deaths per year), often at immense, individual suffering and social cost? Why has the WHO—in spite of its unprecedented powers under Article 22 of its Constitution to impose binding legal obligations without a state's express assent—'not passed a single resolution on the right to health' since the entry into force of the WHO Constitution in 1948?[71] How should reasonable human beings react to the fact that—even though health law, IEL and HRL continue to evolve separately in the context of different worldwide UN, WHO and WTO institutions—the factors responsible for poor global health are largely beyond the control of the health sector? How should economic rights and human rights (eg to health and a clean environment) be reconciled, for instance in those constitutional democracies (like Australia, Brazil and Mexico) that have banned the sale and importation of electronic cigarettes and are increasingly challenged by tobacco industries claiming reparation for damage caused by tobacco control legislation?

In contrast to many diseases whose biological agents *decrease* as living conditions improve, the global burden and threat of non-communicable diseases (NCDs, eg resulting from consuming tobacco, alcohol and unhealthy food) are at risk of *increasing* with economic growth, international trade and the spread of unhealthy lifestyles promoted by industries that produce unhealthy commodities and combat legal limitations on 'business as usual'.[72] In view of the complex regulatory challenges of health governance

[71] Cf LO Gostin, *Global Health Law* (Cambridge, MA, Harvard UP, 2014) 120.

[72] During the 19th century, cigarette smoking was uncommon and often socially unacceptable (eg several US states prohibited the sale of cigarettes).

and conflicts with powerful industries, the 2013 WHO Global Action Plan for the Prevention and Control of NCDs 2013–2020, like the preceding 2011 UN Political Declaration of the High-Level Meeting of the General Assembly on the Prevention and Control of NCDs, emphasized the need for multi-sectoral 'whole-of-government and whole-of-society efforts' at regulating the risk factors of tobacco use, unhealthy diets and abuse of alcohol across diverse sectors such as public health, trade and environmental protection.[73] The required 'governance for health' is recognized as an advocacy and public policy function that also influences governance in non-health sectors (like education, foreign policy, democratic and judicial accountability mechanisms) that can have a positive impact on health protection.

Just as UN HRL and WTO law can serve 'constitutional functions' for empowering citizens and governments to protect human rights and liberal trade against 'rent-seeking' industry pressures, the WHO FCTC is being invoked by ever more civil society groups and governments for justifying national health protection measures vis-à-vis the vested interests of the concentrated tobacco industries.[74] Also in countries that have not ratified the WHO FCTC (like the USA), a federal US district court held in 2006 that tobacco companies 'knew there was a consensus in the scientific community that smoking caused lung cancer and other diseases by at least January 1964', and that they nonetheless engaged in a campaign to 'mislead the public about the health consequences of smoking'. The same court order indicated that the tobacco industry would be required to publish several 'corrective statements' explaining the truth to the public. Yet it was only in May 2012—following six years of judicial appeals by the tobacco industry—that the district court finally specified the corrective statements the tobacco companies were required to publish, each presaged by a statement that 'A Federal Court has ruled that the Defendant tobacco companies deliberately deceived the American public ... and has ordered those companies to make this statement. Here is the truth', for instance that

> Smoking kills, on average, 1,200 Americans. Every day.
>
> Secondhand smoke kills over 3,000 Americans each year.
>
> More people die every year from smoking than from murder, AIDS, suicide, drugs, car crashes and alcohol combined.

[73] Cf UN Doc A/RES/66/2 of 22 January 2012.

[74] Over the past few decades, the tobacco industry has become increasingly dominated by six companies. Four of these are privately owned (ie Philip Morris International, British American Tobacco, Imperial Tobacco, and Indian Tobacco Company); Japan Tobacco is 50% owned by the Japanese Government; China National Tobacco Company is entirely owned by the Chinese Government.

> When you smoke, the nicotine actually changes the brain—that's why quitting is so hard.[75]

Tobacco companies and tobacco-exporting WTO members have initiated an increasing number of disputes in national, regional and worldwide jurisdictions and investor-state arbitrations challenging the legal consistency of tobacco control measures—such as Australia's 'Tobacco Plain Packaging' legislation and regulations—with international trade, investment and intellectual property law. The defendant countries and NGOs tend to justify tobacco-control measures by invoking public health provisions in IEL, domestic constitutional laws, public health legislation, human rights law and the WHO FCTC ratified by 177 UN member states and the EU. The following overview of multilevel health governance illustrates why multilevel judicial administration of justice in tobacco control disputes requires judicial cooperation in applying 'constitutional methodologies' so as to avoid incoherent judgments, for instance regarding:

- the 'balancing' of competing rights;
- proportionality of restrictions;
- reasonable judicial justifications promoting 'public reason';
- mutually 'consistent interpretations' (eg based on the 'integration principle' limiting legal 'fragmentation'); and
- 'judicial comity' (eg regarding the rule of law, respecting 'margins of appreciation', protecting 'access to justice').

i. Multilevel Health Governance in the WHO

Virtually all UN member states are members of the WHO and have recognized in the 1946 WHO Constitution 'the enjoyment of the highest attainable standard of health [as] one of the fundamental rights of every human being' (Preamble) and an objective of the WHO (Article 1), which is also 'basic to the happiness, harmonious relations and security of all peoples' (Preamble). Every UN and WHO member state has ratified one or more of the UN human rights conventions that recognize and protect the 'right of everyone to the enjoyment of the highest attainable standard of physical and mental health' (Article 12 ICESCR). Additionally, more than 160 UN member states have also ratified the 1966 ICCPR and ICESCR, thereby recognizing additional human rights (like rights to life, civil and political freedoms, access to food, housing, water, education, employment and a clean

[75] On 'adversarial legalism' and industry challenges of US health regulation limiting tobacco, alcohol and unhealthy food consumption, see SD Sugarman, 'United States' in T Voon, AD Mitchell and J Liberman (eds), *Regulating Tobacco, Alcohol and Unhealthy Foods. The Legal Issues* (Cheltenham, Elgar, 2014) 193 ff.

environment) that have proved to be social determinants of health and to promote social engagement and political accountability in health protection policies.[76] Both General Comment 14, elaborated by the UN Committee on Economic, Social and Cultural Rights, and General Comment 15, elaborated by the UN Committee on the Rights of the Child, adopted a 'holistic approach' that recognizes such related human rights as 'integral components of the right to health', thereby emphasizing the synergies (also of not explicitly mentioned rights like access to water and sanitation) with private and public health protection. This rights-based approach has contributed to the unprecedented constitutional powers of the WHO, such as the power to adopt international treaties by a two-thirds vote (Article 19), thereby requiring members to 'take action' by accepting or rejecting the agreement (eg the 2003 FCTC) within 18 months of adoption by the World Health Assembly (Article 20). The WHO can also adopt international health regulations (Article 21) that enter into force for all members unless they notify their rejection within a specified time (Article 22). The rights-based approach has facilitated successful regulation and litigation for health protection in many countries, and the proliferation of non-governmental foundations (eg the Gates Foundation supporting AIDS medication), stakeholder constituencies (like pharmaceutical industry and trade associations) and private-public partnerships cooperating in health protection activities.[77]

Political, legal and judicial health reforms inside many countries have been possible, notwithstanding the fact that the right-to-health framework remains based on standards that are often imprecise, only progressively realizable (cf Article 2 ICESCR) and judicially not always enforceable. The results of multilevel health governance differ enormously among countries, depending on their local government systems and resources; constitutional democracies (including less-developed countries like Brazil, Colombia, India and South Africa) increasingly protect enforceable health rights. With the entry into force in 2013 of the 2008 Optional Protocol to the ICESCR, individuals and groups are also empowered (in the states ratifying this Protocol) to submit complaints about rights violations to the UN Committee on Economic,

[76] Cf Arts 11 and 12 ICESCR and Art 6 ICCPR (right to life); according to the UN Human Rights Committee, the right to life 'should not be interpreted narrowly' and also requires states to 'take all possible measures to reduce infant mortality and to increase life expectancy', especially by eliminating malnutrition and epidemics (General Comment 6 of 30 April 1982, paras 1, 5). See also Art 25 UDHR, 'Everyone has the right to a standard of living adequate for the health and well-being of himself and of his family, including food, clothing, housing and medical care and necessary social services, and the right to security in the event of unemployment, sickness, disability, widowhood, old age or other lack of livelihood in circumstances beyond his control.'

[77] Cf Gostin (n 71); J Tobin, *The Right to Health in International Law* (New York, OUP, 2012); J Harrington and M Stuttaford (eds), *Global Health and Human Rights: Legal and Philosophical Perspectives* (New York, Routledge, 2010).

Social and Cultural Rights after having exhausted domestic remedies and either demonstrated harm, or shown that their complaint 'raises a serious issue of general importance' (Article 4).

ii. Worldwide Recognition of Rights to Health Protection

The moral and legal foundations for *transnational* health protection duties often remain contested (eg who owes what to whom?), for instance if health sector corruption is not adequately regulated and lower-income countries with non-democratic rulers do not provide necessary resources for protecting public health. General Comment 14 defines the right to health as including 'minimum core obligations' for health facilities, health goods and services, nutritious and safe food, basic shelter, housing, sanitation, safe and potable water, and essential drugs that are also subject to international trade and intellectual property regulations. Hence, health protection, human rights and mutually beneficial trading systems are recognized as mutually reinforcing, without any established hierarchy of the legally separate treaty regimes and organizations involved. Rights to AIDS treatment and tobacco control measures, for instance, have been subjects on the agendas of many WTO meetings and of regional organizations like the African Union, whose 2007 Conference of Ministers of Health agreed on a common African Union Health Strategy for 2007–15, with enforceable rights to health protection. The UN Special Rapporteur on the Right to Health has been charged with promoting a global dialogue; like other UN Special Rapporteurs on human rights (eg to food), he also participated in WTO meetings and discussions on reconciling trade regulation with human rights. In the context of regional human rights conventions, both the African Commission on Human and Peoples' Rights and the Inter-American Court of Human Rights have issued significant rulings on the right to health.[78] More than 130 national Constitutions protect rights to health that are increasingly invoked by civil society in national courts and litigation; this demonstrates the justiciability of health rights, despite their only progressive implementation and budgetary implications.[79] In such national litigation (eg in Brazil, Colombia, India, Peru, South Africa), the litigants and related advocacy networks also frequently invoke international health regulations by the WHO (like the 2003 FCTC), pertinent trade and intellectual property regulations by the WTO and WIPO, and UN human rights rules as relevant context or an integral part of the applicable domestic law.

[78] Cf Gostin (n 71) 260 ff.

[79] For a survey of such litigation, see *ibid*, 264 ff; and AE Yamin and S Gloppen (eds), *Litigating Health Rights: Can Courts Bring More Justice to Health?* (Cambridge, MA, Harvard UP, 2012).

iii. Worldwide Recognition of WHO Health Regulations

The WHO's International Health Regulations (IHR, 2005) constitute—with 196 member states—one of the world's most widely adopted treaties, recognizing a state's 'sovereign right to legislate and to implement legislation in pursuance of their health policies' (Article 3). Even though they recognize national rights to restrict trade for health purposes, they also require such restrictions to be based on scientific evidence and necessary for averting or reducing health risks. Hence, unlike HRL, both the WHO and WTO law recognize the need to reconcile health regulations with international trade law in ways that protect mutually beneficial trade, open markets and transparent, non-discriminatory trade regulation (cf Article 42 IHR). Hence, the 'IHR (2005) represent a landmark in global governance, with their three-pronged strategy on health security, international trade, and human rights'.[80] This is similarly true for the WHO FCTC, aimed at protecting people from death and chronic diseases as a result of smoking. The adoption of the FCTC in 2003, its ratification by more than 175 states (yet not by the USA) and the 2012 FCTC Protocol on Illicit Trade in Tobacco Products were made possible by the fact that most developed countries had adopted tobacco control measures since the 1990s. Tobacco industries could no longer deny the strong evidence and risks of tobacco becoming a worldwide pandemic.

Even though the FCTC encourages tobacco control measures, it also stipulates that such regulations must remain 'in accordance with international law' (Article 2). Hence, tobacco companies and tobacco-exporting countries have initiated national and international court proceedings challenging the consistency of tobacco control measures (like Australia's legislation on plain-packaging of cigarettes) with legal obligations under WTO law, WIPO conventions and international investment agreements.[81] As discussed in Chapter 1, the customary rules of international treaty interpretation and adjudication require mutually consistent, legal and judicial interpretations of 'overlapping' treaty obligations, with due respect for 'margins of appreciation' under HRL. The increasing national and international jurisprudence discussed below suggests that the comparatively higher 'weight' of health protection over economic rights (like the trademarks owned by tobacco companies, freedom of 'commercial speech') and the quasi-universal acceptance of the FCTC obligations (eg to reduce tobacco demand and supply, limit tobacco advertising and tobacco smoking in public places and workplaces) can justify non-discriminatory restrictions on market access rights

[80] Gostin (n 71) 202.

[81] Cf T Voon *et al* (eds), *Public Health and Plain Packaging of Cigarettes* (Cheltenham, Elgar, 2012); AD Mitchell and T Voon (eds), *The Global Tobacco Epidemic and the Law* (Cheltenham, Elgar, 2014).

for tobacco, intellectual property rights and investor rights under investment treaties.

B. Administration of Justice in National Tobacco Control Disputes?

Due to the universal recognition of rights to protection of health and of 'access to justice',[82] constitutional commitments to 'the improvement of public health' (eg in Article 47 of the Constitution of India) and to judicial independence (eg in India, the third largest consumer of tobacco) have prompted many countries to use the WHO FCTC in domestic legal systems so as to further prioritize tobacco control as a public health task. This is prescribed by the FCTC obligations to 'reduce continually and substantially the prevalence of tobacco use and exposure to tobacco smoke' by adopting and implementing 'effective legislative, executive, administrative and/or other measures'. The FCTC thereby assists political institutions to resist political lobbying from the tobacco industries by invoking the FCTC—and its grounding on the human right to health—as justification for new tobacco control measures.

i. Tobacco Litigation in India, China and the USA

Governmental tobacco control measures have been supported in India by active civil society advocacy and by 'judicial activism'. As early as 2001, the Supreme Court—acknowledging the health hazards of second-hand smoking and the constitutional rights of individuals (under Article 21) to breathe in a pollution-free environment—mandated all public places to be smoke-free and called upon the legislature to enact a comprehensive tobacco control law.[83] Following the enactment of the Cigarettes and other Tobacco Products Act in 2003, the Indian Supreme Court has often adopted a proactive role in supporting 'public interest litigation' aimed at—in the words of former Chief Justice Bhagwati—'finding turn around situations in the political economy for the disadvantaged and other vulnerable groups', so as to 'ensure that the activities of the state fulfill the obligations of the law under which they exist and function'.[84] Departing from traditional adversarial

[82] On 'access to justice' in HRL and IEL, see Francioni (n 18); EUPetersmann, 'Judicial Administration of Justice in Multilevel Commercial, Trade and Investment Adjudication?' in W Shan and J Su (eds), *China and International Investment Law. Twenty Years of ICSID Membership* (Leiden, Brill, 2014) 56–115.

[83] Cf A Yadav and D Singh, 'Tobacco Control in India' in Mitchell and Voon (eds) (n 81) 302 ff.

[84] P Bhagwati, 'Judicial Activism and Public Interest Litigation' (1985) 23 *Columbia Journal of Transnational Law* 561, 569.

court procedures, where each party produces its own evidence, with cross-examination by the other side and the judge deciding as a neutral umpire, the Supreme Court has relaxed the requirements of *locus standi*, allowing any party to initiate court actions on behalf of vulnerable groups. It further appoints independent commissioners to gather evidence in support of the complaints, and monitors the procedures. In the 2010 case of *Ankur Gutkha v Indian Asthama Care Society & others*, for instance, the Court ordered the Department of Health and Family Welfare to present findings on the health benefits of banning smokeless tobacco products. After this evidence demonstrated the health risks of these products (eg causation of oral cancer), six states banned gutka and other tobacco foods, citing the Supreme Court of India's leadership on this issue. In another 2011 case, *Miraj Products Pvt Ltd v Indian Asthama Care Society & others*, concerning the Government's lack of enforcement of a 2008 law requiring health warnings and pictures on tobacco products in conformity with the FCTC requirements, the Court requested and received from the Government evidence of the harmful effects of tobacco products on the health of consumers, and on the necessity for labelling and packaging restrictions aimed at limiting those dangers.

In China and the USA (ie the two biggest tobacco-consuming countries), the domestic legal and judicial experiences with tobacco-control measures have been very different from those in India. Following the ratification of the FCTC by China in 2005, the Convention's emphasis on taking gender inequalities seriously in the design and implementation of tobacco control policies prompted China to introduce gender-specific tobacco control measures so as to reduce the exposure of women to second-hand smoke (97 per cent of smokers in China are men). Yet in view of the absence of an independent judiciary in China, the Chinese tobacco control policies often rely on the WHO's 'naming, blaming, shaming and praising strategy' and related human rights arguments (eg based on China's ratification of the ICESCR) in prioritizing national tobacco control measures.[85]

The refusal by the US Congress to ratify the FCTC as well as UN human rights conventions protecting economic and social human rights to health (eg the ICESCR) meant that the US tradition of 'legal and judicial adversarialism'—eg in terms of a 'particular style of policymaking, policy implementation, and dispute resolution by means of lawyer-dominated litigation'[86]—in the field of US tobacco control measures evolved in more libertarian ways, reflecting 'the litigious nature of US society and the

[85] Cf LA Jacobs, 'Global Tobacco Control Law and Trade Liberalization: New Policy Spaces?' in D Drache and LA Jacobs (eds), *Linking Global Trade and Human Rights: New Policy Space in Hard Economic Times* (Cambridge, CUP, 2014) 131, 142 f.

[86] R Kagan, *Adversarial Legalism: The American Way* (Cambridge, MA, Harvard UP, 2003) 3.

propensity of the courts to be wary of interference with business interests'.[87] The complex, often overlapping allocation of local, state and federal competences for health measures, and the different lobbying powers of local health advocacy groups and concentrated industry interests, have prompted US tobacco industries to challenge many public health measures on grounds of 'legal pre-emption' (eg weak state or federal laws occupying the field, and thereby blocking stronger local or state legislation), improper legal authority (eg of executive departments like the Food and Drug Administration) and other constitutional claims (eg successfully invoking First Amendment protection of 'commercial free speech' against state restrictions limiting tobacco advertising). In the 1992 *Cipollone* case,[88] for instance, the majority in the US Supreme Court decided that claims in tort by smokers for damages based on state 'failure to adequately warn' of the health risks of cigarette smoking were pre-empted by section 5(b) of the Federal Cigarette Labelling and Advertising Act of 1965. Compared with other constitutional democracies, the 'political lobbying power' of the tobacco industries (eg in influencing US legislation and the US Chamber of Commerce) and their 'adversarial litigation strategies' aimed at preventing, or delaying, US restrictions on the supply and consumption of tobacco seem to be stronger in the US in view of the comparatively weak constitutional, legislative and judicial protection of human rights to health inside the US, and the non-ratification of related UN and WHO conventions by the US Congress.

ii. Tobacco Litigation in Australia and other Commonwealth Countries

Australia was one of the first countries to sign and ratify the WHO FCTC, and to implement comprehensive tobacco control measures (eg tax increases, social education campaigns, smoke-free policies) at national, state and local levels in spite of strong industry opposition. Its Tobacco Plain Packaging Act 2011 was also the first national legislation by any country, mandating plain packaging for tobacco products as from 2012. This legislation has been legally challenged by tobacco industries in national courts as well as in investor-state arbitration (eg based on claims of illegal takings of property rights). Tobacco-exporting countries have also challenged the Australian legislation in WTO dispute settlement proceedings (eg based on claims of 'lack of evidence' justifying the necessity for Australia's restrictions on intellectual property rights).

The legal action in the High Court of Australia had been brought by Japan Tobacco International and British American Tobacco, with Philip

[87] Sugerman (n 75) 193.

[88] *Cipollone v Ligett Group Inc*, 505 US 504 (1992). For an overview of relevant US jurisprudence, see Sugerman (n 75).

Morris Ltd and Imperial Tobacco intervening in the dispute in support of the complainants. The claim was based on the ground that the Tobacco Plain Packaging Act amounted to an acquisition of property on less than just terms in contravention of section 51(xxxi) of the Australian Constitution, and that it was therefore invalid. In its judgment of 15 August 2012, the High Court of Australia rejected the challenges to the validity of the legislation by a majority of six to one.[89] The judgment focused on the particular context of 'taking' and 'acquisition of property on just terms' under Australian constitutional law, rather than on the necessity for plain packaging in limiting the harmful effects of smoking. The judicial reasoning (eg regarding the scope and 'taking' of the affected trademarks and their 'advertising functions' under Australian law) had no impact on the ICSID investment award of December 2015, rejecting the admissibility of similar challenges by tobacco producers to the same Australian legislation. The judicial justification of government regulation of tobacco advertising, packaging and labelling implementing the WHO FCTC is in line with the jurisprudence of other national courts (eg a 2012 judgment by the South African Supreme Court), and is likely to influence the judicial practice in other countries that are following the example of Australia's plain packaging legislation.[90]

Many common law countries continue to provide for 'strong-form judicial review' only regarding restrictions on civil and political rights, where courts are empowered to declare legislative acts unconstitutional and to order injunctions against further enforcement of the statute by executive officials. Those Commonwealth countries that have also enacted economic, social, cultural or environmental rights (as, for example, contained in the Canadian Charter of Rights of 1982, the New Zealand Bill of Rights Act 1990, the UK Human Rights Act 1998) often only provide for 'weak-form judicial review' of economic and social rights due to limited judicial powers to enforce such rights against legislative restrictions, even if the latter are found to be inconsistent with constitutional norms.[91] Canada's 1985 Tobacco Products Control Act was held, in a 1995 decision of the Supreme Court, to be an unjustified infringement on freedom of expression. The new legislative restrictions on tobacco advertising were, however, upheld by the Supreme Court in a 2007 judgment that explicitly also referred to Canada's

[89] Cf *JT International SA v Commonwealth; British American Tobacco Australasia Ltd v Commonwealth* HCA 2012, 43 (5 October 2012).

[90] Cf M Rimmer, 'The High Court of Australia and the Marlboro Man: The Battle over the Plain Packaging of Tobacco Products' in Voon, Mitchell and Liberman (eds) (n 75) 337, 352. On the challenges to tobacco control measures in South African courts, see R Kitonyo-Devotsu, 'Africa' in Voon, Mitchell and Liberman (eds) (n 75) 276 ff.

[91] Cf M Tushnet, *Weak Courts, Strong Rights. Judicial Review and Social Welfare Rights in Comparative Constitutional Law* (Princeton, NJ, Princeton UP, 2008).

international obligations, under the WHO FCTC, to comprehensively ban promotion of tobacco.[92]

iii. Tobacco Litigation in Latin American Countries

With the exception of Argentina, Cuba and El Salvador, all Latin American countries had ratified the WHO FCTC by the end of 2012; with the additional exception of Bolivia, they had also adopted smoke-free and other tobacco control measures. Yet due to resistance from tobacco industries and to litigation aimed at obstructing tobacco control, the implementation of tobacco control legislation has remained weak or delayed in many Latin American countries.[93] Litigation has been used to further tobacco control, for instance through individual complaints against the state of Mexico for failing to protect individual rights to health. Following a 2011 amendment of Article 1 of Mexico's Constitution, which recognizes the principle of progressive realization of human rights and grants constitutional hierarchy to international human rights obligations ratified by Mexico, Mexico's Supreme Court explicitly identified the WHO FCTC as a human rights treaty, which could claim constitutional hierarchy justifying tobacco control measures.[94]

In a constitutional challenge to a Colombian law banning advertising, promotion of tobacco products and sponsorship of sporting events by tobacco companies, the Colombian Constitutional Court decided in 2010 that the legislative limitations on the constitutional guarantees of free enterprise and of freedom of commercial expression were justifiable on the ground of protection of health.[95] In response to a direct action brought by 5,000 Peruvian citizens challenging the constitutionality of a legislative prohibition on smoking in certain public places, the Constitutional Court of Peru decided on 19 July 2011 that the limitation of the constitutional guarantees of personal and economic freedoms was proportionate and justified by the right to health, as confirmed by the WHO FCTC.[96] Tobacco litigation in Latin America seems to confirm the constitutional justifiability of legislative tobacco control measures, and the positive impact of the WHO FCTC on

[92] For a discussion of these two Supreme Court decisions, see B von Tigerstrom, 'Canada' in Voon, Mitchell and Liberman (eds) (n 75) 212, 222 ff.

[93] For case studies of tobacco legislation and tobacco litigation in Latin American countries, see F Alonso and A Madrazo, 'Latin America' in Voon, Mitchell and Liberman (eds) (n 75) 232 ff.

[94] Cf *ibid*, at 250. On the similar jurisprudence by Peru's Constitutional Tribunal, see OA Cabrera and J Carballo, 'Tobacco control in Latin America' in Mitchell and Voon (eds) (n 81) 235, 245.

[95] On this judgment C-830/10 of 20 October 2010, see Alonso and Mardrazo (n 93) 251.

[96] Cf *ibid*, at 251.

legislative and 'judicial balancing' of competing rights and obligations. Yet the lack of administrative and judicial enforcement of tobacco control policies aimed at reducing tobacco supply and consumption through regulation of markets, products and consumer habits remains a major challenge.

iv. Tobacco Control Litigation in Europe

The EU and, to a lesser degree, the EEA remain the only regional organizations providing for multilevel constitutional, legislative, administrative and judicial protection of common economic markets, common health regulation and of comprehensive civil, political, economic and social constitutional and human rights that promote the mutual coherence of economic law, health law and HRL. In spite of the limited EU powers, the TFEU prescribes that '[a] high level of human health protection shall be ensured in the definition and implementation of all Union policies and activities' (Article 168:1 TFEU). In conformity with the EU action programs in the field of public health, the EU has ratified both the WHO FCTC and the additional FCTC Protocol to Eliminate Illicit Trade in Tobacco Products, in addition to the ratifications of these WHO conventions by individual EU member states. Yet the EU's 2001 Tobacco Products Directive, the 2003 Tobacco Advertising Directive and the 2014 Directive on the Approximation of the Laws, Regulations and Administrative Provisions of the Member States Concerning the Manufacture, Presentation and Sale of Tobacco and Related Products, were primarily justified by the functionally limited empowerment of the EU to 'adopt the measures for the approximation of the provisions laid down by law, regulation or administrative action in Member States which have as their object the establishment and functioning of the internal market' (Article 114 TFEU).

In view of the limited EU competence in public health matters, the legality of EU tobacco control measures—such as EU information disclosure requirements, marketing restrictions, product and production regulations, and fiscal regulations (like minimum rates of excise duties on cigarettes)—depends on their compliance with the EU legal principles on limited delegation of powers (eg in Articles 114 and 168 TFEU), subsidiarity, proportionality of EU measures and EU protection of fundamental rights.[97] The jurisprudence

[97] Cf A Alemanno and A Garde, 'The Emergence of an EU Lifestyle Policy: The Case of Alcohol, Tobacco and Unhealthy Diets' (2013) 50 *CML Rev* 1745–86. More recently, see also EU Directive 2014/40/EU of 3 April 2014 on the approximation of the laws, regulations and administrative provisions of the Member States concerning the manufacture, presentation and sale of tobacco and related products and repealing Directive 2001/37/EC, OJ L 127; the authorization in the 2014 Directive for stricter packaging requirements was subsequently used by Ireland (2014) and the UK (2015) for introducing 'plain packing requirements' for the marketing of tobacco products, in spite of judicial challenges of this 2014 Directive by tobacco industries in the CJEU.

of both the CJEU and the European Free Trade Area (EFTA) Court on the regular judicial challenges of tobacco control measures has confirmed the regulatory discretion of EU legislation (eg regarding the content, labelling or packaging of tobacco products) to pursue internal market and public health objectives simultaneously.[98] In a judgment of 4 May 2016 relating to the 2014 EU Directive, the CJEU confirmed that the EU acted within its powers when it adopted an EU-wide ban on menthol cigarettes, extensive standardization of packaging of cigarettes and special limitations on electronic cigarettes. In view of the significant divergences between the regulatory systems of EU member states regarding cigarette flavourings, the CJEU concluded that the prohibition of menthol cigarettes facilitated the smooth functioning of the internal market for tobacco and related products, and was at the same time appropriate for ensuring a high level of protection of human health, especially for young people. The standardization of labelling and packaging of tobacco products, the ban on promotional texts and national legislation on 'plain packaging' were intended to protect consumers against the risks associated with tobacco use without going beyond what was necessary in order to achieve the objectives pursued. The requirements that manufacturers ensure e-cigarettes do not exceed a maximum level of nicotine, report ingredients of new products to member states and report annually about sales volumes of e-cigarettes were found to be proportional and legitimate. A few weeks after this judgment by the CJEU, the High Court in London also rejected a legal challenge by the tobacco industry against the plain-packaging legislation adopted by the UK Parliament.

The EU tobacco control policies aim to go beyond the minimum standards of the WHO FCTC (cf Article 2) and include pricing and tax policies, smoking bans in public places and work places, advertising bans (eg regarding misleading descriptions like 'mild' and 'light') and consumer information. An increasing number of EU member states (like France, Hungary and Ireland) have already made public their intention to also introduce plain packaging of tobacco. As the EUCFR also guarantees 'a high level of human health protection' as a human right (cf Article 35), the CJEU and the EFTA Court have never annulled EU tobacco control measures on grounds of other fundamental rights protected by EU law (like freedoms of expression and information, freedom to conduct a business, rights to property).

[98] On this jurisprudence (such as the Tobacco Advertising judgments of the CJEU of 2000 and 2006, the advisory opinion by the EFTA Court of 2011 at the request of a Norwegian court in a dispute brought by Philip Morris), see A Alemanno and A Garde, 'European Union' in Voon, Mitchell and Liberman (eds) (n 75) 259, 264 ff. On the EU jurisprudence on the 'suitability', 'necessity' and 'proportionality *stricto sensu*' of health protection measures, which tends to engage in more intensive review of restrictive measures adopted by a member state than in the case of EU legislation, and the judicial deference vis-à-vis regulatory discretion (except in the case of 'manifest disproportionality'), see also A Alemanno and E Bonadino, 'Plain packaging of cigarettes under EU law' in Voon *et al* (eds) (n 81) 214, 224 ff, 234 f.

National constitutional guarantees inside EU member states of maximum equal freedoms (eg in Article 2:1 German Basic Law) remain subject to democratic legislation that may limit personal freedoms (including 'freedoms to smoke') and economic freedoms (eg of tobacco companies) on the ground of protection of public health.

C. Administration of Justice in WTO Tobacco Disputes?

The WHO has so far negotiated only three multilateral treaties for enhancing health-promoting norms (ie the IHR, the FCTC and a related Protocol, the Nomenclature Regulations). This reflects the preference of WHO member states for WHO 'soft instruments' (like resolutions, global strategies, codes of best practices) that are less constraining of national sovereignty over health protection regulations.[99] Apart from the fact that the WHO dispute settlement provisions (eg for access to the ICJ and the Permanent Court of Arbitration (PCA)) have hardly ever been used, tobacco companies and tobacco-exporting countries seem to prefer challenging tobacco control measures in trade and investment jurisdictions that may be less inclined to prioritize HRL and health law over economic rights and IEL.

i. The Complaints against Australia's Legislation on Plain Packaging of Tobacco Products

In 2012/13, five WTO members (Cuba, Dominican Republic, Honduras, Indonesia, Ukraine) requested consultations and, subsequently, the establishment of dispute settlement panels in order to review the WTO consistency of certain Australian measures concerning trademarks, geographical indications and other plain-packaging requirements applicable to tobacco products.[100] According to the complainants, Australia's plain-packaging measures are inconsistent with Australia's WTO obligations under the TRIPS Agreement, the Technical Barriers to Trade (TBT) Agreement and the GATT 1994, especially:

— Article 20 TRIPS Agreement, because Australia unjustifiably encumbers the use of trademarks for tobacco products in the course of trade through the imposition of special requirements (eg that trademarks relating to tobacco products be used in a special form and in a manner that is detrimental to their capability to distinguish tobacco products of one undertaking from tobacco products of other undertakings);

[99] For details see Gostin (n 71) 64 ff.
[100] Cf WTO Docs DS434, 435, 441, 458 and 467.

— Article 2.1 TRIPS Agreement read with Article 10*bis*, paras 1 and 3 of the Paris Convention for the Protection of Industrial Property (as amended by the Stockholm Act of 1967), because Australia does not provide effective protection against unfair competition;
— Article 2.1 TRIPS Agreement read with Article 6*quinquies* of the same Paris Convention, because trademarks registered in a country of origin outside Australia are not protected by Australia 'as is';
— Article 3.1 TRIPS Agreement, because Australia accords to nationals of other Members treatment less favourable than it accords to its own nationals with respect to the protection of intellectual property;
— Article 15.4 TRIPS Agreement, because the nature of the goods to which a trademark is to be applied forms an obstacle to the registration of trademarks in Australia;
— Article 16.1 TRIPS Agreement, because Australia prevents owners of registered trademarks from enjoying the rights conferred by a trademark;
— Article 22.2(b) TRIPS Agreement, because Australia does not provide effective protection against acts of unfair competition with respect to geographical indications of tobacco products in foreign countries;
— Article 24.3 TRIPS Agreement, because Australia is diminishing the level of protection afforded to foreign geographical indications as compared with the level of protection that existed in Australia prior to 1 January 1995;
— Article 2.1 TBT Agreement, because Australia imposes technical regulations that accord to imported tobacco products treatment less favourable than that accorded to like products of national origin;
— Article 2.2 TBT Agreement, because Australia imposes technical regulations that create unnecessary obstacles to trade and are more trade-restrictive than necessary to fulfil a legitimate objective taking into account the risks that non-fulfilment would create;
— Article III:4 GATT 1994, because Australia accords to imported tobacco products treatment less favourable than that accorded to like products of national origin;
— Article IX:4 GATT 1994, because Australia imposes requirements relating to the marking of imported cigar products that materially reduce their value and/or unreasonably increase their cost of production.

In view of the systemic legal issues concerning the balance between health and other interests in tobacco regulation, more than 61 WTO members (including the EU and 28 EU member states) requested to join the consultations and to intervene as third parties in the WTO panel proceedings. In April 2014, the Dispute Settlement Body (DSB) established five panels on the basis of a 'Procedural Agreement between Australia and Ukraine, Honduras, the Dominican Republic, Cuba and Indonesia', providing for each of the five panels to be composed by the WTO Director-General of the same three panellists and for the harmonization of the timetables for each of the five panel proceedings. In May 2014, the Director-General announced the composition of the panels. In view of the exceptional legal complexity and involvement of more than 65 WTO members, the Panel later announced that it did not expect to be able to conclude these five parallel panel proceedings before late in 2016. Judging from past GATT/WTO jurisprudence, there appear to be good reasons to assume that the panel will dismiss all the above-mentioned legal challenges to Australia's plain-packaging legislation:

— If Australia can prove its claim that its plain-packaging laws (eg prohibiting the use of promotional colours, graphics and logos on tobacco products, and allowing the identification of brands and variants only in a standardized font, colour and size) apply on a non-discriminatory basis to all tobacco products from all countries including Australia, there will be no violations of Article 2.1 TBT Agreement or Article III:4 GATT. This dispute seems to differ from previous tobacco control disputes in GATT and the WTO, where the USA was found to have violated Article 2.1 TBT Agreement because of its discrimination between prohibited clove cigarettes (mainly imported from Indonesia) and domestic 'like products' (menthol cigarettes mainly produced in the USA),[101] or where GATT-inconsistent import restrictions on tobacco products were found to be not 'necessary' for the protection of health (in terms of Article XX(b) GATT) in view of the lack of restrictions on domestic tobacco products.[102]
— If Australia can prove its claim that the WHO FCTC is an 'international standard' in terms of Article 2.2 TBT Agreement, the incorporation of which into Australia's plain-packaging regulations has already contributed to reducing tobacco consumption in Australia,[103] there is also a presumption that Australia's plain-packaging regulations are 'not more trade-restrictive than necessary' to fulfil a legitimate health protection objective, as permitted by Article 2.2 TBT Agreement. The WTO panel could also follow the jurisprudence of the EFTA Court by recognizing that—even if evidence-based, scientific studies on the empirical impact of specific tobacco control measures were not yet available—governments could not be prevented from exercising their

[101] Cf Appellate Body Report, *US—Measures Affecting the Production and Sale of Clove Cigarettes*, WT/DS406/AB/R (adopted 24 April 2012).

[102] Cf GATT panel report on *Thailand—Restrictions on importation of and internal taxes on cigarettes*, BISD 37S/200 (adopted on 7 November 1990).

[103] Cf L Gruszczynski, 'The WHO FCTC as an international standard under the WTO Agreement on Technical Barriers to Trade' in Mitchell and Voon (eds) (n 81) 105–25.

regulatory duty to protect public health by non-discriminatory tobacco control measures that 'by their nature' are suitable to limit, 'at least in the long run, the consumption of tobacco products'.[104]

— Plain packaging does not prevent the registration of new trademarks, nor the use of registered trademarks for preventing 'all third parties not having the owner's consent from using in the course of trade identical or similar signs for goods or services which are identical or similar to those in respect of which the trademark is registered where such use would result in a likelihood of confusion' (Article 16:1 TRIPS Agreement). As the Paris Convention and the TRIPS Agreement leave states considerable scope to refuse registration of trademarks, they seem to imply an even greater regulatory power to limit the use of trademarks if 'necessary for public health' protection as acknowledged in Article 8 of the TRIPS Agreement. If, as suggested by the WHO and by the agreed implementing guidelines for the FCTC, non-discriminatory plain-packaging legislation is 'necessary to protect public health', Australia's burden of proving the 'necessity' of its public health measures in terms of Article 8:1 of the TRIPS Agreement could be reversed by a legal presumption based on the FCTC that plain packaging does not contravene international obligations under the TRIPS Agreement or the Paris Convention in relation to the protection of trademarks.[105] If Australia's plain-packaging regulations should be found to go beyond what is necessary for public health within the meaning of Article 8 TRIPS Agreement, they could also be found to 'unjustifiably encumber' the 'use of a trademark in the course of trade' in violation of Article 20 TRIPS Agreement. Yet, according to past WTO and also EU jurisprudence, the Paris Convention and Article 16 TRIPS Agreement confer on trademark owners only a 'negative right' to prevent unauthorized third parties from using the registered trademark.[106] The EC—Trademarks Panel emphasized that

> a fundamental feature of intellectual property protection inherently grants Members freedom to pursue legitimate public policy objectives since many

[104] *Philip Morris Norway AS v Ministry of Health and Care Services* (E-16/10), EFTA 2011 (Advisory Opinion of 12 September 2011) para 84.

[105] See, however, Chang-fa Lo, 'Guidelines and protocols under the framework convention' in Mitchell and Voon (eds) (n 81) 32, 44 ('treaty-interpreters might not be able to infer from the guidelines alone that the adoption of plain packaging requirements is strictly necessary and that there is no appropriate alternative for countries to consider').

[106] Cf Appellate Body Report on *US—Section 211 Appropriations Act*, WT/DS176/AB/R, paras. 186-188 (adopted 1 February 2002); Panel Report on *EC—Protection of Trademarks and Geographical Indications. Complaint by Australia*, WT/DS290/R, para 7.246 (adopted 20 April 2005). On the WTO and CJEU jurisprudence, see also Alemanno and Bonadino (n 98) 230 ff.

measures to attain the public policy objectives lie outside the scope of intellectual property and do not require an exception under the TRIPS Agreement.[107]

Similarly, the Advocate-General, in the CJEU dispute on the validity on the Tobacco Products Directive, stated that

the essential substance of a trademark right does not consist in an entitlement as against the authorities to use a trademark unimpeded by provisions of public law. On the contrary, a trademark right is essentially a right enforceable against other individuals if they infringe the use made by the holder.[108]

It appears unlikely, therefore:

— that Article 20 TRIPS Agreement can be construed as protecting a more comprehensive 'positive right' to use a trademark that limits the sovereign right to 'adopt measures necessary to protect public health' (Article 8 TRIPS Agreement);
— that such a positive, private right could override any 'justifiable encumbrance' for public health reasons, notwithstanding the recognition in Article 7 TRIPS Agreement of the need to protect intellectual property rights 'in a manner conducive to social and economic welfare, and to a balance of rights and obligations'; and
— that the complainants can rebut the legal presumption that Australia's implementation of the WHO FCTC does not 'unjustifiably encumber' the 'use of a trademark in the course of trade'.[109]

The Paris Convention and the TRIPS Agreement recognize sovereign rights to refuse registration and limit use of trademarks on non-economic grounds. The practice and jurisprudence of the WTO recognize the protection of human life and health as 'both vital and important in the highest degree'.[110] Hence, non-discriminatory plain-packaging requirements in conformity with the WHO FCTC regulations are also unlikely to distort competition or violate any other TRIPS provisions. As stated in the 2001 Doha Declaration on the TRIPS Agreement and Public Health, the TRIPS Agreement 'can and should be interpreted and implemented in a manner supportive of WTO Members' right to protect public health'.[111]

[107] WT/DS290/R (n 106) para 7.246.

[108] Case C-491/01*The Queen v Secretary of State for Health, ex parte British American Tobacco Ltd and Imperial Tobacco Ltd* [2002] ECR I-11453, Opinion of Advocate-General Geelhoed, para 266.

[109] Cf M Davison, 'The Legitimacy of Plain Packaging under International Intellectual Property Law: Why there is no right to use a trademark under either the Paris Convention or the TRIPS Agreement' in Voon *et al* (eds) (n 81) 81–108.

[110] Cf Appellate Body Report on *EC—Asbestos*, WT/DS135/AB/R, para 172 (adopted 5 April 2001).

[111] Cf WT/MIN(01)/DEC/2 of 20 November 2001, paras 4 and 5(a). This unanimous WTO Ministerial Declaration is widely recognized as a 'subsequent agreement between the parties regarding the interpretation of the treaty or the application of its provisions' that must be taken into account in interpreting the TRIPS Agreement pursuant to Art 31:3(a) of the VCLT.

ii. 'Balancing Methods' used in WTO Tobacco Control Disputes

In *US—Clove Cigarettes*, the Appellate Body noted:

> The balance set out in the preamble of the TBT Agreement between, on the one hand, the desire to avoid creating unnecessary obstacles to international trade and, on the other hand, the recognition of Members' right to regulate, is not, in principle, different from the balance, set out in the GATT 1994, where obligations such as national treatment in Article III are qualified by the general exceptions provision of Article XX.[112]

This 'systemic interpretation' of the TBT Agreement was justified in view of the recognition of sovereign rights 'to protect public health' and 'promote the public interest in sectors of vital importance to socio-economic development' in numerous WTO provisions (like GATT Article XX, the Preamble to the TBT Agreement, Article 8 TRIPS Agreement). The dispute over Australia's tobacco regulations offers an important opportunity to further clarify to what extent the legal methodology for ensuring 'a balance of rights and obligations' (Article 7 TRIPS Agreement) and 'security and predictability in the multilateral trading system' (Article 3 DSU), in the context of the TBT and TRIPS Agreements, must follow the WTO jurisprudence on the 'necessity test' in WTO exception clauses like GATT Article XX and GATS Article XIV, by considering

> the relevant factors, particularly the importance of the interests or values at stake, the extent of the contribution to the achievement of the measure's objective, and its trade restrictiveness. If this analysis yields a preliminary conclusion that the measure is necessary, this result must be confirmed by comparing the measure with possible alternatives ... This comparison should be carried out in the light of the importance of the interests or values at stake.[113]

> It rests upon the complaining Member to identify possible alternatives ... [I]n order to qualify as an alternative, a measure ... must be not only less trade restrictive than the measure at issue, but should also 'preserve for the responding Member its right to achieve its desired level of protection with respect to the objective pursued' ... If the responding Member demonstrates that the measure proposed ... is not a genuine alternative or is not 'reasonably available', ... the measure at issue is necessary.[114]

From the perspective of the customary law requirements to interpret treaties and settle related disputes 'in conformity with principles of justice and international law', the judicial reconciliation ('balancing') of economic freedoms with public health protection should not be prejudged by:

- 'forum shopping' among competing jurisdictions; or by
- 'rules shopping' regarding specific WTO agreements, using 'objectives' (like the Preamble to the TBT Agreement, Article 7 TRIPS Agreement),

[112] Appellate Body Report, *US—Clove Cigarettes* (n 101), para 96.
[113] Appellate Body Report on *Brazil—Retreaded Tyres*, WT/DS332/AB/R, para 178 (adopted 17 December 2007).
[114] *Ibid*, para 156.

'principles' (like Article 8 TRIPS Agreement), 'basic rights' (as in Article 2 Sanitary and Phytosanitary Measures (SPS) Agreement), general treaty provisions (like Article 2 TBT Agreement) or 'exceptions' (like Article XX GATT; Article XIV GATS) for protecting sovereign rights of WTO members and corresponding constitutional rights to health protection.

Just as national courts tend to 'balance' economic and health rights on the basis of constitutional principles of non-discrimination, good faith, necessity and proportionality of governmental restrictions, regional and WTO dispute settlement jurisdictions also must interpret IEL 'in conformity with principles of justice' and 'human rights and fundamental freedoms' as accepted by all WTO members. The differences among the applicable laws in different jurisdictions may entail different procedures (eg regarding burden of proof, judicial standards of review) and legitimately different interpretations of HRL, constitutional laws, health law and IEL.[115] The WTO panel should therefore repeat and clarify in respect of the TRIPS Agreement what the Appellate Body has already indicated with regard to the TBT Agreement, ie that the legal and judicial 'balancing methods' for interpreting the specific WTO agreements should proceed from the same 'principles of justice' that underlie WTO law, as well as the human rights obligations of WTO members, ie:

1. *Relative importance of the competing policy values?* The economic and public health objectives and underlying values must be identified, compared and 'weighted' in conformity with the WTO, WHO, EU law and human rights principles recognizing sovereign rights to prioritize human health protection over WTO market access commitments and other economic rights.[116]
2. *Contribution of the contested measure?* The health protection measure restricting economic rights must 'bring about a material contribution to the achievement of its objective', rather than only a 'marginal or insignificant contribution', based on a 'genuine relationship of ends and means between the objective pursued and the measure at issue'.[117]

[115] On the need for judicial deference, see L Gruszczynski and W Wouter (eds), *Deference in International Courts and Tribunals: Standard of Review and Margin of Appreciation* (Oxford, OUP, 2014), including the contribution by EU Petersmann, 'Judicial Standards of Review and Administration of Justice in Trade and Investment Law and Adjudication', *ibid*, 19–37.

[116] On the decision by the CJEU that 'the protection of public health ... must take precedence over economic considerations', see Case C-183/95 *Affish* [1997] ECR I-4362, para 43. On methodologies for 'weighting', see F Schauer, 'Proportionality and the Question of Weight' in G Huscroft, BW Miller and G Webber (eds), *Proportionality and the Rule of Law. Rights, Justification and Reasoning* (Oxford, OUP, 2014) 173.

[117] Cf the Appellate Body Report on *Brazil—Retreaded Tyres* (n 113), paras 150–51; according to the Appellate Body, the degree of the contribution may be assessed 'either in

3. *Impact on economic rights?* As non-discriminatory product and packaging requirements are unlikely to distort international trade and competition (eg among competing trademarks), the weighing and balancing of their impact on economic rights with their contribution to reducing tobacco advertising and tobacco consumption seem to be consistent with 'a balance of rights and obligations' that is 'conducive to social and economic welfare' (as required by Article 7 TRIPS Agreement) and to avoiding 'unnecessary obstacles to international trade' (as required by GATT and the TBT Agreement).
4. *Reasonably available alternatives?* The WHO FCTC and its ratification by 177 countries confirm the view, also expressed by the WTO Appellate Body, that 'certain complex public health or environmental problems may be tackled only with a comprehensive policy comprising a multiplicity of interacting measures'.[118] As '[s]ubstituting one element of this comprehensive policy for another would weaken the policy by reducing the synergies between its components, as well as its total effect',[119] the WTO and WHO principles of preserving for each WTO and WHO member 'its right to achieve its desired level of protection with respect to the [health] objective pursued'[120] should prevail in both WTO and WHO law, as also suggested by Article 31:3 VCLT.

The 'integration' and 'consistent interpretation' requirements of the customary rules of treaty interpretation must not be rendered ineffective by the fact that—in view of the non-state WTO members—no UN treaty has the same membership as WTO agreements. From the perspective of citizens and their human rights, legitimate legal, democratic and judicial 'balancing' of economic and non-economic rules must remain justifiable by an inclusive 'reasonable equilibrium' rather than merely by 'instrumental rationality' of diplomats and economists. The criteria of reasonableness and their respective weight may differ depending on the concrete circumstances (eg in WTO disputes among members that have accepted the same UN legal obligations and relevant legal context for interpreting WTO rules and principles like 'sustainable development'). Democracies should promote consumer welfare through trade liberalization, trade regulation, protection of human rights,

quantitative or in qualitative terms' (cf paras 145–46), without being 'obliged, in setting health policy, automatically to follow what ... may constitute a majority scientific opinion' (Appellate Body Report on *EC—Asbestos* (n 110) para 178). Hence, even though the FCTC does not legally require 'plain packaging', the agreed implementing guidelines recommending governments to 'consider adopting ... plain packaging' as a tobacco control measure lend support to Australia's legal argument that its plain-packaging regulations aim at reducing tobacco advertising and consumption; cf T Voon and AD Mitchell, 'Implications of WTO law for plain packaging of tobacco products' in Voon *et al* (eds) (n 81) 109, 127.

[118] Appellate Body Report on *Brazil—Retreaded Tyres* (n 113), para 151.
[119] *Ibid*, para 172.
[120] Cf n 116 above.

and compliance with UN and WTO agreements approved by parliaments for the benefit of citizens, even without reciprocity by foreign rulers.

D. Administration of Justice in Investor-State Tobacco Disputes?

In 2010, at the request of several Philip Morris affiliates registered in Switzerland, the ICSID established an investor-state arbitral tribunal to examine whether Uruguay's tobacco-packaging measures of 2009 were consistent with Uruguay's obligations under a BIT with Switzerland.[121] Previously, the Philip Morris affiliates had challenged the regulations in Uruguay's domestic courts, but the Supreme Court upheld them as constitutional. In July 2013, the ICSID arbitral tribunal decided that it had jurisdiction to hear this case and instructed the parties to prepare substantive arguments.[122] The tribunal also decided to admit an *amicus curiae* submission from the WHO and its FCTC Secretariat in support of Uruguay's justifications of tobacco control measures. The final award was rendered on 8 July 2016; it not only rejected the claims of the complainants, but also ordered Philip Morris to pay Uruguay's fees and other costs in excess of $7 million.[123] The arbitral tribunal upheld the two specific regulations adopted by Uruguay, which (i) prohibited tobacco companies from marketing cigarettes in ways that falsely represent some cigarettes as less harmful than others; and (ii) required tobacco companies to use 80 per cent of the front and back of cigarette packs for graphic warnings of the health hazards of smoking. In addition, the tribunal also ruled that Uruguay's courts did not violate Philip Morris's rights, or deny it justice, when it challenged the regulations before those courts. More specifically:

— Uruguay's regulatory measures did not 'expropriate' Philip Morris's property. They were *bona fide* exercises of Uruguay's sovereign police power to protect public health, developed by highly trained tobacco control experts and physicians in the Ministry of Public Health with the support of experts from civil society.
— The measures did not deny Philip Morris 'fair and equitable treatment' because they were not arbitrary; instead, they were reasonable measures strongly supported by the scientific literature, and had received broad support from the global tobacco control community.
— The measures did not 'unreasonably and discriminatorily' deny Philip Morris the use and enjoyment of its trademark rights, because they

[121] *Philip Morris Brand Sarl v Uruguay* (Notice of Arbitration, ICSID Arbitral Tribunal Case No ARB/10/7, 19 February 2010).
[122] Decision on Jurisdiction of 2 July 2013, ICSID Case No ARB/10/7.
[123] Award of 8 July 2016, ICSID Case No ARB/10/7.

were enacted in the interests of legitimate policy concerns and were not motivated by an intention to deprive Philip Morris of the value of its investment.

— Uruguay's courts did not 'deny justice' to Philip Morris. Instead, the tribunal found that Philip Morris received due process and fair treatment from the Uruguayan courts.

In 2012, Philip Morris Asia (PMA) commenced arbitral proceedings pursuant to UNCITRAL arbitration rules against Australia, challenging the consistency of Australia's plain-packaging regulations with Australia's legal obligations under a BIT between Hong Kong and Australia, using the PCA as registry.[124] According to PMA, the plain-packaging regulations—by mandating every aspect of the retail packaging of tobacco products, including the appearance, size and shape of tobacco packaging, prohibiting the use of trademarks, symbols, graphic and other images, and mandating that brand names and variants must be printed in a specified font and size against a uniform drab brown background—virtually eliminate its branded business by expropriating intellectual property, transforming it from a manufacturer of branded products to a manufacturer of commoditized products, with the consequential effect of substantially diminishing the value of PMA's investments in Australia. In April 2014, the arbitral tribunal issued Procedural Order No 8, granting Australia's request to have the proceedings bifurcated between arguments on jurisdiction and arguments on the merits. According to Australia, the tribunal lacks jurisdiction on three grounds:

— First, Australia alleges that PMA's investment in Australia was not admitted in accordance with the BIT, because PMA's statutory notice pursuant to Australia's foreign investment rules contained false and misleading assertions as to the purpose of the investment. Australia alleges that PMA's true purpose—which should have been stated on the statutory notice—was to place itself in a position where it could bring this claim under the BIT.
— Secondly, Australia alleges that PMA's claim falls outside the BIT because it relates to a pre-existing dispute; or, alternatively, that it amounts to an abuse of right because PMA restructured its investments with the express purpose of bringing this claim, after the Australian Government had announced its intention to implement plain packaging.
— Thirdly, Australia alleges that PMA's assets—being only its shares in Philip Morris companies registered in Australia—are not 'investments' in Hong Kong that enjoy the protection of the BIT.

124 *Philip Morris Asia Ltd v Australia* (Procedural Order by the PCA of 31 December 2012), Case No 2012-12.

The tribunal ruled that Australia's first and second jurisdictional arguments should be bifurcated and be heard at a jurisdictional meeting in February 2015. The third jurisdictional argument should be joined with the merits. As PMA had acquired its interest in Philip Morris Australia only some 10 months after Australia's plain-packaging measures were announced, and the tobacco industries acknowledged their support for the simultaneous WTO complaints against Australia's plain-packaging measures, the parallel complaints in specialized investment and WTO jurisdictions increased widespread concerns against globally integrated tobacco companies. For by using their enormous financial resources for multilevel litigation strategies based on 'forum shopping', 'rules-shopping' and legal restructuring of multinational companies so as to use investor-state jurisdictions under the most favourable BIT, tobacco companies could delay tobacco control measures and threaten notably less-developed countries with litigation risks, related costs and 'regulatory chill'. As regards the substantive complaints, Australia has rejected each of them, notably:

- that the Australian packaging requirements amount to expropriation of the investments by PMA, which justify compensation claims in the order of 'billions' of dollars (eg by undermining the 'brand value' based on the 'Marlboro' trademark);
- that Australia failed to provide these investments with 'fair and equitable treatment' and 'unreasonably impaired' the investments; and
- that Australia failed to accord the investments 'full protection and security'.

According to Australia, all claims should be rejected on grounds of jurisdiction, but are also unfounded on the merits. Australia emphasizes the non-discriminatory nature of its plain-packaging regulations, and their justification by public health reasons and the 'police powers exception' recognized in international investment law. The above-mentioned ICSID award in favour of Uruguay, and the support expressed by both the WHO and the FCTC Secretariat for Australia's plain-packing regulations, bolster Australia's claim that plain packaging is a justifiable and proportionate limitation of investor rights for reducing the adverse health effects of tobacco products. On 17 December 2015, the website of the PCA indicated that the investment tribunal had issued a decision on jurisdiction and admissibility dismissing the investor's claim of breach of the BIT.[125] The award called the complaint an 'abuse of rights' and declined jurisdiction over the case. While the tribunal rejected Australia's first two preliminary objections to jurisdiction, it upheld the third objection by concluding that

[125] The tribunal's award was published on the PCA website only in May 2016.

> the initiation of this arbitration constitutes an abuse of rights, as the corporate restructuring by which the claimant acquired the Australian subsidiaries occurred at a time when there was a reasonable prospect that the dispute would materialise and as it was carried out for the principal, if not the sole purpose of gaining Treaty protection. Accordingly, the claims raised in this arbitration are inadmissible and the Tribunal is precluded from exercising jurisdiction over this dispute.

In view of the challenges to tobacco control measures in investor-state tribunals, Article 29.5 of the TPP, signed in February 2016, provides for a 'carve-out', allowing each of the 12 contracting states to unilaterally exempt challenges to tobacco control measures from the TPP rules on investment protection and investor-state arbitration. The increasing number of national and regional court judgments and investor-state arbitral awards on tobacco control regulations raise numerous questions, for instance on whether 'umbrella clauses' in BITs can transform WTO obligations into applicable and enforceable law in investment disputes. Even if an investment tribunal should ever conclude that tobacco restrictions amount to compensable expropriation of tobacco companies, the latter might find it difficult to enforce such an award, for instance in view of the 'execution immunity' of foreign state property serving public functions ('*jure imperii*' rather than '*jure gestionis*') and the national and regional jurisprudence protecting non-discriminatory and proportionate tobacco control regulations.

E. Conclusion: Multilevel 'Integration Law' and Judicial Comity Can Promote Multilevel Legal Coherence of Human Rights Law, Health Law and International Economic Law

According to the 'general rule of interpretation' codified in Article 31:1 VCLT, a 'treaty shall be interpreted in good faith in accordance with the ordinary meaning to be given to the terms of the treaty in their context and in the light of its object and purpose'. The customary law requirement of interpreting treaties and settling related disputes 'in conformity with the principles of justice and international law' (Preamble and Article 31 VCLT) is consistent with Dworkin's theory of 'law as integrity', explaining why a reading of the 'black letter rules' may not enable the 'best understanding' unless the interpreter also explores the 'principles' underlying the rules in order to justify why a certain interpretation 'fits best' with the objectives of the legal system concerned.[126] Yet 'member-driven governance' in UN and WTO institutions entails that governments—as legislators and administrators of UN/WTO rules—often insist on the same power-orientated and state-centered interpretations that they advocate when negotiating and administering the relevant international law rules.

[126] Cf R Dworkin, *Justice in Robes* (Cambridge, MA, Harvard UP, 2006) 22 ff.

Judicial disputes arise because the parties interpret the applicable rules in conflicting ways, and request impartial and independent judges to apply and clarify the law by 'administering justice', leading to a legally binding judgment. While the object of judicial interpretations is politics (eg trade policy rules) and ICJ/WTO judgments inevitably have political effects (eg for the 'winning' and 'losing' governments in the dispute concerned), the judicial procedures, applicable rules and methods of interpretation are legal and aim at rationalizing and depoliticizing the dispute (eg through 'due process of law' and impartial, judicial justification of the reasoning). Arguably, the legal requirement in Article 3 DSU—ie the 'dispute settlement system of the WTO ... serves to preserve the rights and obligations of Members under the covered agreements, and to clarify the existing provisions of those agreements in accordance with customary rules of interpretation of public international law'—is applied in WTO practices in conformity with Dworkin's rejection of 'judicial discretion': WTO dispute settlement bodies justify their legal findings as the most coherent interpretation of WTO rules without asserting discretionary powers. Similarly, investment arbitration also aims at the most convincing, effective interpretation and legally binding dispute settlement, even if judicial interpretations of indeterminate rules (eg on 'fair and equitable treatment' of foreign investors) may be influenced by HRL and pertinent 'margins of appreciation' of government regulators. No legal system can specifically answer all future legal questions concerning the interpretation of legal rules and principles. Also the multilevel trading and legal system cannot be based on legislation, administration and 'member-driven WTO governance' alone, without judicial rule clarification 'providing security and predictability to the multilateral trading system' (Article 3 DSU). As a global 'aggregate PG', the multilateral trading system is composed of local, national, regional and global markets and jurisdictions: WTO law regulates (sub)national, regional and global rule-making, and protects 'access to justice' at (sub)national, regional and WTO levels of trade governance as a precondition for multilevel rule of law.[127] As '[e]ach Member shall ensure the conformity of its laws, regulations and administrative procedures with its obligations as provided in the annexed Agreements' (Article XVI:4 WTO Agreement), 'consistent interpretations' and 'judicial comity' of domestic courts vis-à-vis WTO dispute settlement bodies are integral requirements of WTO law. Arguably, the selfish requests by many governments that domestic courts should not allow citizens to invoke WTO legal obligations in domestic judicial proceedings, run counter to the explicit WTO legal requirements to protect individual access to justice in domestic

[127] On WTO rules protecting individual access to judicial remedies in domestic courts, and the refusal by WTO governments to offer citizens effective legal and judicial remedies in domestic courts against arbitrary violation of GATT/WTO rules, see Petersmann (n 25) 19 ff, 233 ff.

legal systems inside WTO members too, for instance in the field of GATT (cf Article X), the WTO Antidumping Agreement (cf Article 13), the WTO Agreement on Customs Valuation (cf Article 11), the Agreement on Pre-shipment Inspection (cf Article 4), the Agreement on Subsidies and Countervailing Measures (cf Article 23), the General Agreement on Trade in Services (cf Article VI GATS), the Agreement on Trade-Related Intellectual Property Rights (cf Articles 41–50, 59 TRIPS) and the Agreement on Government Procurement (cf Article XX).

i. The Framework Convention on Tobacco Control as a Rights-Based Model of 'Integration Law' Clarifying 'Law as Integrity'

Similar legal guarantees of individual access to judicial remedies and of 'consistent interpretations' are also part of multilevel HRL, as well as of intellectual property law and investment law. Yet in many of the national and international dispute settlement proceedings over tobacco control measures, the applicable trade, investment, intellectual property and human rights provisions—such as the pertinent WTO rules in Articles III and IX GATT, Article 2 TBT Agreement, Articles 2, 3, 15, 16, 22 and 24 TRIPS Agreement—do not specifically answer whether the legal claims by tobacco companies challenging public health measures are justified. As explained by Dworkin, in 'hard cases' too—where the applicable legal rules do not specifically answer the disputed legal questions—it 'remains the judge's duty ... to discover what the rights of the parties are, not to invent new rights retrospectively'.[128] As judges have been mandated to clarify indeterminate, 'interpretive legal concepts' and to decide disputes in legally binding ways, 'in conformity with the principles of justice', including 'human rights and fundamental freedoms for all' (Preamble and Article 31 VCLT), courts of justice should not limit the relevant 'interpretative legal community' to governments without regard to civil society and citizens as 'democratic principals' and 'agents of justice'. The fact that WTO law only exceptionally protects *individual rights* to invoke and enforce WTO rules in domestic courts (eg pursuant to Article XX WTO Agreement on Government Procurement), or *individual access* to international arbitration (as provided for in Article 4 of the WTO Agreement on Pre-shipment Inspection), does not detract from the judicial obligation to interpret the 'systemic nature' of WTO law—notably of its 'dispute settlement system' (cf Article 3 DSU) and 'basic principles ... underlying this multilateral trading system' (Preamble WTO Agreement)—in conformity with the human rights obligations of UN and WTO member states. As the FCTC has been ratified by almost all WTO members, and integrates

[128] R Dworkin, *Taking Rights Seriously* (London, Duckworth, 1977) 81.

HRL, trade and investment law, intellectual property law and health law in mutually coherent ways with regard to health and tobacco regulation, the systemic integration principle of the customary rules of treaty interpretation justifies judicial interpretations of trade and investment rules in conformity with the FCTC and the WHO mandate to interpret its multilevel health regulations.

The more globalization transforms *national* into *international PGs*, the more national democratic legislation becomes substituted and pre-determined by international agreements for the collective supply of international PGs. Their democratic legitimacy and control do not depend on parliamentary approval alone. Even more important than *ex post* parliamentary approval and implementation of agreements negotiated among government executives is that HRL and constitutional democracy require international 'PGs agreements' to be interpreted as protecting equal freedoms and rights enabling citizens to hold governments legally, democratically and judicially accountable. Dworkin's conception of 'law as integrity'—which 'asks judges to assume, so far as this is possible, that the law is structured by a coherent set of principles about justice and fairness and procedural due process, and it asks them to enforce these in the fresh cases that come before them, so that each person's situation is fair and just according to the same standards'[129]—also needs to be applied to multilevel regulation of PGs for the benefit of citizens. 'Hobbesian interpretations' of multilevel UN and WTO governance are inconsistent with HRL in the twenty-first century, as rightly emphasized in the '*Kadi* jurisprudence' of the CJEU, recognizing that UN Security Council regulations and their implementation inside the EU also remain constitutionally restrained by 'inalienable' human rights.

ii. The Framework Convention on Tobacco Control as an Example of 'Constitutionalization' of International Economic Law?

The historical evolution of constitutional democracies confirms the much older 'republican experience' that collective protection of PGs—and the effectiveness of republican 'civic virtues' and agreed 'principles of justice' (eg in the 1776 US Declaration of Independence, the 1948 UDHR)—depends on the constant transformation of republican rights of citizens into constitutional, legislative, administrative and international rules, their judicial protection, and institutionalization of 'public reason' so that citizens can invoke and enforce their constitutional rights vis-à-vis multilevel governance institutions and voluntarily comply with rules they recognize as legitimate. European trade law illustrates how rights-based interpretations of trade and competition rules, and their decentralized enforcement by self-interested citizens—through national and European trade and competition authorities

[129] R Dworkin, *Law's Empire* (Cambridge, MA, Harvard UP, 1986) 225, 243.

and courts—have limited 'market failures' as well as 'governance failures' in welfare-increasing transnational markets. Similar to the decentralized enforcement of international commercial law through multilevel judicial protection of economic freedoms (like freedom of contract, property rights, mutually agreed arbitration), 'cosmopolitan interpretations' of the now more than 3,000 international investment agreements—ie as protecting individual investor rights and their decentralized enforcement through investor-state arbitration—have also improved judicial remedies and the legal accountability of governments in international law more effectively than power-orientated 'Westphalian methods' of diplomatic protection and inter-state disputes in the ICJ. The transformation of European economic and human rights treaties among states into 'constitutional instruments' protecting fundamental rights of citizens beyond state borders through multilevel legislation, administration and adjudication, illustrates that functionally limited, multilevel constitutional protection of transnational PGs is a 'realistic utopia' if citizens, democratic governments and courts of justice insist on transforming principles of justice into international rules and institutions. This section has argued that the FCTC—by transforming universally recognized health rights into mutually coherent, multilevel health, trade, investment, intellectual property and human rights regulations—contributes to 'constitutionalizing' IEL in conformity with the human rights obligations of UN and WTO member states.

If modern IEL must be construed, as argued in Chapter 1, from a democratic citizen perspective as deriving its legitimacy from protecting 'constitutional justice', rather than only from 'state sovereignty' and 'Kaldor-Hicks efficiency', then multilevel trade governance must prioritize the equal freedoms and constitutional rights of citizens and engage in judicial 'balancing' of whether governmental protection of health rights (eg to breathe air free from toxic tobacco smoke) justifies related restrictions on economic rights (like trademarks of tobacco companies). In their task of interpreting and reconciling health law, economic law and human rights in mutually coherent ways, judges must distinguish 'rules' (based on 'if-then commands' determining the outcome of the dispute) and 'principles' (characterized by a dimension of weight that must be optimized in a more-or-less fashion) as sub-categories of legal norms.[130] A rule with a limited scope of application (like the human right to protection of health) and a principle representing the same value (like protection of health as a general governmental duty) may coexist as overlapping legal norms. Alleged conflicts among rules are resolved by determining their respective scope of application (eg of trademarks as merely 'negative rights'). Collisions among principles are resolved by favouring the principle that weighs more in the dispute (eg protection of

[130] R Alexy, *A Theory of Constitutional Rights* (Oxford, OUP, 2002).

health), whilst also optimizing the competing principle to the extent that its simultaneous application is legally and factually possible (eg by limiting only certain uses of intellectual property to the extent necessary for protection of health).

iii. The Need for Clarifying the 'Constitutional Functions' of Courts of Justice

The judicial power to review (inter)national legislation reflects a constitutional conception of democracy, according to which majority decisions must also remain constitutionally restrained by the rule of law and by its judicial clarification in specific disputes. Even if judges may disagree among themselves, their judicial mandate requires them to justify their judicial interpretations and decisions in terms of the applicable law and relevant 'principles of justice'. 'Constitutional conceptions' of IEL emphasize the 'constitutional functions' of courts of justice to protect equal rights of citizens with due respect for the reality and justifiability of 'constitutional pluralism'. In its Opinion 2/13 on EU accession to the ECHR, the CJEU emphasized the need for protecting 'the autonomy of EU law in the interpretation and application of fundamental rights': 'fundamental rights, as recognized in particular in the Charter, must be interpreted and applied within the EU in accordance with the constitutional framework' of EU law.[131] Diverging interpretations of WTO legal obligations by national, regional and WTO dispute settlement bodies—like diverging interpretations of human rights obligations—call for 'judicial dialogues' rather than for arbitrary disregard of WTO obligations and WTO dispute settlement rulings at the request of trade diplomats. Diverse national jurisprudence can induce private and public litigants to struggle for the 'best legal interpretation'; it can thereby contribute to institutionalizing 'public reason' in WTO jurisprudence. Unconvincing national court decisions can be limited and corrected, for instance through 'preliminary rulings' by the CJEU inside the EU and 'advisory opinions' by the EFTA Court inside the EEA; they may prompt WTO dispute settlement findings that clarify judicial reasoning and, in cooperation with domestic courts, protect transnational rule of law in multilevel trade governance.

In contrast to the comprehensive WTO jurisprudence on reciprocal rights and obligations among WTO members, the legal duties of governments 'in providing security and predictability to the multilateral trading system'—and in protecting individual 'access to justice' for the benefit of citizens and non-governmental economic actors—have been neglected so far. They need to be clarified in cooperation with national and regional courts requested to review diplomatic claims to prioritize rights of governments over rights of

[131] Opinion 2/13 of the Court of 18 December 2014, paras 177–78.

citizens. Arguably, just as health law and the WHO FCTC give priority to the human right to health over non-discriminatory restrictions of tobacco trade and related intellectual property rights, multilevel judicial governance of international trade must respect the 'margins of appreciation' of each WTO member in limiting toxic tobacco consumption for the benefit of citizens and their human rights. Also, WTO judges should recognize that state-centered and utilitarian justifications of WTO rules derive their ultimate legitimacy from 'constitutional justice' and respect for the human rights of citizens as 'democratic principals' of all multilevel governance institutions, including the WTO. In view of the limited effectiveness of UN and WTO law in reducing unnecessary poverty and abuses of power inside so many UN and WTO member states, multilevel judicial cooperation and protection of the domestic 'conformity of laws, regulations and administrative procedures' with WTO law (cf Article XVI:4 WTO) can help citizens to protect themselves against the manifest injustices of 'tobacco trade as usual'. Multilevel judicial protection of WTO guarantees of equal freedoms, non-discriminatory conditions of competition and transnational rule of law in international trade can enhance 'public reason' and 'democratic capabilities' bottom-up, by empowering citizens to assume their 'republican responsibilities' for collective supply of international PGs like 'the optimal use of the world's resources in accordance with the objective of sustainable development' (WTO Preamble). State-centered 'Westphalian conceptions' of WTO law—by treating citizens as mere objects rather than legal subjects, and depriving citizens of effective judicial remedies—often serve the self-interests of politicians in avoiding legal and judicial accountability for illegal trade restrictions that tax domestic citizens and redistribute domestic income in favour of rent-seeking interest groups (eg European banana-trading companies that successfully lobbied for illegal EU import restrictions from 1991–2012, redistributing billions of dollars as in a banana republic). Prioritizing the human right to protection of health, and the corresponding government duties to restrict consumption of toxic tobacco products—as universally acknowledged in WHO law and its FCTC, offers a better interpretation of the WTO trade, intellectual property and health protection rules in view of its coherence with international health law and the human rights obligations of all WTO members, and the reasonable, human needs of citizens.

iv. Judicial Clarification of General Principles of Law and Cosmopolitan Rights

Similar to the judicial task of a coherent 'principled reconciliation' of trade and public health provisions in the more than 60 specific WTO Agreements (including WTO accession protocols) as discussed above, investment arbitral tribunals should likewise aim at reconciling the general principles of law underlying the more than 3,000 investment treaties with the governmental duties to protect public health not only on the basis of specific treaty commitments, but also with due regard to the progressive judicial clarification of their underlying 'principles of justice', acknowledging sovereign rights to give priority to existential public health values over utilitarian justifications of trade and investment law. While some BITs include general 'exception clauses' similar to GATT Article XX, other BITs follow the drafting technique of the TBT or TRIPS Agreements by including treaty objectives or 'general principles' that acknowledge the regulatory discretion of the host state in protecting non-economic public interests like public health.[132] Many BIT provisions are vaguely drafted without specifically clarifying whether tobacco control regulations on demand reduction, passive smoking, the contents of tobacco products, their disclosure, mandatory health warnings, the prohibition of deceptive labels and of other tobacco advertising and sales restrictions may conflict with, say, obligations of 'fair and equitable treatment', 'full protection and security', prohibitions of performance requirements, or other BIT provisions and related concession contracts. By clarifying indeterminate rules through legally binding interpretations and judicial 'gap-filling', investment arbitral awards—similar to other jurisprudence—progressively develop the law and its underlying 'general principles';[133] governments increasingly respond to investment arbitration by modifying their 'model BITs' and clarifying their 'rights to regulate' in new investment treaties. The legal requirements to interpret IEL rules in conformity with human rights and other obligations of states (eg global health law adopted by the WHO) justify judicial deference (eg towards national legal restrictions on smoking and their judicial justification by human health protection as a 'higher value' than the trademarks of cigarette producers). They thereby promote coherence of HRL, health law, IEL, and 'security and predictability' in the multilateral trading system (Article 3 DSU).

The tobacco disputes discussed above illustrate the political and democratic need to establish 'stakeholder democracy' that supports participatory, multilevel governance of international PGs. They also illustrate the need for adjusting legal and economic regulation to the different 'contexts of justice', such as the different roles of citizens as (i) *private citizens* responsible for individual self-realization and family life; (ii) *economic citizens* responsible for producing private goods and services necessary for human welfare;

[132] Cf J Chaisse, 'Exploring the Confines of International Investment and Domestic Health Protections—Is a General Exceptions Clause a Forced Perspective?' (2013) 39 *American Journal of Law and Medicine* 332–60.

[133] Cf A Stone Sweet and G della Cananea, 'Proportionality, General Principles of Law, and Investor-State Arbitration: A Response to José Alvarez' (2014) 46 *New York University Journal of International Law and Politics* 911–54. On the different cultures and legal understandings of judicial 'balancing' and 'proportionality review', see also Huscroft, Miller and Webber (eds) (n 116).

(iii) *political citizens* responsible for collective supply of national PGs; and (iv) *cosmopolitan citizens* responsible for collective supply of transnational PGs like public health protection. From the perspective of adversely affected citizens (eg in their role as 'passive smokers' and taxpayers responsible for the public health costs of smoking), there is a need for additional rights and judicial remedies protecting citizens against the existing 'asymmetries' in tobacco litigation procedures. Neither the focus of international law on states and governments, nor the one-sided IEL privileges for powerful business actors (eg direct access to investor-states arbitration) justify restrictions in judicial protection of citizens as holders of legitimate 'constituent power', who are responsible for holding multilevel governance institutions accountable for their governance failures (eg in regulating the commercial sale of toxic tobacco products). The multilevel tobacco litigation illustrates how constitutional conceptions of multilevel economic and health regulation can strengthen constitutional rights and transnational rule of law for the benefit of all citizens.

v. Need for Multilevel Judicial Protection of 'Cosmopolitan Constitutionalism'

Chapter 1 explained why the universal recognition of human rights and of corresponding 'duties' to protect global PGs requires reinterpretation of the 'rules of recognition' of international law in favour of citizens and peoples as 'agents of justice', legitimate holders of 'constituent powers' and democratic principals of multilevel governance agents. This chapter has argued that constituting, limiting, regulating and justifying multilevel governance of transnational 'aggregate PGs' requires stronger legal and judicial protection of cosmopolitan rights of citizens so as to hold multilevel governance agents more accountable vis-à-vis citizens for complying with their limited 'constituted powers'. The case study of the FCTC illustrates how multilevel recognition and protection of cosmopolitan health rights and related judicial remedies offers decentralized incentives to challenge multilevel governance failures, for instance by identifying exposures to risk factors of NCDs and preventing or limiting harmful uses of tobacco, alcohol and unhealthy diets that are offered and distributed across frontiers by TNCs. More equal 'access to justice' in order to challenge 'market failures' (like disinformation by tobacco industries concealing the addictiveness of nicotine) and related 'governance failures' helps national and international courts of justice to overcome the artificial 'fragmentation' of multilevel health, economic and human rights regulations by interpreting HRL, health and economic law in mutually coherent ways that clarify the 'constitutional principles' common to these interrelated fields of law and governance. The increasing 'horizontal cooperation' and joint reports by the WHO, WTO and WIPO acknowledge the need—in UN HRL, WHO law, WIPO law and also WTO law—to give 'priority to the right to protect public health' (Preamble FCTC) so as to interpret HRL, health law and IEL in mutually coherent ways.[134] Courts of justice can help citizens to limit and 'constitutionalize' the 'regulatory capture' of UN and WTO governance by government executives and powerful industry lobbies interested in treating citizens as mere legal objects of UN and WTO law rather than as 'democratic owners' of all governance institutions and ultimate sources of all legal values.

Just as the 'European public international law' system prior to World War II was abused by 'power politics in disguise' (eg in the context of imperial politics) that harmed citizens (eg by not preventing World Wars I and II and the inter-war economic crises), citizens must assume their democratic responsibilities to limit power politics and defend their human and constitutional rights vis-à-vis abuses of UN and WTO law and governance. As parliaments approve UN, WHO and also WTO agreements for the benefit of citizens, and legal compliance with these 'PGs regimes' has enabled governments to increase human welfare for the benefit of citizens enormously, courts of justice should protect the rights of adversely affected citizens through 'consistent interpretations' and judicial protection of transnational rule of law as defined by constitutional rules and democratic legislation. The FCTC illustrates how trade, foreign investments and intellectual property may contribute to 'market failures' (like transmission of disease and lifestyle risks, making prices of essential medicines unaffordable for the poor) and related 'governance failures' that must be limited by protecting human, constitutional and 'countervailing rights' of citizens. Hence, Article 19 of the WHO FCTC recommends taking legislative action to establish domestic systems of civil and criminal liability consistent with the obligations under the FCTC. The FCTC also acknowledges the increasing need to involve NGOs, civil society and domestic legislative, administrative and judicial institutions in multilevel governance of tobacco control in order to limit 'market failures' (eg exploited by tobacco industries) and 'governance failures' (eg in 'indirect governance through intermediaries' like regulatory agencies and 'corporate social responsibilities' of companies). As producers and traders of tobacco, alcohol and unhealthy diets tend to justify their commercial activities by invoking economic freedoms and private property rights, cosmopolitan 'countervailing rights' and judicial remedies for adversely affected consumers and other citizens to invoke—in case of

[134] On the WTO's 'coherence mandate' and cooperation with UN Specialized Agencies, see *The WTO at 20: Challenges and Achievements* (Geneva, WTO, 2015) 69 ff. As an example of the common reports by the WTO, WHO and WIPO on mutual coherence of WTO, WIPO and WHO law with human rights, see *Promoting Access to Medical Technologies and Innovation. Intersections between public health, intellectual property and trade* (Geneva, WTO/WHO/WIPO, 2012) 40 ff.

national, transnational and international disputes—their rights to health, food, consumer protection, access to justice and compensation for injuries are essential for 'rebalancing access to justice' and litigation strategies.

Article 4:7 of the WHO FCTC emphasizes that civil society participation is 'essential in achieving the objective of the Convention and its protocols'. As the democratic capability for protecting PGs depends on institutionalizing 'public reason' in order to limit 'discourse failures' (eg in intergovernmental power politics) and promote compliance with the rule of law, legal empowerment of civil society is a precondition for democratic governance and more effective protection of transnational PGs. The increasing references to human rights (eg to health protection)—notably by host states and non-governmental third parties, but occasionally also by complainants and judges on their own initiative—in international courts and investment arbitration reflect increasing judicial willingness to limit *state-centered principles of justice* (eg based on international state responsibility) by *person-centered principles of justice* in judicial balancing of public and private interests.[135] Investor-state arbitration was designed in the 1960s in order to protect foreign investors against inadequate administration of justice in less-developed countries. Even though BITs have been successful in 'exporting principles of justice' that limit governance failures in less-developed, capital-importing countries, their provisions on investor-state arbitration risk undermining constitutional and judicial guarantees in investment disputes in constitutional democracies with well-functioning judicial systems. Hence, developed countries increasingly recognize the need to review whether legal and judicial privileges of foreign investors are still justifiable in FTAs among developed countries (like Canada, the EU and the USA), or unduly circumvent domestic jurisdictions, public and transparent adjudication and appellate review.

In their 'judicial balancing' and 'weighting' of competing rights and obligations, national and international courts, investment tribunals and WTO dispute settlement bodies have to construe similar constitutional principles, like non-discrimination, fair and equitable treatment, good faith, human and constitutional rights, proportionality of governmental restrictions (eg in terms of suitability, necessity and 'proportionality *stricto sensu*' of health protection measures) and state responsibility for violations of international law. Notably in European economic, health and human rights law, and in international criminal law, cooperation among national and international jurisdictions (eg in terms of 'judicial comity', respect for national 'margins of appreciation', 'consistent interpretations') has proved to be of crucial importance for the effectiveness of multilevel legal, political and judicial

[135] Cf V Kube and EU Petersmann, 'Human Rights Law in International Investment Arbitration' in (2016) 11 *AJWH* 65–115.

governance of transnational PGs like transnational rule of law. The increasing 'horizontal cooperation' among UN (eg FAO, WHO, WIPO) and WTO institutions, and the repeated references by WTO dispute settlement panels and investment tribunals (eg in *PMA v Uruguay*) to the obligations under the WHO FCTC,[136] need to be supplemented by stronger 'vertical cooperation' among national, regional and WTO dispute settlement bodies in 'providing security and predictability to the multilateral trading system' (Article 3 DSU) in conformity with 'principles of justice' and 'human rights and fundamental freedoms for all', as required by international law. This is particularly urgent in the field of multilevel health protection against tobacco use as one of the largest causes of preventable death worldwide. Multilevel adjudication should recognize this legal and judicial task as a matter of justice, rather than only as a matter of intergovernmental UN and WTO politics and of governmental discretion that, in too many UN member states, continues to neglect human and cosmopolitan rights of citizens to hold governments accountable for their often shocking failures to protect public health and reduce unnecessary poverty for the benefit of citizens. Like HRL, global health law and IEL will also become more effective and more legitimate if all adversely affected citizens have equal 'access to justice' and to judicial remedies protecting citizens against toxic products, the global risks of NCDs and other social injustices of allegedly 'efficient economic regimes'. As the effectiveness of the rights and obligations under *international* health, economic and human rights law depends on their *domestic* implementation so as to enable 'every individual and every organ of society' to strive for universal observance of human rights (as called for in the Preamble to the 1948 UDHR), legal empowerment of citizens by cosmopolitan rights is a matter of procedural, distributive and corrective justice in multilevel governance of international PGs.

IV. HOW TO 'CONSTITUTIONALIZE' MULTILEVEL TRADE GOVERNANCE BEYOND THE EU AND EEA? FAILURES OF TRANSATLANTIC FREE TRADE AGREEMENTS

According to Article 21:1 TEU, the

> Union's action on the international scene shall be guided by the principles which have inspired its own creation, development and enlargement, and which it seeks

[136] Cf the Panel Reports on *US—Clove Cigarettes*, WT/DS406/R, adopted 24 April 2012; on *Dominican Republic—Measures Affecting the Importation and Internal Sale of Cigarettes*, WT/DS302/R, adopted 19 May 2005; and also the finding by the Appellate Body in *US—Clove Cigarettes* (n 101), 'We do not consider that [any WTO agreement should] be interpreted as preventing Members from devising and implementing public health policies generally and tobacco-control policies in particular … Moreover, we recognize the importance of Members' efforts in the World Health Organization on tobacco control' (para 235). See also the ICSID Award of 8 July 2016 in ICSID Case No ARB/10/7 discussed above (n 123).

> to advance in the wider world: democracy, the rule of law, the universality and indivisibility of human rights and fundamental freedoms, respect for human dignity, the principles of equality and solidarity, and respect for the principles of the United Nations Charter and international law.

Chapter 1 argued that the EU's 'constitutional foreign policy mandate' (eg in Articles 3:5, 21 TEU and the EUCFR) was a justified extension to EU external relations of the 'human rights constitutionalism', 'republican' and 'democratic' constitutionalism, and 'regulatory competition' mandated by UN HRL and progressively realized inside and beyond the EU:

1. *Multilevel 'human rights constitutionalism'*. Both UN law and EU law proceed from the same 'constitutional principles' of human rights, self-determination and democratic governance of peoples, state sovereignty and peaceful settlement of disputes based on transnational rule of law. The customary law requirement of interpreting treaties 'in conformity with the principles of justice' requires examination of the extent to which the person-centered 'constitutional interpretations' and judicial clarifications of EU law (eg in terms of recognizing citizens as legal subjects, protecting their fundamental rights and limiting delegation of governance powers through common constitutional principles) should also guide the EU's interpretations of UN and WTO law (cf Chapter 1, section II).
2. *Republican constitutionalism and regulatory competition*. The UN and EU legal guarantees of sovereign equality of states, popular and individual self-determination and other 'equal freedoms' (eg 'inalienable' and 'indivisible' civil, political, economic, social and cultural rights and freedoms) entail individual and collective responsibilities to protect PGs and regulatory competition. Often, UN and GATT/WTO law develop through 'fragmented reforms' (eg through regional implementation of the 1948 UDHR by the ECHR of 1950, the separate UN Law of the Sea Conventions of 1958, the UN human rights conventions of 1966 separating civil and political from economic, social and cultural human rights, the 1964 Kennedy Round and 1979 Tokyo Round Agreements of GATT contracting parties) that enabled later 'multilateralization', legal 'reintegration' (eg through the 1982 UNCLOS, the 1989 UN Convention on the Rights of the Child, the 1994 WTO Agreement) and dialectic reforms of international law (cf Chapter 1, section III). Similar 'dialectic reform methods' underlay the progressive transformation of the initially fragmented European integration agreements (eg establishing the ECSC, EEC and EURATOM) into common EU constitutional and institutional law (eg as codified in the 2007 Lisbon Treaty) that explicitly promotes 'enhanced cooperation' between limited numbers of EU member states (eg among 19 Eurozone member states in the context of the EU's monetary union).

3. *Democratic constitutionalism.* The 'human rights imperative' of recognizing citizens as 'constituent powers', 'democratic principals' and 'agents of justice' (eg entitled to individual 'access to justice' and democratic self-governance) has been implemented beyond national constitutional democracies through EU constitutional law, EU jurisprudence and EU citizenship; it needs to be extended to other regional and worldwide 'PGs treaties' in order to hold multilevel governance of PGs legally, democratically and judicially more accountable, for instance by embedding international law and its institutions into stronger democratic, republican and cosmopolitan constitutionalism (cf Chapter 1, section IV).
4. Hence, the *EU's 'cosmopolitan foreign policy constitution'* (eg in Articles 3, 21 TEU, and the EUCFR) rightly mandates the EU to extend and 'export' the successful European integration law principles in the EU's external relations with third countries, albeit with due respect for legitimate 'constitutional pluralism' and diverse democratic preferences in other countries. This made the successive EU enlargements to (now) 28 EU member states and the EU's 'neighbourhood policies' vis-à-vis the EFTA countries the most successful EU foreign policies, which succeeded in transforming centuries of intergovernmental power politics among these European countries into multilevel republican and cosmopolitan constitutionalism (cf Chapter 1, section V). If human and fundamental rights are also recognized as constituting general principles of law (cf Article 6:3 TEU) and foreign policy objectives to protect international PGs through international treaties and their domestic legal implementation and judicial protection, the EUCFR specifies and limits the foreign policy powers of the EU (eg under Article 21 TEU), yet without modifying the constitutional requirement of an appropriate legal basis for foreign policy actions of the EU (eg under Articles 206–208 TFEU) and without extending the scope of the EU's limited powers (Article 51 EUCFR).

In addition to the common 'constitutional foundations' of UN and European law (like 'human rights constitutionalism', rule of law principles, 'regulatory competition'), the Lisbon Treaty prescribes additional, more specific 'constitutional principles' for the external policies of the EU (section IV.A below). The EU's international agreements respond to the diverse constitutional and legal contexts in third countries by actively promoting transnational 'constitutional pluralism' (section IV.B), for instance through (i) extending the EU's 'multilevel constitutional democracy' to accession countries, (ii) providing for multilevel protection of cosmopolitan rights and judicial remedies in the EEA Agreement with EFTA states, and (iii) concluding more decentralized FTAs (eg with Switzerland), customs union agreements (eg with Turkey) and association agreements (eg with other neighbouring countries) if the third country is either unwilling (like Switzerland) or incapable of accepting the EU's multilevel constitutionalism (*acquis communautaire*). Section IV.C below criticizes the CETA and TTIP negotiations of the EU for disregarding the EU's 'cosmopolitan foreign policy constitution', and for unnecessarily undermining the rights and judicial remedies of citizens in transatlantic market regulations without adequate justification (eg in terms of the proportionality requirement of Article 52 EUCFR).

A. How to Evaluate the EU's Participation in Multilevel Governance of Public Goods? Republican, Democratic and Cosmopolitan Constitutionalism

As explained in Chapter 1, section V, the EU rules and principles constituting, limiting, regulating and justifying the conferral of limited EU foreign policy powers (eg in Articles 3, 21 TEU; Articles 205 et seq TFEU; the EUCFR) for multilevel protection of transnational PGs can be construed as a 'cosmopolitan foreign policy constitution' based, *inter alia*, on the following principles for the EU external relations policies:

1. *Multilevel rights constitutionalism.* The inclusion of 'human rights clauses' in more than 130 EU agreements with third countries,[137] and the multilevel judicial protection of rights of citizens (eg through the '*Kadi* jurisprudence' of the CJEU annulling EU regulations that implement UN Security Council 'smart sanctions' against alleged terrorists in violation of human rights[138]), have enhanced the legitimacy and effectiveness of EU Treaty commitments to 'protection of its citizens' and of their human and constitutional rights in the EU's external relations (cf Articles 3, 21 TEU; Articles 15–17, 47 EUCFR).
2. *Multilevel legal commitments to the 'rule of law'* (Article 2 TEU) and to effective judicial remedies at national levels of governance (cf Article 47 EUCFR), European levels of governance (cf Article 19 TEU), and beyond the EU in regional PGs treaties (eg by the ECtHR and the EFTA Court) and worldwide PGs treaties (eg by the WTO dispute settlement bodies and the UNCLOS dispute settlement bodies) aim at 'strict observance of international law' (Article 3 TEU), without delegation of EU powers to violate international treaties approved by parliaments for the benefit of EU citizens.

[137] Cf EU Petersmann, 'Integrating Human Rights into EU Trade Relations—The EU as a Global Role Model?' in T Takacs, A Ott and A Dimopoulos (eds), *Linking Trade and Non-Commercial Interests: The EU as a Global Role Model?*, CLEER Working Paper (Amsterdam, 2013/4).

[138] This jurisprudence was discussed in ch 1; for extensive analysis, see M Avbel, F Fontanelli and G Martinico (eds), *Kadi on Trial* (London, Routledge, 2014).

3. *EU Treaty commitments to parliamentary, participatory and deliberative democracy* in internal and external policy-making protect multilevel, democratic governance, as illustrated by parliamentary co-decision powers (eg of the directly elected European Parliament) and individual rights that go far beyond the more limited parliamentary and democratic powers provided for in other multilateral treaties.[139]
4. *EU membership in worldwide and regional organizations.*
5. *Incorporation into EU law of related 'PGs treaties'* (like the WTO Agreement, the UNCLOS, the UN Convention on Climate Change) illustrates new kinds of multilevel integration law and governance of transnational PGs. Treaties concluded by the EU become 'integrating parts of the Community legal system', and justify legal presumptions that precise and unconditional treaty obligations of the EU (eg under the EEA and other free trade and association agreements) can also be invoked by citizens in domestic courts as relevant legal context, thereby strengthening individual rights (eg as protected by the CJEU in EU trade relations with EFTA countries, Russia and Turkey), in spite of the increasing limitations by the CJEU and by the political EU institutions of such legal presumptions and individual rights.

Chapter 1 argued that the explicit 'foundation' (Article 2 TEU) of both internal and external EU law—and the legal definition of 'the Union's aim' (Article 3 TEU)—in terms of protection of human rights, the rule of law, democratic governance and specific PGs (like the single market, a monetary union), excludes path-dependent claims that the EU external relations law 'lacks a *telos*' and sets no specific goals limiting the EU's foreign policy discretion.[140] For instance, EU constitutional law protects fundamental rights in the external relations of the EU too (eg 'the freedom to conduct a business in accordance with Union law' pursuant to Article 16 EUCFR, property rights as protected in Article 17 EUCFR); it permits limitations 'on the exercise of the rights and freedoms recognised by this Charter ... only if they are necessary and genuinely meet objectives of general interest recognised by the Union or the need to protect the rights and freedoms of others' (Article 52 EUCFR), subject to 'an effective remedy before a tribunal' (Article 47 EUCFR). Such 'cosmopolitan and republican constitutionalism' justifies not only legal and judicial review of foreign policy restrictions on rights and freedoms of citizens, as illustrated by the *Kadi* jurisprudence. The EU commitments to liberal

[139] See the example of the European Parliament's rejection of the draft ACTA and SWIFT agreements (cf n 15 above and related text).

[140] The 'absence of a *telos*' and the 'open-ended characteristics' in EU external policies are emphasized notably by Anglo-Saxon lawyers from countries with 'parliamentary sovereignty' traditions; see M Cremona, 'A Reticent Court? Policy Objectives and the Court of Justice' in M Cremona and A Thies (eds), *The European Court of Justice and External Relations Law. Constitutional Challenges* (Oxford, Hart Publishing, 2014) 29, 31.

trade policies, monetary stability, 'sustainable development' and protection of human rights also exclude claims that 'the EU's external policy objectives are non-teleological, non-prioritised, open-ended, and concerned more with policy orientation than goal-setting'.[141] Just as the ECHR was designed as a regional implementation and progressive development of UN HRL (as illustrated by the explicit Preamble references to the UDHR), so can EU law be construed as a regional 'constitutionalization' of the human rights obligations accepted by EU member states. As the 'multilevel rights constitutionalism' and 'multilevel constitutional democracy' underlying EU law and its EUCFR go far beyond UN human rights constitutionalism, European constitutional law can serve as a model for how UN HRL may be 'constitutionalized' and implemented in multilevel governance of international PGs—with due respect for 'constitutional pluralism'. Chapter 1 mentioned numerous other examples of EU leadership towards reforming international law and governance institutions, such as EU membership in worldwide agreements and institutions (like the FAO, WTO, UNCLOS), and the leading role of the EU in adopting and implementing the 1997/2005 Kyoto Protocol, in enabling the 2015 'Paris Agreement' on climate change prevention, and in setting decentralized incentives for reducing carbon emissions through the European carbon emissions trading system and its inclusion of foreign airlines flying to and from the EU.[142] Yet Chapter 1, section IV also discussed why the EU's multilevel 'foreign policy constitution' has not prevented 'governance failures' of EU institutions, such as:

- EU non-compliance with 'strict observance of international law' (contrary to Article 3 TEU) and with the prohibition on 'disproportionate' restrictions of fundamental rights (eg through illegal and welfare-reducing market restrictions persistently violating the EU's WTO obligations and the 'freedom to conduct a business in accordance with Union law', cf Article 16 EUCFR);
- the power-orientated refusal by European courts to protect EU citizens and their 'right to an effective remedy' (Article 47 EUCFR) against arbitrary EU violations of international treaty obligations;
- the authoritarian 'disempowerment' of EU citizens by EU institutions' excluding individual rights and judicial remedies in international trade and investment agreements, contrary to the requirement of 'protection of its citizens' in EU external relations (Article 3 TEU) and of placing 'individuals at the heart of its activities' (Preamble EUCFR);

[141] Cremona (n 140). This view overlooks that human rights constitute not only individual rights and 'general principles of the Union's law' (Article 6 TEU), but also PGs (like public health protection) that must be protected in the exercise of internal and external EU powers.

[142] Cf Bartels (n 20); G Falkner and P Müller (eds), *EU Policies in a Global Perspective. Shaping or Taking International Regimes* (London, Routledge, 2014); D Kochenov and F Amtenbrink (eds), *The European Union's Shaping of the International Legal Order* (Cambridge, CUP, 2014).

— non-transparent and non-inclusive 'executive dominance' in many EU foreign policy areas, contrary to the requirement in Article 10 TEU for taking decisions 'as openly and as closely as possible to the citizen'; and
— inadequate parliamentary and democratic participation in, and control of, EU negotiations on international 'PGs treaties' (eg during the secretive CETA negotiations from 2009 to 2014, and the preceding FTA negotiations with Korea and other trading partners).[143] The fiscal, debt, economic growth and rule of law crises in some EU member states reflect not only *national* governance failures (eg to respect the agreed EU fiscal, debt and economic convergence disciplines),[144] but also EU governance failures in protecting the 'rule of law' (eg compliance with the EU's fiscal and debt disciplines, the Schengen and Dublin rules on treatment of immigrants and refugees at the EU's external borders) throughout the EU.[145]

Chapter 1 argued that—contrary to claims that economic globalization and international legal restraints on national policy autonomy are inconsistent with national democratic autonomy[146]—democratic approval of, and compliance with, international 'PGs treaties' can strengthen and enhance 'individual' and 'democratic self-government', 'constitutional democracy' and social welfare of citizens in a globally interdependent world, for instance by protecting the rule of law and other PGs across national borders and limiting harmful practices of other states.[147] As discussed in section IV.B below, the 1992 Agreement establishing the European Economic Area (EEA) between EU and EFTA member states illustrates how the EU's republican and 'constitutional foreign policy objectives' can also be promoted effectively in external relations with third countries whose peoples do not wish to accede to the EU in view of their different constitutional traditions.

[143] On this 'Lockean dilemma' of inadequate constitutional control of discretionary foreign policy powers, see P Hilpold, 'The "Politicization" of the EU's Common Commercial Policy—Approaching the "Post-Lockean" Era' in Cremona *et al* (eds) (n 15) 21–36.

[144] Cf C Bastasin, *Saving Europe. How National Politics Nearly Destroyed the Euro* (Washington, DC, Brookings Institution Press, 2012).

[145] On the need for transforming international into cosmopolitan communities based on human and democratic rights and responsibilities, see also J Habermas, *The Crisis of the European Union. A Response* (London, Polity Press, 2012) 53 ff.

[146] Cf D Rodrik, *The Globalization Paradox: Democracy and the Future of the World Economy* (New York, Norton, 2011).

[147] On the need for justifying international guarantees of freedom, non-discrimination, the rule of law and protection of other PGs in terms of their contribution to corresponding legal guarantees in *domestic constitutional systems*, and their promotion of mutual synergies in terms of transnational aggregate PGs for the benefit of citizens with due respect for legitimate 'constitutional pluralism', see Petersmann (n 69).

B. 'Cosmopolitan Constitutionalism' in Legal and Judicial EU Cooperation with the EFTA States

European integration law illustrates various successful methods for progressively reconciling the legitimate reality of 'constitutional pluralism' in international cooperation among constitutional democracies with diverse constitutional traditions, such as:

1. the *'multilevel constitutional democracy approach'* underlying the progressive extension of EU law to the more than 20 European countries that acceded to the European Community since the 1970s: the EU 'provisions on democratic principles' (Articles 9–12 TEU) indicate that the EU derives democratic legitimacy not only *indirectly* from the consent to EU law by democratically elected, national and EU governance institutions (including the directly elected European Parliament), but also *directly* from EU citizenship, from protection of the constitutional rights of EU citizens, their democratic participation and deliberation in the democratic governance of the EU;
2. the *'cosmopolitan foreign policy approach'* underlying the extension of the EU's constitutional rights and judicial remedies of citizens to the EFTA countries, which focuses on multilevel constitutional, democratic and judicial protection of cosmopolitan rights in the context of the 'two pillars system' of the EEA (see below); unlike multilevel constitutional democracy inside the EU, the more deferential EEA model focuses on representative democracy at the level of EFTA member states, deliberative democratic justification of EEA law-making (eg the incorporation of EU 'secondary law' into EEA law by the EEA institutions), and on multilevel judicial protection of common market rights, constitutional rights of citizens and 'homogeneity' between EU and EEA law through the EFTA Court and national courts in EFTA member states;
3. the *'national constitutional democracy approach'* underlying the EU's bilateral FTAs (eg with Switzerland) and customs union agreements (eg with Turkey) avoids multilevel governance institutions and protects cosmopolitan rights and judicial remedies in the context of bilateral trade agreements that can be invoked by citizens in domestic and European courts;
4. the *'majoritarian intergovernmentalism'* characteristic of the EU's 'new FTAs' since 2006, by contrast, explicitly excludes rights and effective judicial remedies of citizens in domestic and international courts, and circumvents effective parliamentary and judicial control of governmental regulations and of EU violations of international law; this approach also dominates the transatlantic FTAs with NAFTA states, and reflects the 'legal dualism' and 'hegemonic power politics' by the US Congress as well as by US governments, which often assert their constitutional

powers to ignore international treaty obligations inside the USA on the ground that majoritarian democratic self-governance—even if driven by 'parochial interest group politics' ignoring democratic demand for transnational PGs—should take priority over multilevel protection of transnational rule of law and of other international PGs. The TTIP negotiations raise doubts over how such 'constitutional nationalism' can be reconciled with the EU's multilevel constitutionalism for coherent protection of transnational 'aggregate PGs'.

The EEA Agreement, which was concluded on 2 May 1992 between the EC and its member states on the one hand and the EFTA states on the other hand, extends the free movement of goods, services, persons and capital to the EEA/EFTA states (Iceland, Liechtenstein and Norway—Switzerland did not ratify the EEA Agreement following a negative popular referendum).[148] Fair conditions of competition and non-discrimination on grounds of nationality in EEA member states are protected by EEA law and its EFTA Court. The successful operation of the EEA builds on a two-pillar system of supervision (involving the European Commission, the EFTA Surveillance Authority and national authorities) and of judicial control (involving the CJEU, the EFTA Court and national courts). As EU and EEA law constitute separate legal orders and the 'EEA law on the books' includes numerous indeterminate provisions, Article 6 EEA prescribes the following 'homogeneity obligations':

> Without prejudice to future development of case law, the provisions of this Agreement, in so far as they are identical in substance to corresponding rules of the Treaty establishing the European Economic Community and the Treaty establishing the European Coal and Steel Community and to acts adopted in application of these two Treaties, shall, in their implementation and application, be interpreted in conformity with the relevant rulings of the Court of Justice of the European Communities given prior to the date of signature of this Agreement.

Article 3:2 of the 1992 Agreement among the EFTA states on the establishment of a Surveillance Authority and the EFTA Court of Justice adds the following, additional homogeneity obligation:

> In the interpretation and application of the EEA Agreement and this Agreement, the EFTA Surveillance Authority and the EFTA Court shall pay due account to the principles laid down by the relevant rulings by the Court of Justice of the European

[148] For a survey of EEA law, see E Mendez Pinedo, *EC and EEA Law. A comparative study of the effectiveness of European law* (Groningen, Europa Law Publishing, 2009); C Baudenbacher, *The EFTA Court in Action* (Stuttgart, German Law Publishers, 2010); EFTA Court (ed), *The EEA and the EFTA Court. Decentered integration* (Oxford, Hart Publishing, 2014); C Baudenbacher (ed), *The Handbook of EEA Law* (Heidelberg, Springer, 2015).

> Communities given after the date of signature of the EEA Agreement and which concern the interpretation of that Agreement or of such rules of the Treaty establishing (the EEC and the ECSC) ... in so far as they are identical in substance to the provisions of the EEA Agreement ...

i. Judicial Deference and 'Contrapunctual Integration Law' in the EEA

In view of the different (eg more 'dualist') constitutional traditions of EFTA states and their limited influence on EU legislation that becomes binding on the EFTA states through EEA law (eg due to incorporation of EU rules into EEA law by the EEA Joint Committee) and its judicial clarification by the EFTA Court, the EEA objectives of legislative, judicial and institutional homogeneity—and the legal relationships between EEA law and the national legal systems in EFTA countries—were interpreted and developed by the EEA member states and the EFTA Court in more deferential and 'pluralist' ways compared to the EU constitutional principles of 'legal primacy', 'direct effect' and 'direct applicability' by individuals of precise and unconditional EU rules. The EFTA Court characterized EEA law as a 'distinct legal order'; some legal scholars advocated interpreting EEA law in conformity with the EU principles of legal primacy and direct effect, so as to realize the 'legal homogeneity' obligations and protect rights of private market actors. Yet the main legal doctrines elaborated by the EFTA Court in close legal and judicial dialogue with EEA member governments, national courts and EU institutions acknowledged lack of supranational primacy and direct effect of EEA law. All EEA governments recognized the more deferential 'judge-made principles' of 'quasi-primacy' and 'indirect effect' of implemented EEA rules inside national legal systems, consistent interpretation requirements, state liability and principles of loyalty, as they were progressively developed in the jurisprudence of the EFTA Court and its 'judicial dialogues' with national courts and governments in EEA member states. As a result of these 'multilevel constitutional dialogues' over a period of more than 20 years of EEA legal practices, conflicts between EU law and EEA law were successfully avoided.[149] The dynamically emerging 'cosmopolitan constitutionalism' in the multilevel governance among the 31 EEA member states also revealed how 'the classical dualist paradigm appears to be increasingly inadequate—descriptively as well as normatively—to explain

[149] But such conflicts remain possible in the very rare cases where a national act of parliament asserts legal primacy vis-à-vis international obligations based on the constitutional doctrine of *lex posterior legi priori derogat*; cf OI Hannesson, *Giving Effect to EEA Law—Examining and Rethinking the Role and Relationship between the EFTA Court and the Icelandic National Courts in the EEA Legal Order* (Florence, EUI doctoral thesis, 2012) ch 6.

how the EEA Agreement, an international treaty *sui generis* comprising its own specific legal order, fits into domestic practice'.[150] Even though national governments and courts initially advocated 'nationalist approaches' to interpreting EEA law, the EEA's institutionalization of multilevel legal and judicial dialogues among national, EEA and EU institutions regarding the interpretation and progressive development of EEA law increasingly emphasized the need for protecting rights and judicial remedies of EEA citizens with due respect for 'constitutional pluralism' and 'counterpoint legal techniques', as explained by EU Advocate-General Maduro:

> The discovery that different melodies could be heard at the same time in a harmonious way was one of the greatest developments in musical history and greatly enhanced the art and pleasure of music. In law too, we have to learn how to manage the non-hierarchical relationship between different legal orders and institutions and to discover how to gain from the diversity and choices that are offered to us without generating conflicts that ultimately will destroy those legal orders and the values they sustain.[151]

Similarly, as explained in Chapter 1, the 'consistent interpretation' requirements of customary international law require interpreting 'overlapping PGs treaties' in mutually consistent ways, with due respect for their diverse 'principles of justice' and legitimately diverse constitutional traditions. In multilevel judicial cooperation and interpretation of multilevel regulation of transnational 'aggregate PGs', national and international judges must cooperate like musicians discovering the most harmonious ways of performing orchestral music, especially if there is not one single conductor of the orchestra. As emphasized in Chapter 1, the common human rights obligations of constitutional democracies require multilevel legal and judicial protection and clarification of rights and remedies of citizens by 'balancing'—in the context of 'contrapuntal legal interpretations'—the rights and other constitutional principles of the legal systems involved, with due respect for legitimate 'constitutional pluralism', ie that no single legal system can legitimately impose its own constitutional traditions and prescribe a 'single voice' for the law in disregard of the many dissonances among diverse jurisdictions, peoples and citizens in multilevel governance of transnational aggregate PGs.[152]

[150] OI Hannesson, 'Legal Pluralism in the EEA Legal Order: The EFTA Court's Role in a Broader Institutional Context' in Cremona *et al* (eds) (n 15) 81–95, 81.

[151] MP Maduro, 'Contrapunctual Law: Europe's Constitutional Pluralism in Action' in N Walker (ed), *Sovereignty in Transition* (Oxford, Hart Publishing, 2003) 501–37, 524 f.

[152] Cf Hannesson (n 150); see also N Lavranos, 'The Systemic Responsibility of the ECJ for Judicial Comity towards International Courts and Tribunals' in Cremona *et al* (eds) (n 15) 51–64.

C. 'Transformative' Transatlantic Free Trade Agreements without Rights and Remedies of Citizens?

In 2006, the lack of progress in the Doha Round negotiations prompted the EU to launch a new 'Global Europe' trade and investment strategy aimed at concluding 'deep and comprehensive' FTAs with economically and strategically important partner countries in Asia (eg Korea, Singapore and Vietnam) and in the Americas. The CETA and TTIP negotiations were launched on the promise to elaborate 'transformative FTAs' that—similar to other mega-regional FTAs, like the 'Trans-Pacific Partnership' (TPP) agreement signed in February 2016 among 12 Pacific trading countries producing more than 40 per cent of global GDP[153]—would liberalize and regulate trade in goods and services far beyond WTO rules, thereby assuming 'geo-political importance' by setting new standards for multilateral trade, investment, environmental, labour and consumer protection regulation. The TTIP focuses on the following four objectives that are discussed and progressively clarified in 24 joint EU–US working groups on the TTIP, which aim at finalizing a draft agreement before the end of 2016:[154]

1. Ambitious, reciprocal liberalization of market access for goods, services, investments and public procurement at all levels of government. Market access for goods and services aims at removing customs duties on goods and restrictions on services, gaining better access to public markets and making it easier to invest. The exclusion of audio-visual services, of general free movement of workers and of other citizens illustrates that the TTIP remains less ambitious than the EEA Agreement.
2. Reducing non-tariff trade barriers and enhancing the compatibility of regulatory regimes through a permanent system of regulatory cooperation. Improved regulatory coherence and cooperation in dismantling unnecessary regulatory barriers (eg due to bureaucratic duplication of procedures) will go beyond the WTO TBT and SPS Agreements, for instance by means of specific sectorial agreements for textiles, chemicals, pharmaceuticals, cosmetics, medical devices, cars, electronics/information and communications technology, machinery/engineering and pesticides.

153 They include Australia, Brunei Darussalam, Canada, Chile, Japan, Malaysia, Mexico, New Zealand, Peru, Singapore, USA and Vietnam.

154 All the following details on the TTIP negotiations are based on information available on the website of the European Commission, Directorate-General for Trade, at <http://trade.ec.europa.eu/doclib/press>. On the normative conflicts underlying TTIP negotiations and their impact on non-trade issues, see F De Ville and G Siles-Brügge, *TTIP—The Truth about the Transatlantic Trade and Investment Partnership* (Cambridge, Polity Press, 2016).

3. Developing common rules (eg for consumer, labour, investment, social and environmental protection, civil society involvement, parliamentary cooperation) to address shared, global trade challenges. The improved international cooperation in setting international standards (eg for energy and raw materials, labour and environment, trade and sustainable development, public procurement, intellectual property, competition policy, small and medium-sized enterprise, trade remedies, customs and trade facilitation) aims at making TTIP countries global 'standard-setters' rather than 'standard-takers'.
4. Institutional structures for progressively implementing the TTIP. While the proposed dispute settlement and ISDS provisions remain less ambitious than in the EEA Agreement (eg its EFTA Court), the TTIP Regulatory Council could introduce innovative procedures for harmonisation, mutual recognition agreements and common minimum (equivalence) standards aimed at making the TTIP a 'standard-setter' also for third countries exporting to TTIP countries and complying with TTIP standards.

Evaluations of the CETA and the TTIP depend on their respective legal, economic and political methodologies for multilevel governance of PGs like a transatlantic market that could—in future—include all three NAFTA states, the 31 EEA member states and additional states (like Switzerland, Turkey and the UK following its 'Brexit'). From utilitarian economic perspectives, transatlantic FTAs offer important economic welfare gains, for instance in terms of reducing the costs of production, trade and consumption, and enhancing productivity and competitiveness of European industries and consumer welfare. They also offer geopolitical gains, eg in terms of:

— promoting energy security in Europe;
— setting global standards for regulation of the 'interface' between economic and non-economic PGs (like health protection, climate change prevention); and
— preparing future reforms of WTO law, for instance by 'multilateralizing' mega-regional FTAs, which could ultimately replace the ineffective WTO system for consensus-based, global trade liberalization with a more ambitious 'WTO II legal system' (similar to the replacement of GATT 1947 with the WTO Agreement).

Yet economic integration gains, their social distribution and the democratic acceptability of legal reforms will depend largely on persuading and empowering citizens to cooperate in multilevel protection of transnational rule of law, so that citizens can challenge, for instance, the long-standing market failures and governance failures in transatlantic relations that have given rise to numerous transatlantic economic disputes over the past decades.[155] From the point of view of the EU's 'cosmopolitan foreign policy constitution' (as discussed in section IV.A above) and of the successful 'cosmopolitan constitutionalism' in the EU's external relations with EFTA states (cf section IV.B above), the democratic and 'republican governance problems' in the EU's transatlantic relations with NAFTA countries risk undermining the constitutional rights of EU citizens. This is illustrated by:

— the intergovernmental exclusion of rights and effective judicial remedies of citizens (eg in Article 30.6 CETA);
— the lack of transparency and parliamentary control of the EU's negotiations of the CETA and of previous FTAs (see below section IV.D);
— the provision of legal and judicial privileges to foreign investors and related 'negative discrimination' against EU citizens in transatlantic economic cooperation (see below section IV.E); and
— the intergovernmental neglect of the EU guarantees of the rule of law (see below section IV.F), as illustrated by the neglect of the EUCFR and by the US criticism that EU proposals for authorizing EU member states to restrict genetically modified organisms (GMOs), without scientific evidence of their potential health risks, run counter to WTO law and to the need to promote global food security, scientific progress and 'public reason' in conformity with transatlantic rule of law.

The very limited participation of national parliaments, the European Parliament and of European civil society in the CETA negotiations revealed not only inadequate 'democratic input legitimacy' in transatlantic rule-making dominated by government executives; the intergovernmental exclusion of equal rights and remedies of EU citizens (eg in Article 30.6 CETA) also illustrates inadequate 'democratic output legitimacy' and inadequate protection of transatlantic PGs (like the rule of law). The systemic 'governance failures' in the 'Transatlantic Partnership' since the 1990s had triggered numerous transatlantic economic and legal disputes over EU import restrictions on bananas, safeguard measures, antidumping and countervailing duties, industrial subsidies (eg for US 'foreign sales corporations'), European agricultural subsidies, EU import restrictions on hormone-fed beef and GMOs, technical barriers to trade (eg on 'hushkits' for US airplanes), extraterritorial application of competition laws, US interferences with transatlantic data protection, discriminatory US practices in fields like government procurement and intellectual property rights, and inadequate regulatory cooperation in environmental policies, telecommunications, shipping and air transport.[156]

[155] Cf EU Petersmann and M Pollack (eds), *Transatlantic Economic Disputes. The EU, the US and the WTO* (Oxford, OUP, 2003).

[156] Cf the numerous case studies and cross-sectoral studies, *ibid*.

Many of these disputes confirmed Kagan's claim that—with regard to international law and policy cooperation—'Americans are from Mars and Europeans are from Venus'.[157] For instance, the 'constitutional nationalism' and hegemonic power politics cultivated by US politicians favour 'legal dualism' and US scepticism towards international law (eg prompting the US Congress to exclude rights of citizens to invoke and enforce international treaty obligations of the US in US courts). European integration is built on using international law in multilevel governance of international PGs. American and European approaches to international economic governance often differ, as illustrated by the comparatively lesser participation of US regulatory agencies in international standard-setting organizations, and US reluctance to ratify international human rights treaties, labour law, criminal law and environmental conventions. The stronger US preferences for science-based risk assessment procedures (as internationally agreed in the WTO SPS Agreement) are linked to the comparatively stronger parliamentary control of US regulatory agencies and their avoidance of some of the health and phytosanitary crises (like mad cow diseases) that undermined consumer confidence in Europe regarding science-based risk assessments of product and production standards.[158]

i. Constitutional Nationalism and its Limits in the EU's Free Trade Agreements

All EU member states are committed to human rights, the rule of law and democracy as 'values ... common to the Member States in a society in which pluralism, non-discrimination, tolerance, justice, solidarity and equality between women and men prevail' (Article 2 TEU); yet their national constitutional systems differ enormously. The 'homogeneity obligations' of EFTA states vis-à-vis the EU legal order entail an asymmetric legal structure of EEA law and unilateral rights of the EU to restrict access to the EU's single market if EFTA states do not comply with their legal obligation to maintain the consistency of their national and EEA market regulations with the dynamically evolving EU common market law. In the EEA, national courts, the CJEU and the EFTA Court interpret EEA law from the diverse perspectives of their national, EU and EFTA jurisdictions. Their judicial independence and mutual duties of 'judicial comity' induce the courts to cooperate in clarifying common constitutional principles and adjusting their diverse national, EU and EEA legal doctrines (eg by rejecting the EU doctrine of

[157] Cf R Kagan, *Of Paradise and Power: America and Europe in the New World Order* (New York, Knopf, 2003) 3.

[158] Cf the numerous case studies on American and European approaches to multilevel economic governance in C Joerges and EU Petersmann (eds), *Constitutionalism, Multilevel Trade Governance and International Economic Law* (Oxford, Hart Publishing, 2011).

'direct effect' in the different context of the EEA legal system, so as to accommodate the 'dualist constitutional traditions' in the Nordic EFTA states). In accordance with the 'contrapuntal methodology' discussed above, EU, EEA and national governance institutions cooperate in protecting legitimately diverse constitutional, legal and judicial methodologies justified by their diverse constitutional contexts. Vis-à-vis Switzerland, whose population rejected joining the EEA, the EU has concluded even more deferential FTAs that reconcile EU law with Swiss law by respecting Switzerland's different constitutional system (eg direct 'popular *referenda*') and adjusting the EU–Switzerland FTA to the dynamically evolving EU secondary law. If third trading partners of the EU (like Switzerland) do not accept the jurisdiction of the CJEU (eg as provided for in the EU–Turkey association agreement) or of the EFTA Court for the settlement of disputes, the EU decides unilaterally on whether restrictions by these trading partners (eg Swiss 'safeguard measures' limiting free movement of persons) can be accepted as consistent with the more deferential 'homogeneity obligations' in bilateral FTAs.

The transatlantic FTAs go far beyond reciprocal trade liberalisation by acknowledging common constitutional principles like human rights, transnational rule of law and democratic governance in transatlantic relations. Their treaty objectives to promote a permanent framework for regulatory cooperation and harmonize economic and non-economic regulations through common rules—although fundamentally different from the EEA objectives of extending the EU's common market regulations to third trading partners—require 'constructing a We'[159] so as to justify collective rule-making and reciprocal protection of rule of law, even if transatlantic FTAs are not supposed to change national and European legislative procedures. How can—and should—the 'constitutional nationalism' in the USA be reconciled with the EU's multilevel constitutionalism?

The EU Treaty requirements (eg in Articles 3 and 21 TEU) to base external FTAs on the constitutional 'values' and 'principles' that successfully govern market regulation and competition throughout Europe, reflect the insight that the more international treaties assume legislative functions for protecting *transnational PGs* that no single state can unilaterally protect without international law and institutions, the more domestic institutions must apply and protect international treaties approved by national parliaments for the benefit of citizens. Inside the EU and the EEA, citizens invoking and enforcing their rights in domestic jurisdictions—as 'market citizens' (eg producers, investors, traders, consumers), 'social citizens' (eg family members of workers moving across the EU), 'democratic principals' of multilevel governance agents (eg electing the European Parliament) and 'agents of justice'

[159] Cf P Lomba, 'Constructing a "We": Collective Agency and the European Union' in Cremona *et al* (eds) (n 15) 97–110.

entitled to challenge abuses of public and private powers in national and European courts—have been among the most important drivers for democratic acceptance, progressive development and decentralized enforcement of economic integration law, as reflected in the case law of European courts on individual rights under EU and EEA law. The multilevel judicial protection by national and European courts of the economic and constitutional rights of private plaintiffs against violations of EU law—as in the leading EU case law triggered by complaints from the Dutch transporter Van Gend en Loos, the Italian lawyer Costa, the German vine grower Hauser, or the Belgian stewardess Defrenne—illustrated that constitutional rights and judicial remedies of citizens offer powerful, legitimate 'republican instruments' for protecting multilevel compliance with treaties approved by parliaments for the benefit of citizens. Similar disputes are bound to arise in transatlantic market relations—also beyond traditional, international movements of goods, services and investments. For instance, similar to the expansion of legal protection of EU citizenship rights in the EU 'area of freedom, security and justice' (Articles 67–89 TFEU), EU criticism of inadequate legal and judicial protection of privacy rights in the USA has become a major obstacle to transatlantic cooperation.[160] Hence, rather than limiting judicial remedies of citizens to investor-state arbitration that risks circumventing domestic constitutional restraints, transatlantic FTAs should protect democratic 'compliance constituencies' and transnational rule of law for the benefit of all citizens.[161] Respect for the fundamental rights of EU citizens as codified in the EUCFR—such as 'freedom to conduct a business in accordance with Union law' (Article 16) and the 'right to an effective remedy and to a fair trial' (Article 47)—can empower citizens to protect 'strict observance of international law' (Article 3 TEU) across national boundaries, for instance in transnational economic, social and other civil society cooperation. This 'emancipatory function' of FTAs among democracies—eg for extending multilevel protection of equal rights of citizens against abuses of foreign policy powers—has been unduly neglected in the secretive CETA and TTIP negotiations. Civil society and parliaments increasingly resist such 'disconnected intergovernmentalism'. International treaties with 'legislative functions' for protecting transnational PGs must be governed democratically and protect

[160] Cf n 39 above.

[161] The need for limiting power-orientated foreign policies (eg perceiving international treaties as breakable contracts between governments rather than as instruments for protecting transnational rule of law for the benefit of citizens) by stronger rule-of-law institutions, reducing transaction costs and protecting equal rights of citizens and other transnational PGs, is also increasingly recognized by American academics; cf K Alter, *The New Terrain of International Law: Courts, Politics, Rights* (Princeton, NJ, Princeton UP, 2014). Stronger judicial remedies can empower 'compliance supporters' (notably civil society actors) and 'compliance partners' (eg domestic and international institutions) to pressure governments to comply with treaty obligations approved by parliaments for protecting transnational PGs for the benefit of citizens.

transnational rights and remedies of citizens, so as to enable the 'democratic principals' to hold governance agents and their limited 'constituted powers' more accountable for the ubiquity of 'market failures' and 'governance failures' that continue to distort transatlantic relations, the rule of law and consumer welfare.[162] The fact that 'dualist', democratic traditions prompt parliaments in Canada and the USA to avoid incorporating international treaties into domestic legal systems, offers no justification for EU diplomats to undermine the more 'monist' legal traditions in EU law with FTA provisions excluding rights of EU citizens to invoke FTA provisions in European jurisdictions.

ii. Need for Protecting Democratic, Republican and Cosmopolitan EU Citizenship Rights

The EUCFR protects fundamental freedoms across national frontiers (such as the economic freedoms protected in Articles 15–17 EUCFR); 'limitations may be made only if they are necessary and genuinely meet the objectives of general interest recognised by the Union or the need to protect the rights and freedoms of others' (Article 52 EUCFR). Hence, EU citizens are entitled to know whether EU restrictions can be justified:

- on constitutional grounds, like the protection of equal freedoms as the 'first principle of justice' (as explained in theories of justice from Kant to Rawls) and democratic 'discourse justifications' convincing reasonable citizens to accept legal rules as 'just' (eg justified by procedural and substantive reasons that citizens cannot reasonably reject);
- on other 'republican grounds', like promotion of general consumer welfare through open markets and non-discriminatory conditions of competition; and
- in view of the EU's 'values' as defined in Articles 2 and 3 TEU; for democratic governance depends on institutionalizing 'public reason' and the republican virtues of citizens, 'civil servants' and parliamentarians struggling to transform agreed 'principles of justice' into democratic legislation, judicial administration of justice and multilevel protection of PGs.

Such republican conceptions of multilevel governance of PGs—as being dependent on a '*démocratie de tous les jours*' in support of 'aggregate PGs' demanded by citizens—seemed to be absent during the secretive CETA negotiations. Citizens of the EU following the occasional press conferences

[162] Cf D Cardoso *et al* (eds), *The Transatlantic Colossus. Global Contributions to Broaden the Debate on the EU–US Free Trade Area* (Bertelsmann e-book, 2015).

on these negotiations were amazed by the discrepancy between the EU 'law in the books' and the 'law in action'. According to EU law:

— '[D]ecisions are taken as openly as possible and as closely as possible to the citizen' (Article 1 TEU); the 'institutions shall, by appropriate means, give citizens and representative associations the opportunity to make known and publicly exchange their views in all areas of Union action' (Article 11:1). Yet from 2009 the CETA was negotiated in almost complete secrecy. Following the publication of the draft text in September 2014, EU Trade Commissioner de Gucht responded to criticism from parliaments and civil society by rejecting renegotiation of the treaty provisions on investor-state arbitration as being 'now too late'.
— 'In its relations with the wider world, the Union shall … contribute to the protection of its citizens' (Article 3:5 TEU), for, according to the EUCFR, the EU 'places the individual at the heart of its activities' (Preamble). Yet citizens—if they can read the more than 1,600 pages of English treaty texts—can discover in Article 30.6 CETA that under the Agreement they will have neither private rights nor judicial remedies in domestic courts against treaty violations adversely affecting domestic citizens.
— In its external relations, the Union shall 'contribute to … the strict observance of international law' (Article 3:5 TEU) in view of the lack of any conferral of EU powers to violate international treaties enacted by national and EU parliaments for the benefit of citizens. Yet, as discussed below, the CJEU refuses to enforce EU compliance with UN and WTO dispute settlement rulings without offering EU 'violation victims' and 'retaliation victims' effective legal and judicial remedies or financial compensation of their injuries suffered from, say, illegal trade restrictions by the EU;[163] similarly, citizens are denied rights to invoke CETA obligations in domestic courts and in the CJEU so as to protect them against harmful violations of the rule of law.
— Even though EU law protects the right of 'everyone … to an effective remedy' (Article 47 EUCFR), only foreign investors have privileged access to investor-state adjudication under the CETA. Investment arbitrators may order governments to grant financial compensation in the order of billions of euros through special judicial proceedings that circumvent the constitutional constraints under EU law.[164] Similar to the assertion by EU institutions of exclusive rights to invoke and enforce

[163] Cf A Thies, *International Trade Disputes and EU Liability* (Oxford, OUP, 2013).

[164] An example is the pending arbitration at the request of the Swedish nuclear company Vattenfall, demanding €3.5 billion of damages from Germany as compensation for its lost profits due to the German decision to phase out the production of nuclear energy in Germany in the aftermath of Japan's nuclear disaster at Fukushima; ICSID Arbitration Case no ARB/12/12. The revised 2016 CETA rules on the composition and procedures of investment tribunals do

WTO obligations vis-à-vis EU member states in EU courts, without corresponding rights of citizens and of EU member states to judicial protection of the 'strict observance of international law' (Article 3 TEU) by the EU itself,[165] Article 30.6 CETA excludes effective judicial remedies of EU citizens against EU violations of CETA law and dispute settlement rulings under the CETA.

iii. Why the CETA and the TTIP Risk Undermining Rights of Citizens In Transatlantic Relations

According to the consolidated text of Article 30.6 CETA on 'Private Rights' (as published online in the final text of February 2016):

> Nothing in this Agreement shall be construed as conferring rights or imposing obligations on persons other than those created between the Parties under public international law, nor as permitting this Agreement to be directly invoked in the domestic legal systems of the Parties.
>
> A Party shall not provide for a right of action under its domestic law against the other Party on the ground that a measure of the other Party is inconsistent with this Agreement.

This provision goes beyond similar provisions in other recent FTAs of the EU, such as Article 17.15 on 'No Direct Effect' in the EU–Singapore FTA initialed and published online in September 2013:

> For greater certainty, nothing in this Agreement shall be construed as conferring rights or imposing obligations on persons, other than those created between the Parties under public international law.

While the EU rightly insists on protecting its *acquis communautaire* vis-à-vis EFTA states and other associated trading partners, Article 30.6 CETA—by excluding individual rights under the CETA and effective judicial remedies of citizens against violations of CETA rules—risks undermining the EU treaty obligations (eg in Articles 2, 3 and 21 TEU) to protect citizens, the rule of law and other 'EU values' and 'constitutional principles' in the EU's external relations too.

The EU Commission has never publicly explained why—contrary to the EU Treaty requirement to contribute 'in its relations with the wider

not change the facts that the judgment remains an arbitral award, and national and EU law cannot be invoked as applicable law (cf Art 8.31 CETA on 'applicable law and interpretation' in investment adjudication).

[165] Cf EU Petersmann, 'Why Do the EU and its Court of Justice Fail to Protect the "Strict Observance of International Law" (Article 3 TEU) in the World Trading System and in other Areas of Multilevel Governance of International Public Goods?' in C Herrmann *et al* (eds), *Trade Policy between Law, Diplomacy and Scholarship: European Yearbook of International Economic Law* (Heidelberg, Springer, 2015) 145–89.

world ... to the protection of its citizens' (Article 3:5 TEU) in conformity with the 'principles which have inspired (the EU's) own creation, development and enlargement' (Article 21 TEU) and the transnational rights of citizens under EU constitutional law[166]—it has begun excluding its legal and judicial accountability vis-à-vis EU citizens for violations of FTA rules and obligations. Unofficially, EU officials admit their desire to benefit—similar to Canadian and US trade politicians—from lack of judicial accountability for their non-compliance with FTA and WTO obligations and for injuries caused to EU citizens thereby.[167] Officially, the EU's main argument against the 'direct effect' of WTO rules and against 'consistent interpretations' of EU law in conformity with WTO dispute settlement rulings is its power-orientated claim to 'political freedom of manoeuvre'.[168] Arguably, such 'Hobbesian claims'—even though they have been accepted by the CJEU in order to justify its judicial self-restraint in not reviewing the legality of EU acts in the light of WTO law and UN conventions (like UNCLOS, UN air transport and environmental conventions)—are inconsistent with:

- the EU's constitutional requirements for 'strict observance of international law' (Article 3 TEU) and judicial protection of the rule of law (Article 19 TEU);
- the 'coherence' and 'consistent interpretation' requirements of domestic and international legal systems (eg Article 21 TEU; Article XVI:4 WTO; Article 3 DSU);
- the 'network conception' linking global trading communities (eg interested in reducing transaction costs for global supply chains and 'providing security and predictability to the multilateral trading system' as prescribed in Article 3 DSU);
- multilevel judicial administration of justice and judicial comity among domestic and international courts committed to protecting the rule of law;
- the EU principles of 'conferral' of limited competences and of their 'proportionate' use (cf Article 5 TEU); and
- the constitutional rights of EU citizens (eg under Articles 16, 47, 52 EUCFR).

[166] Apart from the 'common market freedoms', see the additional rights protected by the EUCFR, such as transnational economic freedoms 'in conformity with Union law' (Art 16), rights of access to documents (Art 42) and rights to effective judicial remedies (Art 47).

[167] On the legal incoherence of the various claims by EU advocates (eg that GATT/WTO rules are less precise and less unconditional than EU customs union rules, or that WTO safeguard, reciprocity and dispute settlement provisions exclude 'direct effect'), see Petersmann (n 165).

[168] Cf n 179 in ch 1 and related text.

As illustrated by the '*Kadi* jurisprudence' of the CJEU emphasizing the constitutional restraints of UN and EU actions,[169] EU power politics ignoring 'strict observance of international law' (Article 3 TEU) to the detriment of equal rights of citizens lacks constitutional justification. It runs counter to the EU's legal obligations (eg under WTO and EU law) to terminate illegal trade restrictions and protect the rule of law and judicial remedies of citizens.[170] Persistent EU violations of 'PGs treaties' risk undermining not only general consumer welfare but also democracy, the rule of law and transnational 'aggregate PGs'. To regain legitimacy and enhance accountability for abuses of power, the EU must 'contribute to the protection of its citizens' through 'strict observance of international law' (Article 3:5 TEU), including treaties approved by parliaments in order to protect transnational PGs through rules-based cooperation among citizens. Respect for the 'constitutional nationalism' and 'dualist legal traditions' in North-American democracies, and for the 'executive dominance' of their NAFTA institutions, offers no justification for the EU institutions to disregard Article 52 EUCFR by using FTAs to undermine individual rights and judicial remedies of EU citizens vis-à-vis EU institutions.

D. Transparent, Democratic Governance of Transatlantic Market Regulations?

'Transparency' refers not only the the public disclosure and accessibility of information, but also to its readability and comprehensibility. Most EU citizens risk remaining 'rationally ignorant' vis-à-vis online publications of draft treaty texts in the English language, with more than 1,600 pages on technical and complex legal issues (like product and production standards and market access commitments in diverse services sectors), and vis-à-vis related claims by EU diplomats that their foreign policy discretion, diplomatic privileges and secretive diplomatic traditions justify their confidential treaty negotiations. If citizens—as suggested by Rawls—'think of themselves as if they were legislators and ask themselves what statutes, supported by what reasons satisfying the criterion of reciprocity, they would think it most reasonable to enact',[171] they have good reasons to resist non-transparent,

[169] Cf Avbelj, Fontanelli and Martinico (eds) (n 138).

[170] Cf Petersmann (n 165). The EU's invocation of Art 22 DSU is misleading in this context: Art 22 envisages mutually agreed compensation only as an option for avoiding lawful sanctions without justifying the maintenance of illegal trade restrictions.

[171] J Rawls, 'The Idea of Public Reason Revisited' (1997) 64 *Chicago Law Review* 765, 769 (citizens 'fulfil their duty of civility and support the idea of public reason by doing what they can to hold government officials to it').

'intergovernmental domination' and to insist on transparent, democratic rule-making. For instance, 'anti-citizen clauses' (as in Article 30.6 CETA) should be replaced with explicit FTA rules on 'protection of citizens', as required by Articles 3 and 21 TEU, such as:

> This Agreement aims at placing Canadian [US] and EU citizens at the heart of CETA [TTIP] by protecting their rights and rule of law in transatlantic cooperation, including rights under the EU Charter of Fundamental Rights.

Such a provision would demonstrate that diplomats pay more than lip service to the few references—notably in the Preamble to the CETA—to 'human rights and the rule of law'. Placing citizens at the heart of the CETA would respond to the 'cosmopolitan foreign policy mandate' in Article 21 TEU by empowering citizens:

— to act as transnational 'agents of justice';
— to be protected as main economic actors in transatlantic economic cooperation; and
— to assume their cosmopolitan responsibilities for collective protection of transatlantic PGs.

Citizen-orientated FTA provision would set incentives for national, European and transatlantic dispute settlement bodies to interpret transatlantic FTAs in conformity with the rights of citizens, and prevent disputes through mutually 'consistent interpretations' of multilevel regulation of transatlantic cooperation for the benefit of citizens. Even if citizens may reasonably disagree on which rights they are owed as a matter of justice in multilevel governance of PGs, the democratic ideal of a self-legislating, political community cannot be realized without empowering citizens to invoke international 'PGs treaties', as recognized in European integration law.

i. EU Citizen Rights to Transparent, Democratic Self-Governance

Discussion of democracy since Plato and Aristotle has not produced a universally accepted 'mainstream theory' on the prescriptive (normative) and descriptive (empirical) definitions of the concept.[172] Claims of 'representative democracy' remain deeply contested, for instance in view of the public choice insight that public officials tend to represent rational self-interests and powerful lobbying interests no less than alleged community interests. Globalization and its shift from national 'governments' to multilevel 'governance' entail national 'democracy deficits' that are difficult to compensate at international governance levels. For instance, UN law and UN human rights

[172] If defined as 'government by discussion' based on 'power of the people', democracy has even been described as 'a high-flown name for something that does not exist': G Sartori, *The Theory of Democracy Revisited: Part One* (London, Chatham House, 1987) 7.

conventions neither precisely define nor effectively enforce their 'principles of democracy';[173] as many governments of UN and WTO member states are not democratically elected and do not effectively represent the republican interests of all their citizens (eg in protecting human rights and other PGs), UN and WTO governance practices lack 'democratic input legitimacy' (eg in terms of constitutional, participatory and deliberative democracy) and acquire 'democratic output legitimacy' only to the extent that UN law is democratically implemented in constitutional democracies for the benefit of all citizens.[174] The Lisbon Treaty prescribes 'democratic principles' (eg in Articles 2, 6, 9–12 TEU) in terms of multilevel constitutional, parliamentary, deliberative and participatory democracy; these principles complement the diverse national democratic traditions in order to protect the constitutional and democratic values in EU law and governance, such as protection of individual and democratic autonomy of EU citizens and of 'the peoples of Europe' (Article 1 TEU) in multilevel governance of PGs.[175] To the extent that EU governance (eg by the ECB) prevails over the democratic and legal authority of national government institutions (eg as acknowledged by the CJEU and by the German Constitutional Court in their 'OMT judgments' discussed above), it must protect the constitutional and democratic rights of EU citizens in order to assert democratic input- as well as output-legitimacy.[176]

Most external EU agreements include human rights provisions aimed at justifying and enforcing 'human rights conditionality' vis-à-vis third states.

[173] See, eg, Art 21(3) UDHR: 'The will of the people shall be the basis of the authority of government; this shall be expressed in periodic and genuine elections which shall be by universal and equal suffrage and shall be held by secret vote or by equivalent free voting procedures.' The UDHR guarantees of freedom of expression (Art 19), freedom of assembly (Art 20) and democratic participation (Art 21) are confirmed in many UN and regional human rights conventions and national constitutions, and render non-democratic governance powers illegitimate.

[174] UN human rights law recognizes citizens and peoples as holders of constituent powers who delegate only limited 'constituted powers' to governments, subject to 'inalienable' human and democratic rights, including the entitlement of 'everyone ... to a social and international order in which the rights and freedoms set forth in this Declaration can be fully realized' (Art 28 UDHR). The UN Democracy Fund financially supports 'democracy-building' as 'one of the universal and indivisible core values and principles of the United Nations'. Yet UN practices refrain from imposing 'democratic conditionality' vis-à-vis the many UN member states that lack democratic governance.

[175] Cf A von Bogdandy, 'The European Lesson for International Democracy: The Significance of Articles 9–12 EU Treaty for International Organizations' (2012) 23 *EJIL* 315–34. On democratic nation states, EU citizenship, cosmopolitan rights and civil society actors as complementary bases for the democratization of multilevel governance, see A Peters, 'Dual Democracy' in J Klabbers, A Peters and G Ulfstein (eds), *The Constitutionalisation of International Law* (Oxford, OUP, 2009) 153 ff.

[176] This need for justifying multilevel governance in terms of the democratic and human rights of citizens, inclusive representation, democratic participation, deliberation and accountability was explained in ch 1; see also A Mulieri, 'Can we democratize global governance?' in J Wouters *et al* (eds), *Global Governance and Democracy. A Multidisciplinary Analysis* (Cheltenham, Elgar, 2015) 15–36.

As national and European parliaments have given no mandate to EU diplomats to exclude individual rights and judicial remedies in FTAs, 'anti-citizen clauses' (like Article 30.6 CETA) run counter to the 'cosmopolitan foreign policy mandate' in Articles 3 and 21 TEU, for example by undermining democratic citizen participation in multilevel protection of PGs. The 'executive dominance' and inadequate 'democratic public reason' in intergovernmental FTA negotiations illustrate how national and European parliaments neglect their democratic responsibilities to protect the equal rights and democratic representation of EU citizens. As already emphasized in the French *Declaration of the Rights of Man and the Citizen* (1789),[177] prioritization of the rights of governments, 'disempowerment' of citizens, and inadequate judicial 'checks and balances' risk provoking government failures to protect PGs (like the rule of law in transatlantic economic cooperation). Comparative institutionalism confirms through empirical evidence that citizen-driven 'cosmopolitan legal regimes' with multilevel judicial remedies—like international commercial law, investment law, regional HRL, European single market and competition law, rights-based FTAs, international consular and criminal law conventions—have realized their legal objectives more effectively through multilevel judicial protection of cosmopolitan rights than Westphalian 'top-down' treaty regimes prioritizing the rights of governments without protecting the rights of citizens.[178]

Constitutional democracies and European law increasingly promote 'internal transparency' (eg duties pursuant to Article 218:10 TFEU to inform the European Parliament of the EU's international treaty negotiations), 'external transparency' (eg duties of EU institutions pursuant to Article 11:2 TEU to engage in 'civil society dialogues'), and 'legal' and 'institutional' transparency, in order to justify law and governance vis-à-vis citizens and enhance the legitimacy of intergovernmental rule-making through democratic participation, accountability of governments and predictability of rules. For example:

— Article 1 TEU defines the EU as 'an ever closer union among the peoples of Europe, in which decisions are taken as openly as possible and as closely as possible to the citizen'.

[177] Cf its Preamble, 'Considering that ignorance, forgetfulness, or contempt of human rights are the sole causes of public misfortune and government depravity'.

[178] Cf Petersmann (n 13) 145 ff; F Wilman, *Private Enforcement of EU Law Before National Courts* (Cheltenham, Elgar, 2015). On the applicability of the EUCFR to the EU's external relations powers, see V Moreno-Lax and C Costello, 'The Extraterritorial Application of the EU Charter of Fundamental Rights: From Territoriality to Facticity, the Effectiveness Model' in S Peers *et al* (eds), *The EU Charter of Fundamental Rights: A Commentary* (Oxford, Hart Publishing, 2014) 1657–83; V Kube, 'The EU's External Human Rights Commitment: What is the Legal Value of Article 21 TEU?', *Working Papers Law* 2016/10 (Florence, EUI, 2016).

- Article 10:3 TEU adds that 'Every citizen shall have the right to participate in the democratic life of the Union. Decisions shall be taken as openly and a closely as possible to the citizen.'
- Article 11 TEU specifies related legal obligations of the EU institutions, which:
  - 'shall ... give citizens and representative associations the opportunity to make known and publicly exchange their views in all areas of Union action' (para 1),
  - 'shall maintain an open, transparent and regular dialogue with representative associations and civil society' (para 2), and
  - 'shall carry out broad consultations with parties concerned in order to ensure that the Union's actions are coherent and transparent' (para 3).

Article 15:3 TFEU and Article 42 EUCFR supplement these transparency principles by recognizing corresponding individual rights: 'Any citizen of the Union, and any natural or legal person residing ... in a Member State, shall have the right of access to documents of the Union institutions, bodies, offices and agencies ... subject to the principles and the conditions to be defined in accordance with this paragraph.' The implementing Regulation 1049/2001 regarding public access to EU documents aims 'to ensure the widest possible access to documents'. It is supplemented by rules of the EU institutions protecting the confidentiality of certain documents, as clarified in the jurisprudence of European courts on the legal and judicial 'balancing' of the transparency and confidentiality requirements.[179] Over the past few years, many international organizations—including UN bodies, the WTO, ICSID and UNCITRAL—have actively promoted public access to trade, investment and other legal documents, to economic and human rights adjudication, and the rights of third parties (eg *amici curiae*) to make submissions to transnational dispute settlement bodies, thereby strengthening 'rights to know' and corresponding transparency obligations as integral parts of ever more national and international legal systems.[180]

ii. The EU Commission's 'Transparency Initiative' and 'Cosmopolitan Public Reason'

Lack of information on confidential treaty negotiations by the EU Commission prompted the European Parliament twice to veto international

[179] Cf C Herrmann, 'Transleakancy' in Herrmann *et al* (eds) (n 165) 39–46.

[180] On transparency in international law-making and adjudication, see Bianchi and Peters (eds) (n 27).

draft agreements (ie the SWIFT agreement in February 2010 and the Anti-Counterfeiting Trade Agreement in July 2012). Following repeated complaints from the European Parliament, civil society and from the European Ombudsman over the excessive confidentiality of TTIP negotiations and related documents, in March 2014 the European Commission launched a public consultation on investment protection and investor-state dispute settlement (ISDS) rules; it received almost 150,000 replies, mostly opposing the proposed investment protection and ISDS rules. In response to these democratic pressures, in October 2014 the EU Council finally disclosed its TTIP negotiations mandate of 2013. EU Trade Commissioner Malmström launched a new 'transparency strategy' in November 2014, aimed at helping 'to ensure greater access to trade documents by the general public and the European Parliament, and legitimacy of EU trade policy at large'.[181] The European Parliament's resolution of 8 July 2015 includes very detailed recommendations by the Parliament to the European Commission on many aspects of the TTIP negotiations, including proposals to replace the ISDS mechanism with a new system of public law courts.

Chapter 1, section IV argued that in order to limit 'democracy deficits' in intergovernmental market regulation, constitutional, parliamentary, participatory and deliberative democracy empowering national and EU citizens needs to be supplemented by 'cosmopolitan democracy', also empowering transnational 'stakeholder communities' through 'republican rights' to hold multilevel governance institutions more accountable, for instance by interpreting international treaties with legislative functions for transnational PGs similar to democratic legislation as also protecting rights of citizens, the rule of law and 'access to justice' in conformity with national and EU constitutional law. Just as 'constitutional democracy' inside states enables citizens to challenge 'market failures' as well as 'governance failures' through countervailing rights and remedies, so 'cosmopolitan democracy' can contribute to promoting 'public reason' and equal cosmopolitan rights by enabling citizens to invoke and progressively clarify—'as openly as possible and as closely as possible to the citizen' (Article 1 TEU)—international PGs regimes with due respect for diverse democratic contexts. Citizen-orientated interpretations of international trade rules increase the accountability and democratic capability of the EU to protect its constitutional values of freedom, equality, the rule of law, non-discrimination and justice (cf Article 2 TEU) in transnational trade relations with other constitutional democracies through multilevel legal rights and judicial remedies.[182] Intergovernmental conceptions

[181] European Commission, *Communication concerning transparency in TTIP negotiations*, 25 November 2014 (C 2014 9052 final).

[182] On public reason as a 'collective capability', see: EI Kelly, 'Public Reason as a Collective Capability' (2012) 43 *Rutgers Law Journal* 295–316. 'Public reason' is less demanding than the 'discourse principle' of J Habermas, *The Inclusion of the Other: Studies in Political Theory* (Cambridge, MA, MIT Press, 1998) 39 ff: 'Only those norms can claim validity that

of FTAs—by treating citizens as mere objects rather than legal subjects of FTAs and depriving citizens of effective judicial remedies in domestic courts (eg by excluding the 'direct applicability' of FTA rules)—disfranchise and alienate citizens; they weaken the legal capacity of democratic governance institutions to resist rent-seeking interest group pressures to redistribute domestic income through welfare-reducing trade restrictions favouring powerful interest groups (eg European banana trading companies, which successfully lobbied for illegal EU import restrictions from 1992–2012, redistributing billions of dollars each year, as in a banana republic).

The absence of any public discussion so far—by EU citizens, national and European parliaments—of the 'disempowerment' of citizens through the EU's recent FTAs illustrates why increased transparency of FTA negotiations is a precondition for more effective democratic control and accountability of international law-making. Violations of international rule of law have become systemic in ever more areas of European integration since the global financial crisis in 2008, the debt and euro crises since 2010, and the EU's border protection and immigration crises since 2014, resulting in persistently decreasing confidence of EU citizens in EU governance.[183] The secretive CETA negotiations and the intergovernmental exclusion of rights and effective remedies of adversely affected citizens (other than powerful foreign investors) reinforce fears in civil society that FTAs risk legitimizing regulatory 'top-down harmonization' of product and production standards in response to special interest advocacy (eg by agricultural and biotech lobbies). By-mid 2016, about 3.5 million EU citizens had signed a petition to stop TTIP and CETA, and almost 1,900 cities, municipalities and regions throughout Europe had declared themselves 'TTIP-free zones'.

iii. Democratic Legitimacy of Free Trade Agreement Negotiations, Ratification and Implementation?

Evaluation of the democratic legitimacy of FTAs must distinguish between intergovernmental negotiations, and the conclusion and implementation of FTAs like the CETA and the TTIP.

a. Negotiations

At the stage of *treaty negotiations*, constitutional, representative, participatory and 'deliberative' democracy requires parliaments and civil society to

could meet with the acceptance of all concerned in practical discourse.' Arguably, Habermas's requirement of 'fully inclusive, real discourse' is difficult to reconcile with the 'rational ignorance' and limited, cognitive capacities of individuals regarding collective supply of global PGs affecting billions of people in diverse countries with diverse democratic preferences; cf A Kuper, *Democracy Beyond Borders: Justice and Representation in Global Institutions* (Cambridge, CUP, 2004) 194 ff.

[183] Cf J Zalc, 'Overcoming Democratic Breakdown in the EU' in Fondation Robert Schuman, *European Issues* No 333 of 18 November 2014 (n 176 in ch 1 and related text).

insist on taking decisions 'as openly and as closely as possible to the citizen' (Article 10:3 TEU), and on respecting the 'cosmopolitan mandate' of Article 21 TEU to protect equal rights and remedies of citizens as 'democratic principals' and main economic actors in FTAs. Inclusive consultations during FTA negotiations must go beyond 'stakeholder consultations' with selected business representatives, 'civil society dialogues' with selected civil society representatives, EU press conferences and incomplete EU website information. The new 'transparency initiative' for the EU's common commercial policy is to be welcomed not only in view of the existential importance of transatlantic FTAs for the jobs, income, rights and welfare of millions of EU citizens;[184] the subsequent renegotiation of CETA's investment chapter also confirms how participatory democracy can successfully limit abuses of diplomatic powers. Exclusion of direct invocation of FTA provisions in domestic legal systems (eg by Article 30.6 CETA) risks rendering domestic legal and judicial remedies ineffective for resolving transatlantic disputes; it illustrates why—from the point of view of citizens and their constitutional rights—secretive intergovernmental negotiations are far more dangerous than transparent parliamentary legislation. If FTA provisions cannot be invoked in domestic judicial proceedings, domestic courts will be incapable of administering justice in disputes over compliance with FTA rights and obligations, and over their consistency with constitutional rights of citizens.

b. Ratification

At the level of *treaty ratification*, many EU member states have criticized the legal position of the EU Commission to conclude CETA as a 'Community agreement'; they claim that the broad regulatory scope of transatlantic FTAs (eg regarding subsidies, investments, movements and professional qualifications of natural service suppliers, telecommunications, intellectual property, labour rights, environmental protection) and their criticism in civil society require approval of the CETA and the TTIP by national parliaments as 'mixed agreements'. The national parliaments in both Europe and in the USA (eg in view of the trade promotion authority granted by the US Congress for 'fast track approval' of FTAs) and the European Parliament are likely to focus on (dis)approval of the draft treaty as a whole, without insisting on renegotiation of specific treaty provisions. Parliamentary approval of the CETA and the TTIP as 'mixed agreements' could delay their entry into force by years, especially if national parliaments link ratification to other political demands (eg Bulgarian parliamentarians having already requested visa-free travel between Bulgaria and the USA as a condition for ratifying the TTIP). Approval by the European Parliament might be preceded by

[184] This importance is illustrated by the CJEU judgment of October 2015 annulling the EU–US 'safe harbour agreement' on the ground of violating privacy rights of EU citizens (see n 39 above).

another request for an opinion from the CJEU on the consistency of FTAs with EU law (pursuant to Article 218:11 TFEU).[185] Civil society opposition to the TTIP has so far focused on vague fears of its leading to a 'race to the bottom' in levels of product and production standards, by-passing parliamentary decision-making, and giving undue weight to trade and investment rather than to health, environmental, social, labour and consumer interests. Such fears are countered by claims of the EU Commission that the TTIP will neither lower the existing level of EU protection of social rights, public health and the environment, nor prejudge the sovereign 'freedom to regulate' at levels of protection decided democratically.

c. Implementation

As regards the *implementation* of future FTAs, citizens and parliaments should insist on their republican experience that multilevel democratic and judicial rights and remedies of citizens—including EU law 'rights to an effective remedy and a fair trial' (Article 47 EUCFR) and duties to publicly justify 'any limitation on the exercise of rights and freedoms' (Article 52 EUCFR; Article 296 TFEU)—have proved to be the most effective guarantees of the rule of law, 'protection of citizens' and 'strict observance of international law' (Article 3 TEU). The transformation of the 1995 'New Transatlantic Agenda' into the 1998 'Transatlantic Economic Partnership' led to the establishment of intergovernmental, inter-parliamentary and civil society institutions without an adequate legal framework for protecting open markets and preventing or settling transatlantic disputes. As TTIP negotiations are committed to maintaining the regulatory autonomy and democratic law-making procedures in both the EU and the USA, it is through reliance on their common traditions of 'multilevel bottom-up constitutionalism' that the past 'disconnected top-down governance' in transatlantic relations should be 'constitutionalized' by protecting cosmopolitan rights, democratic responsibilities and judicial remedies of citizens. Like other democratic legislation, parliamentary approval of 'PGs treaties' justifies presumptions that precise and unconditional treaty guarantees of equal freedoms, non-discrimination, the rule of law and judicial remedies can be invoked by citizens in domestic jurisdictions.

E. Investor-State Arbitration Rather Than General Rights of Citizens to Effective Remedies?

The negotiation directives for the TTIP, which were unanimously approved by the EU Council in June 2013, also called for investment protection and

[185] Such a request was made by the EU Commission in respect of the EU–Singapore FTA; the opinion had not yet been given by the CJEU by mid-2016, thereby delaying the entry into force of this FTA.

ISDS on the condition that the final outcome meets the EU interests. In view of the strong public interest in this issue, the EU Commission launched a public consultation—from March to July 2014—on the proposed EU approach, in order to seek feedback on the following 12 key issues:

1. Scope of the substantive investment protection provisions.
2. Non-discriminatory treatment for investors.
3. Fair and equitable treatment.
4. Expropriation.
5. Ensuring the right to regulate and investment protection.
6. Transparency in ISDS, multiple claims and relationship to domestic courts.
7. Arbitrators' ethics.
8. Conduct and qualifications.
9. Reducing the risk of frivolous and unfounded cases.
10. Allowing claims to proceed (filter).
11. Guidance by the parties on the interpretation of the agreement.
12. Appellate mechanism and consistency of rulings.

The Commission's Report on these consultations[186] acknowledged that 97 per cent of the almost 150,000 submissions made by EU citizens, companies and NGOs revealed a 'huge scepticism' by civil society as to the proposed treaty provisions on investor protection. Critics argue, *inter alia*, that arbitration procedures risk limiting the regulatory discretion of states by circumventing existing domestic legal standards and judicial procedures so as to privilege foreign investors at potentially immense costs for domestic taxpayers. The Report identified four areas in particular for further improvement of ISDS:

— the protection of the right to regulate;
— the establishment and functioning of arbitral tribunals;
— the relationship between domestic judicial systems and ISDS; and
— the review of ISDS decisions through an appellate mechanism.

i. Investor-State Dispute Settlement Risks Undermining Constitutional 'Rule of Law'

As briefly discussed in Chapter 1, section III, following the 1960s, ISDS emerged as a substitute for the perceived weaknesses of judicial systems inside less-developed capital-importing countries. Inside TTIP countries, there is no constitutional justification for preventing access by all investors

[186] Cf EU Commission, *Report on Online public consultation on investment protection and investor-to-state dispute settlement in TTIP*, Staff Working Document of 13 January 2015.

to the highly developed, domestic judicial systems to ensure the 'rule of law', including precise and unconditional FTA rules as integral parts of EU law.[187] Hence, a large number of the respondents to the EU's online consultation considered that domestic courts should be used exclusively to settle disputes between states and foreign investors, in view of the fact that the EU and the USA have democratic legal systems and experienced judicial systems that protect property rights and other fundamental rights, including the rights of foreigners. The TTIP negotiators should focus on improving domestic legal and judicial remedies (eg in order to prevent 'negative discrimination' against local companies, avoid parallel proceedings, and ensure application of international investment rules by domestic courts). They should follow the precedent of the 2004 FTA between Australia and the USA, which abstained from providing for investor-state arbitration because of the fact that both countries have developed legal systems for resolving disputes between foreign investors and government. Reference is also made to investor-state arbitration practices (eg the *Loewen v United States* and *Mondev v United States* arbitral awards under Chapter 11 NAFTA) as evidence that investor-state arbitration may not offer foreign investors effective remedies against alleged failures in US local judiciaries.[188] The pending *Vattenfall v Germany* arbitration under the Energy Charter Treaty is cited as evidence for the dangers of foreign arbitrators circumventing national and European constitutional law by possibly awarding compensation claims amounting to billions of euros. As EU and US law recognize legal presumptions that precise and unconditional treaty provisions protecting individual rights may be invoked by private parties in domestic courts as 'self-executing', 'directly applicable' rules, or as relevant legal context for 'consistent interpretations' of applicable domestic law, TTIP negotiators should secure the effectiveness of domestic legal and judicial remedies for the benefit of all citizens, rather than engage in reverse discrimination of *domestic investors* in international treaties with legislative functions for multilevel protection of transnational PGs. They could leave it to domestic courts of justice to decide which treaty rules can be invoked in the diverse domestic jurisdictions by adversely affected citizens so as to protect their rights. A non-discriminatory 'constitutional approach' to investment protection would promote both international

[187] The legal situation may be different for Canada; see A de Mestral, 'Investor-State Arbitration Between Developed Democratic Countries', *Investor-State Arbitration Series Paper No 1* (Waterloo Ontario, Center for International Governance Innovation, September 2015), according to whom most of the 31 NAFTA investor-state arbitration complaints against Canada might have received lesser legal and judicial protection (eg due to the constitutional protection of 'parliamentary sovereignty', the lack of constitutional guarantees of investor rights) if they had been decided in Canadian courts.

[188] The *Loewen* case was about procedural biases in local US courts against a Canadian investor; the *Mondev* case challenged an immunity clause preventing the foreign investor from

investment law (eg by promoting domestic enforceability of international investment treaties in domestic courts) and multilevel 'republican governance' of transnational PGs based on international 'PGs regimes'.[189] Supporting the jurisdiction of domestic courts—not only for foreign investors, but for all citizens adversely affected by FTA rules and practices—would also avoid the risk that the CJEU—in view of its increasing reluctance to approve limitations on its jurisdiction and on the autonomous interpretation of EU law by national and EU courts in view of the risk of international jurisdictions (like a European Patent Court, the ECtHR) misconstruing EU law[190]—might find TTIP provisions on transnational ISDS to be incompatible with EU law.

On 12 November 2015, the EU Commission released a new proposal for TTIP provisions on ISDS, replacing investor-state arbitration with a new 'investment court system' based on a Tribunal of First Instance (composed of 15 public law judges: five judges from EU member states, five judges from the USA, and five judges from third countries) and a permanent Appeal Tribunal composed of six public law judges (two from EU member states, two from the USA, and two from third countries).[191] In contrast to Article 42 of the ICSID Convention, which defines the applicable law in investor-state arbitration comprehensively as including the domestic law of the host state, international law and the investor-state concession contracts, the applicable law in this proposed 'investment court system' is limited to the TTIP (CETA) investment rules and 'other rules and principles of international law applicable between the Parties' (Article 8.31 CETA). As simultaneous proceedings before domestic and international courts are excluded, such 're-fragmentation' of the applicable law and jurisdictions—ie domestic jurisdictions that are prevented from applying the agreed treaty rules and principles, and international investment courts that are prevented from applying the domestic law of the host state, the investor-state contracts and EU law (eg Articles 16, 17 and 47 EUCFR protecting economic freedoms, property rights and effective remedies)—risks repeating the procedural and

suing the Boston Redevelopment Authority. For discussion of these two ICSID disputes from the perspective of 'denial of justice', see RD Bishop, J Crawford and WM Reisman, *Foreign Investment Disputes. Cases, Materials and Commentary* (The Hague, Kluwer, 2005) 953 ff.

[189] Cf M Kumm, 'An Empire of Capital. Transatlantic Investment Protection as the Institutionalization of Unjustified Privilege' *ESIL Newsletter* vol 4 (2015), issue 3, available at <http://www.esil-sedi.eu/node/944>.

[190] Cf B de Witte, 'A Selfish Court? The Court of Justice and the Design of International Dispute Settlement Beyond the European Union' in M Cremona and A Thies (eds), *The European Court of Justice and External Relations Law. Constitutional Challenges* (Oxford, Hart Publishing, 2014) 33–46.

[191] For an analysis of these rules, which were subsequently incorporated into the revised CETA text published in February 2016, see A Reinisch, 'The EU and ISDS: From Investor State Arbitration to a Permanent Investment Court', *Investor-State Arbitration Series Paper No 2* (Waterloo Ontario, Center for International Governance Innovation, March 2016).

substantive legal disadvantages that Article 42 of the ICSID Convention was designed to avoid, for instance many years of litigation in domestic courts over the domestic law dimensions of the dispute, followed by additional years of litigation in international courts over the different international law dimensions of the same dispute. The practice of EU executives, since about 2006, to prevent domestic courts from holding governments accountable for violations of FTA obligations, and the proposed appointment of more than 20 international judges for each investment treaty of the EU, risk undermining the effectiveness of ISDS. Non-discriminatory legal and judicial remedies of all citizens against harmful violations of FTA rules in domestic courts are more consistent with constitutional principles of justice than procedural privileges of foreign investors in specialized investment courts, whose 'jurists of recognised compentence' (cf Article 10:7 EU draft proposal of 12 November 2015) may be ignorant of domestic constitutional law systems. Citizens and the CJEU have good reasons to oppose the EU's zeal to provide legal privileges to foreign investors alone and prevent domestic courts from applying FTA rules.

More problematic than the unjustified discrimination in favour of foreign investors is the failure of the EU proposals to protect the 'rule of law' as a constitutional restraint on 'rule by law' so as to 'ensure that in the interpretation and application of the Treaties the law is observed' (Article 19 TEU) and the EU constitutional principles of 'respect for human dignity, freedom, democracy, equality ... and respect for human rights' (Article 2) are protected, including 'strict observance of international law' (Article 3 TEU). Provisions like Article 30.6 CETA aim at preventing citizens and domestic courts from holding governments and foreign investors accountable for violating FTA obligations. As the 'Union's action on the international scene shall be guided by the principles which have inspired its own creation, development and enlargement' (Article 21 TEU), and private enforcement of common market rules and fundamental rights in domestic courts has proved to be the most effective and democratic, decentralized remedy in European integration practices, the EU commitment to 'strict observance of international law' (Article 3 TEU) could be secured more effectively, for instance, by:

- protecting everyone's 'right to an effective remedy before a tribunal' (Article 47 EUCFR) through individual access to *domestic judicial remedies for everybody* based on consistent interpretations and direct applicability of precise and unconditional FTA rules in domestic courts that are better placed to address investor-state disputes than specialized investment lawyers, who risk being unfamiliar with national and European constitutional law;
- protecting individual access by all citizens adversely affected by FTA violations to a Transatlantic Market Court with a more general jurisdiction for protecting the 'rule of law' and composed of public law

judges with qualifications for appointment to the highest judicial offices in their own countries; and

— promoting 'judicial comity' and 'judicial dialogues' between national and international judges through preliminary rulings or advisory opinion procedures, empowering national judges to request legal interpretations of FTA rules and principles from such a TTIP Court.

If the 'rule of law' requirements of the Lisbon Treaty are construed in conformity with the famous *Les Verts* judgment of the ECJ, to the effect that the EU is 'a community based on the rule of law' to the extent that neither the member states nor the EU institutions can avoid review of the conformity of their acts with European constitutional law,[192] then the EU commitments to protecting 'strict observance of international law' and to 'exporting its values' in external EU relations must remain consistent with the constitutional rights and remedies of EU citizens, even if third countries—like the NAFTA countries in their FTAs with the EU—may not be willing to limit their national jurisdictions through transatlantic common market courts.[193] As illustrated by the 'constitutional pluralism' in the EU relations with EFTA states as discussed above, the EU can and must protect its constitutional principles (like individual rights to effective remedies pursuant to Article 47 EUCFR) as restraints on the exercise of EU public powers, even if judicial remedies and access to courts within the jurisdiction of the EU's trading partners may be regulated differently in view of their diverse constitutional traditions.

F. Disfranchisement of Citizens Enhances the Risks of Regulatory Cooperation

The EU's 'textual proposal' of February 2015 for the TTIP Chapter on 'Regulatory Cooperation' emphasizes that the provisions—as they 'concern predominantly procedures for cooperation' and 'cannot be interpreted or applied as to oblige either Party to change its fundamental principles governing regulation in its jurisdiction, for example in the areas of risk assessment

[192] Cf Case 294/83 *Les Verts v Parliament* [1986] ECR 1339, para 23. In the *Kadi I* and *II* cases, the CJEU stressed the importance of reviewing 'any Community measure' in the light of the fundamental rights of citizens in order to ensure 'a Community based on the rule of law'. In the *E & F* case of 2010, the CJEU confirmed the constitutional character of the rule of law principle by referring to the 'Union based on the rule of law': Case C-550/09, *E & F* [2010] ECR I-6209, para 44.

[193] In Case C-336/10 *Air Transport Association of America v Secretary of State for Energy* [2011] ECR I-13755, para 101, the CJEU confirmed, 'Under Article 3(5) TEU, the European Union is to contribute to the strict observance and the development of international law. Consequently, when it adopts an act, it is bound to observe international law in its entirety, including customary international law, which is binding upon the institutions of the European Union.'

and management'—'may not lend themselves to the application of dispute settlement rules'. Yet experience with product standards inside the EU demonstrates that EU standards may later be challenged as inadequately protecting public interests (eg Mercedes Benz challenging an EU standard for automobile coolers as posing a risk of causing fire and injuring people). The different cultures of *national* risk regulation in the US and *international risk regulation* and domestic risk aversion inside the EU, and the interest-driven nature of economic regulation notably in the USA (as illustrated by the disproportionate influence of the US gun and tobacco lobbies on preventing public health legislation), have given rise to numerous transatlantic regulatory conflicts over the past decades. Conflict prevention through inclusive representation (eg of trade, investment, consumer, labour and environmental interests), transparent negotiations and the design of the TTIP as a 'living agreement' enabling regulators to add and implement 'sectorial regulation annexes', must be supplemented by democratic scrutiny and judicial remedies, so as to take into account a maximum of information that may not be available to central regulators and changes over time. The 'new trade strategy' announced by EU Commissioner Malmström in October 2015[194] claims that the TTIP and other EU trade agreements will maintain or improve consumer protection levels, and will not amend the legislative and democratic decision-making procedures, so that the scope for autonomous rule-making by the Commission and other regulatory agencies remains limited.[195] Yet such claims are inconsistent with the denial of effective legal and judicial remedies of citizens against harmful treaty violations. As the past regulatory conflicts (eg regarding use of growth hormones and GMOs) will not magically disappear through the TTIP, inclusive regulatory processes, regulatory compatibility assessments and stakeholder participation in the TTIP's Regulatory Cooperation Council must be complemented by rights and remedies of citizens as the ultimate sources of values and the guardians of the rule of law in constitutional democracies. European Union diplomats have not offered convincing reasons why the EU constitutional law requirements for the 'rule of law' and 'rights to an effective remedy before a tribunal' (Article 47 EUCFR) should no longer be protected in FTAs, despite the past EU experience that such judicial remedies are crucial for realizing the EU Treaty objectives of 'protection of its citizens' and of 'strict observance of international law' (Article 3:5 TEU) in the EU's internal and external relations. Many of the past transatlantic disputes could have

[194] *Trade for All. Towards a More Responsible Trade ad Investment Policy*, EU Commission 2015.

[195] For detailed studies see C Gerstetter *et al*, *Regulatory Cooperation under TTIP—A Risk for Democracy and Regulation?* (Berlin, H Böll Stiftung, 2014); A Alemanno, *The TTIP and the Parliamentary Dimension of Regulatory Cooperation*, European Parliament 2014.

been avoided by stronger legal and judicial accountability of trade politicians vis-à-vis citizens, for instance if domestic courts had protected citizens against harmful violations of WTO dispute settlement rulings and WTO legal obligations approved by parliaments for the benefit of citizens.[196]

Since the 1960s, the internal EU common market rules and external FTAs based on GATT Article XXIV had been consistently interpreted and protected by national and European courts in terms of equal freedoms and rights of citizens, rather than only as reciprocal rights of governments. Such consistent interpretations and 'direct applicability' of liberal trade rules for the benefit of private economic actors and citizens were supported by the comprehensive GATT/WTO guarantees of individual access to judicial remedies, for instance in the field of GATT (Article X), the WTO Antidumping Agreement (Article 13), the WTO Agreement on Customs Valuation (Article 11), the Agreement on Pre-shipment Inspection (Article 4), the Agreement on Subsidies and Countervailing Measures (Article 23), the General Agreement on Trade in Services (Article VI GATS), the Agreement on Trade-Related Intellectual Property Rights (Articles 41–50, 59 TRIPS) and the Agreement on Government Procurement (Article XX). In contrast to this long-standing jurisprudence granting 'direct effect' to precise and unconditional FTA provisions approved by parliaments in order to enhance equal freedoms of citizens and general consumer welfare, from 2006 the political EU institutions began explicitly to restrain the 'direct effect' of more recent FTAs, for instance by:

- general clauses in the 'final provisions' of the agreement precluding 'direct effect';
- treaty clauses that FTA dispute settlement rulings 'shall be binding on the Parties and shall not create any rights or obligations for natural or legal persons';
- clauses in the schedules to commitments to liberalize services to the effect that 'the rights and obligations arising from the list shall have no self-executing effect and thus confer no rights directly to natural or juridical persons'; or
- provisions in the Council Decision approving the FTA that 'the agreement shall not be construed as conferring rights or imposing obligations which can be directly invoked before Union or Member State courts and tribunals'.[197]

This study has argued that the EU's neglect of its constitutional obligation of 'strict observance of international law' (eg through persistent violations

[196] Cf the numerous case studies in Petersmann and Pollack (eds) (n 155).

[197] Cf A Semertzi, 'The Preclusion of Direct Effect in the Recently Concluded EU Free Trade Agreements' (2014) 51 *CML Rev* 1125–58.

of GATT/WTO rules and dispute settlement findings) is just one illustration of 'systemic deficiencies' in the rule of law among and inside EU member states (like Bulgaria, Romania, Greece and Italy) that undermine multilevel EU governance by persistent violations of EU budget and debt disciplines, and of EU border protection and immigration rules.[198] Without the rule of law, democratic majority politics becomes increasingly opportunistic and devoid of legitimacy, as also illustrated by the past transatlantic 'banana disputes', anti-dumping disputes, 'subsidy competition' (eg from agricultural products to aircraft), disputes over growth hormones, GMOs, technical barriers to trade, discrimination in government procurement, telecommunications practices, air transport regulation and intellectual property rights.[199] Instead of designing transformative, transatlantic FTAs as 'an empire of laws and not of men' (using James Harrington's classic (1656) expression), the 'executive dominance' of CETA and TTIP negotiations and their intergovernmental 'disempowerment' of citizens risk making both Europe and the USA less democratic.[200]

V. CONCLUSION: COURTS OF JUSTICE MUST PROMOTE LEGAL CONSISTENCY IN MULTILEVEL DISPUTE SETTLEMENT IN CONFORMITY WITH COSMOPOLITAN RIGHTS

Chapter 1 argued that, when it comes to 'foreign policy', many international lawyers and politicians neglect the customary law requirement to interpret treaties and settle related disputes 'in conformity with the principles of justice and international law', including 'human rights and fundamental freedoms for all'. The more 'international PGs treaties' take over the 'constitutional functions' of democratic legislation by protecting equal freedoms, transnational rule of law and judicial remedies across national frontiers, the stronger become constitutional and republican arguments for interpreting precise and unconditional treaty rules—especially if they are incorporated into domestic legal systems as an 'integrating part of the Community legal system'[201] with legal primacy over national and EU secondary law inside the EU—as also protecting the equal rights of citizens. This chapter has used the examples of multilevel health, trade and investment regulations

[198] Cf A von Bogdandy and M Ioannidis, 'Systemic Deficiency in the Rule of Law: What it is, What has been done, What can be done' (2014) 51 *CML Rev* 59–96.

[199] On these past transatlantic disputes, see the case studies in Pollack and Petersmann (eds) (n 155).

[200] See also J Kopstein and S Steinmo (eds), *Growing Apart? America and Europe in the 21st Century* (Cambridge, CUP, 2008).

[201] This legal term for the 'domestic law effects' of international agreements concluded by the EC was coined by the ECJ in Case 181/73 *Haegeman v Belgium* [1974] ECR 449.

and related adjudication for explaining why transformation of *international* into *multilevel dispute settlement* can empower citizens to enforce human rights, liberal trade, investment and other treaty rules in decentralized ways, by holding governments accountable in domestic courts. Compared with intergovernmental dispute settlements, such empowerment of the 'democratic principals' to hold governance agents accountable for complying with the law approved by democratic parliaments is a more democratic, more efficient and more rules-based policy instrument in conformity with the 'subsidiarity' and 'proportionality principles' of EU law (eg Article 5 TEU). Power-orientated 'Hobbesian interpretations' of the EU's foreign policy constitution require justification beyond power politics ('freedom of manoeuvre') and utilitarianism ('Community interests') in view of the constitutional limitations of EU law by 'respect for human dignity, freedom, democracy, equality, the rule of law and respect for human rights' (Article 2 TEU).

This chapter has used the two case studies of multilevel tobacco regulation and transatlantic FTAs to argue that:

— EU law also requires protection of constitutional rights of EU citizens in multilevel regulation of transnational PGs (like health protection and transatlantic markets) on the basis of constitutional, parliamentary, deliberative and participatory 'principles of democratic governance', in conformity with the EU principles of the rule of law, limited delegation of powers, subsidiarity, proportionality and reasonable justifications of restrictions of individual freedoms;
— the inadequate parliamentary control of intergovernmental treaty-making must be compensated by constitutional, participatory and 'deliberative democracy', so as to empower citizens to invoke, challenge or enforce precise and unconditional 'PGs treaties' for transnational protection of equal freedoms, non-discriminatory competition and the rule of law in domestic courts, thereby restraining discretionary foreign policy powers and their frequent abuses in response to rent-seeking interest group pressures;
— transatlantic FTAs with the federal democracies in North America—like other democratic legislation—derive their democratic legitimacy from protecting equal rights of citizens, democratic autonomy and PGs demanded by citizens; rights-based interpretations and decentralized enforcement of FTA rules are likely to contribute to limiting 'market failures' as well as 'governance failures' in transatlantic relations, including the selfish exclusion of legal and judicial accountability of governments vis-à-vis citizens adversely affected by violations of FTA guarantees of equal freedoms, non-discrimination and transnational rule of law.

As 'the demands of justice can be assessed only with the help of public reasoning', citizens rightly insist on more inclusive discussion of transatlantic

FTAs, so as to promote more accountability and substantive justice in transatlantic relations.[202] Article 30.6 CETA and 'ISDS privileges' of foreign investors are inconsistent with the EU's 'cosmopolitan mandate' of protecting the rights of EU citizens equally and democratically. The lack of transparency of CETA and TTIP *negotiations* has prevented citizens from voicing their concerns at such 'legal protectionism' and 'agency capture' by interest groups. Citizens must now—during the parliamentary and democratic debates about *conclusion* and *implementation* of the CETA—assume their democratic and 'cosmopolitan responsibilities' for protecting the rights of all citizens, so as to enhance 'human and democratic capabilities' in mutually beneficial, transatlantic cooperation. If politics is the art of making possible tomorrow what seems impossible today, citizens should insist on reforming 'Hobbesian power politics' by limiting discretionary foreign policy powers through stronger constitutional rights and remedies of citizens. Who else could provide leadership for such 'cosmopolitan reforms' of intergovernmental power politics than citizens and constitutional democracies in Europe and North America? Their past 'democratic experience' confirms that 'republican FTAs' (like the EEA Agreement) based on cosmopolitan rights and their decentralized 'bottom-up enforcement'—beginning with a limited number of transnational rights of citizens (eg to justification of governmental restrictions, non-discriminatory market access, individual 'access to justice' and judicial remedies in domestic courts)—tend to be more effectively supported and enforced for the benefit of citizens.

A. Beyond Liberalism and Communitarianism: the Human Right to Justification

As explained in Chapter 1, the more global communications, division of labour and international movements of persons make the cosmopolitan paradigm of human beings as a world community a social reality, the more important becomes the universal recognition in HRL (eg Article 29 UDHR) and constitutional law (eg Article 52 EUCFR) that governmental limitations of individual freedoms must be justifiable in terms of procedural and substantive 'due process of law', 'human rights and fundamental freedoms for all'. The universal recognition that '[a]ll human beings are born free and equal in dignity and rights' and are 'endowed with reason and conscience' (Article 1 UDHR) justifies a conception of justice as being based on a human right to justification; as 'justificatory human beings', citizens

[202] Cf A Sen, *The Idea of Justice* (Cambridge, MA, Harvard UP, 2009) 326, 349 (eg pointing out that public criticism and accountability of politicians have contributed to avoiding famines and promoting gender equality and public education in democratic countries).

have moral duties to 'discursively construct and justify' constitutional law and challenge injustices by insisting on the public use of human 'reason and conscience'.[203] Chapter 1 also explained why the universal recognition of the 'inalienable' and 'indivisible' nature of civil, political, economic, social and cultural human rights leaves each state democratic 'margins of appreciation' that entail legitimate 'constitutional pluralism', requiring respect for diverse democratic preferences and constitutional traditions. For instance, the interpretation of national and European constitutional guarantees of equal freedoms as the 'first principle of justice' (in terms of Kantian and Rawlsian constitutional theories) remains contested by communitarian legal and democratic traditions. Chapter 1 and this chapter have argued that—in order to protect multilevel governance of transnational aggregate PGs—the 'intermediate PGs' inside constitutional democracies (like the 'trias' of constitutional rights, the rule of law, democratic self-government) need to be extended beyond national frontiers, for instance by multilevel judicial protection of cosmopolitan and 'republican' rights, regardless of whether domestic democracies prioritize 'liberal' or 'communitarian' constitutional traditions. This conclusion was justified in Chapter 1 by the need for interpreting 'principles of justice' with due regard to their diverse contexts; under-theorized 'PGs treaties' need to be clarified for the benefit of citizens entitled to more effective legal protection of reasonably justified, cosmopolitan rights and other transnational PGs.

As 'constitutional justice' requires recognition of citizens as the authors and addressees of legal self-government, the exclusion of individual rights and judicial remedies in recent intergovernmental trade negotiations by the EU was criticized as an illustration of how 'principles of justice'—as justifications of 'just relations among persons'—continue to be procedurally and substantively neglected in multilevel governance of transnational PGs. The EU's 'cosmopolitan foreign policy mandate' was construed as requiring limitation of *state-centered, international* by *person-centered multilevel dispute settlement*, so as to protect the equal freedoms of citizens in their mutually beneficial cooperation in the external relations of the EU too. The 'contexts of justice' in the EU's external relations differ depending on the specific 'PGs treaties' and foreign policy objectives. For example:

— the EU's multilevel *legal protection of human rights* in its external relations (eg by including human rights clauses into more than 130 trade and cooperation agreements with third countries) strengthens civil society struggles for human rights and the rule of law in transnational relations, and justifies EU responses to violations of human rights by its treaty partners;

[203] Cf R Forst, *The Right to Justification. Elements of a Constructivist Theory of Justice* (New York, Columbia University Press, 2012).

— the multilevel *judicial protection of human rights and the rule of law*—eg by means of the *Kadi* jurisprudence of the CJEU and the '*Solange* jurisprudence' of national constitutional courts and of the ECtHR—has contributed to multilevel governance reforms (eg in UN Security Council practices through the institution of an 'ombudsman' reviewing private challenges by persons listed as potential terrorists);
— even if the EU's legal obligations (eg under Article 21 TEU and the EUCFR) 'to advance ... human rights and fundamental freedoms' also in the Union's external actions do not provide for additional foreign policy powers, the EU institutions infer from these constitutional obligations procedural rights and duties (eg to conduct a human rights impact assessment) that—in the case of manifest errors of assessment—may call into question the validity of EU acts. For instance, in the recent Case T-512/12 *Frente Polisario v Council* of 10 December 2015, the General Court annulled the Council's decision to conclude a trade agreement with Morocco that could have violated the fundamental rights protected under the EUCFR and Article 21 TEU.[204] Similarly, in response to a complaint by two NGOs in the context of the FTA between the EU and Vietnam, the EU Ombudsman derived from Article 21 TEU a procedural duty to conduct a human rights impact assessment.[205] Depending on the legal context, multilevel judicial protection of transnational trading, investment and intellectual property rights may be justifiable in view of corresponding constitutional rights of citizens and explicit treaty clauses (eg in EU law, WTO law, WIPO conventions and BITs) protecting rights and remedies of citizens beyond national frontiers.

Chapter 1 construed the universal recognition of 'inalienable' and 'indivisible' civil, political, economic, social and cultural rights as acknowledging the human entitlement to 'ethical autonomy' (eg to define one's individual identity and conception of a 'good life'), 'social autonomy' (eg to develop one's individual human capacities in social communities), legal autonomy (eg to be recognized and protected as an equal person and a legal subject), political autonomy (eg to be recognized and legally protected as a 'democratic principal' and an 'agent of justice') and universal moral autonomy

[204] Case T-512/12 *Frente Polisario v Council*, EU:T:2015:953 (nyr and under appeal before the CJEU).

[205] This Decision by the EU Ombudsman of 26 February 2016 (Case 1409/2014/MHZ) is discussed by Kube (n 178) 27 ff. The EUCFR protects the rights of 'everyone', as well as additional rights of EU citizens or EU residents. While the term 'human rights' is today mostly used in international law, EU law and EU institutions use the term 'fundamental rights' for specifying human rights within EU constitutional contexts. Unlike some human rights conventions, the EUCFR's applicability does not follow the distinction between applying rights inside the state territory and in extra-territorial relations (cf Moreno-Lax and Costello, n 178).

(eg as a human being, to be treated with all due respect for one's human dignity and 'cosmopolitan responsibilities'). Yet these diverse dimensions of individual autonomy as a human right must be justified, reconciled and regulated through social, legal and democratic discourse, and reciprocal recognition of individuals as free and equal citizens in their respective communities, preferably without one-sided focus on 'liberalism' or 'communitarianism'.[206] In multilevel governance of transnational PGs, EU citizens are entitled to multilevel judicial protection of 'strict observance of international law' (Article 3 TEU) so that they can hold multilevel governance 'agents' with limited mandates legally, democratically and judicially accountable. Violations by the EU of international 'PGs treaties' approved by parliaments risk undermining the rule of law and equal rights of EU citizens inside and beyond the Union. 'Cosmopolitan interpretations' of the external relations law of the EU are not only more consistent with the text, context and objectives of the Lisbon Treaty than 'statist paradigms' of discretionary power politics in EU foreign policies; the deliberate non-conferral of EU powers to violate international treaties for republican supply of international PGs justifies legal presumptions that—in a transnational rule of law community like the EU, with constitutionally limited powers based on principles of conferral, subsidiarity and proportionality (Article 5 TEU), and committed to 'protection of its citizens' and 'strict observance of international law' in the EU's external relations too (Article 2 TEU)—international dispute settlement obligations of the EU must be legally presumed to derive their constitutional legitimacy from protecting the equal rights of EU citizens and judicial remedies (cf Article 47 EUCFR). Similar to the constitutional obligations of national courts (eg pursuant to the jurisprudence of the German Constitutional Court) to interpret fundamental rights with due regard to their interpretation and protection by the CJEU and by the ECtHR,[207] the 'consistent interpretation' requirements of EU law and international law may require national and EU courts to protect transnational rights of citizens with due regard to international dispute settlement rulings binding on the EU and its member states. It is necessary for EU law to balance state-centered and person-orientated 'principles of justice' with due respect for 'due process of law' guarantees and judicial remedies in the EU's external relations too, so as to 'support democracy, the rule of law, human rights' and 'consistency' between its internal and external actions (cf Article 21 TEU). This calls for multilevel legal protection of civil society cooperation and democratic self-government among free and equal citizens beyond

[206] Cf R Forst, *Contexts of Justice: Political Philosophy beyond Liberalism and Communitarianism* (Berkeley, CA, University of California Press, 2002).

[207] Cf *Görgülü v Germany* (2004) 2 BvR 1481/04.

national frontiers, for instance in the global division of labour and in related 'compliance communities' benefitting from transnational rule of law.

B. Unjust Treatment of EU Citizens as Mere Legal Objects

In *internal* EU and EEA law, citizens continue to be recognized as 'market citizens', 'democratic principals', and subjects of constitutional and cosmopolitan rights and related judicial remedies in national and European courts. In the *external* relations of the EU with non-European countries, however, the EU policies deny legal and judicial rights of citizens to invoke and enforce in national and European courts 'PGs treaties' approved by parliaments for the benefit of citizens (like UN and WTO agreements, and FTAs). From the point of view of the EU 'values' as defined in Article 2 TEU and confirmed for EU external relations in Articles 3 and 21 TEU and the EUCFR, this 'disrespect' for the human autonomy of EU citizens and for their rights—as 'agents of justice' and 'democratic principals' of EU governance agents—to be treated as the authors and addressees of EU rule-making was criticized in Chapter 1 and this chapter as undermining the EU's 'cosmopolitan foreign policy mandate' and transnational rule of law inside the EU too. For instance, discriminatory import restrictions in violation of WTO rules are also bound to discriminate between domestic importers and consumers by distorting market access, prices and market shares. As market freedoms and the 'liberty rights' protected in the EUCFR permeate not only internal EU law, but also the EU's customs union obligations under WTO law (eg Article XXIV) and EU law (Articles 30 et seq TFEU), it was suggested that the corresponding transnational rights of citizens (eg the 'freedom to conduct a business in accordance with Union law' pursuant to Article 16 EUCFR) and the constitutional commitments to 'protection of its citizens' and 'free and fair trade' in external relations (Article 3 TEU) should be interpreted as protecting the freedom of EU citizens beyond EU borders too, for instance by prohibiting discriminatory non-tariff trade barriers violating GATT/WTO obligations of the EU and its member states. Empirical evidence confirms that the successful internal development of the EU (eg its single market law) was largely due to its multilevel judicial protection of fundamental freedoms, the rule of law and democratic governance. Also the EU's 'foreign policy constitution' requires multilevel judicial protection of equal freedoms, 'strict observance of international law' and democratic governance, so as to realize the explicit EU objective 'to advance in the wider world: democracy, the rule of law … and … human rights and fundamental freedoms' (Article 21 TEU). As the exclusion of rights and remedies of EU citizens in transatlantic FTAs is not convincingly justified, and EU treaty violations to the detriment of EU citizens tend to be arbitrary, reasonable citizens should resist the EU's intergovernmental power politics.

The EU participates in international dispute settlement proceedings mainly in the context of UN agreements (eg the International Tribunal for the Law of the Sea), WTO agreements (the WTO dispute settlement system), and EU trade and investment agreements (eg third-party intervention by the EU in investor-state arbitration). All these UN, WTO, trade and investment agreements are approved by national and European parliaments so as to protect transnational transactions (eg trade, investments, shipping) of EU citizens, for instance by providing 'security and predictability to the multilateral trading system' (Article 3 DSU), reducing private transaction costs, and protecting individual rights and market access in the global division of labour. The EU Trade Barriers Regulation offers legal procedures empowering EU citizens to request diplomatic and legal protection by the EU vis-à-vis 'illicit trade barriers' by third countries. A large number of the more than 600 complaints submitted by GATT/WTO members since 1948 continue to be triggered indirectly by requests from industries on the basis of domestic legal safeguards, as reflected in the names of many GATT/WTO disputes (eg 'Kodak/Fuji', 'Havana Club', 'EU bananas', 'Boeing/Airbus aircraft disputes', GMO disputes). More importantly, the 'dispute settlement system of the WTO' (Article 3 DSU) also prescribes and protects judicial remedies for individuals and non-governmental actors in *domestic legal systems* against rule violations by their own governments. Violations of international trade, investment, transport and communication rules regularly affect the equal freedoms and welfare of EU citizens—for instance, their 'freedom to conduct a business in accordance with Union law and national laws' (Article 16 EUCFR) and their 'right to own, use, dispose of and bequeath [their] lawfully acquired possessions' (Article 17 EUCFR). Hence, judicial protection of 'consistent interpretations' of multilevel economic regulations and individual rights to invoke international rules protecting equal freedoms, non-discrimination and the rule of law in domestic courts, have been among the most successful EU principles for promoting rule of law inside the EU. Also in the EEA and other FTAs, the 'direct applicability' of free trade rules has meant that *international* trade disputes among states have rarely arisen in the CJEU, the EFTA Court and other FTA dispute settlement procedures, due to their avoidance through decentralized, depoliticized rule enforcement by citizens. 'Direct applicability' of WTO rules in domestic legal systems (as required by Article XX of the WTO Agreement on Government Procurement), 'consistent interpretation' of WTO rules, or their 'indirect applicability' by domestic courts (as required by the above-mentioned WTO guarantees of judicial remedies and by Article XIV:4 WTO Agreement on good faith-implementation of WTO obligations) could similarly promote decentralized implementation of WTO rules by economic operators and domestic institutions, thereby preventing and depoliticizing power-orientated dispute settlement proceeding with third WTO members.[208] Rights-based participation of citizens in providing PGs also promotes 'participatory' and 'deliberative democracy' and 'republican virtues'. By empowering citizens to challenge abuses of public and private powers, it helps to 'constitutionalize' law and transform the 'constitutional law in the books' into 'law in action' and social reality. The more UN and WTO 'decisions affect the lives of ordinary men and women all over the world',[209] the more it becomes necessary to interpret democratic legislation and related 'PGs treaties' in mutually consistent ways for the benefit of citizens.

C. 'Access to Justice' Requires Multilevel Dispute Settlement in the EU's External Relations Law

Chapter 1 identified 'access to justice' as one of the core 'principles of justice', HRL and constitutional law, as recognized in numerous EU Treaty provisions (eg Articles 47, 52 EUCFR, Article 296 TFEU: 'Legal acts shall state the reasons on which they are based'). Past arguments invented by EU politicians for justifying their non-compliance with GATT/WTO legal and dispute settlement obligations, and for preventing citizens from invoking GATT/WTO rules in domestic courts—such as the alleged indeterminacy of GATT obligations, the existence of GATT safeguard clauses, the reciprocity of trade liberalization in GATT, and the political possibility of avoiding trade sanctions by third countries through voluntarily agreed compensation—lacked convincing legal reasoning;[210] they have been progressively abandoned in favour of political claims by EU institutions that the 'nature and purpose of WTO law' justify 'freedom of manoeuvre' to violate WTO rules. Yet such claims are inconsistent with:

— the unconditional GATT/WTO obligations to terminate illegal measures (eg as specified in the customary rules on state responsibility and enforced through the WTO's DSU);
— the lack of conferral of EU powers to engage in welfare-reducing violations of WTO rules, which all national parliaments and the European

[208] Cf Petersmann (n 25) 233 ff; C Heidfeld, *Die denzentrale Durchsetzung des WTO-Rechts in der EU* (Baden-Baden, Nomos, 2012).

[209] WTO Director-General Moore, in his opening speech to the first 'Public Forum' inside the WTO, which has continued to be organized annually in the WTO since 2001, with the participation of thousands of civil society representatives and NGOs; cf *The WTO at 20: Challenges and Achievements* (Geneva, WTO, 2015) 81.

[210] Cf EU Petersmann, 'Application of GATT by the Court of Justice of the European Communities' (1983) 20 *CML Rev* 397–437.

Parliament approved for the benefit of EU citizens so as to protect rule of law inside and beyond the EU;

— the legal primacy of international agreements concluded by the EU—as 'integral' and 'integrating' parts[211] of the EU legal system—over other 'secondary EU law';
— the often precise and unconditional nature of WTO guarantees of freedom of trade, non-discrimination and the rule of law; and
— the multilevel 'nature and purpose' of the GATT/WTO dispute settlement system, as illustrated by the explicit GATT/WTO legal obligations to protect legal and judicial remedies against GATT/WTO violations in *domestic jurisdictions* too, in order to provide 'security and predictability' for traders.[212]

The GATT/WTO jurisprudence of the CJEU further disregards:

— the 'constitutional mandate' of EU courts (eg as specified in Articles 19, 21 TEU) to 'ensure that in the implementation and application of the Treaties the law is observed' so as to 'ensure effective legal protection' (Article 19 TEU) in the EU's participation in multilevel governance of international PGs like a rules-based world trading system; and
— the 'democratic' and 'republican functions' of international 'PGs treaties', which increasingly take over functions of democratic legislation so as to protect 'aggregate PGs' for the benefit of citizens, for example by requiring '[e]ach Member [to] ensure the conformity of its laws, regulations and administrative procedures with its obligations as provided in the annexed Agreements' (Article XVI:4 WTO Agreement).

According to the settled case law of the CJEU, 'the principle of proportionality requires that acts of the EU institutions be appropriate for attaining the legitimate objectives pursued by the legislation at issue and do not go beyond what is necessary in order to achieve those objectives';[213] EU compliance with WTO guarantees of equal freedoms, non-discriminatory trade conditions and 'strict observance of international law' in mutually beneficial trade transactions offers more efficient, lawful policy instruments than discriminatory, welfare-reducing and illegal EU trade distortions in violation of WTO rules. At least in the trade policy area, EU constitutional law and the large 'policy space' reserved by WTO law exclude 'political question justifications' of EU violations of WTO obligations to the detriment of EU citizens. Contrary to the claims by EU institutions, the 'nature and purpose' of WTO rules require 'providing security and predictability to the multilateral trading system' (Article 3 DSU) and individual access to justice for private

211 Cf n 201 above.

212 Cf Petersmann (n 165) and related text.

213 Cf Case C-59/11 *Kokopelli*, EU:C:2012:447, and the case law cited in para 38.

economic actors who are adversely affected by illegal EU disregard for WTO law and dispute settlement rulings. When the GATT Secretariat hired me in 1981 as the first 'legal officer' ever employed by GATT, I was told that the GATT Directors-General had so far not dared to establish a 'GATT Office of Legal Affairs' due to opposition from the EC and its preference for political (ie power-orientated) rather than judicial settlement of the many GATT challenges of EC restrictions/distortions in agricultural trade.[214] In the early 1980s, lawyers from the EC Legal Services were not allowed to participate in GATT panel procedures; and EC Trade Commissioner Willy de Clerq continued to give speeches to the effect that 'GATT must never be transformed into a trade court'. Even after the successful conclusion of the Uruguay Round negotiations on the WTO and its DSU establishing a worldwide, compulsory jurisdiction for the settlement of WTO disputes, the EC Council Decision of 22 December 1994 on the conclusion of the WTO agreements claimed that 'by its nature, the Agreement establishing the World Trade Organization, including the Annexes thereto, is not susceptible to being directly invoked in Community or Member State courts'.[215] Just as, during the 1980s, EU trade politicians responded to industry pressures by concluding dozens of secretive 'voluntary export restraint agreements' in violation of GATT and EU law, the 20 years (1991–2012) of illegal EU import restrictions on bananas reflected the unwillingness of EU trade politicians to defend the rule of law vis-à-vis rent-seeking pressure groups. Other persistent violations of EU law—eg of the budget and debt disciplines imposed by Article 126 TFEU for the European Economic and Monetary Union, or of the 'Schengen' and 'Dublin' procedures for foreign asylum seekers and economic migrants—reveal systemic rule-of-law problems of periodically elected politicians inside the EU. The more the EU 'law in the books' is persistently violated, the weaker political institutions become (eg due to their 'capture' by rent-seeking interest groups they have to satisfy to secure majority support) and the more EU citizens complain about the 'democratic deficit' of illegal EU actions that ignore the law approved by national and European parliaments on behalf of citizens.

D. Constitutional EU Safeguards of Individual Freedoms do not Depend on Reciprocity

Constitutional EU guarantees to 'everyone' of 'an effective remedy before a tribunal' are not conditioned on reciprocity (cf Article 47 EUCFR). Human

[214] Cf EU Petersmann, 'The Establishment of a GATT Office of Legal Affairs and the Limited Public Reason in the GATT/WTO Dispute Settlement System' in G Marceau (ed), *A History of Law and Lawyers in the GATT/WTO. The Development of the Rule of Law in the Multilateral Trading System* (Cambridge, CUP, 2015) 182–207.

[215] Cf Petersmann (n 25) 21.

rights law and European constitutional law provide that '[a]ny limitation on the exercise of the rights and freedoms recognized by this Charter must be provided for by law and respect the essence of those rights and freedoms', subject to constitutional safeguards of 'necessity' and 'proportionality' (Article 52 EUCFR). This constitutional justification must also be respected by national and EU institutions in the external relations law of the EU whenever individual freedoms—like the economic freedoms 'to choose an occupation' (Article 15 EUCFR), 'to conduct a business in accordance with Union law' (Article 16 EUCFR), and to own and use private property (Article 17 EUCFR)—are protected by EU constitutional law across national and EU frontiers. In a multilevel rule of law community with constitutionally limited powers, the 'consistent interpretation' requirements of EU law and international law require national and EU courts to protect transnational rights of citizens with due regard to multilevel adjudication binding on the EU and its member states. The shared legal obligations and 'constitutional functions' of national, EU and international dispute settlement bodies to interpret treaties and settle related disputes 'in conformity with the principles of justice and international law', including 'universal respect for human rights and fundamental freedoms for all' (Preamble and Article 31 VCLT), require multilevel judicial comity in their common mission of administering justice, including 'individual justice' for citizens participating in transnational cooperation and protection of PGs. As:

- EU citizens and national 'peoples' remain the 'constituent powers' in the EU;
- the European Parliament exercises only limited legislative, budgetary and political powers (cf Article 14 TEU); and
- 'the Union is founded on the indivisible, universal values of human dignity, freedom, equality and solidarity', 'the principles of democracy and the rule of law', and 'places the individual at the heart of its activities' (Preamble EUCFR);

'constitutional' and 'cosmopolitan' interpretations of EU law better fit its multilevel constitutional structures than statist, power-orientated paradigms of foreign politics. The policy argument by EU trade diplomats—ie that they exclude individual rights to invoke FTA provisions and WTO legal obligations in domestic courts in view of the similar practices in the EU's trading partners like Canada, Singapore and the USA—is inconsistent with the EU's 'foreign policy constitution', just as denial of protection of human rights and labour rights in the context of FTAs cannot be justified on the ground that foreign trading partners (like the USA) have not ratified UN human rights and ILO labour rights conventions that were ratified by EU member states.

As '[e]veryone whose rights and freedoms guaranteed by the law of the Union are violated has the right to an effective remedy before a tribunal' (Article 47 EUCFR), the EU must also protect equal freedoms, the rule of law and effective judicial remedies in international dispute settlement proceedings over EU violations of the 'strict observance of international law'. Article 3 TEU—by stating that the 'Union's aim is to promote peace, its values and the well-being of its peoples' and specifying these objectives by a list of PGs (like the internal market, the 'area of freedom, security and justice', a 'highly competitive social market economy', an economic and monetary Union)—reflects the republican nature of EU law, ie the conferral by citizens and peoples of limited powers to EU institutions in order to protect PGs beneficial for all EU citizens. Articles 3 and 21 TEU explicitly commit the EU to 'republican constitutionalism' (eg 'democracy, the rule of law, human rights and fundamental freedoms', and other specific PGs) in its external relations too. Similarly, the EU's foreign policy mandates emphasize the need for respecting 'uniform principles' (Article 207 TFEU), and define agreed PGs like 'progressive abolition of restrictions on international trade and on foreign investments' (Article 206 TFEU) in the context of the EU's common commercial policy, or 'reduction and ... eradication of poverty' as a 'primary objective' of the EU's development cooperation policy (Article 208 TFEU).

Welfare-reducing treaty violations are neither 'necessary' nor 'proportionate' instruments for realizing legitimate EU policy objectives. Hence, citizens and courts of justice must challenge the widening gap between the 'EU law in the books' and EU legal practices, so as to enhance the EU's 'democratic capabilities' to comply with the rule of law. Rights-based empowerment of citizens is not only a matter of justice and of promoting 'republican virtues' and 'democratic vigilance' against abuses of governance powers; 'countervailing rights' of adversely affected citizens are also the most efficient, decentralized instrument for counteracting rule violations. In citizen-driven areas of transnational economic, democratic and civil society cooperation, the EU's subsidiarity requirement—ie 'to ensure that decisions are taken as closely as possible to the citizens of the Union' (cf Article 1 and the TEU Protocol on the Application of the Principles of Subsidiarity and Proportionality)—reflects historical lessons from centuries of civil society struggles for republican constitutionalism, eg that multilevel judicial cooperation in human rights, commercial, common market and criminal law adjudication can protect the equal rights of citizens, judicial remedies, transnational rule of law and 'republican compliance communities' more effectively across national frontiers than intergovernmental power politics. Also in international commercial, trade and investment law, criminal and maritime law, HRL, and intellectual property law and adjudication, the increasing number of international courts and of their cases[216] respond to demands from civil society and related 'legal communities' for limiting 'governance failures' through international courts. The 'new strategy' advocated by EU Trade Commissioner Malmström in response to the EU citizen protests against the secretive TTIP negotiations, confirms, once again, that struggles for justice by EU citizens may be crucial for transforming an 'international community of states' (Article 53 VCLT) into a cosmopolitan community of citizens, peoples and democratic governments respecting their legal duties to 'uphold and promote' the EU's internal values and also 'contribute to the protection of its citizens' (Article 3:5 TEU) in multilevel governance of global PGs.

[216] Cf G De Baere and J Wouters (eds), *The Contribution of International and Supranational Courts to the Rule of Law* (Cheltenham, Elgar, 2015); K Alter, *The New Terrain of International Law: International Courts in International Politics* (Princeton, NJ, Princeton UP, 2013).

3

Civilizing and Constitutionalizing 'Disconnected' UN, WTO and EU Governance Require 'Cosmopolitan Constitutionalism': Legal Methodology Challenges

THE INTRODUCTION TO this book briefly described how the constitutional principles of democracy, republicanism, access to justice and cosmopolitan rights—since their emergence in ancient Greek and Roman legal and political philosophy, and notwithstanding their frequent disregard in legal and judicial practices (like the trial of Jesus in ancient Jerusalem, the trial of Gallileo Gallilei in the Vatican at the end of the Renaissance)—not only have gradually evolved into integral parts of UN law; the long-standing civil society struggles for 'democratic', 'republican' and 'cosmopolitan constitutionalism' aimed at democratic protection of PGs have also—following World War II—progressively succeeded in 'constitutionalizing' ever more national and regional governance systems for the benefit of citizens, including functionally limited fields of international regulation such as commercial, trade, investment, intellectual property, labour law and Internet regulation. Yet in many UN member states, the universal human rights obligations of all UN member states and related 'top-down' and 'bottom-up processes' of progressive 'constitutionalization' have failed to transform the 'UN law in the books' into effective 'law in action' and 'cosmopolitan legal cultures' protecting human rights for all human beings.

I. FROM 'CONSTITUTIONALISM 1.0' TO 'CONSTITUTIONALISM 4.0'

Chapter 1 briefly discussed the impact of the globalization of markets and of related security risks on the transformation of national Constitutions in terms of Somek's distinction between '*constitutionalism 1.0*' (like the post-revolutionary, emancipatory US and French 'constitutions of liberty' during the eighteenth century establishing legislative, executive and judicial powers for democratic self-government), '*constitutionalism 2.0*' (like the post-World War II democratic 'human rights constitutions', committed to the protection of human dignity and civil, political, economic and social rights for everybody) and '*constitutionalism 3.0*' (like the national 'cosmopolitan Constitutions' of EU member states supporting multilevel constitutionalization of multilevel governance of transnational PGs like the single market among 31 EEA member states based on common market rights, other fundamental rights and non-discrimination of citizens on grounds of nationality). The constitutional principles of liberty, equality and solidarity have become universally recognized parts of UN HRL; multilevel regulation of 'market failures' and 'governance failures', and judicial powers of review of legislative and administrative restrictions of fundamental rights, continue to increase in national and international jurisdictions (eg by resorting to multilevel 'proportionality review' rather than only to the more limited judicial review of whether government institutions pursue legitimate ends through rational means within their limited powers). Yet even if global constitutionalism and global democracy remain *utopias* in the twenty-first century, Somek's claim that the modern 'constitutional pluralism' and disabling effects of 'rampant market integration' and 'global capitalism' reflect a 'law of the jungle' and the demise of rules-based, democratic self-government was criticized.[1] Chapters 1 and 2 of this book focused rather on the opportunities for using 'cosmopolitan constitutionalism' for 'bottom-up' and 'top-down' constitutionalization of multilevel governance of functionally limited, transnational PGs like human rights, transnational rule of law, citizen-driven market competition, public health and protection of scarce environmental resources. European economic and human rights laws since the 1950s were described as the most successful 'civilization project' in history. Arguably, globalization requires the transformation of *national* democratic and republican constitutionalism into *multilevel cosmopolitan* and *republican constitutionalism* supported by citizens and non-citizens alike. This political need for constitutionalizing multilevel governance of transnational PGs—and the legal possibility of promoting '*multilevel constitutionalism 4.0*' through empowering citizens, civil society, parliamentary and judicial cooperation in multilevel governance across national frontiers—is unduly

[1] See A Somek, *The Cosmopolitan Constitution* (Oxford, OUP, 2014) 21 ff and my criticism at n 215 and related text in ch 1. According to Somek: 'Constitutionalism 3.0 is, therefore, witness to the return of *political* constitutionalism. Effective constraints emerge not from law but from more or less subtle equilibria of power ... The overall constitution of the multilevel system ceases to be law altogether. It is a factum, not a norm'; 'a form of political constitutionalism' and 'authoritarian liberalism' that fails to effectively control 'transnational fora of executive governance' and global markets owing to the lack of information and expertise of national parliaments; 'the real constraints on governance are economic'; 197 ff ('pluralism confronts us ... with the law of the jungle').

neglected in Somek's account of 'constitutionalism' (eg by neglecting 'constitutional failures' in 'constitutionalism 3.0' and how they have partly been overcome through European constitutional law). The universal recognition of human rights by UN member states has not brought about 'the end of history', 'social justice' for all least-advantaged members of society, and effective democratic control of the ever more expansive 'executive governance' and its 'administrative rationality' (eg relying on 'experts'), which threatens both the 'freedom of the ancients' (eg self-government) as well as modern social freedoms of 'cosmopolitan strangers' unless citizens use their human, constitutional and cosmopolitan rights for 'constitutionalizing' UN/WTO and regional governance of PGs.

In Europe and North America, democratic constitutionalism in the twenty-first century is no longer only about emancipation of 'peoples' and citizens inside nation states and the 'constitutionalization' of the 'executive power grab' inside most states; it is also about the emancipation of 'market citizens' and 'social citizens' living as foreigners abroad (eg EU citizens) and invoking transnational rights (eg under the EUCFR, the ECHR) as limitations on 'market failures' and 'governance failures' (eg in transatlantic market relations, related violations of international law, international economic migration). If cosmopolitans leave their country and live abroad as foreigners, their cosmopolitan rights (eg under EU law and HRL) assume existential importance as the legal foundation of their self-determination in a foreign polity, economy and society. Nation states often deny foreigners adequate representation and engage in harmful regulation adversely affecting foreigners. Hence, the limitation of discrimination on grounds of nationality remains the chief objective of international commercial, trade, investment and other 'cosmopolitan' agreements. Non-discriminatory cosmopolitan law enhances 'public reason' and morality over the rationality of popular, national majority politics, for instance by limiting adverse 'external effects' beyond national borders. Yet, as discussed in Chapter 2 in the context of EU FTAs with non-European countries, constitutional rules on 'inclusive decision-making' and on the 'protection of citizens' in external relations (eg Articles 3, 21 TEU) are often disregarded in 'executive governance' and 'interest group politics', for instance by 'disempowering citizens' (eg in Article 30.6 CETA) and undermining their fundamental rights and judicial remedies (eg contrary to Article 47 EUCFR). Democratic criticism by parliaments and civil society of such 'disconnected', multilevel governance of PGs and of 'market failures' (eg bankers selling financial products they do not understand) is increasing in Europe and North America too.

As discussed throughout this book, 'public choice analyses' demonstrate the idealist assumptions of the project of constraining political power through constitutional law (eg that government officials will maximize 'public interests', and 'separation of powers' will result in *equilibria* as envisaged by 'legal constitutionalism'). 'Political constitutionalism' and globalization require civil society struggles for 'constitutionalizing' abuses of power through multilevel guarantees of cosmopolitan freedoms inside states, among states and vis-à-vis foreign states. Kant convincingly rejected utopias of a 'world state' and emphasized the inadequacy of merely coordinating foreign policies through international 'congresses' and a 'League among sovereign states' ('*Völkerbund*'). His proposals for a republican, multi-state confederation ('*Völkerstaat*') and 'cosmopolitan constitution' acknowledged the non-ideal reality of international relations and the need for experimenting with diverse kinds of transnational 'cosmopolitan law' and 'institutional pluralism'.[2] The Introduction explained why—just as national constitutional democracies succeeded in 'constitutionalizing' human rights protection only by integrating the diverse democratic, republican and cosmopolitan constitutional traditions—the 'disconnected intergovernmentalism' in UN, WTO and regional governance of transnational PGs requires integrating democratic, republican and cosmopolitan constitutionalism through 'constitutional' treaty interpretations and adjudication that must reconcile state-centered and person-centered 'principles of justice'. In determining the 'rules of recognition' and interpreting international law, citizens and democratic peoples must be recognized as 'constituent powers' and 'agents of justice'; the legally required respect for human dignity, legal autonomy and 'access to justice' of all persons affected by UN/WTO law must be more effectively protected through transparent and inclusive 'discourse justifications', 'constitutional interpretations' and judicial remedies of citizens in multilevel legal practices. 'State sovereignty', 'international law among sovereign states' and power politics will remain foundations of international relations. As globalization transforms national into transnational PGs, the central legal challenge of the twenty-first century is the constitutional and republican design of more effective and more democratic multilevel rules and governance institutions for the collective supply of PGs demanded by citizens. In view of the rational egoism and 'animal instincts' of human beings, multilevel constitutionalism, republican constructivism and learning from comparative institutionalism were described as necessary methodologies for protecting and progressively extending the 'trias' of constitutional rights, rule of law and democracy in multilevel governance of 'aggregate PGs'.

[2] On Kantian legal and constitutional philosophy, see EU Petersmann, *International Economic Law in the 21st Century. Constitutional Pluralism and Multilevel Governance of Interdependent Public Goods* (Oxford, Hart Publishing, 2012) ch III. On Kant's 'cosmopolitan international law' and its openness for 'institutional pluralism', see also C Corradetti, 'Kant's Legacy and the Idea of a Transitional *Jus Cosmopoliticum*' (2016) 29 *Ratio Juris* 105–21.

Hence, this book has rejected nationalist claims by 'realist politicians' and by some constitutional lawyers to perceive multilevel regulation of international PGs as mere politics.[3] Chapters 1 and 2 explained why international 'PGs treaties' approved by parliaments for the benefit of citizens can protect interdependent 'aggregate PGs' better if their incorporation or transformation into domestic legal systems protects cosmopolitan rights and judicial remedies that enable citizens to assume their democratic, republican and cosmopolitan responsibilities for democratic, administrative, judicial and 'cosmopolitan' enforcement of multilevel PGs regimes. Contrary to the claims by Krisch,[4] multilevel cosmopolitan constitutionalism remains a highly 'pluralistic' rather than hierarchical legal system; international 'PGs treaties' must be construed with due respect for national 'margins of appreciation' and for competing 'overlapping jurisdictions' with specialized 'institutional competences' and diverse democratic preferences.[5] Nationalist democratic rejection (eg in the USA) of many international PGs regimes (eg US non-ratification of UN human rights conventions, the WHO FCTC, ILO conventions, multilateral environmental agreements) risks undermining multilevel governance of aggregate PGs. National 'cosmopolitan constitutions' (like the German Basic Law of 1949) can protect cosmopolitan rights and PGs beyond national frontiers only through multilevel PGs regimes (eg multilevel trade governance based on national law, regional and WTO agreements). Hence, it was proposed to conceptualize cosmopolitan constitutionalism—contrary to Somek[6]—as *multilevel legal* rather than merely *political constitutionalism*. Chapters 1 and 2 emphasized that empowerment of citizens by 'cosmopolitan citizenship rights'—as decentralized instruments for constituting, limiting, regulating, justifying and enforcing transnational PGs regimes and supplementing national citizenship—is a necessary part of 'cosmopolitan constitutionalism' so as to enable citizens to assume 'republican responsibility' for multilevel supply of aggregate PGs. This concluding chapter summarizes the 'constitutional functions' of cosmopolitan rights (section II) and the need for multilevel 'integration law' (section III) that must remain embedded in constitutional, representative, deliberative and participatory democracy (section IV) and multilevel judicial protection of cosmopolitan rights (section V).

[3] See my criticism of the recent books by Kissinger in the Introduction and of Somek in ch 1 (nn 178 and 215 and related texts).

[4] N Krisch, *Beyond Constitutionalism. The Pluralist Structure of Postnational Law* (Oxford, OUP, 2013).

[5] See *Handyside v United Kingdom* [1979] 1 EHRR 737, para. 48 (national authorities are better positioned to strike the balance between individual rights and the public good since they are 'in direct and continuous contact with the vital forces of their countries').

[6] Cf Somek (n 1), 21 (the 'overall constitution of the multilevel system ceases to be law altogether').

II. FOUR 'CONSTITUTIONAL FUNCTIONS' OF COSMOPOLITAN RIGHTS AND THE EMERGENCE OF 'COSMOPOLITAN INTERNATIONAL LAW'

Chapters 1 and 2 used the emergence of 'cosmopolitan international law conceptions'—notably in European economic integration and human rights law, international commercial, trade and investment law, multilevel tobacco regulation based on the UN FCTC, international criminal law and consular protection—to demonstrate that the 'collective action problems' in multilevel governance of transnational 'aggregate PGs' can be addressed more effectively by taking into account that justice, HRL and globalization require 'constitutionalizing' multilevel governance of PGs through stronger legal and judicial protection of human rights and other cosmopolitan rights, as increasingly also practised in many other fields of international law (like intellectual property law and labour law). The 'implementation deficits' of UN, WTO and regional legal systems, and the indeterminate nature of many 'constitutional principles' (like human rights, the rule of law, democracy, sovereignty, non-discrimination, fair and equitable treatment, necessity, proportionality, subsidiarity), require stronger incentives for 'constitutionalizing' and 'socializing' legal systems by citizens as 'constituent powers', 'democratic principals', main economic and 'republican actors', and 'agents of justice', who must hold multilevel governance institutions legally, democratically and judicially more accountable. Cosmopolitan rights serve four 'constitutional functions' for transforming 'disconnected' UN, WTO and regional governance by 'connecting' the functional interrelationships and 'constitutional principles' that underlie constitutional democracies and UN/WTO law.

A. 'Empowering Functions' of Cosmopolitan 'Citizenship Rights'

Civil, political, economic, social and cultural human rights, and constitutional and legislative rights are necessary for protecting the ethical, moral, social, legal and political autonomy and human capacities of individuals in a globally integrating and interdependent world. International economic law, for instance, is increasingly interpreted and developed in terms of legal and judicial protection of individual trading rights (eg based on the WTO Protocol for the Accession of China), investor rights (eg based on BITs), intellectual property rights (eg based on WIPO conventions and the TRIPS Agreement), labour rights (eg based on ILO conventions) and other cosmopolitan rights (like health rights and individual access to justice protected by HRL); they reinforce the transnational 'cosmopolitan legal culture' based on international contract, commercial and arbitration law, and induce citizens to insist that economic rights must be reconciled and 'balanced' with all other constitutional rights of citizens. Cosmopolitan rights empower citizens to challenge abuses of power (eg due to information asymmetries, distortions of competition or cognitive weaknesses of consumers). By doing justice to the foundational 'values of respect for human dignity, freedom, democracy and equality' as recognized in national and European constitutional law (eg Article 2 TEU) and HRL, autonomy rights also protect the 'moral powers' of individuals[7] to pursue diverse conceptions for a 'good life', for legal and social justice, and for collective supply of PGs through democratic self-governance. Without such autonomy rights and citizen-driven 'struggles for justice', citizens cannot freely determine the 'basic legal structures' of their constitutional law, the 'public choices' and alternatives in democratic self-government, economic and social cooperation inside and beyond states. All the examples of 'cosmopolitan international law' discussed in Chapters 1 and 2—like HRL, European economic integration law, international commercial, trade, investment and health regulation—resulted from civil society struggles to limit abuses of power like monarchical and feudal powers, power politics among European states, colonialism, welfare-reducing border discrimination and other abuses of economic power (eg tobacco companies inducing consumers to buy toxic products with large social costs, as discussed in Chapter 2, section III; trade negotiators treating citizens as mere objects rather than as legal subjects of FTAs, as discussed in Chapter 2, section IV). Chapters 1 and 2 proposed strengthening the 'empowering functions' of cosmopolitan rights by recognizing 'cosmopolitan citizenship rights' (eg to invoke and enforce in domestic courts international 'duties to protect PGs') as integral parts of national citizenship, so that citizens can assume more 'cosmopolitan responsibility' for multilevel governance of transnational aggregate PGs essential for individual and democratic self-development. The more international agreements take over functions of democratic legislation in protecting PGs, the more agreements approved by parliaments for the benefit of citizens must be legally presumed to confer rights on those citizens to invoke and enforce precise and unconditional treaty guarantees of equal freedoms, non-discrimination and the rule of law in domestic courts.

As explained by Kantian moral philosophy, multilevel 'republican' and 'cosmopolitan' constitutionalism must be recognized as a 'moral imperative' and 'reasonable mind-set', rather than only as a multilevel framework of rules and institutions.[8] Chapter 1 explained why 'constitutionalization' of multilevel governance of 'aggregate PGs' depends on 'republican virtues'

[7] On the 'two moral powers' and the need for recognizing that 'justice is prior to the good in the sense that it limits the admissible conceptions of the good', see J Rawls, *Collected Papers* (S Freeman (ed)) (Cambridge, MA, Harvard UP, 1999) 312, 386.

[8] See Petersmann (n 2), ch III. Empowering citizens to use cosmopolitan rights and judicial remedies for enforcing transnational rule of law promotes self-enforcing constitutions limiting the 'disconnect' of UN/WTO and regional governance vis-à-vis citizens, as explained in ch 1.

by law-complying citizens assuming 'republican responsibilities' for collective supply of PGs. Just as national citizenship, constitutional rights and 'constitutional patriotism' (Habermas) have become recognized as constitutional foundations and incentives for democratic supply of *national PGs* inside constitutional democracies, so must cosmopolitan citizenship and cosmopolitan rights—as integral parts of national citizenship rights and of 'cosmopolitan Constitutions'—be recognized as constitutional foundations and incentives for collective supply of *transnational PGs* based on 'principles of distributive, corrective, commutative justice and equity' that justify multilevel PGs regimes for the benefit of citizens. The 'constitutional coherence' of the fragmented UN and WTO rules and institutions must be promoted by recognizing citizens and democratic peoples as 'constituent powers', entitled to transnational rule of law and to hold the limited 'constituted powers' of multilevel governance institutions more accountable for their widespread disregard of the customary law requirements of treaty interpretation and adjudication. Just as citizens have constitutional rights to invoke and enforce democratic legislation that protects *national PGs* for the benefit of citizens in domestic courts, so do the constitutional rights of citizens to multilevel protection of PGs (eg transnational rule of law) call for recognition of cosmopolitan citizenship rights to invoke and enforce precise and unconditional obligations under international PGs regimes (eg UN and WTO obligations) for the benefit of citizens in domestic courts. Chapters 1 and 2 argued that legal recognition of 'cosmopolitan citizenship'—as the 'external dimension' of state citizenship, empowering and requiring citizens to assume individual and democratic responsibility for multilevel governance of transnational aggregate PGs—is justifiable by multilevel HRL and constitutional law. If citizens conceive of themselves as the authors and addressees of 'constitutional contracts' and democratic law-making, they have strong reasons to insist on additional rights and responsibilities of citizens for multilevel governance of transnational aggregate PGs. 'Cosmopolitan citizenship rights' are essential for transforming 'constitutional nationalism' into multilevel constitutionalism protecting transnational PGs for the benefit of citizens and their human and constitutional rights, as illustrated by the contribution of EU citizenship rights and constitutional rights (as codified in the EUCFR) to the development of European constitutional law.[9] Cosmopolitan rights need to be specified through reciprocal international treaties and multilevel judicial clarification of the 'cosmopolitan constitutionalism' underlying modern HRL.[10]

[9] Cf H van Eijken, *EU Citizenship and the Constitutionalisation of the European Union* (Groningen, Europa Law Publishing, 2015).

[10] As democracy can enact democratic laws only for the citizens and *demos* that authorize them, *cosmopolitan constitutionalism* inevitably differs from *democratic constitutionalism*. On the obstacles in democratic legal systems impeding 'constitutionalization' of

Like Constitutions in federal states, international 'PGs treaties' should no longer be construed only as contractual relations among states, but also as democratic self-government, deriving democratic legitimacy from protecting the rights of citizens and transnational rule of law by multilevel governance institutions. As international 'PGs treaties' are not about creating a 'global nation' or 'world constitution', cosmopolitan rights are better understood as integral parts of national and regional constitutional and citizenship rights (eg in the EU) than as 'UN or WTO rights', even if they are legally specified in UN and WTO agreements (like UN human rights conventions, WTO guarantees of individual access to judicial remedies).

B. 'Limiting' and 'Enforcement Functions' of Cosmopolitan Rights

The 'human condition' of rational egoism, limited reasonableness and animal instincts calls for limiting social conflicts through 'constitutional self-commitments' to rules and morality. The historical experiences with law and governance since the Athenian democracy during the fifth century BC confirm that neither national nor international PGs can be effectively and legitimately protected without constitutional rights of citizens and democratic peoples to hold the limited, 'constituted powers' of multilevel governance institutions legally, democratically and judicially accountable for failures to protect the equal rights of citizens and PGs demanded by citizens. Hence, Chapter 1 criticized 'Hobbesian conceptions' of 'international law among sovereign states' as being inconsistent with modern HRL and with citizen-orientated 'constitutional contract interpretations' (eg since Rousseau and Kant) as voluntary subordination of men to political self-government by reasonable individuals and a democratic people using 'government agents' with limited, delegated and separated 'constituted powers' that must always remain subordinated to the power of the people. In the twenty-first century, democratic Constitutions and international PGs regimes must be construed as also protecting cosmopolitan rights to participate in collective supply of PGs and hold multilevel governance institutions accountable for transnational rule of law.

Chapters 1 and 2 explained why—even beyond the specific recognition (eg in HRL and IEL) of individual rights of 'access to justice'—the constitutional recognition of human dignity and equal autonomy rights are limited by 'rights to justification' (eg through constitutional rules, democratic legislation and judicial clarification) of the inherent 'reasonable limitations' of equal freedoms and corresponding government duties to protect

foreign policies through protection of cosmopolitan rights, see A Nollkaemper, *National Courts and International Rule of Law* (Oxford, OUP, 2011).

PGs. Where such 'rules of reason' are not specified through legislation (eg in national and European competition laws), they must be progressively clarified through democratic discourse and adjudication, balancing and reconciling public and private rights and interests as a reciprocal principal-agent relationship between citizens and governments. As constitutional democracies must interpret the limited powers of multilevel governance institutions as being constitutionally restrained by duties to protect and fulfil the equal constitutional and human rights of citizens, 'judicial dialogues' between national and international jurisdictions were welcomed as a necessary part of multilevel governance. Complementary national and international 'duties to protect PGs' must be linked by stronger legal, democratic and judicial remedies that hold governments more accountable for abuses of powers. In a globally interdependent world, national rule of law based on reciprocal rights and duties of citizens inside states can no longer be guaranteed without transnational rule of law beyond the state based on national, transnational and international legal and judicial accountability mechanisms, as explained in Kantian legal theory.

Chapter 2 criticized the unnecessary poverty and inadequate protection of human rights in so many UN member states as empirical evidence that the moral cosmopolitanism[11] underlying UN HRL (eg the UDHR) must be transformed into legal constitutionalism so as to render PGs regimes more effective. Chapter 2, section III showed how multilevel health regulation and adjudication based on the WHO FCTC enabled rights-based reforms of multilevel governance of international PGs in cooperation with human rights institutions; similar public-private partnerships mobilizing civil society support and multilevel judicial protection of cosmopolitan rights exist in other areas, like international criminal law.[12] Both public health regulation and criminal justice were strengthened by citizen-orientated reforms of international law (eg the entry into force of the Statute of the International Criminal Court (ICC) in 2002 and of the WHO FCTC in 2005) and judicial remedies enabling citizens to challenge abuses of power in national and international courts. Chapter 2, section II engaged in additional, comparative evaluations of multilevel governance institutions in regional and worldwide PGs regimes; it concluded that—similar to the citizen-driven enforcement of international commercial law, investment law, regional economic integration, environmental and human rights law in Europe—multilevel WTO

[11] Cf D Held, *Cosmopolitanism: Ideals and Realities* (Cambridge, Polity Press, 2010).

[12] Cf the case studies of the ICC, and of its cooperation with national criminal courts on the basis of principles of complementarity and accountability, in chs 8 and 9 of R Pierik and W Werner (eds), *Cosmopolitanism in Context. Perspectives from International Law and Political Theory* (Cambridge, CUP, 2010) 179 ff. Following the narrow judicial interpretation by the US Supreme Court (in *Kiobel v Royal Dutch Petroleum Company*, 133 SCt 1659 (2013)) of the jurisdiction under the US Alien Torts Act, some victims of corporate human rights abuses and their lawyers have filed claims before the ICC on the ground that, eg, violent, widespread and systematic land seizures by the Cambodian Government and Government-linked foreign businesses amount to crimes against humanity.

and free trade rules and governance at worldwide, regional, national and sub-national levels of governance (eg inside autonomous customs territories like Hong Kong, Macao and Taiwan) must likewise be strengthened through mutually 'consistent interpretations', judicial review of illegal acts, 'judicial comity' and other modes of judicial cooperation among WTO, regional and domestic dispute settlement procedures, so as to protect the existing guarantees of 'access to justice' and transnational rule of law more effectively for the benefit of citizens. 'Cosmopolitan reinterpretations' of IEL can be constitutionally and democratically justified through 'consistent interpretations' of existing 'principal-agent regulations' (eg existing EU and WTO legal guarantees of individual access to justice justifying 'cosmopolitan countervailing rights' and judicial remedies of citizens) so as to limit abuses of governance powers more effectively. By recognizing such rights of citizens to mutually consistent interpretations of national and international government obligations, the 'disconnected' UN and WTO governance could become functionally 'connected' and legally accountable. As the 'consistent interpretation' requirements are already part of the 'rule of law' requirements and 'principles of justice' of existing national and international legal systems, such constitutional reforms of IEL could be politically realized without changing UN and WTO rules, ie by taking the existing legal principles of 'consistent interpretations' of multilevel regulation of PGs more seriously in conformity with international treaties approved by parliaments. As legal restraints on foreign policy powers, cosmopolitan rights are necessary for transforming and enforcing the emerging 'multilevel human rights constitution' (as described in Chapter 1) and for realizing the human right to 'a social and international order in which the rights and freedoms set forth in this Declaration can be fully realized' (Article 28 UDHR).[13] This 'human right' to a 'global PG' illustrates the functional interrelationships between constitutional rights, general principles of law (cf Article 6:3 TEU) and the need for their legislative, administrative and judicial institutionalization as PGs (eg a public health system protecting health rights in national and international legal systems).

[13] Resolving this central 'constitutional problem' of the 21st century by recognizing human, constitutional and other cosmopolitan rights of citizens as the 'constitutional foundation' of both national and international law, is in line with a long tradition in international law doctrine that challenges 'states-only conceptions' with 'individualistic conceptions' of international law; cf H Lauterpacht, 'The Subjects of the Law of Nations' in E Lauterpacht (ed), *International Law: Being the Collected Papers of Hersch Lauterpacht* (Cambridge, CUP, 1975) 526 f: 'There is no rule of international law which precludes individuals and bodies other than States from acquiring directly rights under customary or conventional international law and, to that extent, becoming subjects of the Law of Nations. … The conferment of such rights may cover either particular rights or the so-called fundamental rights of the individual in general. With regard to the latter, there is room for the view that having regard to the inherent purposes of international law, of which the individual is the ultimate unit, he is in that capacity a subject of international law … [T]here has been an increasing realization that the direct subjection of the individual to the rule of international law is an essential condition of the strengthening of the ethical basis of international law.'

C. 'Regulatory' and 'Integrating Functions' of Cosmopolitan Rights

Chapter 1 explained why, in a constitutional democracy, citizens are the 'constituent powers' responsible for regulating and reconciling the interrelationships between 'overlapping PGs', like equal civil, political, economic, social and cultural human rights, and additional constitutional and legislative rights. All public governance results from complex interactions between citizens as 'democratic principals', multilevel 'governance agents', and democratic, administrative and judicial discourses on how to realize legally defined 'policy mandates and targets'. As 'communicative reasons' (eg justifying the economic efficiency of alternative government policies) must also acknowledge their contribution to 'intermediate PGs' like the equal rights of citizens, the rule of law and 'republican morality' that is 'owed' to all human persons in the polity, research and democratic discourse on multilevel governance of PGs must be interdisciplinary. Cosmopolitan rights also rest on the insight that individual moral autonomy remains constitutive for 'republican virtues' and 'public reason' in regulating the polity and economy and 'integrating indivisible human rights'. For instance, European constitutional law protects the constitutive importance of cosmopolitan rights for the proper functioning of economic markets (eg freedom of contract and arbitration, private property rights, market access rights, privacy rights, individual rights to decentralized enforcement of competition, environmental and social market regulations limiting 'market failures'), as well as of democratic 'political markets' (eg freedoms of expression, association and participation in democratic decision-making). Enlarging national citizen rights by transnational cosmopolitan rights (eg EU citizenship rights) has proved to be the most effective instrument for promoting non-discriminatory conditions of competition and decentralized correction of 'market failures' (like anti-competitive agreements, environmental pollution) and 'governance failures' by self-interested citizens. As illustrated by the overview of tobacco litigation in national and international courts and investment tribunals, the current asymmetries in allocating rights and judicial remedies favour powerful interest groups to the detriment of general consumer and citizen interests.

The comparative study of diverse multilevel governance regimes (in Chapter 2, section II) illustrated diverse approaches to using cosmopolitan rights for multilevel governance of PGs (like labour rights in the ILO, human rights in UN human rights bodies, intellectual property rights in WIPO conventions, rights to food in FAO law, rights to health protection in WHO law, rights to education in UNESCO law) and for 'integrating' multilevel constitutionalism through cosmopolitan rights. Almost all UN member states have adopted national Constitutions as well as functionally limited 'treaty constitutions' (eg establishing the ILO, UNESCO, WHO and FAO, whose constitutive agreements are explicitly called 'constitutions') that regulate multilevel governance of transnational PGs by:

— protecting citizen rights to multilevel protection of PGs like public health (the 'enabling function' of constitutions);
— subjecting multilevel governance to constitutional restraints and institutional 'checks and balances' (the 'limiting function' of constitutions);
— committing multilevel governance agents to constitutionally defined objectives and regulatory instruments (the 'regulatory function' of constitutions); and
— legitimizing law and governance by democratic consent and other 'principles of justice' (the 'justificatory function' of constitutions).

The more national Constitutions become 'partial constitutions' due to their increasing dependence on international 'PGs treaties' and institutions, the more important the functional interdependencies become between 'big "C" Constitutionalism' (constituting national polities) and 'small "c" constitutionalism' for protecting functionally limited 'aggregate PGs' beyond national frontiers. Human rights law and national Constitutions say little about transnational regulation and multilevel protection of PGs (eg in UN, WTO and regional governance institutions). Hence, Chapter 2, section II emphasized the need for learning through comparative institutional research why multilevel governance institutions (eg in UN, WTO and regional legal systems) are often designed and cooperate in such diverse ways. All democratic constitutions—including functionally limited 'treaty constitutions' (eg establishing rule-making, executive and judicial powers and citizen rights in the EU, EEA and ECHR)—acknowledge the need for six basic types of rulemaking (ie constitutional, legislative, administrative, judicial, international and private) and of corresponding institutions necessary for democratic self-governance and 'deliberative democracy' based on inclusive, public deliberation. One defining element of constitutional democracies is that all six types of rule-making and related institutions interact as multilevel governance systems that compete in their search to protect human rights and other 'principles of justice'. Yet the institutionalization and evolution of 'public reason' necessary for maintaining democratic self-governance differ among countries depending on their historical experiences, legal cultures and democratic preferences, for instance regarding their choice of 'parliamentary democracy' (eg in commonwealth countries like England and Australia) rather than 'constitutional democracy' (eg following the example of US and German constitutional law).

D. 'Justificatory Functions' of Cosmopolitan Rights

It is up to citizens and peoples to autonomously constitute, limit, regulate and justify governance systems, and explain the primacy of what is 'morally right' for every citizen over what individuals choose as 'ethically good' for their individual lives. Cosmopolitan rights and judicial remedies are essential for clarifying the 'values' (cf Article 2 TEU) and 'principles of justice' governing the relationships between citizens and multilevel governance agents. They structure the decision-making procedures and related principles (like 'conferral', subsidiarity and proportionality prescribed in Article 5 TEU, the 'democratic principles' defined in Articles 9–12 TEU) governing the exercise of governance powers (eg resulting from democratic elections, legislative, administrative and judicial procedures) for 'weighing', 'balancing' and reconciling competing rights and corresponding duties of governments in a world of scarce resources and often conflicting interests of individuals and peoples. For instance, the public controversies about the judicial 'balancing' of single market freedoms and discriminatory uses of trade union rights by the CJEU in the 2007 *Laval* and *Viking* disputes,[14] or about the exclusion of certain collective agreements from the scope of EU competition disciplines in the *Albany* and *Wouters* judgments of the CJEU,[15] promoted 'deliberative democracy' on how to reconcile diverse 'social models' inside EU member states. Cosmopolitan 'countervailing rights' and remedies can thereby contribute to the social acceptance of market regulations and inclusive decision-making that is necessary for protecting an 'overlapping consensus' among governments and citizens with diverse conceptions of justice on the overall legal coherence of the hundreds of multilevel PGs regimes. The 'Brexit' referendum of June 2016 was also justified by principles of democratic governance. As the Lisbon Treaty makes it clear (eg in Articles 3, 21 TEU) that EU diplomats have no democratic mandate to arbitrarily exclude rights of citizens under FTAs based on claims of 'Kaldor-Hicks efficiency', Chapter 2, section IV criticized the one-sided commercial focus of CETA and TTIP negotiators for ignoring the historical lessons from American and European 'republican constitutionalism' that rights of citizens to participate in FTAs and customs unions (eg among US states in the eighteenth century, German and Swiss states in the nineteenth century, the EU customs union and FTAs in the twentieth century), and to challenge arbitrary government restrictions of trade and private restraints of competition, were crucial for

[14] Cf L Azoulai, 'The Court of Justice and the Social Market Economy: The Emergence of an Ideal and the Conditions for its Realization' (2008) 45 *CML Rev* 1335–56.

[15] Cf LS Rossi and SJ Curzon, 'An Evolving "Rule of Reason" in the European Market' in G Bongiovanni, G Sartor and C Valentini (eds), *Reasonableness and Law* (Berlin, Springer, 2009) 405–19.

the PG of rules-based, common markets and for constitutional accountability of rulers. The entry into force of CETA and TTIP rules will depend less on intergovernmental economic bargaining than on convincing citizens and parliaments that these 'PGs agreements' protect the general interests of all citizens. Democratic insistence on renegotiating CETA and TTIP provisions for the benefit of citizens should not be seen—as wrongly pretended by former EU Trade Commissioner de Gucht—as provoking a transatlantic crisis; it rather offered a strategic opportunity to protect citizens through republican governance reforms (eg by revising the investment and ISDS rules in the 2016 CETA text).[16] Even if the TTIP will not change American and European constitutional law, multilevel TTIP institutions need to be designed so as to limit the past 'governance failures' in transatlantic relations.[17]

E. Lessons from 'Comparative Institutionalism' for 'Republican Constructivism'

The former EU High Representative for Foreign Affairs, Cathy Ashton, interpreted the EU treaty commitments to multilevel protection of human rights as 'the promise of the Lisbon Treaty [for] a more coherent, more consistent and hence more effective EU foreign policy ... [H]uman rights, democracy and the rule of law ... will run like a silver thread through everything we do externally'.[18] The EU's multilevel legal, parliamentary and judicial protection of cosmopolitan rights, remedies and responsibilities remains alien to the 'constitutional nationalism' prevailing in many third countries (eg NAFTA countries), as illustrated by US opposition to free movements of workers inside NAFTA, to many human rights conventions, ILO agreements, the Kyoto climate change convention, and to protection of health rights by the WHO FCTC. Also the multilevel legal and judicial protection and decentralized, citizen-driven enforcement of EU customs union and single market rules in terms of fundamental rights and transnational rule of law for the benefit of citizens is fundamentally different from 'Hobbesian

[16] Similar claims by another, former EU Trade Commissioner (Willy de Clerq) during the 1980s—that 'GATT should never have a compulsory dispute settlement jurisdiction'—were, likewise, proved strategically wrong by the compulsory WTO dispute settlement system, now celebrated as the 'crown jewel' of the world trading system.

[17] See the more than a dozen of detailed case-studies of past transatlantic disputes in EU Petersmann and M Pollack (eds), *Transatlantic Economic Disputes. The EU, the US and the WTO* (Oxford, OUP, 2003).

[18] C Ashton, Speech to the European Parliament on human rights on 16 June 2010. For a comprehensive analysis see M Golabek, *'Weaving a Silver Thread'. Human Rights Coherence in EU Foreign Affairs and Counter-Terrorism* (Florence, EUI doctoral thesis, January 2013).

interpretations' of US trade policy powers.[19] The 'chessboard conception' dominating 'realist' US foreign policies prompts US governments to prevent domestic courts from applying most international treaty rules as the 'supreme Law of the Land' (Article VI US Constitution). Such 'disconnected multilevel governance' (as illustrated by US legislation and US courts disregarding WTO obligations) differs from the EU's 'cosmopolitan foreign policy constitution', which has made EU enlargement policies the most successful foreign policies of the EU. Just as EU membership of UN institutions (such as the FAO, UNCLOS, UN environmental conventions) necessitates overcoming political obstacles inside and outside the EU, the EU initiatives for 'transformative FTAs' with all NAFTA countries must aim at promoting not only *economic welfare*, but also democratic reforms of multilevel governance of transnational PGs protecting rights of citizens.

Comparative institutionalism confirms how legal and judicial protection of the rights of citizens (eg in EU and US common market, competition, investment, environmental and labour law) has been crucial for promoting competitive markets, the rule of law, 'participatory democracy' and 'public reason' supporting multilevel governance of transnational 'aggregate PGs' in Europe and North America. Past research explains why many of the 'governance failures' in EU–US initiatives for establishing a *new transatlantic market place* during the 1990s could have been avoided through 'cosmopolitan restraints' on 'transatlantic governance failures'.[20] For instance:

— non-transparent politics has raised many unjustified fears (such as the 'chlorinated chickens issue') and impeded civil society support;
— 'institutional failures' of the existing 'Transatlantic Partnership' (eg regarding the transatlantic 'legislators' dialogue', 'early warning system', regulatory cooperation) could have been avoided by stronger civil society involvement based on 'republican rights' to protect PGs;[21] and

[19] See, eg, *Buttfield v Stranahan*, 192 US 470, 493 (1904), where the Supreme Court held 'that no one has a vested right to trade with foreign nations, which is so broad in character as to limit and restrict the power of Congress to determine what articles ... may be imported into this country and the terms upon which a right to import may be exercised'. While this decision could have been construed as part of a democratic 'principal-agent relationship' to imply a limited 'right to import' subject to Congressional regulation, subsequent US Court decisions have inferred from this Supreme Court decision 'that no one has a vested right to trade with foreign nations': 'When the people granted Congress the power "to regulate Commerce with foreign Nations" ... they thereupon relinquished at least whatever right they, as individuals, may have had to insist upon the importation of any product' (*Arjay Associates Inc v Bush*, 891 F 2d 981, 898 (Fed Cir 1989)). Such denial of citizen rights in parliamentary trade regulation (similar to a 'master-slave interpretation' of the ruler/subject relationship) is inconsistent with European constitutional traditions.

[20] Cf Petersmann and Pollack (eds) (n 17), eg chs 1, 3, 11, 12, 16 and 26.

[21] Cf *ibid*, eg chs 2, 10, 13, 15 and 27.

— cosmopolitan rights, stronger inter-parliamentary cooperation and judicial remedies could have protected the PG of a transatlantic market more effectively than mere intergovernmental 'transatlantic dialogues'.

Citizens in Europe and North America can reasonably expect their governments to demonstrate to the world that citizen-driven 'republican governance' of transatlantic FTAs can protect international PGs (like a mutually beneficial world trading system) more effectively and legitimately than the authoritarian 'top-down governance' in most multilevel governance institutions outside Europe and North America, for instance by taking into account that:

— 'market failures' (like abuses or private power, external effects, information asymmetries, social injustice) require multilevel regulation far beyond existing UN/WTO rules;
— democratic 'governance failures' (like 'majority' or 'minority' biases in majoritarian regulation and deregulation) require multilevel constitutional restraints far beyond current UN/WTO governance;
— intergovernmental dispute settlement procedures can be rendered more effective through citizen-driven, 'judicial administration of justice'; and
— intergovernmental 'top-down governance' of PGs can become more effective, more legitimate and less costly by using private initiatives and resources through 'public-private partnerships' and rights-based 'network governance' (eg in global supply chains).

The design of multilevel governance of transnational 'aggregate PGs' requires *republican constructivism* based on jurisprudential clarification, doctrinal connection and empirical justification of the diverse 'principles of justice' justifying national, regional and worldwide legal systems for multilevel governance of PGs and transnational protection of republican rights of citizens, as discussed in Chapter 1. The EU example of 'cosmopolitan citizenship rights'—derived from national citizenship rights (eg free movement of persons inside the EU) so as to empower EU citizens to participate in multilevel governance of transnational PGs—illustrates how decentralized participatory and enforcement rights can transform 'disconnected top-down governance' (eg of GATT's FTA rules) into more powerful and more efficient 'democratic governance' of PGs (eg based on the EU single market freedoms and related social rights). The World Bank and other international financial institutions define their 'development' objectives no longer only in terms of economic growth, but also as including the rule of law and human rights protection.[22] The multilevel WTO trading, legal and dispute

[22] Cf P Dann, *The Law of Development Cooperation: A comparative analysis of the World Bank, the EU and Germany* (Cambridge, CUP, 2013); J Wolfensohn, 'Some reflections on

settlement system could, similarly, realize its citizen-orientated treaty objectives—like 'providing security and predictability to the multilateral trading system' (Article 3 DSU), protecting 'access to justice' at national, regional and WTO levels of trade governance, and inducing each WTO member to 'ensure the conformity of its laws, regulations and administrative procedures with its obligations' under the WTO Agreement (cf Article XVI:4)—more effectively and more legitimately if citizens could invoke and enforce precise and unconditional treaty obligations in domestic courts, just as citizens can invoke national democratic legislation protecting PGs for the benefit of citizens. Transatlantic FTAs should exercise leadership for democratic reforms of multilevel governance of transnational PGs by promoting citizen-driven economic, democratic, legal and judicial governance methods, empowering citizens through decentralized rights and remedies, including 'countervailing rights', to challenge transnational 'market failures' and 'governance failures' condoned by intergovernmental power politics. Democratic, republican and cosmopolitan constitutionalism require limiting the 'executive dominance' in transatlantic regulation and its one-sided prioritization of rights of governments to the detriment of citizen-driven governance methods.

III. NEED FOR INTEGRATING THE COMPETING CONCEPTIONS OF INTERNATIONAL ECONOMIC LAW: FROM FRAGMENTATION TO CONVERGENCE IN INTERNATIONAL LAW

What is the legal significance of jurisprudential 'principles of justice' for designing legal and judicial doctrines (eg on treaty interpretation)? Chapter 1 criticized the substantive, institutional and methodological 'fragmentation' in multilevel governance practices, and welcomed the increasing recourse by international courts (like the ICJ, the WTO Appellate Body, regional economic and human rights courts, investment tribunals) to person-centered rather than only state-centered 'principles of justice' in interpreting international law.[23] As UN governance has avoided 'human rights constitutionalism', and human rights discourse is even more resisted in UN economic and GATT/WTO institutions, Chapter 1 argued for embedding

human rights' in P Alston and M Robinson (eds), *Human Rights and Development: Towards Mutual Enforcement* (Oxford, OUP, 2005).

[23] Cf also M Andenas, 'Reassertion and Transformation: From Fragmentation to Convergence in International Law' (2015) 46 *Georgetown Journal of International Law* 685–734; M Andenas and E Bjorge (eds), *A Farewell to Fragmentation. Reassertion and Convergence in International Law* (Cambridge, CUP, 2015).

constitutional democracies and their multilevel governance of PGs in stronger forms of multilevel republican and cosmopolitan constitutionalism. Chapter 2 used the WHO FCTC as an illustration of how national, regional and worldwide courts and arbitral tribunals use 'consistent interpretations' and 'judicial comity' for promoting the overall legal coherence of fragmented yet 'overlapping' treaties and jurisdictions (eg WHO, WTO, EU, national and transnational jurisdictions for reconciling economic tobacco regulations with health regulations). In view of the limited judicial powers, legislation clarifying the interrelationships between tobacco trade regulations, health law and human rights (eg through parliamentary approval and implementation of the FCTC) is democratically preferable. Yet, as illustrated by the transatlantic FTAs discussed in Chapter 2, section IV, intergovernmental treaty negotiations and democratic majority politics risk being biased and less impartial and independent than 'judicial administration of justice'. Moreover, as illustrated by the WTO's 1994 'coherence mandate' and by the so far limited involvement of UN institutions in WTO law-making,[24] the limited mandates and expertise of UN and WTO diplomats favour legal fragmentation rather than 'democratic integration law' clarifying the contested interrelationships between human rights and international PGs treaties. Hence, as international 'principles of justice' and their relationships to domestic 'principles of justice' remain disputed, diplomats prefer to pragmatically pursue narrow procedural conceptions of justice—eg as a balanced settlement of conflicting claims[25]—without linking economic and environmental agreements to UN human rights conventions and their underlying 'constitutional principles of justice', as illustrated by the absence of any explicit references to human rights in WTO law and the only scarce references to some human rights in some of the 'treaty constitutions' (*sic*) establishing UN Specialized Agencies (like the ILO, WHO, UNESCO and FAO). China's power-based rejection of the unanimous award of 12 July 2016 by the arbitral tribunal constituted at the request of the Philippines under Annex VII of the UNCLOS, which found 'no legal basis' for China's expansive territorial claims for 85 per cent of the South China Sea,[26] is a recent reminder that—even in worldwide 'PGs treaties' (like UNCLOS) with compulsory jurisdiction—power politics remains a reality.

[24] Cf A Pitaraki, *Institutional Linkages: WTO—IMF, World Bank, WIPO, WHO. A Global Administrative Law Approach as a Means for Supplying Public Goods* (Florence, EUI doctoral thesis, 2014).

[25] Cf C Albin, *Justice and Fairness in International Negotiation* (Cambridge, CUP, 2001).

[26] See Permanent Court of Arbitration Case No 2013-19 in the matter of the South China Sea Arbitration (The Republic of the Philippines v The Peoples Republic of China), award of 12 July 2016. The award is published on the PCA website at <https://www.pcacases.com/web/view/7>.

This section illustrates the need to reconcile and 'balance' state-centered and person-centered 'principles of justice' (as discussed in Chapter 1)—and to respond to claims of 'special legal regimes' by promoting legal convergence through 'consistent interpretations' and 'judicial administration of justice' adjusting authoritarian conceptions of 'international law among sovereign states' to the democratic 'principal-agent conceptions' of modern HRL and constitutional democracies—by a brief discussion of the necessary integration of the competing conceptions of IEL. Legal textbooks tend to describe and analyse IEL in diverse ways, for instance as (i) part of public 'international law among states', (ii) global administrative law (GAL), (iii) multilevel economic regulation, (iv) international private and 'conflicts law', and (v) multilevel constitutional regulation.[27] Such partial conceptions risk contributing to doctrinal incoherencies and to the study of worldwide monetary, financial, trading, investment, environmental, development and commercial law systems as 'fragmented sub-systems', without adequate regard to 'vertical multilevel governance' problems and 'horizontal interface problems' (like the trade-distorting effects of currency manipulations, and investment-distorting effects of financial, environmental and social under-regulation of 'market failures'). The competing 'narratives'[28] of existing IEL reflect different rationalities, value premises and disagreements on 'theories of justice' to justify IEL (eg in terms of 'state interests' rather than general citizen interests like consumer welfare and transnational PGs). As illustrated by the inadequate responses to the financial crises since 2008, state-centered 'Westphalian conceptions' of IEL, GAL conceptions, 'economic utilitarianism' (eg in NAFTA regulation driven by interest-group politics), 'nationalist realism' and 'legal pluralism' offer diverse and often incoherent advice for the required reforms of multilevel governance of transnational PGs. Just as utilitarian 'GDP approaches' and 'Kaldor-Hicks efficiency' concepts (underlying the Bretton Woods institutions and the WTO) are challenged by 'human development approaches' that focus on basic needs and 'capabilities' of citizens, so the prevailing 'Westphalian justifications' of intergovernmental decision-making in UN and WTO institutions (eg veto powers in the UN Security Council and in consensus-based WTO negotiations) are criticized by civil societies for their failures to protect human rights and legal,

[27] For a detailed discussion of these five competing conceptions of IEL, see Petersmann (n 2) 78 ff. The following overview focuses on the diverse 'principles of justice' underlying the diverse conceptions of IEL, and on how to reconcile them from the point of view of human rights and constitutional democracies.

[28] The term 'narrative' is used here in the Platonic sense that human ideas and ideals are part of reality influencing human actions. Unlike the 'social idealism' underlying Plato's *The Republic* (eg the belief in the capacity of 'philosopher kings' to make the political future conform to their ideals), Plato's last book on *The Laws* embraced a more sceptical 'constitutionalism', taking into account his own experiences with advising the rulers of Syracuse (and being sold in the slave market after having fallen from grace).

democratic and judicial accountability of multilevel governance vis-à-vis citizens. The current controversies over the 'blocking' of the appointment of WTO Appellate Body judges, and over whether investor-state dispute settlement should be included in a TTIP agreement between the EU and the USA (as discussed in Chapter 2, section IV), are illustrative of these increasing demands by constitutional democracies for a 'paradigm change' in transnational economic regulation. Claims to autonomy and specificity of IEL regimes often reflect special interests and 'tunnel visions', rather than 'public reason' respecting and balancing the constitutional rights of all citizens.

A. International Economic Law as 'Public International Law Regulating the Economy'?

The state-centered 'Westphalian conception' of international law and 'political realism', which emerged from the power struggles against the Church, the Holy Roman Empire and colonialism in support of a new system of states with 'sovereign equality' (Article 2 UN Charter), continues to dominate UN law in spite of the increasingly comprehensive human rights obligations acknowledged by all UN member states in hundreds of UN and regional human rights instruments. Most textbooks on IEL focus on its 'Westphalian conception' as consisting primarily of 'horizontal', international rights and duties among states and international organizations, regulating governmental restrictions of international movements of goods, services, persons, capital and related payments among states.[29] The 1944 Bretton Woods Agreements establishing the IMF and the World Bank, the 1945 UN Charter, GATT 1947, UN institutions (like UNCTAD) and UN Specialized Agencies regulating international services (like the Universal Postal Union, the International Telecommunications Union, the International Civil Aviation Organization, the International Maritime Organization) were all negotiated by diplomats representing states, under the leadership of the most powerful industrialized countries. As 'nothing contained in the Charter shall authorize the United Nations to intervene in matters which are essentially within the domestic jurisdiction of any State' (Article 2:7 UN Charter), UN law leaves it to each government to decide on the ratification and domestic implementation of international treaties in order to advance 'state interests'. State sovereignty, the 'weighting' of voting in the Bretton Woods institutions according to the financial contributions by states, and the 'consensus' practices in most UN, GATT and WTO decision-making processes entail

[29] See, eg, AH Qureshi and A Ziegler, *International Economic Law* (London, Sweet & Maxwell, 2007) ix: 'This book focuses on that branch of Public International Law which is concerned with international economic relations between States'.

power-orientated intergovernmental bargaining (eg on reciprocal tariff liberalization in GATT and the WTO) prioritizing rights among states over duties vis-à-vis citizens inside states. For instance, as documented in the Trade Policy Review Mechanism (TPRM) reports of the WTO Secretariat, it took many years until most African WTO members began adjusting their domestic legislation to their legal obligations under the WTO Agreement; and most WTO members do not protect effective rights of citizens to enforce WTO obligations in domestic courts. Due to 'diplomatic privileges', confidentiality of diplomatic negotiations and 'general treaty exceptions' enabling each government unilaterally to depart from treaty obligations to protect domestic interests (eg pursuant to Articles XIX to XXI GATT), intergovernmental rule-making often identifies 'state interests' with those of powerful, domestic interest groups (eg agricultural and industry lobbies demanding subsidies and 'safeguard measures'). The diverse legal structures of UN Specialized Agencies (eg exclusive membership of states, 'tripartite membership' of workers, employers and governments only in the ILO) and of the WTO (eg WTO membership of some sub-state 'customs territories' like Hong Kong, Macao and Taiwan) are due to power politics (eg the strong political influence of trade unions after World War I when the ILO was created) no less than to 'principles of justice'.

The 'public international law conception' of IEL is criticized for its 'dangerously naive tendency towards legalism—an idealistic belief that law can be effective even in the absence of legitimate institutions of governance'.[30] Its 'black box conception' of states and of leaving domestic rule implementation to the discretion of governments neglects:

— the influence of domestic politics (eg rent-seeking) on foreign policies even if international obligations are incorporated into domestic legal systems and protected through 'constitutional checks and balances' (as inside the EU);
— the decentralized, market-driven governance of production, trade and consumption of goods and services, investments and related payments (eg inside and among thousands of TNCs with 'global supply chains');
— the 'principal-agent relationships' between citizens and multilevel governance agents with limited 'delegated powers' and duties to protect constitutional rights, general consumer welfare and other PGs;
— the legal, economic and political interdependencies of 'overlapping aggregate PGs', for instance if discretionary *foreign policy* powers

[30] EA Posner, *The Perils of Global Legalism* (Chicago, IL, Chicago UP, 2009), who claims that 'most European scholars are global legalists' with an 'excessive faith in the efficacy of international law' who lose 'sight of the social function of law' (at xii); Posner justifies the 'pattern of American international lawbreaking' (at xi) on grounds of national cost–benefit analyses by the foreign policy elites.

(eg to tax and restrict domestic consumers through import restrictions, to increase domestic debt through international loans, to block access of citizens to foreign Internet websites) are abused for the benefit of rulers and undermine rule of law inside states and other domestic PGs (like freedom of information and expression in the Internet).[31]

Arguably, such one-sided focus on reciprocal rights, obligations and bargaining among states and governments explains why most worldwide agreements have failed to protect human rights and other global PGs effectively.

B. International Economic Law as 'Global Administrative Law'?

An increasing number of administrative lawyers from the USA and Europe argue that

> [m]uch global regulatory governance—especially in fields such as trade and investment, financial and economic regulation—can now be understood as administration, by which we include all forms of law-making other than treaties or other international agreements on the one hand and episodic dispute settlement on the other.[32]

As multilevel economic governance aims at regulating the conduct not only of states but also of private actors, it is acknowledged that the traditional inter-state paradigm of international law needs to be adjusted to the pluralistic and cosmopolitan regulatory realities. Global administrative law (GAL) approaches seek to ensure that 'global regulatory decision-makers are accountable and responsive to all of those who are affected by their decisions'. For instance, 'the challenges faced by the WTO can be addressed by greater application of GAL decision-making mechanisms of transparency, participation, reason-giving, review and accountability to the WTO's administrative bodies including its councils and committees and the Trade Policy Review Body'. To this end, GAL principles and procedures should be strengthened in three dimensions:

1. The efficacy and legitimacy of the internal WTO governance structures and decision-making procedures could be improved by strengthening transparency, participation, reason-giving and the law-making role of the WTO's regulatory, administrative and adjudicatory bodies.

[31] See, eg, the WTO Appellate Body Report, *China—Publications and Audiovisual Products* (WT/DS363/ABR) adopted 19 January 2010.

[32] R Stewart and RM Ratton Sanchez Badin, 'The WTO and Global Administrative Law' in C Joerges and EU Petersmann (eds), *Constitutionalism, Multilevel Trade Governance and International Economic Law* (Oxford, Hart Publishing, 2011) ch 16. The following quotations in the text are from these authors.

2. In the vertical interrelationships between the WTO and its regulation of members' domestic administrations, the incorporation of GAL principles and procedures into domestic administrative rules and procedures could strengthen the rule of law, transparency of trade regulation, uniform and impartial administration, due process of law and judicial review.
3. In the increasingly close 'horizontal linkages' among different global regulatory institutions, the WTO should recognize (eg pursuant to the WTO Agreements on SPS and TBT) regulatory standards issued by other global regulatory bodies only if generated through transparent procedures and 'regulatory due process', affording rights of participation and based on 'public reason' supported by the decisional record and reflecting fair consideration of all affected interests. Interpreting and applying the 'Washington consensus' that underlies the law of the Bretton Woods institutions and GATT/WTO law in conformity with the 'Geneva consensus', which underlies UN HRL and the law of some other UN Specialized Agencies, would promote common GAL principles, and strengthen and legitimize multilevel governance of 'overlapping PGs'.

The focus of 'GAL norms' on the procedural elements of administrative law has 'served not only to secure implementation of the substantive norms of liberalized trade but also to promote broader goals including open administration, even-handed treatment of foreign citizens, and the rule of law'. The standards seek 'to provide safeguards against abuse of power, counter-factional capture, and temper the tunnel vision of specialized regulatory bodies', as pragmatic responses to the 'accountability gaps' in the administrative practices of international institutions and the recognition that the ultimate aim of many of these regimes is to regulate the conduct of private actors rather than states. Yet GAL proponents acknowledge that due to the absence of democratic legislation and democratic accountability at the global level:

— procedural mechanisms alone may be relatively ineffective in overcoming disparities in power and the biases of specialized mission-orientated organizations;
— the legal status of GAL principles—whether as general principles of law, customary law or 'principles' underlying international treaty law—often remains contested in view of the different context of administrative activities of international organizations compared with national constitutional and administrative laws;
— GAL proposals by US administrative lawyers fail to explain why—as the constitutional constraints and parliamentary control of administrative law inside constitutional democracies are absent from the law of worldwide organizations—US constitutional and administrative law

principles (such as limited judicial review pursuant to the 'Chevron doctrine' in view of congressional regulation and oversight of delegated administrative powers) should be appropriate for worldwide organizations that elude effective parliamentary control at the international level as well as inside most states;

— worldwide organizations offer few effective judicial remedies for adversely affected citizens,[33] and are often dominated by intergovernmental coordination rather than by independent administration; their review and dispute settlement procedures—like the 'compliance procedures' of multilateral environmental agreements identifying, reviewing and restricting harmful activities—are sometimes politicized and lack independent 'administration of justice';

— the 'primary' and 'secondary law' of international organizations also lack a uniform 'constitutional foundation' or 'rule of recognition' to determine GAL principles and rules; hence, GAL remains less developed than 'European administrative law' based on common 'administrative constitutionalism' constituting and limiting national and European administrative practices in the implementation of EU and EEA law;[34]

— some GAL claims reflect wishful thinking rather than methodologically convincing determinations of positively existing international law; for instance, Kingsbury's concept of 'law' in GAL research[35] has been rightly criticized as a 'natural law interpretation'[36] of the 'general principles of public law' without methodologically convincing determinations of positively existing law. Kingsbury admits that the 'legal constitution of the global administrative body' by 'a kind of constitution-making' amounts to an international exercise of 'constitutive power' and 'constitutionalist commitment to publicness'.[37] Yet, rather than exploring the constitutional principles that govern the 'primary law' and 'secondary law' of international organizations and of their judicial interpretation

[33] Exceptions include, *inter alia*, the UN and ILO Administrative Tribunals protecting international civil servants, Part XI of the UN Law of the Sea Convention regarding deep seabed mining, WIPO arbitration concerning disputes over Internet domain names, and World Bank inspection panels.

[34] Cf E Fisher, 'Beyond the Science/Democracy Dichotomy: The WTO Sanitary and Phytosanitary Agreement and Administrative Constitutionalism' in Joerges and Petersmann (eds) (n 32) ch 11.

[35] According to B Kingsbury, 'The Concept of "Law" in Global Administrative Law' (2009) 20 *EJIL* 23, 32–33, 'requirements of publicness in GAL' include the principles of legality, rationality, proportionality, the rule of law and basic human rights, ie basic constitutional principles (called 'constitutive administrative law' in Kingsbury's terminology). Yet Kingsbury fails to identify to what extent his 'general principles of public law' are already part of the positive law of international organizations or merely proposals *de lege ferenda*.

[36] Cf A Somek, 'The Concept of "Law" in Global Administrative Law: A Reply to B Kingsbury' (2009) 20 *EJIL* 985, 990 f.

[37] Cf Kingsbury (n 35) 34–36.

at regional and worldwide levels,[38] Kingsbury claims: 'Constitutionalism implies a coherence of structure which global legal and institutional arrangements do not currently have ... While constitutive power is certainly exercised internationally, international constitutionalism in its richer forms is still, at most, in *statu nascendi*.' Arguably, Kingsbury neglects the common constitutional principles underlying HRL that are also reflected in the administrative law practices in functionally limited, international organizations.[39]

C. International Economic Law as 'Multilevel Economic Regulation' Embedded into 'Constitutional Nationalism'?

Conceptions of IEL as multilevel economic regulation underlie many international trade and investment agreements that focus on the economic rationality and functional unity of private and public, national and international regulation of the economy.[40] They emphasize the advantages of decentralized forms of market regulation (eg of national antitrust regulation in NAFTA member states) and of dispute settlement (eg as provided for in Chapter 11 of NAFTA, as well as in EEA law), and the need to embed economic regulation into the law of constitutional democracies. In contrast to the multilevel constitutionalism inside the EU, constitutionalism in NAFTA member states (Canada, Mexico, USA) focuses on 'constitutional nationalism' (eg in terms of national foreign policy discretion to pursue 'national interests'), subject to only few international legal constraints by NAFTA law and by the comparatively small and politically weak NAFTA institutions.

In conformity with the economic theory of 'optimal intervention' (eg through non-discriminatory internal taxes, product and production regulation rather than through trade-distorting subsidies and border discrimination) and political principles of 'subsidiarity' of economic regulation (ie as closely as possible to the affected citizens), multilevel economic regulation in NAFTA emphasizes the efficiency gains and democratic legitimacy gains of citizen-driven market competition and potential synergies of public–private partnerships (eg in environmental regulation, decentralized settlement of investor-state disputes through commercial arbitration). It stresses the need for supplementing and complementing incomplete, intergovernmental

[38] Cf N Blokker and H Schermers, *International Institutional Law*, 5th edn (Leiden, Nijhoff, 2011).

[39] The constitutional principles and rules identified by Blokker and Schermers (*ibid*) as part of the law of international organizations seem to contradict the claims by Kingsbury.

[40] For instance, the textbook by JH Jackson, WJ Davey and AO Sykes (eds), *Legal Problems of International Economic Relations*, 5th edn (St Paul, MN, West Publishing, 2008), adopts an interdisciplinary 'regulatory approach' (at 2), including private law, national law and international regulation of international economic relations.

regulations by private regulations, decentralized accountability and enforcement mechanisms like arbitration or Article 1904 NAFTA dispute settlement panels, which are established at the request of private complainants in order to limit the risks of 'protectionist biases' in domestic judicial review of antidumping and countervailing duty orders in NAFTA countries. Private–public co-regulation is promoted to enhance private expertise in the elaboration of technical and sanitary standards, the effectiveness of economic regulation, and its legal and democratic accountability; it may justify legal presumptions—as is the case in the WTO Agreements on TBT and SPS—that privately agreed production standards, product standards and sanitary standards are consistent with public international law unless they are successfully challenged in intergovernmental dispute settlement proceedings.[41] Yet private–public partnerships also risk facilitating 'protectionist collusion' and restrictive business practices, to the detriment of consumer welfare.

Multilevel economic regulation at public and private levels lacks a single unifying rule of recognition in view of its broad coverage of private and public, national and international sub-systems of IEL. It understands IEL as interdependent regulatory practices, including the 'private ordering' of the international division of labour among billions of producers, investors, traders and consumers, and millions of corporate actors, in 193 UN member states. The synergies, functional interrelationships and 'optimal levels' of public regulation (eg by means of competition law, banking law, investment law, labour law, environmental law) and private regulation (such as 'corporate governance' of the ever larger share of world trade carried out inside multinational corporations) are perceived as major regulatory challenges. 'Multilevel economic regulation' approaches tend to be critical of authoritarian 'top-down conceptions' of intergovernmental economic regulation. They draw attention to the ineffectiveness of most intergovernmental commodity agreements (eg for coffee, cocoa and tin) aimed at guaranteeing 'stable, fair and remunerative' commodity prices. Yet they recognize (eg in NAFTA Chapter 19 on multilevel judicial review of national antidumping and countervailing duty determinations, NAFTA Chapter 11 on investor-state arbitration) that international legal and procedural guarantees may be necessary to limit 'protection biases' in national laws and institutions.

Identifying the 'optimal level of legal regulation', and promoting mutual synergies between private and public, national and international economic regulation, may differ among jurisdictions with different legal and political systems. Due to its emphasis on 'constitutional nationalism' and on 'law and economics', multilevel economic regulation lacks coherent legal and

[41] On the many problems of such legal presumptions, see the contributions by Hüller, Maier, Howse, Schepel and others to Joerges and Petersmann (eds) (n 32) chs 9 to 14.

political approaches to multilevel governance of transnational PGs. Further, its focus on promoting *decentralized systems* for self-governance across borders (eg based on national contract law, company law, competition law, tort law, 'conflicts law')[42] neglects effective remedies of citizens against transnational 'market failures' (eg due to under-regulation of financial markets, environmental pollution, labour rights), related multilevel 'governance failures' and 'constitutional failures' (eg inadequate protection of rights of citizens vis-à-vis abuses of discretionary foreign policy powers, welfare-reducing discrimination against foreigners). 'Law and economics' also offers no coherent legal and political theory for protecting the 'input legitimacy' and 'output legitimacy' of international governance of transnational PGs, for protecting rights of citizens in global cooperation beyond state borders, and for limiting the 'collective action problems' in multilevel governance of PGs (as discussed in chapter 2, section II).

D. International Economic Law as 'Conflicts Law' and Private International Transactions Law?

Since the ancient trading and commercial practices (eg of the Phoenicians, the Greeks, the Romans and the Arabs) based on private property and contract law, the Roman *jus gentium* governing trade with foreigners and the medieval *lex mercatoria*, transnational commercial law has continued to evolve dynamically. This happens, for instance, through modern codifications of national and international private and commercial law, and their application and further development through thousands of national court decisions and commercial arbitral awards supervised and enforced by national courts. Some textbooks on IEL therefore proceed from the 'bottom-up' perspective of private contract law that regulates international trade, financial services, investment and related transactions,[43] and promotes decentralized coordination of the global division of labour across hundreds of national and international legal systems. The thousands of governmental and non-governmental regulations impact international trade and comparative advantages of producers, investors and countries competing to attract investments and other scarce resources. This competition, rivalry and decentralized legal coordination make some private lawyers emphasize:

— the reality of conflict and contestation in transnational society;
— the inevitable limits of 'top-down global governance';

[42] See the examples discussed by R Wai, 'Conflicts and Comity in Transnational Governance: Private International Law as Mechanism and Metaphor for Transnational Social Regulation' in Joerges and Petersmann (eds) (n 32) 229–62.

[43] An example is B Schöbener, J Herbst and M Perkams, *Internationales Wirtschaftsrecht* (Heidelberg, Müller, 2010).

— lessons from private international law for coordinating and resolving conflicts among jurisdictions, among government regulations and among transnational governance mechanisms; and
— the advantages of using private international law concepts for resolving 'conflicts among multiple systems of rules of both state and private ordering'.[44]

The 'conflict of laws' approaches also draw attention to the social functions and *public policy* goals of private law and private litigation by private 'attorneys general', who—through the pursuit of their own interests—may also serve social purposes of regulation. For example, individuals may promote *public interests* by claiming compensation in litigation related to product liability, environmental harms, restrictive business practices, abuses of intellectual property rights and corporate accountability for human rights violations. The increasing influence in IEL of transnational '*private advocacy networks*' and transnational, *private* litigation against multinational companies, human rights violators and host states of foreign direct investors, illustrates the systemic importance of 'adversarial legalism' as a tool of transnational governance. Private 'conflict of laws' doctrines (like the effects doctrine, judicial restraint doctrines, principles for mutual recognition of foreign standards and court judgments) may assist in resolving the coordination problems that result from competing private and public regulation systems. They may also facilitate cooperation among regulatory authorities, representation in national regulatory bodies of all adversely affected foreign interests, and reduce other regulatory gaps favouring business interests in transnational private ordering (for instance, through contracts and international commercial arbitration privileging the asymmetric mobility of business actors as compared with consumers and workers). Private law approaches often argue for mediating 'conflicts of normative orders' among national and international public law regimes by use of 'judicial comity'. National courts may show deference not only to their own legislatures in the case of cross-jurisdictional conflicts of policy, but also to legitimate interests of foreign jurisdictions and transnational governance procedures. Such conflict rules may promote judicial protection of transnational 'principles of cosmopolitan justice'.[45]

Yet does this increasing confrontation of private and public international law with common regulatory problems—such as the need for overcoming 'methodological nationalism' and parochial legacies of discriminating

[44] Wai (n 42) 230.

[45] Cf Wai (n 42), emphasizing 'the value of both conflict and comity in the relationship among regulatory orders, whether they be public or private, domestic or foreign, or international or transnational' (at 262).

against foreigners—justify the conceptualization of IEL as 'conflicts law'?[46] Arguably, the recognition by all UN member states of human rights obligations and other constitutional restraints of governance powers requires justifying IEL in terms of human and constitutional rights of citizens, rather than only in terms of private law principles and economic utilitarianism. 'Conflicts law principles' of private law for determining whether foreign jurisdictions, conflicting government regulations and transnational governance mechanisms 'deserve recognition' are no substitute for the necessary review of the 'human rights coherence' of IEL. They cannot replace legal and judicial 'balancing' of constitutional principles and human rights in applying and interpreting IEL 'in conformity with principles of justice' and the human rights obligations of governments, as explicitly required by the customary rules of treaty interpretation (as codified in the Preamble to and Article 31 of the VCLT) as well as by many other national and international legal regimes.[47] Private law doctrines offer no coherent answers for the constitutional and 'collective action problems' of multilevel governance of transnational PGs.

E. Multilevel Constitutional Conceptions of International Economic Law?

The more territorially based national sovereignty is transformed by functionally limited, multilevel governance of transnational aggregate PGs, the stronger the need becomes to reconceive sovereignty in terms of duties of governments to protect human rights and transnational 'aggregate PGs' demanded by citizens. Both territorially limited *national governments* and functionally limited *transnational governance* must be reconstituted, limited, regulated and justified more coherently in terms of the constitutional rights and duties of citizens and of their democratic self-governance beyond traditional state borders. 'Multilevel constitutional approaches to IEL' emphasize that the legitimacy and effectiveness of IEL—as an instrument for promoting consumer welfare and human rights of domestic citizens—depend on its consistency with HRL and other constitutional obligations

[46] As suggested by C Joerges, 'Three-Dimensional Conflicts Law as Constitutional Form' in Joerges and Petersmann (eds) (n 32) ch 15.

[47] For my criticism of Joerges' proposals for reinterpreting IEL as 'conflicts law', see EU Petersmann, 'The Future of International Economic Law: A Research Agenda' in Joerges and Petersmann (eds) (n 32) ch 18. On the need for defining law not only by authoritative issuance and social efficacy of rules, but also by principles of justice as integral parts of modern positive legal systems, see R Alexy, *The Argument from Injustice* (Oxford, OUP, 2010). In order to protect legal security, only 'extreme injustice' and violations of human rights may affect the validity of legal rules.

of governments. Such approaches are practised by the CJEU, the EFTA Court and the ECtHR in cooperation with national courts, parliaments and governments throughout Europe. They interpret and develop an increasing number of IEL rules as 'cosmopolitan law', and protect transnational rule of law for the benefit of citizens (eg investors, migrant workers and their families, the property rights and due process rights of alleged terrorists like Mr Kadi), with due respect for the legitimate diversity of constitutional democracies.[48] The legal primacy of constitutional rules over post-constitutional rule-making prompts many states to grant international treaties only an *infra*-constitutional legal rank in domestic legal systems, and to exclude 'direct applicability' of international law rules in domestic courts. As international law's claim (as codified in Article 27 VCLT) to legal primacy over domestic law must remain subject to constitutional restraints, constitutional democracy may require higher levels of *national* protection of human rights than the minimum standards prescribed in UN HRL.

Yet whenever *international guarantees* of freedom, non-discrimination and rule of law go beyond those of *national legal systems*—as in many areas of IEL—constitutional democracy may justifiably use IEL to limit 'constitutional failures' and 'government failures' of nation states that practise border discrimination against foreign goods, services, persons and investments to the detriment of domestic consumer welfare. European economic law, for instance, empowers European citizens to invoke and enforce common market freedoms and other fundamental rights of European law in national courts vis-à-vis welfare-reducing, *national restrictions* of mutually beneficial economic cooperation among citizens across frontiers. Human rights law justifies the practice of virtually all national Constitutions to subject the incorporation of international rules into the domestic legal system to constitutional safeguards, like respect for human rights and parliamentary approval of treaties, often subject to 'later-in-time rules' that protect the sovereign right of parliaments to override the domestic law effects of international treaties by later legislation. In Europe, multilevel economic regulation is designed and judicially reviewed in 'multilevel constitutional systems' that legitimately vary, for instance in:

— multilevel judicial review by national and EU courts of national restrictions by the 28 EU member states;

[48] Cf Petersmann (n 2), ch III; and A Stone Sweet, 'A Cosmopolitan Legal Order: Constitutional Pluralism and Rights Adjudication in Europe' (2012) 1 *Global Constitutionalism* 53–90, who defines a 'cosmopolitan legal order' as 'a transnational legal system in which all public officials bear the obligation to fulfil the fundamental rights of every person within their jurisdiction, without respect to nationality or citizenship' (at 53). Constitutional protection of economic freedoms is more widespread in European countries protecting broadly defined equal freedoms as the 'first principle of justice' (eg as justified by Kantian and Rawlsian theories of justice) than in common law countries prioritizing 'parliamentary sovereignty' over 'common law freedoms'.

— multilevel judicial review by national and EFTA Courts of national restrictions by EFTA and EEA member states;
— multilevel judicial review by national courts and the ECtHR of the legal consistency of national restrictions (eg 'regulatory takings' of private property, violations of privacy rights by competition investigations) by the 47 ECHR member states; or
— multilevel judicial review by national and transnational arbitral tribunals of actions by states participating in BITs or the Energy Charter Treaty.

Legal and judicial assessments may differ depending on whether economic regulations are governed by EU constitutional law as interpreted by the CJEU, EEA law as interpreted by the EFTA Court, the ECHR as interpreted by the ECtHR in close cooperation with national courts, or by multilevel investment rules as applied by transnational investment tribunals. Yet all national and European courts acknowledge the emergence of 'constitutional principles' that are common to the national and international jurisdictions concerned and limit economic regulation in Europe. *Cosmopolitan constitutionalism* claims that only citizen-orientated 'constitutional approaches' to IEL can effectively protect human rights—including the right 'to a social and international order in which the rights and freedoms set forth in this Declaration can be fully realized' (Article 28 UDHR), as reconfirmed in numerous UN Resolutions on the 'right to development' as a human right of citizens and of peoples. Just as national economic law is recognized as a multilevel legal system composed of private and public, constitutional and administrative law levels of legal regulation so as to protect citizens comprehensively, so constitutional approaches to multilevel IEL rules and principles can coherently limit the 'collective action problems' in the supply of international PGs, for instance by linking governmental duties to protect PGs to corresponding rights of citizens, judicial remedies and other 'accountability mechanisms', and by protecting—also in times of economic crisis—fundamental rights and the welfare especially of the poorest and most vulnerable.[49] Cosmopolitan constitutionalism suggests that the successive procedures to progressively develop and clarify principles of justice for multilevel governance of international aggregate PGs—through 'constitutional contracts' (eg based on mutual recognition of inalienable human rights), constitutional conventions, democratic legislation, administration, adjudication, international agreements, multilevel governance institutions and private civil society practices—are understood best as 'deliberative', 'participatory' and legally limited 'constitutional' and 'cosmopolitan democracy'.

[49] Cf *Protecting Fundamental Rights during the Economic Crisis*, EU Agency for Fundamental Rights, Working Paper, December 2010.

Its success depends on 'active citizenship' supporting 'republican values', 'constitutional patriotism' and democratic struggles against abuses of power ('*democratie de tous les jours*').

The common market and rule-of-law systems of the 31 EEA member countries illustrate the potential variety of combining diverse national and international constitutional rules and institutions. Without linking international rules to their domestic 'constitutional foundations', top-down 'public international law conceptions' of IEL risk failing to protect consumer welfare and human rights effectively. As human rights protect *individual* as well as *collective exercises* of fundamental freedoms (eg property rights owned by corporations, collective labour rights exercised by trade unions, democratic rights of peoples), human rights and constitutional law must also protect the institutions necessary for such collective exercises of fundamental rights. For instance, they must safeguard private property, private companies, private newspapers and private markets as 'dialogues about values' among producers and consumers and citizen-driven information mechanisms coordinating supply and demand. Without constitutional, legislative and administrative protection and regulation of market competition and judicial protection of individual rights (eg privacy rights that prompted the CJEU—in a judgment of 6 October 2015[50]—to annul the EU's participation in the EU–US agreements on the transfer of private data in view of their inadequate data protection inside the USA), the ubiquitous conflicts between private and public interests cannot be effectively prevented or resolved in global markets.

F. Justifying International Economic Law by 'Principles of Justice' May Vary Depending on the Actors, Institutions, Legal Contexts and Regulatory Objectives

Chapter 1 argued that—in exploring the customary law requirement of settling disputes over the interpretation of treaties 'in conformity with the principles of justice and international law', and clarifying, for example, the 'basic principles and objectives underlying this multilateral trading system' (Preamble to the WTO Agreement)—regard must be had to a large number of diverse principles of formal justice, procedural justice, distributive, corrective, commutative justice and equity recognized in national and international legal systems. It was also emphasized that political and judicial government bodies use diverse political and judicial procedures for clarifying such principles of justice. Different private and public, national and

[50] Cf CJEU Press Release No 117/15 of 6 October 2015 concerning Case C-362/14 *Schrems v Data Protection Commissioner*, nyr.

international actors and different institutions (eg national and international legislatures, administrations, courts, regulatory agencies) may prioritize different principles of justice depending on the legal context and regulatory objectives. For instance:

- even though all courts have to administer justice (eg by respecting 'due process of law' and equal procedural rights of the disputing parties), the different applicable laws in national and international jurisdictions are bound to entail differences in:
  - the legal reasoning of national and international courts,
  - their institutional constraints,
  - normative preferences, and
  - systemic and teleological understandings of multilevel regulatory problems.

  Such coordination problems may be resolved in a coherent manner only through protection of 'rights to justification' and through multilevel 'judicial dialogues', as illustrated by the increasing number of 'preliminary ruling'—or 'advisory opinion'—procedures in regional legal communities (eg in the EU, EEA, Mercosur, Andean Common Market) promoting cooperation among national and regional courts;[51]
- different polities—such as UN and WTO member states (eg China), sub-national WTO members (like Hong Kong, Macao, Taiwan) and supra-national WTO members (like the EU)—may justify their different membership right in international PGs regimes from diverse legal perspectives, as illustrated by requests from third states to clarify (eg through 'declarations of competences') the limited powers of international organizations participating in UN bodies (eg EU declarations and UN regulations specifying the limited observer rights of the EU in UN bodies, and the limited membership rights of the EU in FAO and UNCLOS bodies).

Hence, as discussed in Chapter 1, respect for the legitimate reality of constitutional and legal pluralism requires legal and judicial deference towards competing justifications of governance, for instance towards diverse definitions of:

- '*constitutional justice*' inside nation states (eg as defined by national parliaments and courts of justice depending on their national Constitutions);

[51] Cf M Poiares Maduro, 'Courts and Pluralism: Essay on a Theory of Judicial Adjudication in the Context of Legal and Constitutional Pluralism' in JL Dunoff and JP Trachtman (eds), *Ruling the World? Constitutionalism, International Law and Global Governance* (Cambridge, CUP, 2009) 356–79.

— '*Westphalian justice*' and 'equity principles' in international border disputes among sovereign states (eg as defined through judicial proceedings in the ICJ);
— '*distributive*' and '*commutative*' *justice* in disputes among states about the interpretation of their trade agreements on reciprocal market access commitments (eg as clarified by WTO dispute settlement bodies in violation, non-violation and 'situation complaints' pursuant to GATT Article XXIII);
— '*administrative justice*' vis-à-vis individuals and non-governmental actors (eg as clarified by UN and ILO Administrative Tribunals, World Bank inspection panels, investor-state arbitral tribunals);
— '*multilevel constitutional justice*' in multilevel human rights regimes and regional integration treaties (eg as clarified by the CJEU, the EFTA Court and the ECtHR); or
— '*multilevel economic justice*' in multilevel economic and investment regulations (eg as clarified in NAFTA Chapter 11 and 19 dispute settlement panels concerning judicial review of investment and antidumping measures).

As justice is ultimately about reasonable justification of law and governance vis-à-vis citizens with due regard to the diverse 'contexts of justice', there are dynamic interrelationships between competing principles of justice. For instance, in view of the inevitable 'democracy deficit' in global UN and WTO governance, this study argues for compensating for the inadequate parliamentary control of UN and WTO decision-making processes by stronger commitments to republican and cosmopolitan constitutionalism (eg in terms of cosmopolitan rights to transnational rule of law and other PGs). Different 'justice paradigms' dominating particular disputes in particular institutional settings applying different legal standards and procedures also interact in multilevel adjudication, as illustrated by the increasing importance of human rights arguments in ICJ disputes among sovereign states and in investor-state arbitration.[52] Justification in terms of 'principles of justice' aims at promoting 'universalizable', albeit often antagonistic, arguments, as well as overall 'structural coherence' in complex, multilevel governance systems based on a multiplicity of competing value principles. Just procedures aim at elaborating justified results that are usually not known to anyone before the beginning of political negotiations (eg on transatlantic FTAs, as discussed in Chapter 2, section IV) or judicial proceedings (eg on litigation challenging tobacco control regulations, as discussed in

[52] Cf the discussion of the recent ICJ jurisprudence on human rights (eg in the *Diallo* and *Germany v Italy* cases) by Andenas (n 23). See also V Kube and EU Petersmann, 'Human Rights Law in International Investment Arbitration' (2016) 11 *AJWH* 65–115.

Chapter 2, section III). For example, the German Constitutional Court's insistence on parliamentary, democratic control of the limited scope of EU competences (as emphasized by the German Constitutional Court in the Court's 'OMT decision' of January 2014 requesting a preliminary ruling from the CJEU) risks colliding with the different EU Treaty principles on democratic governance (cf Articles 9–12 TEU) and authoritative interpretation of EU rules by the CJEU.[53] Principled disagreements among some UN member states, governments, peoples and citizens likewise exist in respect of some UN conventions that collide with different constitutional traditions inside states, as also illustrated by the opposition in democracies (like the USA) to the ratification of certain UN human rights conventions. Yet this reality of legal and methodological 'value pluralism' does not entail that the customary law requirement of interpreting treaties and settling related disputes in conformity with 'principles of justice' and 'human rights and fundamental freedoms for all' offers no useful guidelines for constructing and 'constitutionalizing' multilevel governance of global PGs.

The American leadership after World War I in creating the League of Nations, and after World War II in establishing the UN legal system, like the French–German leadership in progressively developing European integration law since the Treaty of Paris establishing the European Coal and Steel Community, illustrates the obvious need for political leadership in containing power politics and interest-group politics that dominate Westphalian 'billiard ball conceptions' of 'international law among states'. As argued in Chapters 1 and 2, neither constitutional and parliamentary democracies nor multilevel governance of transnational PGs can remain stable over time without also protecting constitutional and cosmopolitan rights of citizens in multilevel governance of transnational PGs. The five competing conceptions of IEL discussed above suggest that the global PG of a just international economic order must also be based on constitutional and cosmopolitan 'principles of justice' rather than only on fragmented principles of 'Westphalian justice', 'administrative justice', 'economic justice' and private law principles of justice. As explained in the following section, the customary rules of treaty interpretation and multilevel constitutionalism promote progressive convergence and coherence of initially fragmented legal (sub)systems.

[53] See the judgment by the CJEU of 16 June 2015 in Case C-62/2014 *Gauweiler and others*, in which the CJEU responded to the request by the German Constitutional Court for a preliminary ruling on the ECB 'OMT decisions' by accepting that the relevant EU rules 'must be interpreted as permitting the European System of Central Banks (ESCB) to adopt a programme for the purchase of government bonds on secondary markets, such as the programme announced in the press release' of the Governing Council of the ECB of 5 and 6 September 2012. For details see nn 77–79 in the Introduction to this book and the related text.

G. 'Constitutional' and 'Cosmopolitan Justice' Require Limiting 'Disconnected, Multilevel Governance'

According to Article 28 UDHR, '[e]veryone is entitled to a social and international order in which the rights and freedoms set forth in this Declaration can be fully realized'. This 'entitlement' is limited to a vaguely drafted 'coherence principle' and 'PGs mandate' without specifying a precise rule, similar to the 'consistency requirement' that 'the Union shall ensure consistency between the different areas of its external action and between these and its other policies' (Article 21:3 TEU). Yet the customary 'integration requirements' of 'consistent treaty interpretation' and dispute settlements 'in conformity with the principles of justice and international law', including 'human rights and fundamental freedoms for all' (Preamble to and Article 31 of the VCLT), justify judicial clarifications of what 'legal consistency' and transnational rule of law require in particular disputes. The lack of explicit references to human rights in the Bretton Woods Agreements, GATT, the WTO, and in most international trade and investment agreements does not justify any counter-argument that IEL should not be construed in conformity with the human rights obligations of UN member states. The fact that 'cosmopolitan IEL agreements' (eg on rights-based commercial, investment and intellectual property law, EU and EEA common market law) have tended to protect PGs more effectively than alternative 'Westphalian conceptions' of IEL,[54] rather suggests also defining 'economic welfare' in terms of individual capacities, resources and rights to freely develop one's unique humanity so as to live the life a person has reason to value.

Chapter 1 derived from the universal recognition of human rights the need for 'democratic discourse justifications' of modern international law, which—in order to be voluntarily complied with by civil society and recognized as democratically legitimate—needs to be justified and evaluated from the perspective of reasonable individuals (as ultimate units of moral concerns), the constitutional and human rights of citizens and other 'principles of justice' that have become integral parts of positive international law. As the human condition is also characterized by rational self-interests in individual utility maximization (eg by UN, WTO and EU diplomats limiting their legal accountability by treating citizens as mere legal objects rather than as cosmopolitan and 'democratic principals' of all governance agents), Chapter 2 argued for constituting, limiting, regulating and justifying multilevel governance in conformity with democratic, republican and cosmopolitan 'constitutional principles of justice'. If, as stated in the ILC Report on *Fragmentation of International Law*, 'the whole complex of inter-regime

[54] This claim is substantiated in Petersmann (n 2) 145 ff.

relations is presently a legal black hole',[55] this is essentially due to the dominance of 'intergovernmentalism' in international decision-making, and its selfish rejection of 'constitutional' and 'human rights approaches' to international rule-making and multilevel governance of global PGs.[56] This section has argued that the mutually beneficial, global division of labour based on functionally limited 'integration law' continues to offer the most successful engine for rules-based promotion of economic welfare, poverty reduction and citizen-orientated, legal reforms of multilevel governance of PGs. Promoting the legal coherence, legitimacy and economic efficiency of IEL in terms of 'cosmopolitan principles of justice'—that reasonable citizens can understand and support—was shown to be no less politically important than justifying multilevel governance of the world economy in terms of economic 'Kaldor-Hicks efficiency'. Even though temporary 'fragmentation' of power-orientated international law regimes (like GATT 1947) is justifiable as a 'second-best policy' for promoting 'transitional justice' (eg through the 1979 Tokyo Round and 1994 Uruguay Round agreements, as discussed in Chapter 1, section III), republican and cosmopolitan constitutionalism call for progressive 'reintegration' of legally fragmented PGs regimes, as illustrated by the WTO Agreement. The continuing transition from 'territorial protection of national PGs' towards functionally limited, multilevel governance of transnational aggregate PGs requires moving toward 'cosmopolitan integration law', as illustrated by the case studies on multilevel health protection, transatlantic FTAs and climate change prevention. Justifying and regulating multilevel governance of such interdependent PGs must recognize citizens and their equal rights as 'agents of justice', 'democratic principals' and ultimate moral concerns.

IV. SUCCESSFUL 'CONSTITUTIONALIZATION' OF 'DISCONNECTED DIPLOMATIC GOVERNANCE' THROUGH REFORMS OF INTERNATIONAL INVESTMENT LAW?

Do the recent transformations of international investment law and governance (as discussed in Chapter 1, section III and Chapter 2, section IV) confirm the conclusion of this study that functionally limited, multilevel governance of *transnational aggregate PGs* requires the supplementing of 'constitutional democracies' by multilevel 'republican' and 'cosmopolitan' constitutionalism so as to constitute, limit, regulate and justify multilevel governance of transnational PGs more effectively, notably by enabling

[55] Cf UN Doc A/CN4/L.682, Analytical Report of 13 April 2006, at 253.

[56] For a discussion of the 'human rights approach' to IEL as suggested by UN human rights bodies, see Petersmann (n 2) 407 ff, 456 ff.

citizens to use cosmopolitan rights for holding multilevel governance institutions more accountable for their 'governance failures' to protect transnational PGs effectively for the benefit of citizens? As the 'executive dominance' of 'disconnected UN/WTO governance' impedes 'top-down constitutionalization' (eg following the model of EU single market and constitutional law) of UN and WTO law, this study has argued that the necessary 'bottom-up constitutionalization' must rely on 'deliberative' and 'participatory' democracy, and on judicial protection of constitutional and cosmopolitan rights of citizens limiting abuses of foreign policy powers. In view of the legal obligations to interpret and develop national and international legal systems in conformity with 'human rights and fundamental freedoms for all' and other 'principles of justice', both democratic legislatures and courts of justice must be pressured by civil society and the legal profession to challenge path-dependent justifications of power-orientated UN, WTO and regional legal and governance systems. The more 'international PGs treaties' take over functions of democratic legislation for protecting PGs, the more necessary becomes protection of cosmopolitan rights of citizens to invoke and enforce such PGs treaties in domestic jurisdictions. Multilevel republican and cosmopolitan constitutionalism cannot become effective without challenging traditional approaches to international law and diplomacy. Just as the enlargement of EU treaties was rightly recognized as a matter of extending democracy to (now) 28 EU member states and additional associated states (like EFTA countries and other potential candidates for EU membership), so must UN and WTO membership be progressively constitutionalized by using the 'constitutional principles' underlying HRL and constitutional democracies as justifications for admitting sub-national members (eg like Hong Kong) and supra-national members (eg regional organizations like the EU).

The evolution of international investment law over the past 65 years illustrates how the international investment law regime—based, in the 1950s, essentially on state-centered customary rules of international law—continues to be progressively 'constitutionalized' by using the legal methodologies proposed in this study:

1. temporary legal fragmentation (eg based on thousands of BITs) so as to export 'principles of justice' to less-developed capital-importing countries;
2. civil society challenges of the one-sided focus of 'business-driven reforms' and multilevel judicial protection of investor rights (eg in hundreds of judgments by national courts, transnational arbitration and regional courts of justice);
3. 'reintegration' of reformed investment rules in regional and functional integration regimes (like EU and EEA law, NAFTA Chapter 11, the Energy Charter Treaty); and

4. institutional reforms of investment adjudication and 'democratic discourse justifications' for reforming substantive and procedural investment rules (eg through new TTIP and CETA investment rules, adjustments of 'model BITs' of developed capital-exporting countries, the G20 consensus of 20 July 2016 on 'guiding principles for global investment policymaking').

In HRL and IEL, multilevel 'judicial administration of justice' continuously clarifies and develops the scope of cosmopolitan rights (eg fundamental freedoms recognized in UN law and regional human rights conventions) and of related constitutional safeguards (eg of UN and WTO legal guarantees of transparency, non-discrimination, necessity and proportionality of governmental restrictions, judicial remedies). The structural reforms and progressive 'constitutionalization' of international investment law offer empirical evidence that civil society, democracies and courts of justice can successfully use republican and cosmopolitan 'constitutional principles' for transforming previously 'disconnected UN governance' of international capital movements (eg based on diplomatic protection of investors by their home states, related policies of the World Bank institutions, and ICJ proceedings). The civil society criticism of the CETA investment rules and the parliamentary insistence on reforming the draft TTIP investment rules—as discussed in Chapter 2, section IV—illustrate the diversity of views on how to evaluate the progressive reforms of international investment law since the 1948 Havana Charter for an International Trade Organization. Also, investment regulations are evaluated by the different actors—like producers, investors, traders, consumers, governments, intergovernmental and non-governmental organizations—from different perspectives and value premises. For instance, writing from the perspective of Canadian constitutional law, Professor Schneiderman recently described the legislative and judicial reforms of international investment law as an 'emergent economic constitutional order', even though 'reminiscent of vested rights doctrine and Lochnerism of the nineteenth century'.[57] Compared with the legal and judicial remedies in 'second generation BITs' concluded during the 1990s, the CETA has clarified, *inter alia*, (i) the consultation procedures, (ii) the relationship between domestic and international remedies, (iii) the appointment and conduct of judges, (iv) the rules on cost allocation and (v) the transparency rules.[58] Yet

[57] D Schneiderman, 'Global Constitutionalism and International Economic Law: the Case of International Investment Law' in *European Yearbook of International Economic Law* 7 (2016, forthcoming).

[58] See A Reinisch, 'The EU and ISDS: From Investor State Arbitration to a Permanent Investment Court', *Investor-State Arbitration Series Paper No* 2 (Waterloo Ontario, Center for International Governance Innovation, March 2016); *Investor-State Dispute Settlement Provisions in the EU's International Investment Agreements*, 2 vols (Strasbourg, European Parliament, 2014).

from the perspective of European constitutional law, the CETA provisions on investor-state arbitration do not guarantee 'everyone' the 'right to an effective remedy before a tribunal in compliance with the conditions laid down' in Article 47 EUCFR. As discussed in Chapter 2, section IV, EU citizens can neither invoke the relevant FTA rules in domestic courts nor directly access transnational investment tribunals, whose jurisdiction will be accessible only to foreign investors and only in respect of complaints concerning violations of international investment law. Professor Schneiderman's call for 'pressing the pause button'—rather than for 'deepening constitution-like commitments' in international investment rules—may be influenced by the fact that the NAFTA and CETA investment rules go far beyond the legal guarantees under Canadian law (eg in view of the lack of constitutional guarantees of property rights and investment contracts, and parliamentary powers to expropriate foreign investments even without compensation). Yet many members of European civil society, national parliaments and the European Parliament request additional reforms of the investment rules to be included in the TTIP agreement.[59] Further, the UNCTAD *World Investment Report 2015: Reforming the International Investment Regime* claims that 'from the heated public debate and parliamentary hearing processes in many countries and regions, a shared view is emerging on the need for reform' of the international investment agreement (IIA) regime to ensure that it works for all stakeholders. The UNCTAD Report outlines many desirable reforms based on, *inter alia*, the following key findings:

- the experiences from almost six decades of IIA rule-making suggest a need for improving the potential of IIAs for investment promotion and for limiting their potential risks;
- IIA reforms should aim at:
  - preserving the right to regulate in the public interest,
  - reforming investment dispute settlement procedures,
  - expanding effective investment promotion,
  - ensuring 'responsible investments', and
  - enhancing the overall consistency of the global IIA regime;
- the numerous 'policy options' discussed in the Report need to be considered at national, bilateral, regional and multilateral governance levels through coordinated, transparent and inclusive reform processes aimed at strategic reforms.[60]

[59] Cf S Hindelang and S Wernicke (eds), *Essentials of a Modern Investment Protection Regime—Objectives and Recommendations for Action* (Berlin, Freie Universität, 2015).

[60] *World Investment Report 2015: Reforming the International Investment Regime* (Geneva, UNCTAD, 2015).

Compared with the 'constitutional guarantees' in EU law (like legal supremacy, direct effect, direct applicability, multilevel judicial protection of fundamental rights), international investment law remains far less 'constitutionalized'. Yet multilevel judicial protection of investor rights and their 'judicial balancing' with other public and private rights dynamically improve through treaty-based arbitral jurisprudence, ICJ jurisprudence (notably in the *Diallo* case) and civil society requests for additional reforms of multilevel investment regulation.[61] Initially indeterminate legal principles (like 'fair and equitable treatment' requirements, good faith and 'proportionality' principles) have become clarified through hundreds of multilevel court proceedings, thereby subjecting governments to stricter rule-of-law disciplines without prejudice to sovereign rights to protect public interests like the environment, public health and human rights.[62] The 'judicial reconceptualization' of the contractual, national and international dimensions of multilevel investment regulation—like the 'legislative integration' of investment rules into broader 'integration treaties' (like TTIP)—continues to progressively transform 'disconnected diplomatic governance' (eg based on diplomatic protection and investment disputes in the ICJ) into citizen-driven, multilevel governance of transnational PGs.[63]

V. MARKET CITIZENS, STATE CITIZENS AND COSMOPOLITAN CITIZENS: LOOKING FOR 'HERCULES' IN 'DISCOURSE JUSTIFICATIONS' OF MULTILEVEL GOVERNANCE

Chapter 1 argued that if the universal recognition of human rights justifies claims of citizens to be legally respected as the authors and addressees of legal rules that apply to them, modern international law and 'PGs treaties' also require discursive justifications that all citizens, as free and equal autonomous persons, can reasonably accept. 'Principles of justice'—as basic

[61] This is particularly evident if compared with earlier international jurisprudence like the *Chorsow Factory* case, the *Mavrommatis Concession* case and the *Oscar Chinn* case in the PCIJ, and the *Barcelona Traction* case and the *ELSI* case in the ICJ: see G Jaenicke, 'International Trade Conflicts before the PCIJ and the ICJ' in EU Petersmann and G Jaenicke (eds), *Adjudication of International Trade Disputes in International and National Economic Law* (Fribourg, Fribourg UP, 1992) 43–58.

[62] On the increasing but often still contested references to human rights as relevant context for interpreting investment treaties (eg the regulatory duties of states), see n 56 and PM Dupuy, F Francioni and EU Petersmann (eds), *Human Rights in International Investment Law and Arbitration* (Oxford, OUP, 2009).

[63] On the widely held view that diplomatic protection, vague customary law standards and costly, lengthy and politicized ICJ procedures offer inadequate protection to foreign investments, see P Muchlinski, 'The Diplomatic Protection of Foreign Investors: A Tale of Judicial Caution' in C Binder *et al* (eds), *International Investment Law for the 21st Century. Essays in Honour of C. Schreuer* (Oxford, OUP, 2009) 342–63.

justifications of interpersonal morality ('what we owe to each other') that reasonable agents accept for their individual and social self-governance, for instance in order to 'tie their hands' by reasonable self-commitments in view of the potentially dangerous 'human condition' (eg due to rational egoism, animal instincts and limited reasonableness)—must earn their authority though public justification vis-à-vis all affected citizens.[64] Due to 'global communications' in the modern 'Internet societies', the mega-regional TTIP and TPP negotiations, UN negotiations (eg on climate change agreements) and WTO negotiations (eg on concluding the Doha Development Round) provoke global discourses and civil society pressures to justify international treaty principles and rules more convincingly, so as to make it possible for reasonable citizens to democratically support international rule-making and the protection of PGs. Democratic justification of 'cosmopolitan principles of justice' is no longer limited to philosophers and representative parliamentary assemblies; it has become a practical challenge of 'deliberative', 'participatory' and 'cosmopolitan democracy'.

A. Cosmopolitan Constitutionalism Complements Democratic Constitutionalism

Cosmopolitan rights and judicial remedies are important incentives for citizens to participate in 'democratic discourse justifications' of legal rules, to design inclusive rules respecting equal rights of all affected persons, to institutionalize 'cosmopolitan public reason', and to protect both the private and political autonomy (ie the 'two moral powers') of citizens participating in multilevel governance of transnational PGs. Rather than relying on Rawlsian fictions of reasonable citizens discussing 'principles of justice' in an 'original position', or on Habermasian 'ideal speech situations' (ie enabling all possibly affected persons to agree as participants in rational discourses), republican and cosmopolitan constitutionalism defines transnational PGs in terms of the equal rights of all citizens to participate in multilevel governance of transnational PGs and corresponding government duties to publicly justify restrictions on 'republican freedoms'. As constitutional restraints on multilevel governance, cosmopolitan rights promote inclusive and 'reasonable' decision-making, respecting all human beings as free, equal and responsible for protecting global PGs. They require 'public justifications' vis-à-vis all affected citizens of the priority of 'political' and

[64] For a discussion of Rawls's and Habermas's theories on discursive political legitimation of laws by the 'public use of reason' (rather than only by individual moral reasoning as suggested by Kant's 'categorical imperative'), see R Forst, *The Right to Justification. Elements of a Constructivist Theory of Justice* (New York, Columbia University Press, 2012) chs 7 and 10.

'legal' justice over diverse, individual conceptions of a 'good life'. Cosmopolitan constitutionalism thereby extends the political tradition (eg of Kant, Rawls and Habermas) of principle-orientated and procedure-orientated justifications of liberal-egalitarian constitutionalism beyond state borders for inclusive, multilevel governance of transnational PGs. By rejecting path-dependent 'Hobbesian traditions' in intergovernmental 'disconnected UN/WTO governance' and deriving political legitimacy from respect for the 'co-originality' of human rights and democratic sovereignty, cosmopolitanism complements HRL and national, parliamentary constitutionalism by extending participatory and deliberative forms of democratic self-governance to transnational cooperation. European Union law and its EUCFR illustrate that—by recognizing civil, political, economic, social and cultural rights of citizens beyond the scope of UN HRL, and extending corresponding duties to justify multilevel governance vis-à-vis all affected individuals so that citizens can understand themselves as the authors and addressees of individual and democratic self-government—cosmopolitan constitutionalism helps to identify and limit multilevel governance failures and to improve the reasonableness of democratic discourse.

B. Cosmopolitan Rights Justify 'Constitutional Functions' of Courts of Justice

Cosmopolitan constitutionalism is also of particular importance for limiting the methodological problems of 'judicial administration of justice', as illustrated in the discussion (in Chapter 2, section III) of the five pending WTO disputes challenging Australia's legislation on plain packaging of cigarettes. Are the complainants right that Australia's legislation unjustifiably encumbers the trademarks and other intellectual property rights of tobacco producers, and creates unnecessary obstacles to international trade? As the pertinent WTO rules (notably in Articles III and IX GATT, Article 2 TBT Agreement, Articles 2, 3, 15, 16, 22 and 24 TRIPS Agreement) do not specifically answer these legal claims, are advocates of legal positivism right that WTO judges have discretion in interpreting the relevant WTO rules and deciding this dispute? Is this judicial discretion confirmed by the fact that WTO dispute settlement bodies have so far never explicitly applied the customary law requirement of interpreting international treaties and settling related disputes 'in conformity with principles of justice', including also 'human rights and fundamental freedoms for all'? What are 'the basic principles and ... objectives underlying this multilateral trading system' (Preamble to the WTO Agreement), and justifying it vis-à-vis citizens as 'democratic principals' of all governance agents? Is the American legal philosopher Dworkin right that in 'hard cases'—where the applicable legal rules do not specifically answer the disputed legal questions—it 'remains the judge's duty ... to discover what the rights of the parties are, not to invent new rights retrospectively'?[65] As Dworkin requests judges to act like Hercules in clarifying the law on the basis of a theory that 'best fits' and justifies the applicable rules and principles through constructive interpretations protecting equal rights of citizens rather than judicial discretion and utilitarian policies, why does the extensive WTO jurisprudence on methods of treaty interpretation not reveal a theory of justice vis-à-vis citizens as the constitutional and democratic agents of justice? Should the WTO follow the example of the World Bank and of other UN institutions by recognizing that the 'sustainable development' objectives pursued by UN and WTO institutions aim not only at promoting economic growth, but also at broadly defined 'human development' in conformity with transnational rule of law and the human rights obligations of states? As the World Bank achieved this change in legal interpretation and legal practices at the initiative of its Legal Counsel Ibrahim Shihata in the 1990s without formal amendment of the World Bank agreement, how can we explain the lack of corresponding leadership by WTO lawyers and judges?[66]

Judicial disputes tend to arise if the parties interpret the applicable rules in conflicting ways and request the judge to apply and clarify the law by administering justice, leading to a legally binding judgment. Dworkin's rejection of 'judicial discretion' seems to be confirmed by the explicit WTO mandate that the 'dispute settlement system of the WTO ... serves to preserve the rights and obligations of Members under the covered agreements, and to clarify the existing provisions of those agreements in accordance with customary rules of interpretation of public international law' (Article 3 DSU). Just as health governance derives its legitimacy from protecting the 'enjoyment of the highest attainable standard of health [as] one of the fundamental rights of every human being' (WHO Constitution) that can be enforced by citizens in domestic courts, the multilevel guarantees in WTO law of 'access to justice' and the rule of law require citizens to be treated as legal subjects—rather than mere objects—of WTO law in conformity with the human rights obligations of WTO members. Both multilevel health and trade governance must prioritize the equal freedoms and human rights of citizens, for instance by judicial 'balancing' of whether governmental protection of health rights (eg to breathe air free from toxic tobacco smoke) justifies related restrictions on economic rights (like trademarks of tobacco companies). In their task

[65] R Dworkin, *Taking Rights Seriously* (London, Duckworth, 1977) 81.

[66] For an answer see EU Petersmann, 'The establishment of a GATT Office of Legal Affairs and the limits of "public reason" in the GATT/WTO dispute settlement system' in G Marceau (ed), *A History of Law and Lawyers in the GATT/WTO. The Development of the Rule of Law in the Multilateral Trading System* (Cambridge, CUP, 2015) 182–207.

of interpreting and reconciling health law, economic law and human rights in mutually coherent ways, judges must distinguish 'rules' and 'principles', and must respect the 'margin of appreciation' of citizens in their democratic decision-making on how to reconcile competing civil, political, economic, social and cultural rights. Impartial and independent judicial reasoning may serve as an 'exemplar' of transparent 'proportionality balancing' and mutually 'consistent interpretations' of competing rights and principles in the legally binding settlement of specific disputes. Yet the limited 'dispute settlement function' of courts of justice must defer to the democratic, legislative authority of parliaments and the 'republican' and 'cosmopolitan' responsibilities of citizens for collective supply of PGs. Democratic, republican and cosmopolitan constitutionalism derive their legitimacy from respect for the legal and political autonomy of citizens to construct and justify the basic structures of national and international legal and governance systems through 'constitutional discourse' inside democracies, and through 'cosmopolitan' and 'republican' discourse in multilevel governance of transnational PGs. It is primarily citizens themselves—rather than only 'the state', 'courts of justice' and other multilevel governance institutions—who must assume their legal, democratic and cosmopolitan responsibilities for protecting their equal rights and legal and political autonomy in multilevel governance of transnational PGs.

The increasing cooperation, 'judicial dialogues' and 'jurisprudential cross-fertilization' among national, transnational and international courts—for instance, in fields like HRL, European integration law, international criminal law, commercial, trade and investment law—contribute to judicial clarification and development of common 'constitutional principles' (eg on inherent powers of courts of justice, 'consistent interpretation' and 'judicial comity' requirements, due process of law, 'proportionality balancing' of competing rights and principles) that strengthen the overall coherence, legitimacy and effectiveness of national and international legal systems through impartial 'administration of justice'.[67] More importantly, as justice has to be realized by individuals, the diverse jurisdictions of the thousands of local, national and international tribunals guarding 'access to justice' in multilevel governance of PGs are crucial for protecting the constitutional rights and 'struggles for justice' of citizens in different 'contexts of justice', for instance whenever globalization adversely affects *private freedoms* (eg freedoms of family life, religion and moral humanity vis-à-vis foreigners) or the *legal*, *political* and

[67] See the annual overviews of 'jurisprudential cross-fertilization' among national and international courts in *The Global Community Yearbook of International Law and Jurisprudence* (*GCYILJ*), eg AA Concado Trindade, 'Contemporary International Tribunals: Their Continuing Jurisprudential Cross-Fertilization in their Common Mission of Imparting Justice' (2013) I *GCYILJ* 155–60.

cosmopolitan rights of citizens to participate in transnational communities (eg by seeking asylum abroad).[68]

VI. CONCLUSION: LESSONS FROM DEMOCRATIC, REPUBLICAN AND COSMOPOLITAN CONSTITUTIONALISM

The main conclusion of this study is that reforming ineffective, 'disconnected UN/WTO governance' requires understanding that—in the twenty-first century—multilevel governance of global PGs can no longer be separated from respect for human rights and from their protection through democratic, republican and cosmopolitan constitutionalism as a necessary bulwark against abuses of power. Human rights, the rule of law, democracy and constitutionalism are all 'pure PGs' that complement and strengthen each other (similar to the 'plywood principle'), and have been successfully integrated inside modern, constitutional democracies. In contrast to the hierarchical nature of *national Constitutions*, the functionally limited, *transnational constitutionalism*—driven mainly by HRL, IEL and civil society claims to more effective protection of their rights across national frontiers[69] (eg through the UN 'Guiding Principles of Business and Human Rights' as adopted by the UN Human Rights Council in 2011)—depends on respect for 'heterarchical constitutional pluralism'[70] and cross-fertilization of pluralist constitutional sub-systems with diverse legal, institutional and social contexts that may justify diverse legal interpretations of indeterminate legal rules and principles in 'under-theorized' treaty regimes. Legitimacy of multilevel governance of PGs does not require 'global democracy'; the ineffective UN policies aimed at promoting democracy in UN member states rather illustrate how 'disconnected UN governance' (eg 'smart sanctions' by the UN Security Council against alleged terrorists) risks undermining protection of human rights inside constitutional democracies protecting 'We the people' in particular constitutional contexts.

This study has showed how the separate evolution of democratic constitutionalism (eg focusing on individual and popular freedoms and

[68] Also in this respect, the European history of a transnational *jus civile* and *lex mercatoria* based on Roman law principles accepted as common law and protected by judicial remedies (eg in the jurisprudence of the Imperial Chamber Court of the 'Holy Roman Empire of a German Nation') offers earlier historical lessons that remain valid to date: the rule of law and justice beyond state borders are safeguarded best by empowering not only governments, but also self-interested citizens and NGOs willing to defend their equal and reciprocal cosmopolitan rights by holding abuses of public and private power legally, politically and judicially accountable.

[69] Cf GW Anderson, *Constitutional Rights after Globalization* (Oxford, Hart Publishing, 2005); F Venter, *Global Features of Constitutional Law* (Nijmegen, Wolf Legal Publishers, 2010) 187 ff.

[70] Cf D Halberstam, 'Constitutional Heterarchy: The Centrality of Conflict in the EU and the USA' in Dunoff and Trachtman (eds) (n 51) 326–55.

decision-making processes), republican constitutionalism (eg focusing on the rule of law and other PGs) and cosmopolitan constitutionalism (eg focusing on civil, political, economic, social and cultural human rights, and democratic emancipation beyond state borders) has ushered in modern constitutional democracies integrating democratic, republican and cosmopolitan constitutional rights and duties for the benefit of citizens as 'constituent powers', 'agents of justice' and 'democratic principals'. It has emphasized that—as long as civil society struggles for extending constitutional, representative, participatory and deliberative democracy to multilevel UN/WTO governance of PGs are strongly resisted by many governments in order to limit their accountability vis-à-vis citizens—efforts at 'constitutionalizing' multilevel governance powers should focus on embedding functionally limited 'PGs treaties' into multilevel republican and cosmopolitan constitutionalism, for instance in view of the empirical fact that most international agreements with enforceable rights and remedies of citizens have protected PGs more effectively than state-centered 'Westphalian international treaties among states'. European Union law, EEA law and the ECHR were discussed as empirical evidence that the normative need for 'six-stage constitutionalization' and multilevel protection of (i) human and constitutional rights and related 'principles of justice' through (ii) constitutional and (iii) parliamentary legislation, (iv) administration, (v) adjudication and (vi) international law and institutions can be successfully implemented if citizens invoke and defend their rights.

A. Lessons from Democratic Constitutionalism

This study has argued that constitutional, representative, participatory and deliberative principles of democracy must be extended to multilevel governance of aggregate PGs, with due respect for the reality of constitutional pluralism. Yet the study has also acknowledged that 'global democracy' remains a utopia; the reality of non-democratic states and of diverse, national democracies protecting human and constitutional rights of citizens in diverse ways is an inevitable consequence of the legitimate diversity of democratic preferences, constitutional traditions and values of citizens. The supranational EU constitutionalism, and the more deferential forms of transnational, democratic cooperation in the EEA and in the EU relations with Switzerland, illustrate that multilevel democratic constitutionalism can successfully extend transnational PGs across national borders. Most national and international parliamentary assemblies participate in—and control—multilevel UN, WTO and regional governance in only insufficient ways. Hence, it was suggested that the 'parliamentary democracy deficits' should be compensated for by stronger multilevel rights and remedies of citizens, aimed at promoting more inclusive and more representative multilevel governance through stronger transnational rights of citizens and legal, democratic and judicial accountability of multilevel governance institutions. Multilevel deliberative democracy requires stronger multilevel duties to promote transparency of intergovernmental decision-making and of its public justification vis-à-vis all affected citizens. As democratic citizens are the 'constituent powers', the constitutional principles of conferral, subsidiarity and proportionality (cf Article 5 TEU) also serve 'democratic functions' aimed at limiting the delegation of powers and abuses of the 'constituted powers' of multilevel governance institutions, by protecting individual and democratic freedoms and rights of citizens that enhance 'democratic input legitimacy'. Inside democracies, democratic approval of international law and governance has become a precondition of their legitimacy and legal validity. Yet democratic rights and duties do not require the constitution, limitation, regulation and justification of international institutions in the same way as national democratic institutions; for multilevel governance of PGs may also be justified on republican and cosmopolitan grounds if democratic decision-making is not possible in worldwide and regional organizations.

B. Lessons from Republican Constitutionalism

In view of the universal human rights obligations of all UN member states and the spontaneous supply of *private goods* through private markets, the 'output legitimacy' of governments, multilevel governance institutions, states and international organizations derives from protecting *public goods* demanded by citizens. Human rights, the rule of law, democracy and national Constitutions are 'pure PGs', offering non-excludable and non-exhaustible benefits to the citizens concerned. They limit monarchical and majoritarian governance systems by protecting inclusive 'republican legal systems' (like Roman private law, protected by the republican Constitution and professional lawyers in ancient Rome); yet historical experience confirms that national 'republican Constitutions' (like the German 'Weimar Constitution' of 1919) may not prevent arbitrary abuses of power inside republican democracies and in their external relations. In view of the domination of international institutions by government executives, 'public choices' of defining, prioritizing and legally designing transnational PGs should be decided democratically, rather than being left to utilitarian economics (eg emphasizing that everyone can benefit from PGs) or to diplomatic elites that may prioritize rational self-interests over democratic preferences of the peoples. As illustrated by the 'Paris Agreement' on climate change prevention of December 2015, developed and less-developed countries may legitimately pursue different priorities in reconciling their developmental, environmental and human rights obligations.

Globalization and its transformation of national into transnational 'aggregate PGs' require multilevel republican international law and institutions committed to protecting transnational PGs for the benefit of citizens. This study has criticized the 'disconnected governance' in UN, GATT, WTO institutions, as well as in some of the FTAs concluded by the EU, for 'disempowering citizens' and privileging the rights of powerful interest groups (like foreign investors, and government executives limiting their legal and judicial accountability vis-à-vis citizens). In order to protect constitutional and human rights of citizens and other PGs more effectively, it was suggested that citizens, democratic institutions and courts of justice must constitute, limit, regulate and justify multilevel governance powers more clearly in terms of democratic, republican and cosmopolitan rights of citizens, empowering citizens to enforce the democratic, republican and cosmopolitan restraints on multilevel governance institutions in the EU, the EEA, the ECHR and also in UN law (notably UN human rights law).

C. Lessons from Cosmopolitan Constitutionalism

Moral, legal, political and economic cosmopolitanism and their underlying values (like methodological individualism, equal treatment of human persons, responsibilities vis-à-vis strangers, respect for individual and democratic diversity) say little about the legal design of multilevel governance institutions for the protection of PGs. In order to protect transnational PGs for the benefit of citizens in a globally integrated world without global democracy, national democratic constitutionalism and multilevel republican constitutionalism (eg based on republican rights and corresponding government duties, principles of limited delegation of powers, multilevel 'checks and balances', economic principles of efficiency and separation of policy instruments) must be supplemented by cosmopolitan constitutionalism aimed at multilevel, legal and judicial protection of human rights and additional cosmopolitan rights. In view of the disagreements among UN member states on the scope of their legal obligations to protect civil, political, economic, social and cultural rights as human rights, it may be justifiable that specialized worldwide institutions (like the WTO) avoid controversial 'human rights discourse' in favour of more pragmatic 'rights discourse' (eg regarding judicial remedies, intellectual property rights). Section I of this chapter distinguished four different functions of cosmopolitan rights similar to the constituting, limiting, regulating and justifying functions of international 'PGs treaties' (as discussed in Chapter 2):

- *empowering functions* (eg in commercial, investment law, common market rights, intellectual property law);

— *limiting functions* (eg labour rights, access to justice, judicial remedies, state responsibility, criminal law);
— *regulating functions* (eg in competition law, consumer protection law, social law, environmental law); and
— *justificatory functions* based on private and public rights to justification (eg inclusive 'discourse justifications' of law and democratic governance) and corresponding government duties to justify legislative, administrative and judicial acts.

As noted in Chapter 1, even if the morality of the ancient Greek and Roman constitutionalism was limited (as illustrated by its discrimination as regards women and slaves), its emphasis on the need for 'civic virtues' and 'virtue politics' as 'social drivers' of 'constitutionalization' of legal systems and protection of PGs continues to form part of modern democratic, republican and cosmopolitan constitutionalism.[71] Similarly, just as constitutional discourse in the ancient city republics was always related to theories of justice (eg as developed by Plato, Aristotle, Cicero and Italian Renaissance philosophers), international courts continue to justify their legal findings by constitutional principles of justice, as famously stated by the International Criminal Court for the former Yugoslavia in the *Tadic* case:

> A State sovereignty-oriented approach has been gradually supplanted by a human-being-oriented approach. Gradually, the maxim of Roman law *hominum causa omne jus constitutum est* (all law is created for the benefit of human beings) has gained a firm foothold in the international community as well.[72]

Since Plato's book on *The Republic* (*c* 375 BC), the metaphor of the 'state ship' is used in Western republicanism for describing the legal structure that protects society from the dangerous waters surrounding it. The Chinese proverb attributed to the Confucian philosopher Xunzi (298–220 BC) uses the metaphor of the 'state ship' in a significantly different way: 'The heavens create the people and appoint the ruler. The ruler is like a boat, the people

[71] Cf P Gottleib, *The Virtue of Aristotle's Ethics* (Cambridge, CUP, 2009). The Latin term 'virtue' refers to the 'power' of man (*vir*) to temper his emotions and desires, to confront uncertainty and fear with fortitude, to use rationality and reasonableness prudently, and to govern our human and social nature justly by rendering to each his due (*suum cuique tribuere*). The term 'cardinal virtues' uses the image of hinges (*cardo*) upon which the door of moral life swings. According to Aristotle's *Nicomachean Ethics*, among the four 'cardinal virtues' (prudence, justice, courage and temperance), only prudence requires intelligence rather than will power. The three 'theological virtues' (faith, love and hope) likewise do not require particular intelligence; they support human- rather than state-based 'cosmopolitics'. For a virtue-centered theory of judging ('virtue jurisprudence') based on (i) judicial temperance, (ii) judicial courage, (iii) judicial temperament, (iv) judicial intelligence, (v) judicial wisdom and (vi) justice, see LB Solum, 'Virtue-Jurisprudence: A Virtue-Centered Theory of Judging' (2003) 34 *Metaphilosophy* 178 ff.

[72] *Prosecutor v Dusko Tadic*, Decision on the Defence Motion for Interlocutory Appeal on Jurisdiction, 2 October 1995.

are like the water. The water may support the boat, and it may also capsize it.' In the Western metaphor, society and its rulers are on the ship together, and the captain acts as an *agent* of the people who are the *democratic principal* and 'constituent power'. The Chinese metaphor describes the people as keeping the state afloat without being on board the ship and without being capable of reforming or steering it. How should 'cosmopolitan citizens' inside and outside China respond to this reality of non-democratic states and rulers? This book has argued that—just as a mountain climber must traverse valleys and foothills in order to progress from one mountain peak to the next—citizens can meet the Sisyphean challenge of improving multilevel governance of PGs in the twenty-first century only by building on the lessons of earlier historical struggles for democratic, republican and cosmopolitan 'constitutionalization' of harmful power politics. Life has to be lived going forward, but it can be understood only by looking back and by learning from past 'trials and errors'. China's ratification of the UN Convention on Economic, Social and Cultural Rights and of the UNCLOS illustrates the potential 'constitutional functions' of 'cosmopolitan international law' and of 'access to justice' (eg to UNCLOS Annex VII arbitration in the maritime dispute between the Philippines and China discussed above). Both inside and outside non-democratic states, citizens can invoke cosmopolitan rights (eg the trading rights, intellectual property and judicial remedies protected under China's Protocol of Accession to the WTO) and universally recognized 'principles of justice' (eg those underlying the compulsory WTO and UNCLOS jurisdictions for peaceful settlement of disputes and transnational rule of law) as a 'shield' against abuses of power and as a building-block for constructing 'public reason' by challenging autocratic rulers.[73] The universal recognition of 'inalienable human rights' by all UN member states entails that also international law and transnational governance must be justified vis-à-vis citizens in terms of protecting equal rights and related PGs, with due respect for democratic 'value pluralism' and legitimate 'constitutional pluralism'.

[73] On these 'constitutional functions' of WTO law and UN law for reforming law and governance inside China, see EU Petersmann, 'Constitutional Functions and Constitutional Problems of International Economic Law in the 21st Century' (2010) 3 *Xiamen Academy of International Law: Collected Courses* 155–242 (Leiden, Nijhoff Publishers, 2011).

Index